TORT LAW: CASES AND MATERIALS

TORT LAW

CASES AND MATERIALS

JODI GARDNER
AND
SARAH GREEN

•HART•
OXFORD • LONDON • NEW YORK • NEW DELHI • SYDNEY

HART PUBLISHING

Bloomsbury Publishing Plc

Kemp House, Chawley Park, Cumnor Hill, Oxford, OX2 9PH, UK

1385 Broadway, New York, NY 10018, USA

29 Earlsfort Terrace, Dublin 2, Ireland

HART PUBLISHING, the Hart/Stag logo, BLOOMSBURY and the Diana logo are trademarks of Bloomsbury Publishing Plc

First published in Great Britain 2024

A catalogue record for this book is available from the British Library.

A catalogue record for this book is available from the Library of Congress.

Library of Congress Control Number: 2024934631

ISBN: PB: 978-1-50997-189-3
ePDF: 978-1-50997-191-6
ePub: 978-1-50997-190-9

Typeset by Compuscript Ltd, Shannon
Printed and bound in Great Britain by Ashford Colour Press Ltd

To find out more about our authors and books visit www.hartpublishing.co.uk. Here you will find extracts, author information, details of forthcoming events and the option to sign up for our newsletters.

CONTENTS

TABLE OF CASES

Note: Cases in **bold** feature in 'Key Case' boxes and page numbers with "n" denote Footnotes

A

B

C

D

E

H

I

M

X

Y

Z

ECTHR

EU

AUSTRALIA

CANADA

IRELAND

NEW ZEALAND

SINGAPORE

UNITED STATES OF AMERICA

TABLE OF LEGISLATION

Note: Legislation in **bold** is set out in the text and page numbers with "n" denote Footnotes

E

F

G

H

I

L

M

O

U

TABLE OF UNITED STATES LEGISLATION

TABLE OF INTERNATIONAL MATERIALS

TABLE OF OTHER MATERIALS

Note: Material in **bold** is set out in the text and page numbers with "n" denote Footnotes

Chapter 1 INTRODUCTION

This chapter delves into three of the big-picture debates around tort law – how to define the topic, the compensation culture and feminist perspectives of tort law. It provides a range of materials for you to read and reflect on when considering these issues. However, this is far from a complete picture of the introductory issues that you should consider when starting your journey into tort law. There are many other fascinating debates and challenges, but they are beyond the scope of the current chapter. We encourage you to read this chapter in conjunction with Chapter 1 of Green and Gardner, *Tort Law*, which goes into other issues, such as the aims of tort law, interests provided by tort law, limitations of tort law, tort law and insurance and alternative compensation systems.

1.1 What is tort law?

We understand that studying tort law can be a daunting task. Unlike other aspects of the law that you may be familiar with – for example, criminal law and contract law – tort law can seem difficult to define, and its scope often seems unclear. This can be especially challenging for students considering the topic for the first time.

The starting point is to consider whether the United Kingdom has a system of 'tort law' or the 'law of torts'. As you will see from the chapters of this book, there is a wide range of torts that all work in different ways and protect different interests. Some are statutory in nature; many derive purely from the common law; whilst others can be a combination of both. This book, and the related textbook, look at the most common torts: negligence, occupiers' liability, product liability, land-based torts, economic torts, intentional torts against the person, defamation and privacy – but there are many other torts that are beyond the scope of an undergraduate textbook.

Below are excerpts from three different sources, all of which provide an insight into the complexity and differences associated with tort law: one from a historical perspective, one from a theoretical viewpoint and another considering the impact of judicial decision-making. When reading these excerpts, reflect on the similarities and differences in the discussion and analysis and how it fits in with your own perspectives of tort law, the legal system and society in general.

Arthur Ripstein, 'Theories of the Common Law of Torts', *Stanford Encyclopedia of Philosophy*, 2 June 2022

Ripstein reflects on the theories associated with tort law across the common law legal system as a whole (covering a variety of different jurisdictions):

> Tort is a branch of private law. It focuses on interpersonal wrongdoing primarily between private persons. Unlike the law of contract, tort obligations are not normally entered into voluntarily; unlike the criminal law, the state is not necessarily a party to a tort action. Private persons can often contract around the rights and obligations of tort law; those rights and obligations provide the background against which other private arrangements can be made. Prominent examples of torts include negligent injury, battery, deceit, and defamation. In each case, the existence of the legal right that has been violated does not depend on any prior act of the injured party. Instead, everyone has rights against these types of conduct on the part of others. Tort law engages with two of the most fundamental questions of morality and social life: how people are permitted to treat each other, and whose problem it is when things go wrong.
>
> …
>
> In common law legal systems, as well as in what are often described as 'mixed' common law/civil law systems such as those of Israel and South Africa, most of tort doctrine developed through decisions made by judges addressing private disputes. In the past century and a half, the diversity of common law jurisdictions and the introduction of statutes and competing regulatory regimes have introduced considerable diversity into the common law, in some cases entirely displacing parts of it. Despite such variation, the broad doctrinal structure of the law of torts is fairly clear. It addresses two fundamental questions of human social interaction.
>
> First, tort law lays out the minimal forms of conduct that people are legally entitled to demand of each other, prior to any arrangements that they have made with each other. It does so by identifying and articulating a range of wrongs for which one person can claim against another before a court and, if successful, be awarded a remedy. The most prominent of these wrongs, both in the business of courts and in scholarly (particularly philosophical) discussions, is the tort of negligence, which involves careless injury of one person by another. Other wrongs include defamation, deceit, trespasses to land and chattel, intentional torts against persons (such as battery, false imprisonment and private nuisance) and liability for dangerous or defective products, as well as a range of more specialized torts, such as public nuisance, misfeasance in public office, the tort of statutory breach, and constitutional torts (cases in which a private citizen sues an official for a violation of the citizen's constitutional rights).
>
> Second, tort law addresses a question about whose problem it is when things go wrong by generating and enforcing a remedial structure within which those who have been

wronged can claim a remedy from the person who has wronged them. In order to establish the remedial claim, the complaining party (the 'plaintiff') must establish that the act of the alleged wrongdoer (the 'defendant') satisfies each of the elements of the tort of which they complain.

Tort law protects each person's bodily integrity against both intentional and negligent interference; it protects each person against deceit by others; it protects each person's mental health against intentional infliction of emotional distress and negligent infliction of psychiatric injury; it protects each person's reputation against misstatements by others; it protects privacy and freedom of movement against certain interferences; and it protects property against various forms of interference, including unauthorized use, willful or careless damage and, in the special case of land, against unauthorized entry and loss of usefulness. No less significantly, the common law of torts declines to protect other interests that might be thought equally pressing, such as the interest in adequate resources or a favorable context in which to pursue one's purposes, the interest in assistance in times of urgent need, and the interest in the continued availability of objects and people on which one relies. Different explanations of the principle on which tort law decides which interests to protect will be considered below. It protects the interests that it does by articulating basic norms of conduct, most of which are continuous with familiar moral ideas. For example, the basic norm of negligence requires that people exercise appropriate care around the bodies and property of others, a moral and social norm that figures in warnings given to children at playgrounds. So, too, the basic norm of battery – which in English law is characterized as 'unauthorized touching' and in American law as 'harmful or offensive touching' – reflects the admonition given to children to keep their hands to themselves. In each case, tort law specifies and systematizes these familiar ideas and makes them legal rather than merely social or moral norms.[1]

John Baker, *Introduction to English Legal History*, 5th edn (OUP, 2019)

Baker describes the development of tort law and its separation from contract law:

The law of torts, or civil wrongs, is extensive and its boundaries are not fixed by any unifying general principle. The very word 'tort', which has long been appropriated by lawyers, was not technical in origin. The nearest medieval equivalent to the modern legal term was 'trespass', whereas the old French word tort (*injuria* in Latin) denoted any kind of legal injury and is best translated as 'wrong'. Until the sixteenth century both words overlapped in meaning. In the preceding chapters we followed the development of trespass in the areas of contract and property law, and noticed that in the early sixteenth century there was nothing incongruous about describing a breach of contract as a tort or trespass. But

1 https://plato.stanford.edu/entries/tort-theories/.

when the action of assumpsit became a truly contractual remedy, based on a promise in return for consideration, breaches of contract came to be seen as legally different in a number of ways from other kinds of trespass. ... By the middle of the seventeenth century, contract and tort were seen as being so different that claims in tort and contract could not be joined in the same action. Thus, when an action was brought in 1665 against the hirer of a horse for misusing the animal and for not paying the hire, counsel argued that the joinder of the two causes of action was erroneous because one sounded in tort and the other in 'breach of promise only'. In another case the same year, counsel treated contract and tort as mutually exclusive: 'tort can never be done where there is a special agreement, unless there be duty by statute or common law incumbent'. This is near the modern understanding of the word, and Twisden J in the same case said that 'tort' encompassed malice, fraud, or negligence. Already by the same period legal indexes were classifying 'tort' in the modern sense, as a sub-heading under actions on the case.

As different kinds of trespass action acquired separate characteristics in the sixteenth and seventeenth centuries, further subdivisions of the law of torts were made, some of which survived the abolition of the writ system itself. Since the eighteenth century, however, the law of torts has undergone a gradual rearrangement as a result of the rapid expansion of the tort of negligence. Liability for negligence alone – that is, without reference to other factors such as contract – was rarely imposed before 1700, and even at the beginning of the twentieth century Sir John Salmond was denying the existence of a separate tort of negligence. In the practitioners' book, Clerk and Lindsell on Torts, negligence did not achieve the status of a separate chapter until as late as 1947. It would be easy to conclude from this that negligence has a short history; but this would be misleading. The negligence approach of the modern law determines liability by focusing on the quality of the defendant's act rather than on the kind of harm done to the plaintiff. The reordering of so much of the modern law of tort around the concept of negligence is a consequence of that shift of focus, which was partly a result of abolishing the forms of action. But there is nothing modern about the concept of negligence in itself; what has changed is its primacy. Negligence and fault have always been familiar ideas, and for at least four centuries before 1700 they played a role in law and legal terminology, but their role was subsidiary. A plaintiff might allege negligence alongside other factors, to reinforce liability, or a defendant might rely on the absence of negligence to show that he was not at fault. The concept was not tied to a particular form of action. It was not even confined to actions in tort, in the modern sense of the term, because most actions on the case for negligence before 1700 were for contractual negligence.[2]

2 ch 23 (footnotes omitted).

Jane Stapleton, *Three Essays on Torts* (OUP, 2021)

In this passage, Stapleton addresses the role of what she refers to as 'grand theories' in tort law – these are theories that attempt to apply tort law as a whole, compared to the 'reflexive tort scholar' which responds to the competing issues addressed by this area of the law:

Case law is replete with illustrations of how complex a task it is for judges to analyse the social facts (including legal facts such as the statutory environment), values, and expectations that generate and ground the living common law, not least when the submitted evidence of these matters is thin. As Sir Terence Etherton M.R. has pointed out, these difficulties become more pronounced as society becomes more pluralist. So, to the reflexive tort scholar, it is not unexpected that judges concede that they find judgment of these, often highly contested, matters challenging or have changed their minds about them. Nor is it unexpected that among themselves judges differ in their evaluation of these questions and about what is the best way in which to articulate a common law rule to give expression to them. After all, as Gary Watt puts it, a Herculean judge might believe he or she has found the right answer in a case but then 'perhaps Zeus would find another answer on appeal'.

Even in cases where the members of today's ultimate court of appeal agree about the substance of the relevant social facts, values, and expectations underpinning the law when the parties interacted and the way in which this is best expressed, the court may disagree with how previous courts identified and stated how the law was at that time of interaction. When today's court announces that the previous court should have identified the law at the time of interaction to have had a different content – that the previous court had been 'wrong' – our judges humbly give us, in the words of Lord Mance, 'a pragmatic acknowledgement of the possibility of ... judicial error'.

...

It is my observation that citizens have a heterogeneous range of concerns and that these are reflected in richly textured expectations of law. Citizens are concerned about not only individual entitlements, such as the vindication of their ownership and the quiet enjoyment of their own property, but also public rights, such as the right of their friends, family, and even strangers to pass along a public highway. They are concerned not simply about individual rights but also about social utility, efficiency, deterrence, incentives, and a broad range of other collective, public interest, concerns.

It is often overlooked, but important for the later discussion, that citizens' collective concerns extend beyond those that might be portrayed merely as some aggregate of their own personal interests and embrace public policies that are remote from them. For example, it is readily conceivable that, even if not in business themselves, citizens want their legal system to provide certainty in commercial dealings, to condemn the conduct of passing off as wrongful etc. It is also the case that many duties of affirmative action can be much more securely anchored in the judicial reading of broad social values and expectations than in an artificial assertion that an individual defendant had assumed a relevant legal responsibility to the individual claimant.

If we take judges seriously when they explain that they seek to identify and articulate common law principles that vindicate these social values, we would expect judicial reasoning in tort cases to reflect this diversity in social concerns. We would also expect diversity in tort doctrine across common law jurisdictions and legal change over time, reflecting how this rich heterogeneous range of social concerns varies between different communities and over time. We would not be surprised to see: some tort complaints being actionable only on proof of a loss and others being actionable per se; and some being actionable only on proof of fault while others do not require this; judicial reasoning giving weight to concerns about individual entitlements as well as collective values; and so on. If citizens are sensitive to the interests of the whole community and expect the law to reflect this, we should not be shocked when judges, seeking legitimately to give effect to such rich social values, explicitly note that there will be cases where, in the words of Lord Hope, the 'interests of the wider community must prevail over those of the individual'.

Finally, it is no secret that citizens choose to come together for group purposes in non-human legal entities such as commercial companies, incorporated cooperative societies, charitable trusts, partnerships, so on. Often these non-human legal entities bring claims in the law of torts to vindicate their interests. Among claims concerning property damage well known to first year torts students are ones by a dock company against the corporate charterers of a ship, a yacht-owning company against the Home Office, one oil company against another, a hotel against a borough council, and a water company against a tannery. Even more obviously, defendants in tort claims are very often non-human legal entities including public authorities, banks, and so on.[3]

Question to consider: Do you think it is more accurate to define this area as 'tort law' or 'the law of torts'? Reflect on the similarities and differences between the different causes of actions.

Other resources: Glanville Williams, 'The Aims of Tort Law' (1951) 4(1) *CLP* 137; Robert Stevens, *Torts and Rights* (OUP, 2007), ch 13; Tony Weir, *An Introduction to Tort Law*, 2nd edn (Clarendon Law Series: OUP, 2006); John Murphy, 'The Heterogeneity of Tort Law' (2019) 39 *OJLS* 455; Rebecca Stone, 'The Circumstances of Civil Recourse' (2022) 41 *L & Phil* 39.

3 pp 10–12 (footnotes omitted).

1.2 Compensation versus 'compensation culture'

One of the key aims of tort law is to compensate the victim, placing them in the situation they would have been in had the tort not occurred.[4] Whilst this seems uncontroversial, a number of countries around the world have complained about the development of a 'compensation culture': a situation in which people too frequently sue others for their misfortune instead of either taking personal responsibility for their losses or accepting that accidents sometimes happen that cannot be attributed to anyone's fault.

For example, if someone has a car accident due to a build-up of snow on the roads – is it just bad luck, and they should be utilising their insurance policy, or should they sue the government body responsible for roads for not being more proactive to ensure the roads were safe to drive, or should they take responsibility for driving in potentially unsafe conditions? Would the answer change if the person was driving to the pub for a drink compared to driving a sick child to the hospital? Would it change if the government body had significant funds available and chose to spend them on a lavish Christmas party compared to being severely underfunded and struggling to cover all the required duties?

Lord Sumption, 'Abolishing Personal Injuries Law – A project', Personal Injuries Bar Association Annual Lecture, 16 November 2017

Lord Sumption raised a concern about the development of a compensation culture in a lecture delivered to a prominent bar association in 2017:

> The mounting concern about compensation culture is powered by a number of factors. The main ones are the upward pressure on motor insurance premiums arising from an increase in the number and value of claims, governmental concern about the cost of claims against the National Health Service, and persistent stories in the press (not always strictly accurate) about unmeritorious claims.
>
> …
>
> I suspect that the main reason why most people instinctively approve of the fault principle has nothing to do with utilitarian considerations of this kind. The law is generally sensitive to considerations of economic efficiency, although judges rarely acknowledge the fact. But one area which has been more or less impervious to considerations of economic efficiency is the legal right to bodily integrity. It is a right founded on profound cultural instincts. Questions of cost tend to seem trivial by comparison. The debate about compensation

4 This was outlined by Lord Blackburn, who stated that tort law should award 'that sum of money which will put the party who has been injured, or who has suffered, in the same position as he would have been in if he had not sustained the wrong for which he is now getting his compensation or reparation' (*Livingstone v Rawyards Coal Co* (1880) 5 App Cas 25, 39).

culture really turns on complex cultural issues about moral responsibility and blame which have very little to do with economic efficiency. The public's view is based on two simple moral judgments. One is that he who causes physical injury must make it good financially. The other is that it is a proper function of the courts to find facts and distribute blame, simply as a satisfaction for victims or their relatives.

Personally, I would question whether there really is a moral case for imposing liability in damages on the ground of negligence. One might perhaps make an exception for professional failures where the Defendant has undertaken to exercise an appropriate measure of care and the relationship with the victim, although not actually contractual, is equivalent to contract. Except in that situation, negligence is not morally culpable. It is a normal feature of human behaviour. This is not the place and 6.40 in the evening is certainly not the time to embark on a profound survey of corrective or distributive justice. I will only say this. I can imagine a moral case for imposing an absolute liability on those who cause physical damage to others, simply on the ground that they are the agents of some invasion of the victim's physical integrity. That was the basis of the more limited and now largely redundant tort of trespass to the person. I can also imagine a moral case for imposing liability on those who intentionally or recklessly cause physical damage to others. But liability for negligence does not depend on a person's mere infliction of damage, nor on his state of mind. It depends on his falling below some objective standard of conduct to which he has not usually assented, but which the law imposes upon him. It seems to me that the only possible justification for the law doing that is its social utility. Yet the arbitrary results and incomplete coverage of a fault-based system, combined with its prodigious cost and unwelcome side-effects, seriously undermine the social utility of the law of tort as a way of dealing with personal injury.[5]

Judges also raised these concerns about the harm of the compensation culture in several decisions, which, in many negligence cases, appeared to influence their decision on liability.

Tomlinson v Congleton Borough Council [2003] UKHL 47, [2004] 1 AC 46, [2]–[4], [81]

Lord Hoffmann reflects on the role of compensation and the tort law system when discussing the facts of this case:

2. In rural south-east Cheshire the early May Bank Holiday week-end in 1995 was unseasonably hot. John Tomlinson, aged 18, had to work until midday on Saturday 6 May but then met some of his friends and drove them to Brereton Heath Country Park, between Holmes Chapel and Congleton. The Park covers about 80 acres. In about 1980

5 At 2, 10–11.

Congleton Borough Council acquired the land, surrounding what was then a derelict sand quarry, and laid it out as a country park. Paths now run through woods of silver birch and in summer bright yellow brimstone butterflies flutter in grassy meadows. But the attraction of the Park for John Tomlinson and his young friends was a 14 acre lake which had been created by flooding the old sand quarry. The sandy banks provided some attractive beaches and in hot weather many people, including families with children, went there to play in the sand, sunbathe and paddle in the water. A beach at the far end of the lake from the car park was where in fine weather groups of teenagers like John Tomlinson would regularly hang out. He had been going there since he was a child.

3. After sitting in the hot sun for a couple of hours, John Tomlinson decided that he wanted to cool off. So he ran out into the water and dived. He had done the same thing many times before. But this time the dive was badly executed because he struck his head hard on the sandy bottom. So hard that he broke his neck at the fifth vertebra. He is now a tetraplegic and unable to walk.

4. It is a terrible tragedy to suffer such dreadful injury in consequence of a relatively minor act of carelessness. It came nowhere near the stupidity of Luke Ratcliff, a student who climbed a fence at 2.30 am on a December morning to take a running dive into the shallow end of a swimming pool (see *Ratcliff v McConnell* [1999] 1 WLR 670) or John Donoghue, who dived into Folkestone Harbour from a slipway at midnight on 27 December after an evening in the pub (*Donoghue v Folkestone Properties Ltd* [2003] 2 WLR 1138). John Tomlinson's mind must often recur to that hot day which irretrievably changed his life. He may feel, not unreasonably, that fate has dealt with him unfairly. And so in these proceedings he seeks financial compensation: for the loss of his earning capacity, for the expense of the care he will need, for the loss of the ability to lead an ordinary life. But the law does not provide such compensation simply on the basis that the injury was disproportionately severe in relation to one's own fault or even not one's own fault at all. Perhaps it should, but society might not be able to afford to compensate everyone on that principle, certainly at the level at which such compensation is now paid. The law provides compensation only when the injury was someone else's fault. In order to succeed in his claim, that is what Mr Tomlinson has to prove.

Even stronger words were uttered by Lord Hobhouse who opined:

81. … it is not, and should never be, the policy of the law to require the protection of the foolhardy or reckless few to deprive, or interfere with, the enjoyment by the remainder of society of the liberties and amenities to which they are rightly entitled. Does the law require that all trees be cut down because some youths may climb them and fall? Does the law require the coast line and other beauty spots to be lined with warning notices? Does the law require that attractive water side picnic spots be destroyed because of a few foolhardy individuals who choose to ignore warning notices and indulge in activities dangerous only to themselves? The answer to all these questions is, of course, no.

> But this is the road down which your Lordships, like other courts before, have been invited to travel and which the councils in the present case found so inviting. In truth, the arguments for the claimant have involved an attack upon the liberties of the citizen which should not be countenanced. They attack the liberty of the individual to engage in dangerous, but otherwise harmless, pastimes at his own risk and the liberty of citizens as a whole fully to enjoy the variety and quality of the landscape of this country. The pursuit of an unrestrained culture of blame and compensation has many evil consequences and one is certainly the interference with the liberty of the citizen. The discussion of social utility in the Illinois Supreme Court is to the same effect: *Bucheleres v Chicago Park District* 171 Ill 2d 435, at 457–8.

CBS Songs Ltd v Amstrad Consumer Electronics Plc [1988] AC 1013, 1059 (Lord Templeman)

Similar concerns were raised by the House of Lords when considering a copyright matter where there was also a claim under the tort of negligence:

> Finally B.P.I. submit that Amstrad committed the tort of negligence, that Amstrad owes to all owners of copyright a duty to take care not to cause or permit purchasers to infringe copyright or alternatively that Amstrad owes a duty to take care not to facilitate by the sale of their models or by their advertisement the infringement of copyright. My Lords, it is always easy to draft a proposition which is tailor-made to produce the desired result. Since *Anns v. Merton London Borough Council* [1978] AC 728 put the floodgates on the jar, a fashionable plaintiff alleges negligence. The pleading assumes that we are all neighbours now, Pharisees and Samaritans alike, that forseeability is a reflection of hindsight and that for every mischance in an accident-prone world someone solvent must be liable in damages.

Gorringe v Calderdale Metropolitan Borough Council [2004] UKHL 15, [2004] 1 WLR 1057, [2]

Lord Steyn further highlighted the difficult balance of the courts in this controversial passage:

> 2. There are, however, a few remarks that I would wish to make about negligence and statutory duties and powers. This is a subject of great complexity and very much an evolving area of the law. No single decision is capable of providing a comprehensive analysis. It is a subject on which an intense focus on the particular facts and on the particular statutory background, seen in the context of the contours of our social welfare state, is necessary. On the one hand the courts must not contribute to the creation of a society bent on

litigation, which is premised on the illusion that for every misfortune there is a remedy. On the other hand, there are cases where the courts must recognise on principled grounds the compelling demands of corrective justice or what has been called 'the rule of public policy which has first claim on the loyalty of the law; that wrongs should be remedied': *M (A Minor) v Newham London Borough Council* and *X (Minors) v Bedfordshire County Council* [1995] 2 AC 633, at 663, per Sir Thomas Bingham MR. Sometimes cases may not obviously fall in one category or the other. Truly difficult cases arise.

Despite the wide-ranging concerns regarding the development of a compensation culture, significant academic research highlighted that there was limited – if any – evidence of an over-litigious society.

Kevin Williams, 'State of fear: Britain's "compensation culture" reviewed' (2005) 25 *LS* 499

[I]n 2004, the government's Better Regulation Task Force (the 'Task Force'), drawing on an international review of the cost of just tort claims published two years earlier, listed the UK's expenditure (at 0.6% of GDP) as lower than that of ten other industrialised nations, including Canada (0.8%), Australia (1.1%), Germany (1.3%) and the USA (1.9%); only Denmark spent less. The Task Force report, which government has since largely accepted, denied that Britain is in the grip of a compensation culture, basing itself partly on the opinion of 'almost everyone' who gave evidence to the enquiry and partly on the declining number of personal injury claims registered in recent years.

...

The idea that defendants are beset by ever-increasing numbers of doubtful claims is not proven. Indeed, the 'problem' we started with seems to have come down to this: that whatever may be the *actual* likelihood of irresponsible litigation, many *believe* themselves to be at heightened risk of being unfairly sued. According to the Task Force, this critical misperception or 'urban myth' induces socially and economically damaging risk-averse behaviour. Reputedly, organisations become less innovative, scarce resources that would be better applied elsewhere are unproductively diverted, unnecessarily costly safety precautions are taken, sometimes beneficial activities are fearfully abandoned altogether. It is worth adding that in low trust organisations operating an internal 'blame culture' there is evidence that staff are less likely to report adverse events, while the accuracy of such reports as are made is likely to be questionable.[6]

6 At 501, 508–9 (footnotes omitted).

Annette Morris, 'Spiralling or Stabilising? The Compensation Culture and Our Propensity to Claim Damages for Personal Injury' (2007) 70 *MLR* 349

Much of the public policy debate has focused on whether the compensation culture exists or not. The attraction of the 'compensation culture' sound bite to the media is understandable, but it is an unhelpful medium through which to understand and analyse trends in our propensity to claim. Notions of a compensation culture combine perceived trends with moral and political views. While it is possible to prove or disprove perceived trends, whether these trends are cause for concern is a matter of opinion and interpretation. As such, the compensation culture is not something that does or does not exist. It is all too easy, therefore, for the debate to go round in circles with some denying its existence on one ground and others resurrecting it on another. The Government has sensibly not engaged in a direct discussion about whether the compensation culture exists or not. Nor has it engaged in an in-depth debate about longer-term trends in our propensity to claim and the desirability and sustainability of the tort system. Instead it has focused on short term trends, and as such, has been reassured that there is not an actual problem with overall levels of claiming. The tort system has, for the moment at least, survived the compensation culture debate.

The phenomenon of the 'compensation culture' provides a fascinating case study in *how* our legal consciousness develops. Our knowledge and understanding of trends in our propensity to claim have not developed on the basis of representative and impartial evidence but through a number of inter-related, subtle processes.[7]

The belief in and discussion of a compensation culture, therefore, appears to be much more of a public perception than the reality of tort law in the UK,[8] raising significant issues about the role of public views and the media in our legal system and what factors judges should consider when making their decisions.

Question to consider: Why do you think there was a widespread belief in compensation culture without supportive evidence? Should judges pay attention to these issues in their decisions?

Other resources: Lord Young, 'Common Sense, Common Safety' (Cabinet Office, 2010); Lord Dyson, 'Compensation Culture: Fact or Fantasy?' (Holdsworth Club Lecture, 15 March 2013); Kylie Burns, '"In this Day and Age": Social Facts, Common Sense and Cognition in Tort Law Judging in the United Kingdom' (2018) 45 *JL Society* 226.

7 At 377–78.
8 Morris (op cit).

1.3 Alternative viewpoints of tort law

Tort law is often portrayed as a universal concept, something that protects people's equality regardless of their personal characteristics. In fact, it has often been stated that tort law assists those who are vulnerable to the actions of others – Stapleton argues that this is the 'golden thread' keeping tort law together.

It will come as no surprise to students commencing their studies that the overwhelming majority of voices in the tort law landscape, from both academia and the judiciary, are white male (and often privileged) voices. It *should*, therefore, come as no surprise that this dominance has limited – but not excluded – alternative viewpoints on the role and development of tort law. There is a significant, growing body of academia emphasising the importance of a feminist perspective of tort law. As Chamallas argues:

> If we stop to think about this for a moment, it should come as no surprise that tort law is ripe for feminist analysis. Ever since the writings of the legal realists, we have realized that the major concepts in tort law – duty, negligence, proximate cause and legal injury – are value laden inquiries that cannot be separated from considerations of social policy. Feminist writers are now going beyond the legal realists to investigate the role that gender ideology and unconscious gender bias play in our understanding of these basic tort concepts.[9]

This is not just a theoretical or academic exercise. The role of feminist voices and perspectives can result in different judicial considerations and sometimes different outcomes. In *Michael v Chief Constable of South Wales*, the Supreme Court considered whether the police should be held tortiously liable for the death of a woman at the hands of her violent ex-partner. The police incorrectly labelled the call as not urgent; therefore, the police did not arrive at the victim's house in time to save her. The Supreme Court needed to consider whether the police owed the victim a duty of care in these situations. The majority held that there was no duty owed, with Lord Kerr and Lady Hale providing powerful dissents. In her judgment, Lady Hale – who had previously worked as a family law academic and practitioner – emphasised the important role of human rights and the police in protecting victims of domestic violence.

Michael v The Chief Constable of South Wales Police [2015] UKSC 2, [2015] AC 1732, [196]–[198]

196. Equally, there is no doubt that the police may be liable under the Human Rights Act if they fail in their duties under articles 2 or 3 of the European Convention on Human Rights. This part of the claim is to be sent to trial. The issues under the Human Rights

9 Martha Chamallas, 'Importing Feminist Theories to Change Tort Law' (1997) 11 *Wisconsin Women's LJ* 389, 389.

Act 1998 are not identical to the issues under the law of negligence, but the existence of a human rights claim means that the policy reasons advanced against the imposition of a duty in negligence claim have also 'largely ceased to apply' in a case such as this, where it is alleged that a tragic death would have been averted had the police reacted appropriately to Ms Michael's emergency call.

197. It is for those reasons that I would support the analysis put forward by Lord Kerr: the necessary proximity is supplied if the police know or ought to know of an imminent threat of death or personal injury to a particular individual which they have the means to prevent. Once that proximity is established, it is fair, just and reasonable to expect them to take reasonable care to prevent the harm. This is very close to, though somewhat narrower than, the test proposed by *Tofaris and Steel* (para 189, above). But it is right to acknowledge the strength of the arguments which they so carefully develop, in particular the inter-relationship between the special status and powers of the police to prevent crime and protect people from harm and the limits placed by the law on the ability of people to protect themselves:

> 'A person faced with the threat of violence is permitted by law to take reasonable measures of self-protection, but beyond that her only option is to inform the police. In essence, other than reasonably protecting herself, the law obliges her to entrust her physical safety in the police.' (*Tofaris and Steel*, p 18)

198. However, in developing the law it is wise to proceed on a case by case basis, and the formulation offered by Lord Kerr would be sufficient to enable this claim to go to trial at common law as well as under the Human Rights Act 1998. It is difficult indeed to see how recognising the possibility of such claims could make the task of policing any more difficult than it already is. It might conceivably, however, lead to some much-needed improvements in their response to threats of serious domestic abuse. This continues to be a source of concern to Her Majesty's Inspectorate of Constabulary: see *Everyone's Business: Improving the Police Response to Domestic Abuse* (2014). I very much regret to say that some of the attitudes which have led to the inadequacies revealed in that report may also have crept into the policy considerations discussed in *Smith* (by Lord Carswell at para 107 and Lord Hope at para 76). If the imposition of liability in negligence can help to counter such attitudes, so much the better. But the principles suggested here should apply to all specific threats of imminent injury to individuals which the police are in a position to prevent, whatever their source.

The inclusion of feminist perspectives opens the door to a greater range of voices in developing tort law, which can benefit other marginalised groups. As Conaghan contends, recognising the gendered harm associated with tort law opens the door to consider the membership of a particular class, group, race or gender, which can significantly shape an individual's experiences with the legal system and the harm they suffer.

Joanne Conaghan, 'Gendered Harms and the Law of Tort: Remedying (Sexual) Harassment' (1996) 16 *OJLS* 407

From a social perspective, feminists have argued that women suffer particular harms and injuries *as women*: their experience of pain and injury is distinguishable, to a large extent, from the experience of men. This claim has at least two dimensions. On the one hand pregnancy and childbirth, menstrual and/or ovulation pains are obvious examples of gender-specific 'harms'. Men do not/cannot experience these traumas directly. On the other hand, the concept of gendered harm can also embrace those harms which, although not exclusive to women in any biological sense, are risks which women are more likely to incur than men – the risk of rape, incest, sexual harassment, spousal abuse or, more contentiously, the risk of harmful medical intervention. Although men can and do experience these harms also, they are, arguably, less likely to do so. Moreover, in so far as they do incur such risks, their experience of them as men is different and distinct from how they are experienced by women. As Robin West observes 'the quality of our suffering is different from that of men's, as is the nature of our joy'.

The social claim that women suffer in ways distinct from men translates into a legal critique which evaluates law in terms of its ability to redress harms endured by women. In this context, it is contended that the harms which law recognizes and redresses, whether through tort or other legal mechanisms, are harms suffered, by and large, by men. Harms suffered by women (for example, sexual harassment or the effects of pornography) are not traditionally recognized or remedied by the legal system.

For some, the failure of law to recognize the gender-specificity of harm stems from the liberal content of legal discourse with its accompanying assumption that society is composed of free separate, autonomous individuals, competing with each other in pursuit of their own self-interest. Feminist theory challenges both the notion of separateness and the idea of self-interest as the dominant or even exclusive factor informing human motivation. Feminists have also been deeply sceptical about the value of the traditional liberal preference for non-intervention by the state into social arrangements on the grounds that it conceives of power solely in terms of the effects of the state upon the liberty of the individual and is blind to the way in which social arrangements are shaped and contoured (*inter alia*) by gender. Tort law, viewed as an expression of this liberal preference, has traditionally been blind to the gender dimension in sexual harassment, viewing it simply as a problem (which may or may not give rise to a legal claim) between two individuals rather than as a manifestation of power abuse in gender relations.

Thus, the notion of 'gendered harm' is but one way of recognizing that injury has a social as well as an individual dimension: people suffer harm not just because they are individuals but also because they are part of a particular class, group, race or gender. Moreover, their membership of that particular class, group, race or gender can significantly shape the nature and degree of the harm they sustain. The problem with law then is its failure to recognize that social dimension. Consequently, and in the context of gendered harms, it fails to offer proper redress.[10]

Considering tort law from a feminist perspective could have a remarkable impact in many areas – including police protection, domestic violence, reproductive rights, psychiatric illness and workplace harassment; the list goes on. As you traverse the different topics in your studies, we encourage you to stop and reflect on these issues and the impact that alternative voices can have on the very important debates considered.

Question to consider: How, if at all, would a 'reasonable woman' test differ from the 'reasonable man' test? What implications does this have for tort law?

Other resources: Leslie Bender, 'A Lawyer's Primer on Feminist Theory and Tort' (1988) 38 *J Leg Ed* 3; Janice Richardson and Erika Rackley (eds), *Feminist Perspectives on Tort Law* (Routledge, 2012); Erika Rackley and Kirsty Horsey, 'Tort Law' in Rosemary Auchmuty (ed), *Great Debates in Gender and Law* (Bloomsbury Publishing, 2018); Anita Bernstein, 'Tort as yet another locus of gender injustice in the distribution of money' in Hanoch Dagan and Benjamin C Zipursky (eds), *Research Handbook on Private Law Theory* (Edward Elgar, 2020); Sarah L Swan, 'Tort Law and Feminism' in Deborah Brake, Martha Chamallas and Verna Williams (eds), *The Oxford Handbook of Feminism and Law in the United States* (OUP, 2021).

1.4 Conclusion

Welcome to your tort law studies. We believe it is a fascinating subject full of interesting and important questions. This *Cases and Materials* book aims not only to assist your reading and understanding of the relevant materials but also to broaden your horizons when considering legal and philosophical debates. Tort law requires not just an understanding of the legal principles but also an appreciation of the broader social and political environment and how these two factors relate and interact. Enjoy the journey!

10 At 407–8 (footnotes omitted).

Chapter 2 THE DUTY OF CARE IN NEGLIGENCE

2.1 Establishing a duty of care

Donoghue v Stevenson is a true landmark case. It is the normative foundation on which the tort of negligence is built and, whilst its reasoning alone is no longer sufficient to understand the nuances of the modern tort, its underlying principle remains crucial. In the words that follow, Lord Atkin sets out the very essence of the tort of negligence.

Donoghue v Stevenson [1932] AC 562, 580–81 (Lord Atkin)

> At present I content myself with pointing out that in English law there must be, and is, some general conception of relations giving rise to a duty of care, of which the particular cases found in the books are but instances. The liability for negligence, whether you style it such or treat it as in other systems as a species of 'culpa,' is no doubt based upon a general public sentiment of moral wrongdoing for which the offender must pay. But acts or omissions which any moral code would censure cannot in a practical world be treated so as to give a right to every person injured by them to demand relief. In this way rules of law arise which limit the range of complainants and the extent of their remedy. The rule that you are to love your neighbour becomes in law, you must not injure your neighbour; and the lawyer's question, Who is my neighbour? receives a restricted reply. You must take reasonable care to avoid acts or omissions which you can reasonably foresee would be likely to injure your neighbour. Who, then, in law is my neighbour? The answer seems to be – persons who are so closely and directly affected by my act that I ought reasonably to have them in contemplation as being so affected when I am directing my mind to the acts or omissions which are called in question.

This basic idea, of a duty that potentially applies to all interactions between persons, regardless of whether there is a pre-existing agreement, as there is of course in contract, represented a seismic change in the course of tort law. Before *Donoghue*, tortious liability was restricted to the nominate torts (such as nuisance, defamation or deceit, for example). Therefore, in the absence of a prior contractual agreement, as was the case in *Donoghue* because it was not the injured claimant but her friend who contracted with the retailer, claimants had no general right of redress for the effects of another's negligent conduct. Inevitably, the generality of Lord Atkin's principle soon required development, nuance and qualification. Over half a century later and several cases later, it was reviewed and consolidated at the highest judicial level (which was at the time the Judicial Committee of the House of Lords) in the following case.

Caparo v Dickman [1990] 2 AC 605, 617 (Lord Bridge)

Lord Reid gave a large impetus to the modern approach in Dorset Yacht Co. Ltd. v. Home Office [1970] AC 1004, 1026–1027, where he said:

> 'In later years there has been a steady trend towards regarding the law of negligence as depending on principle so that, when a new point emerges, one should ask not whether it is covered by authority but whether recognised principles apply to it. Donoghue v. Stevenson [1932] AC 562 may be regarded as a milestone, and the well known passage in Lord Atkin's speech should I think be regarded as a statement of principle. It is not to be treated as if it were a statutory definition. It will require qualification in new circumstances. But I think that the time has come when we can and should say that it ought to apply unless there is some justification or valid explanation for its exclusion.'

The most comprehensive attempt to articulate a single general principle is reached in the well known passage from the speech of Lord Wilberforce in Anns v. Merton London Borough Council [1978] AC 728, 751–752:

> 'Through the trilogy of cases in this House – Donoghue v. Stevenson [1932] AC 562, Hedley Byrne & Co. Ltd. v. Heller & Partners Ltd. [1964] AC 465, and Dorset Yacht Co. Ltd. v. Home Office [1970] AC 1004, the position has now been reached that in order to establish that a duty of care arises in a particular situation, it is not necessary to bring the facts of that situation within those of previous situations in which a duty of care has been held to exist. Rather the question has to be approached in two stages. First one has to ask whether, as between the alleged wrongdoer and the person who has suffered damage there is a sufficient relationship of proximity or neighbourhood such that, in the reasonable contemplation of the former, carelessness on his part may be likely to cause damage to the latter – in which case a prima facie duty of care arises. Secondly, if the first question is answered affirmatively, it is necessary to consider whether there are any considerations which ought to negative, or to reduce or limit the scope of the duty or the class of person to whom it is owed or the damages to which a breach of it may give rise: see Dorset Yacht case [1970] AC 1004 *per* Lord Reid at p. 1027.'

But since the Anns case a series of decisions of the Privy Council and of your Lordships' House, notably in judgments and speeches delivered by Lord Keith of Kinkel, **have emphasised the inability of any single general principle to provide a practical test which can be applied to every situation to determine whether a duty of care is owed** and, if so, what is its scope: see Governors of Peabody Donation Fund v. Sir Lindsay Parkinson & Co. Ltd. [1985] AC 210, 239f–241c; Yuen Kun Yeu v. Attorney-General of Hong Kong [1988] A.C. 175, 190e–194f; Rowling v. Takaro Properties Ltd. [1988] AC 473, 501d–g; Hill v. Chief Constable of West Yorkshire [1989] AC 53, 60b–d. **What emerges is that,**

in addition to the foreseeability of damage, necessary ingredients in any situation giving rise to a duty of care are that there should exist between the party owing the duty and the party to whom it is owed a relationship characterised by the law as one of 'proximity' or 'neighbourhood' and that the situation should be one in which the court considers it fair, just and reasonable that the law should impose a duty of a given scope upon the one party for the benefit of the other. But it is implicit in the passages referred to that the concepts of proximity and fairness embodied in these additional ingredients are not susceptible of any such precise definition as would be necessary to give them utility as practical tests, but amount in effect to little more than convenient labels to attach to the features of different specific situations which, on a detailed examination of all the circumstances, the law recognises pragmatically as giving rise to a duty of care of a given scope. Whilst recognising, of course, the importance of the underlying general principles common to the whole field of negligence, I think the law has now moved in the direction of attaching greater significance to the more traditional categorisation of distinct and recognisable situations as guides to the existence, the scope and the limits of the varied duties of care which the law imposes. We must now, I think, recognise the wisdom of the words of Brennan J. in the High Court of Australia in Sutherland Shire Council v. Heyman (1985) 60 A.L.R. 1, 43–44, where he said:

> 'It is preferable, in my view, that the law should develop novel categories of negligence incrementally and by analogy with established categories, rather than by a massive extension of a prima facie duty of care restrained only by indefinable "considerations which ought to negative, or to reduce or limit the scope of the duty or the class of person to whom it is owed."'

On reading these words from Lord Bridge when he handed them down in 1992, one would be forgiven for thinking that his Lordship was making it clear that there is no such thing as a practical test, able to determine on any given facts whether a duty of care in negligence exists. And yet, in an ironic twist, the very judgment in which Lord Bridge seemed to make this explicit was used and referred to over the next couple of decades as just such a test.[1] The '*Caparo* test', as it was often referred to, had the following ingredients (and so was often referred to as the tripartite or threefold test):

- Was the damage reasonably foreseeable?
- Was there a sufficiently proximate relationship between the parties?
- Would it be 'fair, just and reasonable' for the court to impose a duty of care, having regard to policy concerns?

1 See Lord Bingham in *Van Colle v Chief Constable of the Hertfordshire Police (Secretary of State for the Home Department intervening)* [2009] 1 AC 225 at [42], who (in a rare moment of fallibility) describes the *Caparo* considerations as 'the most favoured test of liability'.

This approach to the *Caparo* criteria has gradually changed in recent years: Lord Toulson said in *Michael v Chief Constable of South Wales* (a case to which we will return in detail below):[2]

> In *Caparo Plc v Dickman* [1990] 2 AC 605 Lord Bridge (with whom Lords Roskill, Ackner and Oliver of Aylmerton agreed) emphasised the inability of any single general principle to provide a practical test which could be applied to every situation to determine whether a duty of care is owed and, if so, what is its scope. He said, at pp 617–618, that there must be not only foreseeability of damage, but there must also exist between the party owing the duty and the party to whom it is owed a relationship characterised by the law as one of 'proximity' or 'neighbourhood', and the situation should be one in which the court considers it fair, just and reasonable that the court should impose a duty of a given scope on one party for the benefit of the other. He added that the concepts both of 'proximity' and 'fairness' were not susceptible of any definition which would make them useful as practical tests, but were little more than labels to attach to features of situations which the law recognised as giving rise to a duty of care. Paradoxically, this passage in Lord Bridge's speech has sometimes come to be treated as a blueprint for deciding cases, despite the pains which the author took to make clear that it was not intended to be any such thing.[3]

Three years later, the Supreme Court once more analysed the approach that should be taken to establishing whether a duty of care in negligence should arise in a novel fact situation. The analysis of Lord Reed in particular in this next case is enormously helpful for understanding the current common law concept of the duty of care in negligence. The extracts that follow across this chapter are, as a consequence, fairly extensive, but amount to a crucial account of the current position. Knowing this judgment well will mean that you can master one of the trickiest inquiries in the law of tort.

In the first part extracted here, Lord Reed explains the relevance of, and role played by, the *Caparo* considerations in the duty of care inquiry. In so doing, he also puts it in an historical context:

Robinson v Chief Constable of West Yorkshire [2018] UKSC 4, [2018] 2 WLR 595, [21]–[27], [29]

21. The proposition that there is a Caparo test which applies to all claims in the modern law of negligence, and that in consequence the court will only impose a duty of care where it considers it fair, just and reasonable to do so on the particular facts, is mistaken. As Lord Toulson pointed out in his landmark judgment in *Michael v Chief Constable of South Wales*

2 [2015] UKSC 2.

3 ibid at [106].

Police (Refuge and others intervening) [2015] UKSC 2; [2015] AC 1732, para 106, that understanding of the case mistakes the whole point of Caparo, which was to repudiate the idea that there is a single test which can be applied in all cases in order to determine whether a duty of care exists, and instead to adopt an approach based, in the manner characteristic of the common law, on precedent, and on the development of the law incrementally and by analogy with established authorities.

22. *Caparo* was decided in the aftermath of Lord Wilberforce's attempt in *Anns v Merton London Borough Council* [1978] AC 728, 751–752 to lay down an approach which could be applied in all situations in order to determine the existence of a duty of care. That approach had two stages: first, it was necessary to decide whether there was a prima facie duty of care, based on the foreseeability of harm, and secondly, in order to place limits on the breadth of the first stage, it was necessary to consider whether there were reasons of public policy for excluding or restricting any such prima facie duty. That approach had major implications for public authorities, as they have a multitude of functions designed to protect members of the public from harm of one kind or another, with the consequence that the first stage enquiry was readily satisfied, and the only limit to liability became public policy.

23. *Anns* led to a period during which the courts struggled to contain liability, particularly for economic loss unassociated with physical damage or personal injury, and for the acts and omissions of public authorities. Commenting extra-judicially during that period, Lord Oliver of Aylmerton said that 'what has been seen as a principle of prima facie liability has been prayed in aid in subsequent cases to justify claims for damages which have become progressively more divorced from common sense and as placing on the defendant a burden, sometimes virtually insurmountable, of showing some good reason in "policy" why he should not be held liable': 'Judicial Legislation: Retreat from *Anns*', Third Sultan Azlan Shah Law Lecture (1988). It was in the context of the retreat from *Anns* that emphasis was placed in a number of cases on the concept of 'proximity', and on the idea that it must be fair to impose a duty of care on the defendant.

24. In *Caparo*, Lord Bridge of Harwich noted that, since *Anns*, a series of decisions of the Privy Council and the House of Lords, notably in judgments and speeches delivered by Lord Keith of Kinkel (including his speech in *Hill v Chief Constable of West Yorkshire*), had emphasised 'the inability of any single general principle to provide a practical test which can be applied to every situation to determine whether a duty of care is owed and, if so, what is its scope' (p 617). It is ironic that the immediately following passage in Lord Bridge's speech has been treated as laying down such a test, despite, as Lord Toulson remarked in *Michael*, the pains which he took to make clear that it was not intended to be any such thing:

> 'What emerges [from the post-*Anns* decisions] is that, in addition to the foreseeability of damage, necessary ingredients in any situation giving rise to a duty of care are that there should exist between the party owing the duty and the party to whom it is owed a relationship characterised by the law as one of "proximity" or "neighbourhood" and

> that the situation should be one in which the court considers it fair, just and reasonable that the law should impose a duty of a given scope upon the one party for the benefit of the other. But it is implicit in the passages referred to that *the concepts of proximity and fairness embodied in these additional ingredients are not susceptible of any such precise definition as would be necessary to give them utility as practical tests, but amount in effect to little more than convenient labels to attach to the features of different specific situations which, on a detailed examination of all the circumstances, the law recognises pragmatically as giving rise to a duty of care of a given scope.*' (pp 617–618; emphasis added)

25. Lord Bridge immediately went on to adopt an incremental approach, based on the use of established authorities to provide guidance as to how novel questions should be decided:

> 'I think the law has now moved in the direction of attaching greater significance to the more traditional categorisation of distinct and recognisable situations as guides to the existence, the scope and the limits of the varied duties of care which the law imposes ...'

It was that approach, and not a supposed tripartite test, which Lord Bridge then proceeded to apply to the facts before him.

26. Applying the approach adopted in *Caparo*, there are many situations in which it has been clearly established that a duty of care is or is not owed: for example, by motorists to other road users, by manufacturers to consumers, by employers to their employees, and by doctors to their patients. As Lord Browne-Wilkinson explained in *Barrett v Enfield London Borough Council* [2001] 2 AC 550, 560, 'Once the decision is taken that, say, company auditors though liable to shareholders for negligent auditing are not liable to those proposing to invest in the company ... that decision will apply to all future cases of the same kind'. Where the existence or non-existence of a duty of care has been established, a consideration of justice and reasonableness forms part of the basis on which the law has arrived at the relevant principles. It is therefore unnecessary and inappropriate to reconsider whether the existence of the duty is fair, just and reasonable (subject to the possibility that this court may be invited to depart from an established line of authority). Nor, a fortiori, can justice and reasonableness constitute a basis for discarding established principles and deciding each case according to what the court may regard as its broader merits. Such an approach would be a recipe for inconsistency and uncertainty, as Hobhouse LJ recognised in *Perrett v Collins* [1999] PNLR 77, 90–91:

> 'It is a truism to say that any case must be decided taking into account the circumstances of the case, but where those circumstances comply with established categories of liability, a defendant should not be allowed to seek to escape from liability by appealing to some vaguer concept of justice or fairness; the law cannot be re-made for every case. Indeed, the previous authorities have by necessary implication held that it is fair, just and reasonable that the plaintiff should recover in the situations falling within the principles they have applied.'

27. It is normally only in a novel type of case, where established principles do not provide an answer, that the courts need to go beyond those principles in order to decide whether a duty of care should be recognised. Following *Caparo*, the characteristic approach of the common law in such situations is to develop incrementally and by analogy with established authority. The drawing of an analogy depends on identifying the legally significant features of the situations with which the earlier authorities were concerned. The courts also have to exercise judgement when deciding whether a duty of care should be recognised in a novel type of case. It is the exercise of judgement in those circumstances that involves consideration of what is 'fair, just and reasonable'. As Lord Millett observed in *McFarlane v Tayside Health Board* [2000] 2 AC 59, 108, the court is concerned to maintain the coherence of the law and the avoidance of inappropriate distinctions if injustice is to be avoided in other cases. But it is also 'engaged in a search for justice, and this demands that the dispute be resolved in a way which is fair and reasonable and accords with ordinary notions of what is fit and proper'.

…

29. Properly understood, *Caparo* thus achieves a balance between legal certainty and justice. In the ordinary run of cases, courts consider what has been decided previously and follow the precedents (unless it is necessary to consider whether the precedents should be departed from). In cases where the question whether a duty of care arises has not previously been decided, the courts will consider the closest analogies in the existing law, with a view to maintaining the coherence of the law and the avoidance of inappropriate distinctions. They will also weigh up the reasons for and against imposing liability, in order to decide whether the existence of a duty of care would be just and reasonable. In the present case, however, the court is not required to consider an extension of the law of negligence. All that is required is the application to particular circumstances of established principles governing liability for personal injuries.

Paragraphs 27 and 29, emphasised above, really form the crux of this important judgment. They provide the tools (as opposed to a 'test') for a court to use in establishing whether a duty of care in negligence arises. The process is an incremental one, requiring a court to establish whether the facts before it are similar in a legally significant way to the facts of those cases in which a duty has previously been found. The considerations of fairness, justice and reasonableness can then play a part to allow the court to balance its factual finding against those broader principles.

Before we return to the other salient features of *Robinson*, it makes sense to look at a recent case in which this method was applied, again by the Supreme Court, to a novel duty situation. In the following case, the claimants were police officers who alleged that the Commissioner had been negligent in defending proceedings brought against her by a suspected terrorist. In those proceedings, the suspect claimed that the Commissioner's officers (the claimants) had subjected him to gratuitous violence during his arrest, and that she was vicariously liable for his damage. In not conducting her defence reasonably, the officers claimed that the Commissioner had thereby caused them reputational and economic harm, and that she owed them a duty of care in relation to these interests.

James-Bowen v Commissioner of Police for the Metropolis [2018] UKSC 40, [2018] 1 WLR 4021, [22]–[26], [30]–[33] (Lord Lloyd-Jones)

It begins with an introduction to the duty of care question:

22. In the present case the courts below have proceeded on the basis that, with the exception of the claim in respect of psychiatric injury which is no longer pursued, harm was arguably foreseeable. Furthermore, it was clearly arguable that by virtue of their relationship, akin to that of employer and employee, the parties were in a sufficiently proximate relationship to give rise to a duty of care. The argument therefore focussed on whether the imposition of a duty of care was fair, just and reasonable as indicated in *Caparo*. In *Robinson v Chief Constable of West Yorkshire Police* [2018] UKSC 4; [2018] 2 WLR 595 this court recently held, with regard to this aspect of *Caparo*, that it is normally only in a novel type of case, where established principles do not provide an answer, that the courts need to go beyond those principles in order to decide whether a duty of care should be recognised. Since the police generally owe a duty of care not to inflict physical injury by their actions when such a duty arises under the ordinary principles of the law of negligence, unless statute or other common law principle provides otherwise, there was no requirement in that case to examine whether the recognition of the claimed duty would be fair, just and reasonable. However, this ingredient will be of critical importance in a situation where it is proposed that a duty of care should be imposed in novel circumstances. ...

23. Contrary to the submission of Mr Bowen on behalf of the officers, the present case is very clearly one in which it is sought to extend a duty of care to a new situation. As Lord Reed explained in *Robinson*, in determining whether such a duty should be recognised the law will proceed incrementally and by analogy with previous decisions. ...

The theme was developed by Lord Bingham in *Customs and Excise Comrs v Barclays Bank plc* [2007] 1 AC 181 where he observed at para 7:

> '... I incline to agree with the view ... that the incremental test is of little value as a test in itself, and is only helpful when used in combination with a test or principle which identifies the legally significant features of a situation. The closer the facts of the case in issue to those of a case in which a duty of care has been held to exist, the readier a court will be, on the approach of Brennan J adopted in *Caparo Industries plc v Dickman*, to find that there has been an assumption of responsibility or that the proximity and policy conditions of the threefold test are satisfied. The converse is also true.'

In addition, the proposed duty will be tested against considerations of legal policy and judgement will have to be exercised with particular regard to both the achievement of justice in the particular case and the coherent development of the law.

And here begins the incremental analogy bit:

24. The law protects reputation in a variety of ways in different circumstances. Causes of action such as libel, slander, malicious falsehood and passing off are designed to protect reputation. Moreover, a variety of other causes of action including breach of confidence, misuse of private information and causes of action in relation to data protection and intellectual property may often indirectly achieve this result. The common law does not usually recognise a duty of care in the tort of negligence to protect reputational interests. However, there are exceptions. In *Spring v Guardian Assurance plc* [1995] 2 AC 296 a majority of the House of Lords held that an employer who gave a reference in respect of a former employee owed that employee a duty to take reasonable care in its preparation and would be liable to him in negligence for a breach of duty which caused him economic loss. Lord Lowry, Lord Slynn and Lord Woolf reached this conclusion on the basis of the three ingredients identified by Lord Bridge in *Caparo*. Lord Goff (at p 316E-F) concluded that a duty of care was owed to the former employee on a narrower ground. In his view the source of the duty of care was the principle in *Hedley Byrne & Co Ltd v Heller & Partners Ltd* [1964] AC 465 ie an assumption of responsibility by the authors of the reference to the plaintiff in respect of the reference, and reliance by the plaintiff upon the exercise by them of due care and skill in respect of its preparation. This case was essentially concerned with negligent mis-statement and it may be that assumption of responsibility is the better rationalisation of the recognition of a duty in these circumstances. (See *NRAM Ltd (formerly NRAM plc) v Steel* [2018] UKSC 13; [2018] 1 WLR 1190 per Lord Wilson at para 24 referring also to *Henderson v Merrett Syndicates Ltd* [1995] 2 AC 145 per Lord Goff at p 181 and *Williams v Natural Life Health Foods Ltd* [1998] 1 WLR 830 per Lord Steyn at p 837.)

25. This decision should be contrasted with *Calveley v Chief Constable of the Merseyside Police* [1989] 1 AC 1228. Following their reinstatement, police officers, against whom disciplinary proceedings had been taken, brought actions in negligence against their Chief Constables on the basis that they were vicariously liable for the investigating officers. The claimants alleged that the investigating officers had failed to conduct the proceedings properly or expeditiously and claimed, inter alia, damages in respect of loss of overtime earnings during their suspension and damages for injury to reputation. The House of Lords considered the submission that a duty of care was owed to the claimants to be unsustainable. First, Lord Bridge explained (at p 1238B-G), anxiety, vexation and injury to reputation did not constitute reasonably foreseeable damage capable of sustaining an action in negligence within *Donoghue v Stevenson* [1932] AC 562. Secondly, it was not reasonably foreseeable that the negligent conduct of a criminal investigation would cause injury to the health of the suspect, whether in the form of depressive illness or otherwise. Thirdly, while it is reasonably foreseeable that a suspect may suffer some economic loss which might have been avoided had more careful investigation established his innocence at an earlier stage, such a claim would encounter the formidable obstacles in the path of liability in negligence for purely economic loss. Fourthly, it would be contrary to public

policy to prejudice the discharge by police officers of their public duty of investigating crime by requiring them to act under the shadow of a potential action for damages for negligence by the suspect.

26. To my mind *Calveley* has an important bearing on the present case. If a Chief Constable does not, in principle, owe a duty of care to protect the economic and reputational interests of his officers in respect of the prosecution of an investigation or disciplinary proceedings, it is difficult to see why he should owe a duty to his officers as to the manner in which he defends a claim brought against him by a third party. In the former situation the Chief Constable has himself initiated the investigation or proceedings over which he has at least a substantial measure of control and he is responsible for making allegations against officers. In the latter situation his role is essentially responsive to allegations made by third parties.

And here the balancing consideration in terms of what is 'fair, just and reasonable':

30. The interests of an employer who is sued on the basis that he is vicariously liable for the tortious conduct of his employees differ fundamentally from the interests of those employees. The financial, commercial and reputational standing of the employer may be at stake. It is the employer who will incur the cost of defending the proceedings which, however successful the defence may be, is most unlikely to be recovered in full, and who, if unsuccessful, will bear the liability to the claimant. The employer must be able to make his own investigation into the claim and to assess its strength based on the conduct of his employee and the prospects of a successful defence. In this regard, he will need to form his own view as to the reliability and veracity of his employee and as to how the employee is likely to perform as a witness. The interests of insurers may have to be taken into account. The employer will have to decide what degree of importance he attaches to successfully defending the claim and what financial and other resources should be devoted to its defence. He may consider that, however strong the prospects of a successful defence, he cannot justify the cost and effort of defending the claim and that it should, therefore, be settled. The predominant interest of the employee, by contrast, will be that his reputation should be vindicated. The position will often be complicated further by the existence of inconsistent views or interests between different employees or groups of employees. (See, for example, *Mohidin v Comr of Police of the Metropolis* [2016] EWHC 105 (QB) (Gilbart J) [2016] 1 Costs LR 71, para 14)

31. In cases where an employer is alleged to be vicariously liable for the tortious conduct of his employee, the possibility of contribution proceedings between employer and employee highlights this potential conflict of interests. It is particularly relevant here that claims under the Civil Liability (Contribution) Act 1978 may be brought up to two years after judgment in the original claim or settlement of that claim (Limitation Act 1980, section 10). That the possibility of bringing such a claim is not fanciful, at least in cases where deliberate misconduct is alleged, is demonstrated by *Mohidin v Comr of Police of the Metropolis* where such a claim succeeded.

32. These stark differences between the interests of employer and employee strongly suggest that it would not be fair, just or reasonable to impose on an employer a duty of care to defend legal proceedings so as to protect the economic or reputational interests of his employee. Nor do I consider it realistic to suggest, as do the respondents in the present case, that this potential for conflict can be overcome by the recognition of a duty of care up to the time at which an actual conflict of interests arises, at which point 'timeous notification' by the Commissioner could result in the duty of care ceasing to apply. Where an employer defends a claim against him founded on his vicarious liability for his employees, the potential for conflict is too great to permit such a compromise. Moreover, it would often be totally impracticable. A civil claim and its defence, as they proceed, often develop in unexpected ways. There could be no justification for imposing on an employer the burden of keeping under review at each stage of the proceedings the question whether an actual conflict has arisen. Furthermore, steps taken by the employee as a result of such 'timeous notification' of the emergence of an actual conflict may well be disruptive of the litigation.

33. In the present case, moreover, the Commissioner is not merely in a position analogous to that of an employer. She also holds public office and has responsibility for the Metropolitan Police Service. This adds a further dimension to this appeal because in the conduct of the proceedings against her she must be free to act as she considers appropriate in accordance with her public duty. This duty is, to my mind, totally inconsistent with her owing a duty of care to protect the reputational interests of her employees when defending litigation based on vicarious liability for their alleged misconduct. As we have seen, in *Calveley* the House concluded that it would be contrary to public policy to prejudice the discharge by the police of their public duty to investigate alleged misconduct by officers by imposing a conflicting duty of care to protect the reputational interests of those officers. In the same way in *SXH* this court considered (at para 38) that to recognise a duty of care owed by the CPS to victims or suspects would not be conducive to the best interests of the criminal justice system. These considerations apply with equal force to the present case.

Recent Supreme Court decisions on the question of duty of care provide much assistance to those trying to gain an understanding of it, not least because they deal with the considerations in an express and candid way. They also make fairly extensive reference to each other, making it clear therefore how each can be distinguished from the other and which part each plays. In the case extracted below, Lord Lloyd-Jones sets out clearly the difference between how a court will approach established and novel duty situations.

In this case, the claimant attended the defendant's Accident and Emergency Department, having incurred a head injury. The administrative receptionist on duty informed him that he would have to wait up to four or five hours before being seen by a medical practitioner. In fact, the standard procedure at the hospital was for head injury patients to be seen within 30 minutes by a triage nurse. As a result of being giving misleading information about the likely length of his wait, the claimant decided that he felt too ill to stay in the waiting room, and went home to bed. Had he known that he was likely to be seen within 30 minutes, he would have stayed and been examined. He later had to undergo emergency neurosurgery and was left with permanent brain damage as a result of his injuries. Both the trial judge and the Court of Appeal found in favour of the NHS Trust, the latter by majority on the basis that the hospital owed no duty of care to advise patients about waiting times. The Supreme Court allowed the claimant's appeal, finding that the case fell within an established duty of care situation for NHS Trusts.

Darnley v Croydon Health Services NHS Trust [2018] UKSC 50, [2019] AC 831, [15]–[17], [20], [24]–[27] (Lord Lloyd-Jones)

15. First, we are not here concerned with the imposition of a duty of care in a novel situation. The common law in this jurisdiction has abandoned the search for a general principle capable of providing a practical test applicable in every situation in order to determine whether a duty of care is owed and, if so, what is its scope. (*Caparo Industries plc v Dickman* [1990] 2 AC 605 per Lord Bridge at p 617; *Michael v Chief Constable of South Wales Police (Refuge intervening)* [2015] AC 1732 per Lord Toulson at para 106; *Robinson v Chief Constable of West Yorkshire Police* [2018] 2 WLR 595 per Lord Reed at para 24). In the absence of such a universal touchstone, it has taken as a starting point established categories of specific situations where a duty of care is recognised and it has been willing to move beyond those situations on an incremental basis, accepting or rejecting a duty of care in novel situations by analogy with established categories (*Caparo* per Lord Bridge at p 618 citing Brennan J in the High Court of Australia in *Sutherland Shire Council v Heyman* (1985) 60 ALR 1, at pp 43–44). **The familiar statement of principle by Lord Bridge in *Caparo* at pp 617–618 in which he refers to the ingredients of foreseeability of damage, proximity and fairness does not require a re-evaluation of whether those criteria are satisfied on every occasion on which an established category of duty is applied. In particular, as Lord Reed demonstrated in his judgment in *Robinson* (at paras 26, 27), where the existence of a duty of care has previously been established, a consideration of justice and reasonableness has already been taken into account in arriving at the relevant principles and it is, normally, only in cases where the court is asked to go beyond the established categories of duty of care that it will be necessary to consider whether it would be fair, just and reasonable to impose such a duty.** The recent decision of the Supreme Court in *James-Bowen v Comr of Police of the Metropolis* [2018] 1 WLR 4021 was such a case and it was necessary for the court on that occasion to consider whether extension by analogy of established categories of duty was justified and the policy implications of such an extension. By contrast, *Robinson* itself involved no more than the application of a well-established category of duty of care and all that was required was the application to particular circumstances of established principles.

16. In the present case Jackson LJ observed (at para 53) that to hold the respondent responsible would create 'a new head of liability for NHS health trusts'. To my mind, however, **the present case falls squarely within an established category of duty of care.**

It has long been established that such a duty is owed by those who provide and run a casualty department to persons presenting themselves complaining of illness or injury and before they are treated or received into care in the hospital's wards. The duty is one to take reasonable care not to cause physical injury to the patient (*Barnett v Chelsea and Kensington Hospital Management Committee* [1969] 1 QB 428, per Nield J at pp 435–436). In the present case, as soon as the appellant had attended at the respondent's A & E department seeking medical attention for the injury he had sustained, had provided the information requested by the receptionist and had been 'booked in', he was accepted into the system and entered into a relationship with the respondent of patient and health care provider. The damage complained of is physical injury and not economic loss. This is a distinct and recognisable situation in which the law imposes a duty of care. Moreover, the scope of the duty to take reasonable care not to act in such a way as foreseeably to cause such a patient to sustain physical injury clearly extends to a duty to take reasonable care not to provide misleading information which may foreseeably cause physical injury. While it is correct that no authority has been cited in these proceedings which deals specifically with misleading information provided by a receptionist in an A & E department causing physical injury, it is not necessary to address, in every instance where the precise factual situation has not previously been the subject of a reported judicial decision, whether it would be fair, just and reasonable to impose a duty of care. It is sufficient that the case falls within an established category in which the law imposes a duty of care.

17. Secondly, this duty of care is owed by the hospital trust and it is not appropriate to distinguish, in this regard, between medical and non-medical staff. In the specific context of this case, where misleading information was provided as to the time within which medical attention might be available, it is not appropriate to distinguish between medically qualified professionals and administrative staff in determining whether there was a duty of care. That distinction may well be highly relevant in deciding whether there was a negligent breach of duty; there the degree of skill which can reasonably be expected of a person will be likely to depend on the responsibility with which he or she is charged. In the present circumstances, however, questions as to the existence and scope of a duty of care owed by the trust should not depend on whether the misleading information was provided by a person who was or was not medically qualified. The respondent had charged its non-medically qualified staff with the role of being the first point of contact with persons seeking medical assistance and, as a result, with the responsibility for providing accurate information as to its availability.

…

20. … For the reasons explained earlier in this judgment, in deciding whether a duty of care is owed in the present circumstances it is not necessary to proceed incrementally by analogy with decided cases because no extension of an established category of duty is called for here. …

…

24. The reception desk at the A & E department was the first point of contact between the respondent trust and members of the public seeking medical assistance. It has not been suggested that the respondent was in any way at fault in allocating this responsibility to receptionists who were not medically qualified. Moreover, it has not been suggested that the receptionists should have provided accurate information to each patient on arrival as to precisely when he or she would be seen by a medically qualified member of staff. Anyone who has any experience of A & E departments will know that this would be impossible. The pressures on medical staff are enormous, the demand for attention is constantly fluctuating and priorities are likely to change. However, it is not unreasonable to require receptionists to take reasonable care not to provide misleading information as to the likely availability of medical assistance.

25. The particular role performed by the individual concerned will be likely to have an important bearing on the question of breach of the duty of care. As Mustill LJ explained in *Wilsher v Essex Area Health Authority* [1987] QB 730, 750–751, the legitimate expectation of the patient is that he will receive from each person concerned with his care a degree of skill appropriate to the task which he or she undertakes. A receptionist in an A & E department cannot, of course, be expected to give medical advice or information but he or she can be expected to take reasonable care not to provide misleading advice as to the availability of medical assistance. The standard required is that of an averagely competent and well-informed person performing the function of a receptionist at a department providing emergency medical care.

26. Responding to requests for information as to the usual system of operation of the A & E department was well within the area of responsibility of the receptionists. The two receptionists on duty at the material time were both aware that the standard procedure was that anyone complaining of a head injury would be seen by a triage nurse and they accepted that the usual practice was that such a patient would be told that they would be seen by a triage nurse within 30 minutes of arrival (Mrs Ashley) or as soon as possible (Mrs Reeves-Bristow). No reason has been suggested as to why the appellant was not told of the standard procedure. The hospital was operating within the acceptable range of triage timing agreed by the experts and the actual position was that the appellant, had he remained, would have been seen by a triage nurse within 30 minutes because he was complaining of a head injury. It is not unreasonable to require that patients in the position of the appellant should be provided on arrival, whether orally by a receptionist, by leaflet or prominent notice, with accurate information that they would normally be seen by a triage nurse within 30 minutes.

27. However, instead the appellant was simply told that he would have to wait for up to four or five hours to see a doctor. That information was incomplete and misleading. The Chief Executive of the respondent described it in his letter to the appellant dated 23 March 2011 as 'completely incorrect'. The appellant was misinformed as to the true position and, as a result, misled as to the availability of medical assistance. The trial judge made the critical finding that it was reasonably foreseeable that a person who believes that it may be four or

five hours before he will be seen by a doctor may decide to leave. In the light of that finding I have no doubt that the provision of such misleading information by a receptionist as to the time within which medical assistance might be available was negligent.

One of the principal takeaways from all of these cases is that this is a tricky area. The best (and only) thing that can be done, whether by students or by Supreme Court Justices, is to know the case law and apply it as appropriate to a given set of facts. In the article extracted below, Donal Nolan unpacks the concept and provides some suggestions as to why it is so infamously difficult.

Donal Nolan, 'Deconstructing the Duty of Care' (2013) 129(Oct) *LQR* 559–88

[At 581:] To give a flavour of the malleability of the duty enquiry, consider the following formulations of the notional duty question, all taken from English cases decided since 1995:

- Do those responsible for issuing a company's prospectus owe a duty of care to persons who rely upon it by subsequently buying shares of that company in the market?
- Does the fire brigade owe a duty of care to an owner of property if they respond to an emergency call about a fire at the property, arrive at the scene and start to fight the fire?
- Does a health and safety inspector owe a duty of care to a business in respect of economic loss caused by a notice issued on his advice under the Health and Safety at Work Act 1974?
- Does an insurance company which advises a customer on insurance provision for pension and life cover owe a duty of care to dependants of the customer whose interests are fundamental to the transaction in question not to give the customer negligent advice which will adversely affect their interests as the customer intended them to be?
- Do the professionals involved in compiling reports for adoption agencies on children up for adoption owe a duty of care to prospective adopters?
- Did the British Geological Survey owe a duty of care to the population of Bangladesh not to publish a report which implied by its silence that it believed that the presence of arsenic in the water in that country was so unlikely that it was not necessary to test for it?

The extraordinary malleability of the duty question as revealed by these examples is a disadvantage of the duty concept for three reasons: (1) because it makes it difficult to summarise the law in a given field of negligence with any precision; (2) because it creates a danger that a court will overlook an earlier duty decision which has either resolved or is at least closely analogous to the central question of law raised by the facts of the case; and (3) because the tendency revealed by at least some of these examples to formulate the duty question in an overly specific manner threatens to return negligence law to the 'wilderness of single instances' which characterised the field before the great generalising decision in *Donoghue v Stevenson*.

This last point highlights the perennial tension that runs through much of the common law between certainty and flexibility: common law incrementalism and judicial development often means a more agile approach to shifting social behaviours and mores, but it can also mean, as Nolan points out, that this is achieved at the expense of certainty and predictability.

A duty of care question that has given rise to much discussion over the years is that of public authority liability; that is, when will public bodies have a primary private law duty of care towards individuals?[4] Arguably, this is now one of the duty of care questions in relation to which there is a degree of certainty and predictability, especially in the case of police liability. To illustrate, we will return to a couple of important cases that have already been introduced: *Michael* and *Robinson*. In the first of these, Lord Toulson grasps the nettle in the following paragraphs:

Michael v Chief Constable of South Wales [2015] UKSC 2, [2015] AC 1732, [114]–[116], [118]–[120], [138] (Lord Toulson)

> 114. It does not follow from the setting up of a protective system from public resources that if it fails to achieve its purpose, through organisational defects or fault on the part of an individual, the public at large should bear the additional burden of compensating a victim for harm caused by the actions of a third party for whose behaviour the state is not responsible. To impose such a burden would be contrary to the ordinary principles of the common law.
>
> 115. The refusal of the courts to impose a private law duty on the police to exercise reasonable care to safeguard victims or potential victims of crime, except in cases where there has been a representation and reliance, does not involve giving special treatment to the police. It is consistent with the way in which the common law has been applied to other authorities vested with powers or duties as a matter of public law for the protection of the public. Examples at the highest level include *Yuen Kun Yeu v Attorney-General of Hong Kong* [1988] AC 175 and *Davis v Radcliffe* [1990] 1 WLR 821 (no duty of care owed by financial regulators towards investors), *Murphy v Brentwood District Council* (no duty of care owed to the owner of a house with defective foundations by the local authority which passed the plans), *Stovin v Wise* and *Gorringe v Calderdale Metropolitan Borough Council* (no duty of care owed by a highway authority to take action to prevent accidents from known hazards).
>
> 116. The question is therefore not whether the police should have a special immunity, but whether an exception should be made to the ordinary application of common law principles which would cover the facts of the present case.

Paragraph 116 here is responding to a belief that had grown up in the wake of *Hill v Chief Constable of West Yorkshire*[5] that the police had an 'immunity' to claims in negligence. In that case the claimant's daughter was the last person to be killed by

4 To be distinguished from vicarious (secondary) liability, for which see Chapter 15.
5 [1989] AC 53.

Peter Sutcliffe, the serial killer known as the Yorkshire Ripper. The claim was based on the argument that the police had breached their duty of care in carrying out their investigation and that, had they not done so, Sutcliffe would have been caught before he killed his final victim. The House of Lords held, in agreement with the first instance judge, that the police owed no duty of care to the public to apprehend criminals, and the claim was accordingly struck out. Lord Keith's judgment was significant for two reasons: first, for its account of why there was insufficient proximity on the facts of this case for a duty of care to arise. The second reason was his infamous use of the word 'immunity' when referring to the police and their relationship to the tort of negligence. In the more recent cases examined here, it has been made clear that there is no such immunity (if indeed there ever really was – although Lord Keith used that word, his judgment viewed holistically does not substantiate it). Rather than the police being immune from suit, Lord Toulson makes clear here that the question is really whether they should have a duty of care imposed upon them *because* they are a public body, or whether the inquiry should proceed in relation to them in the same way as it does to private individuals.

118. I recognise fully that the statistics about the incidence of domestic violence and the facts of individual cases such as the present are shocking. I recognise also that the court has been presented with fresh material on the subject. However, I am not persuaded that they should cause the court to create a new category of duty of care for several reasons.

119. If the foundation of a duty of care is the public law duty of the police for the preservation of the Queen's peace, it is hard to see why the duty should be confined to potential victims of a particular kind of breach of the peace. Would a duty of care be owed to a person who reported a credible threat to burn down his house? Would it be owed to a company which reported a credible threat by animal rights extremists to its premises? If not, why not?

120. It is also hard to see why it should be limited to particular potential victims. If the police fail through lack of care to catch a criminal before he shoots and injures his intended victim and also a bystander (or if he misses his intended target and hits someone else), is it right that one should be entitled to compensation but not the other, when the duty of the police is a general duty for the preservation of the Queen's peace? Similarly if the intelligence service fails to respond appropriately to intelligence that a terrorist group is intending to bring down an airliner, is it right that the service should be liable to the dependants of the victims on the plane but not the victims on the ground? Such a distinction would be understandable if the duty is founded on a representation to, and reliance by, a particular individual but that is not the basis of the interveners' liability principle. **These questions underline the fact that the duty of the police for the preservation of the peace is owed to members of the public at large, and does not involve the kind of close or special relationship ('proximity' or 'neighbourhood') necessary for the imposition of a private law duty of care.**

...

Issue 3: should the police be held to have assumed responsibility to take reasonable care for Ms Michael's safety?

138. Mr Bowen submitted that what was said by the Gwent call handler who received Ms Michael's 999 call was arguably sufficient to give rise to an assumption of responsibility on the *Hedley Byrne* principle as amplified in *Spring v Guardian Assurance Plc*. I agree with the Court of Appeal that the argument is not tenable. The only assurance which the call handler gave to Ms Michael was that she would pass on the call to the South Wales Police. She gave no promise how quickly they would respond. She told Ms Michael that they would want to call her back and asked her to keep her phone free, but this did not amount to advising or instructing her to remain in her house, as was suggested. Ms Michael's call was made on her mobile phone. Nor did the call handler's inquiry whether Ms Michael could lock the house amount to advising or instructing her to remain there. The case is very different from *Kent v Griffiths* where the call handler gave misleading assurances that an ambulance would be arriving shortly.

Question to consider: Do you agree with the majority decision in *Michael v Chief Constable of South Wales*? Do you agree that the police do not have sufficient proximity to victims of crimes on the facts of this case?

Other resources: N McBride, 'Michael and the Future of Tort Law' (2016) 32(1) *Professional Negligence* 14; J Conaghan and C Torrible (2017). Policing, professionalism and liability for negligence (2017) 33(2) *Tottel's Journal of Professional Negligence* 86–108; *Brooks v Commissioner of Police for the Metropolis* [2005] UKHL 24; *Hill v Chief Constable of West Yorkshire*.

We will return to the ambulance case of *Kent v Griffiths* below. Further to the inquiry in relation to the police, Lord Reed continues the analysis in ***Robinson***:

Robinson v Chief Constable of West Yorkshire Police [2018] UKSC 4, [2018] AC 736, [50], [55], [64], [70], [72]–[74] (Lord Reed)

50. ... as Lord Toulson noted in *Michael* (para 37), Lord Keith held [in *Hill v Chief Constable of West Yorkshire* [1989] AC 53] that the general duty of the police to enforce the law did not carry with it a private law duty towards individual members of the public. In particular, police officers investigating a series of murders did not owe a duty to the murderer's potential future victims to take reasonable care to apprehend him. That was again in accordance with the general law of negligence. As explained earlier, the common law does not normally impose liability for omissions, or more particularly for a failure to prevent harm caused by the conduct of third parties. Public authorities are not, therefore, generally under a duty of care to provide a benefit to individuals through the performance of their public duties, in the absence of special circumstances such as an assumption of responsibility. This was recognised by Lord Toulson in *Michael*.

...

55. The case of *Hill* is not, therefore, authority for the proposition that the police enjoy a general immunity from suit in respect of anything done by them in the course of investigating or preventing crime. On the contrary, the liability of the police for negligence or other tortious conduct resulting in personal injury, where liability would arise under ordinary principles of the law of tort, was expressly confirmed. Lord Keith spoke of an 'immunity', meaning the absence of a duty of care, only in relation to the protection of the public from harm through the performance by the police of their function of investigating crime.

...

64. In *Smith v Chief Constable of Sussex Police*, the majority of the House were in agreement that, absent special circumstances such as an assumption of responsibility, the police owed no duty of care to individuals affected by the discharge of their public duty to investigate offences and prevent their commission. Lord Hope, with whose reasoning the other members of the majority agreed, followed the approach adopted in *Brooks* in the passage cited in para 61 above, and emphasised the risk that the imposition of a duty of care of the kind contended for would inhibit a robust approach in assessing a person as a possible suspect or victim. He acknowledged that '[t]here are, of course, cases in which actions of the police give rise to civil claims in negligence in accordance with ordinary delictual principles', and cited *Rigby* as an example (para 79). Lord Phillips of Worth Matravers CJ summarised the core principle to be derived from *Hill* and *Brooks* as being that in the absence of special circumstances, the police owe no common law duty of care to protect individuals against harm caused by criminals. Lord Brown approached the matter in a similar way, concluding that, in the absence of an assumption of responsibility towards the eventual victim, the police generally owe no duty of care to prevent injuries deliberately inflicted by third parties, when they are engaged in discharging their general duty of combating and investigating crime. None of the speeches is inconsistent with the existence of a duty of care to avoid causing physical harm in accordance with ordinary principles of the law of negligence.

70. ... **it follows that there is no general rule that the police are not under any duty of care when discharging their function of preventing and investigating crime. They generally owe a duty of care when such a duty arises under ordinary principles of the law of negligence, unless statute or the common law provides otherwise.** Applying those principles, they may be under a duty of care to protect an individual from a danger of injury which they have themselves created, including a danger of injury resulting from human agency, as in *Dorset Yacht* and *Attorney General of the British Virgin Islands v Hartwell*. Applying the same principles, however, **the police are not normally under a duty of care to protect individuals from a danger of injury which they have not themselves created, including injury caused by the conduct of third parties, in the absence of special circumstances such as an assumption of responsibility.**

Questions about the liability of public authorities often involve related questions about omissions liability, to which we will return below. Since the argument in favour of public authority liability is that it had the power to prevent the harm to the claimant but did not use it to do so, the omissions question is usually live when their potential liability is discussed. This happened, somewhat inevitably, in *Robinson*:

> 72. The role of the police in the accident in which Mrs Robinson was injured is not comparable to that of the defendant in the examples commonly given of pure omissions: for example, someone who watches and does nothing as a blind man approaches the edge of a cliff, or a child drowns in a shallow pool. Nor, to cite more realistic examples, is it comparable to that of the police authority in *Hill*, which failed to arrest a murderer before a potential future victim was killed, or the police authority in *Michael*, which failed to respond to an emergency call in time to save the caller from an attack. In such cases the defendant played no active part in the critical events. Nor is this a case in which the chief constable is sought to be made liable for the conduct of a third party. Lord Reid's observation in *Dorset Yacht* (at p 1027) is apposite: 'the ground of liability is not responsibility for the acts of the escaping trainees; it is liability for damage caused by the carelessness of these officers in the knowledge that their carelessness would probably result in the trainees causing damage of this kind'.
>
> 73. In the present case, the ground of action is liability for damage caused by carelessness on the part of the police officers in circumstances in which it was reasonably foreseeable that their carelessness would result in Mrs Robinson's being injured. Her complaint is not that the police officers failed to protect her against the risk of being injured, but that their actions resulted in her being injured. In short, this case is concerned with a positive act, not an omission.
>
> *(4) Did the police officers owe a duty of care to Mrs Robinson?*
>
> 74. It was not only reasonably foreseeable, but actually foreseen by the officers, that Williams was likely to resist arrest by attempting to escape. That is why Willan summoned assistance in the first place, before attempting to arrest Williams, and why it was decided that DS Roebuck and DC Green should be positioned on the opposite side of Williams from Willan and Dhurmea, so as to block his escape route. The place where the officers decided to arrest Williams was a moderately busy shopping street in a town centre. Pedestrians were passing in close vicinity to Williams. In those circumstances, it was reasonably foreseeable that if the arrest was attempted at a time when pedestrians – especially physically vulnerable pedestrians, such as a frail and elderly woman – were close to Williams, they might be knocked into and injured in the course of his attempting to escape. That reasonably foreseeable risk of injury was sufficient to impose on the officers a duty of care towards the pedestrians in the immediate vicinity when the arrest was attempted, including Mrs Robinson.

It is not hard to see why questions of police liability provoke strong opinions. In the following extract, Nick McBride offers a valuable and measured account of how the judicial reasoning has developed in this area. In the full article, he goes on to analyse its implications for tort law in a broader context.

Nicholas McBride, 'Michael and the Future of Tort Law' (2016) 32(1) *Professional Negligence* 14

[T]he law on when a *private* person will owe another a duty of care to save someone from harm is fairly clear. The rule is that no such duty of care will be owed, outside certain exceptional situations, such as where D has put C in danger of suffering harm or where D is in control of a dangerous thing or person that is liable to do harm to C if it escapes from D's control. However, for the past 75 years ... the courts have vacillated over what is the correct approach ... Two approaches to the question of when it would be, in the modern terminology, 'fair, just and reasonable' to find that a public body owed such a duty of care can be distinguished:

(1) *The uniform approach.* On this approach, we determine whether a public body owed a claimant a duty of care to save them from harm by asking – would a private person, equivalently situated, have owed the claimant a duty of care to save them from harm? If not, then no duty of care can have been owed by the public body. It is this approach that prevailed in the majority judgments in the *East Suffolk* case, refusing to find that the defendant board owed the plaintiff farmer a duty of care expeditiously to abate the flooding to which his land was subject: if the plaintiff's neighbours would not have owed the plaintiff such a duty of care, had they offered to help him wall up his land against flooding, there was no basis for finding that the defendant board owed him such a duty of care.

(2) *The policy approach.* Under this approach, in a case where a public body or official (B) has failed to save someone (C) from harm in a situation where B's role or function was to save C from that kind of harm, we should *presume* that B owed C a duty of care to save C from that harm unless there is some reason of public policy why it would be undesirable to find that B owed C such a duty ...

Once one grasps the distinction between these two different approaches, one can see them wax and wane in the case law over the last 75 years on when a public body will owe a duty of care to save someone from harm ...

2.2 Acts v omissions

There is a broader question about the extent to which liability in negligence should attach to omissions, as opposed to positive acts. This is complicated by the extent to which the two can be separated (ie if I run somebody down in my car, is that a positive act of driving, or an omission to brake?). It is also complicated by considerations of the *nature* of the duty in question: if the very purpose of my duty was to perform in some active way (eg to stop a prisoner in my custody doing something destructive), it hollows out that duty if I can claim there should be no liability for my failing so to act. There is also the more philosophical point that duties are usually singular (you must do a particular thing in a reasonable way) but omissions are very open-ended: there are countless ways in which one can not do something. Finally, there is the question of why this defendant? If something has not been done, presumably nobody has done it, so the law needs to justify why liability should be imposed on one individual rather than another.

The basic rule is that individuals do not owe each other a duty of care to act in any positive way. So A does not, for instance, owe B a duty of care to rescue her from the river in which she is apparently drowning. There are, however, as we shall see, several exceptions to this where, for instance, there is a pre-existing duty (so if, in the example just given, B is a minor and A is her parent), where the defendant caused the relevant risk to occur in the first place, or where the defendant assumed a responsibility to the claimant.

Lord Diplock's judgment in the following case is one of the most well-known articulations of the legal principles in this area. The claimant's yacht had been damaged by boys who were, at the relevant time, detainees of an institution for young offenders, and were under the supervision of the Home Office's employees. The boys had a history of behaving in a similar way, a fact that was known to the officers. The House of Lords did not agree with the Home Office's argument that liability cannot be imposed for wrongs done by another who is of full age and capacity, unless that other was acting as a servant or agent of the defendant. It held that where the defendant's duty was to guard against the very risk that eventuated in the harm of which the claimant complains, an omission to prevent that risk from materialising could ground liability in negligence.

Dorset Yacht Co Ltd v Home Office [1970] AC 1004, 1027 (Lord Reed), 1060 (Lord Diplock)

[Lord Reed at 1027] *Donoghue v. Stevenson* [1932] AC 562 may be regarded as a milestone, and the well-known passage in Lord Atkin's speech should I think be regarded as a statement of principle. It is not to be treated as if it were a statutory definition. It will require qualification in new circumstances. But I think that the time has come when we can and should say that it ought to apply unless there is some justification or valid explanation for its exclusion.

[Lord Diplock at 1060] The branch of English law which deals with civil wrongs abounds with instances of acts and, more particularly, of omissions which give rise to no legal liability in the doer or emitter for loss or damage sustained by others as a consequence of the act or omission, however reasonably or probably that loss or damage might have been anticipated. The very parable of the good Samaritan (Luke 10 v. 30) which was evoked by Lord Atkin in *Donoghue* v. *Stevenson* illustrates, in the conduct of the priest and of the Levite who passed by on the other side, an omission which was likely to have as its reasonable and probable consequence damage to the health of the victim of the thieves, but for which the priest and Levite would have incurred no civil liability in English law. Examples could be multiplied. You may cause loss to a tradesman by withdrawing your custom though the goods which he supplies are entirely satisfactory; you may damage your neighbour's land by intercepting the flow of percolating water to it even though the interception is of no advantage to yourself; you need not warn him of a risk of physical danger to which he is about to expose himself unless there is some special relationship between the two of you such as that of occupier of land and visitor; you may watch your neighbour's goods being ruined by a thunderstorm though the slightest effort on your part could protect them from the rain and you may do so with impunity unless there is some special relationship between you such as that of bailor and bailee.

In the next case, which refers to *Dorset Yacht*, the defendants acquired a disused cinema. Vagrants then moved into it and set fire to the building. This fire spread and caused damage to the claimants' neighbouring property, which is what gave rise to the negligence claim. The House of Lords held that there was no liability because the defendants were not responsible in law for the behaviour of third parties. Lord Goff's reasoning emphasised the absence of a duty of care in this situation, owing primarily to the lack of foreseeability of the damage, and it is his judgment which has endured, and been referred to with approval most recently by the Supreme Court in *Michael*.

Smith v Littlewoods Organisation Ltd [1987] AC 241, 249 (Lord Brandon), 272 (Lord Goff)

[Lord Brandon at 249] The first question is what was the general duty owed by Littlewoods, as owners and occupiers of the disused cinema, to the appellants, as owners or occupiers of other buildings near to the cinema. The answer to that question is, in my view, that Littlewoods owed to the appellants a duty to exercise reasonable care to ensure that the cinema was not, and did not become, a source of danger to neighbouring buildings owned or occupied by the appellants.

The second question is whether that general duty encompassed a specific duty to exercise reasonable care to prevent young persons obtaining unlawful access to the cinema, and, having done so, unlawfully setting it on fire. The answer to that question, in accordance with general principles governing alike the law of delict in Scotland and the law of negligence in England, must depend on whether the occurrence of such behaviour was reasonably foreseeable by Littlewoods. It should have been reasonably foreseeable by Littlewoods if they had known of the activities of young persons observed by certain individuals in the locality. But they did not know of such activities because the individuals concerned did not inform either Littlewoods or the police of them, nor did the police themselves observe them. In the absence of information about such activities, either from the individuals referred to or from the police, I am of opinion that the occurrence of the behaviour in question was not reasonably foreseeable by Littlewoods. I conclude, therefore, that the general duty of care owed by Littlewoods to the appellants did not encompass the specific duty referred to above.

...

[Lord Goff at 272] That there are special circumstances in which a defender may be held responsible in law for injuries suffered by the pursuer through a third party's deliberate wrongdoing is not in doubt. For example, a duty of care may arise from a relationship between the parties, which gives rise to an imposition or assumption of responsibility upon or by the defender, as in Stansbie v. Troman [1948] 2 K.B. 48, where such responsibility was held to arise from a contract. In that case a decorator, left alone on the premises by the householder's wife, was held liable when he went out leaving the door on the latch, and a thief entered the house and stole property. Such responsibility might well be held to exist in other cases where there is no contract, as for example where a person left alone in a house has entered as a licensee of the occupier. Again, the defender may be vicariously liable for the third party's act; or he may be held liable as an occupier to a visitor on his land. Again, as appears from the dictum of Dixon J in Smith v. Leurs, 70 C.L.R. 256, 262, a duty may arise from a special relationship between the defender and the third party, by virtue of which the defender is responsible for controlling the third party: see, for example, Dorset Yacht Co. Ltd, v. Home Office [1970] AC 1004. ...

... there is a more general circumstance in which a defender may be held liable in negligence to the pursuer, although the immediate cause of the damage suffered by the pursuer is the deliberate wrongdoing of another. This may occur where the defender negligently causes or permits to be created a source of danger, and it is reasonably foreseeable that third parties may interfere with it and, sparking off the danger, thereby cause damage to persons in the position of the pursuer. The classic example of such a case is, perhaps, Haynes v. Harwood [1935] 1 K.B. 146, where the defendant's carter left a horse-drawn van unattended in a crowded street, and the horses bolted when a boy threw a stone at them. A police officer who suffered injury in stopping the horses before they injured a woman and children was held to be entitled to recover damages from the defendant. There, of course, the defendant's servant had created a source of danger by leaving his horses unattended in a busy street. Many different things might have caused them to bolt – a sudden noise or movement, for example, or, as happened, the deliberate action of a mischievous boy. But all such events were examples of the very sort of thing which the defendant's servant ought reasonably to have foreseen and to have guarded against by taking appropriate precautions. ...

A similar situation, but one in which the intervening act was not that of a third party, received the following judicial treatment.

Reeves v Commissioners of Police for the Metropolis [2000] 1 AC 360, 367 (Lord Hoffmann), 379 (Lord Hope)

[Lord Hoffmann at 367] On the first question, Mr. Pannick relied upon the general principle stated in *Hart and Honoré, Causation in the Law* 2nd ed. (1985), at p. 136:

> 'the free, deliberate and informed act or omission of a human being, intended to exploit the situation created by a defendant, negatives causal connection.'

However, as *Hart and Honoré* also point out, (at pp. 194–204) there is an exception to this undoubted rule in the case in which the law imposes a duty to guard against loss caused by the free, deliberate and informed act of a human being. It would make nonsense of the existence of such a duty if the law were to hold that the occurrence of the very act which ought to have been prevented negatived causal connection between the breach of duty and the loss. This principle has been recently considered by your Lordships' House in *Environment Agency (formerly National Rivers Authority) v. Empress Car Co. (Abertillery) Ltd.* [1998] 2 WLR 350. In that case, examples are given of cases in which liability has been imposed for causing events which were the immediate consequence of the deliberate acts of third parties but which the defendant had a duty to prevent or take reasonable care to prevent.

[Lord Hope at 379] In my opinion it is necessary at the outset to identify the duty which was owed to the deceased by the Commissioner. There is no doubt that the Commissioner was right to concede that he owed a duty of care to the deceased while he remained in police custody. The deceased had been identified as a suicide risk, having on two previous occasions attempted to strangle himself with a belt after being placed in a cell. It was the Commissioner's duty to take reasonable care not to provide him with the opportunity of committing suicide by making use of defects in his cell door. The risk was not that he would injure himself accidentally if given that opportunity, but that he would do so deliberately. That is the nature of an act of suicide by a person who is of sound mind. It is a deliberate act of self-destruction by a person who intends to end his own life. So I think that the Commissioner's duty can most accurately be described as a duty to take reasonable care to prevent the deceased, while in police custody, from taking his own life deliberately.

Regardless of whose act is the proximate cause of the ultimate damage, a defendant will not be able to absolve themselves of liability by pointing to that act, if the very content of their duty was to prevent that act from occurring. Where a defendant has legally acknowledged control over the actions of another, they may well be liable if they fail to exercise it in an active way. This is an important exception to the general rule that a defendant will not be liable for failing to act to prevent harm to another.

Lord Keith in *Hill* made it clear how this element of control was the exception to the rule, and explained how it differed from the general principle:

Hill v Chief Constable of West Yorkshire Police [1989] 1 AC 53, 62 (Lord Keith)

The *Dorset Yacht* case was concerned with the special characteristics or ingredients beyond reasonable foreseeability of likely harm which may result in civil liability for failure to control another man to prevent his doing harm to a third. The present case falls broadly into the same category. It is plain that vital characteristics which were present in the *Dorset Yacht* case and which led to the imposition of liability are here lacking. Sutcliffe was never in the custody of the police force. Miss Hill was one of a vast number of the female general public who might be at risk from his activities but was at no special distinctive risk in relation to them, unlike the owners of yachts moored off Brownsea Island in relation to the foreseeable conduct of the Borstal boys. It appears from the passage quoted from the speech of Lord Diplock in the *Dorset Yacht* case that in his view no liability would rest upon a prison authority, which carelessly allowed the escape of an habitual criminal, for damage which he subsequently caused, not in the course of attempting to make good his getaway to persons at special risk, but in further pursuance of his general criminal career to the person or property of members of the general public. The same rule must apply as regards failure to recapture the criminal before he had time to resume his career. In the case of an escaped criminal his identity and description are known. In the instant case the identity of the wanted criminal was at the material time unknown and it is not averred that any full or clear description of him was ever available. The alleged negligence of the police consists in a failure to discover his identity. But if there is no general duty of care owed to individual members of the public by the responsible authorities to prevent the escape of a known criminal or to recapture him, there cannot reasonably be imposed upon any police force a duty of care similarly owed to identify and apprehend an unknown one. Miss Hill cannot for this purpose be regarded as a person at special risk simply because she was young and female. Where the class of potential victims of a particular habitual criminal is a large one the precise size of it cannot in principle affect the issue. All householders are potential victims of an habitual burglar, and all females those of an habitual rapist. The conclusion must be that although there existed reasonable foreseeability of likely harm to such as Miss Hill if Sutcliffe were not identified and apprehended, there is absent from the case any such ingredient or characteristic as led to the liability of the Home Office in the *Dorset Yacht* case. Nor is there present any additional characteristic such as might make up the deficiency. The circumstances of the case are therefore not capable of establishing a duty of care owed towards Miss Hill by the West Yorkshire Police.

In one of the most well-known and oft-cited judgments on liability for omissions, Lord Hoffmann sets out a number of reasons for the law's general rule. In the following excerpt, his Lordship puts this into the wider context of public authority liability:

Stovin v Wise [1996] AC 923, 942 (Lord Hoffmann)

There are sound reasons why omissions require different treatment from positive conduct. It is one thing for the law to say that a person who undertakes some activity shall take reasonable care not to cause damage to others. It is another thing for the law to require that a person who is doing nothing in particular shall take steps to prevent another from suffering harm from the acts of third parties (like Mrs Wise) or natural causes. **One can put the matter in political, moral or economic terms. In political terms it is less of an invasion of an individual's freedom for the law to require him to consider the safety of others in his actions than to impose upon him a duty to rescue or protect. A moral version of this point may be called the 'why pick on me?' argument. A duty to prevent harm to others or to render assistance to a person in danger or distress may apply to a large and indeterminate class of people who happen to be able to do something. Why should one be held liable rather than another? In economic terms, the efficient allocation of resources usually requires an activity should bear its own costs. If it benefits from being able to impose some of its costs on other people (what economists call 'externalities,') the market is distorted because the activity appears cheaper than it really is. So liability to pay compensation for loss caused by negligent conduct acts as a deterrent against increasing the cost of the activity to the community and reduces externalities.** But there is no similar justification for requiring a person who is not doing anything to spend money on behalf of someone else. Except in special cases (such as marine salvage) English law does not reward someone who voluntarily confers a benefit on another. So there must be some special reason why he should have to put his hand in his pocket.

...

The duty of care at common law is therefore derived from the council's duty in public law to 'give proper consideration to the question whether they should inspect or not.' It is clear, however, that this public law duty cannot in itself give rise to a duty of care. A public body almost always has a duty in public law to consider whether it should exercise its powers, but that does not mean that it necessarily owes a duty of care which may require that the power should actually be exercised. As Mason J. said in *Sutherland Shire Council v. Heyman* (1985) 157 C.L.R. 424, 465:

> '... although a public authority may be under a public duty, enforceable by mandamus, to give proper consideration to the question whether it should exercise a power, this duty cannot be equated with, or regarded as a foundation for imposing, a duty of care on the public authority in relation to the exercise of the power. Mandamus will compel proper consideration of the authority of its discretion, but that is all.'

The distinction made in the next and final case in this chapter is, however, significant. Here, a GP called an ambulance on her patient's behalf. Despite her having made two follow-up calls, the patient lost her baby because the ambulance took 38 minutes to arrive. The defendants argued that they had no duty to respond, but the Court of Appeal took a different view. It was found that the ambulance service, as part of the NHS, did owe a duty of care to individual patients and that, once a call had been accepted, there was only one individual who would be affected by any failure to respond.

Kent v Griffiths [2001] QB 36, 45, 49 (Lord Woolf)

> Here what was being provided was a health service. In the case of health services under the Act the conventional situation is that there is a duty of care. Why should the position of the ambulance staff be different from that of doctors or nurses? In addition the arguments based on public policy are much weaker in the case of the ambulance service than they are in the case of the police or the fire service. The police and fire services' primary obligation is to the public at large. In protecting a particular victim of crime, the police are performing their more general role of maintaining public order and reducing crime. In the case of fire the fire service will normally be concerned not only to protect a particular property where a fire breaks out but also to prevent fire spreading. In the case of both services, there is therefore a concern to protect the public generally. The emergency services that can be summoned by a 999 call do, in the majority of situations, broadly carry out a similar function. But in reality they can be very different. The ambulance service is part of the Health Service. Its care function include transporting patients to and from hospital when the use of an ambulance for this purpose is desirable. It is therefore appropriate to regard the LAS as providing services of the category provided by hospitals and not as providing services equivalent to those rendered by the police or the fire service. Situations could arise where there is a conflict between the interests of a particular individual and the public at large. But in the case of the ambulance service in this particular case, the only member of the public who could be adversely affected was the claimant. It was the claimant alone for whom the ambulance had been called.
>
> ….
>
> So in my judgment here. The fact that it was a person who foreseeably would suffer further injuries by a delay in providing an ambulance, when there was no reason why it should not be provided, is important in establishing the necessary proximity and thus duty of care in this case. In other words, as there were no circumstances which made it unfair or unreasonable or unjust that liability should exist, there is no reason why there should not be liability if the arrival of the ambulance was delayed for no good reason. The acceptance of the call in this case established the duty of care. On the findings of the judge it was delay which caused the further injuries. If wrong information had not been given about the arrival of the ambulance, other means of transport could have been used.

The liability of public authorities in negligence is, as the materials above suggest, rarely straightforward. The general rule, which seems increasingly clear in the light of the authorities set out in this chapter, is helpful to bear in mind. The exceptions can then be learned and applied as appropriate. Professor Deakin analyses the liability of public authorities and the general rule in the following extract, concluding with a question about the extent to which it is satisfactory to try to deal with public authority liability through a private law framework.

Simon Deakin, 'Liability in negligence in providing a public good: really not so different?' (2019) 78(3) *CLJ* 513, 515

The overall message is clear: public bodies are not treated in any fundamentally different way to private parties or entities. Thus they are not generally liable for failing to confer a benefit, or for harms caused by third parties. Conversely, the statutory basis of their powers does not, without more, confer on them any particular immunity. *Robinson v Chief Constable of West Yorkshire* ([2018] A.C. 736, [2018] UKSC 4) ... demonstrates that the tort of negligence is committed where a public or statutory defendant foreseeably causes physical harm to another through a positive act amounting to negligence. The *Caparo* test (*Caparo Industries plc. v Dickman* [1990] 2 A.C. 605), which allows for the adjustment of the scope of a duty of care on (among other things) grounds of policy, has no application to such a case. This was a welcome clarification ...

... it may be difficult to maintain the idea that there are special 'policy' factors limiting the tortious liabilities of public bodies, although some of these may reappear in future under the heading of the 'statutory framing' of the common law duty of care, which continues to be relevant ... But should the liabilities of public and private sector defendants be so closely aligned? Private law, in conjunction with liability insurance, prices risks and entities are generally able to diffuse and absorb the costs of managing them. Local authorities, on the other hand, are providing public goods for which no effective price mechanism exists. They cannot use insolvency law or the corporate form to shield themselves from excessive liabilities in the same way that their private sector counterparts can. Rules on joint liability effectively make them defendants of last resort for risks run by others. It is difficult to see why there shouldn't be a special regime for public torts.

Question to consider: Do you think the distinction between acts and omissions in tortious duties of care is justified, desirable or both?

Other resources: S Steel, 'Rationalising Omissions Liability in Negligence' (2019) 135 *LQR* 484; Richard W Wright, 'Acts and Omissions as Positive and Negative Causes' (2007); *Stovin v Wise* [1996] AC 923; *Sutradhar v National Environmental Research Council* [2006] UKHL 33; *Reeves v Commissioner of Metropolitan Police* [2000] 1 AC 360.

2.3 Conclusion

The principal objective of this chapter has been to substantiate the way in which the duty of care has developed in negligence, as well as how it has been interpreted and analysed by commentators. These cases have shown how it operates as a control device, limiting the liability of those whose actions cause harm to others. The cases concerning public authority liability are, as we have seen, particularly thorny, particularly when dealing with the misfeasance v nonfeasance distinction, and in relation to human rights considerations. This is arguably an inevitable challenge, given that it all plays out at the interface of public and private law. One of the most significant takeaways from this area is that, as both the relevant case law and commentary show, the negligence liability of public bodies is established in any case by common law principles, and, most importantly, remains independent of their statutory authority.

Chapter 3 PURE ECONOMIC LOSS

3.1 General principles

The rules on when a claimant can recover for pure economic loss are the most restrictive in the tort of negligence. It is therefore crucial that you are able clearly to distinguish between pure economic loss and consequential economic loss because the latter is subject to far fewer restrictions. *Pure* economic loss is that loss that sounds only in financial form, such as, for instance, losing investment monies as a result of negligence financial advice. *Consequential* economic loss, on the other hand, is the perfectly orthodox claim one makes when, for instance, one has lost earnings as a result of another, conventional injury, such as a broken arm or a damaged car. The principal policy reason often given for the restrictive treatment of pure economic loss claims is that such damage is *indeterminate* in terms of what a defendant might have been able to foresee. How does this differ from claims for economic loss consequent upon damage to a physical thing? Because the sphere of influence one can physically have on others is necessarily smaller that the effect one can have in terms of pure economic loss. If I drive carelessly, it is the people in physical proximity to me that are the foreseeable victims of my carelessness. But if I broadcast poor financial advice, it is far harder to foresee the range and volume of those likely to suffer loss as a result. Also, pure economic loss can have a knock-on effect in a way that physical harm is unlikely to: if a claimant goes insolvent as a result of a significant economic loss, that is bound to affect the other parties in linked commercial chains, such as suppliers, creditors etc. We will return below to a discussion of this policy argument. Suffice it to say for now that it is the reason most often given for the law's restrictions on recovery for pure economic loss in tort. (Note the important presence of the word 'tort' in that sentence: recovery for pure economic loss is not generally restricted *in law*. Contract law is, for example, concerned almost exclusively with it. But that, in terms of this particular policy argument, is very different, because contracts provide the determinacy that would be lacking in a negligence claim: in a contract, parties always know precisely to whom it is they will be liable!)

There is another, less prosaic, argument as to why there are restrictive rules on recovery for pure economic loss in negligence.[1] And that is an argument relating to

1 R Stevens, *Torts and Rights* (OUP, 2007), ch 3.

rights. We all have, so the argument goes, undoubted rights not to have our physical integrity or our property interfered with. There is, however, no such right not to suffer pure economic loss. In fact, our economic order depends on this. Consider, for instance, market competition: there is no legal obstacle to somebody setting up an online shop, selling exactly the same goods as another shop but for a lower price. This will inevitably cause pure economic loss to the owner of the first shop, but it is not something that is prohibited. In fact, from most quarters, it is a practice that is encouraged. The right not to suffer pure economic loss, then, is one that is highly circumscribed.

The distinction between the types of economic loss is often made with reference to the following case. There, the defendants damaged an electricity cable which, although it belonged to the electricity board, supplied the claimants' factory with power. As a consequence of the damage, the claimants' factory was without electricity until the cable could be repaired. When the power supply was first interrupted, the claimants had to remove molten metal from their furnace, and this 'melt' was therefore ruined. They claimed for the value of the ruined melt and for the profit they would have made had they been able to sell it. Crucially, they also claimed for the profits they would have made on the melts that they *would have produced* had the power supply not been cut off. These latter profits were, of course, not consequential upon physical injury to any tangible thing, since they were purely hypothetical and based on melts that did not actually exist. The Court of Appeal allowed the claimants to recover only for the ruined melt and the lost profit consequential upon damage to that physical asset. It was not prepared to allow recovery for lost profits relating to future, as yet non-existent, melts. These future profits were deemed to be pure economic loss (consequent upon damage caused to the power company's cable, and not any property belonging to the claimants).

Spartan Steel & Alloys v Martin & Co [1973] QB 27, 36–37 (Denning MR)

At bottom I think the question of recovering economic loss is one of policy. Whenever the Courts draw a line to mark out the bounds of duty, they do it as matter of policy so as to limit the responsibility of the defendant. Whenever the Courts set bounds to the damages recoverable – saying that they are, or are not, too remote – they do it as matter of policy so as to limit the liability of the defendants.

In many of the cases where economic loss has been held not to be recoverable, it has been put on the ground that the defendant was under no duty to the plaintiff. Thus where a person is injured in a road accident by the negligence of another, the negligent driver owes a duty to the injured man himself, but he owes no duty to the servant of the injured man – see Best v. Fox (1952) A.C. at page 731: nor to the master of the injured man – Inland Revenue Commissioners v. Hambrook (1956) 2 Q.B. 656 at page 660; nor to anyone else who suffers loss because he had a contract with the injured man – see Simpson v. Thomson (1877) 3 A.C. at page 289: nor indeed to anyone who only suffers economic loss on account of the accident – see Kirkham v. Boughey (1958) 2 Q.B. at page 341. Likewise, when property is damaged by the negligence of another, the negligent tortfeasor owes a duty to the owner or possessor of the chattel, but not to one who suffers loss only because he had a contract entitling him to use the chattel or giving him a right to receive it at some later date – see Elliott Steam Tug Company v. Shipping Controller (1922) 1 K.B. at page 139: Margarine Union G.m.b.H. v. Cambay Prince Steamship Co. Ltd. (1969) 1 Q.B. 219 at page 251/2.

In other cases, however, the defendant seems clearly to have been under a duty to the plaintiff, but the economic loss has not been recovered because it is too remote. Take the illustration given by Mr. Justice Blackburn in Cattle v. Stockton (1875) L.R. 10 Q.B. at page 457, when water escapes from a reservoir and floods a coalmine where many men are working. Those who had their tools or clothes destroyed could recovers but those who only lost their wages could not. Similarly, when the defendants' ship negligently sank a ship which was being towed by a tug, the owner of the tug lost his remuneration, but he could not recover it from the negligent ship: though the same duty (of navigation with reasonable care) was owed to both tug and tow – see Remorquage a Helice v. Bennetts (1911) 1 Q.B. at page 248. In such cases if the plaintiff or his property had been physically injured, he would have recovered: but; as he only suffered economic loss, he is held not entitled to recover. This is, I should think, because the loss is regarded by the law as too remote – see King v. Phillips (1953) 1 Q.B. at pages 439–440.

On the other hand, in the cases where economic loss by itself has been held to be recoverable, it is plain that there was a duty to the plaintiff and the loss was not too remote. Such as when one ship negligently runs down another ship, and damages it, with the result that the cargo has to be discharged and reloaded. The negligent ship was already under a duty to the cargo-owners: and they can recover the cost of discharging and reloading it, as it is not too remote – see Morrison S.S.Co. v. Greystoke Castle (Cargo Owners) (1947) A.C. 265. Likewise, when a banker negligently gives a reference to one who acts on it, the duty is plain and the damage is not too remote – see Hedley Byrne & Co. v. Heller & Partners (1964) AC 465.

The more I think about these cases, the more difficult I find it to put each into its proper pigeon-hole. Sometimes I says 'There was no duty'. In others I say: 'The damage was too remote'. So much so that I think the time has come to discard those tests which have proved so elusive. It seems to me better to consider the particular relationship in hand, and see whether or not, as matter of policy, economic loss should be recoverable, or not.

The only context in which a claimant can recover in the tort of negligence for pure economic loss is for the negligent provision of services, and even this is relatively recent in terms of the tort's overall development. The principal authority is the following case. The claimants were advertising agents who consulted the defendant bankers as to the financial health of a client, on whose behalf the claimants were about to place several orders. The bank gave favourable references for the client company, gratuitously, and with the express disclaimer that they were given 'without responsibility'. When the claimant agents lost £17,000 on the orders as a result of the client's liquidation, they sued the defendant bankers for negligence in giving a favourable reference. The House of Lords found that, although such liability would not attach to the defendant in this particular case because it gave its statement subject to a disclaimer, such facts could in principle give rise to liability in negligence. Liability, said the House, will attach to the negligent provision of a statement where there is a 'special relationship' between the claimant and the defendant. This brings the situation factually closer to that of a contract (although, importantly, a contract is *not* required, as Lord Morris makes clear in the extract below).

Hedley Byrne v Heller [1964] AC 465, 486 (Lord Reid), 502 (Lord Morris), 517 (Lord Devlin)

[Lord Reid at 486] A reasonable man, knowing that he was being trusted or that his skill and judgment were being relied on, would, I think, have three courses open to him. He could keep silent or decline to give the information or advice sought: or he could give an answer with a clear qualification that he accepted no responsibility for it or that it was given without that reflection or enquiry which a careful answer would require: or he could simply answer without any such qualification. If he chooses to adopt the last course he must, I think, be held to have accepted some responsibility for his answer being given carefully, or to have accepted a relationship with the enquirer which requires him to exercise such care as the circumstances require.

...

[Lord Morris at 502] Independently of contract there may be circumstances where information is given or where advice is given which establishes a relationship which creates a duty not only to be honest but also to be careful.

In his speech in *Heilbut, Symons & Co. v. Buckleton* [1913] AC 30 Lord Moulton (at p. 51) said that it was of the greatest importance to 'maintain in its full integrity the principle that a person is not liable in damages for an innocent misrepresentation, no matter in what way or under what form the attack is made.' That principle is, however, in no way impeached by recognition of the fact that if a duty exists there is a remedy for the breach of it. As Lord Bowen said in *Low v. Bouverie* [1891] 3 Ch 82: 'the doctrine that negligent misrepresentation affords no cause of action is confined to cases in which there is no duty, such as the law recognises, to be careful.'

The enquiry in the present case, and in similar cases, becomes, therefore, an enquiry as to whether there was a relationship between the parties which created a duty and if so whether such duty included a duty of care. ...

My Lords, I consider that it follows and that it should now be regarded as settled that if someone possessed of a special skill undertakes, quite irrespective of contract, to apply that skill for the assistance of another person who relies upon such skill, a duty of care will arise. The fact that the service is to be given by means of or by the instrumentality of words can make no difference. Furthermore, if in a sphere in which a person is so placed that others could reasonably rely upon his judgment or his skill or upon his ability to make careful inquiry, a person takes it upon himself to give information or advice to, or allows his information or advice to be passed on to, another person who, as he knows or should know, will place reliance upon it, then a duty of care will arise.

...

[Lord Devlin at 517] This is why the distinction is now said to depend on whether financial loss is caused through physical injury or whether it is caused directly. The interposition of the physical injury is said to make a difference of principle. I can find neither logic nor common sense in this. If irrespective of contract, a doctor negligently advises a patient that he can safely pursue his occupation and he cannot and the patient's health suffers and he loses his livelihood, the patient has a remedy. But if the doctor negligently advises him that he cannot safely pursue his occupation when in fact he can and he loses his livelihood, there is said to be no remedy. Unless, of course, the patient was a private patient and the doctor accepted half a guinea for his trouble: then the patient can recover all. I am bound to say, my Lords, that I think this to be nonsense. It is not the sort of nonsense that can arise even in the best system of law out of the need to draw nice distinctions between borderline cases. It arises, if it is the law, simply out of a refusal to make sense. The line is not drawn on any intelligible principle. It just happens to be the line which those who have been driven from the extreme assertion that negligent statements in the absence of contractual or fiduciary duty give no cause of action have in the course of their retreat so far reached.

In the next case, the House of Lords considered an application of what is now generally known as the *Hedley Byrne* principle in a consumer, as opposed to a commercial, situation. As you will see, the treatment of the disclaimer was consequently somewhat different. The claimants were the purchasers of a modest residential property. The defendants produced a valuation assessment of the house for the claimants' mortgage company and, although the claimants paid for the report, it was the mortgage company who commissioned and relied upon it. When it transpired that the report was inaccurate and had been produced negligently, the claimants sued the defendants for the pure economic loss they suffered as a result of buying the house for more than it was worth. Despite the fact that the report stated expressly that only the mortgage company should rely on the report, the House of Lords found that a surveyor in such a situation does owe a duty of care to the purchasers of the property concerned. In order to reach this conclusion, it was necessary to make the requisite 'assumption of responsibility' survive the existence of the express disclaimer. One of the ways in which the House did this was to deem the disclaimer 'unreasonable' and therefore unenforceable under the Unfair Contract Terms Act 1977.

Smith v Eric S Bush; Harris v Wyre Forest District Council [1990] 1 AC 831, 840 (Lord Templeman)

I agree that by obtaining and disclosing a valuation, a mortgagee does not assume responsibility to the purchaser for that valuation. But in my opinion the valuer assumes responsibility to both mortgagee and purchaser by agreeing to carry out a valuation for mortgage purposes knowing that the valuation fee has been paid by the purchaser and knowing that the valuation will probably be relied upon by the purchaser in order to decide whether or not to enter into a contract to purchase the house. The valuer can escape the responsibility to exercise reasonable skill and care by an express exclusion clause, provided the exclusion clause does not fall foul of the Unfair Contract Terms Act 1977.

...

In general I am of the opinion that in the absence of a disclaimer of liability the valuer who values a house for the purpose of a mortgage, knowing that the mortgagee will rely and the mortgagor will probably rely on the valuation, knowing that the purchaser mortgagor has in effect paid for the valuation, is under a duty to exercise reasonable skill and care and that duty is owed to both parties to the mortgage for which the valuation is made. Indeed, in both the appeals now under consideration the existence of such a dual duty is tacitly accepted and acknowledged because notices excluding liability for breach of the duty owed to the purchaser were drafted by the mortgagee and imposed on the purchaser. In these circumstances it is necessary to consider the second question which arises in these appeals, namely, whether the disclaimers of liability are notices which fall within the Unfair Contract Terms Act 1977.

...

Mrs. Smith did not obtain a structural survey of the property. She relied upon the valuer's report to reveal any obvious serious defects in the house she was purchasing. It is common ground that she was behaving in the same way as the vast majority of purchasers of modest houses. They do not go to the expense of obtaining their own structural survey, they rely on the valuation to reveal any obvious serious defects and take a chance that there are no hidden defects that might be revealed by a more detailed structural survey.

The valuer's report said 'the property has been modernised to a fair standard ... no essential repairs are required' and it valued the property at £16,500. If reasonable skill and care had been employed when the inspection took place, it would have revealed that as a result of removing the chimney breasts in the rooms the chimneys had been left dangerously unsupported. Unaware of this defect and relying on the valuer's report, Mrs Smith bought the house for £18,000 with the assistance of a loan of £3,500 from the building society. ...

We are dealing in this case with a loss which will be limited to the value of a modest house and against which it can be expected that the surveyor will be insured. Bearing the loss will be unlikely to cause significant hardship if it has to be borne by the surveyor but it is, on the other hand, quite possible that it will be a financial catastrophe for the purchaser who may be left with a valueless house and no money to buy another. ...

It must, however, be remembered that this is a decision in respect of a dwelling house of modest value in which it is widely recognised by surveyors that purchasers are in fact relying on their care and skill. It will obviously be of general application in broadly similar circumstances. But I expressly reserve my position in respect of valuations of quite different types of property for mortgage purposes, such as industrial property, large blocks of flats or very expensive houses. In such cases it may well be that the general expectation of the behaviour of the purchaser is quite different. With very large sums of money at stake prudence would seem to demand that the purchaser obtain his own structural survey to guide him in his purchase and, in such circumstances with very much larger sums of money at stake, it may be reasonable for the surveyors valuing on behalf of those who are providing the finance either to exclude or limit their liability to the purchaser.

Far more recently, the Supreme Court has considered the issue once more. The point of real relevance in this context was the extent of the defendant's knowledge as to the identity of the party who will rely on the information it provided. Here, the claimant was the Playboy Club which had, in accordance with its usual practice, sought assurances of creditworthiness from a client's bank before advancing gambling credit. Given the name and reputation of the club, it used a different entity, Burlington, in order to approach clients' banks. It was, therefore, to Burlington to which the assurance was given in this case. When, despite those assurances (which were, in any event, given when the client was not even a customer of BNL) the client defaulted on the credit agreement, the claimant sought to recover its £800,000 loss from BNL on the basis of the *Hedley Byrne* principle.

The Supreme Court held that there was insufficient proximity in this case between BNL and the Playboy Club, because BNL gave the information to Burlington and not to the claimant. This was an instance of what is known as undisclosed agency, under which one party enters into contractual relations on behalf of another. Such a relationship was deemed by the Supreme Court not to be 'akin to contract' in the way that *Hedley Byrne* liability requires and so BNL was not liable to the Playboy Club. We can take from this that a defendant must know to whom its statement is directed if the facts are to give rise to the requisite special relationship under *Hedley Byrne*. In the excerpt that follows, Lord Sumption gives a very useful potted account of the history of the principle.

Banca Nazionale del Lavoro SPA v Playboy Club London Ltd and others [2018] UKSC 43, [2018] 1 WLR 4041, [6]–[8], [10], [11] (Lord Sumption)

6. The decision of the House of Lords in *Hedley Byrne & Co Ltd v Heller & Partners Ltd* was a landmark in the development of the law of tort. Contrary to the ordinary rule as it had previously been understood, it allowed the recovery of a purely economic

loss in negligence where the existence of a special relationship between claimant and defendant made this appropriate. The facts were that Hedley Byrne asked its bank, National Provincial Bank, to obtain a credit reference for a company wishing to place advertising contracts through it. The company's bank, Heller & Partners, supplied the reference to National Provincial. The Appellate Committee inferred as a matter of fact that Heller & Partners must have appreciated that National Provincial was not acting for its own account but wanted the reference for a client intending to do business with Heller's client, even though they did not know who that client was: see, in particular, pp 482 (Lord Reid), 493–494 (Lord Morris of Borth-y-Gest), 530 (Lord Devlin). The ratio of the decision was that the reasonable reliance of Hedley Byrne on the reference, combined with Heller & Partners' appreciation of the fact that they would reasonably rely on it, gave rise to a direct relationship between them involving a duty of care. All five members of the Appellate Committee gave reasoned judgments, but Lord Devlin's analysis has generally been treated in the subsequent case law as most clearly expressing the reasoning. At pp 529–530, Lord Devlin, said this:

> 'I have had the advantage of reading all the opinions prepared by your Lordships and of studying the terms which your Lordships have framed by way of definition of the sort of relationship which gives rise to a responsibility towards those who act upon information or advice and so creates a duty of care towards them ... It is a responsibility that is voluntarily accepted or undertaken, either generally where a general relationship, such as that of solicitor and client or banker and customer, is created, or specifically in relation to a particular transaction. ... Responsibility can attach only to the single act, that is, the giving of the reference, and only if the doing of that act implied a voluntary undertaking to assume responsibility. This is a point of great importance because it is, as I understand it, the foundation for the ground on which in the end the House dismisses the appeal ...
>
> I do not go further than this for two reasons. The first is that I have found in the speech of Lord Shaw in *Nocton v Lord Ashburton* and in the idea of a relationship that is equivalent to contract all that is necessary to cover the situation that arises in this case ... All that was lacking was formal consideration ...
>
> I shall therefore content myself with the proposition that wherever there is a relationship equivalent to contract, there is a duty of care. Such a relationship may be either general or particular. Examples of a general relationship are those of solicitor and client and of banker and customer ... There may well be others yet to be established. Where there is a general relationship of this sort, it is unnecessary to do more than prove its existence and the duty follows. Where, as in the present case, what is relied on is a particular relationship created ad hoc, it will be necessary to examine the particular facts to see whether there is an express or implied undertaking of responsibility.'

7. The principle thus established is capable of development. Indeed it has undergone considerable development since 1964, for example to cover omissions and the negligent performance of services. But these have been incremental changes within a consistent

framework of principle. One area in which the courts have resisted expanding the scope of liability concerns the person or category of persons to whom the duty is owed. The defendant's voluntary assumption of responsibility remains the foundation of this area of law, as this court recently confirmed after a full review of the later authorities in *NRAM Ltd (formerly NRAM plc) v Steel* [2018] 1 WLR 1190, paras 18–24 (Lord Wilson JSC). It is fundamental to this way of analysing the duty that the defendant is assuming a responsibility to an identifiable (although not necessarily identified) person or group of persons, and not to the world at large or to a wholly indeterminate group.

8. In *Caparo Industries plc v Dickman* [1990] 2 AC 605, the Appellate Committee held that foreseeability, although it was a necessary condition for liability, was not necessarily a sufficient one. The foundation of the duty is proximity, which may require more than the mere foreseeability of reliance. The problem before the Appellate Committee was to identify the outer limits of the class of persons whose reliance on a statement could properly be said to give rise to a sufficiently proximate relationship. They found the relevant limiting factors in the defendants' knowledge of (i) the person known to be likely to rely on the statement, and (ii) the transaction in respect of which he was known to be likely to rely on. After reviewing the authorities supporting a duty of care for negligent statements, both before and after *Hedley Byrne*, Lord Bridge (with whom Lord Roskill, Lord Ackner and Lord Oliver agreed), summarised the position as follows at pp 620–621:

> 'The salient feature of all these cases is that the defendant giving advice or information was fully aware of the nature of the transaction which the plaintiff had in contemplation, knew that the advice or information would be communicated to him directly or indirectly and knew that it was very likely that the plaintiff would rely on that advice or information in deciding whether or not to engage in the transaction in contemplation. In these circumstances the defendant could clearly be expected, subject always to the effect of any disclaimer of responsibility, specifically to anticipate that the plaintiff would rely on the advice or information given by the defendant for the very purpose for which he did in the event rely on it. So also the plaintiff, subject again to the effect of any disclaimer, would in that situation reasonably suppose that he was entitled to rely on the advice or information communicated to him for the very purpose for which he required it. The situation is entirely different where a statement is put into more or less general circulation and may foreseeably be relied on by strangers to the maker of the statement for any one of a variety of different purposes which the maker of the statement has no specific reason to anticipate. To hold the maker of the statement to be under a duty of care in respect of the accuracy of the statement to all and sundry for any purpose for which they may choose to rely on it is not only to subject him, in the classic words of Cardozo CJ to 'liability in an indeterminate amount for an indeterminate time to an indeterminate class:' see *Ultramares Corpn v Touche* (1931) 174 N.E. 441, 444; it is also to confer on the world at large a quite unwarranted entitlement to appropriate for their own purposes the benefit of the expert knowledge or professional expertise attributed to the maker of the statement.

> Hence, looking only at the circumstances of these decided cases where a duty of care in respect of negligent statements has been held to exist, I should expect to find that the 'limit or control mechanism … imposed upon the liability of a wrongdoer towards those who have suffered economic damage in consequence of his negligence' rested in the necessity to prove, in this category of the tort of negligence, as an essential ingredient of the 'proximity' between the plaintiff and the defendant, that the defendant knew that his statement would be communicated to the plaintiff, either as an individual or as a member of an identifiable class, specifically in connection with a particular transaction or transactions of a particular kind (eg in a prospectus inviting investment) and that the plaintiff would be very likely to rely on it for the purpose of deciding whether or not to enter upon that transaction or upon a transaction of that kind.'

…

10. The defendant's knowledge of the transaction in respect of which the statement is made is potentially relevant for three purposes: (i) to identify some specific person or group of persons to whom he can be said to assume responsibility; (ii) to demonstrate that the claimant's reliance on the statement will be financially significant; and (iii) to limit the degree of responsibility which the defendant is taken to assume if no financial limit is expressly mentioned. We are presently concerned with its significance for the first of these purposes, which will vary according to what is known about the person or group expected to rely on the statement. **Thus in *Hedley Byrne* itself, the defendant understood that the statement would be relied on by the unidentified, but readily identifiable, client on whose behalf National Provincial Bank was known to be making the inquiry.** It was enough that the proposed transaction was said to be an advertising contract for £8,000 to £9,000. It would probably have been enough even if the transaction had not been identified as an advertising contract but simply as some kind of business transaction. For Lord Morris, for example, it was enough that the person contemplated was 'some one who was contemplating doing business with Easipower Ltd': see pp 493–494. In *Caparo* on the other hand, where the persons said to have been entitled to rely on the defendant's audit report were any potential bidder for the auditor's client, the absence of a specific transaction in the defendant's contemplation assumed decisive significance.

11. Mr Salzedo QC, who appeared for the Playboy Club, accepted that there was no evidence that BNL knew that its reference would be communicated to or relied on by anyone other than Burlington. He also accepted that in the ordinary course where a statement is relied upon by B to whom A has passed it on, the representor owes no duty to B unless he knew that the statement was likely to be communicated to B. That concession was plainly justified. **I would go further and say that the representor must not only know that the statement is likely to be communicated to and relied upon by B. It must also be part of the statement's known purpose that it should be communicated and relied upon by B, if the representor is to be taken to assume responsibility to B.**

Over the years (and, for some reason, in 1995 particularly), the *Hedley Byrne* principle developed to cover situations in which there was also a contract (known as 'concurrent liability') and situations in which the loss was caused by deeds as well as by words. In the first case, the claimants were investors who lost significant amounts of money as a result of massive insurance claims made against Lloyd's in the 1980s. They sued the defendants for negligently managing the syndicates (this is the insurance market term for groups of investors who pool funds in order to insure high value risks) in which they had invested. There were two main issues for the House of Lords to consider: first, whether liability for pure economic loss should attach to the performance of services, as opposed to the narrower action of giving a particular statement, and, second, whether the existence of a contract between claimant and defendant meant that negligence liability would not arise. The Court decided that liability could arise in relation to the provision of a service and that, unless the terms of a contract between the parties excluded liability in tort, the existence of the contract itself did not preclude the existence of such a duty of care. Where there was both a contractual and a tortious duty, the claimant could elect which action to pursue.

Henderson v Merrett Syndicates [1995] 2 AC 145, 194 (Lord Goff), 206 (Lord Browne-Wilkinson)

[Lord Goff at 194] My own belief is that, in the present context, the common law is not antipathetic to concurrent liability, and that there is no sound basis for a rule which automatically restricts the claimant to either a tortious or a contractual remedy. The result may be untidy: but, given that the tortious duty is imposed by the general law, and the contractual duty is attributable to the will of the parties, I do not find it objectionable that the claimant may be entitled to take advantage of the remedy which is most advantageous to him, subject only to ascertaining whether the tortious duty is so inconsistent with the applicable contract that, in accordance with ordinary principle, the parties must be taken to have agreed that the tortious remedy is to be limited or excluded.

[Lord Browne-Wilkinson at 206] The existence of an underlying contract (e.g. as between solicitor and client) does not automatically exclude the general duty of care which the law imposes on those who voluntarily assume to act for others. But the nature and terms of the contractual relationship between the parties will be determinative of the scope of the responsibility assumed and can, in some cases, exclude any assumption of legal responsibility to the plaintiff for whom the defendant has assumed to act. If the common law is not to become again manacled by 'clanking chains' (this time represented by causes, rather than forms, of action), it is in my judgment important not to exclude concepts of concurrent liability which the courts of equity have over the years handled without difficulty. I can see no good reason for holding that the existence of a contractual right is in all circumstances inconsistent with the co-existence of another tortious right, provided that it is understood that the agreement of the parties evidenced by the contract can modify and shape the tortious duties which, in the absence of contract, would be applicable.

In the next case, the question was whether a duty of care was owed to the employee by his employer when writing a reference. These facts are different to *Hedley Byrne* to the extent that the statements in the reference were neither directed to, nor relied upon by, the claimant. This case also gave rise to the question of whether a negligence action should lie on facts which could be covered by the tort of defamation, which is a tort expressly concerned with protecting a claimant's reputation. The problem with such an action, however, is that the giving of a reference is protected by qualified privilege, and therefore actionable only if motivated by malice (and there was no malice on the facts of *Spring*). The House of Lords decided, although not unanimously, in the claimant's favour, thereby extending *Hedley Byrne* further still.

Spring v Guardian Assurance [1995] 2 AC 296, 319 (Lord Goff), 326 (Lord Lowry), 344 (Lord Woolf)

[Lord Goff at 319] The fact that the inquiry in *Hedley Byrne* itself was directed, in a case concerned with liability in respect of a negligent misstatement (in fact a reference), to whether the maker of the statement was liable to a recipient of it who had acted in reliance upon it, may have given the impression that this is the only way in which liability can arise under the principle in respect of a misstatement. But. having regard to the breadth of the principle as stated in *Hedley Byrne* itself. I cannot see why this should be so. Take the case of the relationship between a solicitor and his client, treated implicitly by Lord Morris and expressly by Lord Devlin as an example of a relationship to which the principle may apply. I can see no reason why a solicitor should not be under a duty to his client to exercise due care and skill when making statements to third parties, so that if he fails in that duty and his client suffers damage in consequence, he may be liable to his client in damages. The question whether a person who gives a reference to a third party may, if the reference is negligently prepared, be liable in damages not to the recipient but to the subject of the reference, did not arise in *Hedley Byrne* and so was not addressed in that case. That is the central question with which we are concerned in the present case; and I propose first to consider it in the context of an ordinary relationship between employer and employee, and then to turn to apply the relevant principles to the more complex relationships which existed in the present case.

[Lord Lowry at 326] The entire future prosperity and happiness of someone who is the subject of a damaging reference which is given carelessly but in perfectly good faith may be irretrievably blighted. Against this prospect is set the possibility that some referees will be deterred from giving frank references or indeed any references. Placing full reliance here on the penetrating observations of my noble and learned friend Lord Woolf, I am inclined to view this possibility as a spectre conjured up by the defendants to frighten your Lordships into submission. I also believe that the courts in general and your Lordships' House in particular ought to think very carefully before resorting to public policy considerations which will defeat a claim that ex hypothesi is a perfectly good cause of action. It has been said that public policy should be invoked only in clear cases in which the potential harm to the public is incontestable, that whether the anticipated harm to the public will be likely to occur must be determined on tangible grounds instead of on mere generalities and that the burden of proof lies on those who assert that the court should not enforce a liability which prima facie exists. Even if one should put the matter in a more neutral way. I would say that public policy ought not to be invoked if the arguments are evenly balanced: in such a situation the ordinary rule of law. once established, should prevail.

[Lord Woolf at 344] ... the relationship is one where the employer should, as I have already indicated, appreciate that the terms of any reference which he gives could materially affect the ability of the subject of the reference to find alternative employment. Furthermore, in a contemporary employment context it is appropriate to regard the employer as obtaining an indirect benefit from giving a reference. Employers in industry, commerce and the professions are all dependent on the reciprocity which exists among employers as to the giving of references on prospective recruits. Without that reciprocity recruitment of staff would be more difficult. It would also directly affect an employer's ability to recruit staff if it became known that he was not prepared to assist those he has previously engaged by giving them references. Employees are unlikely to regard as attractive employment at the end of which they would find themselves without a reference.

The final of this trio of cases is probably the most difficult. As such, it is probably better regarded as a problematic and specific situation requiring a remedy, rather than a helpful application of a general principle. A testator had instructed the defendant solicitor to alter his will, so as to reinstate his daughters as named beneficiaries. He had previously removed them from it after a family feud. As a result of the solicitor's failure to do so, the daughters inherited nothing under the will. They, therefore, had suffered pure economic loss. The real conceptual difficulty of the case is that, whilst the defendant clearly owed a duty of care to the testator, the testator/his estate had suffered no loss. And yet, the defendant solicitor could not really be said to have assumed a responsibility towards the claimants, who were the ones who had suffered a loss. Nevertheless, the House of Lords held the solicitor liable for the claimants' loss on the basis that its 'voluntary assumption of responsibility' extended (and is, in a sense, transferred) from the testator to the claimant beneficiaries. Lord Goff's analysis of the situation tends towards an admission that this extension is somewhat artificial, but nonetheless necessary in order to achieve 'practical justice'.

White v Jones [1995] 2 AC 207, 265 (Lord Goff)

I turn next to English law in relation to cases such as the present. **Here there is a lacuna in the law, in the sense that practical justice requires that the disappointed beneficiary should have a remedy against the testator's solicitor in circumstances in which neither the testator nor his estate has in law suffered a loss.** Professor Lorenz (*Essays in Memory of Professor F.H. Lawson*, p.90) has said that 'this is a situation which comes very close to the cases of "transferred loss", the only difference being that the damage due to the solicitor's negligence could never have been caused to the testator or to his executor'.

In the case of the testator, he suffers no loss because (in contrast to a gift by an inter vivos settlor) a gift under a will cannot take effect until after the testator's death, and it follows that there can be no depletion of the testator's assets in his lifetime if the relevant asset is, through the solicitors' negligence, directed to a person other than the intended beneficiary. The situation is therefore not one in which events have subsequently occurred which have resulted in the loss falling on another. It is one in which the relevant loss could never fall on the testator to whom the solicitor owed a duty, but only on another; and the loss which is suffered by that other, i.e. an expectation loss, is of a character which in any event could never have been suffered by the testator. Strictly speaking, therefore, this is not a case of transferred loss.

Even so, the analogy is very close. In practical terms, part or all of the testator's estate has been lost because it has been despatched to a destination unintended by the testator. Moreover, had a gift been similarly misdirected during the testator's lifetime, he would either have been able to recover it from the recipient or, if not, he could have recovered the full amount from the negligent solicitor as damages. In a case such as the present, no such remedies are available to the testator or his estate. The will cannot normally be rectified: the testator has of course no remedy: and his estate has suffered no loss, because it has been distributed under the terms of a valid will. In these circumstances, there can be no injustice if the intended beneficiary has a remedy against the solicitor for the full amount which he should have received under the will, this being no greater than the damage for which the solicitor could have been liable to the donor if the loss had occurred in his lifetime.

A contractual approach

It may be suggested that, in cases such as the present, the simplest course would be to solve the problem by making available to the disappointed beneficiary, by some means or another, the benefit of the contractual rights (such as they are) of the testator or his estate against the negligent solicitor, as is for example done under the German principle of Vertrag mit Schutzwirkung fur Dritte. Indeed that course has been urged upon us by Professor Markesinis in (1987) 103 L.Q.R. 354, 396–397, echoing a view expressed by Professor Fleming in (1986) 4 O.J.L.S. 235, 241. Attractive though this solution is, there is unfortunately a serious difficulty in its way. The doctrine of consideration still forms part of our law of contract, as does the doctrine of privity of contract which is considered to exclude the recognition of a jus quaesitum tertio. To proceed as Professor Markesinis has suggested may be acceptable in German law, but in this country could be open to criticism as an illegitimate circumvention of these long established doctrines; and this criticism could be reinforced by reference to the fact that, in the case of carriage of goods by sea, a contractual solution to a particular problem of transferred loss, and to other cognate problems, was provided only by recourse to Parliament. Furthermore, I myself do not consider that the present case provides a suitable occasion for reconsideration of doctrines so fundamental as these.

The Albazero principle

Even so, I have considered whether the present problem might be solved by adding cases such as the present to the group of cases referred to by Lord Diplock in *The Albazero* [1977] A.C. 774, 846–847. In these cases, a person may exceptionally sue in his own name to recover a loss which he has not in fact suffered, being personally accountable for any damages so recovered to the person who has in fact suffered the loss. Lord Diplock was prepared to accommodate within this group the so-called rule in *Dunlop v. Lambert* (1839) 6 Cl. & F. 600, on the principle that:

> '... in a commercial contract concerning goods where it is in the contemplation of the parties that the proprietary interests in the goods may be transferred from one owner to another after the contract has been entered into and before the breach which causes loss or damage to the goods, an original party to the contract, if such be the intention of them both, is to be treated <u>in law</u> as having entered into the contract for the benefit of all persons who have or may acquire an interest in the goods before they are lost or damaged, and is entitled to recover by way of damages for breach of contract the actual loss sustained by those for whose benefit the contract is entered into.' [Emphasis supplied].

Furthermore, in *Linden Gardens Trust Ltd. v. Lenesta Sludge Disposals Ltd.* [1994] AC 85, your Lordships' House extended this group of cases to include a case in which work was done by the defendants under a contract with the first plaintiffs who, despite a contractual bar against assignment of their contractual rights without the consent of the defendants, had without consent assigned them to the second plaintiffs who suffered damage by reason of defective work carried out by the defendants. It was held that, by analogy with the cases referred to in *The Albazero*, [1977] A.C. 774 the first plaintiffs could recover the damages from the defendants for the benefit of the second plaintiffs. In so holding, your Lordships' House relied upon a passage in Lord Diplock's speech (at p. 847) that 'there may still be occasional cases in which the rule [in *Dunlop v. Lambert*] would provide a remedy where no other would be available to a person sustaining loss which under a rational legal system ought to be compensated by the person who has caused it'.

The decision is noteworthy in a number of respects. First, this was a case of transferred loss; and Lord Diplock's dictum, as applied by your Lordships' House, reflects a clear need for the law to find a remedy in cases of this kind. Second, your Lordships' House felt able to do so in a case in which there was a contractual bar against assignment without consent; and as a result, unlike Lord Diplock, did not find it necessary to look for a common intention that the contract was entered into for the benefit of persons such as the second plaintiffs, which in this case, having regard to the prohibition against assignment, it plainly was not. Third, the consequence was that your Lordships' House simply made the remedy available as a matter of law in order to solve the problem of transferred loss in the case before them.

Even so, the result was only to enable a person to recover damages in respect of loss which he himself had not suffered, for the benefit of a third party. In the present case, there is the difficulty that the third party (the intended beneficiary) is seeking to recover damages for a loss (expectation loss) which the contracting party (the testator) would not himself have suffered. In any event, under this principle, the third party who has suffered the loss is not able to compel the contracting party to sue for his benefit, or to transfer the right of action to him; still less is he entitled to sue in his own name. In the last analysis, this is because any such right would be contrary to the doctrine of privity of contract. In consequence a principle such as this, if it could be extended to cases such as the present, would be of limited value because, quite apart from any other difficulties, the family relationship may be such that the executors may be unwilling to assist the disappointed beneficiary by pursuing a claim of this kind for his benefit. Certainly, it could not assist the plaintiffs in the present case, who very understandably are proceeding against the solicitors by a direct action in their own name.

<u>The tortious solution</u>

I therefore return to the law of ton for a solution to the problem. For the reasons I have already given, an ordinary action in tortious negligence on the lines proposed by Sir Robert Megarry V.-C. in *Ross v. Caunters* [1980] Ch. 297 must, with the greatest respect, be regarded as inappropriate, because it does not meet any of the conceptual problems which have been raised. Furthermore, for the reasons I have previously given, the *Hedley Byrne* principle cannot, in the absence of special circumstances, give rise on ordinary principles to an assumption of responsibility by the testator's solicitor towards an intended beneficiary. Even so it seems to me that it is open to your Lordships' House, as in the *Lenesta Sludge* case [1994] AC 85, to fashion a remedy to fill a lacuna in the law and so prevent the injustice which would otherwise occur on the facts of cases such as the present. In the *Lenesta Sludge* case [1994] AC 85, as I have said, the House made available a remedy as a matter of law to solve the problem of transferred loss in the case before them. The present case is, if anything, a fortiori, since the nature of the transaction was such that, if the solicitors were negligent and their negligence did not come to light until after the death of the testator, there would be no remedy for the ensuing loss unless the intended beneficiary could claim. In my opinion, therefore, your Lordships' House should in cases such as these extend to the intended beneficiary a remedy under the *Hedley Byrne* principle by holding that the assumption of responsibility by the solicitor towards his client should be held in law to extend to the intended beneficiary who (as the solicitor can reasonably foresee) may, as a result of the solicitor's negligence, be deprived of his intended legacy in circumstances in which neither the testator nor his estate will have a remedy against the solicitor. Such liability will not of course arise in cases in which the defect in the will comes to light before the death of the testator, and the testator either leaves the will as it is or otherwise continues to exclude the previously intended beneficiary from the relevant benefit. I only wish to add that, with the benefit of experience during the fifteen years in which *Ross v. Caunters* has been regularly applied, we can say with some confidence that a direct remedy by the intended beneficiary against the solicitor appears to create no problems in practice. That is therefore the solution which I would recommend to your Lordships.

As I see it, not only does this conclusion produce practical justice as far as all parties are concerned, but it also has the following beneficial consequences:

(1) There is no unacceptable circumvention of established principles of the law of contract.
(2) No problem arises by reason of the loss being of a purely economic character.
(3) Such assumption of responsibility will of course be subject to any term of the contract between the solicitor and the testator which may exclude or restrict the solicitor's liability to the testator under the principle in *Hedley Byrne*. It is true that such a term would be most unlikely to exist in practice; but as a matter of principle it is right that this largely theoretical question should be addressed.
(4) Since the *Hedley Byrne* principle is founded upon an assumption of responsibility, the solicitor may be liable for negligent omissions as well as negligent acts of commission: see the *Midland Bank Trust Co.* case [1979] Ch. 384, 416, *per* Oliver J., and *Henderson v. Merrett Syndicates Ltd.* [1994] 3 W.L.R. 761, 777, *per* Lord Goff of Chieveley. This conclusion provides justification for the decision of the Court of Appeal to reverse the decision of Turner J. in the present case, although this point was not in fact raised below or before your Lordships.
(5) I do not consider that damages for loss of an expectation are excluded in cases of negligence arising under the principle in *Hedley Byrne*, simply because the cause of action is classified as tortious. Such damages may in principle be recoverable in cases of contractual negligence; and I cannot see that, for present purposes, any relevant distinction can be drawn between the two forms of action. In particular, an expectation loss may well occur in cases where a professional man, such as a solicitor, has assumed responsibility for the affairs of another; and I for my part can see no reason in principle why the professional man should not, in an appropriate case, be liable for such loss under the *Hedley Byrne* principle.

In the result, all the conceptual problems, including those which so troubled Lush and Murphy JJ. in *Seale v. Perry* [1982] V.R. 193, can be seen to fade innocuously away. Let me emphasise that I can see no injustice in imposing liability upon a negligent solicitor in a case such as the present where, in the absence of a remedy in this form, neither the testator's estate nor the disappointed beneficiary will have a claim for the loss caused by his negligence. This is the injustice which, in my opinion, the judges of this country should address by recognising that cases such as these call for an appropriate remedy, and that the common law is not so sterile as to be incapable of supplying that remedy when it is required.

Lord Goff's approach suggests that, if the law is to be complicated in order to achieve practical justice in a difficult case, then it is better to complicate the law of tort than the law of contract. Given that the English law of contract is famous the world over for its certainty, this is perhaps an understandable means of proceeding. In characteristically crisp terms, Tony Weir has the following to say about this particular extension of the *Hedley Byrne* principle:

Tony Weir, 'A damnosa hereditas?' (1995) 111(Jul) *LQR* 357–62

Now we may ask whether the actual decision was 'exceptional' or principled. All members of the House were clear that the case was not covered by existing authority .... On this Lord Browne-Wilkinson said: '... it is legitimate to extend the law to the limited extent proposed using the incremental approach by way of analogy advocated in *Caparo Industries Plc v. Dickman*'. Lord Keith of Kinkel and Lord Mustill were of the contrary opinion, Lord Mustill ... focused on the four distinctive features of *Hedley Byrne* ... The essence of *Hedley Byrne* he identified as 'mutuality', that the defendant was doing something the plaintiff had asked to be done: 'the undertaking of legal responsibility for careful and diligent performance in the context of a mutual relationship'. That feature was missing in the present case, where the defendant was responding to the testator, not the beneficiary. Lord Goff did not deny this ...

Lord Browne-Wilkinson, on the other hand, thought he could discern in *Hedley Byrne* a principle which covered the present case. He took liability under *Hedley Byrne* to be based on 'a conscious assumption of responsibility for the task rather than a conscious assumption of legal liability to the plaintiff for its careful performance' and said that mutuality, in Lord Mustill's sense, was not required. This last point he sought to support by invoking the fact that trustees are answerable to beneficiaries though they do not act at the beneficiaries' instance. This surprising analogy is not really very persuasive. Nor is this from Lord Nolan:

> 'If the defendant drives his car on the highway, he implicitly assumes a responsibility towards other road users, and they in turn implicitly rely on him to discharge that responsibility. By taking his car on to the road, he holds himself out as a reasonably careful driver. In the same way, as it seems to me, a professional man or an artisan who undertakes to exercise his skill in a manner which, to his knowledge, may cause loss to others if carelessly performed may thereby implicitly assume a legal responsibility towards them.'

It must be said that to see no difference between managing someone else's property and doing some service which might benefit him, or to say that driving and drafting are very much of a muchness, is carrying to rather unreasonable lengths the late twentieth-century horror of discriminating between what ought to be distinguished.

Question to consider: Do you think that the law has struck the right balance in its development of 'voluntary assumption of responsibility'. If not, what issues should be considered by the courts?

Other resources: K Barker, 'Are We Up to Expectations? Solicitors, Beneficiaries, and the Tort/Contract Divide' (1994) 14 *Oxford Journal of Legal Studies* 137; J Hartshorne, 'Contemporary Approaches Towards Pure Economic Loss in the Law of Negligence' (2014) 5 *JBL* 425–42; *White v Jones* [1995] 2 AC 207; *Banca Nazionale del Lavoro SPA v Playboy Club London Ltd and others* [2018] UKSC 43.

3.2 Defective premises

This category of pure economic loss is slightly different from what has gone before. That is because it could be said (and in some jurisdictions is said)[2] to be loss consequent on damage to property. In relatively recent times, the law has changed its mind on the issue of how loss should be classified in relation to defective premises. This can be seen most clearly in the shift in judicial analysis from *Anns v Merton LBC* [1978] AC 728 to *Murphy v Brentwood DC* [1991] UKHL 2. These cases show how the law deals with property which turns out to be defective, but where this does not become apparent until after the claimant has acquired it (for a value greater than what it is actually worth, given the latent defect). In *Anns*, the House of Lords regarded this loss as being a form of property damage. In the subsequent case of *Murphy*, however, a differently constituted House reached a different conclusion. As is obvious from Lord McKay's judgment, one significant reason for the change of direction between *Anns* and *Murphy* was the enactment of the Defective Premises Act 1972. That Act must now be read alongside the Building Safety Act 2022, which extends the limitation period in the 1972 Act from six to 15 years.[3] Such improved statutory protection could be argued to fortify further the view that a common law remedy is not necessary in this context.

Lord Keith, below, sets out another means of reclassifying the loss as purely economic; one based on the *timing* of the damage occurring: that is, if it has already occurred when the property is acquired, it is not damage, but a pre-existing fact about the property.

Murphy v Brentwood DC [1991] AC 398, 457 (Lord McKay), 466 (Lord Keith)

[Lord McKay at 457] ... it is relevant to take into account that Parliament has made provisions in the Defective Premises Act 1972 imposing on builders and others undertaking work in the provision of dwellings obligations relating to the quality of their work and the fitness for habitation of the dwelling. For this House in its judicial capacity to create a large new area of responsibility on local authorities in respect of defective buildings would in my opinion not be a proper exercise of judicial power. I am confirmed in this view by the consideration that it is not suggested, and does not appear to have been suggested in *Anns*, that the Public Health Act 1936, in particular Part II, manifests any intention to create statutory rights in favour of owners or occupiers of premises against the local authority charged with responsibility under the Act. The basis of the decision in *Anns* is that the common law will impose a duty in the interests of the safety and health of owners and occupiers of buildings since that was the purpose for which the

2 See, eg, *Brookfield Multiplex v Owners Corporation Strata Plan 61288* [2014] HCA 36 and *Invercargill City Council v Hamlin* [1996] AC 624.

3 Limitation Act 1980, s 4B.

Act of 1936 was enacted. While of course I accept that duties at common law may arise in respect of the exercise of statutory powers or the discharge of statutory duties I find difficulty in reconciling a common law duty to take reasonable care that plans should conform with byelaws or regulations with the statute which has imposed on the local authority the duty not to pass plans unless they comply with the byelaws or regulations and to pass them if they do.

In these circumstances I have reached the clear conclusion that the proper exercise of the judicial function requires this House now to depart from *Anns* in so far as it affirmed a private law duty of care to avoid damage to property which causes present or imminent danger to the health and safety of owners, or occupiers, resting upon local authorities in relation to their function of supervising compliance with building byelaws or regulations, that *Dutton v. Bognor Regis Urban District Council* should be overruled and that all decisions subsequent to *Anns* which purported to follow it should be overruled. I accordingly reach the same conclusion as do my noble and learned friends.

[Lord Keith at 466] **Consideration of the nature of the loss suffered in this category of cases is closely tied up with the question of when the cause of action arises.** Lord Wilberforce in *Anns* [1978] AC 728, 760 as regarded it as arising when the state of the building is such that there is present an imminent danger to the health or safety of persons occupying it. That state of affairs may exist when there is no actual physical damage to the building itself, though Lord Wilberforce had earlier referred to the relevant damage being material physical damage. So his meaning may have been that there must be a concurrence of material physical damage and also present or imminent danger to the health or safety of occupants. On that view there would be no cause of action where the building had suffered no damage (or possibly, having regard to the word 'material,' only very slight damage) but a structural survey had revealed an underlying defect, presenting imminent danger. Such a discovery would inevitably cause a fall in the value of the building, resulting in economic loss to the owner. That such is the nature of the loss is made clear in cases where the owner abandons the building as incapable of being put in a safe condition (as in Batty), or where he choses to sell it at the lower value rather than undertake remedial works. In *Pirelli General Cable Works Ltd. v. Oscar Faber & Partners* [1983] 2 A.C. 1 it was held that the cause of action in tort against consulting engineers who had negligently approved a defective design for a chimney arose when damage to the chimney caused by the defective design first occurred, not when the damage was discovered or with reasonable diligence might have been discovered. The defendants there had in relation to the design been in contractual relations with the plaintiffs, but it was common ground that a claim in contract was time-barred. If the plaintiffs had happened to discover the defect before any damage had occurred there would seem to be no good reason for holding that they would not have had a cause of action in tort at that stage, without having to wait until some damage had occurred. They would have suffered economic loss through having a defective chimney upon which they required to expend money for the purpose of removing the defect. It would seem that in a case such as

Pirelli where the tortious liability arose out of a contractual relationship with professional people, the duty extended to take reasonable care not to cause economic loss to the client by the advice given. The plaintiffs built the chimney as they did in reliance on that advice. The case would accordingly fall within the principle of *Hedley Byrne & Co. Ltd. v. Heller & Partners Ltd.* [1964] AC 465. I regard *Junior Books Ltd. v. Veitchi Co. Ltd.* [1983] 1 AC 520 as being an application of that principle.

In my opinion it must now be recognised that, although the damage in *Anns* was characterised as physical damage by Lord Wilberforce, it was purely economic loss. In *Council of the Shire of Sutherland v. Heyman*, 157 C.L.R. 424 where, as observed above, the High Court of Australia declined to follow *Anns* when dealing with a claim against a local authority in respect of a defectively constructed house, Deane J. said, at pp. 503–505:

> 'Nor is the respondents' claim in the present case for ordinary physical damage to themselves or their property. Their claim, as now crystallized, is not in respect of damage to the fabric of the house or to other property caused by collapse or subsidence of the house as a result of the inadequate foundations. It is for the loss or damage represented by the actual inadequacy of the foundations, that is to say, it is for the cost of remedying a structural defect in their property which already existed at the time when they acquired it. In *Anns v. Merton London Borough Council* [1978] AC 728, it was held by the House of Lords that a local government authority owed a relevant duty of care, in respect of inspection of the foundations of a building, to persons who subsequently became long term lessees (either as original lessees or as assignees) of parts of the building. Lord Wilberforce, at p. 759, in a speech with which three of the other four members of the House of Lords agreed, expressed the conclusion that the appropriate classification of damage sustained by the lessees by reason of the inadequacy of the foundations of the completed building was "material, physical damage, and what is recoverable is the amount of expenditure necessary to restore the dwelling to a condition in which it is no longer a danger to the health or safety of persons occupying and possibly (depending on the circumstances) expenses arising from necessary displacement." While, in a case where a subsequent purchaser or long term tenant reasonably elects to retain the premises and to reinforce the foundations, one possible measure of the damages involved in the actual inadequacy would (if such damages were recoverable) be that suggested by his Lordship, I respectfully disagree with the classification of the loss sustained in such circumstances as "material, physical damage." **Whatever may be the position with respect to consequential damage to the fabric of the building or to other property caused by susequent collapse or subsidence, the loss or Injury involved in the actual inadequacy of. the foundations cannot, in the case of a person who purchased or leased the property after the inadequacy existed but before it was known or manifest, properly be seen as ordinary physical or material damage. The only property which could be said to have been damaged in such a case is the building. The building itself could not be said to have been subjected to**

"material, physical damage" by reason merely of the inadequacy of its foundations since the building never existed otherwise than with its foundations in that state. Moreover, even if the inadequacy of the foundations could be seen as material, physical damage to the building, it would be damage to property in which a future purchaser or tenant had no interest at all at the time when it occurred. Loss or injury could only be sustained by such a purchaser or tenant on or after the acquisition of the freehold or leasehold estate without knowledge of the faulty foundations. It is arguable that any such loss or injury should be seen as being sustained at the time of acquisition when, because of ignorance of the inadequacy of the foundations, a higher price is paid (or a higher rent is agreed to be paid) than is warranted by the intrinsic worth of the freehold or leasehold estate that is being acquired. Militating against that approach is the consideration that, for so long as the inadequacy of the foundations is neither known nor manifest, no identifiable loss has come home: if the purchaser or tenant sells the freehold or leasehold estate within that time, he or she will sustain no loss by reason of the inadequacy of the foundations. The alternative, and in my view preferable, approach is that any loss or injury involved in the actual inadequacy of the foundations is sustained only at the time when that inadequacy is first known or manifest. It is only then that the actual diminution in the market value of the premises occurs. On either approach, however, any loss involved in the actual inadequacy of the foundations by a person who acquires an interest in the premises after the building has been completed is merely economic in its nature.'

I find myself in respectful agreement with the reasoning contained in this passage, which seems to me to be incontrovertible.

It being recognised that the nature of the loss held to be recoverable in *Anns* was pure economic loss, the next point for examination is whether the avoidance of loss of that nature fell within the scope of any duty of care owed to the plaintiffs by the local authority. On the basis of the law as it stood at the time of the decision the answer to that question must be in the negative. The right to recover for pure economic loss, not flowing from physical injury, did not then extend beyond the situation where the Joss had been sustained through reliance on negligent mis-statements, as in *Hedley Byrne*. There is room for the view that an exception is to be found in *The Greystoke Castle* [1947] A.C. 265. That case, which was decided by a narrow majority, may, however, be regarded as turning on specialties of maritime Jaw concerned in the relationship of joint adventurers at sea.

Further, though the purposes of the Act of 1936 as regards securing compliance with building byelaws covered the avoidance of injury to the safety or health of inhabitants of houses and of members of the public generally, these purposes did not cover the avoidance of pure economic loss to owners of buildings (see *Governors of the Peabody Donation Fund v. Sir Lindsay Parkinson & Co. Ltd.* [1985] AC 210, 241). Upon analysis, the nature of the duty held by *Anns* to be incumbent upon the local authority went very much further than a duty to take reasonable care to prevent injury to safety or health. The duty held to exist may be formulated as one to take reasonable care to avoid putting a future inhabitant owner of a house in a position in which he is threatened, by reason of a defect in the house, with avoidable physical injury to person or health and is obliged, in order to continue to occupy the house without suffering such injury, to expend money for the purpose of rectifying the defect.

As Professor Stapleton makes clear in the extract below, whatever the overall merits of not allowing common law claims for buildings with inherent and latent defects, it is hard to justify that position by reference to the oft-cited 'floodgates' argument. That argument is based on the law guarding against an indeterminate amount to an indeterminate class for an indeterminate time;[4] something that does potentially apply to the negligent causing of a power cut, but does not apply to the building and transfer of defective property.[5]

Jane Stapleton, 'Duty of Care and Economic Loss: A Wider Agenda' (1991) 107 *LQR* 249

The concern is with the unfairness involved in holding defendants liable to an indeterminate number of claimants and/or for claims of indeterminate size ... The indeterminate number of claims problem is exemplified by the consensus that a car manufacturer should not be liable for the potentially massive economic losses caused when one of its defective cars ceases to function in the Dartford Tunnel during the rush hour ... It is *not* an objection to a large number of claims. There is no reluctance to hold defendants liable for personal injuries suffered by a large but foreseeable class of victims, as some of the recent industrial disease litigation illustrates. The concern in the tunnel case centres around the fact that the *volume* of claims is indeterminate: it is unforeseeable when the blockage will occur ... so it is unforeseeable how many vehicles will be held up ... In addition, economic loss can 'ripple' down a chain of parties; for example, the loss of profits which D causes P may in turn cause loss of profits to P's supplier and in turn to that supplier's suppliers, etc. But the extent to which multiple claims will be generated in this way is indeterminate. In the physical damage area, the volume of potential 'first-victim' claims is usually foreseeable even when large. Moreover, it is rare for multiple physical damage claims to ripple down a chain ...

The second form of the floodgates concern is with the indeterminacy of each claim. Again this typically arises in lost profits cases. It is said that each plaintiff is in the best position to foresee the likely extent of his or her lost profits while the defendant will often be unable even to guess at it let alone take preventative action ...

4 See La Forest J in *Winnipeg* [1995] 1 SCR 85 at [48]–[50].

5 See also PS Davies and S Green, '"Pure Economic Loss" and Defective Buildings' in A Robertson and M Tilbury (eds), *Convergence and Divergence in the Common Law* (Hart, 2015).

In the real world, both forms of floodgates problem may be less threatening than is feared even in lost profit cases. More important, there is at least one major class of economic loss case where neither problem arises: this is where the plaintiff has, because of the negligence of the defendant, acquired property which is defective and as a result of which has suffered economic loss consisting of the lowered value of the asset. … – only the owner at the relevant time has suffered the loss described – nor is there a problem of the defendant being held liable for a quantum of loss he could not reasonably foresee.

Question to consider: Is the loss suffered in defective premises cases correctly classified as purely economic loss? In your answer, compare the approach taken by the UK courts to that of other Commonwealth jurisdictions.

Other resources: PS Davies and S Green, '"Pure Economic Loss" and Defective Buildings' in A Robertson and M Tilbury (eds), *Convergence and Divergence in the Common Law* (Hart, 2015); P Benson, 'The Basis for Excluding Economic Loss in Tort Law' in D Owen (ed), *Philosophical Foundations of Tort Law* (OUP, 1995); *Anns v Merton London Borough Council* [1978] AC 728; *Council of the Shire of Sutherland v Heyman* (1985) 157 CLR 424; *Brookfield Multiplex v Owners Corporation Strata Plan 61288* [2014] HCA 36; *Bowen v Paramount Builders (Hamilton) Ltd* [1975] 2 NZLR 546.

3.3 Conclusion

This chapter has dealt with one of the two areas of negligence in which indeterminacy comes into play when limiting a claimant's ability to recover. Since pure economic loss can be caused without physical proximity and passed on indefinitely, recovery needs to be limited if defendants' liability is not going to be out of all proportion to their wrongdoing. The other concern in relation to such potential liability is that it be insurable by the defendant, and indeterminacy makes this very difficult. This case law in this chapter has shown how and why it is important to distinguish between the ways in which pure economic loss can be caused and how it is classified, both in this jurisdiction and others across the common law world. As we have seen, some of the judicial reasoning in this area is tricky to reconcile, but there exists at least a common theme: identifying sufficient proximity between the relevant parties.

Chapter 4 PSYCHIATRIC INJURY

Recovery for psychiatric injury in the tort of negligence is, for a certain set of victims at least, less than straightforward. This is for a number of reasons. First, there is the historical baggage associated with mental illness: the tendency not to regard it as being as recognisable or as detrimental as physical harm. Then there is the Hillsborough disaster, the catastrophic event that gave rise to the claims on which most of the modern law relating to psychiatric injury is based. The unique scale and nature of this event arguably affected the legal approach to its related claims in a way which might have been different had the situation been of a lesser magnitude. Finally, there is the standard legal 'floodgates' argument about indeterminacy: the law's concern about holding defendants liable for an indeterminate time, for an indeterminate amount and to an indeterminate class.[1] This last concern is the reason for the distinction made by the law between primary and secondary victims. This is a crucial distinction because the floodgates argument is not an issue where primary victims are concerned (because, as we shall see, such victims do not constitute an indeterminate class). It is, however, at least potentially very much an issue where secondary victims are concerned.

4.1 Primary victims

The first case makes this distinction in a very accessible way. The defendant negligently caused a minor vehicle collision. The claimant victim had a history of suffering from myalgic encephalomyelitis (ME), a condition characterised by long-term fatigue. His condition became chronic and permanent as a result of the accident, making it unlikely that he would be able to work full-time ever again. The claimant succeeded in his negligence claim at trial, but the Court of Appeal allowed the defendant's appeal on the basis that the claimant's injury was not foreseeable. The House of Lords disagreed, and restored the finding in favour of the claimant.

---

1 See also Chapter 3.

Page v Smith [1996] AC 155, 180 (Lord Jauncey), 182 (Lord Browne-Wilkinson), 190 (Lord Lloyd)

[Lord Jauncey at 180] On no view could it here be suggested that the appellant suffered an acute emotional trauma. Otton J. found that the collision was one of moderate severity. However neither the plaintiff nor the occupants of the other car were injured. The appellant suffered no bruises from his seat belt and did not suggest that he was at any time in fear for his own safety or that of the occupants of the other car. He was able to write down the name and address of the respondent, to telephone his wife quite normally and then drive home. His car sustained damage which resulted in it being written off by his insurers but it appears that it was on the ground of economics due to its age and small value rather than because of the severity of the damage. This case is accordingly far removed from those cases in which foreseeability of nervous shock has been established. A motor car collision in which the only damage is to the vehicles involved neither of which even leave the road is not an event which could normally be expected to produce nervous shock with consequential psychiatric illness to one or more of the occupants. I entirely agree with the views of Ralph Gibson and Hoffmann L.JJ. in the Court of Appeal [1994] 4 All E.R. 522, at pp. 544g and 552h – 553c respectively to the effect that it was not reasonably foreseeable that the appellant would suffer nervous shock as a result of this accident. The appeal must therefore be dismissed.

[Lord Browne-Wilkinson at 182] The law has therefore been established both in England and Scotland for many years that a plaintiff who is a participant in an accident is entitled to recover damages for shock even though he or she has not suffered any tangible physical injury. I can see no good reason to modify this law. The analogy drawn with the more recent development in the law permitting a plaintiff, not a participant in an accident, to recover damages for nervous shock flowing from fear for the safety of others or from the trauma of witnessing the event does not seem to me to touch on the case. **A non-participant plaintiff is outside the ordinary area within which the defendant can foresee causing damage. The only method whereby a non participant plaintiff can establish that the defendant should have foreseen damage to the plaintiff is by showing that he ought to have foreseen nervous shock.** As Lord Lloyd of Berwick has demonstrated, the law as laid down in relation to these non- participant claims for nervous shock damages has not been applied to claims for such damages made by a plaintiff who was himself involved in the accident. In this connection, it is noteworthy that in *Bourhill v. Young* [1943] A.C. 92, 120 Lord Porter, whilst dismissing the pursuer's claim in that case, referred to *Currie v. Wardrop* 1927 S.C. 538 and said 'Undoubtedly, there was in that case a duty to the pursuer (the woman) and a breach of that duty ...' It is clear that Lord Porter at least was drawing a distinction between claims for nervous shock made by a participant in the accident on the one hand and by a non-participant on the other.

I am therefore of opinion that any driver of a car should reasonably foresee that, if he drives carelessly, he will be liable to cause injury, either physical or psychiatric or both, to other users of the highway who become involved in an accident. Therefore he owes to such persons a duty of care to avoid such injury. **In the present case the defendant could not foresee the exact type of psychiatric damage in fact suffered by the plaintiff who, due to his M.E., was 'an eggshell personality'. But that is of no significance since the defendant did owe a duty of care to prevent foreseeable damage, including psychiatric damage. Once such duty of care is established, the defendant must take the plaintiff as he finds him.**

Finally I would endorse Lord Lloyd's remarks about the dangers of the court seeking to draw hard and fast lines between physical illness and its causes on the one hand and psychiatric illness and its causes on the other. Although medical science has not as yet progressed very far in elucidating the processes whereby psychiatric disorders come about, recent developments suggest a much closer relationship between physical and mental processes than had previously been thought. There is a substantial body of informed medical opinion which attributes some mental illness to physical causes such as chemical or hormonal imbalance. In the present case, for example, although all but one of the distinguished doctors who gave evidence were agreed that there was indeed an illness (however mysterious) called M.E. and that the plaintiff suffered from it, they had differing views as to its causes. One thought M.E. was linked to viral infection (physical) and stress (psychological): another to neuroendocrine disturbance (physical) and psychiatric disorder. In cases where distinguished doctors take differing views as to the aetiology of an illness it obviously presents great problems for the court to resolve what was the cause of the recrudescence of such an illness. For the courts to impose different criteria for liability depending upon whether the injury is 'physical' or 'psychiatric' is likely to lead to a growing complication in straight forward personal injury cases. In my judgment, the law will be more effective if it accepts that the result of being involved in a collision may include both physical and psychiatric damage.

[Lord Lloyd at 190] The test in every case ought to be whether the defendant can reasonably foresee that his conduct will expose the plaintiff to risk of personal injury. If so, then he comes under a duty of care to that plaintiff. If a working definition of 'personal injury' is needed, it can be found in section 38(1) of the Limitation Act 1980:

> '"Personal injuries" includes any disease and any impairment of a person's physical or mental condition ...'

There are numerous other statutory definitions to the same effect. In the case of a secondary victim, the question will usually turn on whether the foreseeable injury is psychiatric, for the reasons already explained. In the case of a primary victim the question will almost always turn on whether the foreseeable injury is physical. But it is the same test in both cases, with different applications. There is no justification for regarding physical and psychiatric injury as different 'kinds' of injury. Once it is established that the defendant is under a duty of care to avoid causing personal injury to the plaintiff, it matters not whether the injury in fact sustained is physical, psychiatric or both. The utility of a single test is most apparent in those cases such as *Schneider v. Eisovitch* [1960] 2 Q.B. 430, *Malcolm v. Broadhurst* [1970] 3 All E.R. 508 and *Brice v. Brown* [1984] 1 All E.R. 997, where the plaintiff is both primary and secondary victim of the same accident.

As these excerpts make clear, the fact that claimants are primary victims (in that *physical* injury to them is foreseeable) means that indeterminacy is not a problem: they will be within the defendant's sphere of foreseeability because the class of people to whom one might cause physical injury is determinate. Once a claimant is within that sphere, whether the injury that results in fact is physical or psychiatric is of no relevance (and psychiatric injury is recoverable even if no physical injury has actually occurred, as was the case in *Page*). Where physical injury is not in itself foreseeable, the victim will be classed as secondary because any psychiatric injury will not be the result of a primary risk to them. Generally, this is a fairly straightforward distinction to make: primary victims are those who are in the physical sphere of potential harm, and secondary victims are those not themselves physically at risk of such harm. You will need to be aware, however, of the next case because it is something of an exception to this simple rule.

W v Essex CC [2000] UKHL 17, [2001] 2 AC 592, 599 (Lord Slynn)

The claimants were parents of children who had been sexually abused by a foster child, placed with them by the local council. The claimants had explicitly specified that they were not prepared to foster a child with a history of sexually abusing others, but the council breached its duty in placing such a child with them. The House of Lords was here deciding whether the parents' claim should be struck out. This judgment, therefore, makes no finding one way or another on whether the claimants were actually classed as primary or secondary victims, but it does show that the House unanimously felt that that their case for being primary victims was arguable and had, therefore, a chance of succeeding. It also contains a very useful account of the reasoning involved in making any such distinction.

> ... the law recognises a distinction between 'primary victims' and 'secondary victims.' The former are those who were involved in the event causing the psychiatric injury 'mediately or immediately as [participants]' (*Alcock* [1992] 1 AC 310, 407D-E). Moreover it was only if the parents were within the range of foreseeable physical injury that they were primary victims: *Frost v. Chief Constable of South Yorkshire Police* [1999] 2 AC 455. If such physical injury had been foreseeable then a claim might lie for psychiatric injury even if it was not itself foreseeable: *Page v. Smith* [1996] AC 155. The parents were not participants in this sense in the injury to their children nor was it foreseeable that if G. was placed with the family the parents would suffer physical injury.
>
> A secondary victim on the other hand is 'no more than the passive and unwilling witness of injury caused to others' (*Alcock* p. 407D-E *per* Lord Oliver of Aylmerton) and to be compensatable in damages psychiatric injury must be foreseeable in persons of normal fortitude. Moreover there must be a sufficiently proximate relationship with the person causing physical harm to that other. Here the parents had the necessary ties of love for their children but they were neither near enough in time or space to the acts of abuse and they did not have direct visual or oral perception of the incident or its aftermath as the

House, agreeing with the speech of Lord Oliver, required that they would have to have in order to claim for psychiatric injury. The parents only knew about the incidents after they had happened.

The defendants also reject any suggestion that the parents can claim to be entitled to damages because they feel that they had participated in or contributed to or laid the foundation for the commission of the acts of abuse on their children by arranging for G. to be brought into their home. They were for example much less involved in the accident than the claimant in *Hunter v. British Coal Corporation* [1999] Q.B. 140. The parents are in no different position from a person who suffers shock on being told of the death of a loved one ...

Is it clear beyond reasonable doubt that the parents cannot satisfy the necessary criteria as 'primary' or 'secondary' victims? As to being primary victims it is beyond doubt that they were not physically injured by the abuse and on the present allegations it does not seem reasonably foreseeable that there was risk of sexual abuse of the parents. But the categorisation of those claiming to be included as primary or secondary victims is not as I read the cases finally closed. It is a concept still to be developed in different factual situations. Lord Goff of Chieveley (dissenting) in *Frost* [1999] 2 AC 455, 472G said that Lord Oliver 'did not attempt any definition of this category [i.e. of primary victims] but simply referred to a number of examples.' In *Robertson v. Forth Road Bridge Joint Board* 1995 SCLR 466 at p. 475D Lord President (Hope) said 'Nor is there any basis in the evidence for attributing their illnesses to a belief that they had been the unwitting cause of Smith's death.' That seems to recognise that if there had been such a basis a claim might have been arguable. See also the discussion in *Young v. Charles Church (Southern) Limited*, (unreported), 24 April 1997; (Civil Division) Transcript number 810 of 1997, as to whether the claimant there was a primary or a secondary victim.

I do not consider that any of the cases to which your Lordships have been referred conclusively shows that, if the psychiatric injury suffered by the parents flows from a feeling that they brought the abuser and the abused together or that they have a feeling of responsibility that they did not detect earlier what was happening, prevents them from being primary victims. Indeed, in *Alcock* [1992] 1 AC 310, 408F Lord Oliver said 'The fact that the defendant's negligent conduct has foreseeably put the plaintiff in the position of being an unwilling participant in the event establishes of itself a sufficiently proximate relationship between them and the principal question is whether, in the circumstances, injury of that type to that plaintiff was or was not reasonably foreseeable.'

In the next case, the primary/secondary victim distinction is explored further, as is the decision in *Page v Smith*. The question, answered so clearly and emphatically by Lord Hoffmann below, is what should happen where the event that causes the psychiatric injury has actually occurred (as did the collision in *Page v Smith*), as opposed to when the psychiatric injury is caused by fear/anticipation of that event occurring (as was the case in *Rothwell*, below).

Rothwell v Chemical and Insulating Co Ltd [2007] UKHL 39, [2008] 1 AC 281, [30]–[33] (Lord Hoffmann)

The claimants were employees who had been exposed to asbestos by their defendant employers. As a result, they had developed pleural plaques (patches of scar tissue) on their lungs. Such pleural plaques are not deemed to amount to physical injury for the purposes of grounding a negligence action in its own right: first, the plaques are symptomless; second, although the plaques signify that exposure to asbestos dust has occurred, they do not in themselves mean that those who have them are any more likely to develop an asbestos-related disease than those who have been exposed to asbestos but have not developed pleural plaques. The claimants conceded this much, but based their claim on the existence of those plaques *combined with* the fact that, as a result of becoming aware of the plaques, they had developed anxiety about their risk of sustaining an asbestos-related disease in the future. The House of Lords found that the defendant employers were not liable because the claimants had suffered no more than an increased risk of developing a disease in the future. Unless and until such injury actually occurs, there is nothing recognised by the tort of negligence as forming the gist of an action: mere anxiety about an increased risk is not sufficient. Whilst one of the claimants, Grieves, had suffered more than anxiety, in that he had been diagnosed with a recognised psychiatric illness, this was still found to be insufficient because it was based only on the *risk of* a future injury.

30. In the case of psychiatric illness, the standard description of what should have been foreseen, namely that *the event which actually happened* would have caused psychiatric illness to a person of 'sufficient fortitude' or 'customary phlegm', has been part of the law since the speech of Lord Porter in *Bourhill v Young* [1943] AC 92, 117. It was plainly intended to make the test more difficult to satisfy than whether it was foreseeable that something might happen which would cause someone (or even a person of reasonable fortitude) to suffer psychiatric injury. The latter test would not be hard to satisfy, as is evidenced by the opinion of the majority of the House in *Page v Smith* [1996] AC 155. But in my opinion the latter test was applicable only in the special circumstances of that case, to which I shall in due course return. The general rule still requires one to decide whether it was reasonably foreseeable that the event which actually happened (in this case, the creation of a risk of an asbestos-related disease) would cause psychiatric illness to a person of reasonable fortitude. I think that the Court of Appeal was right to say that there was no basis for such a finding.

Page v Smith

31. Counsel for Mr Grieves submits that even if his psychiatric illness was not foreseeable, the decision of the majority of the House in *Page v Smith* [1996] AC 155 makes such foreseeability unnecessary. It is enough that his employer ought to have foreseen that exposure to asbestos might cause him physical injury, namely, an asbestos-related disease. In *Page v Smith* it was held to be sufficient that the defendant should have foreseen that his negligent driving might cause some physical injury. It did not matter that he could not

have foreseen that the event which actually happened, namely a minor collision, would cause psychiatric injury.

32. Counsel for the defendant invited the House to depart from the decision in *Page v Smith* on the ground that it was wrongly decided. It has certainly had no shortage of critics, chief of whom was Lord Goff of Chieveley in *Frost v Chief Constable of South Yorkshire Police* [1999] 2 AC 455, supported by a host of academic writers. But I do not think that it would be right to depart from *Page v Smith*. It does not appear to have caused any practical difficulties and is not, I think, likely to do so if confined to the kind of situation which the majority in that case had in mind. That was a foreseeable event (a collision) which, viewed in prospect, was such as might cause physical injury or psychiatric injury or both. Where such an event has in fact happened and caused psychiatric injury, the House decided that it is unnecessary to ask whether it was foreseeable that what actually happened would have that consequence. Either form of injury is recoverable.

33. In the present case, the foreseeable event was that the claimant would contract an asbestos-related disease. If that event occurred, it could no doubt cause psychiatric as well as physical injury. But the event has not occurred. The psychiatric illness has been caused by apprehension that the event may occur. The creation of such a risk is, as I have said, not in itself actionable. I think it would be an unwarranted extension of the principle in *Page v Smith* to apply it to psychiatric illness caused by apprehension of the possibility of an unfavourable event which had not actually happened.

In order to make the distinction, then, ask yourself whether the claimant was exposed to an event that could have caused psychiatric injury (in which case they will be a primary victim on the basis of *Page v Smith*) or whether they were exposed to *the risk of* an event happening that could have caused such injury. *Rothwell* is probably best described as a case involving *potential* primary victims, as opposed to actual primary victims. The rule in *Page*, which applies where a claimant has been within the vicinity of an event that has actually occurred, means that they can recover for psychiatric injury even where a person of reasonable fortitude would not have suffered the same way. Where, however, claimants are not in that vicinity but are instead exposed to an increased risk of an event happening in the future (such as the development of an asbestos-related disease), the question of whether a person of reasonable fortitude would have responded in the same way *is* relevant (and recovery will only be allowed when the answer to that last question is yes).

Importantly, a slightly different, and more subjective, approach is taken where the claimant has suffered from psychiatric injury as a result of being exposed by their employer to stress, as opposed to physical risks, at work. In the next case, *Barber v Somerset County Council*, the claimant was a teacher whose doctor had signed him off for three weeks as a result of his suffering from stress and depression. After this period, he returned to work and was promised a greater level of support. Eventually, however, he suffered a mental breakdown and sued his employer in negligence.

The House of Lords found that the defendant employer had been in breach of its duty of care once it knew (or ought reasonably to have known) that he had a particular vulnerability. Although it came to a different conclusion to the Court of Appeal on the facts, the House of Lords endorsed Hale LJ's 'practical propositions':[2]

> (1) There are no special control mechanisms applying to claims for psychiatric (or physical) illness or injury arising from the stress of doing the work the employee is required to do. The ordinary principles of employer's liability apply.
>
> (2) **The threshold question is whether this kind of harm to this particular employee was reasonably foreseeable:** this has two components (a) an injury to health (as distinct from occupational stress) which (b) is attributable to stress at work (as distinct from other factors).
>
> (3) **Foreseeability depends upon what the employer knows (or ought reasonably to know) about the individual employee.** Because of the nature of mental disorder, it is harder to foresee than physical injury, but may be easier to foresee in a known individual than in the population at large. An employer is usually entitled to assume that the employee can withstand the normal pressures of the job unless he knows of some particular problem or vulnerability.
>
> (4) The test is the same whatever the employment: there are no occupations which should be regarded as intrinsically dangerous to mental health.
>
> (5) Factors likely to be relevant in answering the threshold question include:
>
> (a) The nature and extent of the work done by the employee. Is the workload much more than is normal for the particular job? Is the work particularly intellectually or emotionally demanding for this employee? Are demands being made of this employee unreasonable when compared with the demands made of others in the same or comparable jobs? Or are there signs that others doing this job are suffering harmful levels of stress? Is there an abnormal level of sickness or absenteeism in the same job or the same department?
>
> (b) Signs from the employee of impending harm to health. Has he a particular problem or vulnerability? Has he already suffered from illness attributable to stress at work? Have there recently been frequent or prolonged absences which are uncharacteristic of him? Is there reason to think that these are attributable to stress at work, for example because of complaints or warnings from him or others?
>
> (6) The employer is generally entitled to take what he is told by his employee at face value, unless he has good reason to think to the contrary. He does not generally have to make searching enquiries of the employee or seek permission to make further enquiries of his medical advisers.

2 Particularly Lord Scott at 6: Hale LJ in *Sutherland v Hatton* at [2002] ICR 613 at 631–32.

(7) To trigger a duty to take steps, the indications of impending harm to health arising from stress at work must be plain enough for any reasonable employer to realise that he should do something about it.
(8) The employer is only in breach of duty if he has failed to take the steps which are reasonable in the circumstances, bearing in mind the magnitude of the risk of harm occurring, the gravity of the harm which may occur, the costs and practicability of preventing it, and the justifications for running the risk.
(9) The size and scope of the employer's operation, its resources and the demands it faces are relevant in deciding what is reasonable; these include the interests of other employees and the need to treat them fairly, for example, in any redistribution of duties.
(10) An employer can only reasonably be expected to take steps which are likely to do some good: the court is likely to need expert evidence on this.
(11) An employer who offers a confidential advice service, with referral to appropriate counselling or treatment services, is unlikely to be found in breach of duty.
(12) If the only reasonable and effective step would have been to dismiss or demote the employee, the employer will not be in breach of duty in allowing a willing employee to continue in the job.
(13) In all cases, therefore, it is necessary to identify the steps which the employer both could and should have taken before finding him in breach of his duty of care.
(14) The claimant must show that that breach of duty has caused or materially contributed to the harm suffered. It is not enough to show that occupational stress has caused the harm.
(15) Where the harm suffered has more than one cause, the employer should only pay for that proportion of the harm suffered which is attributable to his wrongdoing, unless the harm is truly indivisible. It is for the defendant to raise the question of apportionment.
(16) The assessment of damages will take account of any pre-existing disorder or vulnerability and of the chance that the claimant would have succumbed to a stress related disorder in any event.

As well as endorsing these principles, the House of Lords added further reasoning on the issue:

Barber v Somerset County Council [2004] UKHL 13, [2004] 1 WLR 1089, [67], [68], [70] (Lord Walker)

67. My Lords, the issue of breach of the County Council's duty of care to Mr Barber was in my view fairly close to the borderline. It was not a clear case of a flagrant breach of duty any more than it was an obviously hopeless claim. But the judge, who saw and heard the witnesses (including Mr Barber himself, Mrs Hayward and Mr Gill) came to

the conclusion that the employer was in breach of duty, and in my view there was insufficient reason for the Court of Appeal to set aside his finding. The Court of Appeal was concerned about the timing of the breach, but for my part I do not think there is much room for doubt about that. The employer's duty to take some action arose in June and July 1996, when Mr Barber saw separately each member of the school's senior management team. It continued so long as nothing was done to help Mr Barber. The Court of Appeal evidently considered that Mr Barber was insufficiently forceful in what he said at these interviews, and that he should have described his troubles and his symptoms in much more detail. But he was already suffering from depression, and neither Mrs Hayward nor Mrs Newton was a sympathetic listener. What the Court of Appeal failed to give adequate weight to was the fact that Mr Barber, an experienced and conscientious teacher, had been off work for three weeks (not two weeks, as the Court of Appeal thought at para 160) with no physical ailment or injury. His absence was certified by his doctor to be due to stress and depression. The senior management team should have made inquiries about his problems and seen what they could do to ease them, in consultation with officials at the County Council's Education Department, instead of brushing him off unsympathetically (as Mrs Hayward and Mrs Newton did) or sympathising but simply telling him to prioritise his work (as Mr Gill did).

68. It was argued that the school as a whole was facing such severe problems (with all the teachers stressed and overworked, no budget for more staff, and the Ofsted inspection looming) that there was nothing that the school could have done to help Mr Barber other than advising him to resign, or in the last resort terminating his employment (a point on which the Court of Appeal made some observations in para 34 of its judgment). I would not accept that. At the very least the senior management team should have taken the initiative in making sympathetic inquiries about Mr Barber when he returned to work, and making some reduction in his workload to ease his return. Even a small reduction in his duties, coupled with the feeling that the senior management team was on his side, might by itself have made a real difference. In any event Mr Barber's condition should have been monitored, and if it did not improve, some more drastic action would have had to be taken. Supply teachers cost money, but not as much as the cost of the permanent loss through psychiatric illness of a valued member of the school staff.

…

70. The Court of Appeal also attached weight to the fact that Mr Barber did not make any further complaint during the autumn term. The judge had to assess the significance of that but he evidently (para 56) saw Mr Barber's nervous breakdown in November 1996 as caused by failures on the employer's part which had continued since the summer term. During the autumn term Mr Barber was still ill with depression, and he seems to have concluded, after his experiences in the summer, that further complaint would be pointless. He had also (as he saw it) failed to obtain help when he went to his doctor on 19 September 1996 and his doctor did not advise him not to go to work. But as the senior management team did not know that Mr Barber had been to see his doctor, they cannot

take much comfort from the doctor's opinion. The judge was entitled to form the view that the school's senior management team were in a position of continuing breach of the employer's duty of care, and that that caused Mr Barber's serious nervous breakdown on 12 November 1996.

It is clear from this that, where the claimant is suffering from psychiatric injury as a result of pressure at work, it is the ongoing nature and extent of this pressure that is relevant. This must be taken into account by a court as well as the effect that that pressure had *on the individual claimant before the court* and the defendant's knowledge of this specific effect.

Although the law on primary victims might seem less than straightforward (and it is – so the best way to deal with it is to know your case law so that you can apply the most relevant authority to any facts you might be presented with), the law applicable to secondary victims is even more challenging.

4.2 Secondary victims

As established above, secondary victims are those claimants who were not themselves within the sphere of risk of physical injury. In any problem question, this is the distinction you must make at the outset, because the psychiatric injury of secondary victims is treated very differently in law to that of primary victims, and different authorities apply. In essence, recovery is a lot more restricted in relation to secondary victims than it is to primary victims. This is because, as also established above, the indeterminacy issue does not arise in relation to those within the proximity of physical risk, but potentially is engaged by those who suffer as a result of someone else's physical peril. The most significant cases on this issue are those that arose out of the Hillsborough disaster, in which many people were killed or injured as a result of overcrowding at a football stadium. In the first case below, the claimants were not physically involved in the crush at the stadium, but were connected in some way to people who were, some of whom had died or been injured. These claimants were not therefore primary victims. Images of these highly distressing events were to some extent broadcast on television, both live at the time and repeated several times afterwards. The potential for indeterminate liability on such facts is clear.

Alcock v Chief Constable of South Yorkshire [1992] 1 AC 310, 396 (Lord Keith), 403 (Lord Ackner)

[Lord Keith at 396] It was argued for the plaintiffs in the present case that reasonable foreseeability of the risk of injury to them in the particular form of psychiatric illness was all that was required to bring home liability to the defendant. In the ordinary case of direct physical injury suffered in an accident at work or elsewhere, reasonable foreseeability of the risk is indeed the only test that need be applied to determine liability. But injury by psychiatric illness is more subtle, as Lord Macmillan observed in Bourhill v. Young [1943]

AC 92, 103. **In the present type of case it is a secondary sort of injury brought about by the infliction of physical injury, or the risk of physical injury, upon another person.** That can affect those closely connected with that person in various ways. One way is by subjecting a close relative to the stress and strain of caring for the injured person over a prolonged period, but psychiatric illness due to such stress and strain has not so far been treated as founding a claim in damages. **So I am of the opinion that in addition to reasonable foreseeability liability for injury in the particular form of psychiatric illness must depend in addition upon a requisite relationship of proximity between the claimant and the party said to owe the duty.** Lord Atkin in Donoghue v. Stevenson [1932] AC 562, 580 described those to whom a duty of care is owed as being:

> 'persons who are so closely and directly affected by my act that I ought reasonably to have them in contemplation as being so affected when I am directing my mind to the acts or omissions which are called in question.'

The concept of a person being closely and directly affected has been conveniently labelled 'proximity,' and this concept has been applied in certain categories of cases, particularly those concerned with pure economic loss, to limit and control the consequences as regards liability which would follow if reasonable foreseeability were the sole criterion.

As regards the class of persons to whom a duty may be owed to take reasonable care to avoid inflicting psychiatric illness through nervous shock sustained by reason of physical injury or peril to another, I think it sufficient that reasonable foreseeability should be the guide. I would not seek to limit the class by reference to particular relationships such as husband and wife or parent and child. The kinds of relationship which may involve close ties of love and affection are numerous, and it is the existence of such ties which leads to mental disturbance when the loved one suffers a catastrophe. They may be present in family relationships or those of close friendship, and may be stronger in the case of engaged couples than in that of persons who have been married to each other for many years. It is common knowledge that such ties exist, and reasonably foreseeable that those bound by them may in certain circumstances be at real risk of pyschiatric illness if the loved one is injured or put in peril. **The closeness of the tie would, however, require to be proved by a plaintiff, though no doubt being capable of being presumed in appropriate cases.** The case of a bystander unconnected with the victims of an accident is difficult. Psychiatric injury to him would not ordinarily, in my view, be within the range of reasonable foreseeability, but could not perhaps be entirely excluded from it if the circumstances of a catastrophe occurring very close to him were particularly horrific.

In the case of those within the sphere of reasonable foreseeability the proximity factors mentioned by Lord Wilberforce in McLoughlin v. O'Brian [1983] 1 AC 410, 422, must, however, be taken into account in judging whether a duty of care exists. The first of these is proximity of the plaintiff to the accident in time and space. For this purpose the accident is to be taken to include its immediate aftermath, which in McLoughlin's case was held to cover the scene at the hospital which was experienced by the plaintiff some two hours after the accident. In Jaensch v. Coffey (1984) 155 C.L.R. 549, the plaintiff saw her injured husband at the hospital to which he had been taken in severe pain before and between his undergoing a series of emergency operations, and the next day stayed with him in the intensive care unit and thought he was going to die. She was held entitled to recover damages for the psychiatric illness she suffered as a result. Deane J. said, at p. 608:

> 'the aftermath of the accident extended to the hospital to which the injured person was taken and persisted for so long as he remained in the state produced by the accident up to and including immediate post-accident treatment .... Her psychiatric injuries were the result of the impact upon her of the facts of the accident itself and its aftermath while she was present at the aftermath of the accident at the hospital.'

As regards the means by which the shock is suffered, Lord Wilberforce said in McLoughlin v. O'Brian [1983] 1 AC 410, 423 that it must come through sight or hearing of the event on or of its immediate aftermath. He also said that it was surely right that the law should not compensate shock brought about by communication by a third party. On that basis it is open to serious doubt whether Hevican v. Ruane [1991] 3 All E.R. 65 and Ravenscroft v. Rederiaktiebølaget Transatlantic [1991] 3 All E.R. 73 were correctly decided, since in both of these cases the effective cause of the psychiatric illness would appear to have been the fact of a son's death and the news of it.

[Lord Ackner at 403] *The three elements*

Because 'shock' in its nature is capable of affecting such a wide range of persons, Lord Wilberforce in McLoughlin v. O'Brian [1983] 1 AC 410, 422, concluded that there was a real need for the law to place some limitation upon the extent of admissible claims and in this context he considered that there were three elements inherent in any claim. It is common ground that such elements do exist and are required to be considered in connection with all these claims. The fundamental difference in approach is that on behalf of the plaintiffs it is contended that the consideration of these three elements is merely part of the process of deciding whether, as a matter of fact, the reasonable foreseeability test has been satisfied. On behalf of the defendant it is contended that these elements operate as a control or limitation on the mere application of the reasonable foreseeability test. They introduce the requirement of 'proximity' as conditioning the duty of care.

The three elements are (1) the class of persons whose claims should be recognised; (2) the proximity of such persons to the accident – in time and space; (3) the means by which the shock has been caused.

I will deal with those three elements seriatim.

(1) The class of persons whose claim should be recognised

When dealing with the possible range of the class of persons who might sue, Lord Wilberforce in McLoughlin v. O'Brian [1983] 1 AC 410 contrasted the closest of family ties – parent and child and husband and wife – with that of the ordinary bystander. He said that while existing law recognises the claims of the first, it denied that of the second, either on the basis that such persons must be assumed to be possessed with fortitude sufficient to enable them to endure the calamities of modern life, or that defendants cannot be expected to compensate the world at large. He considered that these positions were justified, that other cases involving less close relationships must be very carefully considered, adding, at p. 422:

> 'The closer the tie (not merely in relationship, but in care) the greater the claim for consideration. The claim, in any case, has to be judged in the light of the other factors, such as proximity to the scene in time and place, and the nature of the accident.'

I respectfully share the difficulty expressed by Atkin L.J. in Hambrook v. Stokes Brothers [1925] 1 K.B. 141, 158-159 – how do you explain why the duty is confined to the case of parent or guardian and child and does not extend to other relations of life also involving intimate associations; and why does it not eventually extend to bystanders? As regards the latter category, while it may be very difficult to envisage a case of a stranger, who is not actively and foreseeably involved in a disaster or its aftermath, other than in the role of rescuer, suffering shock-induced psychiatric injury by the mere observation of apprehended or actual injury of a third person in circumstances that could be considered reasonably foreseeable, I see no reason in principle why he should not, if in the circumstances, a reasonably strong-nerved person would have been so shocked. In the course of argument your Lordships were given, by way of an example, that of a petrol tanker careering out of control into a school in session and bursting into flames. I would not be prepared to rule out a potential claim by a passer-by so shocked by the scene as to suffer psychiatric illness.

As regards claims by those in the close family relationships referred to by Lord Wilberforce, **the justification for admitting such claims is the presumption, which I would accept as being rebuttable, that the love and affection normally associated with persons in those relationships is such that a defendant ought reasonably to contemplate that they may be so closely and directly affected by his conduct as to suffer shock resulting in psychiatric illness.** While as a generalisation more remote relatives and, a fortiori, friends, can reasonably be expected not to suffer illness from the shock, there can well be relatives and friends whose relationship is so close and intimate that their love and affection for the victim is comparable to that of the normal parent, spouse or child of the victim and should for the purpose of this cause of action be so treated. This was the opinion of Stocker L.J. in the instant appeal, ante, p. 376E-G, and also that of Nolan L.J. who thus expressed himself, ante, pp. 384–385:

> 'For my part, I would accept at once that no general definition is possible. But I see no difficulty in principle in requiring a defendant to contemplate that the person

> physically injured or threatened by his negligence may have relatives or friends whose love for him is like that of a normal parent or spouse, and who in consequence may similarly be closely and directly affected by nervous shock ... The identification of the particular individuals who come within that category, like that of the parents and spouses themselves, could only be carried out ex post facto, and would depend upon evidence of the "relationship" in the broad sense which gave rise to the love and affection.'

It is interesting to observe that when, nearly 50 years ago, the New South Wales legislature decided to extend liability for injury arising wholly or in part from 'mental or nervous shock' sustained by a parent or husband or wife of the person killed, injured or put in peril, or any other member of the family of such person, it recognised that it was appropriate to extend significantly the definition of such categories of claimants. Section 4 (5) of the Law Reform (Miscellaneous Provisions) Act 1944 provides:

> '"Member of the family" means the husband, wife, parent, child, brother, sister, half-brother or half-sister of the person in relation to whom the expression is used. "Parent" includes father, mother, grandfather, grandmother, stepfather, stepmother and any person standing in loco parentis to another. "Child" includes son, daughter, grandson, granddaughter, stepson, stepdaughter and any person to whom another stands in loco parentis.'

Whether the degree of love and affection in any given relationship, be it that of relative or friend, is such that the defendant, in the light of the plaintiff's proximity to the scene of the accident in time and space and its nature, should reasonably have foreseen the shock-induced psychiatric illness, has to be decided on a case by case basis. As Deane J. observed in Jaensch v. Coffey, (1984) 155 C.L.R. 549, 601:

> 'While it must now be accepted that any realistic assessment of the reasonably foreseeable consequences of an accident involving actual or threatened serious bodily injury must, in an appropriate case, include the possibility of injury in the form of nervous shock being sustained by a wide range of persons not physically injured in the accident, the outer limits of reasonable foreseeability of mere psychiatric injury cannot be identified in the abstract or in advance. Much may depend upon the nature of the negligent act or omission, on the gravity or apparent gravity of any actual or apprehended injury and on any expert evidence about the nature and explanation of the particular psychiatric injury which the plaintiff has sustained.'

(2) The proximity of the plaintiff to the accident

It is accepted that the proximity to the accident must be close both in time and space. Direct and immediate sight or hearing of the accident is not required. It is reasonably foreseeable that injury by shock can be caused to a plaintiff, not only through the sight or hearing of the event, but of its immediate aftermath.

Only two of the plaintiffs before us were at the ground. However, it is clear from McLoughlin v. O'Brian [1983] 1 AC 410 that there may be liability where subsequent identification can be regarded as part of the 'immediate aftermath' of the accident. Mr. Alcock identified his brother-in-law in a bad condition in the mortuary at about midnight, that is some eight hours after the accident. This was the earliest of the identification cases. Even if this identification could be described as part of the 'aftermath,' it could not in my judgment be described as part of the immediate aftermath. McLoughlin's case was described by Lord Wilberforce as being upon the margin of what the process of logical progression from case to case would allow. Mrs. McLoughlin had arrived at the hospital within an hour or so after the accident. Accordingly in the post-accident identification cases before your Lordships there was not sufficient proximity in time and space to the accident.

(3) The means by which the shock is caused

Lord Wilberforce concluded that the shock must come through sight or hearing of the event or its immediate aftermath but specifically left for later consideration whether some equivalent of sight or hearing, e.g. through simultaneous television, would suffice: see p. 423. Of course it is common ground that it was clearly foreseeable by the defendant that the scenes at Hillsborough would be broadcast live and that amongst those who would be watching would be parents and spouses and other relatives and friends of those in the pens behind the goal at the Leppings Lane end. However he would also know of the code of ethics which the television authorities televising this event could be expected to follow, namely that they would not show pictures of suffering by recognisable individuals. Had they done so, Mr. Hytner accepted that this would have been a 'novus actus' breaking the chain of causation between the defendant's alleged breach of duty and the psychiatric illness. As the defendant was reasonably entitled to expect to be the case, there were no such pictures. Although the television pictures certainly gave rise to feelings of the deepest anxiety and distress, in the circumstances of this case the simultaneous television broadcasts of what occurred cannot be equated with the 'sight or hearing of the event or its immediate aftermath.' Accordingly shocks sustained by reason of these broadcasts cannot found a claim. I agree, however, with Nolan L.J. that simultaneous broadcasts of a disaster cannot in all cases be ruled out as providing the equivalent of the actual sight or hearing of the event or its immediate aftermath. Nolan L.J. gave, ante, pp. 386G-387A, an example of a situation where it was reasonable to anticipate that the television cameras, whilst filming and transmitting pictures of a special event of children travelling in a balloon, in which there was media interest, particularly amongst the parents, showed the balloon suddenly bursting into flames. Many other such situations could be imagined where the impact of the simultaneous television pictures would be as great, if not greater, than the actual sight of the accident.

These three principles, requiring a court to consider in relation to secondary victims how close were their ties of love and affection to the primary victim(s), how close they themselves were to the incident, and the manner in which they apprehended it, are often referred to as the *Alcock* principles. They are the key means of establishing liability for the psychiatric injury of secondary victims and so you should make yourself very familiar with them.

Question to consider: Do you think the *Alcock* criteria were fit for purpose when the case was handed down? Do you think they are fit for purpose now, in light of the technological developments that have occurred since?
Other resources: M Jones, 'Liability for Psychiatric Damage: Searching for a Path Between Pragmatism and Principle' in Jason Neyers et al (eds), *Emerging Issues in Tort Law* (Hart, 2007) at 119; N Mullany and P Handford, 'Hillsborough Replayed' (1997) 113 *LQR* 410.

Sadly, the same disaster gave rise to further civil liability questions. In the next case, the House of Lords was presented with the psychiatric injury claims of police officers who were present in the ground as 'professional rescuers'. Whilst none of the claimants had been working in the immediate area where the crush had occurred (liability to those officers had been admitted), four had been working at the stadium, and a fifth dealt with the bodies at the hospital to which they were taken. By a majority, the House of Lords found in favour of the defendants. In his well-known judgment in this case, Lord Hoffmann examines both the theoretical and practical implications of developing this area of the law, and concludes with some exasperation that the House in *White* could do very little to ameliorate the unsatisfactory state of the common law after *Alcock*. His Lordship suggests that legislative change is called for and points to the Law Commission's work in the area (which has not to date been implemented, leaving *Alcock* and *White* as the last words of highest common law authority on the subject).

White v Chief Constable of South Yorkshire Police [1999] 2 AC 455, 503 (Lord Hoffmann)[3]

The position which the law has reached as a result of *Alcock v. Chief Constable of South Yorkshire* [1992] 1 AC 310 has not won universal approval. The control mechanisms have been criticised as drawing distinctions which the ordinary man would find hard to understand. Jane Stapleton has said that a mother who suffers psychiatric

3 Also commonly referred to as *Frost* – the lead name of the case in the Court of Appeal – as it is in the article excerpt below.

injury after finding her child's mangled body in a mortuary 'might wonder why the law rules her child's blood too dry to found an action': see *The Frontiers of Liability* ed. Peter Birks, O.U.P. (1994) Volume 2, p. 84. Equally, the spectacle of a plaintiff, who has, ex hypothesi, suffered psychiatric illness in consequence of his brother's death or injury, being cross-examined on the closeness of their ties of love and affection and then perhaps contradicted by the evidence of a private investigator, might not be to everyone's taste: see the Law Commission Report on Liability for Psychiatric Illness (Law Com. No. 249) at para. 6.24).

Academic writers have made contradictory but equally radical suggestions for reform. *Mullany and Handford*, in their excellent book *The Liability for Psychiatric Damage* (Sydney, 1993), advocate getting rid of the control mechanisms and, in the light of advances in psychiatric knowledge, equating psychiatric injury to physical injury. Jane Stapleton, on the other hand, would abolish recovery for psychiatric injury altogether and revert to the law as stated in *Victorian Railway Commissioners v. Coultas* (1888) 13 App Cas 222: see the article to which I have already referred.

The appeal of these two opposing proposals rather depends upon where one starts from. If one starts from the proposition that in principle the law of torts is there to give legal force to an Aristotelian system of corrective justice, then there is obviously no valid distinction to be drawn between physical and psychiatric injury. On this view, the control mechanisms merely reflect a vulgar scepticism about the reality of psychiatric injury or a belief that it is less worthy of compensation than physical injury: therein the patient must minister to himself. On the other hand, if one starts from the imperfect reality of the way the law of torts actually works, in which the vast majority of cases of injury and disability, both physical and psychiatric, go uncompensated because the persons (if any) who caused the damage were not negligent, or because the plaintiff lacks the evidence or the resources to prove to a court that they were negligent, or because the potential defendants happen to have no money, then questions of distributive justice tend to intrude themselves. Why should X receive generous compensation for his injury when Y receives nothing? Is the administration of so arbitrary and imperfect a system of compensation worth the very considerable cost? On this view, a uniform refusal to provide compensation for psychiatric injury adds little to the existing stock of anomaly in the law of torts and at least provides a rule which is easy to understand and cheap to administer.

The Law Commission in its recent Report (*supra*) inclines somewhat to the Mullany and Handford point of view by recommending that the condition of close ties of love and affection for secondary victims be retained in a modified form but that the other two be abolished. The reason given for retention of any control mechanism was that:

> 'a review of the medical literature has led us to believe that the adoption of a simple foreseeability test would or could result in a significant increase in the number of claims which, at least at this point in time, would be unacceptable.'

I shall in due course return to this concept of unacceptability and try to analyse what it means. But I shall not enter further into the merits of the various proposals for reform because neither of the radical solutions, or indeed the Law Commission solution, is open to your Lordships. **It is too late to go back on the control mechanisms as stated in *Alcock*. Until there is legislative change, the courts must live with them and any judicial developments must take them into account.**

The control mechanisms were plainly never intended to apply to all cases of psychiatric injury. They contemplate that the injury has been caused in consequence of death or injury suffered (or apprehended to have been suffered or as likely to be suffered) by someone else. In *Page v. Smith* [1996] AC 155, 184 Lord Lloyd of Berwick described such a plaintiff as a 'secondary victim' who was 'in the position of a spectator or bystander.'

...

The ... way in which the plaintiffs put their case is that they were not 'bystanders or spectators' but participants in the sense that they actually did things to help. They submit that there is an analogy between their position and that of a 'rescuer', who, on the basis of the decision of Waller J. in *Chadwick v. British Railways Board* [1967] 1 W.L.R. 912, is said to be treated as a primary victim, exempt from the control mechanisms.

In *Chadwick*, the plaintiff suffered psychiatric injury as a result of his experiences in assisting the victims of a railway accident. He spent twelve hours crawling in the wreckage, helping people to extricate themselves and giving pain killing injections to the injured. Waller J. said (at p. 921) that it was foreseeable that 'somebody might try to rescue passengers and suffer injury in the process.' The defendants therefore owed a duty of care to the plaintiff. He went on to say that it did not matter that the injury suffered was psychiatric rather than physical but in any event 'shock was foreseeable and ... rescue was foreseeable.' Thus the judge's reasoning is based purely upon the foreseeability of psychiatric injury in the same way as in other cases of that time. And I think there can be no doubt that if foreseeability was the only question, the judge's conclusion was unexceptionable.

References in the authorities to rescuers sometimes give the impression that they are a category of persons who would not qualify for compensation under the strict rules of the law of negligence but receive special treatment on grounds of humanity and as a reward for altruism. A florid passage by Cardozo J. in *Wagner v. International Railway Company* 232 N.Y. 176, 180 (1921) is frequently quoted. If rescuers formed a specially privileged category of plaintiff, one would expect that the rule would give rise to a definitional problem about who counted as a rescuer and so qualified for special treatment. In fact, as one can see from the absence of any such problem in the cases, rescuers can be accommodated without difficulty in the general principles of the law of negligence. There are two questions which may arise. The first is whether injury to the rescuer was foreseeable. There is usually no difficulty in holding that if it was foreseeable that someone would be put in danger, it was also foreseeable that someone would go to look for him or try to rescue him or otherwise help him in his distress. The second question is whether the voluntary act of the rescuer, searcher or helper in putting himself in peril negatives the causal connection between the original negligent conduct and his injury. Again, the courts have had equally little difficulty in holding that such a person, acting out of a sense of moral obligation, does not make the free choice which would be necessary to eliminate the causal effect of the defendant's conduct. In the same way, its causal effect is not negatived by an unsuccessful attempt of the person in peril, whose freedom of choice has been limited by the position into which the defendant has put him, to extricate himself from danger: see *The Oropesa* [1943] 140.

The cases on rescuers are therefore quite simple illustrations of the application of general principles of foreseeability and causation to particular facts. There is no authority which decides that a rescuer is in any special position in relation to liability for psychiatric injury. And it is no criticism of the excellent judgment of Waller J. in Chadwick v. British Railways Board [1967] 1 W.L.R. 912 to say that such a question obviously never entered his head. Questions of such nicety did not arise until the Alcock control mechanisms had been enunciated.

There does not seem to me to be any logical reason why the normal treatment of rescuers on the issues of foreseeability and causation should lead to the conclusion that, for the purpose of liability for psychiatric injury, they should be given special treatment as primary victims when they were not within the range of foreseeable physical injury and their psychiatric injury was caused by witnessing or participating in the aftermath of accidents which caused death or injury to others. It would of course be possible to create such a rule by an ex post facto rationalisation of *Chadwick v. British Railways Board* [1967] 1 W.L.R. 912. In both *McLoughlin v. O'Brian* [1983] 1 AC 410 and in *Alcock v. Chief Constable of South Yorkshire* [1992] 1 AC 310, members of the House referred to *Chadwick* with approval. But I do not think that too much should be read into these remarks. In neither case was it argued that the plaintiffs were entitled to succeed as rescuers and anything said about the duty to rescuers was therefore necessarily obiter. If one is looking for an ex post facto rationalisation of *Chadwick*, I think that the most satisfactory is that offered in the Court of Appeal in *McLoughlin v. O'Brian* [1981] 1 Q.B. 599, 622 by my noble and learned friend Lord Griffiths, who had been the successful counsel for Mr. Chadwick. He said:

> 'Mr. Chadwick might have been injured by a wrecked carriage collapsing on him as he worked among the injured. A duty of care is owed to a rescuer in such circumstances ....'

If Mr. Chadwick was, as Lord Griffiths said, within the range of foreseeable physical injury, then the case is no more than an illustration of the principle applied by the House in *Page v. Smith* [1996] AC 155, namely that such a person can recover even if the injury he actually suffers is not physical but psychiatric. And in addition (unlike *Page v. Smith* [1996] AC 155) Waller J. made a finding that psychiatric injury was also foreseeable.

Should then your Lordships take the incremental step of extending liability for psychiatric injury to 'rescuers' (a class which would now require definition) who give assistance at or after some disaster without coming within the range of foreseeable physical injury? It may be said that this would encourage people to offer assistance. The category of secondary victims would be confined to 'spectators and bystanders' who take no part in dealing with the incident or its aftermath. On the authorities, as it seems to me, your Lordships are free to take such a step.

In my opinion there are two reasons why your Lordships should not do so. The less important reason is the definitional problem to which I have alluded. The concept of a rescuer as someone who puts himself in danger of physical injury is easy to understand. But once this notion is extended to include others who give assistance, the line between them and bystanders becomes difficult to draw with any precision.

... the ... reason for not extending the law is that in my opinion the result would be quite unacceptable. I have used this word on a number of occasions and the time has come to explain what I mean. I do not mean that the burden of claims would be too great for the insurance market or the public funds, the two main sources for the payment of damages in tort. The Law Commission may have had this in mind when they said that removal of all the control mechanism would lead to an 'unacceptable' increase in claims, since they described it as a 'floodgates' argument. These are questions on which it is difficult to offer any concrete evidence and I am simply not in a position to form a view one way or the other. I am therefore willing to accept that, viewed against the total sums paid as damages for personal injury, the increase resulting from an extension of liability to helpers would be modest. But I think that such an extension would be unacceptable to the ordinary person because (though he might not put it this way) it would offend against his notions of distributive justice. He would think it unfair between one class of claimants and another, at best not treating like cases alike and, at worst, favouring the less deserving against the more deserving. He would think it wrong that policemen, even as part of a general class of persons who rendered assistance, should have the right to compensation for psychiatric injury out of public funds while the bereaved relatives are sent away with nothing.

...

It may be said that the common law should not pay attention these feelings about the relative merits of different classes of claimants. It should stick to principle and not concern itself with distributive justice. An extension of liability to rescuers and helpers would be a modest incremental development in the common law tradition and, as between these plaintiffs and these defendants, produce a just result. **My Lords, I disagree. It seems to me that in this area of the law, the search for principle was called off in *Alcock v. Chief Constable of South Yorkshire* [1992] 1 AC 310. No one can pretend that the existing law, which your Lordships have to accept, is founded upon principle.** I agree with Jane Stapleton's remark that: (see *The Frontiers of Liability* ed. Peter Birks, O.U.P. (1994) Volume 2, p. 87.

> 'once the law has taken a wrong turning or otherwise fallen into an unsatisfactory internal state in relation to a particular case of action, incrementalism cannot provide the answer.'

Consequently your Lordships are now engaged, not in the bold development of principle, but in a practical attempt, under adverse conditions, to preserve the general perception of the law as system of rules which is fair between one citizen and another.

...

Naturally I feel great sympathy for the plaintiffs, as I do for all those whose lives were blighted by that day at Hillsborough. But I think that fairness demands that your Lordships should reject them. I have also read in draft the speech of my noble and learned friend Lord Steyn and agree with his reasons for taking the same course, which seem to me substantially the same as my own. I would therefore allow these appeals and dismiss the actions.

Lord Hoffmann's reasoning in *White* has been subjected to quite a degree of scrutiny, both judicial and academic. In the following analyses, the authors ask how it relates to the principles of corrective and distributive justice.

Robin Oppenheim, 'The "mosaic" of tort law: the duty of care question' (2003) *JPI Law* (Sep) 151–71

Distributive justice is concerned with the just distribution of burdens and losses, including risks, within a community. This may require members of a community to bear the risk of harm to others even where they are not a fault ...

Lord Hoffmann first introduced the concept into English case law in *Frost*, where in concluding why liability to police officers for psychiatric injury whilst on duty ... should not be permitted, he stated:

> '... I think such an extension would be unacceptable to the ordinary person because (he might not put in this way) it would offend against his notions of distributive justice. He would think it unfair between one class of claimant and another, at best not treating like cases alike and, at worst, favouring the less deserving against the more deserving. He would think it wrong that policemen, even as part of a general class of persons who have rendered assistance, should have the right to compensation for psychiatric injury out of public funds while the bereaved relatives are sent away with nothing.'

There are several contentious aspects to this passage ... There was an obvious point of legal distinction between a bystander and a police officer. The former was owed no duty of care by the chief constable, where the latter was and the law draws no distinction between a duty to protect from physical and psychiatric injury, except as to the demands of foreseeability. This distinction might not command universal public respect either on the London underground or the Clapham omnibus, but the law should not be afraid of marking out the boundaries of recovery based on principle, rather than the fear of public perplexity. If intuition is used in this field, where else in legal endeavour is it to be used and to what end? Here, there was a fundamental contradiction between the demands of corrective justice which led Lord Goff in a powerful dissenting judgment to conclude that the officers were owed a duty of care and Lords Hoffmann and Steyn with whom Lord Browne-Wilkinson agreed. Lord Steyn did not expressly use the language of distributive justice, but concluded pragmatically:

> 'In reality there are no refined analytic tools which will enable the courts to draw lines by way of compromise solution in a way which is coherent and morally defensible'.

Stelios Tofaris, 'Limping into the future: negligence liability for mental injury to secondary victims' (2022) 81(3) *CLJ* 452–56

It is a truth universally acknowledged that the English law on negligence liability for mental injury to secondary victims is unsatisfactory. What is less readily acknowledged is what to do about it …

First, it has long been accepted that *Alcock* is not justified as a matter of principle. Neither 'corrective justice', which provides the structure of tort law, nor 'distributive justice', which operates within that structure, justify treating pure mental injury and physical injury differently. This conclusion is also likely to follow if one were to ask what the public think, as Lord Hoffmann did in *White* under the false banner of 'distributive justice' (p. 510).

Second, policy does not justify the *Alcock* framework. Of the considerations articulated by Lord Steyn in *White* (pp. 493–94), the most potent is 'floodgates' – the notion that a single event will lead to a flood of claims. The reason is that there is no physical immediacy in the causation of pure mental injury to restrict the class of claimants, unlike with physical injury. However, experiences in other jurisdictions show that the concern is overstated. While it may support *some* restrictions, it does not support *Alcock*.

…

If the *Alcock* framework is to go, what should replace it? One option is to hold that the test is whether it is reasonably foreseeable that the claimant would suffer mental injury as a result of the defendant's careless act/omission, and explain that in determining whether that is satisfied, courts can take into account several factors, including the relationship of the claimant with the person imperilled, the physical and temporal proximity to the event, and how her mental injury was caused … Another (less expansive) option is to affirm the test of reasonable foreseeability of mental injury, but discard physical and temporal proximity, direct perception of the event and sudden shock as additional requirements. This would restrict claims to those with close ties of love and affection to the person imperilled (see Law Commission, Rep 249, 1998). In either case, the test would be additional to the requirement for a recognised mental injury …

The ball is now firmly in the Supreme Court's court. It is hoped that it will pick it up and bring the law into line with contemporary societal and medical perceptions. It will no doubt be tempting to conclude again that legislation is the best, perhaps the only, option for reform. Tempting, but wrong.

White is a famously thorny case, both in terms of its facts and in terms of the judicial response to them. It is worth, therefore, knowing in some detail and reflecting on the currents of corrective justice, distributive justice and pragmatism that flow through it. Not only will this set you up well for applying it in a problem question, but it will also give you excellent material on which to base a discursive essay.

Question to consider: Do you think the court let policy concerns override principle in *White v Chief Constable of South Yorkshire Police*?
Other resources: *Chadwick v British Railways Board* [1967] 1 WLR 912; *Ogwo v Taylor* [1988] AC 431; Law Commission, *Report on Liability for Psychiatric Illness* (Law Com Report No 249, 1998); C Hilson, 'Nervous Shock and the Categorisation of Victims' (1998) 6 *Tort L Rev* 37.

After a considerable hiatus, psychiatric injury has again been considered at appellate level, albeit in relation to damaging events caused by medical negligence, as opposed to sudden and horrifying incidents.

Paul v Royal Wolverhampton NHS Trust revisited the time and space question in relation to cases in which the primary victims died in traumatic circumstances a number of months after a negligent misdiagnosis. The defendants argued that the events witnessed by the secondary victim claimants were too far removed in time from the alleged negligence, which, as we have seen, accords with the cases decided so far on this point. A seven member panel of the Supreme Court, by a majority of 6-1 (Lord Burrows dissenting), dismissed the defendant's appeal. It thereby confirmed that no duty is assumed by a hospital to *third parties* (secondary victims) who might be affected by harm caused to a patient (primary victim) by its negligence.[4]

4 See Imogen Goold and Catherine Kelly, 'Time to Start *De Novo*: the *Paul*, *Purchase* and *Polmear* litigation and the temporal gap problem in secondary victim claims for psychiatric injury' (2023) 39 *Professional Negligence* 24 for an illuminating discussion of the issues (cited by the Supreme Court).

Paul v Royal Wolverhampton NHS Trust [2024] UKSC 1, [2024] 2 WLR 417, [107]–[116] (Lord Leggatt and Lady Rose)

[Lord Leggatt and Lady Rose (with whom Lord Briggs, Lord Sales and Lord Richards agreed)]

Why witnessing an accident is legally significant

107. To pursue the comparison further, we will identify three ways in which the occurrence of an accident is integral both to the reasons for recognising the category of claims by secondary victims arising from an accident and in defining the limits of this category.

108. First, an accident is, by definition, a discrete event in the ordinary sense of that word, meaning something which happens at a particular time, at a particular place, in a particular way. Whether someone was present at the scene and whether they directly perceived an accident are in most cases questions which admit of a clear and straightforward answer. These criteria for determining whether a person is eligible to claim compensation as a secondary victim therefore have the great merit of providing legal certainty. The clarity and certainty of these tests have been compromised to some extent by the decision in *McLoughlin* that the claimant in that case had witnessed the 'immediate aftermath' of the accident even though she saw the injured members of her family in a different place from the accident site more than two hours after the accident had occurred. Nevertheless, a reasonably clear line can be drawn if heed is paid to the observations of Lord Wilberforce that allowing the claim in *McLoughlin* (a) was 'upon the margin of what the process of logical progression would allow' (p 419G) and (b) depended critically on the evidence that, when the claimant came upon the members of her family, 'they were in the same condition [as they had been at the roadside], covered with oil and mud, and distraught with pain' (p 419F).

109. Second, witnessing an accident involving a close family member is itself likely to be a disturbing and upsetting event even if that person in fact escapes unharmed and all the more so if that person is physically injured or killed. It is easy to appreciate the psychological trauma caused to a mother who sees her child run down by a car or to a husband who comes upon the badly injured body of his wife immediately after an accident. Most people would, we think, accept that, if a line is going to be drawn between cases where illness consequent on bereavement is compensable and cases where it is not, distinguishing between claimants who suffered the ordeal of actually witnessing the accident in which a close relative was killed and those who did not is an intelligible place to draw it.

110. A third significant feature of accident cases is that it is often difficult or arbitrary in such cases to distinguish between primary and secondary victims. Once the courts accepted that compensation can be recovered for psychiatric injury sustained without any physical impact, no distinction could reasonably be drawn between injury caused by fear for the claimant's own safety and by fear for the safety of a close family member. It was this reasoning which led the Court of Appeal in *Hambrook* to reject the view expressed (obiter) by Kennedy J in *Dulieu* [1901] 2 KB 669, 675, that the right to recover

compensation is limited to cases where psychiatric injury 'arises from a reasonable fear of immediate personal injury to oneself'. In *Hambrook* [1925] 1 KB 141, 157, Atkin LJ said of this suggested limitation:

> 'It would result in a state of the law in which a mother, shocked by fright for herself, would recover, while a mother shocked by her child being killed before her eyes, could not, and in which a mother traversing the highway with a child in her arms could recover if shocked by fright for herself, while if she could be cross-examined into an admission that the fright was really for her child, she could not. In my opinion such distinctions would be discreditable to any system of jurisprudence in which they formed part.'

We agree. We would add that in a case where, for example, both a mother and her child are put in physical peril, it would not only be unjust but practically impossible to distinguish between the mother's emotions of fear for herself and fear for her child.

The contrast with non-accident cases

111. None of these three significant features of the accident cases is applicable where the claimant suffers illness from witnessing physical injury or illness in another person but does not witness any accident.

112. First, as we have seen, in many such cases there is no discrete event comparable to an accident. This is not always true. If a person suddenly and unexpectedly collapses and dies after suffering a cardiac arrest or some other medical crisis as happened in *Paul* and *Novo*, such an event can be identified with the same degree of certainty as an accident can. But the length of time for which symptoms of injury or disease last before a person recovers or dies is entirely variable. It may be minutes, hours, days or weeks. In *Walters*, for example, the period was 36 hours; in *Shorter* it was around 24 hours (measuring from first manifestation of injury rather than the inception of the underlying cause); in *Sion* it was 14 days. This gives rise to uncertainty about what qualifies as an 'event' capable of founding a claim. We have discussed above the intractable difficulties involved in trying to answer that question in a way that is both reasonably certain and not entirely arbitrary. There are no comparable difficulties in determining whether a person has been killed, injured or put in peril in an accident.

113. Second, in cases where the claimant has not witnessed an accident but has witnessed the injury or illness of a close family member, the extent to which this experience is traumatic is also entirely variable. The facts of the present cases are at one extreme, as was *Walters*. But again there is a whole range of possible scenarios. The symptoms of injury or illness witnessed may be more or less severe. Unless the door is to be opened to claims based on direct perception of any symptoms however mild, some criterion is needed to distinguish between claims which are, or are not, admissible. We have discussed above three such criteria which have been applied or proposed: the 'sudden shock', 'horrifying event' and 'first manifestation of damage' tests. For the reasons indicated, none of these,

in our view, is an acceptable test. We have not been shown any cases in which comparable difficulties have arisen where the claim is based on presence at, and direct perception of, an accident.

114. Third, in cases where the claimant was not present at the scene of any accident, no question can arise of the claimant suffering psychiatric harm through fear for her own safety or bodily integrity. Any such harm which the claimant suffers can only be of a secondary nature caused by witnessing the injury, illness or death of another person. Allowing the claimant to recover compensation cannot therefore be justified by the practical impossibility and injustice of otherwise having to distinguish between injury caused by fear for the claimant's own safety and injury caused by fear for the safety of a close family member.

115. For these reasons, we do not consider that an analogy can reasonably be drawn between the situation with which *McLoughlin*, *Alcock* and *Frost* were concerned where illness is caused by witnessing an accident (or its immediate aftermath) involving a victim with whom the claimant has a close tie of love and affection and situations where the claimant does not witness an accident but suffers illness as a result of witnessing such a person suffering a medical crisis.

116. We also agree with the Court of Appeal in *Novo* that to extend the scope of allowable claims by secondary victims to situations where the claimant witnesses the death or illness of a relative from disease would give rise to unacceptable and unfair differences in treatment between different categories of claimant. It would be impossible to explain to an ordinary reasonable person why, for example, damages can be recovered by a daughter who sees her parent die from a heart attack or pulmonary embolism which should have been avoided, but compensation is denied to, say, a mother who did not witness a road accident in which her child was fatally injured or its 'immediate aftermath' but identifies the mutilated body afterwards in the mortuary or is present at the hospital when her child dies many days later from injuries sustained in the accident. Such unjust differences in outcome could, of course, be avoided by removing the second and third requirements for claims by secondary victims established by the House of Lords in *Alcock* and confirmed in *Frost*. But it would not, in our view, be right to contemplate such a radical departure from settled law.

4.3 Conclusion

This chapter has dealt with an area which is widely regarded as containing some of the most challenging reasoning and rules in the common law. As we have seen, the fact that psychiatric injury can be caused remotely removes it from the natural limits created by physical proximity, exposing it to the same risk of potential indeterminacy as recovery for pure economic loss. But the facts of the cases in this area are more harrowing and the human interest a great deal keener; something which might explain why there have been calls for legislative reform here but not in relation to pure economic loss. It is probably also clear by now that the case law in this area does not make complete sense (as Lord Hoffmann says explicitly in *White*). Your strategy as a student, therefore, should be to know the reasoning and how it has been employed. Where necessary, you also need to recognise explicitly the inconsistencies and ambiguities that exist. This will mean that you will be able to apply the principles as analogously as possible to the facts of a problem question – which is of course the exercise that judges themselves engage in.

Chapter 5 BREACH OF DUTY

Once a claimant has established that the defendant owes them a duty of care, the question then remains whether that duty has been breached. It is crucial to remember that these are two separate stages: duties of care abound, but breaches of them are not nearly so common. A GP, for instance, owes a duty of care to every one of their patients, but many will go through their entire careers without it even being alleged that they have breached that duty. It is important, therefore, to establish what standard a defendant is held to when they owe a duty of care; it is only, of course, if they fall below this standard that they will be deemed by a court to be in breach.

5.1 Reasonableness

The standard of care in negligence is an objective one of reasonableness. This means that it holds each defendant to the standard of a reasonable person doing that activity they are doing. Essentially, if a person, by engaging in a particular activity, holds themselves out as having the capability to do that activity, they will be held by the law to the standard of reasonableness that applies to that activity. In other words, if you choose to perform brain surgery on somebody, you will be held to the standard of the reasonable brain surgeon, whether you have the requisite skills and training or not. As the next case shows, it is not a standard that is tailored to what a particular defendant is capable of, nor does it make any allowance for inexperience. In that case, the defendant, a learner driver, injured by driving badly the friend who was teaching her to drive. The question was whether she had breached her duty of care to her passenger-instructor by not driving as well as a reasonable driver would have done. The answer, as we shall see, was yes.

Nettleship v Weston [1971] 2 QB 691, 703 (Salmon LJ)

> [A] learner-driver is responsible and owes a duty in civil law towards persons on or near the highway to drive with the same degree of skill and care as that of the reasonably competent and experienced driver. The duty in civil law springs from the relationship which the driver, by driving on the highway, has created between himself and persons likely to suffer damage by his bad driving. This is not a special relationship. Nor, in my respectful view, is it affected by whether or not the driver is insured. On grounds

of public policy, neither this criminal nor civil responsibility is affected by the fact that the driver in question may be a learner, infirm or drunk. The onus, of course, lies on anyone claiming damages to establish a breach of duty and that it has caused the damages which he claims.

Any driver normally owes exactly the same duty to a passenger in his car as he does to the general public, namely to drive with reasonable care and skill in all the relevant circumstances. **As a rule, the driver's personal idiosyncrasy is not a relevant circumstance. In the absence of a special relationship what is reasonable care and skill is measured by the standard of competence usually achieved by the ordinary driver.**

[Megaw LJ at 708–10] As I see it, if this doctrine of varying standards were to be accepted as part of the law on these facts, it could not logically be confined to the duty of care owed by learner-drivers. There is no reason, in logic, why it should not operate in a much wider sphere. The disadvantages of the resulting unpredictability, uncertainty and, indeed, impossibility of arriving at fair and consistent decisions outweigh the advantages. **The certainty of a general standard is preferable to the vagaries of a fluctuating standard**.

...

Why should the doctrine, if it be part of the law, be limited to cases involving the driving of motor cars? Suppose that to the knowledge of the patient a young surgeon, whom the patient has chosen to operate on him, has only just qualified. If the operation goes wrong because of the surgeon's inexperience, is there a defence on the basis that the standard of skill and care was lower than the standard of a competent and experienced surgeon? Does the young, newly qualified, solicitor owe a lower standard of skill and care, when the client chooses to instruct him with knowledge of his inexperience?

...

In my judgment, in cases such as the present it is preferable that there should be a reasonably certain and reasonably ascertainable standard of care, even if on occasion that may appear to work hardly against an inexperienced driver, or his insurers. The standard of care required by the law is the standard of the competent and experienced driver: and this is so, as defining the driver's duty towards a passenger who knows of his inexperience, as much as towards a member of the public outside the car; and as much in civil as in criminal proceedings.

It is not a valid argument against such a principle that it attributes tortious liability to one who may not be morally blameworthy. For tortious liability has in many cases ceased to be based on moral blameworthiness. For example, there is no doubt whatever that if Mrs. Weston had knocked down a pedestrian on the pavement when the accident occurred, she would have been liable to the pedestrian. Yet so far as any moral blame is concerned, no different considerations would apply in respect of the pedestrian from those which apply in respect of Mr. Nettleship.

When students first encounter this case, they often find it difficult or objectionable, to varying degrees. This is perhaps a combination of a couple of factors: often, such students have only recently learned to drive themselves and they are in the early stages of thinking about the law of tort. Once one bears in mind that, as Megaw LJ underscores, tort (or at least negligence)[1] is not interested in moral culpability and punishment, but instead compensation and redress for harms, the rectitude of the objective standard is obvious. We are all as likely to be defendants in negligence as we are claimants and this is not something we choose. Whilst the objective standard might be regarded as operating harshly towards those with subjectively lower than average abilities, it would be equally (if not more) harsh to expect the seriously injured passenger or pedestrian to shoulder their own losses simply because they had the misfortune to be struck by a novice driver. Claimants do not choose their defendants any more than defendants choose their claimants.[2] The same is true, as we see above, for surgeons. And it is just as true for dentists, architects, engineers and pilots. If it were not, nobody would ever want to be treated, advised, operated on, built for or flown by anyone but an experienced individual.

It remains to be established just how the standard of reasonableness is determined in any given case. The case from which the following excerpt is taken sets out clearly the way in which the courts approach this question. In that case, the claimant was injured by a cricket ball which had been hit out of a cricket ground and into the road in which she was standing. Cricket balls had apparently been hit out of the ground in this way 'five or six times' before, but had not previously caused injury. The question for the House of Lords was whether the club had been in breach of its duty in allowing cricket matches to be played too close to the road and in failing to erect a fence of sufficient height, thereby creating the risk of injury to those nearby. The answer was no.

Bolton v Stone [1951] AC 850, 857 (Lord Porter), 864 (Lord Oaksey), 867 (Lord Reid)

[Lord Porter at 857] But the question remains: Is it enough Jo make an action negligent to say that its performance may possibly cause injury or must some greater probability exist of that result ensuing in order to make those responsible for its occurrence guilty of negligence?

In the present case the Appellants did not do the act themselves, but they are trustees of a field where cricket is played, are in control of it and invite visiting teams to play there. They are, therefore, and are admitted to be responsible for the negligent action of those who use the field in the way intended that it should be used.

1 Deceit, for example, is arguably less morally neutral.

2 See the discussion of the eggshell skull rule in Chapter 7 (Remoteness).

The question then arises: What degree of care must they exercise to escape liability for anything which may occur as a result of this intended use of the field?

Undoubtedly they knew that the hitting of a cricket ball out of the ground was a possible event and, therefore, that there was a conceivable possibility that someone would be hit by it. But so extreme an obligation of care cannot be imposed in all cases. If it were, no one could safely fly an aero- plane or drive a motor car since the possibility of an accident could not be overlooked and if it occurred some stranger might well be injured. But cases of that kind presuppose the happening of an event which the flyer or driver desire to do everything possible to avoid, whereas the hitting of a ball out of the ground is an incident in the game and. indeed, one which the batsman would wish to bring about.

But in order that the act may be negligent there must not only be a reasonable possibility of its happening but also of injury being caused. In the words of Lord Thankerton in *Bourhill* v. *Young* |1943] A.C. 92 at p. 98, the duty is to exercise 'such reasonable care as will avoid the risk of injury to such persons as he can reasonably foresee might be injured by failure to exercise such reasonable care', and Lord Macmillan used words to the like effect at p. 104. So, also, Lord Wright in *Glasgow Corporation* v. *Muir* [1943] A.C. 448 at p. 460, quoted the well-known words of Lord Atkin in *Donoghue* v. *Stevenson* [1932] AC 562 at p. 580: 'You must take reasonable care to avoid acts or omissions which you can reasonably foresee would be likely to injure your neighbour'.

It is not enough that the event should be such as can reasonably be foreseen; the further result that injury is likely to follow must also be such as a reasonable man would contemplate, before he can be convicted of actionable negligence. Nor is the remote possibility of injury occurring enough; there must be sufficient probability to lead a reasonable man to anticipate it. The existence of some risk is an ordinary incident of life, even when all due care has been, as it must be, taken.

[Lord Oaksey at 864] The standard of care in the law of negligence is the standard of an ordinarily careful man, but in my opinion an ordinarily careful man does not take precautions against every foreseeable risk. He can, of course, foresee the possibility of many risks, but life would be almost impossible if he were to attempt to take precautions against every risk which he can foresee. He takes precautions against risks which are reasonably likely to happen. Many foreseeable risks are extremely unlikely to happen and cannot be guarded against except by almost complete isolation. The ordinarily prudent owner of a dog does not keep his dog always on a lead on a country highway for fear it may cause injury to a passing motor cyclist, nor does the ordinarily prudent pedestrian avoid the use of the highway for fear of skidding motor cars. It may very well be that after this accident the ordinarily prudent (committee man of a similar cricket ground would take some further precaution, but that is not to say that he would have taken a similar precaution before the accident.

[Lord Reid at 867] It would take a good deal to make me believe that the law has departed so far from the standards which guide ordinary careful people in ordinary life. In the crowded conditions of modern life even the most careful person cannot avoid creating some risks and accepting others. What a man must not do, and what I think a careful man tries not to do, is to create a risk which is substantial. ... In considering that matter I think that it would be right to take into account not only how remote is the chance that a person might be struck but also how serious the consequences are likely to be if a person is struck: but I do not think that it would be right to take into account the difficulty of remedial measures. If cricket cannot be played on a ground without creating a substantial risk, then it should not be played there at all.

The same year, the House of Lords considered the issue of breach again. The following case shows how the equation changes when the gravity of the harm that is risked is much greater. On those facts, the employee in question only had the use of one eye to begin with. It was material, therefore, in establishing what a reasonable employer should choose to do in relation to such a worker, to set the gravity of that potential harm against the cost of preventing it by providing precautions.

Paris v Stepney Borough Council [1951] AC 367, 384 (Lord Oaksey)

The duty of an employer towards his servant is to take reasonable care for the servant's safety in all the circumstances of the case. The fact that the servant has only one eye if that fact is known to the employer, and that if he loses it he will be blind, is one of the circumstances which must be considered by the employer in determining what precautions if any shall be taken for the servant's safety. The standard of care which the law demands is the care which an ordinarily prudent employer would take in all the circumstances. As the circumstances may vary infinitely it is often impossible to adduce evidence of what care an ordinarily prudent employer would take. In some cases, of course, it is possible to prove that it is the ordinary practice for employers to take or not to take a certain precaution, but in such a case as the present, where a one-eyed man has been injured, it is unlikely that such evidence can be adduced. The court has, therefore, to form its own opinion of what precautions the notional ordinarily prudent employer would take. In the present case the question is whether an ordinarily prudent employer would supply goggles to a one-eyed workman whose job was to knock bolts out of a chassis with a steel hammer while the chassis was elevated on a ramp so that the workman's eye was close to and under the bolt. In my opinion Lynskey, J., was entitled to hold that an ordinarily prudent employer would take that precaution The question was not whether the precaution ought to have been taken with ordinary two-eyed workmen and it was not necessary, in my opinion, that Lynskey, J., should decide that question – nor did he purport to decide it, although it is true that he stated the question in one sentence too broadly as 'whether the employers in adopting this system and not providing or requiring the use of goggles for the workers on this system were taking reasonable care to provide a suitable system of work and to provide a suitable plant'.

The risk of splinters of steel breaking off a bolt and injuring a workman's eye or eyes may be and, I think, is slight and it is true that the damage to a two-eyed workman if struck by a splinter in the eye or eyes may be serious, but it is for the judge at the trial to weigh up the risk of injury and the extent of the damage and to decide whether, in all the circumstances, including the fact that the workman was known to be one-eyed and might become a blind man if his eye was struck, an ordinarily prudent employer would supply such a workman with goggles. It is a simple and inexpensive precaution to take to supply goggles, and a one-eyed man would not be likely, as a two-eyed man might be, to refuse to wear the goggles.

It should by now be abundantly clear that the test is an objective one, based on the hypothetical reasonable defendant rather than the particular defendant before the court. The age of the defendant, *if the defendant is a child*, is, however, relevant to that inquiry. In the following case, the 15-year-old claimant was injured whilst engaged in a plastic ruler 'swordfight' with a classmate of the same age. At first instance, damages were awarded against her fellow pupil (subject to a 50% reduction for contributory negligence), but the Court of Appeal reversed that decision. In the extract below, in the reference to the judgment of Kitto J, we can see how this does not necessarily detract from the objective nature of the process.

Mullin v Richards [1998] 1 WLR 1304, 1308 (Hutchison LJ)

The test of foreseeability is an objective one; but the fact that the first defendant was at the time a 15-year-old schoolgirl is not irrelevant. The question for the judge is not whether the actions of the defendant were such as an ordinarily prudent and reasonable adult in the defendant's situation would have realised gave rise to a risk of injury, **it is whether an ordinarily prudent and reasonable 15-year-old schoolgirl in the defendant's situation would have realised as much**. In that connection both counsel referred us to, and relied upon, the Australian decision in *McHale v. Watson* (1966) 115 C.L.R. 199 and, in particular, the passage in the judgment of Kitto J., at pp. 213–214. I cite a portion of the passage I have referred to, all of which was cited to us by Mr. Lee on behalf of the appellant, and which Mr. Stephens has adopted as epitomising the correct approach:

> 'The standard of care being objective, it is no answer for him, [that is a child] any more than it is for an adult, to say that the harm he caused was due to his being abnormally slow-witted, quick-tempered, absent-minded or inexperienced. **But it does not follow that he cannot rely in his defence upon a limitation upon the capacity for foresight or prudence, not as being personal to himself, but as being characteristic of humanity at his stage of development and in that sense normal. By doing so he appeals to a standard of ordinariness, to an objective and not a subjective standard.'**

Mr. Stephens also cited to us a passage in the judgment of Owen J., at p. 234: 'the standard by which his conduct is to be measured is not that to be expected of a reasonable adult but that reasonably to be expected of a child of the same age, intelligence and experience.' I venture to question the word 'intelligence' in that sentence, but I understand Owen J. to be making the same point essentially as was made by Kitto J. It is perhaps also material to have in mind the words of Salmon L.J. in *Gough v. Thorne* [1966] 1 W.L.R. 1387, 1391, which is cited also by Mr. Stephens, where he said:

> 'The question as to whether the plaintiff can be said to have been guilty of contributory negligence depends on whether any ordinary child of 13½ can be expected to have done any more than this child did. I say "any ordinary child." I do not mean a paragon of prudence; nor do I mean a scatter-brained child; but the ordinary girl of 13½.'

I need say no more about that principle as to the way in which age affects the assessment of negligence because counsel are agreed upon it and, despite the fact that we have been told that there has been a good deal of controversy in other jurisdictions and that there is no direct authority in this jurisdiction, the approach in *McHale v. Watson* seems to me to have the advantage of obvious, indeed irrefutable, logic.

5.2 Professional situations

Courts are often faced with having to decide what is reasonable in a professional situation, or one which calls for the application of specialist knowledge. Most often (certainly in terms of student reading lists), this happens in medical negligence settings. One might well ask how a judge, who is of course highly legally trained, knows what is reasonable for a trained doctor to do in a medical emergency. The answer is that the court asks the profession whether it recognises the defendant's behaviour as being reasonable in the circumstances. Note that, whilst the following case is one concerning medical expertise, the principle that emerges is *not* limited to medical professionals, but applies across all situations of professional expertise. Note also that it is not the case that all members of the given profession need to agree that the defendant's actions were reasonable in the circumstances; only that a recognised body of professional opinion does so.

Bolam v Friern Hospital Management Committee [1957] 1 WLR 582, 586 (McNair J)

In the ordinary case which does not involve any special skill, negligence in law means a failure to do some act which a reasonable man in the circumstances would do, or the doing of some act which a reasonable man in the circumstances would not do; and if that failure or the doing of that act results in injury, then there is a cause of action. How do you test whether this act or failure is negligent? In an ordinary case it is generally said you judge it by the action of the man in the street. He is the ordinary man. In one case it has been said you judge it by the conduct of the man on the top of a Clapham omnibus. He is the ordinary man. **But where you get a situation which involves the use of some special skill or competence, then the test as to whether there has been negligence or not is not the test of the man on the top of a Clapham omnibus, because he has not got this special skill. The test is the standard of the ordinary skilled man exercising and professing to have that special skill. A man need not possess the highest expert skill; it is well established law that it is sufficient if he exercises the ordinary skill of an ordinary competent man exercising that particular art.** I do not think that I quarrel much with any of the submissions in law which have been put before you by counsel. Mr. Fox-Andrews put it in this way, that in the case of a medical man, negligence means failure to act in accordance with the standards of reasonably competent medical men at the time. That is a perfectly accurate statement, as long as it is remembered that there may be one or more perfectly proper standards; and if he conforms with one of those proper standards, then he is not negligent. Mr. Fox-Andrews also was quite right, in my judgment, in saying that a mere personal belief that a particular technique is best is no defence unless that belief is based on reasonable grounds. That again is unexceptionable. But the emphasis which is laid by the defence is on this aspect of negligence, that the real question you have to make up your minds about on each of the three major topics is whether the defendants, in acting in the way they did, were acting in accordance with a practice of competent respected professional opinion. Mr. Stirling submitted that if you are satisfied that they were acting in accordance with a practice of a competent body of professional opinion, then it would be wrong for you to hold that negligence was established. In a recent Scottish case, *Hunter v. Hanley*, Lord President Clyde said:

> **'In the realm of diagnosis and treatment there is ample scope for genuine difference of opinion and one man clearly is not negligent merely because his conclusion differs from that of other professional men, nor because he has displayed less skill or knowledge than others would have shown. The true test for establishing negligence in diagnosis or treatment on the part of a doctor is whether he has been proved to be guilty of such failure as no doctor of ordinary skill would be guilty of, if acting with ordinary care.'**

... **he is not guilty of negligence if he has acted in accordance with a practice accepted as proper by a responsible body of medical men skilled in that particular art.** I do not think there is much difference in sense. It is just a different way of expressing the same thought. Putting it the other way round, a man is not negligent, if he is acting in accordance with such a practice, merely because there is a body of opinion who would take a contrary view. At the same time, that does not mean that a medical man can obstinately and pig-headedly carry on with some old technique if it has been proved to be contrary to what is really substantially the whole of informed medical opinion.

... it is not essential for you to decide which of two practices is the better practice, as long as you accept that what the defendants did was in accordance with a practice accepted by responsible persons.

Whilst this, the '*Bolam* test', is a reasonable means for the court to employ where it does not have the requisite specialist skill itself to conduct the entire inquiry, it is a method that has attracted some criticism for according too much deference to the professions themselves (and the medical profession in particular).[3] There are fears that professional colleagues will 'close ranks' to protect one of their own. However well-founded these fears may have been, the following case is often referred to as limiting the potential of the *Bolam* test to allow such a risk to eventuate. In essence, it emphasises that the court can reject a professional body of opinion if, in its view, it is not logically defensible.

In *Bolitho*, a 2-year-old boy died after suffering a cardiac arrest and respiratory failure. He had, prior to the attack that killed him, suffered two previous respiratory failures whilst in the care of the defendant's hospital. On neither of the previous two occasions did a doctor attend the boy, despite requests from nurses for them to do so. The claimant argued that, had a doctor attended, and had the boy been intubated as a result of these earlier episodes, the final respiratory failure and cardiac arrest could have been prevented. The doctor argued that, even had she attended, she would not have intubated the boy in the circumstances. The question for the court, therefore, was whether omitting to intubate a child in this situation was a reasonable course of action for a doctor to take.

Bolitho v City of Hackney Health Authority [1998] AC 232, 241 (Lord Browne-Wilkinson)

My Lords, I agree with these submissions to the extent that, in my view, the court is not bound to hold that a defendant doctor escapes liability for negligent treatment or diagnosis just because he leads evidence from a number of medical experts who are genuinely of opinion that the defendant's treatment or diagnosis accorded with sound medical practice. In the *Bolam* case itself, McNair J. stated [1957] 1 W.L.R. 583, 587, that the defendant had to have acted in accordance with the practice accepted as proper by a '*responsible* body of medical men.' Later, at p. 588, he referred to 'a standard of practice recognised as proper by a competent *reasonable* body of opinion.' Again, in the passage which I have cited from *Maynard*'s case, Lord Scarman refers to a 'respectable' body of professional opinion. **The use of these adjectives – responsible, reasonable and respectable – all show that the court has to be satisfied that the exponents of the body of opinion relied upon can demonstrate that such opinion has a logical basis.** In particular in cases involving, as they so often do, the weighing of risks against benefits, the judge before accepting a body of opinion as being responsible, reasonable or respectable, will need to be satisfied that, in forming their views, the experts have directed their minds to the question of comparative risks and benefits and have reached a defensible conclusion on the matter.

---

3 See, eg, K Norrie, 'Medical Negligence: Who Sets the Standard?' (1985) 11 *JME* 135. See also the critical literature referred to in M Brazier and J Miola, 'Bye-Bye Bolam: A Medical Litigation Revolution?' (2000) 8 *Med Law Review* 85 at fn 2.

There are decisions which demonstrate that the judge is entitled to approach expert professional opinion on this basis. For example, in *Hucks v. Cole* (a case from 1968 reported in [1993] 4 Med. L.R. 393), a doctor failed to treat with penicillin a patient who was suffering from septic places on her skin though he knew them to contain organisms capable of leading to puerperal fever. A number of distinguished doctors gave evidence that they would not, in the circumstances, have treated with penicillin. The Court of Appeal found the defendant to have been negligent. Sachs L.J. said, at p. 397:

> 'When the evidence shows that a lacuna in professional practice exists by which risks of grave danger are knowingly taken, then, however small the risk, the court must anxiously examine that lacuna – particularly if the risk can be easily and inexpensively avoided. If the court finds, on an analysis of the reasons given for not taking those precautions that, in the light of current professional knowledge, there is no proper basis for the lacuna, and that it is definitely not reasonable that those risks should have been taken, its function is to state that fact and where necessary to state that it constitutes negligence. In such a case the practice will no doubt thereafter be altered to the benefit of patients. On such occasions the fact that other practitioners would have done the same thing as the defendant practitioner is a very weighty matter to be put on the scales on his behalf; but it is not, as Mr. Webster readily conceded, conclusive. The court must be vigilant to see whether the reasons given for putting a patient at risk are valid in the light of any well-known advance in medical knowledge, or whether they stem from a residual adherence to out-of-date ideas.'

Again, in *Edward Wong Finance Co. Ltd. v. Johnson Stokes & Master* [1984] 1 A.C. 296, the defendant's solicitors had conducted the completion of a mortgage transaction in 'Hong Kong style' rather than in the old fashioned English style. Completion in Hong Kong style provides for money to be paid over against an undertaking by the solicitors for the borrowers subsequently to hand over the executed documents. This practice opened the gateway through which a dishonest solicitor for the borrower absconded with the loan money without providing the security documents for such loan. The Privy Council held that even though completion in Hong Kong style was almost universally adopted in Hong Kong and was therefore in accordance with a body of professional opinion there, the defendant's solicitors were liable for negligence because there was an obvious risk which could have been guarded against. Thus, the body of professional opinion, though almost universally held, was not reasonable or responsible.

These decisions demonstrate that in cases of diagnosis and treatment there are cases where, despite a body of professional opinion sanctioning the defendant's conduct, the defendant can properly be held liable for negligence (I am not here considering questions of disclosure of risk). In my judgment that is because, in some cases, it cannot be demonstrated to the judge's satisfaction that the body of opinion relied upon is reasonable or responsible. In the vast majority of cases the fact that distinguished experts in the field are of a particular opinion will demonstrate the reasonableness of that opinion.

In particular, where there are questions of assessment of the relative risks and benefits of adopting a particular medical practice, a reasonable view necessarily presupposes that the relative risks and benefits have been weighed by the experts in forming their opinions. **But if, in a rare case, it can be demonstrated that the professional opinion is not capable of withstanding logical analysis, the judge is entitled to hold that the body of opinion is not reasonable or responsible.**

5.3 Failure to warn patients of risks

This aspect of the doctor–patient relationship requires consideration in its own right. We will return to it in Chapter 6 on Causation, but it is essential that you understand how the warning question feeds into the breach of duty analysis. You will need, therefore, to be very familiar with the following authority. The claimant in this case suffered from diabetes and had a small physical frame. Both of these characteristics increased the risk of complications when she gave birth. Those risks eventuated and her baby son suffered serious injuries as a result. Whilst Mrs Montgomery had expressed concern in the past about the size of her baby, she did not ask about specific risks and her doctor did not volunteer information about specific risks and their consequences. The doctor's decision was based on her judgement that the risk to the baby was small and that, were the mother to be made aware of it, she would likely opt for delivery by caesarean section; something which would not be in her overall interests. Had the claimant been made aware of the risks, she would have opted for a caesarean delivery, it would have been made available to her, and the injuries to her son would not, on the balance of probabilities, have occurred.

The claimant's case had failed in the lower courts on the issue of breach; the lower courts applying the *Bolam* test to the question of whether the doctor had acted reasonably in not disclosing the specific risk in question. Such a failure to disclose would not, on that approach, amount to a breach of duty if an established body of professional opinion would deem it to have been reasonable. The Supreme Court, however, departed from this approach for the purposes of risk disclosure, and made a clear distinction between a doctor's conduct in providing diagnosis or treatment, to which the Bolam test *will* apply, and a doctor's conduct in advising patients about risks and alternative treatments. It is a notable judicial move away from the historically more paternalistic approach to this question, and a move towards greater recognition of, and willingness to protect, patient autonomy.

Montgomery v Lanarkshire Health Board [2015] UKSC 11, [2015] AC 1430, [81]–[89] (Lords Kerr and Reid), [108], [109], [115] (Lady Hale)

[Lords Kerr and Reid] 81. The social and legal developments which we have mentioned point away from a model of the relationship between the doctor and the patient based upon medical paternalism. They also point away from a model based upon a view of the patient as being entirely dependent on information provided by the doctor. What they point towards is an approach to the law which, instead of treating patients as placing themselves in the hands of their doctors (and then being prone to sue their doctors in the event of a disappointing outcome), treats them so far as possible as adults who are capable of understanding that medical treatment is uncertain of success and may involve risks, accepting responsibility for the taking of risks affecting their own lives, and living with the consequences of their choices.

82. In the law of negligence, this approach entails a duty on the part of doctors to take reasonable care to ensure that a patient is aware of material risks of injury that are inherent in treatment. This can be understood, within the traditional framework of negligence, as a duty of care to avoid exposing a person to a risk of injury which she would otherwise have avoided, but it is also the counterpart of the patient's entitlement to decide whether or not to incur that risk. The existence of that entitlement, and the fact that its exercise does not depend exclusively on medical considerations, are important. They point to a fundamental distinction between, on the one hand, the doctor's role when considering possible investigatory or treatment options and, on the other, her role in discussing with the patient any recommended treatment and possible alternatives, and the risks of injury which may be involved.

83. The former role is an exercise of professional skill and judgment: what risks of injury are involved in an operation, for example, is a matter falling within the expertise of members of the medical profession. But it is a *non sequitur* to conclude that the question whether a risk of injury, or the availability of an alternative form of treatment, ought to be discussed with the patient is also a matter of purely professional judgment. The doctor's advisory role cannot be regarded as solely an exercise of medical skill without leaving out of account the patient's entitlement to decide on the risks to her health which she is willing to run (a decision which may be influenced by non-medical considerations). Responsibility for determining the nature and extent of a person's rights rests with the courts, not with the medical professions.

84. Furthermore, because the extent to which a doctor may be inclined to discuss risks with a patient is not determined by medical learning or experience, the application of the *Bolam* test to this question is liable to result in the sanctioning of differences in practice which are attributable not to divergent schools of thought in medical science, but merely to divergent attitudes among doctors as to the degree of respect owed to their patients.

85. A person can of course decide that she does not wish to be informed of risks of injury (just as a person may choose to ignore the information leaflet enclosed with her medicine); and a doctor is not obliged to discuss the risks inherent in treatment with a person who makes it clear that she would prefer not to discuss the matter. Deciding whether a person is so disinclined may involve the doctor making a judgment; but it is not a judgment which is dependent on medical expertise. It is also true that the doctor must necessarily make a judgment as to how best to explain the risks to the patient, and that providing an effective

explanation may require skill. But the skill and judgment required are not of the kind with which the *Bolam* test is concerned; and the need for that kind of skill and judgment does not entail that the question whether to explain the risks at all is normally a matter for the judgment of the doctor. That is not to say that the doctor is required to make disclosures to her patient if, in the reasonable exercise of medical judgment, she considers that it would be detrimental to the health of her patient to do so; but the 'therapeutic exception', as it has been called, cannot provide the basis of the general rule.

86. It follows that the analysis of the law by the majority in *Sidaway* is unsatisfactory, in so far as it treated the doctor's duty to advise her patient of the risks of proposed treatment as falling within the scope of the *Bolam* test, subject to two qualifications of that general principle, neither of which is fundamentally consistent with that test. It is unsurprising that courts have found difficulty in the subsequent application of *Sidaway*, and that the courts in England and Wales have in reality departed from it; a position which was effectively endorsed, particularly by Lord Steyn, in *Chester v Afshar*. There is no reason to perpetuate the application of the *Bolam* test in this context any longer.

87. The correct position, in relation to the risks of injury involved in treatment, can now be seen to be substantially that adopted in *Sidaway* by Lord Scarman, and by Lord Woolf MR in *Pearce*, subject to the refinement made by the High Court of Australia in *Rogers v Whitaker*, which we have discussed at paras 77–73. An adult person of sound mind is entitled to decide which, if any, of the available forms of treatment to undergo, and her consent must be obtained before treatment interfering with her bodily integrity is undertaken. The doctor is therefore under a duty to take reasonable care to ensure that the patient is aware of any material risks involved in any recommended treatment, and of any reasonable alternative or variant treatments. The test of materiality is whether, in the circumstances of the particular case, a reasonable person in the patient's position would be likely to attach significance to the risk, or the doctor is or should reasonably be aware that the particular patient would be likely to attach significance to it.

88. The doctor is however entitled to withhold from the patient information as to a risk if he reasonably considers that its disclosure would be seriously detrimental to the patient's health. The doctor is also excused from conferring with the patient in circumstances of necessity, as for example where the patient requires treatment urgently but is unconscious or otherwise unable to make a decision. It is unnecessary for the purposes of this case to consider in detail the scope of those exceptions.

89. Three further points should be made. First, it follows from this approach that the assessment of whether a risk is material cannot be reduced to percentages. The significance of a given risk is likely to reflect a variety of factors besides its magnitude: for example, the nature of the risk, the effect which its occurrence would have upon the life of the patient, the importance to the patient of the benefits sought to be achieved by the treatment, the alternatives available, and the risks involved in those alternatives. The assessment is therefore fact-sensitive, and sensitive also to the characteristics of the patient.

[Lady Hale] 108: **It is now well recognised that the interest which the law of negligence protects is a person's interest in their own physical and psychiatric integrity, an important feature of which is their autonomy, their freedom to decide what shall and shall not be done with their body** (the unwanted pregnancy cases are an example: see *Rees v Darlington Memorial Hospital NHS Trust* [2003] UKHL 52, [2004] 1 AC 309). Thus, as Jonathan Herring puts it in Medical Law and Ethics (2012), 4th ed, p 170), 'the issue is not whether enough information was given to ensure consent to the procedure, but whether there was enough information given so that the doctor was not acting negligently and giving due protection to the patient's right of autonomy'.

109. An important consequence of this is that it is not possible to consider a particular medical procedure in isolation from its alternatives. Most decisions about medical care are not simple yes/no answers. There are choices to be made, arguments for and against each of the options to be considered, and sufficient information must be given so that this can be done ...

...

115. **In any event, once the argument departs from purely medical considerations and involves value judgments of this sort, it becomes clear, as Lord Kerr and Lord Reed conclude at para 85, that the *Bolam* test, of conduct supported by a responsible body of medical opinion, becomes quite inapposite.** A patient is entitled to take into account her own values, her own assessment of the comparative merits of giving birth in the 'natural' and traditional way and of giving birth by caesarean section, whatever medical opinion may say, alongside the medical evaluation of the risks to herself and her baby. She may place great value on giving birth in the natural way and be prepared to take the risks to herself and her baby which this entails. The medical profession must respect her choice, unless she lacks the legal capacity to decide (*St George's Healthcare NHS Trust v S* [1999] Fam 26). There is no good reason why the same should not apply in reverse, if she is prepared to forgo the joys of natural childbirth in order to avoid some not insignificant risks to herself or her baby. She cannot force her doctor to offer treatment which he or she considers futile or inappropriate. But she is at least entitled to the information which will enable her to take a proper part in that decision.

Montgomery is undoubtedly an emphatic step towards the courts limiting both doctors', and their own, jurisdiction to decide what is in the best interests of patients. In the article extracted below, however, Hobson argues that *Montgomery* has not consigned *Bolam* to history in this context because it still applies on facts giving rise to the 'therapeutic privilege': situations in which medical professionals are entitled to withhold information about risks where to do otherwise would be seriously detrimental to the patient's health.

Clark Hobson, 'No (,) more Bolam please: Lanarkshire v Montgomery Health Board' (2016) 79(3) *MLR* 488–503 at 489

Montgomery is highly significant for numerous reasons. Not only does the decision impact upon the scope of the medical professional's duty to disclose to avoid negligent practice, but it comes amid claims that '[t]he common law no longer sees the professions as somehow sacred or fragile assets of society, which merit special protection'. Linked to this is a pervasive concern throughout the leading joint judgment given by Lord Kerr and Lord Reed, and the ... concurring judgment from Lady Hale, with what has been called the concept of 'jurisdiction'; the demarcation by the Court of a territory to which it alone exclusively possesses the appropriate power to make determinations on matters that arise. This is done by addressing the underlying nature of the issues surrounding risk disclosure. As a result, the Court repeatedly emphasises one broad message: risk disclosure should change to focus on what the patient wants to know rather than what the medical professional may wish to provide ...

The promotion of autonomy ... argument ... rings hollow. How is the patient able to exercise a right to judge whether to undergo treatment, if the medical professional is to gauge how much information to tell the patient on the basis of her medical experience and training?

Question to consider: When, if ever, should the courts be able to override professional opinion on what is reasonable when determining whether there has been a breach of duty?

Other resources: John-Paul Swoboda, 'Bolam: going, going ... gone' (2018) 1 *JPI Law* 9; K Mason and D Brodie, '*Bolam, Bolam* – Wherefore Art Thou *Bolam*?' (2005) 9(2) *Edinburgh Law Review* 298; L Skene and H Luntz, 'Effects of tort law reform on medical liability' (2005) 79 *Australian Law Journal* 345–63.

5.4 Social Action, Responsibility and Heroism (SARAH) Act 2015

Any discussion of breach of duty should now make reference to the Social Action, Responsibility and Heroism (SARAH) Act 2015, which was formulated in response to the perception of a growing compensation culture. A court asking whether a defendant has breached their duty of care now has expressly to consider ss 2–4 of the Act as part of that inquiry. The principal aim of the legislation is to prevent fear of litigation from reducing or stopping socially beneficial activities. It has yet to be the focus of any notable case law.

Social Action, Responsibility and Heroism (SARAH) Act 2015

1 When this Act applies

This Act applies when a court, in considering a claim that a person was negligent or in breach of statutory duty, is determining the steps that the person was required to take to meet a standard of care.

2 Social action

The court must have regard to whether the alleged negligence or breach of statutory duty occurred when the person was acting for the benefit of society or any of its members.

3 Responsibility

The court must have regard to whether the person, in carrying out the activity in the course of which the alleged negligence or breach of statutory duty occurred, demonstrated a predominantly responsible approach towards protecting the safety or other interests of others.

4 Heroism

The court must have regard to whether the alleged negligence or breach of statutory duty occurred when the person was acting heroically by intervening in an emergency to assist an individual in danger.

5.5 Conclusion

The aim of this chapter has been, primarily, to make clear the crucial distinction that must be made between establishing the existence of a duty of care in negligence (Chapter 2) and deciding whether that standard has been breached. It is very common for these two inquiries to be run into one, but this will lead to a problematic and inaccurate analysis, so avoid doing so at all costs! In order to do this, the chapter has set out the significant authorities that establish the objective nature of the reasonableness standard, and how that standard is reached and applied in various factual contexts, including, importantly, the *Bolam* test for professional standards of reasonableness. We have also seen here, however, the limitations of the *Bolam* test and some academic criticism that has been levelled at it. Its application to risk warning cases has already been curtailed; the question remains whether it will in the future be further curtailed by common law development, particularly given the increased contemporary recognition of personal autonomy.

Chapter 6

CAUSATION

> Why is causation important in tort law? One reason is that to insist on causal connection between conduct and harm ensures that in general we impose liability only on those who, by intervening in the world, have changed the course of events for the worse.[1]

The causal part of the negligence inquiry links a defendant's breach of duty with the loss suffered by the claimant. It is often described as being in two parts; variously referred to as either factual causation and legal causation or causation and remoteness. Whatever label is applied, the two parts of the inquiry aim to do the same thing: first, to establish whether the defendant's breach of duty had a historical role to play in the bringing about of the claimant's loss and, second, to determine whether, where it has played such a role, it is a legally relevant role. The first inquiry is often described as being purely factual: 'Did the breach have a part to play in bringing about the loss?' The second part is normative: 'Does the law regard the breach as attracting legal responsibility?' The difference can be illustrated clearly with an oversimplified example. B is run over whilst she is crossing the road. B was on her way to pick up her son from school at the time because he injured himself playing football. A drove into her because he was texting rather than looking at the road and failed to see B. Both A and B's son are undoubtedly factual causes of B's injury because they are part of the historical chain of events leading to the accident. The law will not regard the son's role as being legally relevant (it was a factual but not a legal cause), but it will so regard the actions of A.

6.1 The 'but for' test

The first, factual inquiry is usually[2] conducted by means of the 'but for' test. Basically, in order for a defendant's breach to have been a factual cause of the claimant's loss, the court asks, 'But for the breach, would the claimant's loss have occurred when it did?' Where the answer is no, the breach satisfies this first stage of factual causation

---

1 A Honoré, 'Necessary and Sufficient Conditions' in D Owen (ed), *Philosophical Foundations of Tort Law* (Clarendon Press, 1995), 385.

2 We will come to the exceptions below.

because, in line with the Honoré quotation above, here the defendant has intervened in the claimant's course of events for the worse. Where the answer to the but for question is yes, the loss would have happened anyway, and the defendant's breach is deemed not to be a factual cause. This is what happened in the first case set out here; the classic account of the but for test.

The claimant's husband became ill after drinking tea during his shift. Having attended the defendant's hospital, he was sent home without appropriate diagnosis and treatment, an action which amounted to a breach of the hospital's duty of care. He died a few hours later of what turned out to be arsenic poisoning. The question for the court was whether, even with appropriate medical treatment, he would still have died when he did. The medical evidence was such that, on the balance of probabilities, the outcome would have been the same whether or not treatment had been provided. In other words, it was more likely than not that, but for the defendant's breach, the night watchman would still have died. The defendant was therefore not liable in negligence for the death.

Barnett v Chelsea and Kensington Hospital Management Committee [1969] 1 QB 428, 438 (Nield J)

> It remains to consider whether it is shown that the deceased's death was caused by that negligence or whether, as the defendants have said, the deceased must have died in any event.
>
> …
>
> There has been put before me a timetable which I think is of much importance. The deceased attended at the casualty department at five or 10 minutes past eight in the morning. If the casualty officer had got up and dressed and come to see the three men and examined them and decided to admit them, the deceased (and Dr. Lockett agreed with this) could not have been in bed in a ward before 11 a.m. I accept Dr. Goulding's evidence that an intravenous drip would not have been set up before 12 noon, and if potassium loss was suspected it could not have been discovered until 12.30 p.m. Dr. Lockett, dealing with this, said: 'If this man had not been treated until after 12 noon the chances of survival were not good.'

The standard of proof in civil law is that of the balance of probabilities. The burden of proof lies on the claimant, who has to persuade the court that it is more likely than not that her version of events is correct. In statistical terms, this means that a claimant must show that it is =>50% likely that her account accurately represents what happened. Note that the competing account does not have to be disproved, as long as the proffered account is 'proved'. The burden of proof is on the claimant, but if and when the claimant establishes that it is more likely than not that the defendant caused her injury, the court proceeds as if this were proved as a certainty. Conversely, the case of any claimant who fails to prove her causal submission to this standard, even if she comes very close to the threshold, will be treated as a total failure of proof.

As Lord Hoffmann put it when writing extra-judicially:[3]

> The law operates a binary system in which the only values are 0 and 1. If the evidence that something happened satisfies the burden of proof … then it is assigned a value of 1 and treated as definitely having happened. If the evidence does not discharge the burden of proof, the event is assigned a value of 0 and treated as definitely not having happened. There is no forensic space for the conclusion that something which has to be proved may have happened.

In one sense, therefore, the causal inquiry is one of all or nothing. It is crucial, however, to make a distinction for this purpose between divisible and indivisible injuries. The purpose of damages in the tort of negligence is to put the claimant back into the position that they were in before the defendant's breach intervened and changed their life for the worse. In keeping with this objective, courts recognise that some injuries can be divided up between different causal factors, often meaning that whilst the defendant's breach caused one part of the claimant's loss, it is not the cause of the whole of the ultimate loss. The following case is a clear example of this because it is concerned with a divisible injury: deafness. Deafness is divisible because a person can have varying degrees of deafness, it can get worse with longer exposure to loud noise, and it can therefore be divided up into different causal time periods. This is to distinguish it from, say, death, which is the ultimate indivisible injury: it is binary in that a person is either alive or dead; it does not come in varying degrees of severity and cannot therefore be divided up across identifiable time periods.

Thompson v Smiths Shiprepairers (North Shields) Ltd [1984] QB 405, 438 (Mustill J)

> The starting point for any inquiry into the measure of damages is the principle that the court should so far as possible endeavour to restore the plaintiff to the position in which he would have found himself but for the defendant's wrongful act. The impracticability of giving full effect to this principle must be recognised at every stage of the process. Money can never properly compensate a loss which consists of social impairment rather than financial deprivation. Quantification of damages for personal injury involve the use of conventional measures, the adoption of which at once makes nonsense of any attempts at mathematical accuracy. In a field where the subject matter is people, not contracts, bank balances and abstract rights, the recognition that certain results are unacceptable in human terms must rightly lead to alternative solutions which cannot be easily rationalised. Complete logical rigour cannot be attained.

3 'Causation' in R Goldberg (ed), *Perspectives on Causation* (Hart Publishing, 2011) 8.

Nevertheless, it is instructive at least to begin by adopting the primary rule to which I have referred, and seeing whether it yields sensible results. The first step is to consider the case of a worker, whose hearing has been impaired by excessive noise wrongfully suffered whilst in the service of successive employers A and B. The basic principle suggests that A should be liable in full, but not more than in full, for the impairment existing when the worker leaves his employment. Ideally, this should be assessed by reference to the damage suffered by the structure of his organs of hearing. But this cannot directly be measured, so it is quantified in terms of the decibel hearing loss, and the inquiry can be focussed by asking what would be the result if the worker had issued a writ immediately upon leaving A's employment, and brought the matter very speedily to trial.

...

What of employer B? Principle and common sense demand a recognition of the fact that he has 'taken over' the plaintiff in a condition where his organs of hearing are already damaged, and where he is already subject to actual and potential symptoms. It would be an injustice to employer B to make him liable for damage already done before he had any connection with the plaintiff. His liability, first principles suggest, should be limited to compensation for (a) the perpetuation and amplification of the handicaps already being suffered at the moment when the employment changed hands, and (b) the bringing to fruit in the shape of current hardship those symptoms which had previously been no more than potential.

If this reasoning is followed, the result should be that the recoveries against A and B will amount in total to the award which would have been made if the damage had all been caused by the wrongs of a single employer; and, equally, that the assessment of such an award could form at least the starting point of any quantification of the individual liability of employers A and B.

Next, one must consider how this approach can be applied to a case where either (a) there are two successive employers, of whom only the second is at fault, or (b) there is a single employer, who has been guilty of an actionable fault only from a date after the employment began. Logic suggests that the analysis should be the same. Employer B has, once again, 'inherited' a workman whose hearing is already damaged by events with which that employer has had no connection, or at least no connection which makes him liable in law. The fact that, so far as the worker is concerned, the prior events unfortunately give him no cause of action against anyone should not affect the principles on which he recovers from employer B. Justice looks to the interests of both parties, not to those of the plaintiff alone.

This solution pre-supposes a division of responsibility between A and B, or (in the case of the second example) between non-blameworthy and blameworthy sources of noise.

Importantly, and as illustrated by the following case, the same principle applies where the division amongst factors is done not just between multiple tortfeasors, but also where one (or some) factors are tortious and one (or some) factors are natural causes. The same principle explains both: a tortfeasor should no more be held liable for the effects of natural, non-legally relevant factors than they should for the effects of another's breach of duty. Not only is this fairer to tortfeasors, but it also prevents claimants from getting an unjustified windfall. After all, people do not have a right to compensation for succumbing to natural disease, as the following case makes clear. In this case, the claimant was injured at work as a result of his employer's breach of duty. His back was damaged and his earning capacity thereby reduced. Three years later, and *completely independent of his accident*, Jobling developed a back disease which rendered him completely unfit for work. The House of Lords held that the defendant should not be liable for the claimant's consequential losses after the point at which the disease manifested itself.

Jobling v Associated Dairies Ltd [1982] AC 794, 810 (Lord Russell)

It is well established that in assessing compensation for damage caused to a plaintiff by a tortfeasor among other considerations is the consequent loss or reduction in earning capacity in the working life of the plaintiff. It is also well established that it is appropriate, in arriving at an estimated figure under that head, that some allowance or discount should be made for the ordinary vicissitudes of life. It is also well established that if by the time of trial facts emerge which make known a vicissitude of life as applicable to the plaintiff, that knowledge should replace that which would have been only an estimate: where there is knowledge estimation has no part.

One of these vicissitudes is that a plaintiff might thereafter succumb to a disease (unconnected with the tort) which would abbreviate the plaintiff's working life. Commonly the discount for such a possibility might well be small: but it is not to be ignored. If before trial the plaintiff does so succumb in my opinion the evidence of its abbreviating effect must take the place of estimate, and reduce the amount of compensation for the tortious damage under that head.

6.2 Material contribution to injury

So far, so relatively simple. The inquiry gets more complicated where the injury is (at least practically) indivisible[4] but there are multiple potential factors, some of which result from breaches of duty and some of which do not. On such facts, the courts

4 See *Holmes v Poeton Holdings Ltd* [2023] EWCA Civ 1377 for confirmation by the Court of Appeal that the Material Contribution to Injury analysis applies only to indivisible injuries.

have developed a 'material contribution to injury' analysis. Its roots are most closely associated with the following case, in which the claimant's disease was caused by dust that he inhaled at work. Some dust was released into the atmosphere as a result of the defendant's breach of duty, but some of it was termed 'innocent dust' because it was not discharged as a result of the defendant's wrong. The problem was that the claimant inhaled both sets of dust simultaneously, and the disease he developed was indivisible in the sense that someone either has pneumoconiosis or does not. The question therefore arose: did the defendant's breach cause the disease to occur?

Bonnington Castings Ltd v Wardlaw [1956] AC 613, 621 (Lord Reid)

The medical evidence was that pneumoconiosis is caused by a gradual accumulation in the lungs of minute particles of silica inhaled over a period of years. That means, I think, that the disease is caused by the whole of the noxious material inhaled and, if that material comes from two sources, it cannot be wholly attributed to material from one source or the other. I am in agreement with much of the Lord President's opinion in this case, but I cannot agree that the question is which was the most probable source of the Respondent's disease, the dust from the pneumatic hammers or the dust from the swing grinders. It appears to me that the source of his disease was the dust from both sources, and the real question is whether the dust from the swing grinders materially contributed to the disease. What is a material contribution must be a question of degree. A contribution which comes within the exception *de minimis non curat lex* is not material, but I think that any contribution which does not fall within that exception must be material. I do not see how there can be something too large to come within the *de minimis* principle but yet too small to be material.

[Lord Keith at 626] The disease is a disease of gradual incidence. Small though the contribution of pollution may be for which the defenders are to blame, it was continuous over a long period. *In cumulo* it must have been substantial, though it might remain small in proportion. It was the atmosphere inhaled by the pursuer that caused his illness and it is impossible, in my opinion, to resolve the components of that atmosphere into particles caused by the fault of the defenders and particles not caused by the fault of the defenders, as if they were separate and independent factors in his illness. *Prima facie* the particles inhaled are acting cumulatively, and I think the natural inference is that had it not been for the cumulative effect the pursuer would not have developed pneumoconiosis when he did and might not have developed it at all.

The defendant in *Bonnington*, therefore, was held liable for materially contributing to the claimant's injury. In other words, but for the 'guilty' dust, the claimant's pneumoconiosis would not have been as it was. The contribution of the negligence was found to have been 'material' and therefore legally relevant, even though it could not be quantified.

Professor Stapleton explains how this situation calls for a non-orthodox application of causal considerations:[5]

> *Bonnington* may represent a departure from the … orthodox approach in the context of a particular evidentiary gap: namely, where it is known that the victim's total condition is a divisible one but there is no acceptable evidentiary basis on which the disability due to the separate insults to the body could be apportioned to the individual sources, the claimant is allowed to recover for the total condition … the pursuer could prove an orthodox causal connection between breach and a part of the divisible injury, he just could not quantify it.

6.3 Material contribution to risk

Even more challenging, and requiring an even more exceptional approach, is the situation in which there is, in the words of Lord Bingham, a 'rock of uncertainty' or, as Professor Stapleton calls it, an 'evidentiary gap'. In these situations, the injury is indivisible and there are multiple potential causes of it. But there is *also* insufficient scientific knowledge about the injury in question for the medical experts to be able to say how, or even whether, a causal link can be made[6] between any of the tortious causes and the outcome. They cannot say that there is such a link, but neither can they say that there is not. And the same impossibility also applies, of course, to the non-tortious causes: a rock of uncertainty indeed.

In the first case extracted below, the claimant, who was employed by the defendants to work in brick kilns, had contracted dermatitis. Whilst he worked, his skin was inevitably in contact with brick dust, which was the agent identified as the cause of his illness. His employers were not in breach of their duty of care for exposing him to brick dust whilst he was physically in the kilns, but they were in breach for failing to provide washing facilities to enable him to wash the dust off his skin before cycling home. The real problem here was that the medical experts were unable to determine whether, and if so to what extent, the disease was triggered by brick dust attributable to the breach of duty as opposed to exposure which would have occurred even if showers had been provided for use after work. Therefore, they were simply unable to say whether the dermatitis would have occurred but for the defendant's breach of duty. The House of Lords got around the issue by holding the defendants liable for having materially *increased the risk* of the claimant's developing dermatitis. This is different to material contribution to injury, dealt with above, because here the experts were unable to say that the breach had actually contributed to the injury. In *Bonnington*, they could say that the breach contributed to the injury; just not by how much. Here, the most they could say was that the breach had contributed to the *risk* of the illness developing.

5 Jane Stapleton, 'Unnecessary Causes' (2013) 129 *LQR* 39 at 52–53.
6 On the balance of probabilities.

McGhee v National Coal Board [1973] 1 WLR 1, 7 (Lord Wilberforce), 12 (Lord Salmon)

[Lord Wilberforce at 7] [T]he default here consisted not in adding a material quantity to the accumulation of injurious particles but by failure to take a step which materially increased the risk that the dust already present would cause injury. And I must say that, at least in the present case, to bridge the evidential gap by inference seems to me something of a fiction, since it was precisely this inference which the medical expert declined to make. But I find in the cases quoted an analogy which suggests the conclusion that, in the absence of proof that the culpable addition had, in the result, no effect, the employers should be liable for an injury, squarely within the risk which they created and that they, not the pursuer, should suffer the consequence of the impossibility, foreseeably inherent in the nature of his injury, of segregating the precise consequence of their default.

[Lord Salmon at 12] My Lords, I would suggest that the true view is that, as a rule, when it is proved, on a balance of probabilities, that an employer has been negligent and that his negligence has materially increased the risk of his employee contracting an industrial disease, then he is liable in damages to that employee if he contracts the disease notwithstanding that the employer is not responsible for other factors which have materially contributed to the disease.

The tenor of this decision was really that, where a defendant has materially increased the risk of an injury, where that injury has occurred (liability will not be imposed for pure risk creation where harm has not actually occurred),[7] and where the defendant is unable to prove that its breach did *not* materially increase that risk, liability will be imposed for the creation of that risk. The policy arguments, which are examined more expressly in the following case, focus on the fact that, in these situations, there is a defendant who has, in pursuit of a profit, exposed their employees to risk in a situation over which they have the greater control. Looked at in this way, particularly in the following case, the House of Lords felt that, as between a duty-breaching defendant and an innocent claimant, the latter should not have to bear the consequences of the evidential gap.

In the case that follows, probably one of the most infamous decisions on causation in negligence, the defendants were former employers of individuals who had contracted mesothelioma, and had exposed those individuals to asbestos in breach of their duties of care. It was accepted that, for the purposes of the case, any exposure to asbestos other than that for which the defendants were responsible (such as general environmental exposure) could be discounted. The major complication was that each individual had been exposed to asbestos by more than one employer, and medical

7 See *Rothwell v Chemical and Insulating Co Ltd* [2007] UKHL 39 and S Green, 'Risk Exposure and Negligence' (2006) 122 *LQR* 386 (a note on the Court of Appeal decision, but referred to by the House of Lords at [55]).

knowledge about the way in which mesothelioma occurred was incomplete. The Court was therefore unable to associate the development of the disease with any particular source of asbestos (in other words, with any particular employer):

Fairchild v Glenhaven Funeral Services [2002] UKHL 22, [2003] 1 AC 32, [2], [7], [9], [12], [34] (Lord Bingham)

2. The essential question underlying the appeals may be accurately expressed in this way. If

(1) C was employed at different times and for differing periods by both A and B, and
(2) A and B were both subject to a duty to take reasonable care or to take all practicable measures to prevent C inhaling asbestos dust because of the known risk that asbestos dust (if inhaled) might cause a mesothelioma, and
(3) both A and B were in breach of that duty in relation to C during the periods of C's employment by each of them with the result that during both periods C inhaled excessive quantities of asbestos dust, and
(4) C is found to be suffering from a mesothelioma, and
(5) any cause of C's mesothelioma other than the inhalation of asbestos dust at work can be effectively discounted, but
(6) C cannot (because of the current limits of human science) prove, on the balance of probabilities, that his mesothelioma was the result of his inhaling asbestos dust during his employment by A or during his employment by B or during his employment by A and B taken together,

is C entitled to recover damages against either A or B or against both A and B?

...

7. ... It is accepted that the risk of developing a mesothelioma increases in proportion to the quantity of asbestos dust and fibres inhaled: the greater the quantity of dust and fibre inhaled, the greater the risk. But the condition may be caused by a single fibre,[8] or a few fibres, or many fibres: medical opinion holds none of these possibilities to be more probable than any other, and the condition once caused is not aggravated by further exposure. So if C is employed successively by A and B and is exposed to asbestos dust and fibres during each employment and develops a mesothelioma, the very strong probability is that this will have been caused by inhalation of asbestos dust containing fibres. But C could have inhaled a single fibre giving rise to his condition during employment by A, in which case his exposure by B will have had no effect on his condition; or he could have inhaled a single fibre giving rise to his condition during his employment by B, in which case his exposure by A will have had no effect on his condition; or he could have inhaled fibres

8 In the decade following, the 'single-fibre theory' had been effectively discredited. See *Amaca Pty Ltd v Booth* [2011] HCA 53.

during his employment by A and B which together gave rise to his condition; but medical science cannot support the suggestion that any of these possibilities is to be regarded as more probable than any other. There is no way of identifying, even on a balance of probabilities, the source of the fibre or fibres which initiated the genetic process which culminated in the malignant tumour. It is on this rock of uncertainty, reflecting the point to which medical science has so far advanced, that the three claims were rejected by the Court of Appeal and by two of the three trial judges.

9. … The overall object of tort law is to define cases in which the law may justly hold one party liable to compensate another. Are these such cases? A and B owed C a duty to protect C against a risk of a particular and very serious kind. They failed to perform that duty. As a result the risk eventuated and C suffered the very harm against which it was the duty of A and B to protect him. Had there been only one tortfeasor, C would have been entitled to recover, but because the duty owed to him was broken by two tortfeasors and not only one, he is held to be entitled to recover against neither, because of his inability to prove what is scientifically unprovable. If the mechanical application of generally accepted rules leads to such a result, there must be room to question the appropriateness of such an approach in such a case.

…

12. My noble and learned friend Lord Hoffmann has, on more than one occasion, discouraged a mechanical approach to the issue of causation. In *Environment Agency (formerly National Rivers Authority) v Empress Car Co. (Abertillery) Ltd* [1999] 2 AC 22 at 29, he said:

> 'The first point to emphasise is that common sense answers to questions of causation will differ according to the purpose for which the question is asked. Questions of causation often arise for the purpose of attributing responsibility to someone, for example, so as to blame him for something which has happened or to make him guilty of an offence or liable in damages. In such cases, the answer will depend upon the rule by which responsibility is being attributed.'

34. To the question posed in paragraph 2 of this opinion I would answer that where conditions (1)–(6) are satisfied C is entitled to recover against both A and B. That conclusion is in my opinion consistent with principle, and also with authority (properly understood). Where those conditions are satisfied, it seems to me just and in accordance with common sense to treat the conduct of A and B in exposing C to a risk to which he should not have been exposed as making a material contribution to the contracting by C of a condition against which it was the duty of A and B to protect him. I consider that this conclusion is fortified by the wider jurisprudence reviewed above. Policy considerations weigh in favour of such a conclusion.

Given the period during which asbestos was widely used, and the long time it takes for mesothelioma to materialise in those so exposed, the House of Lords was well aware that it was dealing with a situation that, unlike *McGhee*, was sadly going to be litigated more and more over the following years. Their policy dilemma was therefore a very real one. It was unquestionably a departure from orthodoxy, and one made in favour of claimants. The House was therefore understandably at pains to emphasise just how exceptional an approach it was, and how tightly circumscribed should be its boundaries. It did not take long for the following question about its limits to return to them.

The late Mr Barker had been exposed to asbestos during three periods of his working life: whilst working for an employer other than the defendant; whilst working for the defendant; and also whilst self-employed. The question was thus whether the *Fairchild* principle applied to situations where an individual has been exposed to asbestos dust during periods of self-employment as well as periods of employment by others. The House of Lords was also asked whether *Fairchild* entitled a defendant to have their liability apportioned to reflect the fact that the defendant was responsible for only part of the total exposure. The answer was that the principle would apply in such circumstances, but on the basis of liability apportioned to the relative risk contributions of each defendant. The alternative would have been joint and several liability. This distinction is highly significant for defendants because joint and several liability means that any one defendant can be pursued by the claimant for the full amount of damages. That defendant then has to claim back from its co-defendants their share of the award under the Civil Liability (Contribution) Act 1978. Not only is this time-consuming and expensive, but it puts the risk of any of the other defendants being insolvent or unable to pay on to the defendant who has paid. Apportioning liability, on the other hand, means that the court allocates a set amount to be recovered from each defendant, and this is the upper limit of what they will pay. Under this method, the risk of any defendant being unable to pay falls on the claimant – an element of the decision that, as Lord Hoffmann explains below, balances out the fact that the application of the principle itself favours the claimant. This is also the element of the decision, however, that caused some consternation, and which Parliament later overturned, as we shall see below.

Barker v Corus [2006] UKHL 20, [2006] 2 AC 572, [43], [47] (Lord Hoffmann)

43. In my opinion, the attribution of liability according to the relative degree of contribution to the chance of the disease being contracted would smooth the roughness of the justice which a rule of joint and several liability creates. The defendant was a wrongdoer, it is true, and should not be allowed to escape liability altogether, but he should not be liable for more than the damage which he caused and, since this is a case in which science can deal only in probabilities, the law should accept that position and attribute

liability according to probabilities. **The justification for the joint and several liability rule is that if you caused harm, there is no reason why your liability should be reduced because someone else also caused the same harm. But when liability is exceptionally imposed because you *may* have caused harm, the same considerations do not apply and fairness suggests that if more than one person may have been responsible, liability should be divided according to the probability that one or other caused the harm.**

…

47. Similarly, if the defendant is deemed to have caused the mesothelioma but the claimant, like Mr Barker, was himself responsible for a significant period of exposure, the court may find that he did not take adequate care for his own safety or was in breach of safety regulations and, as Moses J did in the Barker case, reduce the damages for contributory negligence. On the other hand, if liability is several, there is no question of contributory negligence any more than of contribution. A defendant is liable for the risk of disease which he himself has created and not for the risks created by others, whether they are defendants, persons not before the court or the claimant himself.

As alluded to above, the response to this decision from victims' groups and MPs was on the whole not favourable. As a result, the following section was added to the Compensation Act 2003 (a piece of legislation that was already going through Parliament). Its effect is to reverse the apportionment part of *Barker* so that, whenever the *Fairchild* principle is applied, the result will be joint and several liability (so that one defendant can be pursued for the full amount). Note, however, that the *Barker* judgment as a whole is not affected, so that *Fairchild* will still apply where a claimant has worked for those, including themselves, who are not defendants to the negligence action. Note also s 3 (1)(b) below: this statutory reversal applies only to cases involving mesothelioma contracted as a result of asbestos exposure and not any other indivisible injury in relation to which there is an evidential gap.

Compensation Act 2006

3 Mesothelioma: damages

(1) This section applies where—

- (a) a person ('the responsible person') has negligently or in breach of statutory duty caused or permitted another person ('the victim') to be exposed to asbestos,
- (b) the victim has contracted mesothelioma as a result of exposure to asbestos,
- (c) because of the nature of mesothelioma and the state of medical science, it is not possible to determine with certainty whether it was the exposure mentioned in paragraph (a) or another exposure which caused the victim to become ill, and
- (d) the responsible person is liable in tort, by virtue of the exposure mentioned in paragraph (a), in connection with damage caused to the victim by the disease (whether by reason of having materially increased a risk or for any other reason).

(2) The responsible person shall be liable—

(a) in respect of the whole of the damage caused to the victim by the disease (irrespective of whether the victim was also exposed to asbestos—

(i) other than by the responsible person, whether or not in circumstances in which another person has liability in tort, or

(ii) by the responsible person in circumstances in which he has no liability in tort), and

(b) jointly and severally with any other responsible person.

Whilst the expansion of the *Fairchild* principle was kept within narrow parameters, in that it was not accepted as a means of a claimant sidestepping the requirement to prove causation outside of the 'rock of uncertainty' and single agent cases,[9] its boundaries within the asbestos and mesothelioma cases continued to be pushed. In this next case, one of the claimants had been exposed to asbestos whilst employed by the defendant but it differed from *Fairchild* in a significant way: the court accepted that the occupational exposure had been very small. In fact, the trial judge accepted evidence to the effect that her asbestos exposure by the defendant increased her overall risk of developing mesothelioma by only 18%, and that the rest of her exposure was due to background environmental factors not associated with any breach of duty. The major question was therefore whether the exceptional principle applied in situations in which there had been only one tortious exposure to risk.

Sienkiewicz v Grief (UK) Ltd [2011] UKSC 10, [2011] 2 AC 229, [175], [176], [184]–[187] (Lord Brown)

175. The present position, exemplified by the facts of these very appeals, can be simply stated as follows: any person who negligently or in breach of duty exposes another more than minimally to the inhalation of asbestos fibres will be liable to make full compensation if that other develops mesothelioma more than five years later (five years being now thought to be the minimum period between the development of the first malignant cell and the diagnosis of the disease – see Lord Phillips' judgment at para 19(v)). That statement of the position holds true irrespective of whether the victim was exposed by others to even longer and more intensive inhalation (and indeed inhalation of more noxious fibres), whether negligently or not, and irrespective too of any environmental or other exposure (again, however intensive). It requires qualification only if and to the extent that the victim negligently exposed himself to the inhalation of asbestos fibres (when there may be a finding of contributory fault).

…

9 For single agent cases, see *Wilsher*, below.

176. One need hardly stress how radically different such an approach to compensation represents from that followed in all other cases of physical injury. All other cases require that the claimant satisfies the 'but for' test of causation.

…

184. In my judgment it could only be by reversing *Fairchild* and allowing no exception whatever to the normal rule of causation that this Court could now avoid what Lord Phillips (at para 58 of his judgment) rightly describes as the 'draconian consequences' of coupling section 3 to the *Fairchild/Barker* principle: the liability in full even of someone 'responsible for only a small proportion of the overall exposure of a claimant to asbestos dust'. There is in my opinion simply no logical stopping place between the case of successive negligent employers dealt with in *Fairchild* itself (apparently circumscribed though that decision was) and the extreme ('draconian') position now arrived at, well exemplified as it seems to me by the facts of these very appeals. If, because of the 'rock of uncertainty', the law is to compensate by reference to negligence which merely increases the *risk* of such injury as then develops, why should not that relaxation of the normal rule of causation apply equally when, as here, there is but one negligent employer (or negligent occupier) as when there are several? As *Barker* recognised, there can be no rational basis for confining the special rule within narrow bounds, whatever may have been contemplated by the House in *Fairchild*.

185. In short, the die was inexorably cast in *Fairchild* – although, as already suggested, it is doubtful if that was then recognised and it is noteworthy too that, even when in *Barker* it came to be recognised, it was then thought palatable only assuming that compensation was going to be assessed on an aliquot basis. Parliament, however, then chose – although, of course, only in mesothelioma cases – to go the whole hog.

186. The result must surely be this. As I began by saying, mesothelioma cases are in a category all their own. Whether, however, this special treatment is justified may be doubted. True, as Lord Phillips observes at the outset of his judgment, mesothelioma is indeed a hideous disease. (And it is perhaps also the case, as Lord Phillips suggests at para 104, that mesothelioma, after all, may result from the cumulative effect of exposures to asbestos dust.) The unfortunate fact is, however, that the courts are faced with comparable rocks of uncertainty in a wide variety of other situations too and that to circumvent these rocks on a routine basis – let alone if to do so would open the way, as here, to compensation on a full liability basis – would turn our law upside down and dramatically increase the scope for what hitherto have been rejected as purely speculative compensation claims. Although, therefore, mesothelioma claims must now be considered from the defendant's standpoint a lost cause, there is to my mind a lesson to be learned from losing it: the law tampers with the 'but for' test of causation at its peril.

187. There is a rough justice about the law of personal injury liability as a whole. To compensate a claimant in full for a lost finger because there was a 60:40 chance

that he would have worn protective gloves had they been made available to him may be regarded as rough justice for defendants. But it is balanced by the denial of compensation to a claimant who cannot establish that he would probably have worn the gloves – or whose finger the judge concludes was probably already doomed because of frostbite. Save only for mesothelioma cases, claimants should henceforth expect little flexibility from the courts in their approach to causation.

The tenor of this judgment is very much one of having to follow *Fairchild* reasoning through to its logical conclusion, and that if any other result is to be reached on these facts, it would require a reversal of *Fairchild*. Although the facts of *Sienkiewicz* are very different to those in the original case, particularly in terms of the likelihood of any defendant having any role to play in the claimants' injuries, there was nothing in the formulation of the *Fairchild* principle to distinguish it from such facts. In the following excerpt, Professors Steel and Ibbetson analyse the effect of this, suggesting that it is less than satisfactory:

Sandy Steel and David Ibbetson, 'More Grief on Uncertain Causation in Tort' (2011) 70 *CLJ* 451

[T]he law now seems fixed in an unprincipled position. The claimant who succumbs to a deadly cancer potentially due to a doctor's negligence receives nothing, whilst the victim of dermatitis potentially caused by his employer's negligence has access to proportional liability. Yet there is no logical reason why *Barker* should not apply to medical negligence cases where there is a sufficient degree of uncertainty over causation. It takes one little further to say that this would re-write the rules of evidence: that is simply to re-state the question of whether proportional liability should be applied. To say the distinction is one of policy – perhaps protection of limited NHS funds – needs much greater scrutiny to go beyond conjecture.

Whether the inconsistency should be resolved towards the expansion of the exceptional rule or its contraction is a difficult question. The difficulty arises from a fundamental tension ... On the one hand, the traditional, individualist model of tort law dictates that a particular defendant must be shown to have caused harm to a particular claimant in order to come under a duty to compensate. Without the causation of harm, there is nothing to correct and hence no place for corrective justice (hence mere risk is not enough); and without showing that the particular defendant caused harm to the particular claimant, there is no reason to demand the defendant pay compensation. Thus, if individual causation is essential to ground the liability to compensate, and the claimant cannot show it, the claimant should lose. On the other hand, beyond reasons of individual justice, there are also reasons of collective justice, based upon the fair distribution of burdens or losses across groups of individuals. In cases like *Fairchild*, it seems unjust that negligent defendants as a group are privileged over the class of mesothelioma sufferers. This unfair privileging arises from the fact that if the normal evidential rule of causation is applied, there will, in all probability, be far more denials of liability than there ought to be – claimants as a whole will lose more than they ought – though we cannot tell in an individual case whether there should be liability or not. This privileging seems almost unbearable when the defendant has actually been shown to have caused harm as in the American drug manufacturer cases, where each defendant has been shown to have caused much harm but the claimant cannot identify his injurer.

Question to consider: How should the law deal with scientific and factual uncertainties in causation? Has a fair balance been struck in this area of law?

Other resources: J Morgan, 'The English – and Scottish – Asbestos Saga' in R Goldberg (ed), *Perspectives on Causation* (Hart, 2011), 67; and S Green, 'Risk Exposure and Negligence' (2006) 122 *LQR* 386; L Hoffmann, 'Fairchild and After' in A Burrows, D Johnston and R Zimmermann (eds), *Judge and Jurist: Essays in Memory of Lord Rodger of Earlsferry* (OUP, 2013), 64; *Durham v BAI (Run-off) Ltd* [2012] UKSC 14; *AB v Ministry of Defence* [2013] 1 AC 78.

6.4 Multiple agent cases

What is clear is that the exceptional *Fairchild* principle will not apply outside of the single agent-indivisible injury-rock of uncertainty cases. Most notably, and as stated by the House of Lords in *Fairchild* itself,[10] it will not apply in cases in which there is more than one potential causal agent. In *Fairchild*-type cases, there is only one causal agent: asbestos. In the following case, whose authority was expressly preserved by Lord Rodger in *Fairchild*, the claimant's injury was an eye condition that had five possible causes, only one of which was the result of the defendant's breach and none of which could be proven on the balance of probabilities to be the cause of the ultimate damage.

Wilsher v Essex Area Health Authority [1988] AC 1074, 1090 (Lord Bridge)

In the Court of Appeal in the instant case Sir Nicolas Browne-Wilkinson V.-C., being in a minority, expressed his view on causation with understandable caution. But I am quite unable to find any fault with the following passage in his dissenting judgment [1987] Q.B. 730, 779:

10 See Lord Rodger in *Fairchild* at [170].

'To apply the principle in *McGhee v. National Coal Board* [1973] 1 W.L.R. 1 to the present case would constitute an extension of that principle. In the *McGhee* case there was no doubt that the pursuer's dermatitis was physically caused by brick dust: the only question was whether the continued presence of such brick dust on the pursuer's skin after the time when he should have been provided with a shower caused or materially contributed to the dermatitis which he contracted. There was only one possible agent which could have caused the dermatitis, viz., brick dust, and there was no doubt that the dermatitis from which he suffered was caused by that brick dust.

In the present case the question is different. There are a number of different agents which could have caused the RLF. Excess oxygen was one of them. The defendants failed to take reasonable precautions to prevent one of the possible causative agents (e.g. excess oxygen) from causing RLF. But no one can tell in this case whether excess oxygen did or did not cause or contribute to the RLF suffered by the plaintiff. The plaintiff's RLF may have been caused by some completely different agent or agents, e.g. hypercarbia, intraventricular haemorrhage, apnoea or patent ductus arteriosus. In addition to oxygen, each of those conditions has been implicated as a possible cause of RLF. This baby suffered from each of those conditions at various times in the first two months of his life. There is no satisfactory evidence that excess oxygen is more likely than any of those other four candidates to have caused RLF in this baby. To my mind, the occurrence of RLF following a failure to take a necessary precaution to prevent excess oxygen causing RLF provides no evidence and raises no presumption that it was excess oxygen rather than one or more of the four other possible agents which caused or contributed to RLF in this case.

The position, to my mind, is wholly different from that in the *McGhee* [1973] 1 W.L.R. 1, case where there was only one candidate (brick dust) which could have caused the dermatitis, and the failure to take a precaution against brick dust causing dermatitis was followed by dermatitis caused by brick dust. In such a case, I can see the common sense, if not the logic, of holding that, in the absence of any other evidence, the failure to take the precaution caused or contributed to the dermatitis. To the extent that certain members of the House of Lords decided the question on inferences from evidence or presumptions, I do not consider that the present case falls within their reasoning. A failure to take preventative measures against one out of five possible causes is no evidence as to which of those five caused the injury.'

It is very important, therefore, that, in cases in which there are multiple potential causal agents, the *Wilsher* rule is applied and liability is not therefore imposed on a defendant unless and until the claimant has proved that the defendant's breach has caused the loss in question.

6.5 Loss of a chance

Thorny causation problems do not end with the distinction between single and multiple agents. In the next set of cases, we see a return to the all-or-nothing principle that underlies the balance of probabilities standard of proof: that is, if a claimant proves their case to =>50%, they will recover in full but, if they manage to prove it only to 49%, they get nothing. In the first case here, the claimant's argument was formulated as a means of getting around this by offering an alternative formulation. It did not succeed.

The claimant had fallen from a tree and injured his left hip. The defendant hospital negligently failed to diagnose or treat him correctly for five days. Ultimately, he went on to suffer avascular necrosis (which means that the bone tissue in his hip died due to insufficient blood supply), disability of the hip joint and was left with the virtual certainty he would develop osteoarthritis. The trial judge found that, even if the injury had been properly diagnosed and treated in a timely manner, there remained a 75% risk that avascular necrosis would develop anyway. Nonetheless, he went on to award the claimant damages corresponding to the 25% chance of which the defendant's negligence had supposedly deprived him. Whilst the Court of Appeal agreed, the House of Lords did not, holding instead that a finding that, at the time of the fall there had already been a 75% chance of avascular necrosis developing, amounted to a finding on the balance of probabilities that the fall was the sole cause of the injury. However, the Court did not expressly exclude the possibility that 'loss of a chance' could ever form the basis of a successful claim in negligence in the future.

Hotson v East Berkshire Area Health Authority [1987] AC 750, 782 (Lord Bridge)

The plaintiff's claim was for damages for physical injury and consequential loss alleged to have been caused by the authority's breach of their duty of care. In some cases, perhaps particularly medical negligence cases, causation may be so shrouded in mystery that the court can only measure statistical chances. But that was not so here. On the evidence there was a clear conflict as to what had caused the avascular necrosis. The authority's evidence was that the sole cause was the original traumatic injury to the hip. The plaintiff's evidence, at its highest, was that the delay in treatment was a material contributory cause. This was a conflict, like any other about some relevant past event, which the judge could not avoid resolving on a balance of probabilities. Unless the plaintiff proved on a balance of probabilities that the delayed treatment was at least a material contributory cause of the avascular necrosis he failed on the issue of causation and no question of quantification could arise. But the judge's findings of fact, as stated in the numbered paragraphs (1) and (4) which I have set out earlier in this opinion, are unmistakably to the effect that on a balance of probabilities the injury caused by the plaintiff's fall left insufficient blood vessels intact to keep the epiphysis alive. This amounts to a finding of fact that the fall was the sole cause of the avascular necrosis.

> The upshot is that the appeal must be allowed on the narrow ground that the plaintiff failed to establish a cause of action in respect of the avascular necrosis and its consequences. Your Lordships were invited to approach the appeal more broadly and to decide whether, in a claim for damages for personal injury, it can ever be appropriate, where the cause of the injury is unascertainable and all the plaintiff can show is a statistical chance which is less than even that, but for the defendant's breach of duty, he would not have suffered the injury, to award him a proportionate fraction of the full damages appropriate to compensate for the injury as the measure of damages for the lost chance.
>
> There is a superficially attractive analogy between the principle applied in such cases as *Chaplin v. Hicks* [1911] 2 K.B. 786 (award of damages for breach of contract assessed by reference to the lost chance of securing valuable employment if the contract had been performed) and *Kitchen v. Royal Air Force Association* [1958] 1 W.L.R. 563 (damages for solicitors' negligence assessed by reference to the lost chance of prosecuting a successful civil action) and the principle of awarding damages for the lost chance of avoiding personal injury or, in medical negligence cases, for the lost chance of a better medical result which might have been achieved by prompt diagnosis and correct treatment. I think there are formidable difficulties in the way of accepting the analogy. But I do not see this appeal as a suitable occasion for reaching a settled conclusion as to whether the analogy can ever be applied.

As Croom-Johnson LJ had put it in the Court of Appeal:[11]

> … If it is proved statistically that 25 per cent. of the population have a chance of recovery from a certain injury and 75 per cent. do not, it does not mean that someone who suffers that injury and who does not recover from it has lost a 25 per cent. chance. He may have lost nothing at all. What he has to do is prove that he was one of the 25 per cent. and that his loss was caused by the defendant's negligence. To be a figure in a statistic does not by itself give him a cause of action. If the plaintiff succeeds in proving that he was one of the 25 per cent. and that the defendants took away that chance, the logical result would be to award him 100 per cent. of his damages and not only a quarter, but that might be left for consideration if and when it arises … a mere statistical chance will not be enough. The chance must be something lost to the individual patient.

Croom-Johnson LJ's reasoning here is helpful: the idea of a 75% chance belonging to a particular individual is a misrepresentation of what those statistics mean. A '75% chance' in this context really means 'Out of 100 people with your condition, 75 will get avascular necrosis and 25 will not'. The point is that any given individual will either be one of the 75% *or* one of the 25% – there is no way of knowing at the point that the fall occurs, but their individual chance will actually be 100% or 0%.

11 At 728. Although note that the Court of Appeal ultimately dismissed the defendant's appeal against liability.

The balance of probabilities standard is the law's means of splitting the difference between claimant and defendant. The argument was made in both that case and the following case that, given that the claimant's claim is based on this 'lost chance' rather than on the whole of the ultimate injury, the damages should not be all or nothing, but should represent the percentage value of the 'chance lost'. This would amount to a move away from the orthodox means of establishing causation, as Lord Hoffmann made clear when the House of Lords was once more presented with the argument in the following case:

> What we lack is knowledge and the law deals with that lack of knowledge by the concept of the burden of proof.[12]

In *Gregg*, the defendant GP in November 1994 diagnosed a lump in the claimant's armpit as a benign growth. It was not until November 1995 that a biopsy carried out by order of a specialist surgeon revealed that the claimant actually had non-Hodgkin's lymphoma, a form of cancer. By failing to refer the claimant to a specialist at the point of the initial (incorrect) diagnosis, the defendant was held to have been in breach of his duty of care. At trial, the claimant's chance of being 'cured' (defined in this context as a period of ten years' remission) was found to have been 42% when he first visited the defendant, but that the nine-month delay consequent upon the defendant's breach reduced his chance of being cured to 25%. As the claimant had only a 42% chance of a cure in the first place, he was unable to prove on the balance of probabilities that the defendant's negligence caused him to be in a worse state than he would have been in without the delay. The claimant therefore had to argue that he had suffered the loss of a chance of being cured as a result of the defendant's negligence.

By a majority of three to two (Lord Hope and Lord Nicholls dissenting), the House of Lords dismissed the claimant's appeal because the claimant had not proved on the balance of probabilities that the defendant's negligence had caused his life expectancy to be reduced.

Gregg v Scott [2005] UKHL 2, [2005] 2 AC 176, [71], [79], [80], [90] (Lord Hoffmann)

71. I respectfully think that this formulation begs more than one question. It is true that the delay caused an early spread of the cancer and that this reduced his percentage chance of survival for more than 10 years. But to say that the claimant can therefore obtain damages for the reduction in his chances of survival assumes in his favour that a reduction in the *chance* of survival is a recoverable head of damage; an issue raised by the claimant's second argument which Latham LJ said (at paragraph 41) that he did not need to decide. On the other hand, if the claim is for actually depriving him of survival for more than 10 years, the

12 *Gregg v Scott* [2005] UKHL 2 at [79].

question is whether the spread of the cancer caused it. The judge's finding was that it did not. It was likely that his life would have been shortened to less than 10 years anyway.

79. What these cases show is that, as Helen Reece points out in an illuminating article ('Losses of Chances in the Law' (1996) 59 MLR 188)[13] the law regards the world as in principle bound by laws of causality. Everything has a determinate cause, even if we do not know what it is. The blood-starved hip joint in *Hotson*, the blindness in *Wilsher*, the mesothelioma in *Fairchild*; each had its cause and it was for the plaintiff to prove that it was an act or omission for which the defendant was responsible. The narrow terms of the exception made to this principle in *Fairchild* only serves to emphasise the strength of the rule. The fact that proof is rendered difficult or impossible because no examination was made at the time, as in *Hotson*, or because medical science cannot provide the answer, as in *Wilsher*, makes no difference. There is no inherent uncertainty about what caused something to happen in the past or about whether something which happened in the past will cause something to happen in the future. Everything is determined by causality. What we lack is knowledge and the law deals with lack of knowledge by the concept of the burden of proof.

80. Similarly in the present case, the progress of Mr Gregg's disease had a determinate cause. It may have been inherent in his genetic make-up at the time when he saw Mr Scott, as *Hotson's* fate was determined by what happened to his thigh when he fell out of the tree. Or it may, as Mance LJ suggests, have been affected by subsequent events and behaviour for which Dr Scott was not responsible. Medical science does not enable us to say. But the outcome was not random; it was governed by laws of causality and, in the absence of a special rule as in *Fairchild*, inability to establish that delay in diagnosis caused the reduction in expectation in life cannot be remedied by treating the outcome as having been somehow indeterminate.

90. ... a wholesale adoption of possible rather than probable causation as the criterion of liability would be so radical a change in our law as to amount to a legislative act. It would have enormous consequences for insurance companies and the National Health Service.

Question to consider: Do you think that the decision in *Gregg v Scott* is correct? How are the facts materially different from *Hotson*?

Other resources: J Morgan, 'A Chance Missed to Recognise Loss of a Chance in Negligence' (2005) 3(Aug) *LMCLQ* 281–90; E Peel, 'Loss of a Chance in Medical Negligence' (2005) 121 *LQR* 364; H Reece, 'Losses of Chances in the Law' (1996) 59 *MLR* 188; S Green, 'Loss of a Chance as a Commercial Remedy' in G Virgo and S Worthington (eds), *Commercial Remedies: Resolving Controversies* (CUP, 2016); *Allied Maples v Simmons & Simmons* [1995] 1 WLR 1602 (loss of chance in a financial setting).

13 This is a fantastic article (authors' footnote, not Lord Hoffmann's, although he clearly liked it too).

It is important to note, however, that it is sometimes perfectly possible to recover for the loss of a chance in tort, as the next case demonstrates. Where the chance in question is that of making a financial gain, and depends on the hypothetical actions of a third party, recovery is possible. The defendants were solicitors whose negligence in drafting a contract deprived the claimants of the opportunity to negotiate more advantageous terms. The Court of Appeal allowed them to recover for this, and determined that damages should be quantified according to the chance that the claimants would have succeeded in the negotiation had the defendants not been negligent. It concluded that, as long as there was a real (as opposed to speculative) chance of success, there was no need for a positive outcome to be more likely than not in order for the claimant to be able to recover for the chances of that outcome occurring. Stuart-Smith LJ explains why here:

Allied Maples v Simmons & Simmons [1995] 1 WLR 1602, 1609 (Stuart-Smith LJ)

In these circumstances, where the Plaintiffs' loss depends upon the actions of an independent third party, it is necessary to consider as a matter of law what it is necessary to establish as a matter of causation, and where causation ends and quantification of damage begins.

1. What has to be proved to establish a causal link between the negligence of the Defendants and the loss sustained by the Plaintiffs depends in the first instance on whether the negligence consists on some positive act or misfeasance, or an omission or non feasance. In the former case, the question of causation is one of historical fact. The Court has to determine on the balance of probability whether the defendant's act, for example the careless driving, caused the plaintiff's loss consisting of his broken leg. Once established on balance of probability, that fact is taken as true and the plaintiff recovers his damage in full. There is no discount because the judge considers that the balance is only just tipped in favour of the plaintiff; and the plaintiff gets nothing if he fails to establish that it is more likely than not that the accident resulted in the injury.

Questions of quantification of the plaintiff's loss, however, may depend upon future uncertain events. For example, whether and to what extent he will suffer osteoarthritis, whether he will continue to earn at the same rate until retirement, whether, but for the accident, he might have been promoted. It is trite law that these questions are not decided on a balance of probability, but rather on the court's assessment, often expressed in percentage terms, of the risk eventuating or the prospect of promotion, which it should be noted depends in part at least on the hypothetical acts of a third party, namely the plaintiff's employer.

…

Although the question is a hypothetical one, it is well established that the plaintiff must prove on balance of probability that he would have taken action to obtain the benefit or avoid the risk. But again, if he does establish that, there is no discount because the balance is only just tipped in his favour. In the present case the Plaintiffs had to prove that, if they had been given the right advice, they would have sought to negotiate with Gillow to obtain protection. The Judge held that they would have done so.

…

3. In many cases the plaintiff's loss depends on the hypothetical action of a third party, either in addition to action by the plaintiff, as in this case, or independently of it. In such a case does the plaintiff have to prove on balance of probability, as Mr Jackson submits, that the third party would have acted so as to confer the benefit or avoid the risk to the plaintiff, or can the plaintiff succeed provided he shows that he had a substantial chance rather than a speculative one, the evaluation of the substantial chance being a question of quantification of damages?

…

… in my judgment, the plaintiff must prove as a matter of causation that he has a real or substantial chance as opposed to a speculative one. If he succeeds in doing so, the evaluation of the chance is part of the assessment of the quantum of damage, the range lying somewhere between something that just qualifies as real or substantial on the one hand and near certainty on the other. I do not think that it is helpful to seek to lay down in percentage terms what the lower and upper ends of the bracket should be.

All that the plaintiffs had to show on causation on this aspect of the case is that there was a substantial chance that they would have been successful in negotiating total or partial (by means of a capped liability) protection.

6.6 Failure to warn

In causation terms, this is something of a standalone category (although the question of warning in a medical context has given rise to some recent litigation around the breach of duty question). Although it is covered by only one House of Lords authority, it is a very well-known decision about which several commentators disagree. The advantage of this is that its very particular facts, involving the failure to warn of a risk, are easy to spot in problem questions.

In this case, the defendant operated on the claimant to alleviate her severe back pain. Although he did so without negligence, she suffered significant nerve damage and was consequently left partially paralysed. The defendant breached his duty of care by failing to warn his patient of the 1–2% risk inherent in such operation, howsoever performed. The causal problem arose because the claimant did not argue that, had she been warned of the risk, she would never have had the operation, or even that, duly warned, she would have sought out another surgeon to perform the operation. Her argument was simply that, had she been properly warned of the risks inherent in the procedure, she would not have consented to having the surgery within three days of her appointment, and would have sought further advice on alternatives.

The House of Lords (Lords Bingham and Hoffmann dissenting) held the defendant liable on the basis that, since the ultimate injury suffered by the claimant was due to the very risk of which she should have been warned, it could be regarded as having been caused by the failure to warn. This was despite the fact that the defendant's breach had not been established, on the balance of probabilities, to have played any historical role in the claimant's injury because, but for the failure to warn, she would have run exactly the same risk (the 1–2% risk inherent in the procedure itself) on a different day.

Chester v Afshar [2004] UKHL 41, [2005] 1 AC 134, [28]–[32] (Lord Hoffmann, in dissent), [87] (Lord Hope), [97], [98], [101] (Lord Walker)

[Lord Hoffmann (dissenting)] 28. The purpose of a duty to warn someone against the risk involved in what he proposes to do, or allow to be done to him, is to give him the opportunity to avoid or reduce that risk. If he would have been unable or unwilling to take that opportunity and the risk eventuates, the failure to warn has not caused the damage. It would have happened anyway.

29. The burden is on a claimant to prove that the defendant's breach of duty caused him damage. Where the breach of duty is a failure to warn of a risk, he must prove that he would have taken the opportunity to avoid or reduce that risk. In the context of the present case, that means proving that she would not have had the operation.

30. The judge made no finding that she would not have had the operation. He was not invited by the claimant to make such a finding. The claimant argued that as a matter of law it was sufficient that she would not have had the operation at that time or by that surgeon, even though the evidence was that the risk could have been precisely the same if she had it at another time or by another surgeon. A similar argument has been advanced before this House.

31. In my opinion this argument is about as logical as saying that if one had been told, on entering a casino, that the odds on No 7 coming up at roulette were only 1 in 37, one would have gone away and come back next week or gone to a different casino. The question is whether one would have taken the opportunity to avoid or reduce the risk, not whether one would have changed the scenario in some irrelevant detail. The judge found as a fact that the risk would have been precisely the same whether it was done then or later or by that competent surgeon or by another.

32. It follows that the claimant failed to prove that the defendant's breach of duty caused her loss.

[Lord Hope] 87. To leave the patient who would find the decision difficult without a remedy, as the normal approach to causation would indicate, would render the duty useless in the cases where it may be needed most. This would discriminate against those who cannot honestly say that they would have declined the operation once and for all if they had been warned. I would find that result unacceptable. The function of the law is to enable rights to be vindicated and to provide remedies when duties have been breached. Unless this is done the duty is a hollow one, stripped of all practical force and devoid of all content. It will have lost its ability to protect the patient and thus to fulfil the only purpose which brought it into existence. On policy grounds therefore I would hold that the test of causation is satisfied in this case. The injury was intimately involved with the duty to warn. The duty was owed by the doctor who performed the surgery that Miss Chester consented to. It was the product of the very risk that she should have been warned about when she gave her consent. So I would hold that it can be regarded as having been caused, in the legal sense, by the breach of that duty.

[Lord Walker] 97. Was this enough to justify the judge in finding a sufficient causal link between the surgeon's omission to warn and the nerve damage which ensued? My noble and learned friend Lord Hoffmann would reject that view. He puts forward a vivid analogy from roulette. But the 1 in 37 chance of a particular number coming up (assuming the roulette wheel to be properly made and operated) is a matter of simple and precise mathematical calculation. By contrast the chance of nerve damage occurring (without negligence) during lumbar surgery can be calculated only with hindsight, as a more or less accurate approximation, by compiling and analysing statistics as to the outcome of that type of surgery. The risk no doubt varies with the skill and experience of the surgeon, the severity of the patient's condition, and the precise type of surgery undertaken (for instance whether there is an operation on only one disc level, a point on which the judge made a detailed review of the expert evidence). There may be other less easily identifiable factors which also affect the risk.

98. I would not accept, on the strength of the roulette analogy, that these should be regarded as changing the scenario only in some irrelevant detail.

...

101. Nevertheless there are real difficulties (especially, perhaps, for a conscientious claimant aware of the fallibility of hindsight) in a claimant asserting that (if warned of the risks) she would never in any circumstances have submitted to surgery. There would be a danger, as Lord Hope points out, of an honest claimant finding herself without a remedy in circumstances where the surgeon has failed in his professional duty, and the claimant has suffered injury directly within the scope and focus of that duty. I agree with Lord Steyn and Lord Hope that such a claimant ought not to be without a remedy, even if it involves some extension of existing principle, as in *Fairchild v Glenhaven Funeral Services Ltd* [2003] 1 AC 32 (see especially the speech of my noble and learned friend Lord Bingham of Cornhill at paras 8–13). Otherwise the surgeon's important duty would in many cases be drained of its content.

There is little doubt that the effect of this decision is to vindicate the claimant's autonomy and protect a patient's right to choose. Whether this is best achieved circuitously through massaging the rules of the causal inquiry in negligence remains an open question.

6.7 Conclusion

This chapter has dealt with the element of the negligence inquiry that is almost always deemed to be the most challenging. The only really effective way to understand and deal with it is to have a sound grasp of the relevant case law. It is a good idea to follow a similar structure to the one in this chapter, beginning with the simpler tests proceeding to the more complicated and exceptional approaches only if and when necessary. A common mistake that students make is to identify a causal issue and attempt straightaway to apply a causal test that was not formulated for that scenario, but you should always aim to apply the simplest causal test that is relevant on the facts. The case law above began with basic causal principles at one end of the spectrum and the exceptional (and extraordinary) *Fairchild* line of cases at the other. This topic is undoubtedly tricky, but it can also be approached systematically, along the lines suggested by this chapter, which will make its analysis a lot clearer. That is not to suggest that all issues will become easy or easily resolved; the law in this area is not perfectly coherent and some of the cases are difficult to reconcile. The answer to this is to be aware of where this happens, and state it in your application of them. Such inconsistencies and difficulties make excellent ammunition for writing critical analyses of the area in essays.

Chapter

7 REMOTENESS

7.1 Introduction

Once a court has established that a defendant's breach had a historical role in the course of events leading to a claimant's loss, there is then another step in the inquiry. That is to decide whether the historically relevant breach is also legally relevant. In order to establish this, the court asks whether the damage is too remote from the breach in question. It would be neither workable nor fair for individuals to be held legally liable for every consequence of their actions down an infinite chain of events. Prior to the first case dealt with here, known to lawyers as *The Wagon Mound (No 1)*, the remoteness test in negligence was the same as it was for intentional torts (such as, for instance, deceit). That test asked whether the claimant's loss was a consequence that flowed directly from the defendant's breach (*Re Polemis and Furness Withy & Co*).[1] In *The Wagon Mound*, however, the House of Lords, as you will see, decided that the test for non-intentional torts such as negligence should be more restrictive than this. The current test is indeed different: it is to ask whether the claimant's loss was of a reasonably foreseeable *type*, given the defendant's breach of their duty of care.

The defendant in *The Wagon Mound* was responsible for the leakage of oil from a ship that damaged the claimant's wharf. That oil later ignited on coming into contact with sparks from welding work. This caused further (fire) damage to the claimant's wharf. Significantly, however, the latter incident caused damage of a different *type* to the first: the oil damage was distinguished from fire damage. The trial judge, with whom the Privy Council ultimately agreed, found that, whilst oil damage was a reasonably foreseeable consequence of the defendant's breach of duty, fire damage was not reasonably foreseeable. The claimant could only recover, therefore, for the oil damage.

The Wagon Mound (No 1) [1961] AC 388, 422 (Viscount Simonds)

> [I]t does not seem consonant with current ideas of justice or morality that for an act of negligence, however slight or venial, which results in some trivial foreseeable damage the actor should be liable for all consequences however unforeseeable and however grave, so long as they can be said to be 'direct.' It is a principle of civil liability, subject

1 [1921] 3 KB 560.

only to qualifications which have no present relevance, that a man must be considered to be responsible for the probable consequences of his act. To demand more of him is too harsh a rule, to demand less is to ignore that civilised order requires the observance of a minimum standard of behaviour.

This concept applied to the slowly developing law of negligence has led to a great variety of expressions which can, as it appears to their Lordships, be harmonised with little difficulty with the single exception of the so-called rule in *Polemis*. For, if it is asked why a man should be responsible for the natural or necessary or probable consequences of his act (or any other similar description of them) the answer is that it is not because they are natural or necessary or probable, but because, since they have this quality, it is judged by the standard of the reasonable man that he ought to have foreseen them. Thus it is that over and over again it has happened that in different judgments in the same case, and sometimes in a single judgment, liability for a consequence has been imposed on the ground that it was reasonably foreseeable or, alternatively, on the ground that it was natural or necessary or probable. The two grounds have been treated as coterminous, and so they largely are. But, where they are not, the question arises to which the wrong answer was given in *Polemis*. For, if some limitation must be imposed upon the consequences for which the negligent actor is to be held responsible – and all are agreed that some limitation there must be – why should that test (reasonable foreseeability) be rejected which, since he is judged by what the reasonable man ought to foresee, corresponds with the common conscience of mankind, and a test (the 'direct' consequence) be substituted which leads to no-where but the never-ending and insoluble problems of causation. 'The lawyer,' said Sir Frederick Pollock, 'cannot afford to adventure himself with philosophers in the logical and metaphysical controversies that beset the idea of cause.' Yet this is just what he has most unfortunately done and must continue to do if the rule in *Polemis* is to prevail A conspicuous example occurs when the actor seeks to escape liability on the ground that the 'chain of causation' is broken by a 'nova causa' or 'novus actus interveniens.'

It is crucial, however, that you understand exactly what this test means. First, and most significantly, it says nothing about the foreseeability (or otherwise) of the *extent* of the claimant's loss. It refers only to *type*. Once the claimant's damage has been deemed to be of a reasonably foreseeable type, its extent is irrelevant and the defendant will be liable for it in full. This is so, even if that extent was not reasonably foreseeable. This is often referred to as the thin skull principle: if the claimant who is injured as a result of a defendant's negligence happens to be particularly vulnerable or weak (hence, thin skull), meaning that the damage they suffer is greater than it would be had the same defendant (committing the same breach) injured a more robust individual, the defendant is nonetheless liable for the full loss. This is simply a question of moral luck. It is tempting to think of it as a principle that operates unfairly from a defendant's perspective, but it is worth bearing in mind that everyone is as likely to be a claimant in negligence as they are a defendant, meaning that implications always fall to be considered from both perspectives. That being the case, it is also worth bearing in mind that negligence is not a tort concerned with punishment but instead with compensation, and why should a vulnerable individual have to bear some of their own loss when injured by another's negligence when a person of average fortitude can recover in full?

The following case illustrates the thin (or eggshell) skull principle. The claimant's husband burnt his lip at work, owing to the defendant employer's negligence. This burn became cancerous and it turned out that he had had a predisposition to cancer. Although the defendant argued that the cancer was not a reasonably foreseeable consequence of failing to prevent an industrial skin burn, it was made clear at trial that, notwithstanding *The Wagon Mound (No 1)*, a defendant takes her victim as she finds him. Consequently, as long as the type of damage was reasonably foreseeable, it was irrelevant that the victim's pre-existing susceptibility rendered the extent of the damage much greater than it would have been had the victim not had that weakness.

Smith v Leech Brain and Co Ltd [1962] 2 QB 405, 415 (Lord Parker CJ)

> The Judicial Committee were, I think, disagreeing with the decision in the *Polemis* case that a man is no longer liable for the type of damage which he could not reasonably anticipate. The Judicial Committee were not, I think, saying that a man is only liable for the extent of damage which he could anticipate, always assuming the type of injury could have been anticipated. I think that view is really supported by the way in which cases of this sort have been dealt with in Scotland. Scotland has never, so far as I know, adopted the principle laid down in *Polemis*, and yet I am quite satisfied that they have throughout proceeded on the basis that the tortfeasor takes the victim as he finds him.
>
> In those circumstances, it seems to me that this is plainly a case which comes within the old principle. The test is not whether these employers could reasonably have foreseen that a burn would cause cancer and that he would die. The question is whether these employers could reasonably foresee the type of injury he suffered, namely, the burn. What, in the particular case, is the amount of damage which he suffers as a result of that burn, depends upon the characteristics and constitution of the victim.

Question to consider: Is the 'eggshell skull' rule justified? Is it acceptable that the breach of duty can lead to vastly different damages depending on the personal characteristics of the claimant?

Other resources: *The Liesboch* [1933] AC 449; *Lagden v O'Connor* [2004] 1 AC 1067; Tony Honoré, *Responsibility and Fault* (Oxford: Hart Publishing, 1999); John CP Goldberg and Benjamin C Zipursky, 'Tort Law and Moral Luck' (2007) 92 *Cornell L Rev* 1123.

Neither is it the case that the *Wagon Mound* test restricts the *manner* in which the damage must have occurred in order for it to be linked to the defendant's breach. Again, and as the next case demonstrates, once the damage has been deemed by the court to be of a reasonably foreseeable type, the exact way in which it occurred does not have to have been foreseen for the defendant to be held liable for it. In *Hughes*, below, the defendant had left warning paraffin lamps around an unsupervised excavation in the pavement. The claimant was an 8-year-old boy who entered the tent surrounding the hole and knocked one of the lamps into it. The resulting explosion caused severe burns to the boy. Although the defendant argued that the damage which the boy suffered was not of a reasonably foreseeable kind, the House of Lords disagreed, finding instead that burns are precisely the type of damage that is the reasonably foreseeable consequence of leaving paraffin lamps accessible to children. The way in which those burns came about was irrelevant, as was the fact that the injury was ultimately more severe than could reasonably have been foreseen.

Hughes v Lord Advocate [1963] AC 837, 845 (Lord Reid)

> The appellant's injuries were mainly caused by burns, and it cannot be said that injuries from burns were unforeseeable. As a warning to traffic the workmen had set lighted red lamps round the tent which covered the manhole, and if boys did enter the dark tent it was very likely that they would take one of these lamps with them. If the lamp fell and broke it was not at all unlikely that the boy would be burned and the burns might well be serious. No doubt it was not to be expected that the injuries would be as serious as those which the appellant in fact sustained. But a defender is liable, although the damage may be a good deal greater in extent than was foreseeable. He can only escape liability if the damage can be regarded as differing in kind from what was foreseeable.
>
> So we have (first) a duty owed by the workmen, (secondly) the fact that if they had done as they ought to have done there would have been no accident, and (thirdly) the fact that the injuries suffered by the appellant, though perhaps different in degree, did not differ in kind from injuries which might have resulted from an accident of a foreseeable nature. The ground on which this case has been decided against the appellant is that the accident was of an unforeseeable type. Of course, the pursuer has to prove that the defender's fault caused the accident, and there could be a case where the intrusion of a new and unexpected factor could be regarded as the cause of the accident rather than the fault of the defender. But that is not this case. The cause of this accident was a known source of danger, the lamp, but it behaved in an unpredictable way.

It is therefore clear that, for remoteness purposes, the only thing that needs to be reasonably foreseeable is the type of damage suffered by the claimant. Even this apparently simple question, however, is not necessarily easy to answer. Most notably, the inquiry demands that a court identify type boundaries and decide when a particular outcome is in fact the same type of outcome as that which could have been foreseen. This was precisely the issue in the following case, in which the claimant's husband suffered a head injury as a result of his employer's negligence, which caused him to develop a depressive illness and eventually, six years after the accident, to commit suicide. The question for the court was whether suicide is a reasonably foreseeable consequence of a head injury. The House of Lords held that, since depression is a reasonably foreseeable consequence of a head injury and suicide a reasonably foreseeable consequence of that, the ultimate death of the employee was damage of a reasonably foreseeable type, meaning that the claimant succeeded.

Corr v IBC Vehicles Ltd [2008] UKHL 13, [2008] AC 884, [10], [16] (Lord Bingham)

10. ... The law does not generally treat us as our brother's keeper, responsible for what he may choose to do to his own disadvantage. It is his choice. But I do not think that the submission addresses the particular features of this case. The employer owed the deceased the duty already noted, embracing psychological as well as physical injury. Its breach caused him injury of both kinds. While he was not, at the time of his death, insane in *M'Naghten*'s terms, nor was he fully responsible. He acted in a way which he would not have done but for the injury from which the employer's breach caused him to suffer. This being so, I do not think his conduct in taking his own life can be said to fall outside the scope of the duty which his employer owed him.

...

16. In the present case Mr Corr's suicide was not a voluntary, informed decision taken by him as an adult of sound mind making and giving effect to a personal decision about his future. It was the response of a man suffering from a severely depressive illness which impaired his capacity to make reasoned and informed judgments about his future, such illness being, as is accepted, a consequence of the employer's tort. It is in no way unfair to hold the employer responsible for this dire consequence of its breach of duty, although it could well be thought unfair to the victim not to do so.

7.2 Scope of duty

There is another important way in which a defendant's liability can be deemed insufficiently causally relevant to the claimant's loss. This is by means of the scope of duty analysis: under which the court asks whether the loss that actually eventuated was within the *scope* of the defendant's duty. Essentially, this aims to separate those losses that result from the risk that the defendant's duty was designed to guard against, and those losses that result from other, non-tortious risk sources. The modern form of this analysis can be traced back to the following case, and it is consequently often referred to in contemporary case law as the *SAAMCO* principle.

The defendants had negligently overvalued properties on which the claimant lenders had advanced funds. By the time the borrowers defaulted, the property market had crashed. The lenders, therefore, suffered both loss as a result of the properties *never* having been worth that value, but also additional loss because, after the crash, those properties were not even worth what their true market value had been. The Court of Appeal allowed the claimants to recover for the full extent of their loss: the difference between the negligent valuations and the value of the properties *after the crash*. The House of Lords disagreed with this analysis, and held the defendants liable only for the foreseeable consequences of their valuations being wrong: that is, the lenders were able to recover only the difference between the negligent overvaluation and the true market value of the properties *before the crash*. The fall in value owing to the crash was not held to be within the scope of the defendant's duty, and so not recoverable: it resulted from a wholly different (and non-tortious) source of risk. Lord Hoffmann's judgment is particularly notable for its illustration of this distinction, and has been referred to numerous times since:

South Australia Asset Management Corporation v York Montague Ltd [1996] UKHL 10, [1997] AC 191, [9], [14], [18]–[20], [22], [23] (Lord Hoffmann)

9. ... Before one can consider the principle on which one should calculate the damages to which a plaintiff is entitled as compensation for loss, it is necessary to decide for what kind of loss he is entitled to compensation. ...

...

14. A duty of care such as the valuer owes does not however exist in the abstract. A plaintiff who sues for breach of a duty imposed by the law (whether in contract or tort or under statute) must do more than prove that the defendant has failed to comply. He must show that the duty was owed to him and that it was a duty in respect of the kind of loss which he has suffered. Both of these requirements are illustrated by Caparo Industries Plc. v. Dickman [1990] 2 A.C. 605.

...

18. Rules which make the wrongdoer liable for all the consequences of his wrongful conduct are exceptional and need to be justified by some special policy. Normally the law limits liability to those consequences which are attributable to that which made the act wrongful. In the case of liability in negligence for providing inaccurate information, this would mean liability for the consequences of the information being inaccurate.

The following 'mountaineer' example is the part of this judgment that is so often referred to by courts considering scope of duty issues. It is a very helpful illustration of the point:

> 19. I can illustrate the difference between the ordinary principle and that adopted by the Court of Appeal by an example. A mountaineer about to undertake a difficult climb is concerned about the fitness of his knee. He goes to a doctor who negligently makes a superficial examination and pronounces the knee fit. The climber goes on the expedition, which he would not have undertaken if the doctor had told him the true state of his knee. He suffers an injury which is an entirely foreseeable consequence of mountaineering but has nothing to do with his knee.
>
> 20. On the Court of Appeal's principle, the doctor is responsible for the injury suffered by the mountaineer because it is damage which would not have occurred if he had been given correct information about his knee. He would not have gone on the expedition and would have suffered no injury. On what I have suggested is the more usual principle, the doctor is not liable. The injury has not been caused by the doctor's bad advice because it would have occurred even if the advice had been correct.
>
> …
>
> 22. Your Lordships might, I would suggest, think that there was something wrong with a principle which, in the example which I have given, produced the result that the doctor was liable. What is the reason for this feeling? I think that the Court of Appeal's principle offends common sense because it makes the doctor responsible for consequences which, though in general terms foreseeable, do not appear to have a sufficient causal connection with the subject matter of the duty. The doctor was asked for information on only one of the considerations which might affect the safety of the mountaineer on the expedition. There seems no reason of policy which requires that the negligence of the doctor should require the transfer to him of all the foreseeable risks of the expedition.
>
> 23. I think that one can to some extent generalise the principle upon which this response depends. It is that a person under a duty to take reasonable care to provide information on which someone else will decide upon a course of action is, if negligent, not generally regarded as responsible for all the consequences of that course of action. He is responsible only for the consequences of the information being wrong. A duty of care which imposes upon the informant responsibility for losses which would have occurred even if the information which he gave had been correct is not in my view fair and reasonable as between the parties. It is therefore inappropriate either as an implied term of a contract or as a tortious duty arising from the relationship between them.

The principle was further refined by Lord Sumption in the case that follows. His Lordship had been counsel for the applicants in *SAAMCO*. The claimant[2] had lent £200,000 to the defendant, believing that those funds were to be used for property development. The defendant never intended to use them for that purpose, but instead to discharge various debts. The claimant's solicitors negligently included in the loan documentation the terms which confirmed this mistaken belief. When the development project failed, the claimant sued his solicitors for the full extent of his loss (£200,000). At first instance, he succeeded on the basis that, but for the solicitors' negligence, he would not have lent the money and so not suffered any loss at all. The Court of Appeal reduced his damages to nil on the basis that, even had the money been used for the purposes he believed they would be, the project would still have failed and he would still therefore have lost all of his money. The Supreme Court agreed, and confirmed the *SAAMCO* distinction between a duty to provide information and a duty to advise: where, as here, a defendant had a duty *to provide information*, it would be liable only for the consequences of that information being wrong. Where, by contrast, a defendant has a duty *to advise*, it will be liable for the consequences of that course of action being taken. This is so, even where the defendant knows that the information it supplies is critical to the claimant's decision.

Hughes-Holland v BPE Solicitors [2017] UKSC 21, [2018] AC 599, [20], [55] (Lord Sumption)

20. 'Courts of law', said Lord Asquith of Bishopstone in *Stapley v Gypsum Mines Ltd* [1953] AC 663, 687, 'must accept the fact that the philosophic doctrine of causation and the juridical doctrine of responsibility for the consequences of a negligent act diverge'. What Lord Asquith meant by the philosophic doctrine of causation, as he went on to explain, was the proposition that any event that would have not have occurred but for the act of the defendant must be regarded as the consequence of that act. In the law of damages, this has never been enough. It is generally a necessary condition for the recovery of a loss that it would not have been suffered but for the breach of duty. But it is not always a sufficient condition. The reason, as Lord Asquith pointed out, is that the law is concerned with assigning responsibility for the consequences of the breach, and a defendant is not necessarily responsible in law for everything that follows from his act, even if it is wrongful. A variety of legal concepts serves to limit the matters for which a wrongdoer is legally responsible. Thus the law distinguishes between a mere precondition or occasion for a loss and an act which gives rise to a liability to make it good by way of damages.

…

2 Technically, the claimant was the trustee in bankruptcy of the lender.

55. On the footing that BPE was not legally responsible for Mr Gabriel's decision to lend the money, but only for confirming his assumption about one of a number of factors in his assessment of the project, the next question is what if any loss was attributable to that assumption being wrong. The answer is that if it had been right, Mr Gabriel would still have lost his money because the expenditure of £200,000 would not have enhanced the value of the property. The development would have been left incomplete, the loan unpaid and the property substantially worthless when it came to be sold into a depressed market under the chargee's power of sale. None of the loss which Mr Gabriel suffered was within the scope of BPE's duty. None of it was loss against which BPE was duty bound to take reasonable care to protect him. It arose from commercial misjudgments which were no concern of theirs.

Very recently, the principle has been applied by the Supreme Court to the medical negligence context. In *Khan*, the defendant had negligently advised the claimant that she did not need to undergo genetic testing to establish whether she was the carrier of the haemophilia gene. When the claimant's son was born with haemophilia and then later diagnosed with autism, she sued on the basis that she would not have proceeded with the pregnancy, had she known that she was a carrier of the haemophilia gene. The Supreme Court held that the haemophilia was within the scope of the GP's duty because it was a risk against which that duty was imposed to protect. The risk of autism, however, was an entirely different risk and so was not within the scope of the relevant duty.

Khan v Meadows [2021] UKSC 21, [2022] AC 852, [62], [65] (Lord Hodge DPSC and Lord Sales JSC)

62. First, there is no principled basis for excluding clinical negligence from the ambit of the scope of duty principle. Nor is there any principled basis for confining the principle to pure economic loss arising in commercial transactions. As we have already observed, Lord Sumption JSC stated in *Hughes-Holland* [2018] AC 599, para 47, that the principle is a general principle of the law of damages. It is therefore not relevant to its applicability whether a claim is characterised as one for economic loss consequent upon a physical injury or as pure economic loss. That distinction may on the other hand be relevant to the outcome of the application of the principle because in cases where there is a duty to take care to avoid causing physical injury, the economic loss consequent upon that injury will generally be within the scope of duty and will be recoverable if it is not excluded by the legal filters which we have described in our discussion of the sixth question.

65. ... the foreseeability of the possibility of a boy being born with both haemophilia and an unrelated disability, such as autism, which is a risk in any pregnancy, is a relevant consideration when addressing the scope of the duty of care undertaken by a defendant. That is because the absence of foreseeability would militate against there being a duty

of care in relation to such a risk. But the foreseeability of such unrelated disability is in no sense determinative of the question of the scope of the duty of care. That is because the scope of duty question depends principally upon the nature of the service which the defendant has undertaken to provide to the claimant. One asks: 'what is the risk which the service which the defendant undertook was intended to address?' Where a medical practitioner has not undertaken responsibility for the progression of the pregnancy and has undertaken only to provide information or advice in relation to a particular risk in a pregnancy, the risk of a foreseeable unrelated disability, which could occur in any pregnancy, will not as a general rule be within the scope of the clinician's duty of care. Foreseeability is, of course, also relevant to the legal filters such as remoteness of damage, which arise once it has been established that the defendant's duty of care extends beyond particular risks in the pregnancy.

The *SAAMCO* principle, whether it is applied to financial, medical, or any other type of risk, aims to prevent a defendant from being held liable for losses which arise in way that is coincidental to, as opposed to consequential on, their breach of duty. As such, it is an important element in the causal inquiry in negligence. Note that its application to negligence is also significant: where the tort committed by the defendant is an intentional one (such as deceit), the principle does not apply and the defendant will instead be liable for all of the consequences flowing directly from their breach.

In one of her most well-known articles, Professor Stapleton argues for a distinction to be made between a 'scope of duty' analysis and one that refers instead to the 'scope of liability for consequences'. In favouring the latter, she makes the point that failing to make the distinction has the effect of confusing the duty inquiry with its effects.

Jane Stapleton, 'Cause-in-Fact and Scope of Liability for Consequences' (2003) 119 *LQR* 388

The area is analytically complex and resists the traditional common law method of bottom-up case law synthesis because the legal reasoning on which past case law was based is often obscure …. The duty of care should not be framed as being a duty only with respect to particular kinds of consequence. This 'scope of the *duty*' or 'scope of the *risk*' approach which asks 'what kind of harm was it the defendant's duty to guard against' at best conflates inquiries that it is clearer to keep separate and at worst encourages circular reasoning. It is preferable to keep 'duty' as the issue that considers general concerns relating to whether the obligation of care should be recognised between the parties and without regard to the consequences of breach in the particular case. Where it is owed, the 'scope of the duty' is simply to act reasonably in the circumstances. The breach analysis considers what reasonableness entails in the circumstances. Cause-in-fact provides the link between the breach and C suffering actionable damage. Finally, 'scope of *liability*' then considers which of the stream of consequences of the tort that happened on this particular occasion should be judged to be within the scope of D's liability.

7.3 *Novus actus interveniens* or intervening act

In determining whether a claimant's loss is too remote from a defendant's breach of duty, the court will also ask whether any sort of intervention has occurred that *breaks the chain of causation* between the breach of duty and the ultimate damage of which the claimant complains. This inquiry aims to identify any other factors whose effect on the claimant's course of events is so substantial that they override the effect of the defendant's breach.

In the case extracted below, the defendant's negligence caused a traffic accident. The claimant was a police officer who, on the instructions of the senior officer at the scene, rode his motorcycle against the flow of traffic in order to erect a hazard barrier to prevent traffic approaching. In doing so, he was injured by a vehicle. The question for the court was whether the defendant, whose breach of duty was clearly a factual cause of the claimant's injury, should be liable. The Court of Appeal held that the intervening act of the senior police officer broke the chain of causation between the defendant's breach and the claimant's injury, with the result that the defendant was not liable for it. The Court reasoned that the more negligent the act of the third party, and (therefore) the more independent the intervening action from the breach of the defendant, the more likely it is that the intervention in question will break the causal link between the claimant and defendant.

Knightley v Johns [1982] 1 WLR 349, 367 (Stephenson LJ)

[T]he inspector's negligence was not a concurrent cause running with the first defendant's negligence, but a new cause disturbing the sequence of events leading from the first defendant's overturning of his car to the plaintiff's accident and interrupting the effect of it. This would, I think, have been so had the inspector's negligence stood alone. Coming as it did on top of the muddle and misunderstanding of Mr. Williams's telephone call and followed by the inspector's order to remedy his own negligence by a dangerous manoeuvre, it was the real cause of the plaintiff's injury and made that injury too remote from the first defendant's wrongdoing to be a consequence of it.

In the long run the question is, as Lord Reid said in the *Dorset Yacht Co.* case [1970] A.C. 1004, one of remoteness of damage, to be answered as has so often been stated, not by the logic of philosophers but by the common sense of plain men ... **In my judgment, too much happened here, too much went wrong, the chapter of accidents and mistakes was too long and varied, to impose on the first defendant liability for what happened to the**

> **plaintiff in discharging his duty as a police officer, although it would not have happened had not the first defendant negligently overturned his car.** The ordinary course of things took an extraordinary course. The length and the irregularities of the line leading from the first accident to the second have no parallel in the reported rescue cases, in all of which the plaintiff succeeded in establishing the original wrongdoer's liability. It was natural, it was probable, it was foreseeable, it was indeed certain, that the police would come to the overturned car and control the tunnel traffic. It was also natural and probable and foreseeable that some steps would be taken in controlling the traffic and clearing the tunnel and some things be done that might be more courageous than sensible. The reasonable hypothetical observer would anticipate some human errors, some forms of what might be called folly, perhaps even from trained police officers, and some unusual and unexpected accidents in the course of their rescue duties. But would he anticipate such a result as this from so many errors as these, so many departures from the common sense procedure prescribed by the standing order for just such an emergency as this?

It is clear from Stephenson LJ's reasoning here that the more extraordinary the course of events following the defendant's breach, the more likely they are to have the effect of negating the causal effect of that breach on the claimant. This makes sense in the context of negligence, in which corrective justice principles are so important: it is not the case that injured claimants should recover through the law of tort for all of their losses, but only for those that they have suffered as a result of another's breach of duty. The causal inquiry is the means by which this is achieved, and the remoteness element is an important part of that.

Significantly, the *novus actus interveniens* principle (often just referred to as '*novus actus*') applies even where the intervening act is that of the claimant themselves. In the following case (which has already been discussed in Chapter 2 for what it tells us about the duty of care in negligence), the question for the Court was whether the prisoner's suicide broke the chain of causation between the police's breach of duty in failing properly to supervise him, and his ultimate death. The crucial point here is the independence of the claimant's intervention from the defendant's breach. In *Reeves*, as we saw in the earlier account of it, the principal point of relevance was the *content* of the defendant's duty: it was an intrinsic part of the police's duty as custodian to keep such prisoners safe from themselves. They could not, therefore, argue either that the prisoner's self-harm was not a result of their breach of duty, nor could they argue that it was an *independent intervention* between their breach and the resultant death.

Reeves v Commissioner of Police of the Metropolis [2000] 1 AC 360, 374 (Lord Jauncey), 379 (Lord Hope)

[Lord Jauncey at 374] Professor Glanville Williams in his *Joint Torts and Contributory Negligence* (1951) stated at para. 2-24 that:

> 'if a particular consequence of the defendant's wrongdoing is attributable to some independent act or event which supersedes the effect of the tortious conduct, the defendant's responsibilities may not extend to the consequences of the supervening act or event.'

He went on to state that the novus actus interveniens 'must constitute an event of such impact that it rightly obliterates the wrongdoing of the defendant.' The reference to an independent act superseding the effect of the tortious conduct must, in my view, relate to an act which was outwith the contemplated scope of events to which the duty of care was directed. **Where such a duty is specifically directed at the prevention of the occurrence of a certain event I cannot see how it can be said that the occurrence of that event amounts to an independent act breaking the chain of causation from the breach of duty, even although it may be unusual for one person to come under a duty to prevent another person deliberately inflicting harm on himself. It is the very thing at which the duty was directed.**

...

[Lord Hope at 379] In my opinion it is necessary at the outset to identify the duty which was owed to the deceased by the Commissioner. There is no doubt that the Commissioner was right to concede that he owed a duty of care to the deceased while he remained in police custody. The deceased had been identified as a suicide risk, having on two previous occasions attempted to strangle himself with a belt after being placed in a cell. It was the Commissioner's duty to take reasonable care not to provide him with the opportunity of committing suicide by making use of defects in his cell door. The risk was not that he would injure himself accidentally if given that opportunity, but that he would do so deliberately. That is the nature of an act of suicide by a person who is of sound mind. It is a deliberate act of self-destruction by a person who intends to end his own life. **So I think that the Commissioner's duty can most accurately be described as a duty to take reasonable care to prevent the deceased, while in police custody, from taking his own life deliberately.**

It is unusual for a person to be under a duty to take reasonable care to prevent another person doing something to his loss, injury or damage deliberately. On the whole people are entitled to act as they please, even if this will inevitably lead to their own death or injury. As a general rule the common law duty of care is directed towards the prevention of accidents or of injury caused by negligence. The person to whom the duty is owed is, of course, under a corresponding duty to take reasonable care for his own safety. If he is in breach of that duty, his damages may be reduced on the ground of his contributory negligence. But if he injures himself by intentionally doing deliberately the very thing which the defendant is under a duty to prevent him doing negligently, he may find that he is unable to recover any damages. He may be found to have assumed the risk of injury, on the principle of volenti non fit injuria. Or it may be held that the chain of causation was broken by his deliberate act, in which case his claim will be defeated on the principle of novus actus interveniens. Or it may simply be that his loss, injury and damage will be held to have been caused wholly by his own fault, with the result that there will be no room even for a reduced award on the ground of contributory negligence.

But the duty of care may sometimes extend to preventing people injuring themselves deliberately. The person to whom the duty is owed may be unaware of the risks to which he will expose himself by his deliberate act.

Question to consider: Why do the courts distinguish between intentional and non-intentional torts for the purposes of remoteness? Do you think this distinction is justified?

Other resources: *The Wagon Mound (No 1)* [1961] AC 388; J Stapleton, 'Cause-in-Fact and Scope of Liability for Consequences' (2003) 119 *LQR* 388; *Quinn v Leathem* [1901] AC 495; *Scott v Shepherd* (1772) 2 Wm Bl 892.

The next case provides a useful account of how courts will consider the acts of claimants that follow a defendant's breach of duty towards them. On the facts that follow, the claimant had been injured by the negligence of the defendants and, in between the accident and the trial, then suffered further loss related to that initial injury. The question of whether, ultimately, a defendant is liable for the further effects of the injury they cause is answered again by reference to the concept of independence: the more independent the claimant's act is from the result of the defendant's breach, the more likely that act is to break the chain of causation and bar liability. The converse is of course also true: the closer the connection between the result of the breach and the claimant's act, the less likely their intervention will be deemed to break the chain of causation. In *McKew*, the act of the claimant, knowing that his leg was weak and likely to give way, was considered by the court to be both unreasonable and avoidable. As a consequence, it *was* regarded as having broken the chain of causation between the defendant's breach and the claimant's ultimate injury. Had this not been the case, and had the claimant's actions been both a reasonable response and an unavoidable consequential action, the same result would not have been reached (as can be seen by reference to *Wieland v Cyril*

Lord Carpets Ltd,[3] a case in which the injured claimant was deemed to have acted reasonably, and whose actions were regarded therefore as not having broken the chain of causation).

McKew v Holland & Hannen & Cubitts (Scotland) Ltd [1969] UKHL 12, [1969] 3 All ER 1621, [25] (Lord Reid)

25. In my view the law is clear. If a man is injured in such a way that his leg may give way at any moment, he must act reasonably and carefully. It is quite possible that in spite of all reasonable care his leg may give way in circumstances such that as a result he sustains further injury. Then that second injury was caused by his disability, which in turn was caused by the defender's fault. But if the injured man acts unreasonably, he cannot hold the defender liable for injury caused by his own unreasonable conduct. His unreasonable conduct is *novus actus interveniens*. The chain of causation has been broken and what follows must be regarded as caused by his own conduct and not by the defender's fault or the disability caused by it. Or one may say that unreasonable conduct of the pursuer and what follows from it is not the natural and probable result of the original fault of the defender or of the ensuing disability. I do not think that foreseeability comes into this. A defender is not liable for a consequence of a kind which is not foreseeable. But it does not follow that he is liable for every consequence which a reasonable man could foresee. What can be foreseen depends almost entirely on the facts of the case, and it is often easy to foresee unreasonable conduct or some other *novus actus interveniens* as being quite likely. But that does not mean that the defender must pay for damage caused by the *novus actus*. It only leads to trouble if one tries to graft on to the concept of foreseeability some rule of law to the effect that a wrongdoer is not bound to foresee something which in fact he could readily foresee as quite likely to happen. For it is not at all unlikely or unforeseeable that an active man who has suffered such a disability will take some quite unreasonable risk. But if he does, he cannot hold the defender liable for the consequences.

7.4 Conclusion

The materials in this chapter set out how the law limits liability in negligence for those who have breached their duty of care and are thereby a factual cause of a claimant's damage. The basic point is of course that breaches of duty will not necessarily incur liability in negligence where the actionable damage in question is deemed by the court to be too remote from the defendant's breach. These rules recognise and

3 [1969] 3 All ER 1006.

underline the difference between intentional and non-intentional torts by imposing a stricter test on the former (which are subject to greater moral culpability). In most tort courses at undergraduate level, the test most often encountered by students is the test for negligence: reasonable foreseeability of the *type of loss* ultimately suffered by the claimant. Remember that you also need to understand how this dovetails with the thin skull principle: the idea that you take your victim as you find them. Crucially, this means that the extent of the loss ultimately caused to the claimant does *not* have to be reasonably foreseeable in order to be recoverable in a negligence action. This latter point is another very common mistake made by students, so do your very best to familiarise yourself with these cases and avoid it!

Chapter 8 OCCUPIERS' LIABILITY

8.1 Introduction

Occupiers' liability law is a statutory form of negligence, which imposes duties on people who have control of premises. It is largely governed by two statutes which, confusingly, have the same name – the Occupiers' Liability Act 1957 (OLA 1957) and the Occupiers' Liability Act 1984 (OLA 1984). The OLA 1957 applies to visitors and people who have permission to be on the premises, whereas the OLA 1984 applies to non-visitors, more commonly thought of as trespassers. The different Acts have differing corresponding duties, which will be explored in this chapter. It is often incorrectly stated that the Acts require occupiers to keep their premises 'safe', but this is not a correct representation of the law. It is difficult, if not impossible, to make certain premises safe – think about a surf beach, a ski resort, or a skate park. The duty is to do what is 'reasonable' in the circumstances. The occupiers' liability cases and literature raise a number of interesting questions about when and how duties of care should be owed, sometimes to vulnerable people.

8.2 Who is an occupier?

The first question to ask is 'who is an occupier?'. Both Acts use the same term, which is one based on 'control' as opposed to specific legal relationships.

Occupiers' Liability Act 1957

1 Preliminary

(2) The rules so enacted shall regulate the nature of the duty imposed by law in consequence of a person's occupation or control of premises and of any invitation or permission he gives (or is to be treated as giving) to another to enter or use the premises, but they shall not alter the rules of the common law as to the persons on whom a duty is so imposed or to whom it is owed; and accordingly for the purpose of the rules so enacted the persons who are to be treated as an occupier and as his visitors are the same (subject to subsection (4) of this section) as the persons who would at common law be treated as an occupier and as his invitees or licensees.

> The focus of determining who is an 'occupier' is based on who has control of the premises.

> The rules developed by the common law are explicitly referred to in the Act.

Occupiers' Liability Act 1984

1 Duty of occupier to persons other than his visitors

(2) For the purposes of this section, the persons who are to be treated respectively as an occupier of any premises (which, for those purposes, include any fixed or movable structure) and as his visitors are—

(a) any person who owes in relation to the premises the duty referred to in section 2 of the Occupiers' Liability Act 1957 (the common duty of care), ...

The definition of 'occupier' in the Occupiers' Liability Act 1984 specifically refers to the definition in the 1957 Act.

In both Acts, the focus is on who has control of the premises. The question then arises: can there be multiple occupiers who have control over different parts of a single premises? This was discussed and decided in *Wheat v Lacon*.

Wheat v Lacon [1966] AC 552, 564 (Lord Denning)

My Lords, The 'Golfers' Arms' at Great Yarmouth is owned by the brewery company, E. Lacon & Co. Ltd. The ground floor was run as a public-house by Mr. Richardson as manager for the brewery company. The first floor was used by Mr. and Mrs. Richardson as their private dwelling. In the summer Mrs. Richardson took in guests for her private profit. Mr. and Mrs. Wheat and their family were summer guests of Mrs. Richardson. About 9 p.m. one evening, when it was getting dark, Mr. Wheat fell down the back staircase in the private portion and was killed. Winn J. held that there were two causes: (i) the handrail was too short because it did not stretch to the foot of the stairs; (ii) someone had taken the bulb out of the light at the top of the stairs.

The case raises this point of law: did the brewery company owe any duty to Mr. Wheat to see that the handrail was safe to use or to see that the stairs were properly lighted? That depends on whether the brewery company was 'an occupier' of the private portion of the 'Golfers' Arms,' and Mr. Wheat its 'visitor' within the *Occupiers' Liability Act, 1957*: for, if so, the brewery company owed him the 'common duty of care.'

In order to determine this question we must have resort to the law before the Act: for it is expressly enacted [in s 1(2)] that the Act

> 'shall not alter the rules of the common law as to the persons on whom a duty is so imposed or to whom it is owed: and accordingly ... the persons who are to be treated as an occupier and as his visitors are the same ... as the persons who would at common law be treated as an occupier and as his invitees or licensees.'

At the outset, I would say that no guidance is to be obtained from the use of the word 'occupier' in other branches of the law: for its meaning varies according to the subject-matter.

In the *Occupiers' Liability Act, 1957*, the word 'occupier' is used in the same sense as it was used in the common law cases on occupiers' liability for dangerous premises. It was simply a convenient word to denote a person who had a sufficient degree of control over premises to put him under a duty of care towards those who came lawfully on to the premises. Those persons were divided into two categories, invitees and licensees: and a higher duty was owed to invitees than to licensees. But by the year 1956 the distinction between invitees and licensees had been reduced to vanishing point. The duty of the occupier had become simply a duty to take reasonable care to see that the premises were reasonably safe for people coming lawfully on to them: and it made no difference whether they were invitees or licensees: see *Slater v. Clay Cross Co. Ltd.* The Act of 1957 confirmed the process. It did away, once and for all, with invitees and licensees and classed them all as 'visitors'; and it put upon the occupier the same duty to all of them, namely, the common duty of care. This duty is simply a particular instance of the general duty of care which each man owes to his 'neighbour.' When Lord Esher first essayed a definition of this general duty, he used the occupiers' liability as an instance of it: see *Heaven v. Pender*; and when Lord Atkin eventually formulated the general duty in acceptable terms, he, too, used occupiers' liability as an illustration: see *Donoghue v. Stevenson*, and particularly his reference to *Grote v. Chester Railway Company*. Translating this general principle into its particular application to dangerous premises, it becomes simply this: wherever a person has a sufficient degree of control over premises that he ought to realise that any failure on his part to use care may result in injury to a person coming lawfully there, then he is an 'occupier' and the person coming lawfully there is his 'visitor': and the 'occupier' is under a duty to his 'visitor' to use reasonable care. In order to be an 'occupier' it is not necessary for a person to have entire control over the premises. He need not have exclusive occupation. Suffice it that he has some degree of control. He may share the control with others. Two or more may be 'occupiers.' And whenever this happens, each is under a duty to use care towards persons coming lawfully on to the premises, dependent on his degree of control. If each fails in his duty, each is liable to a visitor who is injured in consequence of his failure, but each may have a claim to contribution from the other.

…

In the light of these cases, I ask myself whether the brewery company had a sufficient degree of control over the premises to put them under a duty to a visitor. Obviously they had complete control over the ground floor and were 'occupiers' of it. But I think that they had also sufficient control over the private portion. They had not let it out to Mr. Richardson by a demise. They had only granted him a licence to occupy it, having a right themselves to do repairs. That left them with a residuary degree of control which was equivalent to that retained by the Chelsea Corporation in *Greene*'s case. They were in my opinion 'an occupier' within the Act of 1957, Mr. Richardson, who had a licence to occupy, had also a considerable degree of control. So had Mrs. Richardson, who catered for summer guests. All three of them were, in my opinion, 'occupiers' of the private portion of the 'Golfer's Arms.' There is no difficulty in having more than one occupier at one and the same time, each of whom is under a duty of care to visitors.

8.3 Liability to visitors

The test for 'occupier' is the same under the OLA 1957 and OLA 1984. However, this next section solely focuses on the liability owed to visitors under the OLA 1957. Liability to non-visitors under the OLA 1984 will be discussed at 8.4.

> The duty is related to the 'state of the premises' as opposed to activities undertaken on the premises. It also refers to positive acts and omissions (failure to act).

> This is a very wide definition of premises, which has been interpreted to include a ladder, as well as a range of natural environments such as beaches and lagoons.

> The same duty is now owed to all visitors, compared to the previous common law approach of different duties depending on visitor category.

> The Act specifically allows occupiers to 'extend, restrict, modify or exclude' liability by agreement or otherwise. Understandably, occupiers were keen to exclude or restrict their duty as much as possible, including through notices and exclusion clauses.

> Focus is on what is 'reasonable' in the circumstances, looking at the purpose that the visitor was involved or permitted into the premises.

> A higher standard of care is specified for children entering premises.

> A lower standard of care is specified for professionals acing in the 'exercise of their calling'.

Occupiers' Liability Act 1957

1 Preliminary

(1) The rules enacted by the two next following sections shall have effect, in place of the rules of the common law, to regulate the duty which an occupier of premises owes to his visitors in respect of dangers due to the state of the premises or to things done or omitted to be done on them.

(3) The rules so enacted in relation to an occupier of premises and his visitors shall also apply, in like manner and to the like extent as the principles applicable at common law to an occupier of premises and his invitees or licensees would apply, to regulate—

(a) the obligations of a person occupying or having control over any fixed or moveable structure, including any vessel, vehicle or aircraft; and

(b) the obligations of a person occupying or having control over any premises or structure in respect of damage to property, including the property of persons who are not themselves his visitors.

2 Extent of occupier's ordinary duty

(1) An occupier of premises owes the same duty, the 'common duty of care', to all his visitors, except in so far as he is free to and does extend, restrict, modify or exclude his duty to any visitor or visitors by agreement or otherwise.

(2) The common duty of care is a duty to take such care as in all the circumstances of the case is reasonable to see that the visitor will be reasonably safe in using the premises for the purposes for which he is invited or permitted by the occupier to be there.

(3) The circumstances relevant for the present purpose include the degree of care, and of want of care, which would ordinarily be looked for in such a visitor, so that (for example) in proper cases—

(a) an occupier must be prepared for children to be less careful than adults; and

(b) an occupier may expect that a person, in the exercise of his calling, will appreciate and guard against any special risks ordinarily incident to it, so far as the occupier leaves him free to do so.

(4) In determining whether the occupier of premises has discharged the common duty of care to a visitor, regard is to be had to all the circumstances, so that (for example)—

(a) where damage is caused to a visitor by a danger of which he had been warned by the occupier, the warning is not to be treated without more as absolving the occupier from liability, unless in all the circumstances it was enough to enable the visitor to be reasonably safe; and

(b) where damage is caused to a visitor by a danger due to the faulty execution of any work of construction, maintenance or repair by an independent contractor employed by the occupier, the occupier is not to be treated without more as answerable for the danger if in all the circumstances he had acted reasonably in entrusting the work to an independent contractor and had taken such steps (if any) as he reasonably ought in order to satisfy himself that the contractor was competent and that the work had been properly done.

(5) The common duty of care does not impose on an occupier any obligation to a visitor in respect of risks willingly accepted as his by the visitor (the question whether a risk was so accepted to be decided on the same principles as in other cases in which one person owes a duty of care to another).

(6) For the purposes of this section, persons who enter premises for any purpose in the exercise of a right conferred by law are to be treated as permitted by the occupier to be there for that purpose, whether they in fact have his permission or not.

The OLA 1957 specifically allows occupiers to warn of risks but requires any warning to be sufficient to enable the visitor to be reasonably safe.

If the occupier engages someone for market value (as opposed to suspiciously low) with no knowledge of repeated adverse reports, the duty will, in effect, be delegated to that contractor.

If a warning is held to be sufficient, the claimant will be deemed to have voluntarily assumed liability for the risk and will be prevented from making a claim against the occupier.

8.3.1 Who is a 'visitor'?

As outlined in the legislation above, a visitor is someone who has express or implied permission to be on the premises. This test was considered further in *McGeown v Northern Ireland Housing Executive* and *Phipps v Rochester* in the context of public rights of ways and children.

McGeown v Northern Ireland Housing Executive [1995] 1 AC 233, 243

The claimant lived with her husband, who was a tenant of the defendant housing authority. There were paths across the housing estate, over which the public had acquired a right of way. The claimant was injured whilst using one of the paths, owing to the fact that its surface had been allowed to lapse into disrepair. The claimant sued the defendant housing authority under the OLA (Northern Ireland) 1957. The House of Lords held that the user of a public right of way was not a visitor for the purposes of the OLA (Northern Ireland) 1957 or the OLA 1957 of England and Wales, since her use was one of right.

Lord Keith of Kinkel, with whom the other judges agreed, stated that the rule excluding a duty is:

> ... in my opinion undoubtedly a sound and reasonable one. Rights of way pass over many different types of terrain, and it would place an impossible burden upon landowners if they not only had to submit to the passage over them of anyone who might choose to exercise them but also were under a duty to maintain them in a safe condition. Persons using rights of way do so not with the permission of the owner of the solum but in the exercise of a right. There is no room for the view that such persons might have been licensees or invitees of the landowner under the old law or that they are his visitors under the British and Northern Irish Acts of 1957. There may indeed be a question whether the owner of the solum is occupier of the right of way for the purposes of these Acts. Doubts about that were expressed in *Holden v. White* but it is unnecessary for present purposes to decide it.
>
> It is, however, necessary to consider next whether the common duty of care under the Act of 1957 was owed by the defendants to the plaintiff by reason that the pathway where she sustained her injuries formed part of a means of access to and from her husband's dwelling house. In *Fairman v Perpetual Investment Building Society* [1923] A.C. 74, the defendants owned a block of flats which they let to various tenants, retaining possession and control of the common staircase leading to the flats. The plaintiff, who lodged with one of the tenants, while descending the staircase, caught her heel in a depression in one of the steps and fell, sustaining injuries. The House of Lords held that the plaintiff was a licensee of the defendants and that they owed her a duty of care accordingly, but decided by a majority that there had been no breach of the duty. In *Jacobs v London County Council* [1950] A.C. 361 the plaintiff tripped over a protruding stopcock situated in a forecourt lying between a public street and a shop which the plaintiff was seeking to approach. The forecourt was in the ownership and occupation of the defendants, who were landlords of the shop. The House of Lords held that the facts were indistinguishable from those in *Fairman*'s case, and that the plaintiff was a licensee of the defendants. However, it was decided that the defendants were not in breach of the duty which they owed to the plaintiff as their licensee. It is likely that in both these cases, had they arisen after the passing of the Act of 1957, the defendants would have been held to have been in breach of the common duty of care owed to visitors under it.
>
> If the pathway on which the plaintiff fell in the present case had not become subject to a public right of way it seems clear that the defendants would have owed her the common duty of care under the Act of 1957 and would have been liable accordingly. The question is whether the licence to use the pathway which the defendants would have been held to have granted the plaintiff before it became subject to the public right of way is to be held to have become merged in that right of way and so been extinguished, or whether it can be treated as having a continued existence.
>
> ...

> The concept of licensee or visitor involves that the person in question has at least the permission of the relevant occupier to be in a particular place. Once a public right of way has been established, there is no question of permission being granted by the owner of the solum to those who choose to use it. They do so as of right and not by virtue of any licence or invitation. In the present case the pathway upon which the plaintiff fell had not been adopted by the highway authority, and it was therefore not responsible for the maintenance of it. Adjoining areas had been so adopted, in particular the strip of ground immediately adjoining the terrace where the plaintiff and her husband lived, and which she had to cross in order to get to or from his house. If the plaintiff was the licensee of the defendants upon the pathway where she fell she was equally their licensee upon that strip of ground. The circumstance that the highway authority was responsible under public law for its maintenance cannot logically make any difference to the position. The defendants would still owe a personal duty to the plaintiff to maintain the pathway in a reasonably safe condition, and be liable to her if she suffered injury owing to the area not being in such condition. That unreasonable result can be avoided if it is held that dedication as a public highway puts an end to any duty which might otherwise be owed by the housing executive.

The finding in *McGeown v Northern Ireland Housing Executive* did, however, receive academic criticism. In the article below, Barker and Parry argue that the finding is unjustified, particularly as non-visitors have the benefit of statutory protection under the OLA 1984. The authors believe that there should be statutory reform to create more inclusive public property rights, using the OLA (Scotland) 1960 as a potential model.

F Barker and N Parry, 'Private Property, Public Access and Occupiers' Liability' (1995) 15 *Legal Studies* 335, 353–54

> As Lord Keith protested in *McGeown v Northern Ireland Housing Executive*, they would suffer 'an impossible burden … if they not only had to submit to the passage over them of anyone who might choose to exercise them but also were under a duty to maintain them in a safe condition'.
>
> There are two main responses that might be made to this objection. First, it merely assumes and asserts, rather than offers any justification for, the primacy of private property values in land, and, given that this paper seeks to evaluate critically precisely this stance, it arguably contributes little to the present discussion. Second, the suggested new framework would be based on an approach that has operated in Scotland since 1960 without evident problems, and would be unlikely to impose massive, indeterminate liability on those with private property rights in land since it would continue to be based on 'reasonableness'. The precise steps required to discharge the new, 'universal' duty in any given case would

depend upon the prevailing circumstances, with one of the most relevant issues almost certainly being the status of the entrant: on this basis, an occupier would normally have to do more to discharge his duty in the case of an express invitee than in the case of a public right of way user, and more to protect the latter than a burglar.

It might be argued that this does not represent much of an advance on the current occupiers' liability framework since most of this is already based on duties of 'reasonable care' of one kind or another. However, the proposed approach would help to rationalise the current complex, piecemeal legal framework in this area, consolidating two statutes and a residual body of common law, and would extend the scope of statutory protection to those on land on public rights of way, thereby abolishing the arguably outmoded rule in *Gautret v Egerton*. Suggesting a comprehensive occupiers' liability statute is not to advocate rationalisation for its own sake. As long as the current English legal framework governing this area remains inconsistent and confusing, it may act as a deterrent to those seeking effective public access to land, and thereby frustrate efforts to establish a broader, reformulated conception of private property in land. Rationalisation would largely end the distinction between negligent nonfeasance and misfeasance in this context, and with it the potential for confusion as a result of having a different legal framework applicable in each case. It could help to encourage the effective enforcement of rights of access to land, and would ensure that those exercising them enjoy the kind of protection they arguably deserve in a society where rights-based public access to land is the subject of growing social, political and legal concern.

In *Phipps v Rochester Corporation*, a 5-year-old boy, accompanied by his 7-year-old sister, was blackberry-picking on an area of grassland that was at the relevant time a building site being developed by the defendant. The boy fell into a deep trench that had been dug to accommodate a sewer, and was injured. Since children had been known to play on the land, and the defendant had done nothing to prevent this, the question was therefore whether the child was a trespasser or not.

Phipps v Rochester Corporation [1955] 1 QB 450, 454

Devlin J held that children as a class had implied permission to be on the site (although, as we will see when we return to this case below, the defendant was held not to have been in breach of its duty on the facts). In coming to this conclusion, His Honour stated:

I have first to inquire whether the child is a licensee or a trespasser. It has been argued on his behalf that even if he was a trespasser, there was in this case such a reckless disregard of ordinary humanity as to impose liability upon the corporation. The point was not taken with much confidence, and it seems to me to be putting the case altogether too strongly. If the child was a trespasser, the defendants, in my judgment, succeed. If he was a licensee, I have to consider whether the duty owing to an infant licensee has been broken. As the argument developed, it became apparent that the two points were not entirely separate. But I shall begin by considering them separately, and shall deal first of all with the facts which are said by the plaintiffs to be sufficient to constitute an implied licence.

The evidence on both sides shows that children were in the habit of playing or trying to play in the houses that were under construction.

...

I am satisfied that throughout the summer of 1951 children from the neighbouring houses resorted to this open space. There is no evidence that they did so in great numbers, or that they swarmed over it or that it was anything like an organized playground. But I accept the evidence that they did go on it for the ordinary purposes for which children might be expected to use it. I think that this must have been apparent to the defendants' officials at the time, though I have no doubt that they have now forgotten it. I think that they must have seen enough of what was going on during the working day to make it plain to them, without using more than ordinary powers of imagination, that there would probably be quite a considerable use made of it at week-ends and in the evenings. I therefore find that the defendants did know that children were using the land.

But knowledge is not of itself enough to constitute a licence; there is a distinction between toleration and permission. The owner of moorland or downland, for example, in any favoured part of the country may know quite well that people are walking on his land for pleasure, but he cannot be held merely by that fact to licence them to do so. As it is put in Salmond on Torts, 11th ed., p. 571: 'An occupier who resigns himself to the occasional and perhaps inevitable presence of trespassers on his property does not thereby take upon himself the obligations of a licensor.' I have to ask myself how the matter would be regarded by the reasonable man. There must be something more than casual trespassing by individuals who come once and perhaps never again. There must be a class of people who form something of a habit; and then one must ask oneself whether a reasonable owner would feel that unless he acted to stop the trespass, the belief would naturally be induced in those who used the land that they had his tacit permission to do so. This is a matter of degree which in the present case I do not find it easy to evaluate. It can be and has been argued that this was a short user, that there is no real evidence of any use before the Spring of 1951, and that it was a use that was temporary in character since the land was in process of being built over. But, on balance, I think that there is enough evidence to satisfy the test that I have propounded. It seems after all a very natural thing to allow children to play on open grass land which is not immediately required for any other purpose and which is just beside their homes, and I do not think that more than has been proved in this case is necessary to give rise to the assumption in the mind of the reasonable man that unless he does something to stop it, children will take it for granted that they are acting unobjectionable.

With this conclusion the stage is reached which was expressed by Lord Porter in Edwards v. Railway Executive in these terms: '... no doubt where the owner of the premises knows that the public or some portion of it is accustomed to trespass over his land he must take steps to show that he resents and will try to prevent the invasion.'

On the facts of the present case the plaintiffs have, in my judgment, only to reach this stage to succeed on the point, for there is no evidence that the defendants in this case took any steps at all. I have already expressed the view that the instructions which they gave were intended and understood to be confined to the building plots. There is no evidence that any child was ever chased off the open space, and it would seem such a harsh measure that I think, if it had been done, that it would have been remembered. The fact is that the defendants have already lost this point by staking their case on the contention that there never were any children to chase off. It follows that they never took any steps to show that they resented the invasion.

8.3.2 What are 'premises'?

As outlined in the legislation above, the definition of 'premises' is very wide and refers to 'occupying or having control over any fixed or moveable structure, including any vessel, vehicle or aircraft'. As a result, in *Wheeler v Copas*, Chapman J held that a ladder could be premises, and other cases have included premises such as bouncy castles, bungee runs and similar fairground attractions, abandoned boats, fire escapes and scaffolding.[1]

8.3.3 What is the content of the occupier's duty under the 1957 Act?

The core duty is contained in s 2(2). It is the 'common duty of care' which is 'a duty to take such care as in all the circumstances of the case is reasonable to see that the visitor will be reasonably safe in using the premises for the purposes for which he is invited or permitted by the occupier to be there'. The legislation highlights that the relevant duty is dependent on the nature of the visitor, the purposes of the visit and what is reasonable the circumstances. It is therefore important to understand the case law and be able to draw analogies with problem question facts. There are some specific principles to remember.

First, the occupier will have obligations with regards to the 'state of the premises' under s 1(3), and not the activities occurring on the premises (which are potentially covered by other torts). This was confirmed by the Court of

1 [1981] 3 All ER 405.

Appeal in *Fairchild v Glenhaven Funeral Services Ltd.*[2] The facts of this case are outlined in detail in Chapter 6 (Causation) and will not be repeated here; it is, however, important to remember that the occupiers' liability point did not go up to the House of Lords and therefore the Court of Appeal should be cited for this particular point of law.

Second, it must be shown not only that a duty is owed, but that it has been *breached*. In deciding this, the court will look at the actions of both the visitor and the occupier. For example, in *Portsmouth Youth Activities Committee v Poppleton*, the defendant was the occupier of a climbing wall facility which the claimant was visiting when he was severely injured.[3] He was attempting to jump from one wall to another when he fell and was rendered a tetraplegic. He alleged in his claim that the defendant was liable as an occupier because it had failed to supervise his activities, or to provide an appropriate warning that the matting provided, whilst very thick, would not be sufficient to preclude the possibility of all injuries. The Court of Appeal found that the conduct of the claimant was the cause of the claimant's injuries, rather than the state of the premises, and declined therefore to hold the defendant liable.

Portsmouth Youth Activities Committee v Poppleton [2008] EWCA Civ 646, [2009] PIQR P1, [16]–[20] (May LJ)

16. In my view, the heart of the matter on the respondents' cross-appeal is whether the appellants were under a duty to train or supervise adults whom they admitted to use the climbing wall; and on the appeal whether the judge was correct to hold that the appellants had a duty to warn Mr Poppleton that there was a risk of injury notwithstanding the presence of entirely suitable matting. I put the first of these compendiously as a duty to train or supervise since that, in my view, comprises the kernel of the various aspects of the wider duty of care for which Mr Sharp contends.

17. *Tomlinson v Congleton Borough Council* [2004] 1 AC 46 is a decision mainly about the application of the Occupiers Liability Act 1984. But the speech of Lord Hoffmann in particular has dicta relevant to policy considerations underlying the scope of duties which may be owed in cases such as this. Agreeing in paragraph 26 with the judgment of Lord Phillips of Worth Matravers MR in *Donoghue v Folkestone Properties* [2003] QB 1008 that Mr Tomlinson suffered his injury because he chose to indulge in activity which had inherent dangers, not because the premises were in a dangerous state, Lord Hoffman said at paragraph 27 that Mr Tomlinson was a person of full capacity voluntarily and without any pressure or inducement engaged in an activity which had an inherent risk. Lord Hoffman repeated, in paragraph 44 under the heading 'free will', that Mr Tomlinson was freely and voluntarily undertaking an activity which inherently involved some risk. He then said

2 [2001] EWCA Civ 1881.

3 [2008] EWCA Civ 646.

in paragraph 45 that it would be extremely rare for an occupier of land to be under a duty to prevent people from taking risks which are inherent in the activities they freely chose to undertake. If people want to climb mountains, go hang gliding or swim or dive into ponds or lakes, that is their affair. The land owner may take a paternalistic view and prefer people not to undertake risky activities on his land. But the law does not require him to impose conditions. Lord Hoffmann then said at paragraph 46 that a duty to protect against obvious risk or self inflicted harm exists only in cases in which there is no genuine or informed choice. I add that a duty may also exist where the defendant has in some relevant way assumed responsibility for the claimant's safety, as in *Fowles v Bedfordshire County Council* CA 17.5.95- see especially Millett LJ at pages 20 to 24. The same may be said of *Perrett v Collins* and *Watson v British Board of Control* [2001] PIQR 16, in each of which the relevant defendant was exercising a degree of regulatory control. By contrast, in *Evans v Kosmar Villa Holidays* [2007] EWCA Civ 1003, it was held, following the approach in *Tomlinson*, that the defendants' duty of care did not extend to a duty to guard the claimant against the risk of diving into the pool and injuring himself. That was an obvious risk of which he was well aware.

18. It is, therefore, in my view, necessary to consider whether the risk in the present case was inherent and obvious. The risk of falling from the wall was plainly obvious. The judge held in effect that the risk that the matting might not in every case protect a climber who fell from serious injury was not obvious. But I do not consider that this finding is sustainable, not least in the light of Mr Poppleton's own evidence. Evidence apart, it is to my mind quite obvious that no amount of matting will avoid absolutely the risk of possibly severe injury from an awkward fall and that the possibility of an awkward fall is an obvious and inherent risk of this kind of climbing. Mr Poppleton's evidence was that he did not think it was *that* risky, indicating that he knew that there was a risk.

19. I reach this conclusion, giving all due weight to the advice in the HSE video and the views of the experts. But I do not consider that, in this instance, this advice and these views dictate the result. As Lord Hoffmann said at paragraph 47 in *Tomlinson:*

> 'It is of course understandable that organisations like the Royal Society for the Prevention of Accidents should favour policies which require people to be prevented from taking risks. Their function is to prevent accidents and that is one way of doing so. But they do not have to consider the cost, not only in money but also in deprivation of liberty, which such restrictions entail. The courts will naturally respect the technical expertise of such organisations in drawing attention to what can be done to prevent accidents. But the balance between risk on the one hand and individual autonomy on the other is not a matter of expert opinion. It is a judgment which the courts must make and which in England reflects the individualist values of the common law.'

20. There being inherent and obvious risks in the activity which Mr Poppleton was voluntarily undertaking, the law did not in my view require the appellants to prevent him from undertaking it, nor to train him or supervise him while he did it, or see that others did so. If the law required training or supervision in this case, it would equally be required for a multitude of other commonplace leisure activities which nevertheless carry with them a degree of obvious inherent risk – as for instance bathing in the sea. It makes no difference to this analysis that the appellants charged Mr Poppleton to use the climbing wall, nor that the rules which they displayed could have been more prominent. ...

Third, the legislation provides a higher standard of care in relation to children. Under s 2(3)(a), 'an occupier must be prepared for children to be less careful than adults'. This was a reflection of the case law that already existed, for example *Glasgow Corporation v Taylor*. In this case the defendant was an occupier of a botanical garden where a 7-year-old died after eating poisonous berries. The House of Lords held that the failure to restrict access to children was a breach, particularly as the berries could have been an 'allurement' for children.

Glasgow Corporation v Taylor [1922] 1 AC 44, 52 (Lord Atkinson)

[Do the facts] establish that a duty lay upon the defenders to take reasonably adequate precautions to protect on August 20, 1919, the pursuer's son from the danger by which the child lost his life?

In my opinion that question should be answered in the affirmative. If so, it is not contended that the duty was discharged. They did nothing to protect the child, and contend they were not bound to do anything. There is, in my view, no resemblance between this case and those cases where mischievous boys sustain injury by interfering with or misusing natural objects, such as trees in public parks up which they may be tempted to climb, or water, ornamental or other, into which they may accidentally fall or be tempted deliberately to enter. The appearance of such objects as these is well known and unmistakable. There is nothing deceptive or misleading about them. They cannot well be mistaken for things other than, or different from, what they really are. Whereas, if the averments in the condescendences be true, there was in this belladonna plant, with the deadly berries which it bore, something in the nature of a trap. The berries looked alluring and as harmless as grapes or cherries.

It is averred that the defenders and their agents knew this, and also knew which the deceased child did not – that the berries were, if eaten, highly poisonous. The defenders were, therefore, aware of the existence of a concealed or disguised danger to which the child might be exposed when he frequented their park, a danger of which he was entirely ignorant, and could not by himself reasonably discover, yet they did nothing to protect him from that danger or even inform him of its existence.

Question to consider: How should the courts respond to the challenges of children on premises? When should the duty be owed by the parents and when should it be owed by the occupier?

Other resources: R Kidner, 'The Duty of Occupiers towards Children' (1988) 39 *NILQ* 150; *Phipps v Rochester Corporation* [1955] 1 QB 450; *West Sussex CC v Pierce* [2013] EWCA Civ 1230.

Fourth, there is a higher standard of care in relation to professionals attending premises in the 'exercise of their calling'. This is justified on the basis that occupiers can expect professionals to guard against risks themselves. It does not absolve the occupier of liability, as shown in *Salmon v Seafarer Restaurants Ltd*,[4] as the question will still be whether the occupier had acted reasonably before the specialist attended the premises. The professional will only ever be expected to assume the risks inherent in their professional calling and not the risk of negligent occupier actions.

The extent of the duty was highlighted in *Roles v Nathan*. In this case the defendant was the occupier of a building heated by an old coke boiler. When the boiler produced a great deal of smoke, two brothers, who were chimney sweeps, were called in to clear the flues. The defendant determined that the boiler room was dangerous and ordered everyone out. The sweeps ignored his warning, but were removed by force. Nonetheless, the sweeps were later found to be working there. When found, they said that they had nearly completed their work but could not quite finish because they had not enough cement to do so. They then said that they would return on Saturday. In fact they returned to complete their work that night, and both were found dead in the boiler room on Saturday morning. Their wives sued the defendant for breach of its duty as occupier. The Court of Appeal held that the warnings given to the chimney sweeps were enough to keep them 'reasonably safe' according to the duty outlined in the OLA 1957 and that they should have had a better professional appreciation of the risks to which they subjected themselves.

Roles v Nathan [1963] 1 WLR 1117, 1123

Lord Denning MR held that there was no liability, stating that:

> ... in the case of a chimney sweep who comes to sweep the chimneys or to seal up a sweep-hole. The householder can reasonably expect the sweep to take care of himself so far as any dangers from the flues are concerned. these chimney sweeps ought to have known that there might be dangerous fumes about and ought to have taken steps to guard against

4 [1983] 1 WLR 1264.

them. They ought to have known that they should not attempt to seal up the sweep-hole whilst the fire was still alight. They ought to have had the fire withdrawn before they attempted to seal it up, or at any rate they ought not to have stayed in the alcove too long when there might be dangerous fumes about. All this was known to these two sweeps; they were repeatedly warned about it, and it was for them to guard against the danger. It was not for the occupier to do it, even though he was present and heard the warnings. When a householder calls in a specialist to deal with a defective installation on his premises, he can reasonably expect the specialist to appreciate and guard against the dangers arising from the defect. The householder is not bound to watch over him to see that he comes to no harm. I would hold, therefore, that the occupier here was under no duty of care to these sweeps, at any rate in regard to the dangers which caused their deaths. If it had been a different danger, as for instance if the stairs leading to the cellar gave way, the occupier might no doubt be responsible, but not for these dangers which were special risks ordinarily incidental to their calling.

8.3.4 How can the duty be discharged?

There are many different ways in which the duty to visitors can be discharged. The first is by making the premises safer, ie installing safety railing, protective mats, providing safety equipment to visitors etc. The second is by restricting or not permitting access to the unacceptably dangerous parts of the premises.

A third way that the duty can be discharged is by providing a warning the visitors. Effective and appropriate warnings allow visitors to either avoid or assume the relevant risk themselves. The ability to include a warning is specifically outlined in s 2(4)(a) of the OLA 1957, which requires the occupier to ensure any warning is sufficient to enable the visitor to be reasonably safe. Not all warnings will, however, be sufficient, as outlined in *Intruder Detection & Surveillance Ltd v Fulton* [2008] EWCA Civ 1009.

Intruder Detection & Surveillance Ltd v Fulton [2008] EWCA Civ 1009, [2008] 6 WLUK 646, [3]–[5], [12], [13]

Smith LJ set out the facts of the case:

3. On 26 May 2003, the relevant staircase contractors removed the temporary barriers and carried out a trial fitting of the new banister and balustrade. They then removed the new banister and balustrade to take away for cosmetic finishing. They were to be permanently installed two or three days later. Before they left, Mr Fulton told them that they need not put the temporary barriers back in place. He so decided despite the fact that he and his family were living in the house and, as the judge apparently accepted, without them the staircase and landing were unsafe.

4. The following morning the Defendant's engineer, Mr Mark Smith, arrived at Picktree Manor with two apprentices, including the Claimant, to carry out some work on the alarm

installation contract. It appears that at least some of the work was to be done upstairs. They were greeted by Mr Fulton, who had not expected them to arrive that day. He told them that he did not wish them to work at the premises that day. His wife and family did not wish to be disrupted by workmen. That was how the case was pleaded in the third party defence. In evidence Mr Fulton was to suggest, somewhat obliquely, that he had been reluctant to let the men in because 'things were not in the state they should be'. However, the judge held that the reason for Mr Fulton's objection was to safeguard his family's privacy. Following Mr Fulton's initial objection, there was a discussion in which Mr Smith said that the team (himself and the two apprentices) had no other work to do. Eventually Mr Fulton said that they could come in. He did not say that they could not go upstairs; indeed it appears that he contemplated that they would or might do so, as he warned them that the staircase and landing were unguarded – a fact which was plain to see. Mr O'Sullivan, who appears today for Mr Fulton, accepted that, in effect, he had given the men permission to go upstairs. Mr Fulton then left them to get on with their work. He was not involved in supervising it in any way.

5. Sometime later the claimant, who had been working upstairs, decided to come down. Exactly what happened is not entirely clear because he never had to give evidence, but in some way he fell from the top of the stairs or the landing to the hall floor below, a distance of about three metres. He suffered quite serious injuries. He sued his employers, alleging breaches of various statutory duties, which amounted in summary to an allegation that his place of work had been unsafe, as it manifestly was. The employer, in turn, sued the occupier, alleging a breach of section 2 of the Occupiers' Liability Act 1957.

The judge then considered whether the warning was sufficient, determining that anyone working on that part of the premises could not be made reasonably safe and therefore the warning was not sufficient.

12. In my view, Mr Fulton did breach his common duty of care towards the claimant. He had played a significant role in these events. He had permitted the men to enter and to go upstairs, well knowing that the stairs and landing were dangerous. The warning he gave was not sufficient to make the claimant reasonably safe. In particular it could not protect him from the kind of danger which arises on an unguarded staircase or landing, namely the danger that the visitor will inadvertently make a false step.

13. In the circumstances of this case, the fact that the claimant was with Mr Smith, who was the representative of his employer, had duties of his own towards the claimant, could not of itself amount to a reason why the occupier was absolved of his personal duty. I do accept that there will be cases in which the extent to which one visitor may reasonably be expected to supervise the actions of another will be highly relevant to the question of whether the occupier has breached his duty of care. For example, where a supervised

apprentice climbs out onto an unguarded windowsill, the occupier might properly say that he was entitled to expect the supervisor to prevent the apprentice from doing such a dangerous thing. But here no amount of supervision will prevent a visitor – whether an apprentice or a supervisor or a member of the occupier's family – from making the kind of inadvertent false step, which can so easily lead to an accident on an unguarded staircase or landing.

If a warning is determined to be sufficient under s 2(5), the occupier's liability will be absolved because the visitor will have voluntarily assumed the relevant risk. For an example of this, see *Darby v National Trust*.[5]

A fourth way that an occupier can discharge the duty of care to visitors is to engage a reputable contractor to work on the premises. By doing this, the duty will be delegated to the contractor, provided that the requirements of s 2(6)(a) are met; an example of this is *Maguire v Sefton MBC*.[6] The obligation can also include checking that the subcontractor has adequate insurance documentation in place.

Gwilliam v West Hertfordshire Hospitals NHS Trust [2002] EWCA Civ 1041, [2003] QB 443, [12]–[17] (Lord Chief Justice)

12. The next critical issue is whether the hospital discharged this duty. Although the example in s.2(4)(b) is not directly applicable, I have no doubt that the hospital could fulfil its duty if it employed an appropriate, competent, independent contractor. But, on the other hand, if the hospital had not taken the steps which it should, in order to satisfy itself that the contractor was competent, the hospital would not have discharged the duty which it owed to the claimant. In deciding whether the contractor was competent the hospital had to take into account the nature of the task that the contractors, here Club Entertainments, was required to perform. This involved, in this case, being satisfied that Club Entertainments were sufficiently experienced and reliable to be entrusted with ensuring that members of the public would be reasonably safe using the 'splat-wall'.

13. Whether the hospital had taken reasonable steps to satisfy itself as to Club Entertainments's competence depended upon the evidence of Mr Wynne, confirmed as it is by the evidence by Mr Petherick, Mr Cane's expert. The evidence was brief. As to the evidence, the judge stated as follows:

> 'The statement of Mr Wynne and the evidence of Mr Petherick, simply confirmed, in my judgment, the common sense proposition that if you are organising a fete at which equipment is to be used which might lead to a person or persons being injured, it is

5 [2001] EWCA Civ 189.
6 [2006] EWCA Civ 316.

prudent to see to it that the operator of that equipment or the organisers of the fete are covered by insurance against the possibility of a claim. A professional organiser of such an event, such as Mr Wynne, would be under a duty, in my view to his employer to take steps to see that that is done. But that is not at all the same thing as there being a duty upon the event organisers to ensure that there is insurance in force for the benefit of people using the equipment or indeed even a duty to take reasonable steps to see that there is such insurance in force for the benefit of such people. The reason why organisers of fetes and fairs take such insurance is to protect themselves against the possibility of a claim.'

14. I agree with the judge in relation to his common sense proposition that prudence required the position as to the insurance to be checked. However, I consider the judge came to the wrong conclusion about the significance of this. Because the judge had not appreciated that the hospital owed a duty to the claimant under section 2 of the 1957 Act, he did not consider whether the existence of insurance could reflect on Club Entertainments's competence.

15. While Mr Wynne may have been primarily concerned to protect the hospital by taking the action which he did to ensure that insurance was in place, the purpose of the insurance was to meet any claim of the sort which was in fact made by the claimant against the hospital. Mr Wynne realised, as did Mr Petherick, that if you are engaging a small firm like Club Entertainments to provide an entertainment such as the 'splat-wall', it is important that the operators of the equipment should be insured. The fact of insurance would go to their competence. If the firm did not hold themselves out as being insured this would reflect both on their ability to meet any claim and, in addition, suggest that they were unlikely to be a reputable firm which could properly be entrusted with the responsibility of supplying and operating the 'splat-wall'. If the firm carried insurance this enhanced their standing. It also provided protection for those who would be using their equipment. In these circumstances, on the facts of this case (and these issues are fact specific), in the absence of any other credentials, it seems to me that, in order to discharge the common duty of care, Mr Wynne was under an obligation to enquire into the insurance position of Club Entertainments so as to confirm the firm's suitability to be entrusted with the supply and operation of the 'splat-wall'. The firm had been selected from the phone book and Mr Wynne had no information as to their reliability other than what he was told by Mr Cane. To enquire as to whether the firm was insured would be one simple method of checking the firm's suitability. Certainly there is no authority to which we were referred or which I have been able to ascertain that indicates a contrary conclusion.

16. Mr Wynne did enquire as to the insurance position although it is true that he did not ask to see the policy. However, as the judge found, 'Mr Wynne had no reason to believe that insurance was not in force'. This last conclusion is one which I am prepared to accept on the limited evidence called. If the position was to be otherwise, it would involve finding that the hospital would not only be required to inquire into the insurance position, they

would be required to check the terms of the insurance policy. This I would regard as being an unreasonable requirement. It is to be borne in mind that, even if a policy had been produced which indicated that it would be in force on the date of the fair, there could be circumstances which meant that the policy was not one which was enforceable by the claimant. For example, there could have been a breach of the terms by Club Entertainments.

17. In the result, therefore, I consider that the judge came to the right decision, not because there was no duty but because the duty had been fulfilled.

The approach taken in *Gwilliam* regarding insurance has, however, received both academic and judicial criticism.

J Morgan, 'Tort, Insurance and Incoherence' (2004) 67 *MLR* 384

With respect, the reasoning of both Waller LJ and Lord Woolf CJ is open to question. Waller LJ's approach might seem, at first sight, neat and effective. An occupier's duty when employing independent contractors is not to be seen as an all-or-nothing question, involving strict liability where the contractor is engaged to perform ultra-hazardous activities, but merely the ordinary duty to take care in selecting the contractor, where the activities are not ultra-hazardous. Instead there is to be a gradation; a duty to take care that contractors are not only competent but also solvent or insured or both, in the situation of what we might call 'somewhat hazardous activities'. But such a scheme of rarefied nuance lacks all reality. The line between ordinarily hazardous and ultra-hazardous activities has proved quite impossible to draw, a priori, as witness the difficulties of the Court of Appeal in *Salsbury v Woodland*. Introducing a further tier of the 'somewhat hazardous' seems calculated to produce yet further judicial bemusement, and hair-splitting worthy of medieval scholasticism. Of course, the incoherence of this area of the law was painfully exposed by Professor Glanville Williams, who long ago described the theory of the non-delegable duty as one of the leading sophistries of tort law, and a 'logical fraud'. This hardly provides a firm foundation on which to build such a novel extension of the duty of care.

Both Lord Woolf CJ and Waller LJ treat the extension of duty as a modest, incremental development. The Lord Chief Justice, indeed, tries to limit his decision to the facts, drawing the inference that failure to hold themselves out as being insured would mean that the contractors were unlikely to be a reputable firm. Yet Sedley LJ quite rightly emphasizes, in his dissent, the size of the step which has been taken. There is a very significant difference between protecting visitors from physical harm, and protecting them from inability to recover damages for such harm. This was clearly and explicitly appreciated by the Court of Appeal which decided *Van Oppen v Bedford Trustees*, an apparently inconsistent decision to the effect that that a school had no duty to advise parents to insure their sons against personal injuries sustained while playing rugby football. But the crucial distinction is glossed over by Lord Woolf when he denies at the end of his judgment that the claim against the hospital was for economic loss, even though this was how it was treated by the parties in their presentation of the case. His view would seem to be that the hospital's duty was concerned only with the safety of the visitors and not their financial well-being as such, in the event of contractors proving impecunious. This is hard to understand, for the claim would seem to be that the hospital employed uninsured contractors, and not unsafe ones. The duty to check on contractors' liability insurance arises only by asserting a dubious equivalence between impecunious/uninsured contractors, and incompetent/unsafe contractors. Such assumptions are part of an unconvincing attempt to obscure the 'legal and logical distance' identified by Sedley LJ.[7]

Question to consider: Do you think the presence or absence of insurance should have any bearing on liability in negligence at common law or occupiers' liability in statute? If so, what impact would this have on the objectives of the tort as a whole?

Other resources: Jane Stapleton, 'Tort, Insurance and Ideology' (1995) 58 *MLR* 820; *Salsbury v Woodland* [1970] 1 QB 324; *Bottomley v Todmorden Cricket Club* [2003] EWCA Civ 1575; *Naylor v Payling* [2004] EWCA Civ 560; *Glaister v Appleby-in-Westmoreland Town Council* [2009] EWCA Civ 1325.

8.3.5 Can the duty be excluded?

The next question to ask is whether the duty can be excluded. For this, it is crucial to distinguish between a warning, that prevents liability from arising in the first place, and an exclusion, which attempts to exclude any liability which may arise. The ability of the occupier to exclude liability is impacted by another statutory scheme and the general law of contract.

Under s 2(1) of the OLA 1957, occupiers' liability could be excluded with appropriate notice and with very limited common law protections in place. Therefore, any occupier with an understanding of the law or access to lawyers could effectively remove their liability to visitors with appropriately worded exclusion clauses. An example of this was in *White v Blackmore*. In this case the majority of the Court of Appeal (Lord Denning MR dissenting) held that the occupier had effectively excluded its liability by the use of the words 'howsoever caused' on the warning notices which they were entitled to do by s 2(1) of OLA 1957.

7 Footnotes omitted.

White v Blackmore and others [1972] 3 All ER 158, 170–71 (Buckley LJ)

I think that when the deceased came onto the field in the afternoon he did so in a dual capacity, as a prospective competitor and as a spectator. He was not intending to take part in all the races run on that afternoon, and I can feel no doubt that part of his object in attending the meeting was to enjoy watching those races in which he was not a competitor as well as to compete in those races in which he proposed to compete. There was considerable discussion in the course of the argument as to whether this notice was applicable to the deceased. Mr. Griffiths contended that, if he was wrong about a contract having been entered into in the morning, at least a licence was then granted to the deceased to enter the field in the afternoon for the purpose of competing in the races and Mr. Griffiths contended that such licence was irrevocable until the deceased had completed the purpose for which it was granted, that is to say, until he had completed those races in which he proposed to take part. For my part, I think that no licence was granted to the deceased in the morning beyond an implied licence permitting him to leave his jalopy in the pits coupled with a further implied licence allowing him in due course to remove his jalopy from the field. Whether this be right or not, whatever licence was granted to the deceased by the organisers in the morning was, in my judgment, a gratuitous one. It was not, as was suggested, a licence coupled with an interest. It could consequently be revoked or varied by the organisers at any time subject only to the deceased being given a suitable opportunity to remove his property from the field. In the absence of any express term, a revocable licence can be revoked by whatever notice is reasonable in the circumstances (*Winter Garden Theatre (London) Ltd. v. Millennium Productions Ltd.* [1948] A.C. 173, H.L.(E.)). Since, in my view, the deceased had no legal right to insist upon taking part in the races, there is no reason to regard any licence granted to him in the morning as irrevocable until he had completed those races in which he proposed to take part. In the circumstances of this case I think any licence granted to the deceased in the morning was revocable summarily subject only to his right to recover his jalopy. If it was revocable, it was to a like extent variable.

What then was the effect of the situation which arose when the deceased returned to the field in the afternoon? It is clear that the occupier of land, who permits someone else to enter upon that land as his licensee, can by imposing suitable conditions limit his own liability to the licensee in respect of any risks which may arise while the licensee is on the land (*Ashdown v. Samuel Williams & Sons Ltd.* [1957] 1 Q.B. 409). The *Occupiers' Liability Act 1957*, which in section 2 (1) refers to an occupier excluding his duty of care to any visitor 'by agreement or otherwise' has not altered the law in this respect. Mr. Griffiths concedes that in the present case the notice displayed at the entrance to the ground was sufficient to exclude liability on the part of the organisers of the meeting to all spectators properly so-called, but he contends that a distinction is to be drawn between competitors and spectators for this purpose. It is common ground that the deceased was not a ticket holder within the meaning of the notice, but, in my judgment, he was a spectator.

> The judge so held, and I think that he was right in doing so. The notice was, in my opinion, sufficiently explicit in its application to the deceased. I feel unable to accept the suggestion that the heading 'Warning to the Public' should be read in a restrictive sense excluding competitors. Reading the document as a whole, I think there can be no doubt that it was addressed to all persons answering the descriptions of spectators or ticket holders. The deceased was not even a member of the Severn Valley Jalopy Club. He was, in my opinion, a member of the public. The organisers are, I think, shown to have taken all reasonable steps to draw the condition contained in the notice to the attention of the deceased. The judge found that warnings of this character were a common feature at jalopy races with which the deceased would have been familiar. He also found, as I have already said, that the deceased saw this particular notice and appreciated its character. He also found that the deceased saw a number of other notices in identical terms posted about the field and that he appreciated what these notices were intended to effect. I think that he came onto the field in the afternoon upon the terms contained in the notice displayed at the entrance to the ground.
>
> The liability of the organisers of the meeting to visitors attending it for the purpose of taking part in some races and watching others was in my opinion limited to two respects. Such a visitor, in my judgment, as a competitor and when engaged in the role of a competitor, accepted all the risks inherent in the sport of jalopy racing. The organisers owed no duty to him to protect him against those risks. The express warning to the effect that competitors took part in the races at their own risk, which may have been attached to the signing-on sheet, is consequently, in my view, of little importance. As a spectator, such a visitor was, I think, subject to the condition set out in the warning notice. At the time when the accident occurred the deceased was, in my opinion, a spectator. The limitation on the liability of the organisers in these circumstances is to be found in the notice. The condition set out in the notice was that they were to be absolved from all liabilities arising out of accidents causing damage or personal injury howsoever caused. The use of the words 'howsoever caused' makes clear that the absolution was intended to be of a general character. The effect of the condition must, in my judgment, amount to the exclusion of liability for accidents arising from the organisers' own negligence.

This (unarguably unfair) situation continued until the enactment of the Unfair Contract Terms Act 1977 (UCTA 1977) which placed restrictions on the ability to exclude liability. The regime was later changed – and additional protections provided for consumers – with the Consumer Rights Act 2015 (CRA 2015). The ability for an occupier to exclude or restrict liability will therefore be limited by these two pieces of legislation. They do, however, work in different circumstances.

As a result of the different statutes, it is crucial to establish the capacity in which the occupier allows the visitor to access the premises. If it is in the course of business or professional operations, the context will be one of business liability, even if the visitor's purpose is educational or recreational. The significance of this is that under both UCTA 1977 (where both parties are acting in the course of their business) and under the CRA 2015 (where one is acting in the course of a business (a trader) and one a consumer), it is not possible to limit or restrict liability for death or personal injury caused by negligence.

Unfair Contract Terms Act 1977

1 Scope of Part I

(3) ... liability for breach of obligations or duties arising—

(a) from things done or to be done by a person in the course of a business (whether his own business or another's); or

(b) from the occupation of premises used for business purposes of the occupier; ...

> When the relationship is between two entities acting in their business capacities, UCTA 1977 will apply.

2 Negligence liability

(1) A person cannot by reference to any contract term or to a notice given to persons generally or to particular persons exclude or restrict his liability for death or personal injury resulting from negligence.

> The occupier has no ability to exclude liability for personal injury or death of the visitor.

(2) In the case of other loss or damage, a person cannot so exclude or restrict his liability for negligence except in so far as the term or notice satisfies the requirement of reasonableness.

> Other losses, such as property damage, can only be excluded if the term or notice was reasonable.

(3) Where a contract term or notice purports to exclude or restrict liability for negligence a person's agreement to or awareness of it is not of itself to be taken as indicating his voluntary acceptance of any risk.

> Mere knowledge of and agreement to an exclusion clause is not sufficient to find that a person has voluntarily accepted the risk.

Consumer Rights Act 2015

2 Key definitions

(2) 'Trader' means a person acting for the purposes relating to that person's trade, business, craft or profession ...

(3) 'Consumer' means an individual acting for purposes that are wholly or mainly outside that individual's trade, business, craft or profession.

> Where the relationship is between one party acting in its business capacity (referred to as a 'trader' in the 2015 legislation) and another acting as a consumer, the Consumer Rights Act 2015 (CRA) will apply.

62 Requirement for contract terms and notices to be fair

(1) An unfair term of a consumer contract is not binding on the consumer.

(2) An unfair consumer notice is not binding on the consumer.

> Exclusion of other losses, such as property damage, will only be effective if the notice or term is considered 'fair' under the CRA 2015.

The occupier has no ability to exclude liability for personal injury or death of the visitor.

Mere knowledge of and agreement to an exclusion clause is not sufficient to find that a person has voluntarily accepted the risk.

65 Bar on exclusion or restriction of negligence liability

(1) A trader cannot by a term of a consumer contract or by a consumer notice exclude or restrict liability for death or personal injury resulting from negligence.

(2) Where a term of a consumer contract, or a consumer notice, purports to exclude or restrict a trader's liability for negligence, a person is not to be taken to have voluntarily accepted any risk merely because the person agreed to or knew about the term or notice.

(3) In this section 'personal injury' includes any disease and any impairment of physical or mental condition.

(4) In this section 'negligence' means the breach of—

...

(a) the common duty of care imposed by the Occupiers' Liability Act 1957 or the Occupiers' Liability Act (Northern Ireland) 1957, ...

(5) It is immaterial for the purposes of subsection (4)—

(a) whether a breach of duty or obligation was inadvertent or intentional, or

(b) whether liability for it arises directly or vicariously.

8.4 Liability to non-visitors

The OLA 1957 only applies to people entering premises with permission, namely visitors. Under the common law, non-visitors were owed the basic duty of common humanity, which was largely codified by the OLA 1984.

Occupiers' Liability Act 1984

1 Duty of occupier to persons other than his visitors

(3) An occupier of premises owes a duty to another (not being his visitor) in respect of any such risk as is referred to in subsection (1) above if—

(a) he is aware of the danger or has reasonable grounds to believe that it exists;

(b) he knows or has reasonable grounds to believe that the other is in the vicinity of the danger concerned or that he may come into the vicinity of the danger (in either case, whether the other has lawful authority for being in that vicinity or not); and

(c) the risk is one against which, in all the circumstances of the case, he may reasonably be expected to offer the other some protection.

This section outlines a three part test: the occupier needs: (a) to be aware of or have reasonable grounds to know of the danger, (b) to know or have reasonable grounds to believe that people may be in the vicinity, and (c) it is the type of risk that an occupier would reasonably be expected to offer some protection for.

(4) Where, by virtue of this section, an occupier of premises owes a duty to another in respect of such a risk, the duty is to take such care as is reasonable in all the circumstances of the case to see that he does not suffer injury on the premises by reason of the danger concerned.

Once the three part test in s 1(3) is met, the occupier then has an obligation to take such care as is reasonable in the circumstances.

(5) Any duty owed by virtue of this section in respect of a risk may, in an appropriate case, be discharged by taking such steps as are reasonable in all the circumstances of the case to give warning of the danger concerned or to discourage persons from incurring the risk.

However, the obligation can be discharged by an appropriate warning of the danger in question.

(6) No duty is owed by virtue of this section to any person in respect of risks willingly accepted as his by that person (the question whether a risk was so accepted to be decided on the same principles as in other cases in which one person owes a duty of care to another).

(6A) At any time when the right conferred by section 2(1) of the Countryside and Rights of Way Act 2000 is exercisable in relation to land which is access land for the purposes of Part I of that Act, an occupier of the land owes (subject to subsection (6C) below) no duty by virtue of this section to any person in respect of—

(a) a risk resulting from the existence of any natural feature of the landscape, or any river, stream, ditch or pond whether or not a natural feature, or

(b) a risk of that person suffering injury when passing over, under or through any wall, fence or gate, except by proper use of the gate or of a stile.

(6AA) Where the land is coastal margin for the purposes of Part 1 of that Act (including any land treated as coastal margin by virtue of section 16 of that Act), subsection (6A) has effect as if for paragraphs (a) and (b) of that subsection there were substituted 'a risk resulting from the existence of any physical feature (whether of the landscape or otherwise).'

These sections ensure that the OLA 1984 also covers those exercising a right of way under the Countryside and Rights of Way Act 2000. This piece of legislation was passed in an attempt to open up large parts of the countryside to ramblers and recreational walkers. In asking private landowners to gratuitously grant access to their land, it seems more reasonable to subject them to the level of care expected under the 1984 Act.

(6B) For the purposes of subsection (6A) above, any plant, shrub or tree, of whatever origin, is to be regarded as a natural feature of the landscape.

(6C) Subsection (6A) does not prevent an occupier from owing a duty by virtue of this section in respect of any risk where the danger concerned is due to anything done by the occupier—

(a) with the intention of creating that risk, or

(b) being reckless as to whether that risk is created.

(7) No duty is owed by virtue of this section to persons using the highway, and this section does not affect any duty owed to such persons.

Those using the highway are excluded from the OLA 1984; however, ferries and waterways are excluded from the definition of 'highway'.

The OLA 1984 specifically excludes the ability for non-visitors to claim compensation for loss of or damage to property. This is because the legislation is designed to cover the most important basic rights but does not extend to protecting the property of injured parties.

(8) Where a person owes a duty by virtue of this section, he does not, by reason of any breach of the duty, incur any liability in respect of any loss of or damage to property.

(9) In this section –

- 'highway' means any part of a highway other than a ferry or waterway;
- 'injury' means anything resulting in death or personal injury, including any disease and any impairment of physical or mental condition; and
- 'movable structure' includes any vessel, vehicle or aircraft.

The liability to people without permission – non-visitors or 'trespassers' – was left to the common law until the OLA 1984 was passed. This was because of the legal and societal push-back against the idea that someone could be committing a legal wrong (trespass of land) and still have a duty owed to them. This is more of a moral quandary in theory than practice, as many people can 'innocently trespass' (I personally have taken many shortcuts through private land in my time!) and a significant number of the cases involve child trespassers who cannot be expected to understand the geographical or legal boundaries. An example of this is *British Railways Board v Herrington*, where Lord Reid held that there was a duty of care owed to the child trespasser.

British Railways Board v Herrington [1972] 1 All ER 749, 753, 756–57

My Lords, on 7 June 1965 the respondent, then a child of six years old, was playing with other children on National Trust property at Mitcham which is open to the public. Immediately adjoining this property the appellants have an electrified railway line a few yards from the boundary. Their boundary is marked by a fence which, if it had been in good repair, would have sufficed to prevent the respondent from reaching the railway line. But it was in very bad repair so that when the respondent strayed away from his playmates he was able to get through or over it. He then went a few yards farther and came in contact with the live electrified rail. Fortunately he was rescued but he had already sustained severe injury. His age was such that he was unable to appreciate the danger of going on to the railway line and probably unable to appreciate that he was doing wrong in getting over the fence.

I have no doubt that if the appellants owed to potential child trespassers any duty of care to take steps for their safety, they were in breach of any such duty. Enquiry soon after the accident showed that this was by no means the only place where their fence was defective and a well trodden track leading to the point where the respondent got on to their property showed that a considerable number of trespassers must have crossed the line at this point to other National Trust property on the other side. The appellants led no evidence at the trial and it cannot be inferred that they knew about these trespassers before the accident. The only evidence of their knowledge was a report produced by them which showed that they knew that a few weeks before the accident some children had been seen on the line at some point not very far away. But in my view the evidence was sufficient to show either that there was no systematic inspection of their fence or that if there was any system it was not operated or enforced.

...

Child trespassers have for a very long time presented to the courts an almost insoluble problem. They could only be completely safeguarded in one or other of two ways. Either parents must be required always to control and supervise the movements of their young children, or occupiers of premises where they are likely to trespass must be required to take effective steps to keep them out or else to make their premises safe for them if they come. Neither of these is practicable. The former course was practicable at one time for a limited number of well-to-do parents but that number is now small. The latter, if practicable at all, would in most cases impose on occupiers an impossible financial burden.

Legal principles cannot solve the problem. How far occupiers are to be required by law to take steps to safeguard such children must be a matter of public policy.

The OLA 1984 creates limited obligations on occupiers to protect non-visitors, but – as seen from the case law – unless a child is involved, it is very unlikely to have a successful claim under the Act.

8.4.1 Who is a non-visitor?

A non-visitor is someone who does not have permission, implied or express, to be on the premises. This is often referred to as a 'trespasser' but that is not technically correct, as the 1984 Act also covers 'ramblers' and recreational walkers under the Countryside and Rights of Way Act 2000.

It is also possible for the same person to move from being a visitor to being a non-visitor and therefore move from being covered under the OLA 1957 to being covered by the OLA 1984. An example of this was in *Tomlinson v Congleton Borough Council*, where Mr Tomlinson initially entered as a visitor but when he entered the lake to swim against the instructions of the occupier exceeded his authority and became a non-visitor.

Tomlinson v Congleton Borough Council [2003] UKHL 47, [2003] 3 All ER 1122, [7], [8], [11], [13] (Lord Hoffmann)

7. At first Mr Tomlinson claimed that the council was in breach of its common duty of care under section 2(2). His complaint was that the premises were not reasonably safe because diving into the water was dangerous and the council had not given adequate warning of this fact or taken sufficient steps to prevent or discourage him from doing it. But then a difficulty

emerged. The county council, as manager of the park, had for many years pursued a policy of prohibiting swimming or the use of inflatable dinghies or mattresses. Canoeing and windsurfing were allowed in one area of the lake and angling in another. But not swimming; except, I suppose, by capsized canoeists or windsurfers. Notices had been erected at the entrance and elsewhere saying 'DANGEROUS WATER. NO SWIMMING'. The policy had not been altogether effective because many people, particularly rowdy teenagers, ignored the notices. They were sometimes rude to the Rangers who tried to get them out of the water. Nevertheless, it was hard to say that swimming or diving was, in the language of section 2(2), one of the purposes 'for which [Mr Tomlinson was] invited or permitted by the occupier to be there'. The council went further and said that once he entered the lake to swim, he was no longer a 'visitor' at all. He became a trespasser, to whom no duty under the 1957 Act is owed. The council cited a famous bon mot of Scrutton LJ in *The Carlgarth* [1927] P 93, 110: 'When you invite a person into your house to use the staircase, you do not invite him to slide down the banisters'. This quip was used by Lord Atkin in *Hillen v ICI (Alkali) Ltd* [1936] AC 65, 69 to explain why stevedores who were lawfully on a barge for the purpose of discharging it nevertheless became trespassers when they went on to an inadequately supported hatch cover in order to unload some of the cargo. They knew, said Lord Atkin, at pp 69–70, that they ought not to use the covered hatch for this purpose; 'for them for such a purpose it was out of bounds; they were trespassers'. So the stevedores could not complain that the barge owners should have warned them that the hatch cover was not adequately supported. Similarly, says the council, Mr Tomlinson became a trespasser and took himself outside the 1957 Act when he entered the water to swim.

8. Mr Tomlinson's advisers, having reflected on the matter, decided to concede that he was indeed a trespasser when he went into the water. Although that took him outside the 1957 Act, it did not necessarily mean that the council owed him no duty. At common law the only duty to trespassers was not to cause them deliberate or reckless injury, but after an inconclusive attempt by the House of Lords to modify this rule in *Herrington v British Railways Board* [1972] AC 877, the Law Commission recommended the creation of a statutory duty to trespassers: see its Report on Liability for Damage or Injury to Trespassers and Related Questions of Occupiers' Liability (1976) (Law Com No 75) (Cmnd 6428). The recommendation was given effect by the 1984 Act.

...

11. The case has therefore proceeded upon a concession that the relevant duty, if any, is that to a trespasser under section 1(4) of the 1984 Act and not to a lawful visitor under section 2(2) of the 1957 Act. On one analysis, this is a rather odd hypothesis. Mr Tomlinson's complaint is that he should have been prevented or discouraged from going into the water, that is to say, from turning himself into a trespasser. Logically, it can be said, that duty must have been owed to him (if at all) while he was still a lawful visitor. Once he had become a trespasser, it could not have meaningful effect. In the Court of Appeal, ante, p 63f–g, para 52, Longmore LJ was puzzled by this paradox:

> 'At what point does he become a trespasser? When he starts to paddle, intending thereafter to swim? There was no evidence that Mr Tomlinson in fact swam at all. He dived from a position in which swimming was difficult, if not impossible. I would be troubled if the defendants' duty of care differed depending on the precise moment when a swim could be said to have begun.'
>
> ...
>
> 13. As a matter of logic, I see the force of these observations. But I have nevertheless come to the conclusion that the concession was rightly made. The duty under the 1984 Act was intended to be a lesser duty, as to both incidence and scope, than the duty to a lawful visitor under the 1957 Act. That was because Parliament recognised that it would often be unduly burdensome to require landowners to take steps to protect the safety of people who came upon their land without invitation or permission. They should not ordinarily be able to force duties upon unwilling hosts. In the application of that principle, I can see no difference between a person who comes upon land without permission and one who, having come with permission, does something which he has not been given permission to do. In both cases, the entrant would be imposing upon the landowner a duty of care which he has not expressly or impliedly accepted. The 1984 Act provides that even in such cases a duty may exist, based simply upon occupation of land and knowledge or foresight that unauthorised persons may come upon the land or authorised persons may use it for unauthorised purposes. But that duty is rarer and different in quality from the duty which arises from express or implied invitation or permission to come upon the land and use it.

8.4.2 What is the nature of the duty?

To determine the nature of the OLA 1984 duty, two issues must be considered: (a) when will a duty arise, and (b) what is the content of the duty?

The first question is answered by s 1(3)(a)–(c) of the OLA 1984, which states that a duty will be owed when three requirements are met:

(a) the occupier is aware/has reasonable grounds to believe that danger exists;
(b) the occupier knows/has reasonable grounds to believe that the non-visitor will come within the vicinity of danger; and
(c) the risk is one against which, in all the circumstances of the case, the occupier can reasonably be expected to offer the non-visitor some protection.

Even if these requirements are met, there are two key exclusions to be aware of – those using the highway under s 1(7) and all claims for property damage under s 1(8).

The content of the duty is contained in s 1(4), which states that 'the duty is to take such care as is reasonable in all the circumstances of the case to see that [the non-visitor] does not suffer injury on the premises by reason of the danger concerned'. It is therefore a relatively low duty, and the courts have explicitly stated that it does not include an obligation to warn of obvious dangers; see Lord

Hoffmann in *Tomlinson*.[8] What is an obvious risk will, however, depend on the age of the non-visitor as shown in *Keown v Coventry Healthcare NHS Trust*. In this case the claimant was an 11-year-old boy who was injured when he fell from a fire escape. The claim was rejected on a number of bases, including that the injury arose from the claimant's actions and not the state of the premises. The court did, however, accept that when determining what is an 'obvious risk', the age of the non-visitor is relevant.

Keown v Coventry Healthcare NHS Trust [2006] EWCA Civ 39, [2006] 1 WLR 953, [11], [12] (Longmore LJ)

11. These authorities would conclude the question in Mr Porter's favour if the Claimant was an adult. Does it make any difference that the claimant was a child when the accident occurred?

12. The answer is that premises which are not dangerous from the point of view of an adult can be dangerous for a child but it must be a question of fact and degree. In paragraph 46 of *Tomlinson* Lord Hoffmann said that a duty to protect against obvious risks exists only in cases where there was no genuine and informed choice as in the case of some lack of capacity such as the inability of children to recognise danger. Thus injury suffered by a toddler crawling into an empty and derelict house could be injury suffered by reason of a danger due to the state of the premises where injury suffered by an adult in the same circumstances might not be. But it would not be right to ignore a child's choice to indulge in a dangerous activity in every case merely because he was a child. Mr Keown was 11 at the time he decided to climb the fire escape; the judge's finding was (paras. 15 and 42) that he appreciated not only that there was a risk of falling but also that what he was doing was dangerous and that he should not have been climbing the exterior of the fire escape. In these circumstances it cannot be said that Mr Keown did not recognise the danger and it does not seem to me to be seriously arguable that the risk arose out of the state of the premises which were as one would expect them to be. Rather it arose out of what Mr Keown chose to do.

8.4.3 How can the duty be discharged?

The occupier must behave reasonably in relation to non-visitors. There is little guidance provided on what this actually entails, but some general principles can be highlighted. The easier the premises are to access, particularly for children, the more likely the occupier will have a duty to take positive steps to mitigate the risk of harm. Similar to the OLA 1957, the most appropriate and effective way that this duty can be fulfilled is through issuing a warning; this is specifically outlined in s 1(6) of the 1984 Act.

8 [2003] 3 All ER 1122.

Ratcliff v McConnell [1997] EWCA Civ 2679, [1999] 1 WLR 670, [46], [47] (Stuart-Smith LJ)

46. The plaintiff was a very frank witness. The admissions he made in my judgment make it impossible for him to succeed. He had been told expressly by the defendants that the pool was closed and contained dangerous chemicals. He was not drunk, and he knew what he was doing. He deliberately climbed the wall. He did not notice the light. He intended to make a shallow dive. He had a wide knowledge of swimming pools. He knew there was no standard pool and there was no standard depth profile. All pools are different. He knew that diving could be dangerous and that it was necessary to make sure that there was enough water available before diving. He did not know where the variations in depth might be, and did not know whether or where it might be safe to dive. He knew he had to take great care to control the angle of the dive. He knew that alcohol might affect his judgment. He must have dived deeper than he intended. He was aware that access to the pool was prohibited. He did not know what notices were posted in the pool or changing room. He paid no regard to the prohibition of access and was going to do what he wanted anyway. He ignored the notice at the gate, though he saw the word 'Warning,' disregarding the rest of the notice. He did not consider that the water level might be low, as in fact it was. He did not look at any signs and probably would not have read any different signs.

47. In my judgment it is quite plain that the plaintiff was aware of the risk and willingly accepted it. Accordingly, I would hold that the defendants were under no duty towards him. I cannot accept the judge's conclusion that they ought to have told him that he should not dive in the pool because of its configuration. Still less can I accept the judge's conclusion that the defendants should have made it clear, by punishing offenders, that the rule of non-access would be enforced. That goes far beyond discouragement. In any event, so far as is known to the defendants, there were no known abuses in the autumn term, 1994 by students, so I do not understand how they could make an example to discourage the plaintiff. I would add that I am very doubtful whether on the true facts the plaintiff satisfied section 1(3)(b) as to the state of the defendants' knowledge; but I am content for the purpose of this judgment to assume that he did.

Question to consider: Has the law achieved the correct balance between rights of occupiers and rights of non-visitors?

Other resources: R Buckley, 'The Occupiers' Liability Act 1984 – Has Herrington Survived?' (1984) *Conv* 413; M Jones, 'The Occupiers' Liability Act 1984' (1984) *MLR* 713; J Murphy, 'Public Rights of Way and Private Law Wrongs' [1997] *Conv* 362; *Donoghue v Folkstone Properties* [2003] QB 1008; *Swain v Puri* [1996] PIQR P442.

8.5 Conclusion

The duties owed by occupiers to visitors and non-visitors raise a number of interesting, important and sometimes difficult questions regarding the nature of tort law. Whilst this is a subject that is often used for problem question materials in exams, the theoretical and philosophical debates – particularly around duties to trespassers, obligations to protect children, and treatment of the vulnerable – should not be overlooked. The judgments highlight a rich and interesting array of approaches and opinions, providing students with the opportunity to deepen their understanding not only of this area of the law but also general questions on liability and compensation.

Table 8.1: Overview of the Occupiers' Liability Act 1957 and the Occupiers' Liability Act 1984: similarities and differences

Occupiers' Liability Act 1957	Occupiers' Liability Act 1984
Applies to visitors.	Applies to non-visitors (trespassers and those exercising rights to roam).
Premises are 'any fixed or moveable structure'.	Premises are 'any fixed or moveable structure'.
Occupier defined by *Wheat v Lacon.*	Occupier defined by *Wheat v Lacon.*
Covers property damage.	Excludes property damage.
Duty is owed to all visitors.	Duty only owed where the conditions in s 1(3) are satisfied: the occupier knows or has reasonable grounds to believe that the danger exists, knows or has reasonable grounds to believe that the non-visitor might be in the vicinity of danger, and the risk is one which in all the circumstances of the case the occupier could reasonably be expected to guard against.
Duty to all visitors to take such care that the visitor is reasonably safe while using the premises for the purposes for which they are invited.	Duty to non-visitors to take such care as is reasonable in all the circumstances of the case to see that the non-visitor does not suffer injury on the premises.
An occupier can exclude, restrict or modify its duty insofar as it is able, subject to UCTA 1977 and the CRA 2015.	Uncertain: no express provision and no case law. The lack of provision might be a result of the already minimal duty to which the Act gives rise. It may be that Parliament felt that this minimal duty should not be restricted further.

Chapter 9

PRODUCT LIABILITY

9.1 Introduction

When people, particularly students, think of product liability in tort law, they often go straight to the Consumer Protection Act 1987 (CPA 1987). Whilst this is the key piece of legislation in this area of tort law, it must be recognised that there are two other potential routes for recovery of damage caused by a defective product. The first is an implied term of quality in the Sale of Goods Act 1979 and the Consumer Rights Act 2015. The other is through common law negligence for breach of the relevant duty of care. The final one is the CPA 1987, which was designed to create a 'strict liability' regime for defective consumer products. This means that liability can be found without the need to identify a moral wrong. The difference between strict liability and fault liability is outlined by Peter Cane.

P Cane, 'Responsibility and Fault' in P Cane and J Gardner (eds), *Relating to Responsibility* (Hart Publishing, 2001), 100–101

My argument so far is that the distinction between responsibility for fault and strict responsibility turns neither on the role of luck in our lives, nor on the presence or absence of fault. So what is the difference between them? It is this: responsibility for fault rests on a judgment that the responsible person failed to meet a specified standard of conduct, whereas strict responsibility rests on no such judgment. As Honoré puts it, a person may be strictly responsible for their conduct and its consequences even though their conduct was perfectly 'permissible'. Suppose, for instance, that a statute creates liability for selling adulterated food. The liability will be fault-based if it depends on a judgment that the sale of adulterated food was a result of failure by the seller to meet some relevant specified standard of conduct; or that it would not have occurred if the seller had met all relevant specified standards of conduct. Conversely, the liability will be strict if it can be imposed regardless of whether the sale was the result of failure by the seller to meet specified standards of conduct; or of whether it would have occurred if the seller had met all specified standards of conduct. Fault liability is liability for conduct that fails to measure up to relevant specified standards of conduct. Strict liability is liability for conduct regardless of whether it falls short of specified standards of conduct.

It follows that the imposition on shortcomers of responsibility for failure to comply with standards of conduct that they could not meet (because of lack of general competence) is not a form of strict liability. It is fault liability based on a judgment that the shortcomer failed to comply with a specified standard of conduct. The fact that the shortcomer could not have complied is irrelevant to the issue of fault, and raises a different issue about sensitivity to luck. Conversely, strict liability does not depend on a judgment that the person subject to it failed to comply with specified standards of conduct; and so, of course, the issue of whether they could have complied with specified standards of conduct is irrelevant to their liability. If a person unluckily lacks the capacity to comply with required standards of conduct, we may want to relieve them of strict liability as much as of fault liability. This is why, for instance, minimum capacity is a precondition of tort liability for harm, whether fault-based or strict; and why, in Honoré's view, it is a precondition of the fairness of holding a person responsible for the outcomes of their conduct that they were able to understand the concept of responsibility.[1]

When going through this chapter, we encourage you to reflect on the different aspects of the regime and consider whether it could be classified as truly 'strict' product liability.

9.2 Contractual remedies

There are benefits and detriments to the different potential causes of action relevant to product liability. Tort law has a significant number of elements – recognised damage, duty, breach, causation, and remoteness. The CPA 1987 has specific remedies restrictions, including overall cost requirements and a prohibition on claiming for the cost of the damage to the good itself. Therefore, provided that the claimant purchased the product as a consumer and the seller is acting in the course of a business, the simplest approach may be a breach of contract claim, relying on one of the implied terms under the Consumer Rights Act 2015 and the Sale of Goods Act 1979.

Sale of Goods Act 1979

13 Sale by description

(1) Where there is a contract for the sale of goods by description, there is an implied term that the goods will correspond with the description.

14 Implied terms about quality or fitness

(1) Except as provided by this section and section 15 below and subject to any other enactment, there is no implied term about the quality or fitness for any particular purpose of goods supplied under a contract of sale.

(2) Where the seller sells goods in the course of a business, there is an implied term that the goods supplied under the contract are of satisfactory quality.

1 Footnotes omitted.

(2A) For the purposes of this Act, goods are of satisfactory quality if they meet the standard that a reasonable person would regard as satisfactory, taking account of any description of the goods, the price (if relevant) and all the other relevant circumstances.

(2B) For the purposes of this Act, the quality of goods includes their state and condition and the following (among others) are in appropriate cases aspects of the quality of goods—

(a) fitness for all the purposes for which goods of the kind in question are commonly supplied,
(b) appearance and finish,
(c) freedom from minor defects,
(d) safety, and
(e) durability.

(2C) The term implied by subsection (2) above does not extend to any matter making the quality of goods unsatisfactory—

(a) which is specifically drawn to the buyer's attention before the contract is made,
(b) where the buyer examines the goods before the contract is made, which that examination ought to reveal, or
(c) in the case of a contract for sale by sample, which would have been apparent on a reasonable examination of the sample.

15 Sale by sample

(1) A contract of sale is a contract for sale by sample where there is an express or implied term to that effect in the contract.

(2) In the case of a contract for sale by sample there is an implied term—

(a) that the bulk will correspond with the sample in quality;
(b) ...
(c) that the goods will be free from any defect, making their quality unsatisfactory, which would not be apparent on reasonable examination of the sample.

Consumer Rights Act 2015

9 Goods to be of satisfactory quality

(1) Every contract to supply goods is to be treated as including a term that the quality of the goods is satisfactory.

(2) The quality of goods is satisfactory if they meet the standard that a reasonable person would consider satisfactory, taking account of—

(a) any description of the goods,
(b) the price or other consideration for the goods (if relevant), and
(c) all the other relevant circumstances (see subsection (5)).

(3) The quality of goods includes their state and condition; and the following aspects (among others) are in appropriate cases aspects of the quality of goods—

(a) fitness for all the purposes for which goods of that kind are usually supplied;
(b) appearance and finish;
(c) freedom from minor defects;
(d) safety;
(e) durability.

10 Goods to be fit for particular purpose

(3) The contract is to be treated as including a term that the goods are reasonably fit for that purpose, whether or not that is a purpose for which goods of that kind are usually supplied.

11 Goods to be as described

(1) Every contract to supply goods by description is to be treated as including a term that the goods will match the description.

(2) If the supply is by sample as well as by description, it is not sufficient that the bulk of the goods matches the sample if the goods do not also match the description.

9.3 Common law negligence

The cause of action under the Consumer Protection Act 1987 does not displace the common law of negligence; therefore, both causes can arise on the same facts. In fact, in a lot of situations where there is a defective product, there will be an arguable case that some party has breached their duty of care. The quintessential tort law case, *Donoghue v Stevenson*, was about a defective consumer product. Read through the words of Lord Atkin and think about if and how they are relevant to the current challenges of product liability.

Donoghue v Stevenson [1932] AC 562, HL, 11–12 (Lord Atkin)

At present I content myself with pointing out that in English law there must be, and is, some general conception of relations giving rise to a duty of care, of which the particular cases found in the books are but instances. The liability for negligence, whether you style it such or treat it as in other systems as a species of 'culpa,' is no doubt based upon a general public sentiment of moral wrongdoing for which the offender must pay. But acts or omissions which any moral code would censure cannot in a practical world be treated so as to give a right to every person injured by them to demand relief. In this way rules of law arise which limit the range of complainants and the extent of their remedy. The rule that you are to love your neighbour becomes in law, you must not injure your neighbour; and the lawyer's question, Who is my neighbour? receives a restricted reply. You must take reasonable care to avoid acts or omissions which you can reasonably foresee would be likely to injure your neighbour. Who, then, in law is my neighbour? The answer seems to be – persons who are so closely and directly affected by my act that I ought reasonably to have them in contemplation as being so affected when I am directing my mind to the acts or omissions which are called in question.

…

I think that this sufficiently states the truth if proximity be not confined to mere physical proximity, but be used, as I think it was intended, to extend to such close and direct relations that the act complained of directly affects a person whom the person alleged to be bound to take care would know would be directly affected by his careless act. That this is the sense in which nearness of 'proximity' was intended by Lord Esher is obvious from his own illustration in *Heaven v. Pender* of the application of his doctrine to the sale of goods.

…

'This' (i.e., the rule he has just formulated) 'includes the case of goods, etc., supplied to be used immediately by a particular person or persons, or one of a class of persons, where it would be obvious to the person supplying, if he thought, that the goods would in all probability be used at once by such persons before a reasonable opportunity for discovering any defect which might exist, and where the thing supplied would be of such a nature that a neglect of ordinary care or skill as to its condition or the manner of supplying it would probably cause danger to the person or property of the person for whose use it was supplied, and who was about to use it. It would exclude a case in which the goods are supplied under circumstances in which it would be a chance by whom they would be used or whether they would be used or not, or whether they would be used before there would probably be means of observing any defect, or where the goods would be of such a nature that a want of care or skill as to their condition or the manner of supplying them would not probably produce danger of injury to person or property.' I draw particular attention to the fact that Lord Esher emphasizes the necessity of goods having to be 'used immediately' and 'used at once before a reasonable opportunity of inspection.' This is obviously to exclude the possibility of goods having their condition altered by lapse of time, and to call attention to the proximate relationship, which may be too remote where inspection even of the person using, certainly of an intermediate person, may reasonably be interposed. With this necessary qualification of proximate relationship as explained in *Le Lievre v. Gould*, I think the judgment of Lord Esher expresses the law of England; without the qualification, I think the majority of the Court in *Heaven v. Pender* were justified in thinking the principle was expressed in too general terms. There will no doubt arise cases where it will be difficult to determine whether the contemplated relationship is so close that the duty arises. But in the class of case now before the Court I cannot conceive any difficulty to arise. A manufacturer puts up an article of food in a container which he knows will be opened by the actual consumer. There can be no inspection by any purchaser and no reasonable preliminary inspection by the consumer. Negligently, in the course of preparation, he allows the contents to be mixed with poison. It is said that the law of England and Scotland is that the poisoned consumer has no remedy against the negligent manufacturer. If this were the result of the authorities, I should consider the result a grave defect in the law, and so contrary to principle that I should hesitate long before following any decision to that effect which had not the authority of this House. I would point out that, in the assumed state of the authorities, not only would the consumer have no remedy against the manufacturer, he would have none against any one else, for in the circumstances alleged there would be no evidence of negligence against any one other than the manufacturer; and, except in the case of a consumer who was also a purchaser, no contract and no warranty of fitness, and in the case of the purchase of a specific article under its patent or trade name, which might well be the case in the purchase of some articles of food or drink, no warranty protecting even the purchaser-consumer. There are other instances than of articles of food and drink where goods are sold intended to be used immediately by the consumer, such as many forms of goods sold for cleaning purposes, where the same liability must exist. The doctrine supported by the decision below would not only deny a remedy to the consumer who was injured by consuming bottled beer or chocolates poisoned by the negligence of the manufacturer, but also to the user of what should be a harmless proprietary medicine, an ointment, a soap, a cleaning fluid or cleaning powder. I confine myself to articles of common household use, where every one, including the manufacturer, knows that the articles will be used by other persons than the actual ultimate purchaser – namely, by members of his family and his servants, and in some cases his guests. I do not think so in of our jurisprudence as to suppose that its principles are so remote from the ordinary needs of civilized society and the ordinary claims it makes upon its members as to deny a legal remedy where there is so obviously a social wrong.

9.4 Consumer Protection Act 1987

The CPA 1987 constituted the UK's implementation of EU Council Directive 85/374/EEC (the Product Liability Directive). The aim of the Directive was the creation of a scheme to make producers of products strictly liable for any damage caused by defects in those products. Despite the strict liability aims, the inclusion of defences and the UK's implementation of the Directive have diluted the strength of the strict liability approach.

Consumer Protection Act 1987

1 Purpose and construction of Part I

(1) This Part was enacted for the purpose of making such provision as was necessary in order to comply with the product liability Directive and shall be construed accordingly.

(2) In this Part, except in so far as the context otherwise requires—

- 'producer', in relation to a product, means—

(a) the person who manufactured it;

A producer is defined as the party who manufactured, won, or abstracted the product.

(b) in the case of a substance which has not been manufactured but has been won or abstracted, the person who won or abstracted it;

(c) in the case of a product which has not been manufactured, won or abstracted but essential characteristics of which are attributable to an industrial or other process having been carried out (for example, in relation to agricultural produce), the person who carried out that process;

- 'product' means any goods or electricity and (subject to subsection (3) below) includes a product which is comprised in another product, whether by virtue of being a component part or raw material or otherwise; ...

2 Liability for defective products

(1) Subject to the following provisions of this Part, where any damage is caused wholly or partly by a defect in a product, every person to whom subsection (2) below applies shall be liable for the damage.

(2) This subsection applies to—

(a) the producer of the product;

(b) any person who, by putting his name on the product or using a trade mark or other distinguishing mark in relation to the product, has held himself out to be the producer of the product;

(c) any person who has imported the product into the United Kingdom in order, in the course of any business of his, to supply it to another.

(3) Subject as aforesaid, where any damage is caused wholly or partly by a defect in a product, any person who supplied the product (whether to the person who suffered the damage, to the producer of any product in which the product in question is comprised or to any other person) shall be liable for the damage if—

(a) the person who suffered the damage requests the supplier to identify one or more of the persons (whether still in existence or not) to whom subsection (2) above applies in relation to the product;

(b) that request is made within a reasonable period after the damage occurs and at a time when it is not reasonably practicable for the person making the request to identify all those persons; and

(c) the supplier fails, within a reasonable period after receiving the request, either to comply with the request or to identify the person who supplied the product to him.

This provision was inserted by the Consumer Protection Act 1987 (Product Liability) (Modification) Order 2000 (SI 2000/2771) as a result of the BSE ('mad cow' disease) crisis.

This wide definition of 'product' includes any goods, electricity, and products comprised in another product. However, if the producer of a component part can show that the defect in the final product was 'wholly attributable' to the design of the finished product or to compliance with instructions issued by the producer of the finished product, there will be a defence under s 4(1)(f) of the CPA 1987.

This section highlights the need to show causation between the defect and the suffered harm, which is in accordance with standard common law causation principles.

This section emphasises that more than one party can be held liable for the damage as the legislation states 'every person'.

Liability under the CPA 1987 is narrower than the common law, as specific nominate parties are included as opposed to everyone who may owe the claimant a duty of care. However, the combined effect of ss 1(2) and 2 is to maximise the chances of there being an answerable party for the damage caused by a defective product, even if the manufacturer of the product is hard to identify, contact, or pursue; or if the product was not the result of a manufacturing process at all.

Provided that the requirements in ss (3)(a)–(c) are fulfilled, the party who supplied the product can also be held liable for the damage.

> Where a defective product is made up of several component parts, and one of those parts is defective, s 2(5) tells us that the manufacturers of both the end product and the component part will be jointly and severally liable for any damage caused.

(5) Where two or more persons are liable by virtue of this Part for the same damage, their liability shall be joint and several.

3 Meaning of 'defect'

> 'Defect' is defined in relation to the safety that persons are generally entitled to expect from the product. When determining this, the courts should consider the context of damage to the property and the risks of death or personal injury.

(1) Subject to the following provisions of this section, there is a defect in a product for the purposes of this Part if the safety of the product is not such as persons generally are entitled to expect; and for those purposes 'safety', in relation to a product, shall include safety with respect to products comprised in that product and safety in the context of risks of damage to property, as well as in the context of risks of death or personal injury.

> When determining what is and isn't a 'defect', 'all the circumstances shall be taken into account', which indicates a broad and flexible test. However, the CPA 1987 highlights the following specific issues to consider: (a) the manner in which and the purposes for which the product was marketed, (b) what might be reasonably expected to be done with the product, and (c) the time when the product was supplied to the producer.

(2) In determining for the purposes of subsection (1) above what persons generally are entitled to expect in relation to a product all the circumstances shall be taken into account, including—

(a) the manner in which, and purposes for which, the product has been marketed, its get-up, the use of any mark in relation to the product and any instructions for, or warnings with respect to, doing or refraining from doing anything with or in relation to the product;

(b) what might reasonably be expected to be done with or in relation to the product; and

(c) the time when the product was supplied by its producer to another;

and nothing in this section shall require a defect to be inferred from the fact alone that the safety of a product which is supplied after that time is greater than the safety of the product in question.

4 Defences

(1) In any civil proceedings by virtue of this Part against any person ('the person proceeded against') in respect of a defect in a product it shall be a defence for him to show—

> If a defect arises because the defendant has had to comply with a legal obligation, that will be a defence against liability.

(a) that the defect is attributable to compliance with any requirement imposed by or under any enactment or with any assimilated obligation; or

> This indicates that the product was not supplied at all.

(b) that the person proceeded against did not at any time supply the product to another; or

(c) that the following conditions are satisfied, that is to say—

(i) that the only supply of the product to another by the person proceeded against was otherwise than in the course of a business of that person's; and

> The product was not made or supplied in the course of business.

(ii) that section 2(2) above does not apply to that person or applies to him by virtue only of things done otherwise than with a view to profit; or

(d) that the defect did not exist in the product at the relevant time; or

(e) that the state of scientific and technical knowledge at the relevant time was not such that a producer of products of the same description as the product in question might be expected to have discovered the defect if it had existed in his products while they were under his control; or

(f) that the defect—

(i) constituted a defect in a product ('the subsequent product') in which the product in question had been comprised; and

(ii) was wholly attributable to the design of the subsequent product or to compliance by the producer of the product in question with instructions given by the producer of the subsequent product.

(2) In this section 'the relevant time', in relation to electricity, means the time at which it was generated, being a time before it was transmitted or distributed, and in relation to any other product, means—

(a) if the person proceeded against is a person to whom subsection (2) of section 2 above applies in relation to the product, the time when he supplied the product to another;

(b) if that subsection does not apply to that person in relation to the product, the time when the product was last supplied by a person to whom that subsection does apply in relation to the product.

5 Damage giving rise to liability

(1) Subject to the following provisions of this section, in this Part 'damage' means death or personal injury or any loss of or damage to any property (including land).

(2) A person shall not be liable under section 2 above in respect of any defect in a product for the loss of or any damage to the product itself or for the loss of or any damage to the whole or any part of any product which has been supplied with the product in question comprised in it.

(3) A person shall not be liable under section 2 above for any loss of or damage to any property which, at the time it is lost or damaged, is not—

(a) of a description of property ordinarily intended for private use, occupation or consumption; and

(b) intended by the person suffering the loss or damage mainly for his own private use, occupation or consumption.

The defect occurred after the defendant had supplied the product.

The defence under s 4(1)(e) is known as the 'development risk defence' and has been subject to significant controversy alongside an infringement proceeding brought by the European Commission in the European Court of Justice.

The defence applies to suppliers of component parts, providing them with a special defence if the defect was wholly attributable to either the design of the subsequent product or to the producer of the product in question's compliance with instructions given by the producer of the subsequent product.

Claimants can only recover for death, personal injury, or damage to other property caused by the defective product.

Damage to the defective property itself is classified as pure economic loss; therefore, it cannot be recovered under tort (compare with the contractual claims discussed above).

Liability will only arise if the good is supplied for private use and is intended to be used for the claimant's private use, occupation, or consumption. This is because the Directive was aimed to protect the interests of consumers as opposed to commercial parties.

The value of the claim must exceed £275, which was intended to prevent the court from having to deal with very minor claims. However, despite the Act being passed in 1987, the figure has not changed. It would be worth approximately £740 in 2024.

(4) No damages shall be awarded to any person by virtue of this Part in respect of any loss of or damage to any property if the amount which would fall to be so awarded to that person, apart from this subsection and any liability for interest, does not exceed £275.

(5) In determining for the purposes of this Part who has suffered any loss of or damage to property and when any such loss or damage occurred, the loss or damage shall be regarded as having occurred at the earliest time at which a person with an interest in the property had knowledge of the material facts about the loss or damage.

(6) For the purposes of subsection (5) above the material facts about any loss of or damage to any property are such facts about the loss or damage as would lead a reasonable person with an interest in the property to consider the loss or damage sufficiently serious to justify his instituting proceedings for damages against a defendant who did not dispute liability and was able to satisfy a judgment.

(7) For the purposes of subsection (5) above a person's knowledge includes knowledge which he might reasonably have been expected to acquire—

(a) from facts observable or ascertainable by him; or

(b) from facts ascertainable by him with the help of appropriate expert advice which it is reasonable for him to seek;

but a person shall not be taken by virtue of this subsection to have knowledge of a fact ascertainable by him only with the help of expert advice unless he has failed to take all reasonable steps to obtain (and, where appropriate, to act on) that advice.

In order to bring a claim under the CPA 1987, the claimant must establish that the product in question is defective, and that the defect has caused the relevant loss. This can be broken up into the following issues:

(1) what a product is;
(2) what damage is;
(3) who can be classified as a 'producer';
(4) what a 'defect' is; and
(5) the defences under the CPA 1987

The first three are largely covered by the statute; therefore, you should refer to the annotated CPA 1987 above. However, the final two are significantly more complicated and justify a more detailed analysis and consideration of the relevant case law and academic literature.

9.4.1 What is a defect?

The test of whether there is a defect in the product for the purposes of the CPA 1987 is linked to safety and based on the idea of 'what persons generally are entitled to expect' in terms of safety. This may appear straightforward, but there has been significant academic debate and arguably conflicting case law about what this means in practice. The nature of the product in question must be considered: some products – blow torches, acids, chainsaws – are inherently dangerous; it does not automatically mean that they are defective. The question is not 'is the product safe?' but 'is the product as safe as persons are generally entitled to expect?'

Examples of cases where products were not found defective are *Richardson v LRC Products Ltd*[2] and *Worsley v Tambrands Ltd.*[3] In the former case, a condom split during intercourse causing pregnancy and in the latter a tampon caused toxic shock syndrome. In both cases the court held that in light of the circumstances as a whole, including the relevant warnings, the products were not less safe than people are generally entitled to expect. Therefore, they were not defective and the actions failed. A similar approach was taken in *Tesco Stores Ltd v Pollard*, where a 13-month-old child was injured after eating dishwashing powder sold in a bottle with a child-resistant (but not child-proof) cap.

Tesco Stores Ltd v Pollard [2006] EWCA Civ 393, (2006) 103(17) LSG 23, [15]–[18] (Laws LJ)

15. It will at once be observed that the meaning of 'defect' in the sub-section is not given, or informed, by any cross-reference to any other provisions (such as the British Standard regime) which impose precise objective requirements which have to be met for safety purposes. The test is, and is only, 'what persons generally are entitled to expect'. Certainly, Section 2(3) requires all the circumstances to be taken into account, including the particular matters set out at (a)–(c). Mr Briden submitted that in the present case, and given evidence to which he points to the effect that a CRC was advisedly put onto this bottle design for safety reasons, the terms of Section 3 suffice to import the British Standard torque measure into the content of general public expectation. On the facts, I understand him to say that the dishwasher product in the bottle, being an 'irritant at the severe end of the spectrum' fell just short of giving rise to a mandatory requirement for a CRC under provisions which I need not cite.

16. In developing this argument Mr Briden at first submitted that the public were entitled to expect that the product in question would function in accordance with whatever safety standard might in the particular case be imposed by any relevant public authority. I apprehend that he appreciated this was a step too far, since there is no trace of any reference to the British Standard on the bottle, packaging or get up of this product, and no reason to suppose that members of the public such as Mrs P would have appreciated that

2 (2000) 59 BMLR 185.
3 [1999] EWHC 273 (QB).

any public authority had pronounced upon the matter. Accordingly Mr Briden refined his submission, and ultimately his argument was that under the statute the public are entitled to expect that the product will function to the full extent of the design standard to which it was manufactured. In the present case that meant the same as compliance with the British Standard torque measure.

17. If Mr Briden is right, it means that every producer of a product whose use causes injury effectively warrants to the general public that the product fulfils its design standards. Now, the producer may have no contract with any member of the public, as here, the appellants did not. Members of the public – purchasers like Mrs P – are unlikely to have the faintest idea to what safety standard the product they are buying has been designed, if it has been designed to any. In my judgment Mr Briden's arguments in truth demand a radical rewriting of the statute. They are an attempt to confer on purchasers and users of everyday products a right to sue the product's producers as if there were a contractual warranty as to the safety standard to which the product had been designed. It is quite impossible to get such a result out of the terms of the 1987 Act.

18. What, on the facts here, were 'persons generally entitled to expect' of the safety features of this cap and bottle? In my judgment they were entitled to expect that the bottle would be more difficult to open than if it had an ordinary screwtop. Anything more specific, as a test of public expectation, runs into the difficulties which I have just described. Here, the bottle was more difficult to open than an ordinary screwtop, though not as difficult as it would have been if the British Standard torque measure had been complied with. There was, in my judgment, no breach of the 1987 Act.

Students (and in fact, academics and lawyers!) often struggle to understand why courts find products defective in some cases but not in others. In some cases, the courts have taken a strict approach to the definition of 'defective' that appears to conflict with other cases. An example of this is *Abouzaid v Mothercare (UK) Ltd*, where a 12-year-old boy was injured in the eye trying to strap a sleeping cover to a buggy. Despite the defendant showing that there were no reports of any such accidents, the product was held to be defective.

Abouzaid v Mothercare (UK) Ltd [2000] All ER (D) 2436, CA, [22]–[27] (Pill LJ)

22. In my judgment the case turns on whether there was in the product a defect as defined in section 3 of the Act and Article 6 of the Directive. As the ECJ confirmed in *Commission v United Kingdom*, the statute must be interpreted 'in the light of the wording and the purpose of the Directive so as to achieve the result which it has in view' (paragraph 38 of judgment). The product is to be judged by the standard persons generally are entitled to expect in all the circumstances. In the words of the preamble to the Directive, the

defectiveness of the product should be determined 'by reference not to its fitness for use but to the lack of the safety to which the public at large are entitled to expect'.

...

24. The respondent's case, as accepted by the judge, can be put very simply. The risk arises from the propensity of elastic to spring back. If in the circumstances, that constituted a defect in 1999, it was equally a defect in 1990.

25. Subject to their point under section 4(1)(e), the appellants' reliance upon the passage of time is in my judgment misplaced. The product is to be judged by the expectations of the public at large, as determined by the Court. It is rightly not suggested that public expectations have changed between 1990 and 1999. Elasticated products have been in use for many years and there is no suggestion of any relevant technical advances which might reasonably affect the expectations of members of the public. The court is required to set the standard on the basis of the evidence and all the circumstances.

26. In my view, the judge's comment upon the reasoning of Dr Hayward was justified. I should add that, when preparing his report, Dr Hayward did not have guidance, by way of decided cases, upon the relevance of time in the statutory context. The nature of the defect, if there was a defect, is not such that its existence can depend on the passage of time between 1990 and 1999. The time factor spelt out in section 3(2)(c) as a circumstance to be taken into account has no bearing upon the decision on the present facts.

27. I have come to the conclusion that, though the case is close to the borderline, the product was defective within the meaning of the Act. The risk is in losing control of an elastic strap at a time when it is stretched and eyes are in the line of recoil. The product was defective because it was supplied with a design which permitted the risk to arise and without giving a warning that the user should not so position himself that the risk arose. Members of the public were entitled to expect better from the appellants. A factor in that expectation is the vulnerability of the eye and the serious consequences which may follow from a blunt injury to the eye. Expectations would be different if the worst which could occur was an impact of elastic on the hand. It is not necessary for the Court to determine precisely what more should have been done. It is clear that more could have been done, for example a non-elasticated method of attachment or instructions to fasten the straps from behind the seat unit, together with a warning.

This strict liability approach continued in *A v National Blood Authority*, where Burton J held that the hepatitis-infected blood was a defective product under the CPA 1987. He came to this conclusion despite the fact that at the time of the transfusions, there was no effective test available to distinguish between blood that had been infected with Hepatitis C and blood that had not.

A v National Blood Authority [2001] 3 All ER 289, QBD, [55]–[58] (Burton J)

55. I do not consider it to be arguable that the consumer had an actual expectation that blood being supplied to him was not 100% clean, nor do I conclude that he had knowledge that it was, or was likely to be, infected with Hepatitis C. It is not seriously argued by the Defendants, notwithstanding some few newspaper cuttings which were referred to, that there was any public understanding or acceptance of the infection of transfused blood by Hepatitis C. Doctors and surgeons knew, but did not tell their patients unless asked, and were very rarely asked. It was certainly, in my judgment, not known and accepted by society that there was such a risk, which was thus not *sozialadäquat* (socially acceptable), as Professor Taschner and Count von Westphalen would describe such risks: Taschner/ Riesch *Produkthaftungsgesetz und EG Produkthaftungsrichtlinie* [2nd edn at 291] and von Westphalen loc. cit. at 27. Thus blood was not, in my judgment, the kind of product referred to in the Flesch/Davenant Question and Answer in the European Parliament i.e., '*... a product which by its very nature carries a risk and which has been presented as such (instructions for use, labelling, publicity, etc.)*', '*... risks which are ... inherent in [a] product and generally known*': nor as referred to by Professor Howells (loc. cit.) at 1.17 as being risks which '*consumers can be taken to have chosen to expose themselves to in order to benefit from the product*'.

56. I do not consider that the legitimate expectation of the public at large is that legitimately expectable tests will have been carried out or precautions adopted. Their legitimate expectation is as to the safeness of the product (or not). The Court will act as what Dr Bartl called the *appointed representative of the public at large*, but in my judgment it is impossible to inject into the consumer's legitimate expectation matters which would not by any stretch of the imagination be in his actual expectation. He will assume perhaps that there are tests, but his expectations will be as to the safeness of the blood. In my judgment it is as inappropriate to propose that the public should not 'expect the unattainable' – in the sense of tests or precautions which are impossible – at least unless it is informed as to what is unattainable or impossible, as it is to reformulate the expectation as one that the producer will not have been negligent or will have taken all reasonable steps.

57. In this context I turn to consider what is intended to be included within '*all circumstances*' in Article 6. I am satisfied that this means all relevant circumstances. It is quite plain to me that (albeit that Professor Stapleton has been pessimistic about its success) the Directive was intended to eliminate proof of fault or negligence. I am satisfied that this was not simply a legal consequence, but that it was also intended to make it easier for claimants to prove their case, such that not only would a consumer not have to prove that the producer did not take reasonable steps, or all reasonable steps, to comply with his duty of care, but also that the producer did not take all legitimately expectable steps either. In this regard I note paragraph 16 of the Advocate General's Opinion in Commission v UK at 487 where, in setting out the background to the Directive, he pointed out that:

> 'Albeit injured by a defective product, consumers were in fact and too often deprived of an effective remedy, since it proved very difficult procedurally to prove negligence on the part of the producer, that is to say, that he failed to take all appropriate steps to avoid the defect arising.'
>
> 58. The Court of Justice in its judgment perhaps refers implicitly to this when it states at paragraph 24:
>
> *'In order for a producer to incur liability for defective products under art 4 of the directive, the victim must prove the damage, the defect and the causal relationship between defect and damage, but not that the producer was at fault.'*
>
> It seems to me clear that, even without the full panoply of allegations of negligence, the adoption of tests of avoidability or of legitimately expectable safety precautions must inevitably involve a substantial investigation. What safety precautions or tests were available or reasonably available? Were they tests that would have been excessively expensive? Tests which would have been more expensive than justified the extra safety achieved? Are economic or political circumstances or restrictions to be taken into account in legitimate expectability? Once it is asserted that it is legitimately expectable that a certain safety precaution should have been taken, then the producer must surely be able to explain why such was not possible or why he did not do it; in which case it will then be explored as to whether such tests would or could have been carried out, or were or would have been too expensive or impracticable to carry out. If risk and benefit should be considered, then it might be said that, the more beneficial the product, the lower the tolerable level of safety; but this could not be arrived at without consideration as to whether, beneficial or not, there would have nevertheless been a safer way of setting about production or design.

Burton J made the important distinction between standard and non-standard products (or 'lemons'). This distinction is significant, for example, when dealing with products that are inherently dangerous, like a chainsaw, and those that create a risk simply because they are poorly produced, like flammable children's clothes. The defendants argued that the bags of blood were standard products since they all carried the same risk of being infected with Hepatitis C. This argument was rejected, and Burton J held that they were non-standard as they contained pathogens. Even if they had been standard products, the risks attributable to them should only be borne by users if and when they were known to those users. As a result of this decision, it was easier to establish that a non-standard product was defective. The distinction was, however, significantly criticised in *Wilkes v DePuy International Ltd* in a case brought by a person whose hip replacement fractured after three years.

Wilkes v DePuy International Ltd [2016] EWHC 3096 (QB), [2018] QB 627, [77]–[80], [90]–[94] (Hickinbottom J)

77. The circumstances which are relevant in a particular case is itself a matter of law; but it is to be noted that neither the Directive nor the Act imposes any restriction on the considerations that may be taken into account. The three specific matters set out in section [3(2)] are circumstances which must be considered ('... shall be taken into account ...'); but they are clearly not intended to be an exhaustive list of relevant circumstances, nor are they such that any other circumstance, to be relevant, must be shown to be *eiusdem generis*.

78. There has been a great deal of consideration, before me and in the cases and the academic texts, as to the circumstances which are or are not relevant, and therefore can or cannot be taken into account. However, by whatever criteria 'acceptability' is gauged, assessment of whether the safety of a product is at an acceptable level requires a holistic approach (see paragraphs 13–15 above), involving the application of judgment to the exercise of balancing all relevant considerations. Given the wide range of products (and their intended use) to which the Directive and Act apply, the court must maintain a flexible approach to the assessment of the appropriate level of safety, including which circumstances are relevant and the weight to be given to each, those factors being quintessentially dependent upon the particular facts of any case. That was the intention – and, certainly, the effect – of the Directive ...

79. Accordingly, whilst over time cases may indicate which characteristics may be relevant in particular sets of circumstances (e.g. where the product is a prescription-only medicine), in my view, any attempt at formal rigid categorisation of products for these purposes is in conflict with the inherent flexibility of the Directive, and is likely to be both difficult and unwise. The issue raised by the Act in terms of defect is necessarily one of open-textured judgment, untrammelled by any rigid rules outside the few that appear in the Act itself. It is noteworthy that the Act implements the Directive, which applies to ensure, amongst other things, that competition in respect of the supply of goods is fair across Europe; and so it would be wrong for domestic law to distort the balance of risk-bearing between producers and consumers of products set by the Directive. The Act, reflecting the Directive, simply requires consideration of whether, at the time the producer first put the product into circulation, that product did or did not have the level of safety that persons generally are entitled to expect (in the sense that I have described), taking into account all relevant circumstances including those set out in section 3(2). Like other such questions raised in the law, on the particular facts of a specific case, the assessment may be difficult in practice; but it is conceptually simple. In my view the courts should guard against either over-complicating, or over-analysing, the exercise.

80. Before me, the following circumstances came under particular scrutiny:

i) risk-benefit;
ii) the 'avoidability' (or 'non-avoidability') of the defect;
iii) whether the product is 'standard' or 'non-standard', in accordance with the distinction drawn by Burton J in *A v NBA* (see paragraph 56(ii) above);
iv) the compliance (or non-compliance) with appropriate standards;
v) the compliance (or non-compliance) with any relevant regime under which the product is regulated; and
vi) warnings and other IFU, and the role of any intermediary. ...

Hickinbottom J considered these factors. When discussing the 'standard'/'non-standard' distinction, he stated:

90. Section 2(a), (b) and (c) of the United States Third Restatement on Products Liability classifies defects by reference to traditional types, namely manufacturing, design and warnings; and, as Burton J indicated in *A v NBA* at [39], in the United States, 'there is almost a separate jurisprudence for manufacturing defects as opposed to design defects'.

91. The Directive singularly does not seek to impose this taxonomy; and, at [39], Burton J, noting that to be the case, said that he considered 'there is no place for [these American terms] in the Directive'. He continued:

> '... I am satisfied, and indeed neither Counsel contended to the contrary, that no assistance can be gained from what Mr Underhill [Counsel for the defendants] called the "boxing", or categorisation, of defects in this regard for the purpose of construction of the Directive, or the determination of any of the issues before me ....'

92. Nevertheless, he proceeded to identify two categories of product, namely 'standard' and 'non-standard'. He defined them in the following way (at [36]):

> '... [A] standard product is one which is and performs as the producer intends. A non-standard product is one which is different, obviously because it is deficient or inferior in terms of safety, from the standard product: and where it is the harmful characteristic or characteristics present in the non-standard product, but not in the standard product, which has or have caused the material injury or damage.'

93. In Burton J's view, this categorisation, at least to an extent, then determines the approach to the circumstances which bear upon the definition of 'defect' (see [68]–[73]). For example, as I have said (see paragraph 87 above), Burton J expressly excluded the relevance of risk-benefit in the case of a non-standard product, whereas he appeared to consider that that might be properly relevant in the case of a standard product.

94. In my respectful view, the categorisation of defects into 'standard'/'non-standard', as a classification, is unnecessary and undesirable. It is not, of course, a classification deriving from the Directive or Act. In my judgment, whether a particular product is within the

producer's specification, and is compliant with relevant standards (see paragraphs 97–98 below), may be relevant circumstances in relation to whether the level of safety is that to which persons generally are entitled to expect; but to raise the distinction to a rigid categorisation is positively unhelpful and potentially dangerous.

Question to consider: Can the decisions of *A v National Blood Authority* and *Wilkes v DePuy* be reconciled? If so, how? If not, which decision do you prefer and why?

Other resources: D Nolan, 'Strict Product Liability for Design Defects' (2018) 134 *LQR* 176–81; J Eisler, 'One Step Forward and Two Steps Back in Product Liability: The Search for Clarity in the Identification of Defects' (2017) 76(2) *CLJ* 230–33; J Stapleton, 'Bugs in Anglo-American Product Liability' in D Fairgrieve (ed), *Product Liability in Comparative Perspective* (CUP, 2005), 295; *Gee v DePuy International Ltd* [2018] EWHC 1208 (QB); D Fairgrieve and G Howells, 'Rethinking Product Liability: A Missing Element in the European Commission's Third Review of the European Product Liability Directive' (2007) 70 *MLR* 967; *Bogle v McDonald's Restaurants Ltd* [2002] EWHC 490 (QB).

9.4.2 Relevant defences under the CPA 1987

The CPA has a range of defences under s 4. The majority of these defences are uncontroversial and, therefore, explained in the annotated statute above. However, the 'development risk defence' under s 4(1)(e) requires a more detailed analysis, as it has been a controversial and fought-over defence in the United Kingdom. The wording of the defence in the CPA 1987 was the subject of infringement proceedings brought by the European Commission in the European Court of Justice in *Commission v United Kingdom*. The Product Liability Directive allowed states to include a defence that protects producers from liability if they can show 'that the state of scientific and technical knowledge at the time when he put the product into circulation was not such as to enable the existence of the defect to be discovered'. The Commission argued that the wording of s 4(1)(e) was broader and, therefore, the UK had not correctly implemented the Directive. This claim was not successful, and the ECJ made a number of helpful observations in the product.

Case C-300/95 *Commission v United Kingdom* [1997] ECR I-2663, paras 25–39

25. Several observations can be made as to the wording of Article 7(e) of the Directive.

26. First, as the Advocate General rightly observes in paragraph 20 of his Opinion, since that provision refers to 'scientific and technical knowledge at the time when [the producer]

put the product into circulation', Article 7(e) is not specifically directed at the practices and safety standards in use in the industrial sector in which the producer is operating, but, unreservedly, at the state of scientific and technical knowledge, including the most advanced level of such knowledge, at the time when the product in question was put into circulation.

27. Second, the clause providing for the defence in question does not contemplate the state of knowledge of which the producer in question actually or subjectively was or could have been apprised, but the objective state of scientific and technical knowledge of which the producer is presumed to have been informed.

28. However, it is implicit in the wording of Article 7(e) that the relevant scientific and technical knowledge must have been accessible at the time when the product in question was put into circulation.

29. It follows that, in order to have a defence under Article 7(e) of the Directive, the producer of a defective product must prove that the objective state of scientific and technical knowledge, including the most advanced level of such knowledge, at the time when the product in question was put into circulation was not such as to enable the existence of the defect to be discovered. Further, in order for the relevant scientific and technical knowledge to be successfully pleaded as against the producer, that knowledge must have been accessible at the time when the product in question was put into circulation. On this last point, Article 7(e) of the Directive, contrary to what the Commission seems to consider, raises difficulties of interpretation which, in the event of litigation, the national courts will have to resolve, having recourse, if necessary, to Article 177 of the EC Treaty.

30. For the present, it is the heads of claim raised by the Commission in support of its application that have to be considered.

31. In proceedings brought under Article 169 of the Treaty the Commission is required to prove the alleged infringement. The Commission must provide the Court with the information necessary for it to determine whether the infringement is made out and may not rely on any presumption (see, in particular, Case C-62/89 *Commission v France* [1990] ECR I-925, paragraph 37).

32. The Commission takes the view that inasmuch as section 4(1)(e) of the Act refers to what may be expected of a producer of products of the same description as the product in question, its wording clearly conflicts with Article 7(e) of the Directive in that it permits account to be taken of the subjective knowledge of a producer taking reasonable care, having regard to the standard precautions taken in the industrial sector in question.

33. That argument must be rejected in so far as it selectively stresses particular terms used in section 4(1)(e) without demonstrating that the general legal context of the provision at issue fails effectively to secure full application of the Directive. Taking that context

into account, the Commission has failed to make out its claim that the result intended by Article 7(e) of the Directive would clearly not be achieved in the domestic legal order.

34. First, section 4(1)(e) of the Act places the burden of proof on the producer wishing to rely on the defence, as Article 7 of the Directive requires.

35. Second, section 4(1)(e) places no restriction on the state and degree of scientific and technical knowledge at the material time which is to be taken into account.

36. Third, its wording as such does not suggest, as the Commission alleges, that the availability of the defence depends on the subjective knowledge of a producer taking reasonable care, having regard to the standard precautions taken in the industrial sector in question.

37. Fourth, the Court has consistently held that the scope of national laws, regulations or administrative provisions must be assessed in the light of the interpretation given to them by national courts (see, in particular, Case C-382/92 *Commission v United Kingdom* [1994] ECR I-2435, paragraph 36). Yet in this case the Commission has not referred in support of its application to any national judicial decision which, in its view, interprets the domestic provision at issue inconsistently with the Directive.

38. Lastly, there is nothing in the material produced to the Court to suggest that the courts in the United Kingdom, if called upon to interpret section 4(1)(e), would not do so in the light of the wording and the purpose of the Directive so as to achieve the result which it has in view and thereby comply with the third paragraph of Article 189 of the Treaty (see, in particular, Case C-91/92 *Faccini Dori v Recreb* [1994] ECR I-3325, paragraph 26). Moreover, section 1(1) of the Act expressly imposes such an obligation on the national courts.

39. It follows that the Commission has failed to make out its allegation that, having regard to its general legal context, especially section 1(1) of the Act, section 4(1)(e) clearly conflicts with Article 7(e) of the Directive. As a result, the application must be dismissed.

Question to consider: If the purpose of the CPA 1987 is to be a strict liability regime for products, is there any justification for the development risks defence?

Other resources: C Hodges, 'Development Risks: Unanswered Questions' (1998) 61 *MLR* 560; M Mildred and G Howells, 'Comment on "Development Risks: Unanswered Questions"' (1998) 61 *MLR* 570; *A v National Blood Authority*; P Cane, 'Responsibility and Fault' in P Cane and J Gardner (eds), *Relating to Responsibility* (Hart Publishing, 2001), 100.

9.5 Limitations

Claims under the CPA 1987 receive special attention in terms of the limitations of actions.

> **Limitation Act 1980**
>
> **11A Actions in respect of defective products**
>
> (1) This section shall apply to an action for damages by virtue of any provision of Part I of the Consumer Protection Act 1987.
>
> (2) None of the time limits given in the preceding provisions of this Act shall apply to an action to which this section applies.
>
> (3) An action to which this section applies shall not be brought after the expiration of the period of ten years from the relevant time, within the meaning of section 4 of the said Act of 1987; and this subsection shall operate to extinguish a right of action and shall do so whether or not that right of action had accrued, or time under the following provisions of this Act had begun to run, at the end of the said period of ten years.
>
> (4) Subject to subsection (5) below, an action to which this section applies in which the damages claimed by the plaintiff consist of or include damages in respect of personal injuries to the plaintiff or any other person or loss of or damage to any property, shall not be brought after the expiration of the period of three years from whichever is the later of—
>
> (a) the date on which the cause of action accrued; and
>
> (b) the date of knowledge of the injured person or, in the case of loss of or damage to property, the date of knowledge of the plaintiff or (if earlier) of any person in whom his cause of action was previously vested.

The section creates a 'long-stop' period of 10 years *after the product was put into circulation*. This means that after the expiration of the 10-year period, the right of action is 'extinguished'.

The consequence of this section is that actions for personal injuries and property damage caused by defective products must be brought within three years of the cause of action accruing. 'Accruing' for these purposes means either when the damage is caused, or when it becomes reasonably discoverable by the claimant.

It should be noted that the 'long-stop' period of 10 years under s 11A(3) is unusual, as it does not operate to bar the remedy, but the actual right of action is extinguished. It stops the courts from being able to grant a discretionary extension to the limitation period and has some arguably unfair outcomes for vulnerable claims, an example of which was seen in *O'Byrne v Aventis Pasteur MSD Ltd*.[4]

4 [2010] UKSC 23, [2010] 1 WLR 1412.

9.6 Future of product liability

The final issue to consider is the future of product liability laws, specifically if and how the CPA 1987 would apply to technological developments, particularly software and AI. Like so many things in tort law, the answer is far from clear, and it is an area in desperate need of legislative reform, as we have outlined elsewhere.

Jodi Gardner and Sarah Green, 'Continuing the Product Liability Illusion' in Burns and others (eds), *Tort Law on Three Continents: Honouring Jane Stapleton* (OUP, 2024 forthcoming)

As the previous section has highlighted, the definition of 'defective' has caused political, legal, and social difficulties. This challenge continued and, in fact, deepened when technological developments, particularly software and AI, came onto the consumer market. The Council Directive and CPA were drafted before these types of technologies were appreciated, and in many cases before they were even envisioned. Product liability for new and emerging technologies, and the aim of ensuring that consumers can have recourse to compensation if harmed by products, has in some quarters become an important political issue. In September 2022, the European Commission introduced the draft Artificial Intelligence Liability Directive. This Directive proposal aims to 'adapt private law to the needs of the transition to the digital economy', by which it means making it more likely that consumers will be able to recover compensation when they suffer damage as a result of AI-based products. This was prompted, at least in part, by the increasing difficulty of fitting AI-based products within the established strict liability regime, as a result of scientific and technological developments.

The product liability for medical instruments is something that has drawn particular policy-based attention and analysis. In 2021 for example, the Medicines and Healthcare products Regulatory Agency ran a public consultation on the future regulation of medical products, and the Government's response to the results was published in June 2022. After consultation with multiple stakeholders, including healthcare professionals, manufacturers of medical devices, members of the public, patients, trade associations and businesses, the Government determined that further regulation was required in relation to medical products, particularly the supply and implantation of medical devices. In a similar vein, the Secretary of State for Health and Social Care announced the Equity in Medical Devices Independent Review in November 2021, chaired by Dame Margaret Whitehead. The call for evidence for this review closed in October 2022 and the panel had aimed to provide their advice to the Government in June 2023. At the time of writing, however, no further developments appear to have occurred.

There are also larger changes in the pipeline, all of which suggest a broad political and social desire for increased focus on strict liability for consumer products. From 13 December 2023, a new key instrument – the General Product Safety Regulation (GPSR) – will be implemented in the EU to provide a complete product safety legal framework. The key impetus for the GPSR is to 'increase the protection of EU consumers against dangerous non-food products sold offline or online'. As a result of Brexit, UK consumers will unfortunately not benefit directly from this development. This means that whilst their European counterparts will enjoy increased consumer protection in relation to products, UK consumers will be left behind; something that will only be exacerbated by the impact of the DePuy cases.

There are now several reasons to see consumers in the UK as being in an increasingly unfavourable position when it comes to product liability. First is the apparent trend towards a generally more fault-based approach under the CPA, as set out above. Second is the increasing use of AI and software-based products that are probably out of the remit of the CPA in any event. The final reason is the current deficit in protection afforded to consumers in the UK when compared with that provided in the EU. AI and software-based products, such as automated vehicles for example, have already reinvigorated calls for strict liability. Given the essential novelty of the law having to cater for non-human decision making, and the potential for autonomous products to cause extensive harm to both users and third parties, it is unsurprising that policy arguments in favour of allocating risk to the best-placed insurer have so far won out. Producers of decision-making software are, after all, in a better position than users of that software to evaluate and price the risks of its not behaving according to expectations. Those producers also have much more control over the way in which the software is designed, and in how it operates, than do its consumers.

And yet it is far from clear that such AI and software-based products would be covered by the current (ostensibly stricter than negligence) regime of the CPA in any event. The meaning of 'product' in the CPA has not been considered by a UK court. The courts have however interpreted the meaning of 'goods' under the Sale of Goods Act 1979, the Commercial Agents (Council Directive) Regulations 1993, and at common law. The reasoning in these cases is relevant to the current discussion because 'product' is defined in the CPA by reference to 'goods' ….

After a consideration of the relevant case law on this point, the authors conclude by arguing that 'the UK should follow the EU's lead in reviewing the product liability regime so that it is fit for purpose when applied to AI and software-based products'.

9.7 Conclusion

Product liability in the United Kingdom can occur in three different ways: contractual claims, common law negligence, and through the CPA 1987. This chapter has largely focused on the third process, outlining the background, aims and complexities of this interesting but complicated tort. Whilst it is often labelled as 'strict' liability, it is arguable that the defences under s 4 and the case law interpreting the definition of 'defective' have watered down the strictness of the CPA 1987 regime. Whether or not this is justified and appropriate is a matter of personal opinion. However, it is clear that the legislation, as it is currently positioned, is inadequate to respond to future challenges associated with technological developments, particularly software and AI.

Chapter 10 NUISANCE AND THE RULE IN *RYLANDS v FLETCHER*

10.1 Introduction

This chapter focuses on a range of torts generally designed to protect interests in land. Despite being a 'tort', the actions considered in this chapter are completely different from the tort of negligence and have different rules, aims and remedies. Specifically, the key remedy is an injunction, as those with an interest in land will generally want the interference to stop as opposed to receiving compensatory damages. There is also a gendered component to this topic, as the protection – at least under private nuisance – is limited to those who have an interest in land, which can prevent spouses and children from making a claim. While the key tort of this chapter is private nuisance, the torts of the rule in *Rylands v Fletcher*, public nuisance, and trespass to land will also be briefly discussed. This provides helpful context and a general overview of the land-based torts, and it is important to keep the similarities and differences (not just to private nuisance but to other causes of action considered in this book) in mind when going through the relevant principles.

10.2 Private nuisance

The first tort that will be considered is private nuisance, which responds to the unreasonable interference with the claimant's use and enjoyment of their land. Therefore, it requires a balancing of the interests of different parties, often neighbouring landowners.

10.2.1 What is private nuisance?

To have a successful claim in private nuisance, it has to be shown that (a) the party has title to sue and (b) there has been unreasonable interference with their use and enjoyment of their land.

First, does the claimant have the title to sue in private nuisance? The test here is not the negligence 'duty of care' but whether there is an interest in the land, as highlighted by the majority of the House of Lords in *Hunter v Canary Wharf Ltd*. An impact of this is that private nuisance is not available to remedy personal injuries, as that damage is not related to the claimant's interest in the land. The remedy, as will be discussed further below, is designed to respond to the harm caused to the individual's use and enjoyment of their land.

Hunter v Canary Wharf Ltd [1997] AC 655, HL, 687–88 (Lord Goff), 702–3 (Lord Hoffman), 712–14, 718 (Lord Cooke)

In this case, it was confirmed that claimants must have an 'interest in the land' to have standing to sue in private nuisance.

[Lord Goff at 687–88] I turn next to the question of the right to sue in private nuisance. In the two cases now under appeal before your Lordships' House, one of which relates to interference with television signals and the other to the generation of dust from the construction of a road, the plaintiffs consist in each case of a substantial group of local people. Moreover, they are not restricted to householders who have the exclusive right to possess the places where they live, whether as freeholders or tenants, or even as licensees. They include people with whom householders share their homes, for example as wives or husbands or partners, or as children or other relatives. All of these people are claiming damages in private nuisance, by reason of interference with their television viewing or by reason of excessive dust.

Judge Havery held that the right to sue in private nuisance did not extend to include so wide a class of plaintiffs, but was limited to those with a right to exclusive possession of the relevant property. His decision on this point was however reversed by the Court of Appeal who, in the judgment delivered by Pill L.J., held (see [1996] 2 W.L.R. 348, 365):

> 'A substantial link between the person enjoying the use and the land on which he or she is enjoying it is essential but, in my judgment, occupation of property, as a home, does confer upon the occupant a capacity to sue in private nuisance.'

Against that decision, the defendants in both actions now appeal to your Lordships' House.

The basic position is, in my opinion, most clearly expressed in Professor Newark's classic article on *The Boundaries of Nuisance* in (1949) 65 L.Q.R. 480, when he stated (at p. 482) that the essence of nuisance was that 'it was a tort to land. Or to be more accurate it was a tort directed against the plaintiff's enjoyment of rights over land ...' The historical origin of the tort lay in the fact that (see p. 481):

> 'Disseisina, transgressio and nocumentum [nuisance] covered the three ways in which a man might be interfered with in his rights over land. Wholly to deprive a man of the opportunity of exercising his rights over land was to disseise him, for which he might have recourse to the assize of novel disseisin. But to trouble a man in the exercise of his rights over land without going so far as to dispossess him was a trespass or a nuisance according to whether the act was done on or off the plaintiff's land.'

Later, when distinguishing cases of personal injury, he stated (at pp. 488–489):

> 'In true cases of nuisance the interest of the plaintiff which is invaded is not the interest of bodily security but the interest of liberty to exercise rights over land in the amplest manner. A sulphurous chimney in a residential area is not a nuisance because it makes

householders cough and splutter but because it prevents them taking their ease in their gardens. It is for this reason that the plaintiff in an action for nuisance must show some title to realty.'

Finally, he proclaimed four theses which should be nailed to the doors of the Law Courts and defended against all comers. The first was that:

> 'The term "nuisance" is properly applied only to such actionable user of land as interferes with the enjoyment by the plaintiff of rights in land.'

There are many authoritative statements which bear out this thesis of Professor Newark. I refer in particular to *Sedleigh-Denfield v. O'Callagan* [1940] AC 880, 902–903, *per* Lord Wright; *Read v. Lyons* [1947] AC 156, 183, *per* Lord Simonds; *Tate & Lyle Ltd. v. Greater London Council* [1983] 2 AC 509, 536–537, *per* Lord Templeman; *Fleming, The Law of Torts*, 8th ed. (1992), p. 416.

Since the tort of nuisance is a tort directed against the plaintiff's enjoyment of his rights over land, an action of private nuisance will usually be brought by the person in actual possession of the land affected, either as the freeholder or tenant of the land in question, or even as a licensee with exclusive possession of the land (see *Newcastle-under-Lyme Corporation v. Wolstanton Ltd.* [1947] Ch. 92, 106–108, *per* Evershed J.); though a reversioner may sue in respect of a nuisance of a sufficiently permanent character to damage his reversion.

[Lord Hoffmann at 702–3] The question raised by the preliminary issue is: who can sue? In order to answer this question, it is necessary to decide what exactly he is suing for. Since these questions are fundamental to the scope of the tort of nuisance, I shall deal with them first.

Up to about twenty years ago, no one would have had the slightest doubt about who could sue. Nuisance is a tort against land, including interests in land such as easements and profits. A plaintiff must therefore have an interest in the land affected by the nuisance. In *Sedleigh-Denfield v. O'Callaghan* [1940] AC 880, Lord Wright said:

> 'I do not attempt any exhaustive definition of that cause of action. But it has never lost its essential character which was derived from its prototype, the assize of nuisance, and was maintained under the form of action on the case for nuisance. The assize of nuisance was a real action supplementary to the assize of novel disseisin. The latter was devised to protect the plaintiff's seisin of his land, and the former aimed at vindicating the plaintiff's right to the use and enjoyment of his land. The assize became early superseded by the less formal procedure of an action on the case for nuisance, which lay for damages. This action was less limited in its scope, because whereas the assize was by a freeholder against a freeholder, the action lay also between possessors or occupiers of land. With possibly certain anomalous exceptions, not here material, possession or occupation is still the test.'

In speaking of 'possession or occupation' Lord Wright was in my view intending to refer both to a right to possession based upon (or derived through) title and to de facto occupation. In each case the person in possession is entitled to sue in trespass and in nuisance. …

Lord Cooke took a different approach, and commented that people who are occupying a home (spouses, children, family members) should also have standing.

[Lord Cooke at 712–14, 718] Private nuisance is commonly said to be an interference with the enjoyment of land and to be actionable by an occupier. But 'occupier' is an expression of varying meanings, as a perusal of legal dictionaries shows. Compare, for instance, *Paterson v. Gas Light and Coke Co* [1896] 2 Ch 476, 482; *Regina v. Tao* [1977] Q.B. 141; *Street v. Mountford* [1985] AC 809. In the latter case the expression was used as a neutral one covering either a tenancy or a licence but it was held that, generally speaking, exclusive possession for a fixed or periodic term at a stated rent carries a tenancy. Your Lordships' House does not appear to have been called on hitherto to lay down precisely the meaning to be given to the expression in relation to interference with the amenities of land. There is a dictum by Lord Simonds in *Read v. J. Lyons & Co. Ltd* [1947] AC 156, 183, restricting a lawful claim in nuisance to he who has suffered an invasion of some proprietary or other interest in land; but it was obiter and not focused on interference with amenities. Where interference with an amenity of a home is in issue there is no a priori reason why the expression should not include, and it appears natural that it should include, anyone living there who has been exercising a continuing right to enjoyment of that amenity. Even this would not be exhaustive, as a defendant may not be able to set up the jus tertii against a de facto possessor: see two passages to that effect in *Foster v. Warblington Urban Council* [1906] 1 KB 648 quoted respectively by Clement J.A. in *Motherwell v. Motherwell* (1976) 73 D.L.R. (3d) 62, 77–78, and by Lord Goff of Chieveley in the present case. A temporary visitor, however, someone who is 'merely present in the house' (a phrase used by Fletcher Moulton L.J. in *Malone v. Laskey* [1907] 2 KB 141, 154), would not enjoy occupancy of sufficiently substantial nature.

…

The status of children living at home is different and perhaps more problematical but, on consideration, I am persuaded by the majority of the Court of Appeal in *Khorasandjian v. Bush* [1993] QB 727 and the weight of North American jurisprudence to the view that they, too, should be entitled to relief for substantial and unlawful interference with the amenities of their home. Internationally the distinct interests of children are increasingly recognised. The United Nations Convention on the Rights of the Child, ratified by the United Kingdom in 1991 and the most widely ratified human rights treaty in history, acknowledges children as fully-fledged beneficiaries of human rights. Article 16 declares inter alia that no child shall be subjected to unlawful interference with his or her home and that the child has the right to the protection of law against such interference. International standards such as this may be taken into account in shaping the common law.

The point just mentioned can be taken further. Article 16 of the Convention on the Rights of the Child adopts some of the language of Article 12 of the Universal Declaration of Human Rights and Article 8 of the European Convention for the Protection of Human Rights and Fundamental Freedoms (1953) (Cmd. 8969). These provisions are aimed, in part, at protecting the home and are construed to give protection against nuisances: see *Arrondelle v. United Kingdom*, Application No. 7889/77 (1982) 26 D.R.5 F. Sett. (aircraft noise) and *Lopez Ostra v. Spain* (1994) 20 E.H.R.R. 277 (fumes and smells from a waste treatment plant). The protection is regarded as going beyond possession or property rights: see *Harris, O'Boyle and Warbrick, Law of the European Convention on Human Rights* (1995), p. 319. Again I think that this is a legitimate consideration in support of treating residence as an acceptable basis of standing at common law in the present class of case.

...

Other resident members of the family, including such de facto partners and lodgers as may on the particular facts fairly be considered as having a home in the premises, could therefore be allowed standing to complain of truly serious interference with the domestic amenities lawfully enjoyed by them. By contrast, the policy of the law need not extend to giving a remedy in nuisance to non-resident employees in commercial premises. The employer is responsible for their welfare. On this part of the case I have only to add that normally there should not be any difficulty about sensible compromises with the author of the nuisance. Members of a household impliedly authorise the householder to represent them in such matters.

Question to consider: Do you agree that standing in private nuisance should be limited to people who have an adequate interest in the land? If so, how do you define 'interest in land'? If not, what test would you use instead?

Other resources: *Malone v Laskey* [1907] 2 KB 141, CA; *Khorasandjian v Bush* [1993] QB 727, CA; European Convention on Human Rights, Article 8(1).

The second question to consider is what amounts to unreasonable interference. When determining whether there has been unreasonable interference, it is important to consider the specifics of the land interest in question. There is no limit on what can and should be considered, but there are six key areas to take into account:

(1) *Duration and extent* – the longer the interference continues and/or the higher the level, the more likely it will be unreasonable.[1]

(2) *Time of day* – the more anti-social the time of day of the interference, the more likely it will be unreasonable.[2]

1 *Andreae v Selfridge & Co Ltd* [1938] Ch 1, CA.

2 *De Keyser's Royal Hotel v Spicer Bros* (1914) 30 TLR 257, ChD.

(3) *Locality* – the nature of the locality can have an impact on what is considered unreasonable. However, there is some complicated case law on this issue – discussed further below – and the locality is only relevant when the damage is intangible.
(4) *Motivation* – creating an interference with malicious intent will be a very strong indication that the interference is an unreasonable one.[3]
(5) *Interference with a right* – the defendant's activity must interfere with an established right of the claimant's.[4]
(6) *Claimant's hypersensitivity* – hypersensitivity remains an important consideration in establishing whether an interference has been unreasonable; however, recent case law has taken a more nuanced approach, as will be discussed below.

10.2.1.1 LOCALITY CASES

Thesiger LJ famously declared in *Sturges v Bridgman* that '[w]hat would be a nuisance in *Belgrave Square* would not necessarily be so in *Bermondsey*'.[5] The locality principle means that what is reasonable in one location, for instance, in terms of noise, fumes or smells, might be unreasonable in another. This is not an independent consideration but has a bearing on how other elements of an interference are evaluated, as shown by the Supreme Court in *Lawrence v Fen Tigers Ltd*.

Lawrence v Fen Tigers Ltd [2014] UKSC 13, [2014] AC 822, [59]–[63], [68]–[71] (Lord Neuberger)

59. The assessment of the character of the locality for the purpose of assessing whether a defendant's activities constitute a nuisance is a classic issue of fact and judgment for the judge trying the case. Sometimes, it may be difficult to identify the precise extent of the locality for the purpose of the assessment, or the precise words to describe the character of the locality, but any attempt to give general guidance on such issues risks being unhelpful or worse.

60. However, such questions can give rise to points of principle on which an appellate court can give guidance. Thus, the concept of 'the character' of the locality may be too monolithic in some cases, and a better description may often be something like 'the established pattern of uses' in the locality.

61. In this case, the ground on which the Court of Appeal overturned the judge's decision was that he had wrongly failed to take into account the respondents' activities at the stadium and the track when considering the character of the locality. The appellants contend that the judge was right to disregard those activities.

---

3 *Southwark LBC v Tanner* [2001] 1 AC 1, HL; *Christie v Davey* [1893] 1 Ch 316; *Hollywood Silver Fox Farm Ltd v Emmet* [1936] 2 KB 468.

4 *Bradford Corp v Pickles* [1895] AC 587, HL.

5 (1879) 11 Ch D 852, CA, 865 (Thesiger LJ).

62. The issue therefore is whether, and if so to what extent, the use to which the defendant actually puts his property can or should be relied on when assessing the character of the locality for the purpose of assessing whether the claimant has made out her case that those activities constitute a nuisance.

63. It seems clear that the character of the locality must be assessed by reference to the position as it is as a matter of fact, save to the extent that any departure from reality, or artificial assumption, should be made as a matter of logic or legal requirement (the presumption of reality). Accordingly, in a nuisance claim, I accept that one starts, as it were, with the proposition that the defendant's activities are to be taken into account when assessing the character of the locality.

...

68. The respondents rely on the fact that the activities carried on at the Stadium and the Track had been going on for many years before the judge made his assessment of the character of the neighbourhood. As Jackson LJ put it [2012] 1 WLR 2127, paras 69, 72, these activities were 'an established feature, indeed a dominant feature, of the locality' and 'one of the noise characteristics of the locality' by the time that the appellants brought their claim. However, in so far as those activities were being carried on unlawfully, for instance because they give rise to a nuisance to the claimants making the nuisance claim, they should not be taken into account when assessing the character of the locality, whether they have been going on for a few days or many years.

69. Of course, once the nuisance has been going on for 20 years, the position may be different, as the respondents may well have obtained a right to cause what would otherwise be a nuisance. I should perhaps add that if a defendant's actual activities have been held to be a nuisance by the court, but the court has then decided to refuse an injunction and award damages instead, then, whether or not the activities can be described as 'lawful', it would in my view be proper to take them into account as part of the character of the locality: they have effectively been sanctioned by the court.

70. I do not consider that this conclusion is inconsistent with the reasoning of the Court of Appeal in *Rushmer v Polsue & Alfieri Ltd* [1906] 1 Ch 234; affirmed [1907] AC 121. In my view, the brief opinion of Lord Loreburn LC [1907] AC 121, 122–123 encapsulates the effect of the judgments of Stirling and Cozens-Hardy LJJ in the Court of Appeal, namely that: (i) whether an activity gives rise to a nuisance may depend on the character of the particular locality; (ii) the trial judge rightly directed himself as to the law; and (iii) there was no reason to think that he had not applied his own directions to the facts of the case (and I think that the rather discursive judgment of Vaughan Williams LJ is to much the same effect). The only relevant point for present purposes which I can discern from the reasoning of the Court of Appeal is that an activity can be a nuisance even if it conforms to the character of the locality – a point

made by all three members of the court, perhaps most clearly by Cozens-Hardy LJ [1906] 1 Ch 234, 250–251. But that is entirely consistent with the above analysis.

71. It must be acknowledged, however, that there appears to be an element of circularity in the notion that, when assessing the character of the locality, one has to ignore the defendant's activities if, or to the extent that, they constitute a nuisance, given that the point one is ultimately seeking to decide is whether the defendant's activities amount to a nuisance. However, it seems to me that there should be no real problem in this connection. In many cases, it is fairly clear whether or not a defendant's activities constitute a nuisance once one has established the facts, and nice questions as to the precise identification of the locality or its character do not have to be addressed. In those cases where the precise character of the locality is of importance, the point should not cause much difficulty either. In this case, for example, the question for the judge was the extent to which the noise levels from the Stadium and the Track were or would be acceptable in what was a sparsely populated area, with a couple of small villages and a military airfield between a mile and two miles away, and he answered it by taking the noise levels at other well-established racing circuits elsewhere in the country.

However, it should be noted that tangible interference can never be justified by the nature of the locality: *St Helen's Smelting Co v Tipping*.[6]

10.2.1.2 HYPERSENSITIVITY CASES

Precedent from both the United Kingdom[7] and Canada[8] held that an interference would not be a nuisance because its level of interference had an unreasonable effect simply by virtue of the claimant's particular sensitivity.

However, the approach was questioned in *Network Rail Infrastructure Ltd v Morris*, where the defendant's railway line interfered with the claimant's use of sensitive recording equipment in his studio. The defendant appealed against its liability in nuisance, arguing that the extent of the interference on these facts was from the claimant's hypersensitivity and that it could not have been reasonably foreseen that such damage would occur to this claimant as a result of its operations. The Court of Appeal allowed the appeal, taking a broader approach than the traditional inquiry into hypersensitivity, preferring instead to look at foreseeability as an element of reasonableness.

6 (1865) 11 ER 1483, HL.

7 *Robinson v Kilvert* (1889) 41 ChD 88, CA.

8 *McKinnon Industries Ltd v Walker* [1951] JCJ No 7.

Network Rail Infrastructure Ltd v Morris [2004] EWCA Civ 172, [2004] Env LR 41, [13]–[16], [19] (Lord Phillips MR)

13. The type of private nuisance with which this action is concerned is identified by *Clerk & Lindsell* 18th ed. para.19-06 as 'unduly interfering with his neighbour in the comfortable and convenient enjoyment of his land'. The authors go on to make the following commentary at para 19-11:

> 'A nuisance of this kind, to be actionable, must be such as to be a real interference with the comfort or convenience of living according to the standards of the average man. An interference which alone causes harm to something of abnormal sensitiveness does not of itself constitute a nuisance. A man cannot increase the liabilities of his neighbour by applying his own property to special uses, whether for business or for pleasure.'

14. The authority cited in relation to 'abnormal sensitiveness' is *Robinson v Kilvert* (1889) 41 ChD 88. The relevant issue in that case was whether a landlord, who remained in occupation of a cellar, was liable in nuisance to his tenant, who had leased the premises above for use as a paper warehouse. The landlord had heated the cellar to an extent that resulted in the transmission of heat to the premises above, to the detriment of the tenant's stocks of brown paper, which were particularly sensitive to heat. In the leading judgment at p. 94, Cotton LJ said:

> 'It would, in my opinion, be wrong to say that the doing something not in itself noxious is a nuisance because it does harm to some particular trade in the adjoining property, although it would not prejudicially affect any ordinary trade carried on there, and does not interfere with the ordinary enjoyment of life. Here it is shewn that ordinary paper would not be damaged by what the Defendants are doing, but only a particular kind of paper, and it is not shewn that there is heat such as to incommode the workpeople on the Plaintiff's premises. I am of the opinion, therefore, that the Plaintiff is not entitled to relief on the ground that what the Defendants are doing is a nuisance.'

Lindley LJ gave a judgment to similar effect. Lopes LJ at p. 97 agreed. He said:

> 'I think the Plaintiff cannot complain of what is begin done as a nuisance. A man who carries on an exceptionally delicate trade cannot complain because it is injured by his neighbour doing something lawful on his property, if it is something which would not injure anything but an exceptionally delicate trade.'

15. A similar statement was made by Lord Robertson, giving the advice of the Privy Council in *Eastern and South African Telegraph Company Limited v Cape Town Tramways* [1902] AC 381 in a context closer to that of this appeal. The case concerned a claim based on *Rylands v Fletcher* by the owners of a submarine cable in respect of interference caused to the transmission of messages by the escape of electricity from the defendants' tramway system. The majority of the claim was in respect of expensive remedial measures that had to be taken to prevent the interference. ...

16. The Recorder held that the principle in *Robinson v Kilvert* did not apply to the facts of this case. He held that whether the interference complained of by Mr Morris was capable of constituting a nuisance depended upon whether 'playing the guitar with an amplifier is an important incident of ordinary enjoyment of property'. In this context he had already observed that 'the use of sensitive electric and electronic equipment is so much a feature of modern life that such use cannot be disregarded'. He went on to hold:

> 'I accept that it may not be thought especially important, but it is certainly an ordinary incident of the enjoyment of property. It is the stuff of many young people's pleasure, and is a major part of modern music making'.

Accordingly, he concluded that the electromagnetic interference emitted onto Mr Morris' premises was capable of being a nuisance.

...

19. ... If the authorities to which we have referred in paragraphs 13 to 15 above remain good law, they would lead us to the conclusion that the amplified guitars which were affected by the magnetic field created by Railtrack's installations fell into the category of extraordinarily sensitive equipment which did not attract the protection of the law of nuisance. The evidence to which we are about to turn indicates that the interference suffered by Mr Morris as a result of the use of the TI 21 track circuits was a very rare occurrence indeed. As Buxton LJ's judgment demonstrates, however, the law of nuisance has moved on. If resort must be had to it in order to resolve the competing claims of users of electrical or electronic equipment, the balance may fall to be struck by considering what is reasonable. One thing seems clear, however. Foreseeability is a vital ingredient in the tort of negligence – see *Cambridge Water Co. v Eastern Counties Leather PLC* [1994] 2 AC 264. It was, in this case, common ground that Railtrack could only be liable in nuisance if they should reasonably have foreseen that, by installing the TI 21 track circuits they would cause damage to someone in the position of Mr Morris.

10.2.2 Remedies for private nuisance

Unlike most other torts, the default remedy for private nuisance is an injunction to stop the interference as opposed to the award of damages. The starting point is that, if the claimant can prove private nuisance, an injunction will be awarded unless there is some justification for damages instead. However, this does raise a number of complexities, particularly in cases where there has been planning permission granted for the action creating the nuisance. This situation was discussed by Lord Sumption in *Lawrence v Fen Tigers Ltd.*

Lawrence v Fen Tigers Ltd [2014] UKSC 13, [2014] AC 822, [155]–[161] (Lord Sumption)

155. It is, I think, worth pointing out that the question what impact the grant of planning permission should have on liability in tort for private nuisance and the question what remedies should be available for a nuisance are closely related. They both raise a broader issue of legal policy of some importance, namely how is one to reconcile public and private law in the domain of land use where they occupy much the same space?

156. I agree with Lord Neuberger that the existence of planning permission for a given use is of very limited relevance to the question whether that use constitutes a private nuisance. It may at best provide some evidence of the reasonableness of the particular use of land in question. But planning authorities are concerned with the public interest in development and land use, as that interest is defined in the planning legislation and any relevant development plans and policies. Planning powers do not exist to enforce or override private rights in respect of land use, whether arising from restrictive covenants, contracts, or the law of tort. Likewise, the question whether a neighbouring landowner has a right of action in nuisance in respect of some use of land has to be decided by the courts regardless of any public interest engaged.

157. What saves, or could save the law from anomaly and incoherence is the court's discretion as to remedies. An injunction is a remedy with significant side-effects beyond the parties and the issues in the proceedings. Most uses of land said to be objectionable cannot be restrained by injunction simply as between the owner of that land and his neighbour. If the use of a site for (say) motocross is restrained by injunction, that prevents the activity as between the defendant and the whole world. Yet it may be a use which is in the interest of very many other people who derive enjoyment or economic benefits from it of precisely the kind with which the planning system is concerned. An injunction prohibiting the activity entirely will operate in practice in exactly the same way as a refusal of planning permission, but without regard to the factors which a planning authority would be bound to take into account. The obvious solution to this problem is to allow the activity to continue but to compensate the claimant financially for the loss of amenity and the diminished value of his property. In a case where planning permission has actually been granted for the use in question, there are particularly strong reasons for adopting this solution. It is what the law normally provides for when a public interest conflicts with a proprietary right.

158. The main question, as it seems to me, is not whether the judge in deciding on the appropriate remedy should take account of the public interest or, more generally, of interests which are not before the court. He will usually lack the information to do so effectively, and is in danger of stepping outside his main function of deciding the issue between the parties. The main question is whether the current principles of law governing the availability of injunctions are consistent with the public interest reflected in the successive and increasingly elaborate legislative schemes of development control which have existed in England since 1947.

159. The ordinary principle is that the court does not grant an injunction in a case where there is an adequate legal remedy. In particular, it does not do so where damages would be an adequate remedy. Where an injunction is granted, it is usually because the injury to the claimant is 'irreparable', in the sense that money cannot atone for it. However, this principle has never been consistently followed in cases of nuisance. The leading case is *Shelfer v City of London Electric Lighting Co* [1895] 1 Ch 287 which created a strong presumption in favour of an injunction, to be displaced only in the four narrowly defined categories identified by A L Smith LJ, at pp 322–323. The exceptions applied only to cases where the injury to the claimant was small and the grant of an injunction would be oppressive. In *Colls v Home and Colonial Stores Ltd* [1904] AC 179, 192 Lord Macnaghten wondered why an injunction should be granted 'when substantial damages would be given at law', and there were subsequent attempts to widen the discretion. But the courts have not taken the hint. In *Regan v Paul Properties Ltd* [2007] Ch 135 and *Watson v Croft Promosport Ltd* [2009] 3 All ER 249, the Court of Appeal have reverted to substantially the same position as the Court of Appeal in *Shelfer* more than a century before.

160. The courts might have defended the special treatment of nuisance by pointing to the traditional attitude of equity to land as being unique, an approach which is exemplified in its willingness to grant specific performance of contracts for the sale of land. From this, it might have been concluded that paying the claimant enough to buy a comparable property elsewhere where there was no nuisance was not equivalent to letting him use his existing land free of the nuisance.

…

161. The whole jurisprudence in this area will need one day to be reviewed in this court. There is much to be said for the view that damages are ordinarily an adequate remedy for nuisance and that an injunction should not usually be granted in a case where it is likely that conflicting interests are engaged other than the parties' interests. In particular, it may well be that an injunction should as a matter of principle not be granted in a case where a use of land to which objection is taken requires and has received planning permission. However, at this stage, in the absence of argument on these points, I can do no more than identify them as calling for consideration in a case in which they arise.

However, if there is a social utility in the nuisance continuing, the claimant can be awarded compensatory damages as opposed to an injunction. This recognises that there is an actionable tort interfering with the claimant's rights but that these rights must be balanced against the rights of others. An example of this is *Dennis v Ministry of Defence*.

Dennis v Ministry of Defence [2003] EWHC 793 (QB), [2003] 2 EGLR 121, [44]–[48] (Buckley J)

44. What is the effect of a public interest in an activity continuing, where that activity would otherwise constitute a nuisance? It seems to me that it would be unsatisfactory to attempt a general answer. It will depend on all the circumstances, not least the strength of the public interest in question. If public interest can be a relevant consideration, one solution would be that the particular public interest should be put in the scales at the stage when the court is seeking to balance the competing interests of the parties. As the cases indicate, very often the private interest will prevail. The alternative approach would be to exclude any public interest from consideration of whether a nuisance should be found and consider it as relevant only to remedy.

45. Where there is a real public interest in a particular use of land, I can see no objection in principle to taking that public interest into account, in one way or another, in deciding what is best to be done. Indeed, in effect that happens at present where use is authorised by statute. A recent example is *Marcic v. Thames Water Utilities Ltd.* [2002] EWCA Civ 64, [2002] QB 929. Manifestly a nuisance existed in *Marcic*. Plainly there is a public interest in the continuing operation of sewers and statute recognises that. The common law contribution is to ensure that the operator exercises reasonable care in pursuing its undertaking. The result is that, if due care is exercised, the nuisance continues. The public interest prevails, provided no more damage is done than is reasonably necessary. See also *Allen v. Gulf Oil Refining Ltd.* [1981] AC 1001. The difference in the instant case is that it is left to the common law to provide the answer, no statutory framework is present to assist. However, the public interest in question here, albeit very different, may be considered just as important, if not more so. It could also be thought that the MOD's position, charged as it is with the defence of the realm, should be no less protected than commercial or other undertakings authorised directly by statute.

46. The problem with putting the public interest into the scales when deciding whether a nuisance exists, is simply that if the answer is no, not because the claimant is being over sensitive, but because his private rights must be subjugated to the public interest, it might well be unjust that he should suffer the damage for the benefit of all. If it is to be held that there is no nuisance, there can be no remedy at common law. As this case illustrates, the greater the public interest, the greater may be the interference. If public interest is considered at the remedy stage and since the court has a discretion, the nuisance may continue but the public, in one way or another, pays for its own benefit. The court in *Marcic* was not called upon to make that decision. It was applying the law to an undertaking being pursued with statutory authority and simply holding that the undertaking should be carried on with all due care. However, the comments in paragraphs 111 et seq suggest that it might have favoured the second option, or at least an option that gives effect to public interest but at the public expense, particularly if the common law is to develop consistently with European decisions involving human rights. Allowing a human rights claim but denying a remedy in nuisance would, of course, be another solution, but it would be one that

reflected adversely on the flexibility of the common law. I fear neither Lord Loreburn nor Lord Halisbury would have approved of such an outcome: see *Polsue* at 123.

47. The principles or policy underlying these considerations are that public interest should be considered and that selected individuals should not bear the cost of the public benefit. I am in favour of giving effect to those principles. I believe it is necessary to do so if the common law in this area is to be consistent with the developing jurisprudence on human rights.

48. I therefore hold that a nuisance is established but that the public interest clearly demands that RAF Wittering should continue to train pilots. Mr Wood did raise the possibility of granting the declaration sought, but suspending it to give the MOD time to find an alternative site or, as I understood him, to provide evidence that none existed or none that could be conveniently utilised. I have already commented on the evidence before me and find it sufficient to reach the conclusion that I should not grant a declaration. In reaching that conclusion I have had in mind, in particular, the nature of the public interest, the defence of the realm, the enormous inconvenience and cost of uprooting RAF Wittering and RAF Cottesmore to another location and that, even assuming one might be found away from population, it would probably not be as convenient generally as Wittering/Cottesmore. On the other side, I have considered, particularly, the property rights of Mr Dennis; the fact that he has lived at Walcot Hall since childhood and hopes that one day one of his children will continue to maintain the Estate; and the very considerable noise interference with his enjoyment of it. I have also noted that diminution in the market value of the Estate may be compensated financially and that there has been considerable delay in bringing these proceedings.

10.2.3 Defences in private nuisance

There are a number of defences to private nuisance, including:

- *prescription* – the defendant will need to show that they have performed the interfering action uninterrupted for a period of at least 20 years without complaint, stealth, force, or permission of the landowner;[9]
- *the actions of a stranger* – provided that the defendant has not adopted or continued the nuisance;[10] and
- *statutory authority* – if the action in question has been authorised by Parliament and has been carried out in a reasonable way.

Note that it is no defence to a nuisance that the claimant moved to the nuisance,[11] that the defendant's activities have social utility,[12] or that someone else has a greater interest in the land than the claimant.

9 *Sturges v Bridgman* (1879) 11 Ch D 852, CA.

10 *Sedleigh-Denfield v O'Callagan* [1940] AC 880, HL.

11 *Miller v Jackson* [1977] QB 966, CA.

12 *Dennis v Ministry of Defence* [2003] EWHC 793 (QB).

Question to consider: Does the law of nuisance adequately balance the interests of the parties?

Other resources: M Lee, 'The Public Interest in Private Nuisance: Collectives and Communities in Tort' (2015) 74(2) *CLJ* 329–58; S Steel, 'The Locality Principle in Private Nuisance' (2017) 76(1) *CLJ* 145–67; *Marcic v Thames Water Utilities* [2003] UKHL 66; *Shelfer v City of London Electric Lighting Co* [1895] 1 Ch 287.

10.3 The rule in *Rylands v Fletcher*

The next tort to consider is the rule in *Rylands v Fletcher*, which is much more fashionable and common in undergraduate tort law problem questions than in real-life courtrooms! In the case that created the rule – *Rylands v Fletcher* – the defendant built a reservoir on their land. Their reservoir was built on disused mine shafts which connected with the claimant's mine. When the defendant's reservoir flooded, it subsequently flooded the unused shafts and the claimant's mine.

Rylands v Fletcher LR 1 Exch 265, 279–80 (Blackburn J)

The question of law therefore arises, what is the obligation which the law casts on a person who, like the defendants, lawfully brings on his land something which, though harmless whilst it remains there, will naturally do mischief if it escape out of his land. It is agreed on all hands that he must take care to keep in that which he has brought on the land and keeps there, in order that it may not escape and damage his neighbours, but the question arises whether the duty which the law casts upon him, under such circumstances, is an absolute duty to keep it in at his peril, or is, as the majority of the Court of Exchequer have thought, merely a duty to take all reasonable and prudent precautions, in order to keep it in, but no more. If the first be the law, the person who has brought on his land and kept there something dangerous, and failed to keep it in, is responsible for all the natural consequences of its escape. If the second be the limit of his duty, he would not be answerable except on proof of negligence, and consequently would not be answerable for escape arising from any latent defect which ordinary prudence and skill could not detect.

Supposing the second to be the correct view of the law, a further question arises subsidiary to the first, viz., whether the defendants are not so far identified with the contractors whom they employed, as to be responsible for the consequences of their want of care and skill in making the reservoir in fact insufficient with reference to the old shafts, of the existence of which they were aware, though they had not ascertained where the shafts went to.

We think that the true rule of law is, that the person who for his own purposes brings on his lands and collects and keeps there anything likely to do mischief if it escapes, must keep it in at his peril, and, if he does not do so, is prima facie answerable for all the damage which is the natural consequence of its escape. He can excuse himself by shewing that the escape was owing to the plaintiff's default; or perhaps that the escape was the consequence of vis major, or the act of God; but as nothing of this sort exists here, it is unnecessary to inquire what excuse would be sufficient. The general rule, as above stated, seems on principle just. The person whose grass or corn is eaten down by the escaping cattle of his neighbour, or whose mine is flooded by the water from his neighbour's reservoir, or whose cellar is invaded by the filth of his neighbour's privy, or whose habitation is made unhealthy by the fumes and noisome vapours of his neighbour's alkali works, is damnified without any fault of his own; and it seems but reasonable and just that the neighbour, who has brought something on his own property which was not naturally there, harmless to others so long as it is confined to his own property, but which he knows to be mischievous if it gets on his neighbour's, should be obliged to make good the damage which ensues if he does not succeed in confining it to his own property. But for his act in bringing it there no mischief could have accrued, and it seems but just that he should at his peril keep it there so that no mischief may accrue, or answer for the natural and anticipated consequences. And upon authority, this we think is established to be the law whether the things so brought be beasts, or water, or filth, or stenches.

The application of the rule in *Rylands v Fletcher* has been significantly limited by subsequent cases. For example, the case of *Cambridge Water Co v Eastern Counties Leather plc* added the requirement that the ultimate damage suffered by the claimant had to be foreseeable.

Cambridge Water Co v Eastern Counties Leather plc [1994] 2 AC 264, HL, 302–6 (Lord Goff)

In that passage [in *Rylands v Fletcher*] Blackburn J spoke of 'anything *likely* to do mischief if it escapes'; and later he spoke of something 'which he *knows* to be mischievous if it gets on to his neighbour's [property]', and the liability to 'answer for the natural *and anticipated* consequences'. Furthermore, time and again he spoke of the strict liability imposed upon the defendant as being that he must keep the thing in at his peril; and, when referring to liability in actions for damage occasioned by animals, he referred (p. 282) to the established principle 'that it is quite immaterial whether the escape is by negligence or not'. The general tenor of his statement of principle is therefore that knowledge, or at least foreseeability of the risk, is a prerequisite of the recovery of damages under the principle; but that the principle is one of strict liability in the sense that the defendant may be held liable notwithstanding that he has exercised all due care to prevent the escape from occurring.

There are however early authorities in which foreseeability of damage does not appear to have been regarded as necessary ... *West v Bristol Tramways Co* [1908] 2 KB 14, and the decision of this House in *Rainham Chemical Works Ltd v Belvedere Fish Guano Co Ltd* [1921] 2 AC 465.

...

I feel bound to say that these two cases provide a very fragile base for any firm conclusion that foreseeability of damage has been authoritatively rejected as a prerequisite of the recovery of damages under the rule in *Rylands v Fletcher*.

…

Even so, the question cannot be considered solely as a matter of history. It can be argued that the rule in *Rylands v Fletcher* should not be regarded simply as an extension of the law of nuisance, but should rather be treated as a developing principle of strict liability from which can be derived a general rule of strict liability for damage caused by ultra-hazardous operations, on the basis of which persons conducting such operations may properly be held strictly liable for the extraordinary risk to others involved in such operations. As is pointed out in *Fleming on Torts*, 8th ed., pp 327–328, this would lead to the practical result that the cost of damage resulting from such operations would have to be absorbed as part of the overheads of the relevant business rather than be borne (where there is no negligence) by the injured person or his insurers, or even by the community at large.

…

Like the judge in the present case, I incline to the opinion that, as a general rule, it is more appropriate for strict liability in respect of operations of high risk to be imposed by Parliament, than by the courts. If such liability is imposed by statute, the relevant activities can be identified, and those concerned can know where they stand. Furthermore, statute can where appropriate lay down precise criteria establishing the incidence and scope of such liability.

It is of particular relevance that the present case is concerned with environmental pollution. The protection and preservation of the environment is now perceived as being of crucial importance to the future of mankind: and public bodies, both national and international, are taking significant steps towards the establishment of legislation which will promote the protection of the environment, and make the polluter pay for damage to the environment for which he is responsible – as can be seen from the WHO, EEC and national regulations to which I have previously referred. But it does not follow from these developments that a common law principle, such as the rule in *Rylands v Fletcher*, should be developed or rendered more strict to provide for liability in respect of such pollution. On the contrary, given that so much well-informed and carefully structured legislation is now being put in place for this purpose, there is less need for the courts to develop a common law principle to achieve the same end, and indeed it may well be undesirable that they should do so.

Having regard to these considerations, and in particular to the step which this House has already taken in *Read v Lyons* to contain the scope of liability under the rule in *Rylands v Fletcher*, it appears to me to be appropriate now to take the view that foreseeability of damage of the relevant type should be regarded as a prerequisite of liability in damages under the rule. Such a conclusion can, as I have already stated, be derived from Blackburn J's original statement of the law; and I can see no good reason why this prerequisite should not be recognised under the rule, as it has been in the case of private nuisance.

The rule was limited even further in *Transco plc v Stockport MBC* where the House of Lords held that *Rylands v Fletcher* would only cover instances in which defendants use their land in an ultra-hazardous or extraordinary way.

Transco plc v Stockport MBC [2003] UKHL 61, [2004] 2 AC 1, 11 (Lord Bingham)

[T]he rule in *Rylands v Fletcher* is engaged only where the defendant's use is shown to be extraordinary and unusual. This is not a test to be inflexibly applied: a use may be extraordinary and unusual at one time or in one place but not so at another time or in another place (although I would question whether, even in wartime, the manufacture of explosives could ever be regarded as an ordinary user of land, as contemplated by Viscount Simon, Lord Macmillan, Lord Porter and Lord Uthwatt in *Read v J Lyons & Co Ltd* [1947] AC 156, 169–170, 174, 176–177, 186–187). I also doubt whether a test of reasonable user is helpful, since a user may well be quite out of the ordinary but not unreasonable, as was that of Rylands, Rainham Chemical Works or the tannery in *Cambridge Water*. Again, as it seems to me, the question is whether the defendant has done something which he recognises, or ought to recognise, as being quite out of the ordinary in the place and at the time when he does it. In answering that question, I respectfully think that little help is gained (and unnecessary confusion perhaps caused) by considering whether the use is proper for the general benefit of the community. In *Rickards v Lothian* itself, the claim arose because the outflow from a wash-basin on the top floor of premises was maliciously blocked and the tap left running, with the result that damage was caused to stock on a floor below: not surprisingly, the provision of a domestic water supply to the premises was held to be a wholly ordinary use of the land. An occupier of land who can show that another occupier of land has brought or kept on his land an exceptionally dangerous or mischievous thing in extraordinary or unusual circumstances is in my opinion entitled to recover compensation from that occupier for any damage caused to his property interest by the escape of that thing, subject to defences of Act of God or of a stranger, without the need to prove negligence.

There are several defences available to a claim under the rule in *Rylands v Fletcher*, including:

- *Consent* – if the claimant has consented to the action or situation which caused the interference.[13]
- *Act of God* – if the interference was a result of extraordinary and unpredictable natural forces.[14]
- *Claimant's own fault* – if the interference occurs as a result of the claimant's own fault or action.[15]

13 *Peters v Prince of Wales Theatre (Birmingham) Ltd* [1943] KB 73, CA.

14 *Nichols v Marsland* (1876) 2 Ex D 1, CA.

15 *Ponting v Noakes* [1894] 2 QB 281, DC.

- *Act of a stranger* – if the act was caused by another party; however, this must have been unforeseeable from the defendant's point of view and they must not have been in a position to prevent the damage.[16]
- *Statutory authority* – if a statute imposes on the defendant a duty to carry out the activity in question, this will be a defence.[17]

Question to consider: Should the UK courts have followed Australia's approach instead of narrowing the application of the rule in *Rylands v Fletcher* by overruling *Rylands* completely?

Other resources: K Amirthalingam, 'Rylands Lives' (2004) 63(2) *CLJ* 273–76; R Bagshaw, 'Rylands Confirmed' (2004) 120(Jul) *LQR* 388–92; J Murphy, 'The Merits of Rylands v Fletcher' (2004) 24 *OJLS* 643–69; Donal Nolan, 'The Distinctiveness of Rylands v. Fletcher' (2005) 121 *LQR* 421; *Burnie Port Authority v General Jones Pty Ltd* (1994) 179 CLR 520.

10.4 Public nuisance

Despite the name, public nuisance is a very different tort to private nuisance. It provides for the wider public good as opposed to individual interests in land. It is also primarily a crime, and, therefore, it can only be brought as a civil action in limited circumstances. However, it is important to understand the nature of public nuisance and how it both fits into and contrasts with the more common tort of private nuisance.

There are two stages in a public nuisance claim. The first is whether the nature of the interference meets the definition of a public nuisance; as outlined by Romer LJ in *Attorney General v PYA Quarries*, the interference suffered by the group must be representative of the public interest in that particular area.[18]

Attorney General v PYA Quarries Ltd [1957] 2 QB 169, CA, 184 (Romer LJ)

I do not propose to attempt a more precise definition of a public nuisance than those which emerge from the textbooks and authorities to which I have referred. It is, however, clear, in my opinion, that any nuisance is 'public' which materially affects the reasonable comfort and convenience of life of a class of Her Majesty's subjects. The sphere of the nuisance may be described generally as 'the neighbourhood'; but the question whether the local community within that sphere comprises a sufficient number of persons to constitute a class of the public is a question of fact in every case. It is not necessary, in

16 *Rickards v Lothian* [1913] AC 263, PC.
17 *Dunne v North Western Gas Board* [1964] 2 QB 806, CA.
18 *Attorney-General v PYA Quarries Ltd* [1957] 2 QB 169, CA.

my judgment, to prove that every member of the class has been injuriously affected; it is sufficient to show that a representative cross-section of the class has been so affected for an injunction to issue.

The second is that the individual claimant must have suffered 'special damage' above and beyond that experienced by the rest of the class of people impacted. An example of this is in *Tate & Lyle Industries Ltd v Greater London* Council,[19] where the interference of silting of the river Thames 'caused particular damage' to the claimants, as they had to dredge the river so that their vessels could access a jetty. The requirement for 'special damage' also allows claimants to sue for personal injuries, which is different to the rights of claimants in private nuisance.

The differences between public and private nuisance were further explained in *Re Corby Group Litigation*.

Re Corby Group Litigation [2008] EWCA Civ 463, [2009] QB 335, [27]–[30] (Dyson LJ)

27. It seems to me that it is at least arguable that Professor Newark was wrong to describe a public nuisance as a 'tort to the enjoyment of rights in land'. The definition of the crime of public nuisance says nothing about enjoyment of land and some public nuisances undoubtedly have nothing to do with the interference with enjoyment of land. As Lord Bingham said, the ingredients of the crime and the tort are the same. A public nuisance is simply an unlawful act or omission which endangers the life, safety, health, property or comfort of the public. As was said in *Salmond and Heuston on the Law of Torts*, 21st ed (1996), p 54–55: 'Public and private nuisances are not in reality two species of the same genus at all. There is no generic conception which includes the crime of making a bomb-hoax and the tort of allowing one's trees to overhang the land of a neighbour.'

28. Professor Newark's response seems to be that, because we are mortals and earthbound, the personal injuries we suffer as a result of a public nuisance must necessarily occur while we are exercising rights in land 65 LQR 480, 489. In a sense this is true, if the phrase 'exercising rights in land' is given the generous interpretation for which Professor Newark contends, ie the liberty to exercise rights over land 'in the amplest manner'. It can be said that a person who suffers personal injury must be in some physical place when the injury is caused and, unless he is a trespasser, he is exercising a right over land when he is in that place, even if only as a licensee.

19 [1983] 2 AC 509, HL.

29. But even if that is true, it does not follow that the right which is interfered with in a public nuisance case is properly to be regarded as a right to enjoy property. The essence of the right that is protected by the tort of private nuisance is the right to enjoy one's property. It does not extend to a licensee: see *Hunter's* case [1997] AC 655. The essence of the right that is protected by the crime and tort of public nuisance is the right not to be adversely affected by an unlawful act or omission whose effect is to endanger the life, safety, health etc of the public. This view is reflected in the *American Law Institute, Restatement of the Law, Torts*, 2d (1979), section 821B(h) which states: 'Unlike a private nuisance, a public nuisance does not necessarily involve interference with use and enjoyment of land.'

30. In these circumstances, it is difficult to see why a person whose life, safety or health has been endangered and adversely affected by an unlawful act or omission and who suffers personal injuries as a result should not be able to recover damages. The purpose of the law which makes it a crime and a tort to do an unlawful act which endangers the life, safety or health of the public is surely to protect the public against the consequences of acts or omissions which do endanger their lives, safety or health. One obvious consequence of such an act or omission is personal injury. *The purpose of this law is not to protect the property interests of the public. It is true that the same conduct can amount to a private nuisance and a public nuisance. But the two torts are distinct and the rights protected by them are different.*[20]

10.5 Trespass to land

The final tort to (briefly) consider is trespass to land which, like nuisance, protects claimants' interests in land. A claim in trespass to land involves the following elements:

- a lack of permission from the landowner;
- as with trespass to the person, trespass to land is a tort that can only be committed intentionally – the entering onto another's land must, therefore, be deliberate and not accidental (ie falling or being pushed into another's land);
- there needs to be direct interference as opposed to the indirect interference requirements in private nuisance; and
- the tort is *actionable per se*, meaning that the action will be successful without proof of damage.

The defendant can also successfully invoke a defence of necessity against a claim of trespass to land.[21]

20 Emphasis added.

21 *Southport Corpn v Esso Petroleum Co Ltd* [1956] AC 218.

10.6 Conclusion

The previous chapters of this book have highlighted that tort law can be used to protect a wide range of interests. The focus of this chapter is the torts that protect interests in land – private nuisance, the rule in *Rylands v Fletcher*, and trespass to land. It also briefly considered public nuisance and emphasised the difference between that cause of action and private nuisance. While the focus is on land, the nature of the torts is different – being a combination of strict liability, strict(ish) liability, and intentional torts. We live in a society where interests, particularly those related to land, are likely to come into contact (and often conflict) with one another. Tort law has developed different ways of balancing these rights and obligations; however, many of the legal developments have been subject to criticism. It is important that you consider whether you agree with the principles that have been developed and how the law protects – or does not protect – certain rights and interests.

Chapter 11 ECONOMIC TORTS

11.1 Introduction

The economic torts are in many ways quite different from the other torts dealt with in this book and in most undergraduate courses. They do not, as a group, have an obvious coherent theme[1] and the loss against which they protect is not a straightforward concern of the law of torts. As we saw in the earlier chapter on pure economic loss in negligence, there are difficulties with recognising general rights in persons not to suffer such losses: a competitive market system and economy depend on the causing and creation of such losses, albeit as a means to an end (where the end is, broadly, the most efficient use and distribution of scarce resources). The economic torts, therefore, certainly in their modern guise, have to navigate the boundaries of when the causing of such loss should be unlawful and so generate a remedy for the claimant. Often this will depend on the knowledge of the defendant and the means they employ to cause the relevant loss.

11.2 The law before *OBG v Allan*

An understanding of the modern economic torts depends very much on knowledge of and familiarity with the decision of the House of Lords in *OBG v Allan* [2007].[2] This was a landmark decision, which served to overhaul an area of the common law that had historically developed in a piecemeal way.[3] Much of this chapter will, therefore, focus on this case. Before that, however, it makes sense to look back to the much older case of *Allen v Flood*, extracted below, which sets out some of the fundamental thinking that underpins these torts.

---

1 See J Murphy, *The Province and Politics of the Economic Torts* (Hart, 2022).

2 [2007] UKHL 21.

3 For more detail on this, see H Carty, 'The Economic Torts in the 21st Century' (2008) 124(Oct) *LQR* 641–74. In particular, a 'hybrid' tort had developed during the 20th century, known as 'unlawful interference with contractual relations'. This required no actual breach of contract, and sat somewhere between inducing breach of contract and causing loss by unlawful means, as described below. The House of Lords in *OBG* made it clear that there was to be no such tort.

Allen v Flood [1898] AC 1, 118 (Lord Herschell)

The claimants in this case were shipwrights who were employed to carry out repairs to a ship on which ironworkers were also engaged. The ironworkers objected to the fact that shipwrights worked on both wood and metal and threatened to walk out unless their employers dismissed the shipwrights. When the shipwrights were dismissed to placate the ironworkers, they sued Allen for intentionally causing them economic loss.

Their dismissal, however, did not amount to a breach of contract, either by the employers (they were entitled to dismiss the shipwrights at will) or by the ironworkers (who were not contractually obliged to continue work). The House of Lords therefore concluded that the 'malicious' motivation of the defendant in dismissing the shipwrights did not make unlawful an action that was otherwise lawful.

It is to be observed, in the first place, that the company in declining to employ the plaintiffs were violating no contract – they were doing nothing wrongful in the eye of the law. The course which they took was dictated by self-interest: they were anxious to avoid the inconvenience to their business which would ensue from a cessation of work on behalf of the ironworkers. It was not contended at the bar that merely to induce them to take this course would constitute a legal wrong, but it was said to do so because the person inducing them acted maliciously. The Master of the Rolls declined in the present case to define what was meant by 'maliciously': he considered this. a question to be determined by a jury.[4] But if acts are, or are not, unlawful and actionable, according as this element of malice be present or absent, I think it is essential to determine what is meant by it. I can imagine no greater danger to the community than that a jury should be at liberty to impose the penalty of paying damages for acts which are otherwise lawful, because they choose, without any legal definition of the term, to say that they are malicious. No one would know what his rights were. The result would be to put all our actions at the mercy of a particular tribunal whose view of their propriety might differ from our own. However malice may be defined, if motive be an ingredient of it, my sense of the danger would not be diminished.

The danger is, I think, emphasised by the opinions of some of the learned judges. In a case to which I shall allude immediately the Master of the Rolls included within his definition of malicious acts persuasion used for the purpose 'of benefiting the defendant at the expense of the plaintiff.' Wills J. thinks this 'going a great deal too far,' and that, whether the act complained of was malicious depends upon whether the defendant has, in pursuing his own interests, 'done so by such means and with such a disregard of his neighbour as no honest and fair-minded man ought to resort to.' Here it will be seen that malice is not made dependent on motive. The assumed motive is a legitimate one – the pursuit of one's own interest. The malice depends on the means used and the disregard of one's neighbour, and the test of its existence is whether these are such as no honest and fair-minded man ought to resort to. There is here room for infinite differences of opinion. Some, I dare say, applying this test would consider that a strike by workmen at a time damaging to the

4 Juries are of course no longer used in civil trials in this jurisdiction.

employer, or a 'lock-out' by an employer at a time of special hardship to the workmen, were such means, and exhibited such a disregard of his neighbour as an honest and fair-minded man ought not to resort to. Others would be of the contrary opinion. The truth is, this suggested test makes men's responsibility for their actions depend on the fluctuating opinions of the tribunal before whom the case may chance to come as to what a right-minded man ought or ought not to do in pursuing his own interests. Again, the late Cave J. (whom I cannot name without deploring his loss) expressed the view that the action of the appellant might have been justified on the principles of trade competition if it had been confined to the time when the men were doing ironwork, but that it 'was without just cause or excuse, and consequently malicious,' inasmuch as the respondents were not at the time engaged upon ironwork. On the other hand, it is evident, from the reasoning of some of the learned judges, who think the respondents entitled to succeed, that they would not be prepared to adopt this distinction, and would regard the act as 'malicious' in either case.

…

A study of the case of *Lumley v. Gye* has satisfied me that in that case the majority of the Court regarded the circumstance that what the defendant procured was a breach of contract as the essence of the cause of action. It is true that the word 'maliciously' was to be found in the declaration the validity of which was then under consideration; but I do not think the learned judges regarded the allegation as involving the necessity of proving an evil motive on the part of the defendant, but merely as implying that the defendant had wilfully and knowingly procured a breach of contract. … Upon a review, then, of the judgment in *Lumley v.* Gye, I am satisfied that the procuring what was described as an unlawful act – namely, a breach of contract, was regarded as the gist of the action. I think the judgment would have been precisely the same if, instead of the word 'maliciously,' the words 'wilfully and with notice of the contract,' had been found in the declaration. Every word of the reasoning of the three learned judges would have been equally applicable to that case.

It is clear from this that English courts do not interfere with contractual relations lightly, regarding them as the means by which persons organise their own commercial affairs. Outside of the consumer realm, in which legislation has been passed to make an exception to this general rule in situations in which bargaining power is likely to be unequal, freedom of contract is an important pillar of English commercial law. Lord Herschell's concern about making the outcome dependent on whether the defendant's actions were motivated by malice was that different juries (as were then used in civil trials) might take different views on whether ruthlessly pursuing one's own interest amounts to malice or not. Whilst this danger is certainly reduced in the modern era in which judges deciding such questions of fact can be expected to have far less capricious tendencies, we will see from the more modern authorities that the question of the exact nature of the defendant's intention remains a thorny one.

11.3 A new approach: *OBG v Allan*

OBG Ltd v Allan; Douglas v Hello! Ltd; Mainstream Properties Ltd v Young [2007] UKHL 21, [2008] 1 AC 1, [32], [33], [39]–[44], [47], [49], [51], [62] (Lord Hoffmann)

Two directors of a property company had, in breach of their contracts, diverted a development opportunity to a joint venture in which they had an interest. The defendant knew of their contractual obligations in this respect, but believing that their pursuit of the development opportunity would not amount to a breach, he financed the venture. The claimant therefore argued that the defendant was liable for inducing breach of contract.

In a conjoined appeal, the defendants had been appointed as receivers under a charge which turned out to be invalid. They had been acting in good faith, therefore, when they had taken control of the claimant's business and assets. The claimant brought actions in both unlawful interference with its contractual relations and in conversion.

In the final conjoined appeal, the claimants were well-known celebrities who had contracted with a magazine for the exclusive publication of their wedding photographs. The defendant was a rival publication who published photographs of the event taken surreptitiously, thereby infringing the exclusivity of the claimants' deal. The claimants argued that this was interference by unlawful means with its contractual relations (as well as a breach of its equitable right to confidentiality).

In a highly significant development for this area of the law, the House of Lords held that the tort of intentionally inducing a breach of contract was conceptually distinct from the tort of inflicting harm by unlawful means. As far as intention goes, if the breach of contract was neither an end in itself nor a means to an end, but merely a foreseeable consequence, then it could not be said to have been intended.

The case makes three important points about the economic torts with which it dealt:

- Liability for interference with contractual relations requires a breach of contract and, without such a breach, there will be no liability.
- 'Unlawful means' refers to those acts which are unlawful as against a third party, and which are intended to cause loss to the claimant by interfering with the freedom of a third party.
- Acts against a third party are regarded as 'unlawful means' only if they are actionable at the suit of the third party.

32. In my opinion the principle of accessory liability for breach of contract, the first of Lord Watson's principles of liability for the act of another in *Allen v Flood*, cannot be subsumed in the tort of causing loss by unlawful means (the second of Lord Watson's principles in *Allen v Flood*) simply by classifying 'seduction' as unlawful means. That only adds a pejorative description to a circular argument: see para 18 above. To induce a breach of contract is unlawful means when the breach is used to cause loss to a third party, as in

J T Stratford & Son Ltd v Lindley [1965] AC 269, but it makes no sense to say that the breach of contract itself has been caused by unlawful means. Philip Sales and Daniel Stilitz, in their illuminating article 'Intentional Infliction of Harm by Unlawful Means' (1999) 115 LQR 411, 433, make it clear that *Lumley v Gye* was 'founded on a different principle of liability than the intentional harm tort'. It treats contractual rights as a species of property which deserve special protection, not only by giving a right of action against the party who breaks his contract but by imposing secondary liability on a person who procures him to do so. In this respect it is quite distinct from the unlawful means principle, which is concerned only with intention and wrongfulness and is indifferent as to the nature of the interest which is damaged. I therefore do not think that the two causes of action can be brought within a unified theory and agree with Professor Peter Cane, 'Mens Rea in Tort Law' (2000) 20 Oxford JLS 533, 552, that

> 'The search for "general principles of liability" based on types of conduct is at best a waste of time, and at worst a potential source of serious confusion; and the broader the principle, the more is this so. Tort law is a complex interaction between protected interests, sanctioned conduct, and sanctions; and although there are what might be called "principles of tort liability", by and large, they are not very "general". More importantly, they cannot be stated solely in terms of the sorts of conduct which will attract tort liability. Each principle must refer, as well, to some interest protected by tort law and some sanction provided by tort law.'

33. That said, I would not expect your Lordships to reject the unified theory adopted in *DC Thomson & Co Ltd v Deakin* [1952] Ch 646 unless it had serious practical disadvantages. After all, in *Merkur Island Shipping Corpn v Laughton* [1983] 2 AC 570, 607, Lord Diplock said that for 30 years the judgment of Jenkins LJ had been regarded as authoritative and that no benefit was gained by 'raking over once again the previous decisions', as I must confess to have done. But I do think that it has been a source of confusion in more than one respect and that it would therefore be better to abandon it and return to the two torts identified by Lord Watson in *Allen v Flood* [1898] AC 1.

…

39. To be liable for inducing breach of contract, you must know that you are inducing a breach of contract. It is not enough that you know that you are procuring an act which, as a matter of law or construction of the contract, is a breach. You must actually realize that it will have this effect. Nor does it matter that you ought reasonably to have done so. This proposition is most strikingly illustrated by the decision of this House in *British Industrial Plastics Ltd v Ferguson* [1940] 1 All ER 479, in which the plaintiff's former employee offered the defendant information about one of the plaintiff's secret processes which he, as an employee, had invented. The defendant knew that the employee had a contractual obligation not to reveal trade secrets but held the eccentric opinion that if the process was patentable, it would be the exclusive property of the employee. He took the information in the honest belief that the employee would not be in breach of contract. In the Court of Appeal [1938] 4 All ER 504, 513, MacKinnon LJ observed tartly that in accepting this

evidence the judge had 'vindicated his honesty ... at the expense of his intelligence' but he and the House of Lords agreed that he could not be held liable for inducing a breach of contract.

40. The question of what counts as knowledge for the purposes of liability for inducing a breach of contract has also been the subject of a consistent line of decisions. In *Emerald Construction Co Ltd v Lowthian* [1966] 1 WLR 691 union officials threatened a building contractor with a strike unless he terminated a subcontract for the supply of labour. The defendants obviously knew that there was a contract – they wanted it terminated – but the court found that they did not know its terms and, in particular, how soon it could be terminated. Lord Denning MR said, at pp 700–701:

> 'Even if they did not know the actual terms of the contract, but had the means of knowledge – which they deliberately disregarded – that would be enough. Like the man who turns a blind eye. So here, if the officers deliberately sought to get this contract terminated, heedless of its terms, regardless whether it was terminated by breach or not, they would do wrong. For it is unlawful for a third person to procure a breach of contract knowingly, or recklessly, indifferent whether it is a breach or not.'

41. This statement of the law has since been followed in many cases and, so far as I am aware, has not given rise to any difficulty. It is in accordance with the general principle of law that a conscious decision not to inquire into the existence of a fact is in many cases treated as equivalent to knowledge of that fact: see *Manifest Shipping Co Ltd v Uni-Polaris Insurance Co Ltd* [2003] 1 AC 469. It is not the same as negligence or even gross negligence: in *British Industrial Plastics Ltd v Ferguson* [1940] 1 All ER 479, for example, Mr Ferguson did not deliberately abstain from inquiry into whether disclosure of the secret process would be a breach of contract. He negligently made the wrong inquiry, but that is an altogether different state of mind.

42. The next question is what counts as an intention to procure a breach of contract. It is necessary for this purpose to distinguish between ends, means and consequences. If someone knowingly causes a breach of contract, it does not normally matter that it is the means by which he intends to achieve some further end or even that he would rather have been able to achieve that end without causing a breach. Mr Gye would very likely have preferred to be able to obtain Miss Wagner's services without her having to break her contract. But that did not matter. Again, people seldom knowingly cause loss by unlawful means out of simple disinterested malice. It is usually to achieve the further end of securing an economic advantage to themselves. As I said earlier, the Dunlop employees who took off the tyres in *GWK Ltd v Dunlop Rubber Co Ltd* 42 TLR 376 intended to advance the interests of the Dunlop company.

43. **On the other hand, if the breach of contract is neither an end in itself nor a means to an end, but merely a foreseeable consequence, then in my opinion it cannot for this purpose be said to have been intended.** That, I think, is what judges and writers mean

when they say that the claimant must have been 'targeted' or 'aimed at'. In my opinion the majority of the Court of Appeal was wrong to have allowed the action in *Millar v Bassey* [1994] EMLR 44 to proceed. Miss Bassey had broken her contract to perform for the recording company and it was a foreseeable consequence that the recording company would have to break its contracts with the accompanying musicians, but those breaches of contract were neither an end desired by Miss Bassey nor a means of achieving that end.

44. Finally, what counts as a breach of contract? In *Torquay Hotel Co Ltd v Cousins* [1969] 2 Ch 106, 138 Lord Denning said that there could be liability for preventing or hindering performance of the contract on the same principle as liability for procuring a breach. This dictum was approved by Lord Diplock in *Merkur Island Shipping Corpn v Laughton* [1983] 2 AC 570, 607–608. One could therefore have liability for interference with contractual relations even though the contracting party committed no breach. But these remarks were made in the context of the unified theory which treated procuring a breach as part of the same tort as causing loss by unlawful means. **If the torts are to be separated, then I think that one cannot be liable for inducing a breach unless there has been a breach. No secondary liability without primary liability.** Cases in which interference with contractual relations has been treated as coming within the *Lumley v Gye* tort (like *Dimbleby & Sons Ltd v National Union of Journalists* [1984] 1 WLR 67 and [1984] 1 WLR 427) are really cases of causing loss by unlawful means.

...

47. The essence of the tort therefore appears to be (a) a wrongful interference with the actions of a third party in which the claimant has an economic interest and (b) an intention thereby to cause loss to the claimant.

...

49. In my opinion, and subject to one qualification, acts against a third party count as unlawful means only if they are actionable by that third party. The qualification is that they will also be unlawful means if the only reason why they are not actionable is because the third party has suffered no loss. In the case of intimidation, for example, the threat will usually give rise to no cause of action by the third party because he will have suffered no loss. If he submits to the threat, then, as the defendant intended, the claimant will have suffered loss instead. It is nevertheless unlawful means. But the threat must be to do something which *would* have been actionable if the third party had suffered loss.

...

51. Unlawful means therefore consists of acts intended to cause loss to the claimant by interfering with the freedom of a third party in a way which is unlawful as against that third party and which is intended to cause loss to the claimant. It does not in my opinion include acts which may be unlawful against a third party but which do not affect his freedom to deal with the claimant.

...

62. **Finally, there is the question of intention. In the *Lumley v Gye* tort, there must be an intention to procure a breach of contract. In the unlawful means tort, there must be an intention to cause loss. The ends which must have been intended are different.** *South Wales Miners' Federation v Glamorgan Coal Co Ltd [1905] AC 239* shows that one may intend to procure a breach of contract without intending to cause loss. Likewise, one may intend to cause loss without intending to procure a breach of contract. But the concept of intention is in both cases the same. **In both cases it is necessary to distinguish between ends, means and consequences. One intends to cause loss even though it is the means by which one achieved the end of enriching oneself. On the other hand, one is not liable for loss which is neither a desired end nor a means of attaining it but merely a foreseeable consequence of one's actions.**

OBG v Allan separated inducing breach of contract from causing loss by unlawful means. Prior to this, the two were not distinct. *OBG*'s conceptual distinction has brought at least partial clarity to an area of law long characterised by uncertainty and ad hoc development. The case did not, however, leave the law in this area crystal clear, as the question in the next case makes clear.

11.4 The impact of *OBG v Allan*

Total Network SL v Customs & Excise Commissioners [2008] UKHL 19, [2008] AC 1174, [43]–[45] (Lord Hope)

The question here was whether the defendant was liable in unlawful means conspiracy for claiming, by means of a 'carousel fraud', VAT rebates to which it was not entitled. Specifically, the House of Lords was asked whether it was an essential requirement of the tort that the 'unlawful means' in question should be independently actionable in tort against at least one of the conspirators. Its answer was that criminal conduct used as a means of inflicting harm on the claimant was actionable as the tort of conspiracy, whether or not that conduct, if carried out by an individual alone, would be actionable as a tort. In other words, criminal conduct used as the means of intentionally inflicting harm could constitute unlawful means for the purposes of this tort.

43. In *OBG Ltd v Allan* [2008] 1 AC 1, para 56 Lord Hoffmann said that the courts should be cautious in extending the tort of causing loss by unlawful means beyond the description given by Lord Watson in *Allen v Flood* [1898] AC 1, 96 and Lord Lindley in *Quinn v Leathem* [1901] AC 495, 535, which was designed only to enforce standards of civilised behaviour in economic competition between traders or between employers and labour. I entirely appreciate the point that he makes that caution is needed where the unlawful act is directed against a third party at whose instance it is not actionable because he suffers no loss. There the claimant's cause of action is, as Hazel Carty, *An Analysis of the Economic Torts*, p 274 puts it, parasitic on the unlawful means used by the defendant against another party. As to that situation I would prefer to reserve my opinion. But in this case there was no

third party. The means used by the conspirators were directed at the claimants themselves. This is a case where the claimants were persuaded by the unlawful means to act to their own detriment which, in para 61 of *OBG*, Lord Hoffmann said raises altogether different issues. One has to ask why, in this situation, the law should not provide a remedy.

44. The situation that is contemplated is that of loss caused by an unlawful act directed at the claimants themselves. The conspirators cannot, on the commissioners' primary contention, be sued as joint tortfeasors because there was no independent tort actionable by the commissioners. This is a gap which needs to be filled. For reasons that I have already explained, I do not accept that the commissioners suffered economic harm in this case. But assuming that they did, they suffered that harm as a result of a conspiracy which was entered into with an intention of injuring them by the means that were deliberately selected by the conspirators. If, as Lord Wright said in *Crofter Hand Woven Harris Tweed Co Ltd v Veitch* [1942] AC 435, 462, it is in the fact of the conspiracy that the unlawfulness resides, why should that principle not apply here? As a subspecies of the tort of unlawful means conspiracy, the case is virtually indistinguishable from the tort of conspiracy to injure. The fact that the unlawful means were not in themselves actionable does not seem, in this context at least, to be significant. As Professor Joe Thomson put it in 'An island legacy – The delict of conspiracy', Comparative and Historical Essays in Scots Law, ed Carey Miller and Meyers (1992), p 148, the rationale of the tort is conspiracy to injure. These factors indicate that a conspiracy is tortious if an intention of the conspirators was to harm the claimant by using unlawful means to persuade him to act to his own detriment, even if those means were not in themselves tortious.

45. I would hold that the decision of the Court of Appeal in *Powell v Boladz* [1998] Lloyd's Rep Med 116 was erroneous and that it should be overruled. I would also hold, in agreement with all your Lordships' that criminal conduct at common law or by statute can constitute unlawful means in unlawful means conspiracy. Had it been open to the commissioners to maintain a civil claim of damages the tort of unlawful means would have been available to them, even though the unlawful means relied upon were not in themselves actionable.

The full meaning of 'unlawful means' was not the only element of *OBG* that has since been subjected to further judicial scrutiny. Very recently, in the following case, the Supreme Court was asked to consider the 'dealing requirement' in that case: the distinction made by Lord Hoffmann in relation to the Douglases' claim. The unlicensed photographs taken at their wedding had not, his Lordship said, affected the claimants' *ability to deal* with the third party; they had *reduced the value of that contract*, which is a different thing in law:

> *Hello!* did [not do] anything to interfere with the liberty of the Douglases to deal with *OK!* or perform their obligations under their contract. All they did was to make *OK!*'s contractual rights less profitable than they would otherwise have been.[5]

5 Lord Hoffmann in *OBG* at [129].

Question to consider: Is there sufficient connection between the different causes of action to group them together as 'economic torts', especially as economic harm is experienced in many other tort causes of action?

Other resources: H Carty, 'The Economic Torts in the 21st Century' (2008) 124(Oct) *LQR* 641–74; S Deakin and J Randall, 'Rethinking the Economic Torts' (2009) 72 *MLR* 519; R Bagshaw, 'Can the Economic Torts be Unified?' (1998) 18 *OJLS* 729; J Lee, 'Restoring Confidence in the Economic Torts' (2007) 15 *Tort L Rev* 172.

In *Servier*, below,[6] the Supreme Court stated that 'the dealing requirement' is a necessary limitation on claims for the recovery of economic loss. The Court had been asked to clarify whether the dealing requirement had formed part of the ratio of *OBG v Allan* and, if so, to invoke the 1966 Practice Statement in order to depart from it. In its view, the dealing requirement *did* form part of the ratio of *OBG* and, as it did not depart from that substantive conclusion, there was no need to invoke the Practice Statement. For claims in causing loss by unlawful means to succeed then, we now have confirmation at the highest level that the defendant *must affect a third party's freedom to deal with the claimant.* It underlines that it is committed by striking at one party (the claimant) through actions directed at another (the third party).

Secretary of State for Health v Servier Laboratories Ltd [2021] UKSC 24, [2022] AC 959, [63]–[71], [78]–[83] (Lord Hamblen)

Issue 1 – is the dealing requirement part of the ratio of *OBG*?

63. I agree with the courts below that the dealing requirement is part of the ratio of *OBG* for a number of reasons.

64. **First, it is consistent with Lord Hoffmann's explanation of the rationale of the unlawful means tort as set out in the passage from Lord Lindley's judgment in *Quinn v Leathem* [1901] AC 495 cited at para 46 of his judgment. This passage focuses on 'a person's liberty or right to deal with others' and on wrongful interferences with that 'liberty to deal'.** Mr Jonathan Crow QC on behalf of the appellants questioned whether this was Lord Lindley's view when one considers his judgment as a whole, but what is significant for the purpose of identifying the ratio of *OBG* is that Lord Hoffmann stated it to be the rationale of the tort.

65. Secondly, although Lord Hoffmann does not refer specifically to the dealing requirement when describing the essence of the tort in the first sentence in para 47 of his

6 [2021] UKSC 24, [2022] AC 1158.

judgment, he goes on to explain and expand upon the essence of the tort in the paragraphs which follow. This includes the dealing requirement, as expressly stated by him in para 51.

66. Thirdly, para 51 sets out **Lord Hoffmann's definition of what unlawful means 'consists of'. The second sentence of that paragraph, which sets out the dealing requirement, is part of that definition. It cannot be divorced from the first sentence which is plainly definitional and which it qualifies. As Lord Walker observed, this paragraph sets out Lord Hoffmann's 'proposed test'.**

67. Fourthly, Lord Hoffmann explains and justifies the dealing requirement through his analysis of the cases of *RCA Corpn v Pollard*, *Isaac Oren v Red Box Toy Factory Ltd* and *Lonrho Ltd v Shell Petroleum Co Ltd (No 2)*, all of which he explains by reference to there being no dealings between the claimant and the third party which were affected. It may be that other explanations of those decisions can be advanced, but what matters for present purposes is that this is how Lord Hoffmann analysed and explained them.

68. Fifthly, the dealing requirement is consistent with the authorities in which liability for the unlawful means tort has been established, which, as Lord Hoffmann explained, all involved dealings. As he stated at para 56, no case was cited to the House of Lords in which the tort had been extended beyond the description given by Lord Lindley in *Quinn v Leathem*, focusing as it does on the liberty to deal.

69. Sixthly, the dealing requirement is consistent with and reflects **Lord Hoffmann's concern that the tort be kept within reasonable bounds and that a narrow meaning be given to unlawful means.**

70. Seventhly, it is apparent, and was not disputed by Mr Crow, that the other members of the majority understood Lord Hoffmann's definition of the tort to include a dealing requirement and that they endorsed it. **Thus, Lord Walker said at para 269 that the 'control mechanism' for the tort should be the '*nature of the disruption caused, as between the third party and the claimant*, by the defendant's wrong'. Baroness Hale described the requisite unlawful means at para 306 as involving a 'wrong against the third party inhibiting his *freedom to trade* with the target'. Lord Brown stated at para 320 that the tort is limited to situations in which the defendant 'intentionally injures the claimant's economic interests by unlawfully interfering with *a third party's freedom to deal with him*' (emphasis added).**

71. Eighthly, *OBG* has been understood to impose a dealing requirement by the courts both in this country and elsewhere in the Commonwealth – see, for example, *Emerald Supplies Ltd v British Airways plc (Nos 1 and 2)* [2015] EWCA Civ 1024; [2016] Bus LR 145, para 128 (Court of Appeal); *Intellihub Ltd v Genesis Energy Ltd* [2020] NZHC 807, para 30 (New Zealand High Court, upheld on appeal [2020] NZCA 344); *Wolero Pte Ltd v Lim* [2017] SGHC 89, paras 69–71 and 78 (Supreme Court of Singapore); *Hardie Finance Corpn Pty Ltd v Ahern (No 3)* [2010] WASC 403, paras 720 and 722(iii) (Supreme Court of Western Australia), and *A I Enterprises Ltd v Bram Enterprises Ltd* 2014 SCC 12; [2014] 1 SCR 177, para 87 (Supreme Court of Canada). This has also been the common

understanding of academic commentators – see, for example, Hazel Carty, *An Analysis of the Economic Torts*, 2nd ed (2010), at pp 95–98; Sales and Davies, 'Intentional harm, accessories and conspiracies' (2018) 134 LQR 69–93, at pp 74–75.

...

Issue 2 – should *OBG* be departed from?

78. The appellants put forward three alternative approaches as to how the unlawful means tort can and should be 'refashioned', shorn of the dealing requirement.

79. The first alternative is to reject the dealing requirement as an element of the tort in favour of the requirement that the defendant's conduct must interfere with actions of the relevant third party in which the claimant has an interest.

80. The second alternative is that the dealing requirement should be rejected as part and parcel of a redefinition of the tort, according to which it would be made out wherever a defendant deliberately employs means that the law prohibits (whether or not civilly actionable), with the intention of harming the claimant.

81. The third alternative is that the dealing requirement should be rejected as part and parcel of a redefinition of the tort, according to which it would be made out wherever the defendant employs means that are unlawful (in the sense that they are actionable by a third party, or would be, if the third party had suffered loss) with the intention of harming the claimant.

82. A fundamental difficulty for the appellants is that they need to show that this is an appropriate case for the Supreme Court to depart from *OBG* in accordance with the 1966 Practice Statement: *Practice Statement (Judicial Precedent)* [1966] 1 WLR 1234. I summarised the applicable principles in *Henderson v Dorset Healthcare University NHS Foundation Trust* [2020] UKSC 43; [2020] 3 WLR 1124, para 87 as follows:

> 'As this court has recently emphasised, it will be "very circumspect before accepting an invitation to invoke the 1966 Practice Statement": *Knauer v Ministry of Justice* [2016] AC 908, para 23. It is important not to undermine the role of precedent and the certainty which it promotes. Circumstances in which it may be appropriate to do so include where previous decisions "were generally thought to be impeding the proper development of the law or to have led to results which were unjust or contrary to public policy": per Lord Reid in *R v National Insurance Comr, Ex p Hudson* [1972] AC 944, 966. Even then the court needs to be satisfied that a departure from precedent 'is the safe and appropriate way of remedying the injustice and developing the law' – per Lord Scarman in *R v Secretary of State for the Home Department, Ex p Khawaja* [1984] AC 74, 106.'

83. Whilst the appellants can point to some academic criticism of the decision in *OBG*, they have not provided any real life examples of it causing difficulties, creating uncertainty or impeding the development of the law.

In the following extract, Professor John Murphy, who is a renowned expert on the economic torts, criticises the *Servier* approach to the dealing issue in both formal and substantive terms:

John Murphy, 'Floodgate fears and the unlawful means tort' (2021) 80 *Cambridge Law Journal* 436

This qualification to what counts as 'unlawful means' attracted much academic criticism in the wake of *OBG*. But it remained unchallenged in the courts until *Secretary of State for Health v Servier Laboratories Ltd.* [2021] UKSC 24 [2021] 3 W.L.R. 370 ... In relation to the claim that the dealing requirement formed part of the ratio of *OBG*, Lord Hamblen (who delivered the only full-length judgment) offered various 'reasons' for regarding the dealing requirement this way. He noted, first, that it had been expressly endorsed by most of the members of the panel in *OBG*, albeit only in their general discussion of the tort's ingredients (at [65], [66], [70]). Second, he afforded salience to the fact that the dealing requirement was consistent with the outcomes of, and *obiter dicta* in, numerous earlier cases (at [64], [67], [68]). Third, he pointed to various Commonwealth cases in which the dealing requirement has subsequently been treated as an element of the tort (at [71]). Finally, he adverted to the fact that 'the dealing requirement is consistent with and reflects Lord Hoffmann's concern that the tort be kept within reasonable bounds' (at [69]).

With respect, none of the 'reasons' offers a proper basis for concluding that the dealing requirement formed part of the ratio of *OBG*. The *general discussion* of the tort by the other members of the panel in *OBG* is not where one would expect to find the ratio of the case. One would normally look to the leading judgment and the precise basis on which the appeal was decided ... Third, Lord Hamblen's reference to the outcomes of, and *obiter dicta* in, various earlier cases is, with respect, a red herring. For, by his own admission, 'neither *Allen v Flood* nor any other pre-*OBG* authority holds that the dealing requirement is an essential element of the unlawful means tort' (at [89]) ... In only one of the three appeals heard in *OBG* could the dealing requirement conceivably have formed the ratio: the one in *Douglas v Hello!* But *Douglas* was formally decided as a breach of confidence case, not one involving the unlawful means tort.

There is a very interesting discussion to be had here, as this short excerpt suggests. A reading of the whole article is recommended to get a full idea of the arguments at stake, but there are two related issues. First there is the substantive question about whether the dealing requirement is a necessary limitation on causing loss by unlawful means. But there is also the procedural question of whether that requirement formed part of the ratio of *OBG*. The question of whether *Servier* was an appropriate case for the Supreme Court to invoke the Practice Statement generates a further dimension for discussion.

11.5 Conclusion

The economic torts topic has always been one that lends itself very well to examination by means of essay questions, and this most recent common law analysis, and the academic commentary that it has provoked, is likely only to make essay questions more appealing to examiners. Ensure, therefore, that you are familiar with the House of Lords and Supreme Court authorities, as well as with the views and reasoning of academic commentators. Of course, as always, you should take the time when revising to decide what your views are, and how you can best present and justify them by reference to both primary and secondary legal materials.

Chapter 12 INTENTIONAL TORTS AGAINST THE PERSON

12.1 Introduction

Intentional torts to the person cover a wide range of causes of action designed to protect people's autonomy. As outlined by Goff LJ, '[t]he fundamental principle [of intentional torts], plain and incontestable, is that every person's body is inviolate'.[1] Whilst the six causes of action considered in this chapter are all formally recognised as torts, they work very differently from negligence and other fault-based causes of action. As you may have guessed from the name of these torts, the focus in on the *intention* of the defendant and not whether they have been careless or fallen below a specified standard of care.

12.2 Comparing and contrasting the intentional torts

There is significant divergence between these torts, and the main thing that appears to connect them is a focus on the *intention* of the alleged tortfeasor. This chapter covers six intentional torts against the person – assault, battery, false imprisonment, the tort in *Wilkinson v Downton*,[2] the Protection from Harassment Act 1997 and malicious prosecution. The table below highlights some of the differences and similarities between these torts.

However, an issue arises when there may be a potential negligence claim and an intentional tort. There was historical debate as to whether the same action could be both negligent and intentional; however, in 1964, Denning MR confirmed in *Letang v Cooper*,[3] citing *Fowler v Lanning* with approval,[4] that 'when the injury is not inflicted intentionally, but negligently, … the only cause of action is negligence and not trespass. If it were trespass, it would be actionable without proof of damage; and that is not the law today.'

1 *Collins v Wilcock* [1984] 1 WLR 1172, QB, 1177 (Goff LJ). This specific quote was focused on battery but the concern for autonomy is across all intentional torts against the person in some way.
2 [1897] 2 QB 57.
3 [1965] 1 QB 232, 240.
4 [1959] 1 QB 426.

Table 12.1: Comparing and contrasting the intentional torts

Cause of action	Definition	Intentional tort?	Trespass to the person tort?	Actionable per se?	Recklessness sufficient?
Assault	An intentional threat causing a reasonable expectation of immediate and direct violence	Yes	Yes	Yes	Yes
Battery	Intentionally touching another person without their consent	Yes	Yes	Yes	Yes
False Imprisonment	Confining another against their will without lawful justification	Yes	Yes	Yes	Yes
Tort in *Wilkinson v Downton*	Intentional infliction of physical harm or emotional distress	Yes	No	No, the claimant must prove physical harm or recognised psychiatric illness	No, the claimant must prove specific intention
Protection from Harassment Act 1997	A course of conduct which the individual knows, or ought to know, involves harassment	Yes	No	No, the claimant must prove 'harassment'	Yes
Malicious prosecution	The commencement of criminal proceedings against someone without reasonable grounds	Yes	No	Yes	No, the claimant must prove malice

The claimant was sunbathing on a patch of grass that was also being used as a car park when the defendant drove his car over her legs. The claimant commenced an action for negligence and trespass to the person. At first instance, the claimant was awarded damages for trespass to the person as her claim for negligence was statute-barred by s 2(1) of the Law Reform (Limitations of Actions, etc) Act 1954. The defendant appealed the decision to the Court of Appeal, stating that the entire claim should be statute-barred.

Letang v Cooper [1965] 1 QB 232, CA, 237–40 (Lord Denning MR) (footnotes omitted)

Under the *Limitation Act, 1939*, the period of limitation was six years in all actions founded 'on tort'; but, in 1954, Parliament reduced it to three years in actions for damages for personal injuries, provided that the actions come within these words of section 2 (1) of the *Law Reform (Limitation of Actions, etc.) Act, 1954*: 'actions for damages for negligence, nuisance or breach of duty (whether the duty exists by virtue of a contract or of provision made by or under a statute or independently of any contract or any such provision) where the damages claimed by the plaintiff for the negligence, nuisance or breach of duty consist of or include damages in respect of personal injuries to any person.' The plaintiff says that these words do not cover an action for trespass to the person and that therefore the time bar is not the new period of three years, but the old period of six years.

The argument, as it was developed before us, became a direct invitation to this court to go back to the old forms of action and to decide this case by reference to them. The statute bars an action on the case, it is said, after three years, whereas trespass to the person is not barred for six years.

...

Nowadays, if a man carelessly throws a piece of wood from a house into a roadway, then whether it hits the plaintiff or he tumbles over it the next moment, the action would not be trespass or case, but simply negligence. Another distinction which the old lawyers drew was this: If the driver of a horse and gig negligently ran down a passer-by, the plaintiff could sue the driver either in trespass or in case (see *Williams v. Holland*), but if the driver was a servant, the plaintiff could not sue the master in trespass, but only in case: see *Sharrod v. London and North Western Railway Co.* In either case today the action would not be trespass or case, but only negligence.

If we were to bring back these subtleties into the law of limitation, we should produce the most absurd anomalies; and all the more so when you bear in mind that under the Fatal Accidents Act the period of limitation is three years from the death. The decision of Elwes J. if correct would produce these results: it would mean that if a motorist ran down two people, killing one and injuring another, the widow would have to bring her action within three years, but the injured person would have six years. It would mean also that if a lorry driver was in collision at a cross-roads with an owner-driver, an injured passenger would have to bring his action against the employer of the lorry driver within three years, but he would have six years in which to sue the owner-driver. Not least of all the absurdities is a case like the present. It would mean that the plaintiff could get out of the three-year limitation by suing in trespass instead of in negligence.

> …
>
> The truth is that the distinction between trespass and case is obsolete. We have a different sub-division altogether. Instead of dividing actions for personal injuries into trespass (direct damage) or case (consequential damage), we divide the causes of action now according as the defendant did the injury intentionally or unintentionally. If one man intentionally applies force directly to another, the plaintiff has a cause of action in assault and battery, or, if you so please to describe it, in trespass to the person. 'The least touching of another in anger is a battery,' *per* Holt C.J. in *Cole v. Turner*. If he does not inflict injury intentionally, but only unintentionally, the plaintiff has no cause of action today in trespass. His only cause of action is in negligence, and then only on proof of want of reasonable care. If the plaintiff cannot prove want of reasonable care, he may have no cause of action at all. Thus, it is not enough nowadays for the plaintiff to plead that 'the defendant shot the plaintiff.' He must also allege that he did it intentionally or negligently. If intentional, it is the tort of assault and battery. If negligent and causing damage, it is the tort of negligence.
>
> The modern law on this subject was well expounded by Diplock J. in *Fowler v. Lanning*, with which I fully agree. But I would go this one step further: when the injury is not inflicted intentionally, but negligently, I would say that the only cause of action is negligence and not trespass. If it were trespass, it would be actionable without proof of damage; and that is not the law today.

This case, therefore, reaffirmed the distinction set up in *Fowler v Lanning*: trespass to the person requires intention, and the tort of negligence requires negligence or carelessness. If there is no intentional act, the claim will need to be brought in negligence. There is also a significant difference in the purpose of negligence when compared to the intentional, to-the-person torts. Theoretically, the former is focused on compensation, whereas the latter are designed to protect the claimant's personal autonomy and rights.[5] These distinctions are not, however, clear cut, and there is often overlap and confusion between the two.

> **Question to consider:** Do you think that it is possible, desirable, or both to have a distinction between negligence and intentional torts? Is it possible for harm to be committed intentionally and carelessly?
>
> When thinking through this question, engage in the principles from cases on both negligence and the intentional torts.

5 See comments in *Ashley v Chief Constable of Sussex Police* [2008] UKHL 25, [2008] AC 962, [60] (Lord Scott).

12.3 Assault and battery

The two most commonly considered intentional torts against the person are assault and battery. These torts can be separate but are often considered together, with an assault happening moments before the battery. The difference is outlined by Goff LJ in *Collins v Wilcock*:

> The law draws a distinction, in terms more easily understood by philologists than by ordinary citizens, between an assault and a battery. An assault is an act which causes another person to apprehend the infliction of immediate, unlawful, force on his person; a battery is the actual infliction of unlawful force on another person. Both assault and battery are forms of trespass to the person.[6]

As an example, if someone raises their hand and says, 'I am going to hit you', they have likely committed an assault. If they hit the victim, they have committed a battery. If they do one followed by another, they have committed both. So, in a problem question, make sure to look out for both causes of action, which are sometimes in quick succession!

12.3.1 Assault

For a successful claim under the tort of assault, an individual must show they were subjected to 'an act which causes another person to apprehend the infliction of immediate, unlawful, force on his person'.[7] The defendant must, therefore, have made an intentional threat that gave the claimant the reasonable expectation of immediate and direct violence. This can be divided into the following three elements:

(1) intentional threat;
(2) immediate and direct violence; and
(3) a reasonable expectation by the claimant.

What does the law mean by an 'intentional threat', and can silence ever be a threat? These were the questions raised in *R v Ireland*. The defendant made repeated silent telephone calls to three women, mostly at night. The women suffered psychiatric illness, as the silent telephone calls were combined with a series of harassing activities. Ireland was convicted of assault under the criminal law provisions. He argued, however, that the telephone calls could not be assault as they were silent; there was no intentional threat of violence made to the victims.

6 [1984] 1 WLR 1172, QBD, 1177 (Goff LJ).
7 ibid 1177 (Goff LJ).

R v Ireland [1998] AC 147, 152, 161–62 (Lord Steyn)

[I]t is easy to understand the terrifying effect of a campaign of telephone calls at night by a silent caller to a woman living on her own. It would be natural for the victim to regard the calls as menacing. What may heighten her fear is that she will not know what the caller may do next. The spectre of the caller arriving at her doorstep bent on inflicting personal violence on her may come to dominate her thinking. After all, as a matter of common sense, what else would she be terrified about? The victim may suffer psychiatric illness such as anxiety neurosis or acute depression. Harassment of women by repeated silent telephone calls, accompanied on occasions by heavy breathing, is apparently a significant social problem. That the criminal law should be able to deal with this problem, and so far as is practicable, afford effective protection to victims is self-evident.

From the point of view, however, of the general policy of our law towards the imposition of criminal responsibility, three specific features of the problem must be faced squarely. First, the medium used by the caller is the telephone: arguably it differs qualitatively from a face to face offer of violence to a sufficient extent to make a difference. Secondly, ex hypothesi the caller remains silent: arguably a caller may avoid the reach of the criminal law by remaining silent however menacing the context may be. Thirdly, it is arguable that the criminal law does not take into account 'mere' psychiatric illnesses.

Lord Steyn then discussed the relevant statutes, outlining how it is necessary to show that an 'assault' has occurred for a conviction under s 47 of the Offences against the Person Act 1861.

It is necessary to consider the two forms which an assault may take. The first is battery, which involves the unlawful application of force by the defendant upon the victim.

…

The second form of assault is an act causing the victim to apprehend an imminent application of force upon her: see *Fagan v Metropolitan Police Commissioner* [1969] 1 Q.B. 439, 444D–E.

…

It is to assault in the form of an act causing the victim to fear an immediate application of force to her that I must turn. Counsel argued that as a matter of law an assault can never be committed by words alone and therefore it cannot be committed by silence. The premise depends on the slenderest authority, namely an observation by Holroyd J. to a jury that 'no words or singing are equivalent to an assault:' *Rex v. Meade and Belt* (1823) 1 Lew. 184. The proposition that a gesture may amount to an assault, but that words can never suffice, is unrealistic and indefensible. A thing said is also a thing done. There is no reason why something said should be incapable of causing an apprehension of immediate personal violence, e.g. a man accosting a woman in a dark alley saying. 'Come with me or I will stab you.' I would, therefore, reject the proposition that an assault can never be committed by words.

That brings me to the critical question whether a silent caller may be guilty of an assault. The answer to this question seems to me to be 'Yes, depending on the facts.' It involves questions of fact within the province of the jury. After all, there is no reason why a telephone caller who says to a woman in a menacing way 'I will be at your door in a minute or two' may not be guilty of an assault if he causes his victim to apprehend immediate personal violence. Take now the case of the silent caller. He intends by his silence to cause fear and he is so understood. The victim is assailed by uncertainty about his intentions. Fear may dominate her emotions, and it may be the fear that the caller's arrival at her door may be imminent. She may fear the *possibility* of immediate personal violence. As a matter of law the caller may be guilty of an assault: whether he is or not will depend on the circumstance and in particular on the impact of the caller's potentially menacing call or calls on the victim. …

Note: In the world of mobile phones, it may be difficult to place this decision in context. By answering a landline number, the victim unintentionally informed the accused of their physical whereabouts. In light of the series of harassing activities, there was, therefore, no need for the accused to make any specific comments to the victim to make them reasonably expect immediate and direct violence.

The focus of assault is whether a 'reasonable' person would expect direct and immediate violence. Therefore, the law does not focus on whether the victim actually felt threatened but whether a reasonable person, in their situation, would feel threatened. This creates some difficulties in situations where people may differ from the 'reasonable' person standard. Take the following two scenarios, for example:

- *Example 1:* Xie Li, who is the United Kingdom's jujitsu champion, is walking down the road. She is accosted by two drunk men who threaten to beat her up if she doesn't give them her wallet. In light of her skills and training, Xie Li is not at all frightened by these actions.
- *Example 2:* Owen was a victim of serious physical abuse when he was a child, and this has caused him ongoing psychological harm. His new teacher has a significant physical resemblance to Owen's abuser. One day, while they were doing class presentations, the teacher came behind Owen and said, 'You're next'. These words caused Owen to have a flashback and he feared immediate and direct violence by the teacher, resulting in a panic attack.

Has an assault occurred in either of these cases?

Question to consider: Reflecting on this discussion and the outcome in *R v Ireland*, why do you think the court takes an objective approach to whether a person feels threatened? Why is the focus not on whether the victim actually felt fear of direct and immediate violence? Do you agree with this approach? Why or why not?

Other resources: *Tuberville v Savage* (1669) 86 ER 684; *Thomas v National Union of Mineworkers (South Wales Area)* [1986] Ch 20; *Mbasogo v Logo Ltd* [2006] EWCA Civ 1370, [2007] QB 846; *R v St George* (1840) 9 C & P 483, 493; *Logdon v DPP* [1976] Crim LR 121.

12.3.2 Battery

Assault protects people's mental integrity, whereas battery focuses on their bodily integrity. Battery prevents people from intentionally touching another person without their consent and consists of the following elements:

(1) intention;
(2) direct and immediate force; and
(3) without consent.

'Force' means any unwanted/unconsented touching. Therefore, the claimant does not need to show that the tortfeasor intended to harm them, only that they intended to touch them in some way. For example, in *Williams v Humphrey*, the pushing of a person into a pool as a friendly, practical joke was considered a battery.[8]

There is an ongoing, unsettled question of if and how the touching must be 'hostile' in nature. The case law is unsettled in this area. Some cases indicate that the touching must go beyond being merely intentional and must include a level of hostility, whereas others strongly argue that this would undermine the tort of battery's nature.

Wilson v Pringle [1987] QB 237, CA, 247–48, 252–53 (Croom-Johnson LJ)

The claimant was seriously injured by the defendant, both aged 13, when the latter intentionally jumped on him. The defendant argued that the injury occurred in the course of 'ordinary horseplay'. Judge Wilson Mellor QC held that a battery was committed on the grounds that the defendant admitted they intentionally touched the claimant in a direct and immediate manner without their consent. This decision was appealed to the Court of Appeal where Croom-Johnson LJ stated:

> The first distinction between the two causes of action where there is personal injury is the element of contact between the plaintiff and defendant: that is, a touching of some sort. In the action for negligence the physical contact (where it takes place at all) is normally

8 *The Times*, 20 February 1975.

though by no means always unintended. In the action for trespass, to constitute a battery, it is deliberate. Even so it is not every intended contact which is tortious. Apart from special justifications (such as acting in self-defence) there are many examples in everyday life where an intended contact or touch is not actionable as a trespass. These are not necessarily those (such as shaking hands) where consent is actual or to be implied. They may amount to one of the instances had in mind in *Tuberville v. Savage*, 1 Mod. 3 which take place in innocence. A modern instance is the batsman walking up the pavilion steps at Lord's after making a century. He receives hearty slaps of congratulation on his back. He may not want them. Some of them may be too heavy for comfort. No one seeks his permission, or can assume he would give it if it were asked. But would an action for trespass to the person lie?

Another ingredient in the tort of trespass to the person is that of hostility. The references to anger sufficing to turn a touch into a battery (*Cole v. Turner*, 6 Mod. 149) and the lack of an intention to assault which prevents a gesture from being an assault are instances of this. If there is hostile intent, that will by itself be cogent evidence of hostility. But the hostility may be demonstrated in other ways.

The defendant in the present case has sought to add to the list of necessary ingredients. He has submitted that before trespass to the person will lie it is not only the touching that must be deliberate but the infliction of injury. The plaintiff's counsel, on the other hand, contends that it is not the injury to the person which must be intentional, but the act of touching or battery which precedes it: as he put it, what must be intentional is the application of force and not the injury.

...

In our view, the authorities lead one to the conclusion that in a battery there must be an intentional touching or contact in one form or another of the plaintiff by the defendant. That touching must be proved to be a hostile touching. That still leaves unanswered the question 'when is a touching to be called hostile?' Hostility cannot be equated with ill-will or malevolence. It cannot be governed by the obvious intention shown in acts like punching, stabbing or shooting. It cannot be solely governed by an expressed intention, although that may be strong evidence. But the element of hostility, in the sense in which it is now to be considered, must be a question of fact for the tribunal of fact. It may be imported from the circumstances. Take the example of the police officer in *Collins v. Wilcock* [1984] 1 W.L.R. 1172. She touched the woman deliberately, but without an intention to do more than restrain her temporarily. Nevertheless, she was *acting* unlawfully and in that way was acting with hostility. She was acting contrary to the woman's legal right not to be physically restrained. We see no more difficulty in establishing what she intended by means of question and answer, or by inference from the surrounding circumstances, than there is in establishing whether an apparently playful blow was struck in anger. The rules of law governing the legality of arrest may require strict application to the facts of appropriate cases, but in the ordinary give and take of everyday life the tribunal of fact should find no

> difficulty in answering the question 'was this, or was it not, a battery?' Where the immediate act of touching does not itself demonstrate hostility, the plaintiff should plead the facts which are said to do so.
>
> Although we are all entitled to protection from physical molestation we live in a crowded world in which people must be considered as taking on themselves some risk of injury (where it occurs) from the acts of others which are not in themselves unlawful. If negligence cannot be proved, it may be that an injured plaintiff who is also unable to prove a battery, will be without redress.

There has been mixed treatment of the hostility requirement by the Supreme Court. Lord Hoffmann asserted in *Wainwright v Home Office* that battery was defined as touching someone with 'hostile intent'.[9] However, this approach had been strongly criticised by Lord Goff 14 years earlier in another Supreme Court case, *Re F (Mental Patient: Sterilisation)*.

Re F (Mental Patient: Sterilisation) [1990] 2 AC 1, 53–54 (Lord Brandon), 72–73 (Lord Goff)

The facts were set out by Lord Brandon:

> The material facts relating to F., which are not in dispute, are these. She was born on 13 January 1953, so that she is now 36. She suffers from serious mental disability, probably as a consequence of an acute infection of the respiratory tract which she had when she was about nine months old. She has been a voluntary in-patient at Borocourt Hospital (a mental hospital under the control of the health authority) since 1967 when she was 14. Her mental disability takes the form of an arrested or incomplete development of the mind. She has the verbal capacity of a child of two and the general mental capacity of a child of four to five. She is unable to express her views in words but can indicate what she likes or dislikes, for example, people, food, clothes and matters of routine. She experiences emotions such as enjoyment, sadness and fear, but is prone to express them differently from others. She is liable to become aggressive. Her mother is her only relative and visits her regularly. There is a strong bond of affection between them. As a result of the treatment which F. has received during her time in hospital she has made significant progress. She has become less aggressive and is allowed considerable freedom of movement about the hospital grounds which are large. There is, however, no prospect of any development in her mental capacity.
>
> The question of F. being sterilised has arisen because of a relationship which she has formed with a male patient at the same hospital, P. This relationship is of a sexual nature

9 [2003] UKHL 53, [2004] 2 AC 406, [9] (Lord Hoffman). See discussion of this case at 12.6.1 below.

and probably involves sexual intercourse, or something close to it, about twice a month. The relationship is entirely voluntary on F.'s part and it is likely that she obtains pleasure from it. There is no reason to believe that F. has other than the ordinary fertility of a woman of her age. Because of her mental disability, however, she could not cope at all with pregnancy, labour or delivery, the meaning of which she would not understand. Nor could she care for a baby if she ever had one. In these circumstances it would, from a psychiatric point of view, be disastrous for her to conceive a child. There is a serious objection to each of the ordinary methods of contraception. So far as varieties of the pill are concerned she would not be able to use them effectively and there is a risk of their causing damage to her physical health. So far as an intra-uterine device is concerned, there would be danger of infection arising, the symptoms of which she would not be able to describe so that remedial measures could not be taken in time.

Lord Goff most explicitly considered the role of 'hostility' in battery, commenting:

I start with the fundamental principle, now long established, that every person's body is inviolate. As to this, I do not wish to depart from what I myself said in the judgment of the Divisional Court in *Collins v. Wilcock* [1984] 1 W.L.R. 1172, and in particular from the statement, at p. 1177, that the effect of this principle is that everybody is protected not only against physical injury but against any form of physical molestation.

Of course, as a general rule physical interference with another person's body is lawful if he consents to it; though in certain limited circumstances the public interest may require that his consent is not capable of rendering the act lawful. There are also specific cases where physical interference without consent may not be unlawful – chastisement of children, lawful arrest, self-defence, the prevention of crime and so on. As I pointed out in *Collins v. Wilcock* [1984] 1 W.L.R. 1172, 1177, a broader exception has been created to allow for the exigencies of everyday life – jostling in a street or some other crowded place, social contact at parties, and such like. This exception has been said to be founded on implied consent, since those who go about in public places, or go to parties, may be taken to have impliedly consented to bodily contact of this kind. Today this rationalisation can be regarded as artificial; and in particular, it is difficult to impute consent to those who, by reason of their youth or mental disorder, are unable to give their consent. For this reason, I consider it more appropriate to regard such cases as falling within a general exception embracing all physical contact which is generally acceptable in the ordinary conduct of everyday life.

In the old days it used to be said that, for a touching of another's person to amount to a battery, it had to be a touching 'in anger' (see *Cole v Turner* (1794) 6 Mod. 149, per Holt C.J.); and it has recently been said that the touching must be 'hostile' to have that effect (see *Wilson v Pringle* [1987] Q.B. 237, 253). I respectfully doubt whether that is correct. A prank that gets out of hand; an over-friendly slap on the back; surgical treatment by a surgeon who mistakenly thinks that the patient has consented to it – all these things may transcend the bounds of lawfulness, without being characterised as hostile. Indeed the suggested qualification is difficult to reconcile with the principle that any touching of another's body is, in the absence of lawful excuse, capable of amounting to a battery and a trespass. Furthermore, in the case of medical treatment, we have to bear well in mind the libertarian principle of self-determination which, to adopt the words of Cardozo J. (in *Schloendorff v. Society of New York Hospital* (1914) 105 N.E. 92, 93) recognises that:

> 'Every human being of adult years and sound mind has a right to determine what shall be done with his own body; and a surgeon who performs an operation without his patient's consent commits an assault ...'

This principle has been stated previously by Lord Reid in *S v McC (orse S) and M (D S Intervener)*.[10]

> **Question to consider:** What role, if any, should 'hostility' play in the tort of battery? Why have the courts had such difficulty reconciling this aspect of the tort?

12.3.3 Concluding thoughts on assault and battery

As discussed above, it is important to remember that assault and battery (and, by extension, other intentional torts against the person) have significant differences from negligence. It is often remarked that they aim to vindicate different rights – as outlined by Trindade. Negligence aims to compensate the harmed individual, whereas intentional torts protect the claimant's autonomy and rights.

FA Trindade, 'Intentional Torts: Some Thoughts on Assault and Battery' (1982) 2 *OJLS* 211, 211, 237 (footnotes omitted)

Assault and battery are not fashionable or popular torts in the sense that they are not much used to vindicate rights as is the modern tort of negligence, even when they are capable of being so used. Indeed, it is fairly unusual today to see reported cases of civil assault and battery. Why is this so? First of all, many of the cases of intentional assault and battery are also crimes and recent developments in compensating victims of crimes, which have generally made it easier to obtain compensation, are naturally relied upon by the victims of such crimes rather than the civil actions for assault and battery – especially as there is some evidence to suggest that many of those who commit these intentional torts are impecunious and therefore not in a position to pay the damages that may be awarded against them. Secondly, there is, or so it would seem, a certain confusion, perhaps even ignorance, about the ingredients of the intentional torts of assault and battery. Quite

10 [1972] AC 24 at 43.

recently a Canadian judge expressed the view that 'the distinction between assault and battery had been blurred, and that when we now speak of an assault, it may include a battery'. The requirements of directness, the nature of an 'intentional' act, the kind of contact required for battery, the kind of threat required for assault, the sort of apprehension sufficient for assault, the relevance of the knowledge of the plaintiff and defendant of the assault and battery and the question of consent are all matters which are not dealt with adequately or with sufficient clarity in the textbooks. This may have contributed to what appears to be a certain reluctance in the profession to plead an action in intentional trespass to the person even where it would be proper and appropriate to do so.

…

The tort of battery can be used not only to protect someone from actual physical injury but also to protect him from intentional or reckless contacts with his person which would generally be regarded as objectionable. The tort of assault on the other hand protects a person from threats (by acts or even by words alone) which cause that person to expect an imminent contact with his person by either the person making the threat or by someone acting under his control. This tort is extremely important in protecting the mental integrity of the person because the anticipation of physical harm and sometimes even the anticipation of mere physical contact may be traumatic for the person who is forced to anticipate it.

The torts of assault and battery (together with false imprisonment) not only provide compensation for the victims of these torts but they also have an important role to play in the vindication of constitutional rights. The compensatory function of these torts may be of slightly less significance today in view of certain recent developments in compensating victims of crime, but the other function continues to be of considerable importance. The traditional torts of assault and battery adapted to meet the changing needs of our time are therefore worthy of our consideration and it is well to dispel such ignorance as there is about them.

Question to consider: What are the similarities and differences between assault and battery relative to negligence? Why do you think they are all labelled as 'torts'?

Other resources: Peter Cane, 'Mens Rea in Tort Law' (2000) 20 *OJLS* 533; Nicholas J McBride, 'Trespass to the Person: The Effect of Mistakes and Alternative Remedies on Liability' (2008) *CLJ* 461; Normann Witzleb and Robyn Carroll, 'The Role of Vindication in Torts Damages' (2009) 17 *Tort L Rev* 16.

12.4 False imprisonment

The next intentional tort against the person considered is false imprisonment, which recognises and protects personal autonomy and freedom of movement. Goff LJ defines the tort as 'the unlawful imposition of constraint upon another's freedom of movement from a particular place'.[11] The tort of false imprisonment significantly overlaps with the protection of liberty under Article 5(1) of the European Convention on Human Rights.

12.4.1 Confinement

The basis of false imprisonment is that an individual is confined without their consent. Confinement, however, must be significant and involve more than mere obstruction and inconvenience. For example, in *Bird v Jones*,[12] the sectioning off of part of Hammersmith Bridge in London was not false imprisonment as the claimant had alternative, albeit less convenient, routes they could take. There will also be no false imprisonment if the confinement occurs as a result of the lawful and reasonable enforcement of contractual obligations, such as in *Robinson v Balmain New Ferry Co Ltd*.[13] In this case, the defendant ran a harbour steam ferry and charged customers for entering and exiting the wharf instead of being charged to use the ferry. There was a clear sign stating that all people must pay one penny on entering or leaving the wharf and that no exceptions would be made even if the passenger had not travelled on the ferry. The claimant waited 20 minutes for a ferry and then decided to exit but did not want to pay the penny charge. He argued that it was false imprisonment. The Privy Council rejected this argument, holding that the notice of the terms and conditions formed part of the contract with the defendant, meaning there was no unlawful confinement.

12.4.2 Awareness

One of the controversial questions regarding false imprisonment is whether the confined individual needs to have been aware of the restrictions in place. One particularly complex case considering this issue is *R v Bournewood Community and Mental Health NHS Trust, ex p L*.[14] The claimant in this matter had extreme intellectual disabilities, meaning he was incapable of consenting to medical treatment. He became distressed and was taken by ambulance to the Accident and Emergency Department of a local hospital, where he was sedated and detained in an unlocked mental health ward in the behavioural unit. It was determined that there was no requirement to detain him under the provisions of the Mental Health Act 1983 as he was fully compliant and did not resist admission. The claimant was admitted informally.

Due to the individual's mental state, they were not aware of their confinement. However, this was not relevant for false imprisonment, which is focused on

11 *Collins v Wilcock* [1984] 1 WLR 1172 (QB), 1177.

12 (1845) 7 QB 742.

13 [1910] AC 295.

14 [1999] 1 AC 458.

protecting the liberty of individuals and does not require that the claimant show special damage.[15] By confining someone, even if they are unaware of it, you are harming their liberty, and they will be entitled to claim damages.[16]

> **Question to consider:** Should you have to have an awareness of your confinement to sue for false imprisonment? If you were not aware of the situation, what harm has been suffered?
>
> **Other Resources:** *Meering v Grahame-White Aviation Co Ltd* (1920) 122 LT 44, CA; *Murray v Ministry of Defence* [1988] 1 WLR 692, HL; *Herring v Boyle* (1834) 1 CM & R 377; *GE v Commissioner of An Garda Síochána* [2022] IESC 51.

12.4.3 False imprisonment in the prison system

A significant number of more recent cases of false imprisonment have been based within the prison system. This raises important and interesting questions about the nature of confinement; if an individual is already lawfully confined by the State, when can the confinement become *unlawful*?

R (on the application of Jalloh (formerly Jollah)) v Secretary of State for the Home Department [2020] UKSC 4, [2021] AC 262, [24]–[27] (Lady Hale)

The claimant was granted asylum in 2003 but was convicted of various offences in 2006, and a deportation order was made against him in 2008. There was a further conviction in 2013, and when he completed his custodial sentence, the claimant was issued with a document headed 'NOTICE OF RESTRICTION', imposing several restrictions on him, including reporting to an immigration officer three times a week, living at a specified address, electronic monitoring, and staying at home between 11pm and 7am every day. If he did not comply with these restrictions, there was a potential penalty of a £5,000 fine, six months' imprisonment, or both.

The curfew was in place for 891 days. Although there were a number of occasions when the claimant breached the curfew, either for the entire night or part of it, he generally sought to comply with the restrictions. However, it was determined in 2016 that the Secretary of State lacked the power to impose a curfew by way of restriction. This raised the question of whether a curfew and home detention were sufficient constraints to constitute false imprisonment.

After reviewing the relevant case law and arguments from both sides, Lady Hale held that this was a 'classic detention or confinement' case.

---

15 *Murray v Ministry of Defence* [1988] 1 WLR 692, HL.

16 However, they may only be entitled to limited damages if their confinement was both limited and they were unaware of it; see *R (Lumba) v Secretary of State for the Home Department* [2011] UKSC 12, [2012] 1 AC 245.

24. As it is put in *Street on Torts*, 15th edn (2018), by Christian Witting, p 259, 'False imprisonment involves an act of the defendant which directly and intentionally (or possibly negligently) causes the confinement of the claimant within an area delimited by the defendant.' The essence of imprisonment is being made to stay in a particular place by another person. The methods which might be used to keep a person there are many and various. They could be physical barriers, such as locks and bars. They could be physical people, such as guards who would physically prevent the person leaving if he tried to do so. They could also be threats, whether of force or of legal process. A good example is *R v Rumble* (2003) 167 JP 205. The defendant in a magistrates' court who had surrendered to his bail was in custody even though there was no dock, no usher, nor security staff and thus nothing to prevent his escaping (as indeed he did). The point is that the person is obliged to stay where he is ordered to stay whether he wants to do so or not.

25. In this case there is no doubt that the defendant defined the place where the claimant was to stay between the hours of 11.00 pm and 7.00 am. There was no suggestion that he could go somewhere else during those hours without the defendant's permission. This is not a case like *Bird v Jones* 7 QB 742 where the claimant could cross the bridge by another route or *Robinson v Balmain New Ferry Co Ltd* [1910] AC 295 where he had agreed to go onto the wharf on terms that he could only get out if he paid a penny.

26. The fact that the claimant did from time to time ignore his curfew for reasons that seemed good to him makes no difference to his situation while he was obeying it. Like the prisoner who goes absent from his open prison, or the tunneller who gets out of the prison camp, he is not imprisoned while he is away. But he is imprisoned while he is where the defendant wants him to be.

27. There is, of course, a crucial difference between voluntary compliance with an instruction and enforced compliance with that instruction. The Court of Appeal held that this was a case of enforced not voluntary compliance and I agree. It is not to be compared with those cases in which the claimant went voluntarily with the sheriff's officer. There can be no doubt that the claimant's compliance was enforced. He was wearing an electronic tag which meant that leaving his address would be detected. The monitoring company would then telephone him to find out where he was. He was warned in the clearest possible terms that breaking the curfew could lead to a £5,000 fine or imprisonment for up to six months or both. He was well aware that it could also lead to his being detained again under the 1971 Act. All of this was backed up by the full authority of the State, which was claiming to have the power to do this. The idea that the claimant was a free agent, able to come and go as he pleased, is completely unreal.

Therefore, the claimant was successful in their claim and awarded £4,000 for the false imprisonment by the State.

This approach can be contrasted with *R v Deputy Governor of Parkhurst Prison, ex p Hague*.

R v Deputy Governor of Parkhurst Prison, ex p Hague [1992] 1 AC 58, 162–63 (Lord Bridge)

This case takes a rather different approach to false imprisonment. It considers whether the prisoner's continued segregation in breach of the prison rules amounted to confinement sufficient for false imprisonment.

The starting point is s 12(1) of the Prison Act 1952 which provides:

> 'A prisoner, whether sentenced to imprisonment or committed to prison on remand or pending trial or otherwise, may be lawfully confined in any prison.'

This provides lawful authority for the restraint of the prisoner within the defined bounds of the prison by the governor of the prison, who has the legal custody of the prisoner under section 13, or by any prison officer acting with the governor's authority. Can the prisoner then complain that his legal rights are infringed by a restraint which confines him at any particular time within a particular part of the prison? It seems to me that the reality of prison life demands a negative answer to this question. Certainly in the ordinary closed prison the ordinary prisoner will at any time of day or night be in a particular part of the prison, not because that is where he chooses to be, but because that is where the prison regime requires him to be. He will be in his cell, in the part of the prison where he is required to work, in the exercise yard, eating meals, attending education classes or enjoying whatever recreation is permitted, all in the appointed place and at the appointed time and all in accordance with a more or less rigid regime to which he must conform. Thus the concept of the prisoner's 'residual liberty' as a species of freedom of movement within the prison enjoyed as a legal right which the prison authorities cannot lawfully restrain seems to me quite illusory. The prisoner is at all times lawfully restrained within closely defined bounds and if he is kept in a segregated cell, at a time when, if the rules had not been misapplied, he would be in the company of other prisoners in the workshop, at the dinner table or elsewhere, this is not the deprivation of his liberty of movement, which is the essence of the tort of false imprisonment, it is the substitution of one form of restraint for another.

Mr. Harris seeks to surmount these difficulties by submitting that whenever there is a breach of the rules which is sufficiently 'fundamental' this converts an otherwise lawful imprisonment into an unlawful imprisonment. This, as I understand it, is quite a different concept from that of an infringement of residual liberty. The submission is that any breach of the rules which is sufficiently far reaching in its effect on the prisoner, for example the failure to supply him with clothing 'adequate for warmth and health' pursuant to rule 20(2), undermines the legality of his imprisonment. Logically this would lead to the conclusion that the prisoner who has not been supplied with proper clothing would be entitled to walk out of the prison, but Mr. Harris understandably disclaims any such extravagant proposition. It follows that the authority given by section 12(1) for lawful confinement of the prisoner cannot possibly be read as subject to any implied term with respect to compliance with the *Prison Rules 1964* and this is fatal to any submission which seeks to make the lawfulness of the imprisonment depend in any sense on such compliance.

In my opinion, to hold a prisoner entitled to damages for false imprisonment on the ground that he has been subject to a restraint upon his movement which was not in accordance with the *Prison Rules 1964* would be, in effect, to confer on him under a different legal label a cause of action for breach of statutory duty under the rules. Having reached the conclusion that it was not the intention of the rules to confer such a right, I am satisfied that the right cannot properly be asserted in the alternative guise of a claim to damages for false imprisonment.

Question to consider: How should the law address false imprisonment within the prison system? When can an imprisoned individual be unlawfully detained?

Other resources: Jason NE Varuhas, 'False Imprisonment of Prisoners: Lawful Authority, Omissions and Damages' (2010) 69 *CLJ* 438; Efrat Arbel, 'Devalued Liberty and Undue Deference: The Tort of False Imprisonment and the Law of Solitary Confinement' (2018) 84 *Sup Ct L Rev* 43; *Weldon v Home Office* [1992] 1 AC 58; *R v Governor of Brockhill Prison, ex p Evans (No 2)* [2001] 2 AC 19.

A further question arises in the case of false imprisonment within prison systems – when is 'loss' suffered so that the party has a claim for substantive damages?

R (Lumba) v Secretary of State for the Home Department [2011] UKSC 12, [2012] 1 AC 245, [91]–[96] (Lord Dyson)

In this case, a number of foreign national prisoners, following the completion of their prison sentences, were detained under the Immigration Act 1971. This continued detention was a result of an unpublished policy and did not occur in accordance with the published process. The claimants, who were two of the detailed prisoners, argued that the Secretary of State had unlawfully detained them, and that they were entitled to substantive damages. The Supreme Court agreed that they had been unlawfully detained, but held that they were not entitled to any more than nominal damages, as they had not suffered any loss or damage.

91. Mr Husain and Mr Martin Westgate QC submit that, even if it was inevitable that the appellants would have been detained if the statutory power to detain had been lawfully exercised, they are nevertheless entitled to substantial and not merely nominal damages. They emphasise that false imprisonment is a tort of strict liability which is actionable without proof of special damage. The focus is on the claimant's right rather than the culpability of the defendant's conduct. They rely on two authorities in support of their argument. The first is *Roberts v Chief Constable of the Cheshire Constabulary* ....

92. Clarke LJ gave the leading judgment. He said at p 668D that there was an infringement of the plaintiff's legitimate right to have his case reviewed

'and that, although the outcome may not have been affected by the failure to review in time, this infringement cannot be regarded as a purely nominal matter or a matter compensatable by entirely nominal damages. There are rules, the police must stick to them ...'

93. I do not consider that this case was correctly decided on the issue of damages. I agree that the plaintiff was entitled to be put into the position in which he would have been if the tort of false imprisonment had not been committed .... It seems to me that the fallacy in the analysis in *Roberts* is that it draws no distinction between a detainee who would have remained in detention if the review had been carried out (and therefore no tort committed) and a detainee who would *not* have remained in detention if the review had been carried out. But the position of the two detainees is fundamentally different. The first has suffered no loss because he would have remained in detention whether the tort was committed or not. The second has suffered real loss because, if the tort had not been committed, he would not have remained in detention.

94. The second authority relied on in support of the appellants' case is *Kuwait Airways Corpn v Iraqi Airways Co (Nos 4 and 5)* [2002] 2 AC 883. It was held there that it is no answer to a claim in conversion of goods for a defendant to say that the goods were or would have been subsequently converted by a third party: see the discussion by Lord Nicholls of Birkenhead at paras 81–84 of his speech. But questions of causation in relation to cases of successive conversion by different tortfeasors have no application in the present context.

95. The question here is simply whether, on the hypothesis under consideration, the victims of the false imprisonment have suffered any loss which should be compensated in more than nominal damages. Exemplary damages apart, the purpose of damages is to compensate the victims of civil wrongs for the loss and damage that the wrongs have caused. If the power to detain had been exercised by the application of lawful policies, and on the assumption that the *Hardial Singh* principles had been properly applied (an issue which I discuss at paras 129–148 below), it is inevitable that the appellants would have been detained. In short, they suffered no loss or damage as a result of the unlawful exercise of the power to detain. They should receive no more than nominal damages.

96. I should add that this approach is consistent with the observation by Lord Griffiths in *Murray v Ministry of Defence* [1988] 1 WLR 692, 703A–B: 'if a person is unaware that he has been falsely imprisoned and has suffered no harm, he can normally expect to recover no more than nominal damages.'

This approach was explicitly rejected in Ireland in *GE v Commissioner of An Garda Síochána*.

GE v Commissioner of An Garda Síochána [2022] IESC 51, [35]–[39], [41]–[42] (Hogan J)

35. In *Lumba*, a majority of the UK Supreme Court considered that the damages to be awarded should be so reduced. The *Lumba* majority proceeded on the basis that the damages in English tort law were essentially *compensatory* in nature and – or so the majority reasoned – a plaintiff was not entitled to be compensated for an illegal detention where he had suffered no real loss. In this respect the *Lumba* majority rejected the very notion of what was described as 'vindicatory damages.' ….

36. Other members of the majority in *Lumba* spoke in similar terms. Before proceeding further, however, it may be convenient also to note that the High Court of Australia reached a broadly similar conclusion in *Lewis v. Australian Capital Territory* [2020] HCA 26. This was a case where, it seems, the appellant's sentence in respect of a serious assault had been converted from one of periodic detention into full time detention. That decision of a sentencing board was held to be invalid because it was held the board could not establish that the appellant had been duly served with notice of the proposed alteration to the sentence.

37. The High Court of Australia accepted the broad parameters of *Lumba*, thereby rejecting the notion of vindicatory damages. In essence, just as in *Lumba*, the plaintiff could – or, depending on your point of view, would – have been lawfully detained had appropriate procedures been followed.

38. Yet within the four judgments of the Court (Kiefel C.J. and Keane J.; Gageler, Gordon and Edelman JJ.) there are some subtle (but important) differences and not all aspects of the 'but for' counterfactual assumed in *Lumba* were endorsed. It is again probably unnecessary for me to parse the various judgments in exhaustive detail, as Murray J. has already performed that task in his comprehensive judgment for the Court of Appeal. It is sufficient to point to some of the views expressed on this point by Gaegler, Gordon and Edelman JJ. Thus, for example, Edelman J. differed from the approach taken by Lord Kitchin in Lumba. For Lord Kitchin it was sufficient that the plaintiff 'could' have been lawfully detained, whereas Edelman J. stressed that this is in itself was not enough to justify a purely nominal award of damages: his lawful detention would have to have been inevitable had appropriate procedures been followed for purely nominal damages to be awarded.

39. For my part, I respectfully take a different view to the decisions in *Lumba* or, for that matter, in *Lewis*. I consider that vindicatory damages are indeed an established feature of the common law tradition, at least so far as trespassory torts such as false imprisonment are concerned. Furthermore, such is in principle also required by the very words of … the Constitution which requires the State 'in the case of injustice done' to 'vindicate the life, person, good name and property rights of every citizen.' False imprisonment which is accompanied (as in this case) by the true and actual deprivation of liberty will impact on the person and (depending on the circumstances) may affect his or her good name. Accordingly, the scope of the remedies provided in respect of the tort of false imprisonment must thus be construed in the light of these constitutional guarantees.

…

The vindicatory nature of damages for false imprisonment

41. Since many of these terms are used in a promiscuous and ill-defined way by both judges and by the textbook writers alike, it is important to be clear on what is meant by both nominal damages and vindicatory damages in this context. In *Redmond v. Minister for the Environment (No.2)* [2006] 3 IR 1 at 7, Herbert J. said that nominal damages are not 'be considered to be in any sense, derisory or contemptuous.' Herbert J. then quoted with approval the following dictum of Lord Halsbury LC in *Owners of the Steamship Mediana v. Owners of the Lightship Comet* [1900] AC 113 at 116:

> '… "nominal damages" is a technical phrase which means that you have negatived anything like real damages, but that you are affirming by your nominal damages that there is an infraction of a legal right …'

42. By contrast, so far as vindicatory damages are concerned, I mean damages which are not nominal, but which are nonetheless intended to mark the importance of the right which has been infringed. In this respect they differ from exemplary damages the award of which is generally confined to those cases where the tortfeasor has personally acted oppressively or recklessly or in a high-handed way. The vindicatory element of any damages award is not itself a separate head of damages in the way that, for example, exemplary damages or special damages are, but the sum awarded by way of compensation rather reflects the desire to vindicate the importance of the right which has been infringed.

As a result, despite the factual similarities, in *GE v Commissioner of An Garda Síochána* [2021], substantive damages of €7,500 were awarded to the claimant.

Question to consider: Do you agree with the approach of *R (Lumba) v Secretary of State for the Home Department* or *GE v Commissioner of An Garda Síochána*. Why? How do these cases relate to the concept of 'harm' in the tort of false imprisonment?

Other resources: Jason NE Varuhas, 'The Concept of "Vindication" in the Law of Torts: Rights, Interests and Damages' (2014) 34 *OJLS* 253; *Lewis v Australian Capital Territory* [2020] HCA 26, [2021] 1 LRC 274; *Walker v Commissioner of Police of the Metropolis* [2014] EWCA Civ 897, [2015] 1 WLR 312; Margaret Fordham, 'False Imprisonment and Prisoners: A Question of Justice or Law?' [2003] *SJLS* 444.

12.5 Defences

For a more detailed discussion of defences to tort law generally, please refer to Chapter 16. This section is not intended to provide a full analysis of the relevant defences; instead, it gives the reader a high-level outline of the defences that apply differently in the context of intentional torts against the person. These defences are (1) consent, (2) necessity, (3) self-defence, (4) contributory negligence, and (5) lawful authority.

12.5.1 Consent

One of the requirements of the torts of assault, battery, and false imprisonment is that the wrongdoing occurred without the consent of the victim. For example, if the victim consented to the touching, there would be no claim for battery. Therefore, the lack of consent is an element of the tort in question, meaning consent is not a 'true' defence. The burden will remain on the claimant to show that consent was not given.[17]

There are restrictions and limits placed on what 'consent' must look like. It must be genuinely given, and the victim must have been provided with sufficient information about the situation to provide their consent. This is particularly important in the context of medical treatment, as outlined by *Montgomery v Lanarkshire Health Board*.

Montgomery v Lanarkshire Health Board [2015] UKSC 11, [2015] AC 1430, [87]–[91] (Lord Kerr and Lord Reed)

This case involved a heart-breaking situation of a baby being born with severe disabilities due to complications during delivery. In looking at what consent means in medical situations, Lord Kerr and Lord Reed (delivering a joint judgment with which the rest of the court agreed) highlighted the complex balance that had to be made.

> 87. … An adult person of sound mind is entitled to decide which, if any, of the available forms of treatment to undergo, and her consent must be obtained before treatment interfering with her bodily integrity is undertaken. The doctor is therefore under a duty to take reasonable care to ensure that the patient is aware of any material risks involved in any recommended treatment, and of any reasonable alternative or variant treatments. The test of materiality is whether, in the circumstances of the particular case, a reasonable person in the patient's position would be likely to attach significance to the risk, or the doctor is or should reasonably be aware that the particular patient would be likely to attach significance to it.
>
> 88. The doctor is however entitled to withhold from the patient information as to a risk if he reasonably considers that its disclosure would be seriously detrimental to the patient's health. The doctor is also excused from conferring with the patient in circumstances of necessity, as for example where the patient requires treatment urgently but is unconscious or otherwise unable to make a decision. It is unnecessary for the purposes of this case to consider in detail the scope of those exceptions.
>
> 89. Three further points should be made. First, it follows from this approach that the assessment of whether a risk is material cannot be reduced to percentages. The significance of a given risk is likely to reflect a variety of factors besides its magnitude: for example, the

17 *Freeman v Home Office (No 2)* [1984] 1 QB 524, 537–539 (McCowan J), 557 (Sir John Donaldson MR).

nature of the risk, the effect which its occurrence would have on the life of the patient, the importance to the patient of the benefits sought to be achieved by the treatment, the alternatives available, and the risks involved in those alternatives. The assessment is therefore fact-sensitive, and sensitive also to the characteristics of the patient.

90. Secondly, the doctor's advisory role involves dialogue, the aim of which is to ensure that the patient understands the seriousness of her condition, and the anticipated benefits and risks of the proposed treatment and any reasonable alternatives, so that she is then in a position to make an informed decision. This role will only be performed effectively if the information provided is comprehensible. The doctor's duty is not therefore fulfilled by bombarding the patient with technical information which she cannot reasonably be expected to grasp, let alone by routinely demanding her signature on a consent form.

91. Thirdly, it is important that the therapeutic exception should not be abused. It is a limited exception to the general principle that the patient should make the decision whether to undergo a proposed course of treatment: it is not intended to subvert that principle by enabling the doctor to prevent the patient from making an informed choice where she is liable to make a choice which the doctor considers to be contrary to her best interests.

12.5.2 Necessity

There is also the defence of necessity, which is particularly relevant in the case of rescuers and medical assistance providers. Without this defence, providing medical care to unconscious people or those who cannot actively consent could potentially result in a claim of trespass against the person.

Re F (Mental Patient: Sterilisation) [1990] 2 AC 1, 75 (Lord Goff), 69 (Lord Griffiths)

In this case, F, a severely disabled 36-year-old woman living in a mental hospital, had developed a sexual relationship with another patient. Both her mother and the hospital staff thought it was in her best interest to be sterilised. The concern was whether she could cope with the physical and emotional difficulties of pregnancy and childbirth. Given F's lack of capacity to consent, her mother sought a declaration that the operation would not amount to an unlawful trespass.

When defining necessity, Lord Goff commented that:

[Lord Goff at 75] ... to fall within the principle, not only (1) must there be a necessity to act when it is not practicable to communicate with the assisted person, but also (2) the action taken must be such as a reasonable person would in all the circumstances take, acting in the best interests of the assisted person.

The House of Lords upheld the declaration of lawfulness, finding that it was in the patient's best interests to receive the medical procedure. However, they did reflect on the complex nature of these legal questions, with Lord Griffiths commenting:

> [Lord Griffiths at 69] I agree that those charged with the care of the mentally incompetent are protected from any criminal or tortious action based on lack of consent. Whether one arrives at this conclusion by applying a principle of 'necessity' as do Lord Goff of Chieveley and Lord Brandon of Oakbrook or by saying that it is in the public interest as did Neill L.J. in the Court of Appeal, appear to me to be inextricably interrelated conceptual justifications for the humane development of the common law. Why is it necessary that the mentally incompetent should be given treatment to which they lack the capacity to consent? The answer must surely be because it is in the public interest that it should be so.
>
> In a civilised society the mentally incompetent must be provided with medical and nursing care and those who look after them must do their best for them. Stated in legal terms the doctor who undertakes responsibility for the treatment of a mental patient who is incapable of giving consent to treatment must give the treatment that he considers to be in the best interests of his patient.

Mental Capacity Act 2005

1 The principles

(1) The following principles apply for the purposes of this Act.

(2) A person must be assumed to have capacity unless it is established that he lacks capacity.

The starting point is that a person has capacity, unless it can be shown that they do not under the Mental Capacity Act 2005 or through some other legal mechanism.

(3) A person is not to be treated as unable to make a decision unless all practicable steps to help him to do so have been taken without success.

There is an obligation to assist the person in question to make a decision if that is at all possible, putting a proactive obligation to help those subject to the Act.

(4) A person is not to be treated as unable to make a decision merely because he makes an unwise decision.

The test is, therefore, not on the substance of the decision – people are allowed to make unwise or unreasonable decisions provided they have the capacity to do so.

(5) An act done, or decision made, under this Act for or on behalf of a person who lacks capacity must be done, or made, in his best interests.

The test is always focused on the best interests of the individual in question, as defined in greater detail in s 4; however, there is also a broad requirement to consider 'all relevant circumstances'.

(6) Before the act is done, or the decision is made, regard must be had to whether the purpose for which it is needed can be as

> effectively achieved in a way that is less restrictive of the person's rights and freedom of action.
>
> **2 People who lack capacity**
>
> (1) For the purposes of this Act, a person lacks capacity in relation to a matter if at the material time he is unable to make a decision for himself in relation to the matter because of an impairment of, or a disturbance in the functioning of, the mind or brain.
>
> **3 Inability to make decisions**
>
> (1) For the purposes of section 2, a person is unable to make a decision for himself if he is unable—
>
> (a) to understand the information relevant to the decision,
>
> (b) to retain that information,
>
> (c) to use or weigh that information as part of the process of making the decision, or
>
> (d) to communicate his decision (whether by talking, using sign language or any other means).

Declaring that someone lacks capacity should be treated as a last resort. All other steps should be considered beforehand, as we value people's autonomy, rights, and freedoms.

The threshold test for capacity is whether the person is able to, at the relevant time, make a decision for themselves.

This specifically focuses on impairments and disturbances of the mind or brain as reasons why they cannot make decisions.

There is a relatively prescriptive threshold that will be provided, focusing on the individual's decision-making process.

Question to consider: Do the intentional torts against the person adequately respond to capacity challenges of vulnerable individuals? Consider both the case law and statute in your analysis.

Other resources: Jonathan Herring and Jesse Wall, 'Autonomy, Capacity and Vulnerable Adults: Filling the Gaps in the Mental Capacity Act' (2015) 35 *LS* 698; Nancy J Knauer, 'Defining Capacity: Balancing the Competing Interests of Autonomy and Need' (2003) 12 *Temple Political & Civil Rights L Rev* 321; Cressida Auckland and Imogen Goold, 'Re-Evaluating "Best Interests" in the Wake of *Raqeeb v Barts NHS Foundation Trust & Anors*'(2020) 83(6) *MLR* 1328; *St George's Healthcare NHS Trust v S* [1998] 3 WLR 936; *Re B (Adult: Refusal of Treatment)* [2002] EWHC 429 (Fam); *Re MB (Caesarean Section)* [1997] 2 FLR 426.

12.5.3 Other defences

Whilst necessity and consent are the main defences, there are others that should be briefly outlined:

(1) *Contributory negligence* – it is highly unlikely that contributory negligence would apply to the intentional torts against the person. Under the Law Reform (Contributory Negligence) Act 1945, the definition of contributory negligence is a reflection of the common law, which held that the defence did not apply

to intentional torts. This was because, at common law, contributory negligence was a complete defence, and it was considered inappropriate to have a complete defence available to someone who had committed a deliberate wrong.[18]

(2) *Self-defence and defence of others* – for this defence to apply, the defendant must show that they acted on an honest *and* reasonable belief. This differs from the criminal law, where the belief needs to only have been honestly held. There will also be a restriction that the defence must be proportionate to the original threat.[19]

(3) *Lawful authority* – if enforcement officers are acting lawfully in their detention of an individual, there will be no tortious liability regardless of whether the arrest involved both battery and confinement. However, there are limits to police and other officers' authority under both the common law of torts and the European Convention on Human Rights. In general, there is a requirement to show that the actions were proportionate and the least restrictive means available.[20]

12.6 Other intentional torts

There are three additional intentional torts against the person that should also be considered: the tort in *Wilkinson v Downton*, the Protection from Harassment Act 1997, and malicious prosecution.

12.6.1 The tort in *Wilkinson v Downton*

This tort is generally described as a 'sui generis' cause of action designed to protect people from the intentional infliction of emotional harm. Since the decision in 1897, the tort has been upheld and applied on numerous occasions,[21] but has been subject to some criticisms.[22]

Wilkinson v Downton [1897] 2 QB 57, 59

On the evening that the claimant's husband attended a race meeting, the defendant visited the claimant's house and informed her that her husband had been in an accident and had broken both of his legs. He further stated that the claimant's husband was lying in The Elms public house at Leytonstone, and that he had been sent to fetch the claimant and take her to her husband. All of these statements were false,

---

18 *Pritchard v Co-operative Group Ltd* [2011] 3 WLR 1272, [2011] EWCA Civ 329 (Aikens LJ); John Murphy, 'Misleading Appearances in the Tort of Deceit' (2016) 75 *CLJ* 301.

19 *Lane v Holloway* [1968] 1 QB 379, CA.

20 *Austin v Commissioner of Police of the Metropolis* [2009] UKHL 5, [2009] AC 564.

21 *Janvier v Sweeney* [1919] 2 KB 316, CA; *Khorasandjian v Bush* [1993] QB 727, CA; *Wong v Parkside Health NHS Trust* [2001] EWCA Civ 1721, [2003] 3 All ER 932; *C v D* [2006] EWHC 166 (QB), [2006] All ER (D) 329 (Feb); *Sullivan v Boylan* [2013] IEHC 104, [2013] 1 IR 510.

22 For example, Lord Hoffmann commented that intentional infliction of harm 'has nothing to do with trespass to the person' in *Wainwright v Home Office* [2003] UKHL 53, [2004] 2 AC 406, [47].

and the claimant's husband was fine. However, the claimant believed the comments and became seriously ill from what was, at the time, called 'nervous shock', entailing weeks of suffering and medical expenses. The claimant also incurred the cost of railway fares to see her husband. The defendant stated that the comments were only made as a 'practical joke'. He further claimed that the damage caused to the claimant by way of nervous shock could not be supported as the consequence was too remote.

Wright J awarded both the railway fares and the claim for nervous shock. In relation to the second award, the larger damages for nervous shock, his Honour commented that:

> ... a person who makes a false statement intended to be acted on must make good the damage naturally resulting from its being acted on. Here there is no injuria of that kind. I think, however, that the verdict may be supported upon another ground. The defendant has, as I assume for the moment, wilfully done an act calculated to cause physical harm to the plaintiff – that is to say, to infringe her legal right to personal safety, and has in fact thereby caused physical harm to her. That proposition without more appears to me to state a good cause of action, there being no justification alleged for the act. This wilful injuria is in law malicious, although no malicious purpose to cause the harm which was caused nor any motive of spite is imputed to the defendant.
>
> It remains to consider whether the assumptions involved in the proposition are made out. One question is whether the defendant's act was so plainly calculated to produce some effect of the kind which was produced that an intention to produce it ought to be imputed to the defendant, regard being had to the fact that the effect was produced on a person proved to be in an ordinary state of health and mind. I think that it was. It is difficult to imagine that such a statement, made suddenly and with apparent seriousness, could fail to produce grave effects under the circumstances upon any but an exceptionally indifferent person, and therefore an intention to produce such an effect must be imputed, and it is no answer in law to say that more harm was done than was anticipated, for that is commonly the case with all wrongs. The other question is whether the effect was, to use the ordinary phrase, too remote to be in law regarded as a consequence for which the defendant is answerable. Apart from authority, I should give the same answer and on the same ground as the last question, and say that it was not too remote.

It is difficult to provide a 'test' for the tort from the words Wright J provided in 1897, although it was generally accepted that this case created tortious liability. Helpfully, the Supreme Court in *O (A Child) v Rhodes* provided clarification and guidance, stating that the claimant needed to show:

(1) *a conduct element* – words or conduct directed at the claimant with no justification or excuse;
(2) *a mental element* – requiring an intention to cause emotional distress or severe mental upset;
(3) *a consequence element* – the creation of physical harm or a recognised psychiatric illness.

Due to developments in our understanding of psychiatric illnesses, the test from *Wilkinson v Downton* has developed significantly. The Supreme Court in *O (A Child) v Rhodes* took the opportunity to reflect on the tort and partially clarify how it may apply in modern cases.

O (A Child) v Rhodes [2015] UKSC 32, [2016] AC 219, [51], [73]–[76] (Lady Hale and Lord Toulson)

In this case, Rhodes, a well-known concert pianist, wrote a personal memoir that described the severe abuse he experienced as a child and his subsequent mental health challenges and issues with addiction. His ex-wife sought an injunction preventing publication of the memoir (or a requirement that significant parts be deleted before publication) on the basis that the publication would cause severe emotional distress and harm to their 'psychologically vulnerable' son. The specific question was whether the tort could be used to prevent a person from publishing true information about themselves.

The Supreme Court held that the facts of the case did not fulfil the requirements of the tort in *Wilkinson v Downton* as there was no intentional infliction of harm, and it was not enough to show imputed intention or recklessness. As discussed above, it was held that recklessness is an insufficient basis for imposing liability for the tort in *Wilkinson v Downton*, and, instead, specific intention is necessary.

> 51. *Wilkinson v Downton* [1897] 2 QB 57 has been a source of much discussion and debate in legal textbooks and academic articles but seldom invoked in practice. This may be due to the development of the law of negligence in the area of recognised illness resulting from nervous shock.

After discussing the facts of *Wilkinson*, and some of the cases that applied it, the judges went on to consider what it entailed.

> 73. In *Wilkinson v Downton* Wright J recognised that wilful infringement of the right to personal safety was a tort. It has three elements: a conduct element, a mental element and a consequence element. The issues in this case relate to the first and second elements. It is common ground that the consequence required for liability is physical harm or recognised psychiatric illness. In *Wainwright v Home Office* [2004] 2 AC 406 Lord Hoffmann discussed and left open (with expressions of caution) the question whether intentional causation of severe distress might be actionable, but no one in this case has suggested that it is.
>
> 74. The conduct element requires words or conduct directed towards the claimant for which there is no justification or reasonable excuse, and the burden of proof is on the claimant. We are concerned in this case with the curtailment of freedom of speech, which

gives rise to its own particular considerations. We agree with the approach of the Court of Appeal in regarding the tort as confined to those towards whom the relevant words or conduct were directed, but they may be a group. A person who shouts 'fire' in a cinema, when there is no fire, is addressing himself to the audience. In the present case the Court of Appeal treated the publication of the book as conduct directed towards the claimant and considered that the question of justification had therefore to be judged vis-à-vis him. In this respect we consider that they erred.

75. The book is for a wide audience and the question of justification has to be considered accordingly, not in relation to the claimant in isolation. In point of fact, the father's case is that although the book is dedicated to the claimant, he would not expect him to see it until he is much older. Arden LJ said that the father could not be heard to say that he did not intend the book to reach the child, since it was dedicated to him and some parts of it are addressed to him. We have only found one passage addressed to him, which is in the acknowledgments, but more fundamentally we do not understand why the father may not be heard to say that the book is not intended for his eyes at this stage of his life. Arden LJ also held that there could be no justification for the publication if it was likely to cause psychiatric harm to him. That approach excluded consideration of the wider question of justification based on the legitimate interest of the defendant in telling his story to the world at large in the way in which he wishes to tell it, and the corresponding interest of the public in hearing his story.

76. When those factors are taken into account, as they must be, the only proper conclusion is that there is every justification for the publication. A person who has suffered in the way that the father has suffered, and has struggled to cope with the consequences of his suffering in the way that he has struggled, has the right to tell the world about it. And there is a corresponding public interest in others being able to listen to his life story in all its searing detail. Of course vulnerable children need to be protected as far as reasonably practicable from exposure to material which would harm them, but the right way of doing so is not to expand *Wilkinson v Downtown* [1897] 2 QB 57 to ban the publication of a work of general interest. But in pointing out the general interest attaching to this publication, we do not mean to suggest that there needs to be some identifiable general interest in the subject matter of a publication for it to be justified within the meaning of *Wilkinson v Downton.*

Interestingly, Lady Hale and Lord Toulson noted that even though the tort had not been invoked much in practice, in 'the last 25 years it has had a modest resurgence in the context of harassment'.[23]

23 [2015] UKSC 32 at [55].

12.6.2 Protection from Harassment Act 1997

In the 1990s there was (at the very least) an increase in the awareness of and response to stalking activities. The general consensus was that criminal law did not respond appropriately and that the existing tort toolbox was insufficient to address the challenges. As a result, the Conservative Government introduced the Protection Against Harassment Bill, which came into force in 1997.

HC Deb 17 December 1996, vol 287, col 781–84

[Mr Howard, the Secretary of State for the Home Department, in the Second Reading Speech]

In the past year, a number of highly publicised stalking cases have come to public attention. They have highlighted the need to give the courts more effective powers to deal with stalkers. The Bill covers not only stalkers, but disruptive neighbours and those who target people because of the colour of their skin.

...

The Bill overcomes the difficulty of defining stalking by focusing on the harmful effect that this activity has on its victims. At one level, stalkers cause their victims harassment. The Bill therefore creates civil and – in England and Wales – criminal measures to deal with situations where harassment is caused. That approach is not new – action against harassment was taken in the Public Order Act 1986 – but the present Bill goes much further. It also creates a new civil tort, and provides both the civil and criminal courts with powers to make orders to protect the victims of harassment from future actions by their tormentors.

...

The Bill lays down that the test of guilt in regard to harassment should be whether an offender is committing actions that a reasonable person in the position of the offender would expect to give rise to harassment.

The greatest difficulty that the police find in using existing legislation against stalkers is the need to prove the intention of the stalker. These provisions dispense with that requirement, so that a person who pursues a course of conduct that he ought to have known would cause harassment will commit an offence. A person ought to know that his course of conduct would amount to harassment in circumstances in which a reasonable person, in possession of the same information, would think that that course of conduct would cause the person at whom it was directed the effects of harassment, such as alarm or distress. The maximum sentence for the criminal offence of harassment will be six months' imprisonment and/or a level 5 fine.

We believe that that test gets the balance right between the need to protect victims from the destructive behaviour of stalkers and the need to prevent the courts from being used for the pursuit of frivolous claims. A victim would have to show that harassment had been caused, and that the stalker ought to have known that that would be the effect of his actions – and stalkers will no longer be able to claim as a defence that they did not intend to harass their victims.

By defining the offence in terms of the effect that the actions have on the victim, the proposals in the Bill will catch activity that causes harassment, irrespective of whether it might be termed stalking or something else. I have in mind, in particular, conduct that causes racial harassment. The Bill will catch that conduct if the conduct occurs on more than one occasion, and in circumstances in which the perpetrator ought to have known that his words or behaviour would cause harassment, alarm or distress. Similarly, those who harass their neighbours through a course of conduct would fall within the ambit of this offence, as harassment may be caused in or from a private house. The Bill therefore builds on the provisions of section 4A of the Public Order Act 1986.

The Bill also provides some specific defences. It will be a defence to show that the conduct was pursued for the prevention and detection of crime, or under an enactment or rule of law. Because of the nature of the activities pursued by stalkers, unless special provision is made, some police activities could be caught by the Bill. That, of course, is not our intention. I am also aware that the activities of journalists, salesmen, religious activists, debt collectors, private investigators and even political canvassers might fall within the scope of the Bill. We have therefore provided a defence of acting reasonably in the particular circumstances of the case in order to safeguard these legitimate activities.

We have not defined harassment itself. Harassment as a concept has been interpreted regularly by the courts since 1986. Some 100 cases were dealt with by the courts in 1995 under section 4A of the 1986 Act, 40 leading to a conviction. However, to avoid doubt, the Bill makes it clear that harassment includes causing someone alarm or distress, and that a course of conduct includes speech.

The Protection Against Harassment Act 1997 creates both a civil remedy and a criminal offence for harassment and provides victims the opportunity to seek an injunction and/or restraining order against perpetrators of harassment.

Protection from Harassment Act 1997

1 Prohibition of harassment

(1) A person must not pursue a course of conduct—

(a) which amounts to harassment of another, and

(b) which he knows or ought to know amounts to harassment of the other.

A course of conduct is needed. This is defined as actions that occur on at least two occasions in relation to an individual person or, in relation to two or more persons, conduct on at least one occasion (s 7(3)).

As outlined in the Second Reading Speech discussion above, the definition of harassment was kept open and broad to allow the courts to respond appropriately, being defined as including 'alarming the person or causing the person distress' (s 7(2)).

This protects people from claims regarding activities that may be perceived as harassment by the claimant but would not be considered harassment by an objective and reasonable person (see s 1(2) which states 'if a reasonable person in possession of the same information would think the course of conduct amounted to harassment of the other').

3 Civil remedy

(1) An actual or apprehended breach of section 1(1) may be the subject of a claim in civil proceedings by the person who is or may be the victim of the course of conduct in question.

(2) On such a claim, damages may be awarded for (among other things) any anxiety caused by the harassment and any financial loss resulting from the harassment.

Unlike *Wilkinson v Downton*, there is no need to show a specific psychiatric illness to claim damages.

The Act has been frequently invoked in a wide range of situations, including libel and slander,[24] unwanted sexual advances in the workplace,[25] neighbourhood disputes,[26] banks inundating customers with telephone calls,[27] homophobic remarks and threats,[28] protests against the construction of a facility designed for the conducting of experiments on live animals,[29] publication of personal details of a convicted sex offender,[30] gas companies threatening to cut off gas supplies and report customers to a credit rating agency,[31] and harassment committed by employees during their course of employment.[32]

The Act, therefore, appears to give victims both civil and criminal rights against perpetrators. However, the question remains: has it been effective in stopping these behaviours and making people feel safer? Academic analysis and empirical data do not seem particularly optimistic.

24 *Triad Group plc v Makar* [2019] EWHC 423 (QB); *Levi v Bates* [2016] QB 91, [2015] EWCA Civ 206; *Law Society v Kordowski* [2011] EWHC 3185 (QB).

25 *Piepenbrock v London School of Economics and Political Science* [2018] EWHC 2572 (QB), [2018] ELR 596; the House of Lords also held that employers can be held vicariously liable for these actions: *Majrowski v Guy's and St Thomas's NHS Trust* [2006] UKHL 34, [2007] 1 AC 224.

26 *Worthington v Metropolitan Housing Trust Ltd* [2018] EWCA Civ 1125; *Sheffield City Council v Shaw* [2007] EWCA Civ 42, [2007] HLR 374.

27 *Roberts v Bank of Scotland plc* [2013] EWCA Civ 882, [2013] All ER (D) 88 (Jun).

28 *Jones v Ruth* [2011] EWCA Civ 804, [2012] 1 WLR 1495.

29 *Chancellor, Masters and Scholars of the University of Oxford v Broughton* [2006] EWCA Civ 1305, [2006] All ER (D) 78 (Aug); For similar facts, see *Daiichi UK Ltd and others v Stop Huntingdon Animal Cruelty* [2003] EWHC 2337 (QB), [2004] 1 WLR 1503, [9], which also involved 'threatening letters and telephone calls; … letters containing offensive material … excrement … criminal damage … firebombings … intimidatory home visits'.

30 *CG v Facebook Ireland Ltd* [2016] NICA 54.

31 *Ferguson v British Gas Trading Ltd* [2009] EWCA Civ 46, [2010] 1 WLR 785.

32 *Majrowski v Guy's and St Thomas's NHS Trust* [2006] UKHL 34, [2007] 1 AC 224.

Joanne Conaghan, 'Enhancing Civil Remedies for (Sexual) Harassment: s 3 of the Protection from Harassment Act 1997' (1999) 7 *Fem LS* 203, 211–13 (footnotes omitted)

It is not difficult to conclude that the serious lack of legislative guidance as to exactly what kind of conduct will or will not fall under such a broad and imprecise definition of harassment may well lead the courts back to drawing upon existing common law categories in order to aid their interpretation of the Act and flesh out what kinds of conduct are likely to attract liability. In this context, the Act leaves a host of questions unanswered: for example, how relevant is a victim's consent to the harassing behaviour and how is consent to be determined in this context; to what extent will or should the courts take account of the social situation in which the alleged harassment occurs – are they more likely to find in favour of the plaintiff where a relationship of trust or power has been abused or will they adopt an approach which focuses on the behaviour in relative isolation from its social setting? To what extent does the Act conflict with civil rights to freedom of speech, movement and protest, rights which are soon to be legally and constitutionally enforceable in English law with the passing of the Human Rights Act? Finally, assuming a wide judicial interpretation of harassment (which, while by no means ensured, may be difficult to avoid given the rather skeletal proscriptions embodied in the Act), do the common law torts still have a role to play in remedying acts of harassment and/or abuse?

Obviously, as has already been mentioned, the common law torts, particularly *Wilkinson v. Downton*, will still remain relevant to situations where the conduct complained of is 'one-off'. In this context, the willingness of the courts to develop the Wilkinson principle and resolve the various doubts about its scope and application becomes crucial. Similarly, trespass to person is likely to remain the primary cause of action in the context of serious abuse, including rape or unlawful killing. It is possible, too, that the tort of intimidation as it was applied in *Godwin v. Uzoigwe* will still have a role to play; in a sense, the wrong in Godwin is much more effectively caught by the concept of intimidation than harassment. What is most troubling about what happened to Ms Godwin was the coercion and exploitation to which she was subjected by her 'employer'; this is a very different kind of wrong from that perpetrated by the stalker in *Khorasandjian* or *Burris*. Finally, depending upon the lines which the courts choose to draw round the cause of action under the 1997 Act, the common law will, inevitably be invoked to plug the gaps. For example, conduct which does not strike a reasonable person in the position of the harasser as harassment, or which, while doing so, nevertheless appears to be a reasonable course of conduct, might still constitute an unreasonable interference with the use or enjoyment of another's property for purposes of the tort of nuisance. Similarly, a course of conduct might be deemed to lack the necessary qualities to constitute harassment, but still amount to some kind of intentional infliction of harm, giving rise to an action under *Wilkinson*.

In fact, it is likely that the presence of a statutory tort of harassment will direct Wilkinson arguments towards emotional distress claims which lack an element of harassment, but which nevertheless involve shocking and stress-inducing conduct.

...

Although the 1997 Act was apparently introduced to address the perceived social problem of stalking, its potential scope is much greater. This might be viewed as an advantage to feminists and others seeking to deploy law strategically in pursuit of social or political goals. The danger with the Protection from Harassment Act is that may become a political 'own goal' in that it is capable of being used to suppress rather than enhance the rights and dignities of individuals and groups. In this context, the courts' role in defining and delineating the scope of the Act becomes crucial – with them lies the weighty responsibility of ensuring that law and justice coincide. This poses a troubling prospect for feminists: far from escaping the vagaries of the judicial process through the introduction of tailored legislation, we are ever more reliant upon judges to develop the law in ways which address women's interests but not at the cost of neglecting the legitimate interests and fundamental rights of others. The delicate balancing of rights is a common theme in feminist debate yielding no easy resolution. The Protection from Harassment Act 1997 ensures that it will continue to demand our attention.

Trades Union Congress, 'Still Just a Bit of Banter? Sexual Harassment in the Workplace in 2016' (2016), 7–8 (footnotes omitted)

What we know about the extent of sexual harassment

Measuring the extent of sexual harassment is complicated by the fact that perceptions of sexual harassment vary from person to person, from country to country, and over time. Attempts to quantify incidents of sexual harassment are further complicated by victims' reluctance to share their experiences, even anonymously, or a reluctance to name what happened to them as sexual harassment. Examining official reports of sexual harassment, such as national crime statistics or tribunal data, would be fruitless as research has identified that few victims of sexual harassment take formal action. In 2013, the law firm Slater Gordon commissioned a survey which found that some 60 per cent of women had experienced 'inappropriate behaviour' from a male colleague in the workplace and nearly half of those surveyed had been warned to expect inappropriate behaviour from particular colleagues when they had started their job. Only 27 per cent of those surveyed felt able to report the behaviour to someone senior.

A wide scale European study carried out by the EU Agency for Fundamental Rights in 2014 found that an estimated 83 million to 102 million women (45 per cent to 55 per cent of women) in the EU-28 have experienced sexual harassment since the age of 15.

Of those women who reported having experienced sexual harassment at least once since the age of 15, one third reported that the perpetrator was known to them in a work context – such as a colleague, a boss or a customer.

On International Women's Day (8 March) 2016, the End Violence Against Women (EVAW) coalition published a survey of British women's experience of sexual harassment in public places, which found that 85 per cent of women aged 18–24 had experienced unwanted sexual attention in public places and 45 per cent have experienced unwanted sexual touching.

In 2015 Girlguiding UK found that seventy-five per cent of girls and young women said anxiety about potentially experiencing sexual harassment affects their lives in some way.

Question to consider: Has the law of torts, in both statute and common law, gone far enough to protect people from harassing behaviour? If so, why? If not, what else should it do?

Other resources: Paula Giliker, 'A New Head of Damages: Damages for Mental Distress in the English Law of Torts' (2000) 20 *LS* 19; Emily Finch, 'The Relationship between Freedom of Expression and Harassment' (2002) 66 *JCL* 134; NA Moreham, 'Harassment by Publication' in NA Moreham and Sir Mark Warby (eds), *Tugendhat and Christie: The Law of Privacy and The Media*, 3rd edn (OUP, 2016); *Majrowski v Guy's and St Thomas's NHS Trust* [2006] UKHL 34, [2007] 1 AC 224; *Wainwright v Home Office* [2003] UKHL 53, [2004] 2 AC 406; *Wong v Parkside Health NHS Trust* [2001] EWCA Civ 1721, [2003] 3 All ER 932.

12.6.3 Malicious prosecution

The final tort to consider is malicious prosecution. It has a number of parallels with false imprisonment in that it is also focused on the protection of autonomy and liberty. However, there are two key differences. First, malicious prosecution is not actionable per se; therefore, claimants must show damage from the tortfeasor's actions. Secondly, the focus is not on the imprisoning party but on a third party that created the situation, allowing them to be falsely prosecuted and/or imprisoned.

There are four elements to malicious prosecution:

(1) the prosecution of the victim was initiated by the defendant;
(2) the prosecution was terminated in the claimant's favour;
(3) there was an absence of reasonable and probable cause to commence the prosecution; and
(4) the process was fuelled by malice.

These elements can be surprisingly difficult to prove as the prosecution of individuals occurs by an apparently independent and unbiased third party – making it tricky to show that the prosecution was initiated by the defendant. However, there are circumstances where an action has been made out, such as in *Martin v Watson*.

Martin v Watson [1996] AC 74, 87–88 (Lord Keith)

Where an individual falsely and maliciously gives a police officer information indicating that some person is guilty of a criminal offence and states that he is willing to give evidence in court of the matters in question, it is properly to be inferred that he desires and intends that the person he names should be prosecuted. Where the circumstances are such that the facts relating to alleged offence can be within the knowledge only of the complainant, as was the position here, then it becomes virtually impossible for the police officer to exercise any independent discretion or judgment, and if a prosecution is instituted by the police officer the proper view of the matter is that the prosecution has been procured by the complainant.

…

[T]he trial judge said:

> 'The absence of evidence in this case from Detective Constable Haynes as to the history of the matter leading up to him obtaining the warrant is unfortunate and has made my task more difficult than it otherwise would have been. However, in the light of the defendant's further untruthful accusations about the plaintiff made to Police Constable McKiernan on 7 August and to another officer about an alleged incident on 9 August, when nothing seemed to be happening about executing the warrant, as well as her other wholly unfounded accusations to the police about earlier alleged incidents and her evidence generally, I consider that she was clearly determined that action should be taken and I am prepared to infer that that must have made such an impression on Detective Constable Haynes as to result in him applying for the warrant, notwithstanding the fact that the case depended on her word alone; and of course, as I have said, she was quite willing to give evidence and to accompany Detective Constable Haynes to the magistrates' court on 27 July to assist him in obtaining the warrant.
>
> 'In the circumstances of this particular case, therefore, I find that the defendant was indeed actively instrumental in setting the law in motion against the plaintiff. To hold otherwise would, I consider, be an affront to a proper sense of justice. She wanted the

> plaintiff to be arrested and dealt with from the start, and that is what she achieved in causing Detective Constable Haynes to obtain the warrant from the magistrate. She was, as I say, the only person who could testify about the alleged indecent exposure. I therefore find that the defendant is to be regarded as a prosecutor in setting the law in motion against the plaintiff.'

In my opinion the trial judge reached the right conclusion for the right reasons.

Mr. Munby, for the defendant, mounted a powerful argument to the effect that considerations of policy pointed against a decision in favour of the plaintiff in the present case. Such a decision, so it was maintained, would tend to discourage members of the public from bringing criminal activities to the notice of the police, lest they should find themselves harassed by actions of malicious prosecution in the event that the alleged perpetrator of the offence were acquitted. The logical result, if this argument were accepted, would be to stultify completely the tort of malicious prosecution since the rationale would apply not only to those giving information which resulted in a police prosecution but also to those who themselves signed the charge sheet or laid the information. There is no good ground here for making a distinction between persons who procure a police prosecution and those who are technically prosecutors. It is said that victims of sexual assaults would be particularly discouraged from complaining. This, however, could not be so where the alleged perpetrator was a stranger to the complainant, and where the parties are known to each other a prosecution is unlikely to follow unless there is some evidence other than that of the complainant herself ... there are many other types of offences of which a person may be falsely accused. It is to be kept in mind also that in actions for malicious prosecution the onus lies on the plaintiff to prove malice and want of reasonable cause. This would not be possible in the case of genuine complaints. It is suggested that adequate remedies for false accusations are available by way of prosecution for attempting to pervert the course of justice or wasting the time of the police, and also by way of prosecution for perjury if the complainant has actually given false evidence. But none of these remedies affords any compensation to a person who may have been arrested and imprisoned and perhaps subjected to the ordeal of a trial.

In this case, the House of Lords also reflects on the torts policy implications. Specifically, they highlight the importance of striking a balance between protecting people from being subjected to malicious prosecution and ensuring that others are not scared of being sued under this tort and, therefore, decide not to bring legitimate claims against perpetrators.

12.7 Conclusion

The intentional torts against the person raise a number of important and interesting questions and challenges for tort scholars and students. It is clear from the vast array of statutes, cases, articles, and chapters extracted and referred to in this chapter that there is potential for many different essay questions on these torts. As you progress through these pages, we encourage you to reflect on your opinion of the legal, social, and economic challenges raised, including how and why tort law has responded. It is never too early to develop your own thoughts and opinions!

Chapter 13 DEFAMATION

13.1 Introduction

Defamation law is complicated and complex. These challenges are not helped by the fact that the law has changed considerably over a reasonably short period of time. There have been two different legislative regimes (Defamation Act 1996; Defamation Act 2013). The European Convention on Human Rights (ECHR) (particularly the tension created by the rights to freedom of expression under Article 10 and respect for private and family life under Article 8) has influenced judge-made law and statutory reforms. The internet and social media have profoundly affected how information is published and generate issues about whether and when content hosts, like Facebook, should be liable for communicating defamatory content. More recently, there have been significant questions raised about the chilling effect that defamation could have on victims coming forward with accusations of violence, particularly domestic violence.

There has been an ongoing challenge of balancing people's freedom of expression with their rights not to be defamed, which has caused significant issues for both the common law and statute when trying to address these issues, as outlined by Lord Sumption in *Lachaux v Independent Print Ltd*.

Lachaux v Independent Print Ltd [2019] UKSC 27, [2020] AC 612, [1], [4]–[9] (Lord Sumption)

This case involved a French Aerospace engineer who lived with his British wife in the United Arab Emirates. During divorce proceedings, there were a number of volatile situations including alleged abduction of their son by the wife. The couple were quite high-profile so the media reported on the situation, including allegations that the claimant had been violent and abusive towards his wife, hidden their son's passport to prevent his removal from the UAE and deprived his wife of custody and contact with her son.

1. The tort of defamation is an ancient construct of the common law. It has accumulated, over the centuries, a number of formal rules with no analogue in other branches of the law of tort. Most of them originated well before freedom of expression acquired the

prominent place in our jurisprudence that it enjoys today. Its coherence has not been improved by attempts at statutory reform. Statutes to amend the law of defamation were enacted in 1888, 1952, 1996 and 2013, each of which sought to modify existing common law rules piecemeal, without always attending to the impact of the changes on the rest of the law. The Defamation Act 2013 is the latest chapter in this history. Broadly speaking, it seeks to modify some of the common law rules which were seen unduly to favour the protection of reputation at the expense of freedom of expression. In particular, there had been criticism of a state of the law in which persons resident outside the United Kingdom with only a very limited reputation in the United Kingdom were able to sue here for defamation and obtain substantial damages. One of the principal provisions of the new Act was section 1, which provided that a statement was not to be regarded as defamatory unless it had caused or was likely to cause 'serious harm' to the claimant's reputation.

His Honour then goes on the discuss the facts of the case, before providing a very helpful introduction to the law of defamation.

4. The law distinguishes between defamation actionable per se and defamation actionable only on proof of special damage. But although sharing a common label, these are very different torts with distinct historical origins. Libel, which is always actionable per se, originated in the disciplinary jurisdiction of the ecclesiastical courts and the criminal jurisdiction of the Court of Star Chamber. The gist of the tort is injury to the claimant's reputation and the associated injury to his or her feelings. Defamation actionable per se comprised, in addition to all libels, four categories of slander which were assimilated to libel on account of their particular propensity to injure the reputation of the claimant. These categories were (i) words imputing criminal offences, (ii) words imputing certain contagious or infectious diseases, and (iii) words tending to injure a person in his or her office, calling, trade or profession. The Slander of Women Act 1891 added (iv) words imputing unchastity to a woman. In these cases, the law presumes injury to the claimant's reputation and awards general damages in respect of it. These are not merely compensatory, but serve to vindicate the claimant's reputation. In a frequently quoted passage of his speech in *Broome v Cassell & Co Ltd* [1972] AC 1027, 1071, Lord Hailsham LC acknowledged that this

> '... may put the plaintiff in a purely financial sense in a much stronger position than he was before the wrong. Not merely can he recover the estimated sum of his past and future losses, but, in case the libel, driven underground, emerges from its lurking place at some future date, he must be able to point to a sum awarded by a jury sufficient to convince a bystander of the baselessness of the charge ...'

Special damage, ie pecuniary loss caused by the publication, may be recovered in addition, but must be proved.

5. By comparison, slander which is not actionable per se originated as a common law action on the case, and is governed by principles much closer to those of the law of tort generally. The law does not presume injury to reputation by mere oral statements and treats injury to feelings as insufficient to found a cause of action. Special damage, representing pecuniary loss rather than injury to reputation, must be proved ...

6. For present purposes a working definition of what makes a statement defamatory, derived from the speech of Lord Atkin in *Sim v Stretch* [1936] 2 All ER 1237, 1240, is that 'the words tend to lower the plaintiff in the estimation of right-thinking members of society generally.' Like other formulations in the authorities, this turns on the supposed impact of the statement on those to whom it is communicated. But that impact falls to be ascertained in accordance with a number of more or less artificial rules. First, the meaning is not that which other people may actually have attached to it, but that which is derived from an objective assessment of the defamatory meaning that the notional ordinary reasonable reader would attach to it. Secondly, in an action for defamation actionable per se, damage to the claimant's reputation is presumed rather than proved. It depends on the inherently injurious character (or 'tendency', in the time-honoured phrase) of a statement bearing that meaning. Thirdly, the presumption is one of law, and irrebuttable.

7. In two important cases decided in the decade before the Defamation Act 2013, the courts added a further requirement, namely that the damage to reputation in a case actionable per se must pass a minimum threshold of seriousness.

8. The first was *Jameel (Yousef) v Dow Jones & Co Inc* [2005] QB 946. The Saudi claimant had sued the publishers of the *Wall Street Journal* for a statement published online in Brussels to the effect that he had been funding terrorism. The statement was shown to have reached just five people in England and Wales. The Court of Appeal rejected a submission that the conclusive presumption of general damage was incompatible with article 10 of the Convention for the Protection of Human Rights and Fundamental Freedoms. Lord Phillips of Worth Matravers MR, delivering the leading judgment, observed (para 37) that 'English law has been well served by a principle under which liability turns on the objective question of whether the publication is one which *tends* to injure the claimant's reputation.' But he held that the presumption could not be applied consistently with the Convention in those cases, said to be rare, where damage was shown to be so trivial that the interference with freedom of expression could not be said to be necessary for the protection of the claimant's reputation. The appropriate course in such a case was to strike out the claim, not on the ground that it failed to disclose a cause of action, but as an abuse of process. The Court of Appeal held that it was an abuse of process for the action before them to proceed 'where so little is now seen to be at stake', and duly struck it out. The effect of this decision

was to introduce a procedural threshold of seriousness to be applied to the damage to the claimant's reputation. Two things are clear from the language of Lord Phillips' judgment. One is that the threshold was low. The damage must be more than minimal. That is all. Secondly, the Court of Appeal must have thought that the operation of the threshold might depend, as it did in the case before them, on the evidence of actual damage and not just on the inherently injurious character of the statement in question.

9. The second case was *Thornton v Telegraph Media Group Ltd* [2011] 1 WLR 1985, a decision of Tugendhat J. It arose out of an application by the Defendant newspaper to strike out part of the Particulars of Claim in a libel action on the ground that the statement complained of was incapable of being defamatory. Allowing the application, Tugendhat J held that in addition to the procedural threshold recognised in Jameel, there was a substantive threshold of seriousness to be surmounted before a statement could be regarded as meeting the legal definition of 'defamatory'. The judge's definition (para 96) was that a statement 'may be defamatory of him because it *substantially* affects in an adverse manner the attitude of other people towards him, *or has a tendency so to do*' (the emphasis is the judge's). He derived this formula from dicta of Lord Atkin in *Sim v Stretch* [1936] 2 All ER 1237.

13.2 Statute

In an attempt to address some of the ongoing issues with defamation, the Defamation Act 2013 was enacted, replacing the Defamation Act 1996 and some parts of the common law. It was generally well received, but there remained some concerns and criticisms.

Defamation Act 2013

1 Serious harm

(1) A statement is not defamatory unless its publication has caused or is likely to cause serious harm to the reputation of the claimant.

(2) For the purposes of this section, harm to the reputation of a body that trades for profit is not 'serious harm' unless it has caused or is likely to cause the body serious financial loss.

This additional requirement does not create a separate test above the common law definition of defamation (see *Lachaux v Independent Print Ltd* [2019] UKSC 27, [2020] AC 612, discussed above). However, it does create a higher threshold for commencing an action and proving the elements of defamation.

There is a slightly different test for companies, which have to show that they would suffer actual or likely serious financial loss.

2 Truth

(1) It is a defence to an action for defamation for the defendant to show that the imputation conveyed by the statement complained of is substantially true.

(2) Subsection (3) applies in an action for defamation if the statement complained of conveys two or more distinct imputations.

(3) If one or more of the imputations is not shown to be substantially true, the defence under this section does not fail if, having regard to the imputations which are shown to be substantially true, the imputations which are not shown to be substantially true do not seriously harm the claimant's reputation.

(4) The common law defence of justification is abolished and, accordingly, section 5 of the Defamation Act 1952 (justification) is repealed.

3 Honest opinion

(1) It is a defence to an action for defamation for the defendant to show that the following conditions are met.

(2) The first condition is that the statement complained of was a statement of opinion.

(3) The second condition is that the statement complained of indicated, whether in general or specific terms, the basis of the opinion.

(4) The third condition is that an honest person could have held the opinion on the basis of—

(a) any fact which existed at the time the statement complained of was published;

(b) anything asserted to be a fact in a privileged statement published before the statement complained of.

(5) The defence is defeated if the claimant shows that the defendant did not hold the opinion.

(6) Subsection (5) does not apply in a case where the statement complained of was published by the defendant but made by another person ('the author'); and in such a case the defence is defeated if the claimant shows that the defendant knew or ought to have known that the author did not hold the opinion.

...

There is a defence to an action for defamation if the defendant can show that the imputation conveyed by the statement is 'substantially true' – so the defendant does not need to show that it was completely true. The defendant will, however, need to provide some evidence supporting their assertion of truth, and this must be more than their mere belief in the statement's correctness. Repeating a rumour because you honestly believe it is true is not sufficient to provide a defence under s 2 (*Cookson v Harewood* [1932] 2 KB 478, CA).

The Explanatory Notes provide further information about these sections:

Subsections (2) and (3) replace s 5 of the 1952 Act (the only significant element of the defence of justification which is currently in statute). Their effect is that where the statement complained of contains two or more distinct imputations, the defence does not fail if, having regard to the imputations which are shown to be substantially true, those which are not shown to be substantially true do not seriously harm the claimant's reputation. These provisions are intended to have the same effect as those in s 5 of the 1952 Act, but are expressed in more modern terminology. The phrase 'materially injure' used in the 1952 Act is replaced by 'seriously harm' to ensure consistency with the test in s 1 of the Act.

The previous common law defence of justification has been abolished and replaced with the statutory test of 'truth'.

The Act sets out a three-step test to show how the defence of honest opinion applies.

The defendant's opinion must be based on true facts and they will have an obligation to prove the facts on which their opinion is based.

In addition to the three-step test, the opinion must actually be held by the defendant (s 3(5)). In a situation where the defendant has published a statement made by another author, showing that the author of the statement did not actually hold that opinion, this will defeat the defence (s 3(6)).

(8) The common law defence of fair comment is abolished and, accordingly, section 6 of the Defamation Act 1952 (fair comment) is repealed.

4 Publication on matter of public interest

(1) It is a defence to an action for defamation for the defendant to show that—

(a) the statement complained of was, or formed part of, a statement on a matter of public interest; and

(b) the defendant reasonably believed that publishing the statement complained of was in the public interest.

(2) Subject to subsections (3) and (4), in determining whether the defendant has shown the matters mentioned in subsection (1), the court must have regard to all the circumstances of the case.

(3) If the statement complained of was, or formed part of, an accurate and impartial account of a dispute to which the claimant was a party, the court must in determining whether it was reasonable for the defendant to believe that publishing the statement was in the public interest disregard any omission of the defendant to take steps to verify the truth of the imputation conveyed by it.

(4) In determining whether it was reasonable for the defendant to believe that publishing the statement complained of was in the public interest, the court must make such allowance for editorial judgement as it considers appropriate.

(5) For the avoidance of doubt, the defence under this section may be relied upon irrespective of whether the statement complained of is a statement of fact or a statement of opinion.

(6) The common law defence known as the Reynolds defence is abolished.

Section 3(8) abolished the common law defence of fair comment and repealed s 6 of the Defamation Act 1952 (fair comment). Therefore, the common law requirement that the defence would be defeated if the statement was made with malice no longer applies. Thus, an honest opinion can be made maliciously, provided the three-step test is met.

This defence recognises the importance of people not being deterred from communicating information and their opinions, especially on matters of public interest. The justification is that the public interest is more important than protecting an individual's reputation.

Section 4(2) creates a broad, flexible, and open test to determine what is considered in the public interest, indicating that the court '*must*' consider all relevant circumstances.

Section 4(3) provides a list of considerations for the courts, namely accuracy, impartiality, reasonableness, and the steps taken to verify the statement's truth before making it.

Again, the statute's use of the word '*must*' directs the court to ensure it makes allowances' for editorial judgement.

This defence applies to both statements of fact and statements of opinion.

The Defamation Act 2013 abolished the common law *Reynolds* defence of 'responsible journalism'. The Explanatory Notes (para 35) explain that the abolition of this common law defence occurred because the statutory defence was essentially intended to codify the common law defence. While abolishing the common law defence means the courts are required to apply the statute's words, the current case law constitutes 'a helpful, albeit non-binding, guide' to interpreting how the new statutory defence applies. 'It is expected the courts would take the existing case law into consideration where appropriate,'

5 Operators of websites

(1) This section applies where an action for defamation is brought against the operator of a website in respect of a statement posted on the website.

(2) It is a defence for the operator to show that it was not the operator who posted the statement on the website.

(3) The defence is defeated if the claimant shows that—

(a) it was not possible for the claimant to identify the person who posted the statement,

(b) the claimant gave the operator a notice of complaint in relation to the statement, and

(c) the operator failed to respond to the notice of complaint in accordance with any provision contained in regulations.

[To be read in conjunction with section 10.]

10 Action against a person who was not the author, editor etc

(1) A court does not have jurisdiction to hear and determine an action for defamation brought against a person who was not the author, editor or publisher of the statement complained of unless the court is satisfied that it is not reasonably practicable for an action to be brought against the author, editor or publisher.

(2) In this section 'author', 'editor' and 'publisher' have the same meaning as in section 1 of the Defamation Act 1996.

6 Peer-reviewed statement in scientific or academic journal etc

(1) The publication of a statement in a scientific or academic journal (whether published in electronic form or otherwise) is privileged if the following conditions are met.

(2) The first condition is that the statement relates to a scientific or academic matter.

(3) The second condition is that before the statement was published in the journal an independent review of the statement's scientific or academic merit was carried out by—

(a) the editor of the journal, and

(b) one or more persons with expertise in the scientific or academic matter concerned.

Under the common law, defamation claims could be made against both the parties who had actively published the defamatory material (authors, publishers etc) and the parties who had merely distributed the information (ISPs, booksellers, libraries etc). This section creates a new defence in relation to statements posted on websites.

The website must show that it did not post the allegedly defamatory statement on the website.

The defence will fail if it was not possible for the claimant to have identified the person who posted the statement, the claimant had complained to the website, and the website failed to respond to the complaint.

Together, ss 5 and 10 attempt to strike a balance between allowing freedom of speech on the internet and the protection of reputation. Operators of websites will generally be free from liability if they ensure that parties posting statements can be identified, they respond appropriately to complaints and do not act with any malice.

A court cannot hear an action for defamation brought against someone who is not an 'author, editor or publisher' unless it is not reasonably practicable for an action to be taken against these parties.

This creates a new category of qualified privilege under the Defamation Act 2013.

It has a specific, narrow scope of only applying to scientific and academic matters.

There must have been an element of 'peer review' of the statement.

(4) Where the publication of a statement in a scientific or academic journal is privileged by virtue of subsection (1), the publication in the same journal of any assessment of the statement's scientific or academic merit is also privileged if—

(a) the assessment was written by one or more of the persons who carried out the independent review of the statement; and

(b) the assessment was written in the course of that review.

(5) Where the publication of a statement or assessment is privileged by virtue of this section, the publication of a fair and accurate copy of, extract from or summary of the statement or assessment is also privileged.

(6) A publication is not privileged by virtue of this section if it is shown to be made with malice.

The defence will not apply if the party making the statement acted with malice.

8 Single publication rule

It is important to note that the single publication rule only applies to the *same publisher* and does not address republication by third parties.

(1) This section applies if a person—

(a) publishes a statement to the public ('the first publication'), and

(b) subsequently publishes (whether or not to the public) that statement or a statement which is substantially the same.

Under the common law, a new cause of action arose each time the statement was republished. This rule was substantially changed when s 8 introduced the 'single publication rule'.

(2) In subsection (1) 'publication to the public' includes publication to a section of the public.

(3) For the purposes of section 4A of the Limitation Act 1980 (time limit for actions for defamation etc) any cause of action against the person for defamation in respect of the subsequent publication is to be treated as having accrued on the date of the first publication.

(4) This section does not apply in relation to the subsequent publication if the manner of that publication is materially different from the manner of the first publication.

The limitation does not apply if the publication is 'materially different' from the original publication.

(5) In determining whether the manner of a subsequent publication is materially different from the manner of the first publication, the matters to which the court may have regard include (amongst other matters)—

Section 8(5) provides the definition of materially different, indicating the courts should consider the level of prominence and the extent of the subsequent publication.

(a) the level of prominence that a statement is given;

(b) the extent of the subsequent publication

(6) Where this section applies—

(a) it does not affect the court's discretion under section 32A of the Limitation Act 1980 (discretionary exclusion of time limit for actions for defamation etc), and

(b) the reference in subsection (1)(a) of that section to the operation of section 4A of that Act is a reference to the operation of section 4A together with this section

11 Trial to be without a jury unless the court orders otherwise

(1) In section 69(1) of the Senior Courts Act 1981 (certain actions in the Queen's Bench Division to be tried with a jury unless the trial requires prolonged examination of documents etc) in paragraph (b) omit 'libel, slander,'.

(2) In section 66(3) of the County Courts Act 1984 (certain actions in the county court to be tried with a jury unless the trial requires prolonged examination of documents etc) in paragraph (b) omit 'libel, slander,'.

12 Power of court to order a summary of its judgment to be published

(1) Where a court gives judgment for the claimant in an action for defamation the court may order the defendant to publish a summary of the judgment.

(2) The wording of any summary and the time, manner, form and place of its publication are to be for the parties to agree.

(3) If the parties cannot agree on the wording, the wording is to be settled by the court.

(4) If the parties cannot agree on the time, manner, form or place of publication, the court may give such directions as to those matters as it considers reasonable and practicable in the circumstances

(5) This section does not apply where the court gives judgment for the claimant under section 8(3) of the Defamation Act 1996 (summary disposal of claims).

13 Order to remove statement or cease distribution etc

(1) Where a court gives judgment for the claimant in an action for defamation the court may order—

(a) the operator of a website on which the defamatory statement is posted to remove the statement, or

(b) any person who was not the author, editor or publisher of the defamatory statement to stop distributing, selling or exhibiting material containing the statement.

...

The restriction does not apply if the court exercises its discretion to extend the limitation period.

These sections are procedural in nature, removing the ability for defamation trials by juries without a court order. This was in response to the perception that juries awarded inappropriately large damages, such as the £1.5 million jury award in *Tolstoy Miloslavsky v United Kingdom* (1995) 20 EHRR 442.

These are non-damage based remedies that can be used by the court in an attempt to undo or reduce some of the harm experienced by the claimant. Under s 12 the court can order a summary of its judgment to be published by the defendant. Under s 13 the court, upon giving judgment for the claimant, may order the website operator to remove the defamatory statement.

14 Special damage

(1) The Slander of Women Act 1891 is repealed.

(2) The publication of a statement that conveys the imputation that a person has a contagious or infectious disease does not give rise to a cause of action for slander unless the publication causes the person special damage.

15 Meaning of 'publish' and 'statement'

In this Act—

'publish' and 'publication', in relation to a statement, have the meaning they have for the purposes of the law of defamation generally;

'statement' means words, pictures, visual images, gestures or any other method of signifying meaning.

Traditionally there were four types of slander that were actionable without the need to show special damage:

(1) the imputation of a criminal offence that was punishable by imprisonment;

(2) the imputation of professional unfitness or incompetence;

(3) the imputation of a contagious disease; and

(4) the imputation of unchastity or adultery by a female.

As the distinction between libel and slander has been removed, these categories are now significantly less important. Regardless, s 14 of the Defamation Act 2013 now requires that imputations of a contagious disease and unchastity or adultery by a female cause special damage.

Even though the definition of defamation was purposefully left to the common law, the Defamation Act provides some definitions and guidance. Importantly, 'statement' removes the traditional distinction between libel and slander.

Question to consider: Has the Defamation Act 2013 struck the right balance between freedom of speech and protecting people's reputations? If so, why? If not, what amendments should be made?

Other resources: Douglas W Vick and Linda Macpherson, 'An Opportunity Lost: The United Kingdom's Failed Reform of Defamation Law' (1996) 49 *Fed Comm LJ* 621; J Price QC and F McMahon, *Blackstone's Guide to the Defamation Act 2013* (Oxford University Press, 2013) ch 1; J Townend, 'Freedom of Expression and the Chilling Effect' in H Tumber and S Waisbord (eds), *The Routledge Companion to Media and Human Rights* (Routledge, 2017); Charlie Sewell, 'More Serious Harm than Good? An Empirical Observation and Analysis of the Effects of the Serious Harm Requirement in Section 1(1) of the Defamation Act 2013' (2020) 12 *JML* 47.

13.3 Who can sue?

Not everyone has the right to sue for defamation. Three potential issues could restrict an individual's ability to make a claim: (1) geographical limitations, (2) body corporates, and (3) public authorities.

With regards to the first issue, the Defamation Act 2013 included a geographical element to the right to sue for defamation in the UK, which was designed to address the concern many people had that the country was being used for 'defamation tourism' (ie that people from outside the UK or without legitimate links to the country were commencing actions as they perceived the country to have claimant-friendly laws and legal processes).

Defamation Act 2013

9 Action against a person not domiciled in the UK or a Member State etc

(1) This section applies to an action for defamation against a person who is not domiciled—
   (a) In the United Kingdom;
   (b) in another Member State; or
   (c) in a state which is for the time being a contracting party to the Lugano Convention.

(2) A court does not have jurisdiction to hear and determine an action to which this section applies unless the court is satisfied that, of all the places in which the statement complained of has been published, England and Wales is clearly the most appropriate place in which to bring an action in respect of the statement.

The test for determining the 'most appropriate' jurisdiction was outlined in the Explanatory Notes:

> This means that in cases where a statement has been published in this jurisdiction and also abroad the court will be required to consider the overall global picture to consider where it would be most appropriate for a claim to be heard. It is intended that this will overcome the problem of courts readily accepting jurisdiction simply because a claimant frames their claim so as to focus on damage which has occurred in this jurisdiction only. This would mean that, for example, if a statement was published 100,000 times in Australia and only 5,000 times in England that would be a good basis on which to conclude that the most appropriate jurisdiction in which to bring an action in respect of the statement was Australia rather than England. There will however be a range of factors which the court may wish to take into account including, for example, the amount of damage to the claimant's reputation in this jurisdiction compared to elsewhere, the extent to which the publication was targeted at a readership in this jurisdiction compared to elsewhere, and whether there is reason to think that the claimant would not receive a fair hearing elsewhere.[1]

Should companies be able to sue for defamation? Do they have a right to their reputation in the same way as natural persons? Defamation laws in the UK have continued the right for companies to sue – subject to them showing they will suffer serious financial loss under s 1(2). However, this has not been met with universal acceptance.

1 Explanatory Notes to the Defamation Act 2013, para 66.

Jan Oster 'The Criticism of Trading Corporations and their Right to Sue for Defamation' (2011) 2 *JETL* 255, 255–56, 259–60, 279 (footnotes omitted)

Due to their socio-cultural and political influence, multi-national corporations are subject to close public scrutiny and criticism. The internet, in particular, enables citizens to express their opinions on and experiences with any producer of goods and services to a wide public, ignoring the risk of a defamation lawsuit by potentially defamed companies – a risk to which critical Non-Governmental Organisations (NGOs) and the media are already accustomed. However, it is accepted that the law of defamation is not only an instrument to vindicate the claimant's reputation, but also a tool to reconcile reputation, which is protected as a fundamental right, with the freedom of expression of the defendant, which is likewise protected.

...

In his seminal article on the social foundations of defamation law, Post distinguished three rationales which might serve to explain the concept of reputation: honour, dignity and property. Usually, the three aspects are not clearly distinguishable, yet they complement each other and may explain certain principles of the tort of defamation in their own way. However, it is a distinctive feature of a company's suit for defamation that it may *exclusively* be explained by the conception of reputation as property. Already in 1859, Pollock CB of the English Court of the Exchequer stated: 'it would be very odd if a corporation had no means of protecting itself against wrong; and, if its property is injured by slander, it has no means of redress except by action. Therefore it appears to me clear that a corporation at common law may maintain an action for a libel by which its property is injured.' The notion of reputation as property reflects the image of the market society; individuals, it is argued, are connected to one another through the institution of the market. The value of reputation is therefore determined by the market in the same way as any property loss is measured. Accordingly, reputation is acquired as a result of a person's efforts and labour. Hence, if reputation is injured, the resulting loss is capable of being priced in monetary terms.

By contrast, according to the principle of human dignity, human beings deserve respect and protection due to their mere existence. Yet a commercial enterprise has no personality and no dignity which can be injured. It has no character in its literal meaning and no feelings which are capable of being injured. Companies are entities created for a specific purpose. As a consequence, they may claim legal protection only to the extent that the fulfilment of their function is unlawfully inhibited. It is essentially the purpose of every trading company to operate a business. A trading company's reputation is therefore purely commercial; the 'good name' of a company is an asset of pecuniary value. Companies neither have their own, nor do they participate in their staff's honour or human dignity. That is to say, one has to distinguish between the protection of the reputation of staff members on the one hand and of the company on the other hand. If a company's employee feels injured in his reputation due to a presumed defamation of his company, he may bring his own suit. However, a company may neither sue for the violation of a 'derivative personality right', nor litigate in its own name on behalf of its employees.

The fact that a company's reputation is solely based on the property rationale yields consequences for fundamental rights' protection. As will be shown in the next paragraph, a trading corporation's reputation is not protected by its right to respect for private life according to article 8(1) ECHR, as is the case with regard to individuals, but by the right to protection of property, article 1 of the First Protocol to the ECHR.

...

The presumption of *South Hetton*, *Derbyshire* and *Jameel*, according to which a trading corporation is in the same position as an individual with regard to a defamation claim, needs to be revised. In contrast to individuals, the reputation of a company results exclusively from the conception of reputation as property. As a consequence, the constitutional basis of a company's reputation is article 1(1) of the First Protocol to the ECHR, and *not* article 8(1) ECHR. A publication therefore defames a company only when it is capable of damaging its conduct of its business. However, trading corporations are public figures, and therefore speech about them is per se public speech, enjoying considerable freedom of speech protection that has to be balanced against the company's property right on a case-by-case basis. If the company's property rights prevail in this ad-hoc balancing, a company claimant may, however, only claim economic loss which it has to prove.

Whether public authorities should be able to sue for defamation is a complicated issue which continues to generate debates, as the right to freedom of speech needs to be balanced with protecting reputation and the potential undermining of the democratic process. There were competing cases, with *Manchester Corp v Williams*,[2] and *Bognor Regis Urban District Council v Campion*[3] both providing a local government with the right to sue for defamation; however, this view was criticised as an unjustified restriction on freedom of speech and was overturned by the House of Lords in *Derbyshire County Council v Times Newspapers Ltd*. The Court held in this case that public authorities and government bodies could not sue for defamation as allowing this right could undermine the democratic process.

Derbyshire County Council v Times Newspapers Ltd [1993] AC 534, 547–48 (Lord Keith)

There are, however, features of a local authority which may be regarded as distinguishing it from other types of corporation, whether trading or non-trading. The most important of these features is that it is a governmental body. Further, it is a democratically elected body, the electoral process nowadays being conducted almost exclusively on party political lines. It is of the highest public importance that a democratically elected governmental body, or indeed any governmental body, should be open to uninhibited public criticism. The threat of a civil action for defamation must inevitably have an inhibiting effect on freedom of speech. In *City of Chicago v. Tribune Co.* (1923) 139 N.E. 86 the Supreme Court of Illinois held that the City could not maintain an action of damages for libel. Thompson C.J. said at p. 90:

2 [1891] 1 QB 94.
3 [1972] 2 QB 169.

> 'The fundamental right of freedom of speech is involved in this litigation, and not merely the right of liberty of the press. If this action can be maintained against a newspaper it can be maintained against every private citizen who ventures to criticise the ministers who are temporarily conducting the affairs of his government. Where any person by speech or writing seeks to persuade others to violate existing law or to overthrow by force or other unlawful means the existing government, he may be punished but all other utterances or publications against the government must be considered absolutely privileged.
>
> While in the early history of the struggle for freedom of speech the restrictions were enforced by criminal prosecutions, it is clear that a civil action is as great, if not a greater, restriction than a criminal prosecution. If the right to criticise the government is a privilege which, with the exceptions above enumerated, cannot be restricted, then all civil as well as criminal actions are forbidden. A despotic or corrupt government can more easily stifle opposition by a series of civil actions than by criminal prosecutions.'

After giving a number of reasons for this, he said:

> 'It follows, therefore, that every citizen has a right to criticise an inefficient or corrupt government without fear of civil as well as criminal prosecution. This absolute privilege is founded on the principle that it is advantageous for the public interest that the citizen should not be in any way fettered in his statements, and where the public service or due administration of justice is involved he shall have the right to speak his mind freely.'

These propositions were indorsed by the Supreme Court of the United States in *New York Times Co. v. Sullivan* (1964) 376 U.S. 254, 277. While these decisions were related most directly to the provisions of the American Constitution concerned with securing freedom of speech, the public interest considerations which underlaid them are no less valid in this country. What has been described as 'the chilling effect' induced by the threat of civil actions for libel is very important. Quite often the facts which would justify a defamatory publication are known to be true, but admissible evidence capable of proving those facts is not available. This may prevent the publication of matters which it is very desirable to make public.

Question to consider: Who should have their rights and reputations protected by defamation laws? Draw on at least two of the three issues considered above in your answer.

Other resources: JA Weir, 'Local Authority v Critical Ratepayer – A Suit for Defamation' [1972] 30 *CLJ* 238; *Goldsmith v Bhoyrul* [1998] QB 459; Alastair Mullis and Andrew Scott, 'Something Rotten in the State of English Libel Law? A Rejoinder to the Clamour for Reform of Defamation' (2009) 14 *Comms L* 173; *McLaughlin v Lambeth* [2010] EWHC 2726 (QB); *George v Cannell* [2022] EWCA Civ 1067, [2023] QB 117.

13.4 Elements of defamation

After it has been determined that the claimant has the standing to make a claim for defamation, the next issue to consider is whether their claim will be successful. There are three elements that must be considered: (1) Did the tortfeasor make a defamatory publication? (2) Are there any potential defences that could be applied? (3) What damages are likely to be awarded? It is beyond the scope of this chapter to provide a detailed analysis of these elements as the focus is on developing your critical analysis of underlying issues in the law of defamation. If you would like further information on how to answer a problem question, including sample questions and answer flowcharts, we recommend you refer to Chapter 13 of Green and Gardner, *Tort Law*, 2nd edn (Hart Publishing, 2024).

13.4.1 Defamatory publication

For this requirement, the claimant must show that:

(a) the statement was defamatory;
(b) the statement referred to the claimant by name or otherwise; and
(c) the statement was published to a third party.

For a statement to be defamatory, the claimant must show on the balance of probabilities that it has 'caused or is likely to cause serious harm to the reputation of the claimant'.[4] Interestingly, the Defamation Act 2013 does not include a definition of what constitutes 'defamation' or a 'defamatory statement'; rather, this has been left up to the common law with the restriction under s 1(1) that it must cause 'serious harm' to be actionable.

Lachaux v Independent Print Ltd [2019] UKSC 27, [2020] AC 612, [12]–[16]

The facts of this case have been highlighted above at 13.1. In this section, Lord Sumption considers the impact of the 'serious harm' test on the common law test for defamatory publication.

> 12. Although the Act must be construed as a whole, the issue must turn primarily on the language of section 1. This shows, very clearly to my mind, that it not only raises the threshold of seriousness above that envisaged in *Jameel (Yousef)* and *Thornton*, but requires its application to be determined by reference to the actual facts about its impact and not just to the meaning of the words.
>
> 13. In the first place, the relevant background to section 1 is the common law position, as I have summarised it. Parliament is taken to have known what the law was prior to the enactment. ... The question on these appeals is what are the legal implications of that change, and what necessarily follows from it. Even where some change to the common law was intended, it should not go any further than that. As Lord Reid observed in *Black-Clawson International Ltd v Papierwerke Waldhof-Aschaffenburg AG* [1975] AC 591, 615, Parliament 'can be presumed not to have altered the common law further than was necessary'.

4 Defamation Act 2013, s 1(1).

14. Secondly, section 1 necessarily means that a statement which would previously have been regarded as defamatory, because of its inherent tendency to cause some harm to reputation, is not to be so regarded unless it 'has caused or is likely to cause' harm which is 'serious'. The reference to a situation where the statement 'has caused' serious harm is to the consequences of the publication, and not the publication itself. It points to some historic harm, which is shown to have actually occurred. This is a proposition of fact which can be established only by reference to the impact which the statement is shown actually to have had. It depends on a combination of the inherent tendency of the words and their actual impact on those to whom they were communicated. The same must be true of the reference to harm which is 'likely' to be caused. In this context, the phrase naturally refers to probable future harm. ...

15. Thirdly, it is necessary to read section 1(1) with section 1(2). Section 1(2) is concerned with the way in which section 1(1) is to be applied to statements said to be defamatory of a body trading for profit. It refers to the same concept of 'serious harm' as section 1(1), but provides that in the case of such a body it must have caused or be likely to cause 'serious financial loss'. The financial loss envisaged here is not the same as special damage, in the sense in which that term is used in the law of defamation. Section 1 is concerned with harm to reputation, whereas (as I have pointed out) special damage represents pecuniary loss to interests other than reputation. What is clear, however, is that section 1(2) must refer not to the harm done to the claimant's reputation, but to the loss which that harm has caused or is likely to cause. The financial loss is the measure of the harm and must exceed the threshold of seriousness. As applied to harm which the defamatory statement 'has caused', this necessarily calls for an investigation of the actual impact of the statement. A given statement said to be defamatory may cause greater or lesser financial loss to the claimant, depending on his or her particular circumstances and the reaction of those to whom it is published. Whether that financial loss has occurred and whether it is 'serious' are questions which cannot be answered by reference only to the inherent tendency of the words. The draftsman must have intended that the question what harm it was 'likely to cause' should be decided on the same basis.

16. Finally, if serious harm can be demonstrated only by reference to the inherent tendency of the words, it is difficult to see that any substantial change to the law of defamation has been achieved by what was evidently intended as a significant amendment. The main reason why harm which was less than 'serious' had given rise to liability before the Act was that damage to reputation was presumed from the words alone and might therefore be very different from any damage which could be established in fact. If, as Ms Page submits, the presumption still works in that way, then this anomaly has been carried through into the Act. Suppose that the words amount to a grave allegation against the claimant, but they are published to a small number of people, or to people none of whom believe it, or possibly to people among whom the claimant had no reputation to be harmed. The law's traditional answer is that these matters may mitigate damages but do not affect the defamatory character of the words. ...

Creating a clear definition of 'defamation' has been an ongoing challenge for the courts. Below is a table providing a number of cases, the statements they made, and whether the courts found those statements to be defamatory.

Table 13.1: Key cases on whether statements are defamatory

Case	Statement(s) made	Were the statement(s) defamatory?
Monson v Tussauds Ltd[5]	A wax figure of the claimant was included as part of an exhibit called the 'Chamber of Horrors', which featured predominately notorious murderers but also relics and models of murder scenes. The claimant shot a young man and was tried for murder, but the jury returned a verdict of 'Not proven'.	The wax figure was defamatory. The defendant unsuccessfully argued that they simply exhibited the figure because the claimant was a notorious person, and it did not insinuate anything further. The House of Lords, rejecting this claim, held that the figure and circumstances resulted in 'an actionable wrong, tending to disparage and injure the plaintiff'.
Myroft v Sleight[6]	The defendant said that the claimant, who was a member of the Trade Union, voted in favour of a strike but then asked the employer for work.	The statement was defamatory, as 'an ordinary member of a trade union may claim that the duty of honesty and loyalty rests upon him', and the statement implies that the claimant acted dishonestly.
Cassidy v Daily Mirror Newspapers Ltd[7]	The claimant's husband was featured in a newspaper with another woman, which stated that they were engaged to be married.	The statement was defamatory, as it conveyed the meaning that the claimant and her husband were not legally married and in an 'immoral cohabitation'.
Tolley v JS Fry and Sons Ltd[8]	The defendant published an advertisement without the claimant's consent, which made it appear that the claimant, who was a famous amateur golfer, had agreed to advertise the defendant's products for gain and reward.	The statement was defamatory. People who knew of the claimant's status as being an amateur golfer would believe that he had accepted some sort of consideration from the defendant and, therefore, was 'guilty of conduct unworthy of his status as an amateur golfer'.
Blennerhassett v Novelty Sales Services Ltd[9]	The defendant published an advertisement stating that the claimant, a member of the London Stock Exchange for over 30 years, had such a fascination with the defendant's yo-yo that he became addicted to it.	The statement was not defamatory. Even though the claimant was subjected to a certain level of good-natured teasing at the London Stock Exchange, the advertisement was not serious enough to constitute a defamatory statement.

5 [1894] 1 QB 671, CA.
6 (1921) 37 TLR 646.
7 [1929] 2 KB 331, 340 (Scrutton LJ).
8 [1930] 1 KB 467, CA, 479 (Greer LJ).
9 (1933) 175 LTJ 393.

Case	Statement(s) made	Were the statement(s) defamatory?
Youssoupoff v Metro-Goldwyn-Mayer Pictures Ltd[10]	The claimant had been seduced by and/or raped by Rasputin.	It was defamatory to impute that a woman had been the victim of rape. Even though there is no moral turpitude on the victim, the statement could cause her to be shunned or avoided.
Byrne v Deane[11]	The defendant said, 'But he who gave the game away May he byrnn in hell and rue the day', imputing that the claimant had informed the police about the use of illegal gambling machines.	The statement was not defamatory; reporting illegal activity to the police would not lower the claimant's reputation in the eyes of 'right thinking' members of society.
Lewis v Daily Telegraph Ltd[12]	The claimants were being investigated for fraud and whether that imputed that the claimants were guilty of fraud.	The statements were defamatory but did not impute that the claimants were guilty of fraud as a reasonable person would not 'infer guilt of fraud merely because an inquiry is on foot'.
R v Bishop[13]	An allegation that the claimant had a homosexual affair.	It was defamatory to impute that someone was homosexual.
Shah v Akram[14]	The claimant, a man of the Muslim faith, 'satirically passed such frivolous remarks in the presence of some reliable persons on the respected personality of the Prophet ... that cannot be written down and which are unbearable for a proud Muslim to hear'. The claimant admitted he made a statement the Prophet having married his fourth wife when she was eight years old, but denied it was made satirically.	The statement was defamatory. The Court of Appeal stated that 'the ordinary member of the public, even if he had no religious views of his own or no strongly held views, would not approve of anyone insulting the religious beliefs of others; and anyone who did insult the religious beliefs of other people would, in my judgment, be lowering himself in the estimation of right thinking people'.
Charleston v News Group Newspapers Ltd[15]	A series of digitally manipulated images of the claimants, popular soap opera actors, in pornographic poses, including bondage and sodomy.	The statement was not defamatory as the corresponding text made it clear that the images had been made without the consent of the claimants. The images had to be considered as a whole.

10 (1934) 50 TLR 581, CA.
11 [1937] 1 KB 818, CA.
12 [1964] AC 234, 260 (Lord Reid).
13 [1975] QB 274, CA.
14 [1981] WL 606004, CA.
15 [1995] 2 AC 65.

Case	Statement(s) made	Were the statement(s) defamatory?
Berkoff v Burchill[16]	That the claimant was 'hideous-looking' and that Frankenstein's monster is 'marginally better-looking' than the claimant.	The statement was defamatory, not because it is defamatory that someone is ugly but because the wording could cause the claimant to suffer 'contempt, scorn or ridicule' and/or 'will cause him to be shunned or avoided'.
Cruise v Express Newspapers plc[17]	The claimant, a man married to a woman, was referred to as 'gay'.	This statement was defamatory as it implied that the marriage was a sham to cover up the claimant's homosexuality.
Church v MGN Ltd[18]	The claimant, a famous singer-songwriter, had proposed to her partner after consuming too much alcohol at a karaoke venue.	The statement was defamatory as it attributed drunken behaviour to the claimant. The judge emphasised, however, that whether a statement was defamatory 'depends on the context', so the statement may not have been defamatory if made against another individual.
Monroe v Hopkins[19]	A tweet stating, '@MsJackMonroe scrawled on any memorials recently? Vandalised the memory of those who fought for your freedom. Grandma got any more medals?' This was held to mean that the claimant condoned and approved of vandalising war memorials and monuments commemorating those who fought for the claimant's freedom.	The statement was defamatory. The judge commented that we live '[i]n a diverse society, there are many with views of which some people approve and some disapprove.' Regardless, it was held that an accusation of vandalising war memorials would lower the claimant's reputation in right-thinking members of society as it undermines 'the shared values of our society.'
Lachaux v Independent Print Ltd[20]	A number of statements were made, including that the claimant had been violent and abusive towards his wife, hidden their son's passport to prevent his removal from the UAE, and deprived his wife of custody and contact with her son.	The statements were defamatory, as they fulfilled the 'serious harm' test under s 1(1) of the Defamation Act 2013.

16 [1996] 4 All ER 1008, CA.

17 [1999] QB 931.

18 [2012] EWHC 693 (QB), [2013] 1 WLR 284, [16].

19 [2017] EWHC 433 (QB), [2017] 4 WLR 68.

20 [2019] UKSC 27, [2020] AC 612.

Case	Statement(s) made	Were the statement(s) defamatory?
Stocker v Stocker[21]	Stated on her Facebook page that her husband 'tried to strangle' her.	The judge, at first instance, relied on the dictionary definition of strangle, which stated that 'strangle' must mean try to kill. The Supreme Court held that this was a mistake and the statement did not mean to convey that the husband had attempted to kill the claimant. Therefore, the statement was not defamatory.

Lewis v Daily Telegraph Ltd [1964] AC 234, 237–38, 259–60 (Lord Reid)

In this case, the *Daily Telegraph* and the *Daily Mail* published reports on their front pages stating that Officers of the Fraud Squad were inquiring into the affairs of Rubber Improvement Ltd, with the headlines 'INQUIRY ON FIRM BY CITY POLICE' and 'FRAUD SQUAD PROBE FIRM'. The claimants commenced an action for defamation on the ground that 'the defendants meant and were understood to mean that the affairs of the plaintiffs and/or its subsidiaries were conducted fraudulently or dishonestly or in such a way that the police suspected that their affairs were so conducted'.

In considering this case, Lord Reid provided some helpful comments on the test for a defamatory statement, emphasising that it is what an ordinary person would interpret the statement to be, and not focused on the intention of the statement maker.

The defendants accepted that the publication was defamatory, but argued that the ordinary person would not interpret the statements to mean that the claimants were guilty or suspected of a breach of criminal law. The question therefore was whether there was evidence to support meanings pleaded in the innuendo and whether ordinary people would understand the difference between being investigated for fraud and being guilty of fraud.

> In this case it is, I think, sufficient to put the test in this way. Ordinary men and women have different temperaments and outlooks. Some are unusually suspicious and some are unusually naive. One must try to envisage people between these two extremes and see what is the most damaging meaning they would put on the words in question. So let me suppose a number of ordinary people discussing one of these paragraphs which they had read in the newspaper. No doubt one of them might say – 'Oh, if the fraud squad are after these people you can take it they are guilty.' But I would expect the others to turn on him, if he did say that, with such remarks as – 'Be fair. This is not a police state. No doubt their affairs are in a mess or the police would not be interested. But that could be because Lewis or the cashier has been very stupid or careless. We really must not jump to conclusions.

21 [2019] UKSC 17, [2020] AC 593.

The police are fair and know their job and we shall know soon enough if there is anything in it. Wait till we see if they charge him. I wouldn't trust him until this is cleared up, but it is another thing to condemn him unheard.'

What the ordinary man, not avid for scandal, would read into the words complained of must be a matter of impression. I can only say that I do not think that he would infer guilt of fraud merely because an inquiry is on foot. And, if that is so, then it is the duty of the trial judge to direct the jury that it is for them to determine the meaning of the paragraph but that they must not hold it to impute guilt of fraud because as a matter of law the paragraph is not capable of having that meaning. So there was here, in my opinion, misdirection of the two juries sufficiently serious to require that there must be new trials.

Before leaving this part of the case I must notice an argument to the effect that you can only justify a libel that the plaintiffs have so conducted their affairs as to give rise to suspicion of fraud, or as to give rise to an inquiry whether there has been fraud, by proving that they have acted fraudulently. Then it is said that if that is so there can be no difference between an allegation of suspicious conduct and an allegation of guilt. To my mind, there is a great difference between saying that a man has behaved in a suspicious manner and saying that he is guilty of an offence, and I am not convinced that you can only justify the former statement by proving guilt. I can well understand that if you say there is a rumour that X is guilty you can only justify it by proving that he is guilty, because repeating someone else's libellous statement is just as bad as making the statement directly. But I do not think that it is necessary to reach a decision on this matter of justification in order to decide that these paragraphs can mean suspicion but cannot be held to infer guilt.

Sometimes, it can be relatively straightforward to determine whether a statement is defamatory at face value per the literal meaning of the words. At other times, however, it can be unclear, and it is important to consider the role of innuendo when determining whether a statement is defamatory. It could be that the words convey a negative meaning by implication or inference instead of outright. In the context of defamation, this is referred to as an 'innuendo', and there are two different types. A true (or legal) innuendo occurs where the statements themselves are not sufficient, and the claimant must show that the recipients of the allegations have additional information that would make the statements defamatory.[22] A false (or popular) innuendo occurs when a reasonable member of society with general knowledge could infer the defamatory nature of the statement if they 'read between the lines'.[23]

Byrne v Deane [1937] 1 KB 818, CA, 830–31 (Greer LJ), 832–33 (Slesser LJ), 839–40 (Greene LJ)

The allegedly defamatory statement was a notice put on a public noticeboard that imputed that the claimant (Bryne) had informed the police about the use of illegal

22 See *Tolley v JS Fry and Sons Ltd* [1931] AC 333 for an example of a true innuendo.

23 See *Lewis v Daily Telegraph Ltd* [1964] AC 234, 258 (Lord Reid) for an example of a false innuendo.

gambling machines at a golf club. As a result of this belief, the claimant was excluded from his social circle. The court held that the statement was not defamatory, as reporting illegal activity to police would not lower Byrne's reputation in the eyes of 'right thinking' members of society. The majority, Slesser and Green LLJ, believed that even though it was clear from the evidence that the claimant had suffered as a result of the notice and the innuendo that the claimant was an informant, the claim for defamation could not be sustained.

Slesser LJ commented:

> In my opinion, the words as set out in the statement of claim cannot on any view be taken to be defamatory apart from the innuendo. I do not think that, taken by themselves, they form any ground of complaint, and, as I understand the case, it was treated upon the basis that the innuendo contained the alleged defamatory meaning of these words, and not the words in their natural and ordinary meaning.
>
> ...
>
> I read that innuendo to mean that all the consequent disfavours which it is alleged the plaintiff might suffer at the hands of his fellow members of the club would be due and due only to the fact that he had 'reported to the police the presence of the said machines upon the said premises,' and so, that being the meaning, of course the natural objections on the part of his fellow members would follow.
>
> ...
>
> Now, in my view, to say or to allege of a man – and for this purpose, as my Lord has said, it does not matter whether the allegation is true or is not true – that he has reported certain acts, wrongful in law, to the police, cannot possibly be said to be defamatory of him in the minds of the general public.
>
> We have to consider in this connection the arbitrium boni, the view which would be taken by the ordinary good and worthy subject of the King, and I have assigned to myself no other criterion than what a good and worthy subject of the King would think of some person of whom it had been said that he had put the law into motion against wrongdoers, in considering that such a good and worthy subject would not consider such an allegation in itself to be defamatory.

Green LJ agreed with Slesser LJ, taking a slightly different approach:

> If the allegation that he reported the matter to the police is not defamatory, in my judgment the allegation that in reporting the matter to the police he was guilty of disloyalty cannot be defamatory.
>
> If that be right, the matter resolves itself into this: Are words capable of a defamatory meaning which say of the plaintiff that he reported to the police that on the club premises of which he was a member a criminal offence was being habitually committed?

> Now, it is said that the ordinary sense of society would say of a man who had done that in the case of this particular criminal offence that he had behaved in a disloyal and underhand fashion. It is said that this particular offence is one which can be looked at with an indulgent eye, and that there is something dishonourable in setting in motion the constitutional machinery provided in this country for the suppression of crime.

It was however a split decision, with Greer LJ dissenting. His Lordship emphasised that the innuendo was that the claimant had been disloyal to the club, which was defamatory.

> Was the statement defamatory? There is no question but that it did in fact refer to the plaintiff, and the defamatory part of it, in my judgment, is contained in the words: 'But he who gave the game away May he burn in hell and rue the day.' It does not seem to me that that statement was correctly interpreted in the innuendo, because the plaintiff may rely upon the natural meaning of the words, quite apart from the innuendo. One must distinguish between the question as to what a defamatory statement means, and the question whether that defamatory statement is or is not true. It may well be, if it had been necessary to deal with the matter, that it might have been said by the plaintiff that the defamatory statement was not true because he had not been guilty of any disloyalty to his fellow members because he had only done that which was his duty. But that is not the question. The question is, What is the meaning which any reasonable man would attach to the statement contained in this document? In my judgment the statement in the document in question is a statement that the plaintiff who gave the game away was guilty of disloyalty to his fellow members of the club. Whether that was justified or not is quite another matter. That it would be regarded by any reasonable person as defamatory to say of a man that he was guilty of disloyalty to the fellow members of the club to which he belonged I do not think there is any question. It would in my judgment be a defamatory statement which would entitle him to bring an action in order to recover damages quite independently of the innuendo. But if it is necessary to go to the innuendo I find in the innuendo this statement, that the words meant, amongst other things, that he was guilty of underhand disloyalty to the defendants and his fellow members of the club. In my judgment the words are capable of that meaning, and the learned judge was entitled to decide that that is what they did mean, and we need not consider whether or not the facts when proved would show that that statement was wholly unfounded, that is to say that it was not true. We have not got to consider that. We have only got to consider what the words would convey to an ordinary reasonable member of the club, and in my judgment they would convey either in their natural meaning or as stated in the innuendo that the plaintiff had been guilty of underhand disloyalty to the defendants and his fellow members of the club, and that therefore the learned judge was justified in finding not only that the words were capable of a defamatory meaning but that they were defamatory of the plaintiff.

The next requirement is that the statement refers to the claimant by name or otherwise. This does not require the claimant to be specifically named or identified, but the statement must provide sufficient information such that they could be identified by some members of the public. The identification does not have to occur in the same publication and can occur through a second, linked publication. A recent example occurred when a publication about 'a leading Conservative politician' was combined with a tweet stating, 'Why is Lord McAlpine trending?' to identify Lord McAlpine.[24] Even though the first publication did not specifically mention Lord McAlpine, when combined with the tweet, it was sufficient to identify the claimant by name or otherwise.

The third requirement is that the statement must be published to a third party. Despite the formal wording of 'publication', this does not have to be an official manner of publication. Defamation can occur through the public posting of documents, WhatsApp chats, Twitter/X posts, and group conversations. The focus is on whether the statement was witnessed by a third party or parties regardless of the format.[25]

Question to consider: Do you think the courts have struck the right balance when deciding which statements are defamatory?

Other resources: *Youssoupoff v Metro-Goldwyn-Mayer Pictures Ltd* (1934) 50 TLR 581, CA; *Tolley v JS Fry and Sons Ltd* [1930] 1 KB 467, CA; Thomas Gibbons, 'Defamation Reconsidered' (1996) 16 *OLJS* 587; Ian Loveland, 'A New Legal Landscape? Libel Law and Freedom of Political Expression in the United Kingdom' [2000] *EHRLR* 476; Leslie Kim Treiger-Bar-Am, 'Defamation Law in a Changing Society: the Case of *Youssoupoff v Metro-Goldwyn Mayer*' (2000) 20 *LS* 291.

13.4.2 Defences

The three elements for proving defamation are quite broad; for example, there is no need to show that the comments were untruthful to have a *prima facie* case for defamation. As a result, the defences have a very important role to play in balancing the rights of the claimant and the defendant. Like traditional defences, the burden will be on the defendant (on the balance of probabilities) to show that the elements of the defence are made out.

The Defamation Act 2013 made significant amendments to the common law defences regime, specifically ss 2–7 of the Act. The common law defence of consent is not included in the statute but can still apply to defamation.[26] For a discussion of the statutory aspects of the defences, see the annotated Act at the beginning of this chapter.

24 *Lord McAlpine of West Green v Sally Bercow* [2013] EWHC 1342 (QB), [3], [15].

25 *Loutchansky v Times Newspapers Ltd (Nos 2–5)* [2001] EWCA Civ 1805, [2002] QB 783; *Al Amoudi v Brisard* [2006] EWHC 1062 (QB).

26 *Chapman v Lord Ellesmere* [1932] 2 KB 431, CA.

British Chiropractic Association v Singh [2010] EWCA Civ 350, [2011] 1 WLR 133, [6], [16], [26]–[30]

This case provides an interesting insight into the distinction between fact and opinion. The defendant, a scientist and author, published an article which included the following statement:

> 6. 'This is Chiropractic Awareness Week. So let's be aware. How about some awareness that may prevent harm and help you make truly informed choices? First, you might be surprised to know that the founder of chiropractic therapy, Daniel David Palmer, wrote that, "99% of all diseases are caused by displaced vertebrae". In the 1860s, Palmer began to develop his theory that the spine was involved in almost every illness because the spinal cord connects the brain to the rest of the body. Therefore any misalignment could cause a problem in distant parts of the body.
>
> In fact, Palmer's first chiropractic intervention supposedly cured a man who had been profoundly deaf for 17 years. His second treatment was equally strange, because he claimed that he treated a patient with heart trouble by correcting a displaced vertebra.
>
> You might think that modern chiropractors restrict themselves to treating back problems, but in fact they still possess some quite wacky ideas. The fundamentalists argue that they can cure anything. And even the more moderate chiropractors have ideas above their station. The British Chiropractic Association claims that their members can help treat children with colic, sleeping and feeding problems, frequent ear infections, asthma and prolonged crying, even though there is not a jot of evidence. This organisation is the respectable face of the chiropractic profession and yet it happily promotes bogus treatments.
>
> I can confidently label these treatments as bogus because I have co-authored a book about alternative medicine with the world's first professor of complementary medicine, Edzard Ernst. He learned chiropractic techniques himself and used them as a doctor. This is when he began to see the need for some critical evaluation. Among other projects, he examined the evidence from 70 trials exploring the benefits of chiropractic therapy in conditions unrelated to the back. He found no evidence to suggest that chiropractors could treat any such conditions.'

When determining the distinction between fact and opinion, Lord Judge commented that:

> 16. The critical question, at least for present purposes, is whether its meaning includes one or more allegations of fact which are defamatory of the claimant, or whether the entirety of what it says about the claimant is [honest opinion].

After considering the submissions from the parties and the law, Lord Judge highlighted that:

26. What 'evidence' signifies depends heavily on context. To a literalist, any primary fact – for example, that following chiropractic intervention a patient's condition improved – may be evidence of a secondary fact, here that chiropractic works. To anyone (and not only a scientist) concerned with the establishment of dependable generalisations about cause and effect, such primary information is as worthless as evidence of the secondary fact as its converse would be. The same may equally well be true of data considerably more complex than in the facile example we have given: whether it is or not is what scientific opinion is there to debate. If in the course of the debate the view is expressed that there is not a jot of evidence for one deduction or another, the natural meaning is that there is no worthwhile or reliable evidence for it. That is as much a value judgment as a contrary viewpoint would be.

27. The pleadings in the present case usefully illustrate this. Dr Singh's defence includes, in §8(25), a survey of controlled clinical trials on the efficacy of chiropractic in treating infantile colic, none of which, he contends, affords objective support for the BCA's claim. The BCA, in §9(23) of its reply, relies (among other studies) on a 1989 observational study of 316 children, of which it is said:

> 'This ... measured the number of hours each child spent in crying. It showed a reduction in crying time from 5.2 hours each day to 0.65 hours each day at 14 days. This was a very substantial improvement. There was no control group. However, the study constitutes evidence.'

One need go no further in order to see how value-laden the word 'evidence' is in the present context, let alone to envisage the examination and cross-examination of witnesses called to testify about it, and about the dozens of other reports cited by one side or the other. If Eady J's decision stands, it will not be open to the trial judge to conclude that what they amount to is all a matter of opinion, for it will already have been decided that the existence or non-existence of evidence for the claims made by the BCA is a verifiable fact.

28. Ms Rogers has understandably not sought to make a major issue of the word 'bogus'. In its context the word is more emphatic than assertive. But it is also explicitly supported by the next paragraph of the article, which explains that Dr Singh's co-author Professor Ernst had found in 70 trials no evidence that chiropractic could treat conditions unrelated to the back. It is a paragraph which also underlines the evaluative character of the assertion that there was not a jot of evidence for such claims.

29. The other assertion to which the BCA takes objection is that it 'happily' promotes treatments which, if Dr Singh is right, are bogus. Eady J accepted the BCA's case that this meant, in its context, that the BCA was well aware that there was in reality no evidence to support its claims – 'the plainest allegation of dishonesty', as the judge put it.

30. Once the allegation that there is 'not a jot of evidence' to support the claims is properly characterised as a value judgment, the word 'happily', even if synonymous with 'knowingly', loses its sting. But we respectfully doubt whether the judge was justified in

any event in attributing to the word any significance beyond, say, 'blithely'. The natural meaning of the passage, in other words, was not that the BCA was promoting what it knew to be bogus treatments but that it was promoting what Dr Singh contended were bogus treatments without regard to the want of reliable evidence of their efficacy – a meaning which takes one back to the assertion that there was not a jot of evidence for the BCA's claims.

Banks v Cadwalladr [2022] EWHC 1417 (QB), [2022] 1 WLR 5236, [394]–[399] (Steyn J)

The application of the public interest defence was shown in this case, which involved journalistic allegations by Cadwalladr that the claimant (Banks) had inappropriate Russian connections. In a long and complex judgment, Steyn J highlighted how the successful application of the public interest defence required significantly more than the defendant's belief that the matter was in the public interest. In this case, Cadwalladr had undertaken detailed and meticulous research and had kept detailed records which assisted in showing the reasonableness of her belief that the allegations were made in the public interest.

394. I address the question whether Ms Cadwalladr had reasonable grounds to believe there were grounds to investigate whether the source of Mr Banks's donations was foreign funding, accepted in breach of the law on the funding of electoral campaigns.

395. Based on her investigation, Ms Cadwalladr had reasonable grounds to believe that (i) Mr Banks had been offered 'sweetheart' deals by the Russian government in the period running up to the EU Referendum, although she had seen no evidence he had entered into any such deals; and (ii) Mr Banks's financial affairs, and the source of his ability to make the biggest political donations in UK history, were opaque. Most importantly, when Ms Cadwalladr gave the TED Talk the Electoral Commission had announced, following a one-year investigation, that it had reasonable grounds to suspect that Mr Banks was not the true source of the £8m loans/donations, but rather the source was a non-qualifying company, Rock Holdings, which is based in an off-shore, non-transparent, jurisdiction. In addition, when she gave the TED Talk, the matter had been referred to the NCA and that organisation was investigating.

396. Ms Cadwalladr did not give Mr Banks an opportunity to comment immediately prior to the TED Talk. However, she had sent right-to-reply enquiries earlier, before the articles on which her TED Talk (and in particular the words complained of) was based had been published. Her Russia connection article had conveyed essentially the same allegations, and a very similar meaning to that which she intended to convey in the TED Talk. The primary difference was that the TED Talk was given at a time when Ms Cadwalladr could place reliance on the Electoral Commission's statement of 1 November 2018, and on the ongoing NCA investigation, whereas the Russia connection article pre-dated that statement.

397. Mr McCormick submits that Ms Cadwalladr's approach to her investigation, and in particular to reliance on the views or reports of third parties was one-eyed and flawed. For example, he pointed to her reliance on the openDemocracy report regarding Mr Banks's prospecting site in Lesotho (see para 243 above), disregarding the reported views of Mr Banks's expert, and failing to understand the difference between such a prospecting site and a mine. In my judgment, it was not unreasonable to place more reliance on the view of Mr Whitelock, an expert who was described, even by the claimant's expert, as 'the authority on diamonds in Lesotho' whose word on the topic was 'pretty much gospel', especially given the geological grounds for his view was explained, whereas the logic underlying the claimant's expert's view was not. The report that 'we've recovered diamonds there' was not inconsistent with Mr Whitelock's view that it was geologically impossible to find diamonds 'in commercial quantities' at that site. While Ms Cadwalladr did not appreciate that this was only a prospecting site, that did not undermine the essential point that this was another of Mr Banks's interests which could not have been the source of the exceptionally large donations he made.

398. Although Ms Cadwalladr made clear that she did not understand off-shore structures, in essence, she drew the conclusion that his finances were opaque and it was unclear where he had derived sufficient funds to be able to donate as much as he had to the Brexit campaign. Those limited conclusions that she drew from the wide range of articles she read, and financial journalists and experts she spoke to on this topic, were reasonable.

399. In all the circumstances, I find that the defendant has established that her belief that publishing the TED Talk was in the public interest was reasonable. For the same reasons, if I had found that the serious harm threshold was met in relation to the Tweet, I would also have found that the defendant's belief that publishing the Tweet was in the public interest was reasonable.

13.4.3 Damages (and remedies more generally)

If the claimant can show that the elements of defamation are established, *and* the defendant cannot show that a relevant defence applies, the claim will succeed. The court will then have to decide what remedies are appropriate, including what damages should be awarded to the claimant.

Traditionally, awards of damages were made by juries, but this was effectively abolished by statute. Deciding on an appropriate level of damages for defamation cases has always been a challenge – it is difficult to provide a 'price' on vindicating reputations and compensating hurt feelings and embarrassment. Juries were also accused of making inappropriately high awards of damages, which created concerns about the impact of freedom of speech and press freedom.

Douglas W Vick and Linda Macpherson, 'An Opportunity Lost: The United Kingdom's Failed Reform of Defamation Law' (1996) 49 *Fed Comm LJ* 621, 626–29 (footnotes omitted)

[T]here has been a dramatic rise in the amounts of damages awarded against media defendants in libel cases, with detrimental consequences for press freedom. Defamation law has been exempt from the general trend of removing civil actions from the province of juries. Even with the changes brought by the Defamation Act 1996, juries will continue to decide most of the substantive issues relevant to the outcome of a libel case. More controversially, juries remain vested with the power to determine the level of compensatory and exemplary damages to be awarded to a successful plaintiff. Damage awards (and settlements) for defamation cases routinely surpass £50,000 ($75,000), and a few cases have topped £1,000,000 ($1,500,000). In addition, under the English rule a defeated defendant is responsible for the plaintiff's costs and legal fees, which in libel cases often approach the size of the verdict itself. Despite recent judicial efforts to rein in runaway libel verdicts, the compensation awarded for reputational harms still frequently exceeds that awarded in cases involving serious physical injuries.

The two most conspicuous characteristics of modem libel litigation – the expense involved in pursuing and defending a claim, and the threat of a huge award of damages and costs – have created a system that operates much differently for less wealthy individuals than for the rich and the powerful. Because contingency fee arrangements are unlawful in the United Kingdom, moderate- and low-income persons depend on the state-funded legal aid program to obtain legal representation in civil lawsuits.

Legal aid is unavailable in defamation cases, however, and the cost of pursuing a libel claim has become prohibitive for all but the most wealthy, or those backed by organizations with substantial resources. As a consequence, the press is largely unaccountable in reporting stories involving those individuals financially incapable of bringing a defamation action. On the other hand, a unique combination of substantive and procedural rules makes English defamation law singularly favorable to those plaintiffs who have the resources necessary to pursue a libel action to its conclusion. Little is required to establish a prima facie case of defamation while the defenses intended to protect free expression are plagued by limitations that often undermine their effectiveness, and those who can afford to make the considerable investment required to pursue a libel action are often handsomely rewarded with extravagant monetary awards at the end of the process.

The irony is that the law deters critical reporting of precisely those whose activities most directly affect the public interest. Those who can afford libel litigation are also most likely to be the subject of legitimate comment or journalistic investigation, and are in the best position to rebut negative publicity without needing to resort to the bludgeon of English libel law. Yet the temptation to use the threat of a libel writ to control one's press coverage can be irresistible, and experience shows that many have yielded to this temptation. Particularly litigious individuals, such as Robert Maxwell, have used this threat to discourage inquiry into their activities. The *raison d'être* for the

Goldsmith Libel Fund is to finance libel suits by plaintiffs with conservative sympathies against the 'left-wing' press. English defamation law is frequently criticized for deterring the speech that matters most, and has drawn the censure of the European Court of Human Rights.

In addition to damages, the Defamation Act 2013 allows for further remedies, namely ordering a summary of the court's judgment to be published by the defendant (under s 12) and an order for the removal of statements or ceasing distribution (under s 13).

13.5 Defamation and human rights

There is an important overlay between the laws of defamation and human rights protection. Whilst people should not have their reputations unfairly and inappropriately tarnished, threats of defamation lawsuits can have a chilling effect on the press's freedom and individuals' freedom of speech more generally. This has received increasing attention, particularly in relation to domestic violence and sexual harassment/assault and the impact of 'SLAPP' lawsuits.

The Collation Against SLAAPs in Europe, 'SLAPPS: A Threat to Democracy Continues to Grow: A 2023 Report Update', 2nd edn (The Daphne Caruana Galizia Foundation, 2023) 7[27]

Definition – SLAPP:

SLAPPs: abusive lawsuits filed to shut down acts of public participation, including public interest journalism, peaceful protest or boycotts, advocacy, whistleblowing, academic comments, or simply speaking out against the abuse of power. SLAPPs target anyone who works to hold the powerful to account or engage in matters of public interest: so-called 'public watchdogs'. This broad category includes journalists, activists, rights defenders, whistleblowers, campaigning organisations, unions or trade associations, and academics. Ultimately, the categorisation of a case as a SLAPP is a value judgement, since one can only ever infer an improper purpose from the circumstances of the case.

As a result of these concerns, many countries around the world have implemented anti-SLAPP laws through statute or the common law. The aim of these laws is to provide judges with the power to strike out unmeritorious and/or vexatious claims, potentially disincentivising people from commencing these actions in the first place. The EU is leading this charge and, at the time of writing, is implementing an anti-SLAPP Directive.

27 www.the-case.eu/wp-content/uploads/2023/08/20230703-CASE-UPDATE-REPORT-2023-1.pdf.

Rafał Mańko, 'Legislative Train 11.2023: 6 A New push for European Democracy' (European Parliament, 2023) 2

The Directive includes a number of amendments, including:

- requiring Member States should ensure that natural or legal persons engaging in public participation have access to support measures, including information, advice, legal aid, legal counselling, financial assistance, psychological assistance,
- providing that the court seized should have the power to require the claimant to provide security for costs of the proceedings, including the full costs of legal representation incurred by the defendant and damages, if it considers such security appropriate,
- a natural or legal person who has suffered harm as a result of a SLAPP should be able to claim and to obtain full compensation for that harm, covering material or non-material harm, without the need to initiate separate court proceedings to that end,
- laying down rules on private international law, whereby in defamation claims or other claims based on civil or commercial law which may constitute a claim under the directive, the domicile of the defendant should be considered to be the sole forum, having due regard to cases where the victims of defamation are natural persons. In claims regarding a publication as an act of public participation, the applicable law should be considered to be the law of the place to which that publication is directed,
- providing for a 'one-stop shop' comprising dedicated national networks of specialised lawyers, legal practitioners and psychologists, which targets of SLAPPs can contact, and through which they can receive guidance and easy access to information on, and protection against SLAPPs, including regarding legal aid, financial and psychological support,
- requiring Member States to recommend including the topic of SLAPPs in legal training,
- requiring Member States to cooperate between themselves in combating SLAPPs,

requiring the Member States to establish a publicly accessible national register of court rulings on SLAPPs which would then feed into an EU-wide register run by the Commission.

The push for further anti-SLAPP laws was instigated by Daphne Caruana Galizia, a Maltese investigative journalist, in October 2017. At the time of her death, Daphne was facing 47 open libel cases against her. As a result of her death, the Coalition Against SLAPPs in Europe (CASE), an alliance of over 80 NGOs, was formed.

One of the areas most impacted by SLAPPs is domestic violence and sexual harassment/assault claims. In writing about these changes after the very public *Heard v Depp* defamation lawsuit in the United States of America, Harsey and Freyd highlight the impact that defamation laws can have on victims coming forth and making legitimate accusations against their abusers.

Sarah J Harsey and Jennifer J Freyd, 'Defamation and DARVO' (2022) 23 *Journal of Trauma & Disassociation* 481, 481–82

Violence and trauma are often central features of the news cycle, but some stories attract especially intense and sustained attention. In these instances, the media spotlight often stimulates energetic discussions about interpersonal violence in the public discourse. One such case is actor Johnny Depp's recent defamation trial against his former spouse Amber Heard, which dominated headlines in the spring of 2022. The trial inspired numerous public conversations of varying quality about domestic violence, victim credibility, defamation lawsuits, and DARVO (e.g.: Nolan, 2022).

Depp's legal action against Heard, who is also an actor, began when he sued her over a 2018 op-ed she wrote for the *Washington Post*. According to the lawsuit, Heard defamed Depp when she wrote about witnessing how 'institutions protect men accused of abuse,' (Heard, 2018, para. 5) and when she described herself as 'a public figure representing domestic abuse' (Heard, 2018, para. 3). Even the title of Heard's op-ed ('I spoke up against sexual violence – and faced our culture's wrath. That has to change') was identified in the lawsuit as being defamatory against Depp. Although Heard did not name any perpetrators in the op-ed, Depp's legal team argued she had defamed him and further alleged she had actually been the abusive partner in the relationship. Heard filed a counterclaim against Depp and his attorney after they called her reports of abuse a hoax. The jury sided primarily with Depp, awarding him $10 million in damages and Heard $2 million in damages.

While the Depp v. Heard trial gained much of its attention due in part to its high-profile plaintiff and defendant, it reflects a growing trend in the world of civil litigation: alleged perpetrators of interpersonal violence are filing defamation lawsuits against the individuals who have named them as abusers. In a 2020 article, *Mother Jones* journalist Madison Pauly reported that at least 100 defamation cases had been filed since 2014 by those accused of sexual misconduct (Pauly, 2020). Of these cases, about half were filed in the years following the rise of the 2017 #MeToo movement on social media, indicating a sharp increase in the number of people taking their alleged victims to court. Legal experts have also taken notice of this growing phenomenon. In a 2017 interview for *Buzzfeed*, a lawyer who works with campus sexual assault victims shared that previously only a small fraction – 5% – of her cases included a defamation lawsuit but more recently that number had jumped to about 50% (Kingkade, 2017). Equality Now, a women's rights organization, similarly reports seeing a worldwide increase in perpetrators filing defamation lawsuits against victims of gender-based violence

(Dugan, 2022). Defamation lawsuits against victims have even caught the attention of the U.N. Special Rapporteur for Freedom of Opinion and Expression, Irene Khan. 'In a perverse twist in the #MeToo age,' Khan writes, 'women who publicly denounce alleged perpetrators of sexual violence online are increasingly subject to defamation suits or charged with criminal libel or the false reporting of crimes' (Khan, 2021, p. 8).

It's not just the growing number of cases that's concerning. The threat of such lawsuits against people reporting or disclosing abuse is also something that many victims fear or experience. A survey of 107 sexual assault survivors who reported their assaults to school officials found that 23% were threatened with a defamation lawsuit by either their perpetrator or their perpetrator's attorney (Nesbitt & Carson, 2021). According to this survey, nearly 20% of survivors were also warned by their school that they may be at risk of being sued for defamation.

For victims, the notion of participating in a retraumatizing, expensive, timeconsuming, and hostile legal process is chilling and upsetting. For abusers, these lawsuits are an opportunity to enforce DARVO through civil litigation. DARVO (Deny, Attack, Reverse Victim and Offender) is a perpetrator tactic first described by Freyd (1997). Based on her observations of sex offenders, Freyd (1997) proposed that perpetrators deny committing any wrongdoing, attack their victims' credibility, and cast their victims as the real aggressor and themselves as the real victims when held accountable or confronted with their abusive behavior. DARVO is a tactic used to urge observers to believe that the only real wrongdoing is a false accusation – a terrible injustice brought on by someone pretending to be a victim. The presence of this alternative and oftentimes compelling narrative put forth by an alleged perpetrator can generate confusion – who is really to blame? Did the abuse even happen? By eroding trust in victims, DARVO's purpose is to enable perpetrators to deflect at least some blame and responsibility.

Question to consider: What human rights issues are raised by defamation, and does the law deal with them effectively?

Other resources: Bonnie Docherty, 'Defamation Law: Positive Jurisprudence' (2000) 13 *Harv Hum Rts J* 263; Dan Kozlowski, '"For the Protection of the Reputation or Rights of Others": The European Court of Human Rights' Interpretation of the Defamation Exception in Article 10(2)' (2006) 11 *Comm L & Pol'y* 133; Andrew Nicol, Gavin Millar and Andrew Sharland, *Media Law & Human Rights*, 2nd edn (OUP, 2009); Paul Mitchell, 'Dario Milo, *Defamation and Human Rights*' (2009) 1 *JML* 289; Irene Khan, 'Report of the Special Rapporteur on the promotion and protection of the right to freedom of opinion and expression', A/76/258 (30 July 2021); Gov UK, 'Factsheet: Strategic Lawsuits against Public Participation (SLAPPs)' (26 October 2023).[28]

28 www.gov.uk/government/publications/economic-crime-and-corporate-transparency-bill-2022-factsheets/factsheet-strategic-lawsuits-against-public-participation-slapps.

13.6 Conclusion

Defamation law often does not receive the attention it deserves. It is an area of tort law rich with statutes, interesting case law, and fundamentally important challenges. This chapter has really only scratched the surface of the legal doctrine relevant to the defamation cause of action and instead has focused on the provision of materials designed to increase your understanding of the underlying theoretical aspects of the topic. The balancing of the right to protect an individual's reputation against another's freedom of speech will always be tricky and require a number of considerations – many of which have been outlined in this chapter.

Chapter 14 PRIVACY AND BREACH OF CONFIDENCE

14.1 Introduction

The law of privacy and breach of confidence are inherently connected with defamation; they are both related to harm caused by information. Whilst defamation protects people from the negative impacts of *untrue* statements, privacy aims to protect people from the harmful publication of *true* information that has a confidential or private aspect. Privacy is currently protected in a very piecemeal manner within the UK, with some common law protections, the tort of breach of confidence (also known as misuse of private information), some statutory provisions, some press self-regulation, and human rights provisions. However, these do not provide comprehensive or coherent protection, and there are ongoing calls for both common law and statutory developments in this space. Privacy rights must also often be weighed against competing rights of freedom of speech and freedom of the press, creating a challenging and delicate balance between competing rights and interests.

Committee on Privacy, Younger Report (Cmnd 5012, July 1972), 10

Before continuing any further, it is important to get a clear understanding of what we mean by 'privacy' as it has different meanings in different contexts. Here is one definition, provided by the Younger Report, but this is by no means the sole or only accepted definition available.

37. One of the obstacles to the development of a satisfactory law of privacy has been the difficulty of definition. For instance the formula that 'privacy is the right to be let alone' turns out on closer examination to go so far beyond any right which the individual living in an organised society could reasonably claim, that it would be useless as a basis for the granting of legal protection. Any law which proclaimed this as a general right would have to qualify the right in so many ways that the generality of the concept would be destroyed.

38. We discuss the problem of definition at some length in Chapter 4 of Part I. At this stage it may perhaps be sufficient to say that, for the purposes of this Report, we have conceived of the right of privacy as having two main aspects. The first of these is *freedom from intrusion upon oneself, one's home, family and relationships*. The second is privacy of information, that is the *right to determine for oneself how and to what extent information about oneself is communicated to others*. [emphasis added]

14.2 Current protection of privacy

There is no overriding 'tort of privacy' in the United Kingdom. As discussed in more detail at 14.3, the courts continue to refuse to recognise a freestanding tort protecting people's privacy. However, that does not mean that privacy is not protected in the UK; rather, there is a complicated and piecemeal web of protection arising from various sources.

Wainwright and another v Home Office [2003] UKHL 53, [2004] 2 AC 406, [31] (Lord Hoffman)

> 31. There seems to me a great difference between identifying privacy as a value which underlies the existence of a rule of law (and may point the direction in which the law should develop) and privacy as a principle of law in itself. The English common law is familiar with the notion of underlying values – principles only in the broadest sense – which direct its development.

The following table, from Green and Gardner, *Tort Law*, 2nd edn (Hart Publishing, 2024), highlights the wide range of potential protections in place for privacy – despite the lack of a specific tort of privacy.

Table 14.1: Protections of privacy

Tort in Question	Nature of Right Protection	Potential Privacy Protection	Limitations	Case Example(s)
Defamation	Protects individuals from the publication of untrue statements and representations	Prevents the publication of private information that is defamatory in nature	* Generally restricted to publications of *untrue* statements * Does not provide adequate protection for true but private information	*Cassidy v Daily Mirror Newspapers Ltd* [1929] 2 KB 331
Trespass to Land	Protects people from unwanted intrusion onto land	Prevents individuals from entering the property of others (ie to take photographs)	* Does not protect people from photographs taken in public spaces or other information (ie phone tapping, email hacking etc) * Can still take photos from outside or above property without committing trespass	*Bernstein v Skyviews & General Ltd* [1977] EWHC (QB) 1 *Richard v British Broadcasting Corporation* [2018] 3 WLR 1715

Tort in Question	Nature of Right Protection	Potential Privacy Protection	Limitations	Case Example(s)
Trespass to Person (battery)	Protects the bodily autonomy of individuals	Prevents unwanted touching of others that could constitute an invasion of privacy (ie unjustified strip searches)	* Very limited in scope – only protects the privacy of individuals to the extent that physical touching is necessary	*Wainwright v Home Office* [2003] UKHL 53
Tort of Telephone Harassment	Provides protection for verbal threats and persistent / harassing telephone calls	Prevents unwanted telephone calls that invade the privacy of the recipient	* Considered a 'step too far' in later cases, therefore no longer applicable	*Khorasandjian v Bush* [1993] QB 727 *Hunter v Canary Wharf Ltd* [1997] AC 655
Protection from Harassment Act 1997	Provides for tort liability and criminal sanctions for harassing behaviour	Prevents harassment of individuals in an attempt to obtain information or harassing acts that invade the privacy of others (ie following to take photographs, stalking etc)	* Invasion of privacy must be so severe as to constitute 'harassment' * Actions need to result in a 'course of conduct'	*Hunter v Canary Wharf Ltd* [1997] AC 655 *Fearn v Board of Trustees of the Tate Gallery* [2020] EWCA Civ 104
Nuisance	Protects people from unreasonable interference with their use and enjoyment of land	Prevents people from unreasonably interfering with rights to enjoy land, which can expand to privacy rights when on the land	* Needs a proprietary interest in the land * Recent developments allowing for privacy protection	*Thomas v News Group Newspapers Ltd* [2001] EWCA Civ 1233 *Law Society v Kordowski* [2011] All ER (D) 46 (Dec)
Malicious Falsehoods	Protects people from the malicious publication of false statements which cause financial harm	Prevents the publication of some sorts of private information	* Protected information needs to be of the type that causes financial harm * Only relates to false information, therefore does not prevent the publication of true but private information	*Kaye v Robertson* [1991] FSR 62

Tort in Question	Nature of Right Protection	Potential Privacy Protection	Limitations	Case Example(s)
Breach of Confidence	If people had a reasonable expectation of privacy, it protects them from the unauthorised use of information	Prevents the publication of private information by individuals or the press more generally	* Provides for the protection of private information only – does not protect other forms of privacy * Need to show that there was (a) a reasonable expectation of privacy, and (b) unauthorised use of this information	*Campbell v MGN Ltd* [2004] 2 WLR 1232

Fearn v Board of Trustees of the Tate Gallery [2020] EWCA Civ 104, [2020] 2 WLR 1081, [84]–[85]

The residents of Neo Bankside apartments brought a claim in nuisance and under the Human Rights Act 1998 for protection of their 'rights of privacy'. Their living areas were extensively glassed and looked directly onto the Tate Modern viewing gallery's new extension. Therefore, the people on the viewing gallery could see directly into their windows, and this claimed to be a breach of the residents' privacy. They sought an injunction for the viewing gallery's closure, which was initially denied by the Court of Appeal who held that it was not nuisance's role to protect privacy rights.

Sir Terence Etherton MR, Lord Justice Lewison, and Lady Justice Rose DBE gave a joint judgment stating that:

> 84. [I]t may be said that what is really the issue in cases of overlooking in general, and the present case in particular, is invasion of privacy rather than (as is the case with the tort of nuisance) damage to interests in property. There are already other laws which bear on privacy, including the law relating to confidentiality, misuse of private information, data protection (Data Protection Act 2018), harassment and stalking (Protection of Harassment Act 1997). This is an area in which the legislature has intervened and is better suited than the courts to weigh up competing interests: cf. *Wainwright v Home Office* [2004] 2 AC 406, esp at [33], in which the House of Lords held that there is no common law tort of invasion of privacy and that it is an area which requires a detailed approach which can be achieved only by legislation rather than the broad brush of common law principle.

85. For all those reasons, we consider that it would be preferable to leave it to Parliament to formulate any further laws that are perceived to be necessary to deal with overlooking rather than to extend the law of private nuisance.

This approach was, however, overruled by the Supreme Court, which held that privacy rights can and should be protected when they interfere with the use and enjoyment of land.

Fearn v Board of Trustees of the Tate Gallery [2023] UKSC 4, [2023] 2 WLR 339, [82]–[84] (Lord Leggatt)

82. The judge acknowledged that it is not usually a defence to a nuisance claim to say that the claimant could take remedial steps to avoid the adverse consequences of the defendant's acts. For example, he noted that 'The victim of excessive dust would not be expected to put up additional sealing of doors and windows' and that 'the victim of excessive noise would not be expected to buy earplugs': para 215. However, the judge thought that 'this is an unusual case' and that 'privacy is a bit different' in that it has become acceptable to expect those who want to enhance their privacy to protect their own interests. He saw this as part of the give and take expected of neighbouring property owners and concluded, at para 215: 'Looking at the overall balance which has to be achieved, the availability and reasonableness of such measures is another reason why I consider there to be no nuisance in this case.'

83. It is easy to identify where the judge went wrong here because he himself explained the reason. As he noted, it is not a good defence to a nuisance claim for the defendant to say that the claimant could take remedial steps to avoid the consequences of the defendant's acts. The reason why this is not a good defence is that, far from involving give and take, such an approach is all one way. It places responsibility for avoiding the impact of an activity which causes substantial interference with the ordinary enjoyment of property entirely on the victim rather than on the person who carries out the activity. Arguments of this kind are unsound when relied on to justify any invasion of property rights. It does not avail a trespasser to assert that he would not have wandered onto the claimant's land if the claimant had erected a fence, or a burglar to argue that the claimant's house would not have been burgled if the claimant had installed stronger locks. In the same way it is unsound to argue that the defendant's activity would not violate the claimant's enjoyment of rights in land if the claimant took measures to prevent this.

84. I cannot agree with the judge that 'privacy is a bit different'. In any context it is reasonable to expect those who want more protection from outside interference than the law provides to protect their own interests. For instance, a homeowner may be kept awake or find it impossible to concentrate as a result of noise arising from a normal use of a neighbouring property. If so, then their only recourse is self-protection, for example by using ear plugs. Similarly, someone who cannot stand the smell of their neighbour's

cooking at mealtimes had better close their windows. Visual intrusion is just the same. If the interior of a person's home can be seen from the windows of houses across the street and the occupants wish to avoid being seen, it is for them to draw their blinds or take other measures of the kind suggested by the judge. But in all these cases the person whose activity causes the interference is using their property in a common and ordinary way. What is not acceptable is to place the burden on the claimant to mitigate the impact of a special use of the defendant's property. To do so is inconsistent with the principle of reciprocity that underpins the law of nuisance.

This case shows, at least in the context of privacy and land rights, an increasing acceptance by the courts of their role to protect and uphold people's rights to privacy. However, it is far from a complete protection as this common law approach still requires people to fulfil the 'interest in the land' and 'unreasonable interference' requirements. Therefore, this protection is largely limited to overlooking and has limited application to private information.

Media and the press have been a large source of privacy intrusions – the paparazzi have a terrible reputation for unfairly invading the privacy of various 'celebrities'. A number of scandals, including Princess Diana's fatal car crash and the *News of the World* phone hacking, revealed that the press's self-regulation was not working. This resulted in increased pressure on the government to intervene by providing additional regulation of journalistic activities. The then Prime Minster, David Cameron, announced a public inquiry into these activities with the aim of reviewing the cultural practices and ethics of the press. The final report made 92 recommendations in total, including increasing privacy rights or creating a freestanding right against invasion of privacy. This did not happen, but the Press Complaints Commission was replaced by the Independent Press Standards Organisation (IPSO).

Independent Press Standards Organisation, 'Editors' Code of Practice' (IPSO, January 2021) cls 1–6

[IPSO's Editors' Code of Practice[1] sets out the rules that newspapers and magazines have agreed to follow.]

Preamble

The Code – including this preamble and the public interest exceptions below – sets the framework for the highest professional standards that members of the press subscribing to the Independent Press Standards Organisation have undertaken to maintain. It is the cornerstone of the system of voluntary self-regulation to which they have made a binding contractual commitment. It balances both the rights of the individual and the public's right to know.

As a result of the scandals, the aim was to ensure the 'highest professional standards'.

Continued self-regulation, despite the significant concerns and criticisms.

This approach received quite a bit of criticism as it seemed at odds with the approach of self-regulation.

1 www.ipso.co.uk/media/2032/ecop-2021-ipso-version-pdf.pdf.

To achieve that balance, it is essential that an agreed Code be honoured not only to the letter, but in the full spirit. It should be interpreted neither so narrowly as to compromise its commitment to respect the rights of the individual, nor so broadly that it infringes the fundamental right to freedom of expression – such as to inform, to be partisan, to challenge, shock, be satirical and to entertain – or prevents publication in the public interest.

> Emphasising that the Code is meant to change the nature of press intrusions; therefore, parties should follow the spirit of the document.

> Highlights the need to balance privacy rights with the right to freedom of expression.

It is the responsibility of editors and publishers to apply the Code to editorial material in both printed and online versions of their publications. They should take care to ensure it is observed rigorously by all editorial staff and external contributors, including non-journalists.

> The Code applies widely and is not limited only to journalists but all the parties involved in press publications, applying equally to printed and online materials.

Editors must maintain in-house procedures to resolve complaints swiftly and, where required to do so, co-operate with IPSO. A publication subject to an adverse adjudication must publish it in full and with due prominence, as required by IPSO.

> There must be a complaints resolution process in place that swiftly responds to complaints.

> Any adverse adjudications must be published fully and prominently to try to deter these publications in the first place and to correct any errors.

1. Accuracy

i) The Press must take care not to publish inaccurate, misleading or distorted information or images, including headlines not supported by the text.

> This is designed to ensure that information is accurate and does not mislead readers.

ii) A significant inaccuracy, misleading statement or distortion must be corrected, promptly and with due prominence, and – where appropriate – an apology published. In cases involving IPSO, due prominence should be as required by the regulator.

> Anything incorrect or misleading must result in a correction and, potentially, an apology.

2. Privacy

i) Everyone is entitled to respect for their private and family life, home, physical and mental health, and correspondence, including digital communications.

> A starting point of emphasising the right to privacy.

ii) Editors will be expected to justify intrusions into any individual's private life without consent. In considering an individual's reasonable expectation of privacy, account will be taken of the complainant's own public disclosures of information and the extent to which the material complained about is already in the public domain or will become so.

> Non-consensual intrusions into private life are not prohibited, but they must be justified.

iii) It is unacceptable to photograph individuals, without their consent, in public or private places where there is a reasonable expectation of privacy.

> Again, not an outright ban on non-consensual photographing of individuals, unless they have a reasonable expectation of privacy.

3. Harassment

i) Journalists must not engage in intimidation, harassment or persistent pursuit.

> This is not focused directly on privacy but does have indirect impacts (as intimidating, harassing, or pursuing people will likely impact their privacy).

ii) They must not persist in questioning, telephoning, pursuing or photographing individuals once asked to desist; nor remain on property when asked to leave and must not follow them. If requested, they must identify themselves and whom they represent.

> Specific requirements regarding contact and physical presence that indirectly benefit privacy protections.

iii) Editors must ensure these principles are observed by those working for them and take care not to use non-compliant material from other sources.

> This puts obligations on journalists alongside editors, as the latter cannot publish material that is non-compliant with the ISPO requirements.

6. Children

> A specific focus on protecting children is in line with the common law, which will be discussed in more detail below.

i) All pupils should be free to complete their time at school without unnecessary intrusion.

ii) They must not be approached or photographed at school without permission of the school authorities.

iii) Children under 16 must not be interviewed or photographed on issues involving their own or another child's welfare unless a custodial parent or similarly responsible adult consents.

> In both of these subclauses, children are defined as 'under 16' as opposed to 'under 18' as it usually is in most other areas of the law. Why do you think this is the case? Do you agree with it?.

iv) Children under 16 must not be paid for material involving their welfare, nor parents or guardians for material about their children or wards, unless it is clearly in the child's interest.

v) Editors must not use the fame, notoriety or position of a parent or guardian as sole justification for publishing details of a child's private life.

> Whilst celebrities and people in the public eye are generally expected to 'give up' some of their privacy rights, this does not automatically extend to their children.

Another area where privacy is relevant is under Sch 1 to the Human Rights Act 1998. Here there is a tension between protection of privacy under Article 8 ('Right to respect for private and family life') and Article 10 and s 12 ('Freedom of expression'). This tension creates the balancing test of breach of confidence, which will be discussed at 14.4 below.

Human Rights Act 1998, Sch 1, Arts 8, 10 and s 12

Article 8 – Right to respect for private and family life

1. Everyone has the right to respect for his private and family life, his home and his correspondence.

> This provision has been defined as including a right to privacy, as well as a right to home and family life.

2. There shall be no interference by a public authority with the exercise of this right except such as is in accordance with the law and is necessary in a democratic society in the interests of national security, public safety or the economic well-being of the country, for the prevention of disorder or crime, for the protection of health or morals, or for the protection of the rights and freedoms of others.

> The right to privacy is not absolute or automatic; it must be balanced with a number of other rights and duties.

Article 10 – Freedom of expression

1. Everyone has the right to freedom of expression. This right shall include freedom to hold opinions and to receive and impart information and ideas without interference by public authority and regardless of frontiers. This Article shall not prevent States from requiring the licensing of broadcasting, television or cinema enterprises.

> **People have the right to express themselves freely; this is clearly of fundamental importance to ensure an open and working democracy.**

2. The exercise of these freedoms, since it carries with it duties and responsibilities, may be subject to such formalities, conditions, restrictions or penalties as are prescribed by law and are necessary in a democratic society, in the interests of national security, territorial integrity or public safety, for the prevention of disorder or crime, for the protection of health or morals, for the protection of the reputation or rights of others, for preventing the disclosure of information received in confidence, or for maintaining the authority and impartiality of the judiciary.

> **Similar to Article 8 above, the right to freedom of expression is not absolute and must be balanced with other competing rights and obligations.**

12 Freedom of expression

(1) This section applies if a court is considering whether to grant any relief which, if granted, might affect the exercise of the Convention right to freedom of expression.

> **This section puts safeguards in place to prevent the unjustified undermining of freedom of expression, and specifically relates to relief that may be granted by a court.**

(2) If the person against whom the application for relief is made ('the respondent') is neither present nor represented, no such relief is to be granted unless the court is satisfied—

(a) that the applicant has taken all practicable steps to notify the respondent; or

(b) that there are compelling reasons why the respondent should not be notified.

> **In these hearings, the respondent must either be present to defend the claim, the applicant must have taken all practical steps to notify the respondent, or there must have been strong reasons why it was not appropriate to notify the respondent.**

(3) No such relief is to be granted so as to restrain publication before trial unless the court is satisfied that the applicant is likely to establish that publication should not be allowed.

> **This subsection focuses on interim relief (ie prevention of publication before the full trial has occurred). It requires the applicant to show that they are likely to be successful in the full trial.**

(4) The court must have particular regard to the importance of the Convention right to freedom of expression and, where the proceedings relate to material which the respondent claims, or which appears to the court, to be journalistic, literary or artistic material (or to conduct connected with such material), to—

(a) the extent to which—

(i) the material has, or is about to, become available to the public; or

(ii) it is, or would be, in the public interest for the material to be published;

(b) any relevant privacy code.

> **When the court makes decisions about journalistic, literary, or artistic material, it must consider the extent to which the information is available to the public, the public interest of the material being published, and any relevant privacy code.**

Question to consider: Does the United Kingdom legal regime currently provide sufficient protections for privacy rights?

Other resources: S Warren and L Brandeis, 'The Right to Privacy' (1890) 4 *Harvard LR* 193; *Cassidy v Daily Mirror Newspapers Ltd* [1929] 2 KB 331; *Khorasandjian v Bush* [1993] QB 727; D Feldman, 'Secrecy, Dignity or Autonomy? Views of Privacy as a Civil Liberty' (1994) 47(2) *Current Legal Problems* 41; Annabelle Lever, 'Feminism, democracy and the right to privacy' (2005) (Nov) *Minerva* 1–31.

14.3 Common law and statutory stalemate

As you can see from the numerous sources, the law protects privacy in the United Kingdom in a variety of ways. However, a lack of complete or comprehensive protection is clear, and there are frequent calls to provide a more holistic scheme; the question of whether this should be by common law or statute provides ongoing tension.

The courts have frequently refused to significantly increase privacy rights, including through the creation of a freestanding tort of privacy, stating that Parliament should do so.

Malone v Metropolitan Police Commissioner [1979] 2 WLR 700, 725–26

Sir Robert Megarry VC considered whether there was a privacy right to hold a telephone conversation in one's home without interference. The judge refused to recognise a new privacy right, stating that this was not the role of the court but instead should be done by statute.

> [T]here is the right of privacy. Here the contention is that, although at present no general right of privacy has been recognised by English law, there is a particular right of privacy, namely, the right to hold a telephone conversation in the privacy of one's home without molestation. This, it was said, ought to be recognised and declared to be part of English law, despite the absence of any English authority to this effect. As I have indicated, I am not unduly troubled by the absence of English authority: there has to be a first time for everything, and, if the principles of English law, and not least analogies from the existing rules, together with the requirements of justice and common sense, pointed firmly to such a right existing, then I think the court should not be deterred from recognising the right.
>
> On the other hand, it is no function of the courts to legislate in a new field. The extension of the existing laws and principles is one thing, the creation of an altogether new right is another. At times judges must, and do, legislate; but as Holmes J. once said, they do so only interstitially, and with molecular rather than molar motions: see *Southern Pacific Co. v. Jensen* (1917) 244 U.S. 205, 221, in a dissenting judgment. Anything beyond that must be left for legislation. No new right in the law, fully-fledged with all the appropriate safeguards, can spring from the head of a judge deciding a particular case: only Parliament

can create such a right. The most obvious recent example of this is the so-called deserted wife's equity to occupy the matrimonial home. There was much uncertainty as to the ambit and operation of this right, and whether it arose from desertion alone, or whether there was also a betrayed wife's equity, a battered wife's equity, and so on, or, for that matter, a deserted husband's equity. After some 15 years of controversy and litigation, with its accompanying burden of costs, in *National Provincial Bank Ltd. v. Hastings Car Mart Ltd.* [1965] A.C. 1175 it was held that the equity had never existed. Parliament then enacted the Matrimonial Homes Act 1967, laying down a complete code which the courts could not possibly have laid down by way of judicial decision. The fact that the code has its difficulties does not affect the matter: the point is that the Act dealt with a wide variety of circumstances, and provided a number of safeguards, in a way that no court could properly have done. Where there is some major gap in the law, no doubt a judge would be capable of framing what he considered to be a proper code to fill it; and sometimes he may be tempted. But he has to remember that his function is judicial, not legislative, and that he ought not to use his office to legislate in the guise of exercising his judicial powers.

One of the factors that must be relevant in such a case is the degree of particularity in the right that is claimed. The wider and more indefinite the right claimed, the greater the undesirability of holding that such a right exists. Wide and indefinite rights, while conferring an advantage on those who have them, may well gravely impair the position of those who are subject to the rights. To create a right for one person, you have to impose a corresponding duty on another. In the present case, the alleged right to hold a telephone conversation in the privacy of one's own home without molestation is wide and indefinite in its scope, and in any case does not seem to be very apt for covering the plaintiff's grievance. He was not 'molested' in holding his telephone conversations: he held them without 'molestation', but without their retaining the privacy that he desired. If a man telephones from his own home, but an open window makes it possible for a near neighbour to overhear what is said, and the neighbour, remaining throughout on his own property, listens to the conversation, is he to be a tortfeasor? Is a person who overhears a telephone conversation by reason of a so-called 'crossed line' to be liable in damages? What of an operator of a private switchboard who listens in? Why is the right that is claimed confined to a man's own home, so that it would not apply to private telephone conversations from offices, call boxes or the houses of others? If they were to be included, what of the greater opportunities for deliberate overhearing that they offer? In any case, why is the telephone to be subject to this special right of privacy when there is no general right?

That is not all. Suppose that there is what for brevity I may call a right to telephonic privacy, sounding in tort. What exceptions to it, if any, would there be? Would it be a breach of the right if anyone listened to a telephone conversation in which some act of criminal violence or dishonesty was being planned? Should a listener be restrained by injunction from disclosing to the authorities a conversation that would lead to the release of someone who has been kidnapped? There are many, many questions that can, and should, be asked.

Wainwright and another v Home Office [2003] UKHL 53, [2004] 2 AC 406, [15]–[19] (Lord Hoffman)

Mrs Wainwright and one of her sons visited another of her sons in prison. During their visit, they were subjected to a strip search. This was due to a drug-smuggling problem in the prison. They both agreed to the process but found the experience very upsetting, and the son suffered from post-traumatic stress disorder as a consequence. They both commenced an action against the Home Office for damages. It was found that the strip search was not a proper use of the powers conferred under the Prison Rules 1964, as it was an invasion of their privacy and was not necessary and proportionate to deal with the drug-smuggling problem.

15. My Lords, let us first consider the proposed tort of invasion of privacy. Since the famous article by Warren and Brandeis (*The Right to Privacy* (1890) 4 Harvard LR 193) the question of whether such a tort exists, or should exist, has been much debated in common law jurisdictions. Warren and Brandeis suggested that one could generalise certain cases on defamation, breach of copyright in unpublished letters, trade secrets and breach of confidence as all based upon the protection of a common value which they called privacy or, following Judge Cooley (*Cooley on Torts*, 2nd ed (1888), p 29) 'the right to be let alone'. They said that identifying this common element should enable the courts to declare the existence of a general principle which protected a person's appearance, sayings, acts and personal relations from being exposed in public.

16. Courts in the United States were receptive to this proposal and a jurisprudence of privacy began to develop. It became apparent, however, that the developments could not be contained within a single principle; not, at any rate, one with greater explanatory power than the proposition that it was based upon the protection of a value which could be described as privacy. Dean Prosser, in his work on *The Law of Torts*, 4th edn (1971), p 804, said that:

> 'What has emerged is no very simple matter ... it is not one tort, but a complex of four. To date the law of privacy comprises four distinct kinds of invasion of four different interests of the plaintiff, which are tied together by the common name, but otherwise have almost nothing in common except that each represents an interference with the right of the plaintiff "to be let alone".'

17. Dean Prosser's taxonomy divided the subject into (1) intrusion upon the plaintiff's physical solitude or seclusion (including unlawful searches, telephone tapping, long-distance photography and telephone harassment) (2) public disclosure of private facts and (3) publicity putting the plaintiff in a false light and (4) appropriation, for the defendant's advantage, of the plaintiff's name or likeness. These, he said, at p 814, had different elements and were subject to different defences.

18. The need in the United States to break down the concept of 'invasion of privacy' into a number of loosely-linked torts must cast doubt upon the value of any high-level generalisation which can perform a useful function in enabling one to deduce the rule

to be applied in a concrete case. English law has so far been unwilling, perhaps unable, to formulate any such high-level principle. There are a number of common law and statutory remedies of which it may be said that one at least of the underlying values they protect is a right of privacy. Sir Brian Neill's well known article 'Privacy: a challenge for the next century' in *Protecting Privacy* (ed B Markesinis, 1999) contains a survey. Common law torts include trespass, nuisance, defamation and malicious falsehood; there is the equitable action for breach of confidence and statutory remedies under the Protection from Harassment Act 1997 and the Data Protection Act 1998. There are also extra-legal remedies under Codes of Practice applicable to broadcasters and newspapers. But there are gaps; cases in which the courts have considered that an invasion of privacy deserves a remedy which the existing law does not offer. Sometimes the perceived gap can be filled by judicious development of an existing principle. The law of breach of confidence has in recent years undergone such a process: see in particular the judgment of Lord Phillips of Worth Matravers MR in *Campbell v MGN Ltd* [2003] QB 633. On the other hand, an attempt to create a tort of telephone harassment by a radical change in the basis of the action for private nuisance in *Khorasandjian v Bush* [1993] QB 727 was held by the House of Lords in *Hunter v Canary Wharf Ltd* [1997] AC 655 to be a step too far. The gap was filled by the 1997 Act.

19. What the courts have so far refused to do is to formulate a general principle of 'invasion of privacy' (I use the quotation marks to signify doubt about what in such a context the expression would mean) from which the conditions of liability in the particular case can be deduced.

Privacy: Younger Committee's Report, UK Parliament (July 1972), 34–35, 44

34 For these reasons some of those who gave evidence before the Committee support the view that specific ad hoc remedies of the kind proposed are not enough, and that the law should formally recognise the existence of a general right of privacy and should define as clearly as may be the circumstances in which intrusions into privacy will give rise to civil remedies by way of injunction or an action for damages in tort. On the basis of a law of this kind, it is argued, the courts would have the opportunity to build up a comprehensive law of privacy which would be capable of growth and change as conditions altered. On this view, the well-recognised difficulty of formulating a precise definition of privacy would be by-passed by creating an inherently flexible system, which would leave the courts discretion to apply the general principle to a wide range of differing circumstances.

35 In considering whether a general right of privacy should be declared by statute, it is relevant to note that this has not been the way in which English law in recent centuries has sought to protect the main democratic rights of citizens. Neither the right of free speech nor the right of assembly is embodied in statute law. Reliance has been placed

> on the principle that what is not prohibited is permitted and the main emphasis in the field of civil rights has been placed therefore on keeping within acceptable limits, and providing precise definitions of, the restrictions imposed by the civil and criminal law on the individual's freedom of action.
>
> 44 ... We have concluded that, on balance, there is no need at present for a general law of privacy. We believe that if some of the most substantial anxieties are met by the adoption of the specific proposals recommended by us under the various headings set out in our Report, the extent of the social evil resulting from remaining intrusions into privacy will be much reduced and that it is better to accept the residue of hard cases which may remain than to attempt to deal with them by means of a general measure, whose effect upon other rights of great importance is largely unpredictable but might be serious.

Therefore, the common law refused to further develop privacy into a freestanding right. In light of this lack of development and the multiple scandals experienced, you would expect the legislature to be keen to step in and fill the void. This has not been the case, and multiple attempts to increase protection through statutory mechanisms have failed.

In the 1960s, three Bills aimed at increasing the existing privacy rights were put forward, and they were all unsuccessful. Lord Mancroft's 1961 attempt was withdrawn because it lacked government support; Alexander Lyon's 1967 Bill was rejected on the basis that it was too limited; and Brian Walden's 1969 attempt was rejected as it was widely perceived to encroach too far into freedom of expression.

The Committee on Privacy was appointed in 1970 by the Home Secretary, the Lord Chancellor, and the Scottish Secretary. This Committee was led by the Rt Hon Kenneth Younger and was given the task of considering 'whether legislation is needed to give further protection to the privacy of individuals and companies against intrusions from other individuals and companies'. The Committee outlined the importance of privacy but declined to extend the law of privacy any further, stating it was unjustified and unnecessary. The Committee noted that there were already significant protections in place for privacy, including through legislation, multiple tort law actions (namely defamation, malicious falsehood, trespass to land, and nuisance), breach of contract, copyright, and the criminal law. In the 1980s, two further Bills aimed at providing enhanced privacy rights also failed.

Therefore, the government has repeatedly contended that the development of the law of privacy is the responsibility of the common law and not Parliament. This was particularly evident in the debate regarding the Human Rights Bill, where it was clearly stated that the development of privacy rights was to occur by the common law as opposed to statute.

HL Hansard, 24 November 1997, col 771

> The Bill as drafted would damage the freedom of the press and badly wound the system of tough and effective self-regulation that we have built up to provide quick remedies without cost for ordinary citizens. It would inevitably introduce a privacy law, despite the Government's stated opposition to one.
>
> As will be clear, I speak not as a lawyer but as a layman. From that standpoint, it seems to me that the first problem arises because of the role of the courts as public authorities enforcing the convention and developing the common law. As I understand it, it will therefore be possible for the courts to use the convention not just in respect of disputes between individuals and public authorities but in disputes between private individuals.

Spencer v United Kingdom (1998) 25 EHRR CD 105

The application was introduced by the ninth Earl of Spencer (who is the brother of the late Diana Spencer, former Princess of Wales) and by his wife as she had been photographed in the grounds of a private clinic where she was allegedly receiving treatment for bulimia and alcoholism. The Press Complaints Commission upheld their complaint. They argued in front of the European Commission of Human Rights that their privacy rights had been infringed. Whilst it was found that the claimants had an arguable case, it was held that they had not exhausted their domestic remedies first. During the course of the case, the government provided written submissions.

During the discussion, the Commission commented that:

> The applicants essentially submit that the Government are under a positive obligation to provide effective protection for the rights guaranteed by the Convention. Given the terms of Article 10 (Art. 10) of the Convention, the absence of an effective domestic remedy as regards invasions of privacy by the press constitutes a failure to effectively respect their right to respect for their private lives as guaranteed by Article 8 (Art. 8) of the Convention.
>
> The Government argue that the domestic system as a whole (including remedies in breach of confidence and against trespass, nuisance, harassment and malicious falsehood together with the Press Complaints Commission) provides adequate protection to individuals and an appropriate balance between the often competing rights guaranteed by Articles 8 and 10 (Art. 8, 10) of the Convention.

The development of further privacy rights has not been hindered by a belief that this is not an important or worthy task. Rather, the common law has clearly stated that such developments are a task for statute, and the legislature has determined that no statutory development is needed in light of the existing framework of rights.

14.4 Breach of confidence

One area where privacy laws have seen a significant step forward is in the development of the tort of breach of confidence. To successfully have a claim in this regard, two questions must be considered:

(1) Did the claimant have a reasonable expectation of privacy?
(2) Was there an unauthorised use of this information? Specifically, were the benefits achieved by the information's publication proportionate to the harm that may be done by the interference with the right to privacy?

14.4.1 Development of breach of confidence

The modern concept of the breach of confidence action was developed by the House of Lords in *Campbell v MGN Ltd*. This case was focused specifically on press-related privacy concerns and arose out of an article and photos of supermodel Naomi Campbell when she came out of a Narcotics Anonymous meeting. The Mirror newspaper published an article entitled 'Naomi: I am a drug addict', which included details of Ms Campbell's drug addiction and subsequent attendance at Narcotics Anonymous meetings and counselling sessions. The article included photos of her attending these meetings and quotes from sources about her addiction and recovery.

The House of Lords held that there was no cause of action for invasion of privacy but allowed her claim for breach of confidence for some of the information published. However, the Court determined that Ms Campbell's own actions had removed the protection for certain types of information, showing the fine balance in these cases.

Campbell v MGN Ltd [2004] UKHL 22, [2004] 2 AC 457, [11]–[15] (Lord Nicholls)

11. In this country, unlike the United States of America, there is no over-arching, all-embracing cause of action for 'invasion of privacy': see *Wainwright v Home Office* [2003] 3 WLR 1137. But protection of various aspects of privacy is a fast developing area of the law, here and in some other common law jurisdictions. The recent decision of the Court of Appeal of New Zealand in *Hosking v Runting* (25 March 2004) is an example of this. In this country development of the law has been spurred by enactment of the Human Rights Act 1998.

12. The present case concerns one aspect of invasion of privacy: wrongful disclosure of private information. The case involves the familiar competition between freedom of expression and respect for an individual's privacy. Both are vitally important rights. Neither has precedence over the other. The importance of freedom of expression has been stressed often and eloquently, the importance of privacy less so. But it, too, lies at the heart of liberty in a modern state. A proper degree of privacy is essential for the well-being

and development of an individual. And restraints imposed on government to pry into the lives of the citizen go to the essence of a democratic state: see La Forest J in *R v Dymont* [1988] 2 SCR 417, 426.

13. The common law or, more precisely, courts of equity have long afforded protection to the wrongful use of private information by means of the cause of action which became known as breach of confidence. A breach of confidence was restrained as a form of unconscionable conduct, akin to a breach of trust. Today this nomenclature is misleading. The breach of confidence label harks back to the time when the cause of action was based on improper use of information disclosed by one person to another in confidence. To attract protection the information had to be of a confidential nature. But the gist of the cause of action was that information of this character had been disclosed by one person to another in circumstances 'importing an obligation of confidence' even though no contract of non-disclosure existed: see the classic exposition by Megarry J in *Coco v AN Clark (Engineers) Ltd* [1969] RPC 41, 47–48. The confidence referred to in the phrase 'breach of confidence' was the confidence arising out of a confidential relationship.

14. This cause of action has now firmly shaken off the limiting constraint of the need for an initial confidential relationship. In doing so it has changed its nature. In this country this development was recognised clearly in the judgment of Lord Goff of Chieveley in *Attorney-General v Guardian Newspapers Ltd (No 2)* [1990] 1 AC 109, 281. Now the law imposes a 'duty of confidence' whenever a person receives information he knows or ought to know is fairly and reasonably to be regarded as confidential. Even this formulation is awkward. The continuing use of the phrase 'duty of confidence' and the description of the information as 'confidential' is not altogether comfortable. Information about an individual's private life would not, in ordinary usage, be called 'confidential'. The more natural description today is that such information is private. The essence of the tort is better encapsulated now as misuse of private information.

15. In the case of individuals this tort, however labelled, affords respect for one aspect of an individual's privacy. That is the value underlying this cause of action. An individual's privacy can be invaded in ways not involving publication of information. Strip searches are an example. The extent to which the common law as developed thus far in this country protects other forms of invasion of privacy is not a matter arising in the present case. It does not arise because, although pleaded more widely, Miss Campbell's common law claim was throughout presented in court exclusively on the basis of breach of confidence, that is, the wrongful *publication* by the Mirror of private *information*.

There is ongoing confusion about whether the cause of action should be referred to as 'breach of confidence' or 'misuse of private information', and whether these are the same or different potential actions. Lord Nicholls stated that they are two separate causes of actions protecting different interests in *OBG v Allan*.

OBG Ltd v Allan [2007] UKHL 21, [2008] AC 1, [255]–[258] (Lord Walker)

255. As the law has developed breach of confidence, or misuse of confidential information, now covers two distinct causes of action, protecting two different interests: privacy, and secret ('confidential') information. It is important to keep these two distinct. In some instances information may qualify for protection both on grounds of privacy and confidentiality. In other instances information may be in the public domain, and not qualify for protection as confidential, and yet qualify for protection on the grounds of privacy. Privacy can be invaded by further publication of information or photographs already disclosed to the public. Conversely, and obviously, a trade secret may be protected as confidential information even though no question of personal privacy is involved. This distinction was recognised by the Law Commission in its report on Breach of Confidence (1981) Cmnd 388, pages 5–6.

256. OK's claim is that Hello committed a breach of confidence by publishing a confidential secret. OK's interest was wholly commercial, in maximising the financial advantage flowing from having an exclusive right to publish the authorised pictures. Accordingly, as my noble and learned friend Lord Walker of Gestingthorpe says, OK's claim has to be based on a right to short-term confidentiality for a commercial secret.

257. So the first step is to identify the 'secret'. The secret information cannot lie in the differences between the unapproved photographs and the approved photographs. The secret cannot lie there, because the six unapproved photographs contained nothing not included in the approved photographs. That is common ground. This being so, the inevitable differences, in expression and posture and so on, cannot constitute 'confidential' information for the purposes of this equitable principle. The expression of the bride in one wedding photograph compared with her expression in another is insufficiently significant to call for legal protection. It has not been suggested that the unapproved photographs were embarrassing in any way, or that they were detrimental to the Douglases' image. Accordingly, once the approved pictures were published, albeit simultaneously, publication of the unapproved pictures was not a breach of confidence.

258. OK sought to avoid this difficulty by defining the commercial secret in wider terms. The secret comprised photographic information about the entire wedding as an event, and not just the particular wedding photographs OK was permitted to publish. Publication of the approved photographs did not destroy the confidentiality of the remainder of the information.

14.4.2 Two-stage test for breach of confidence

The distinction between breach of confidence and misuse of private information was recently confirmed by the Supreme Court in *ZXC v Bloomberg LP*, which also reaffirmed the two-stage test for proving breach of confidence claims.

ZXC v Bloomberg LP [2022] UKSC 5, [2022] AC 1158, [45]–[51], [56], [58] (Lord Hamblen and Lord Stephens)

45. In the seminal decision of the House of Lords in *Campbell v MGN Ltd* [2004] 2 AC 457 it was recognised that the values enshrined in articles 8 and 10 had become part of the cause of action for breach of confidence and that in relation to private information 'The essence of the tort is better encapsulated now as misuse of private information' – see the judgment of Lord Nicholls of Birkenhead at para 14. This is a distinct cause of action from breach of confidence. It rests on different legal foundations and protects different interests ...

...

47. In *Murray* the Court of Appeal endorsed the two stage test for whether there has been misuse of private information, as explained in the Court of Appeal decision in *McKennitt v Ash* [2006] EWCA Civ 1714; [2008] QB 73. As stated by Simon LJ at para 42 of his judgment in the present case, at stage one, the question is whether the claimant has a reasonable expectation of privacy in the relevant information; if so, at stage two, the question is whether that expectation is outweighed by the countervailing interest of the publisher's right to freedom of expression. This two stage test is now well established.

(ii) Stage one

48. In relation to both stage one and stage two, general guidance can be found in the growing body of domestic legal precedent and also the jurisprudence of the European Court of Human Rights ('ECtHR') on articles 8 and 10 which the court must take into account. Under section 12(4) of the HRA, where the proceedings relate to material 'which the respondent claims, or which appears to the court, to be journalistic, literary or artistic material (or to conduct connected with such material)' then the court 'must have particular regard' to 'any relevant privacy code'. In relation to newspapers and magazines the relevant privacy code is the Editors' Code of Practice, established by the Editors' Code of Practice Committee and overseen by the Independent Press Standards Organisation – see *Sicri v Associated Newspapers Ltd* [2020] EWHC 3541 (QB); [2021] 4 WLR 9.

49. Whether there is a reasonable expectation of privacy is an objective question. The expectation is that of a reasonable person of ordinary sensibilities placed in the same position as the claimant and faced with the same publicity – see *Campbell* at para 99 per Lord Hope of Craighead; *Murray* at para 35.

50. As stated in *Murray* at para 36, 'the question whether there is a reasonable expectation of privacy is a broad one, which takes account of all the circumstances of the case'. Such circumstances are likely to include, but are not limited to,

the circumstances identified at para 36 in *Murray* – the so-called '*Murray* factors'. These are:

(1) the attributes of the claimant;
(2) the nature of the activity in which the claimant was engaged;
(3) the place at which it was happening;
(4) the nature and purpose of the intrusion;
(5) the absence of consent and whether it was known or could be inferred;
(6) the effect on the claimant; and
(7) the circumstances in which and the purposes for which the information came into the hands of the publisher.

51. Although the *Murray* factors are not exhaustive, and the significance of individual factors will vary from case to case, they have been regularly considered and applied by the courts by way of guidance and the appropriateness of so doing was affirmed by the majority of the Supreme Court in *In re JR38* [2015] UKSC 42 ...

(iii) Stage two

56. Stage two involves a balancing of the claimant's article 8 right to privacy and the publisher's article 10 right to freedom of expression in order to determine which should prevail in the particular circumstances of the case – the so-called 'balancing exercise'.

...

58. In *In re S (A Child) (Identification: Restrictions on Publication)* [2004] UKHL 47; [2005] 1 AC 593, at para 17 Lord Steyn confirmed that neither right has precedence over the other and identified the following considerations as being of particular importance in carrying out the balancing exercise:

(1) 'an intense focus on the comparative importance of the specific rights being claimed in the individual case';
(2) 'the justifications for interfering with or restricting each right'; and
(3) 'the proportionality' of the respective interference or restriction.

14.4.2.1 STAGE ONE: 'REASONABLE EXPECTATION OF PRIVACY'

There are a number of ways that people can show they have a reasonable expectation of privacy. The first is through a relationship of confidence – such as friends, family, employee/employer, therapist, or other confidant. However, it is more common for the expectation of privacy to arise from the nature of the *information* and not from the relationship between the parties. There are certain types of information which are generally private, such as physical and mental health,[2] sexual behaviour and orientation,[3] and financial affairs.[4]

Another way that information can be deemed to create a reasonable expectation of privacy is through contractual arrangements; however, this will not always provide adequate protection for claimants – as outlined in *ABC v Telegraph Media Group Ltd*.

ABC v Telegraph Media Group Ltd [2018] EWCA Civ 2329, [2019] 2 All ER 684, CA, [23]–[24] (Sir Terence Etherton MR, Underhill LJ and Henderson LJ)

The claimants were two companies and a senior executive. Five employees of the companies had previously made serious allegations against the executive. After receiving independent legal advice, the complainants were given substantial payments under settlement agreements. All of these settlements included a non-disclosure agreement to keep the relevant information confidential. A journalist from the defendant media group contacted the claimants to obtain their comments on a story about the complainants' allegations, the settlement, and the non-disclosure agreements. The claimants believed that confidential information had been disclosed, and commenced proceedings preventing the publication of the information, arguing it was a breach of confidence.

23. With regard to the public interest (if any) in the disclosure of private or confidential information, this clearly extends to the disclosure of conduct which, if established at trial, would involve the commission of a criminal offence or some other recognised form of wrongdoing. However, the boundaries of the relevant public interest cannot always be confined within such a narrow formulation. In particular, the public interest must allow for informed debate on the standards of conduct that are required in public or commercial life, and for changing perceptions of the kind of behaviour by people in positions of power that may be regarded as acceptable. In this context, we would respectfully endorse the obiter comments made by Tugendhat J in *Goodwin v News Group Newspapers Ltd* [2011] EWHC 1437 (QB), [2011] EMLR 27, where he said at [133]:

> '... in my judgment it is in the public interest that there should be public discussion of the circumstances in which it is proper for a chief executive (or other person holding public office or exercising official functions) should be able to carry on a sexual relationship with an employee in the same organisation. It is in the public interest

2 *Venables v News Group Newspapers Ltd* [2001] Fam 430.

3 *PG and JH v United Kingdom* (ECtHR, Application 44787/98, Judgment 25 September 2001). See *ABK v KDT* [2013] EWHC 1192 (QB) for the utilisation of privacy rights to obtain an injunction for 'revenge porn'.

4 *Lykiardopulo v Lykiardopulo* [2010] EWCA Civ 1315.

that newspapers should be able to report upon cases which raise a question as to what should or should not be a standard in public life. The law, and standards in public life, must develop to meet changing needs. The public interest cannot be confined to exposing matters which are improper only by existing standards and laws, and not by standards as they ought to be, or which people can reasonably contend that they ought to be.'

24. As we have already explained, the weight which should be attached to an obligation of confidence may be enhanced if the obligation is contained in an express contractual agreement. One type of situation where this consideration is likely to have a significant influence on the balancing exercise which the court has to perform is where the obligation in question is contained in an agreement to compromise, or avoid the need for, litigation, whether actual or threatened. Provided that the agreement is freely entered into, without improper pressure or any other vitiating factor, and with the benefit (where appropriate) of independent legal advice, and (again, where appropriate) with due allowance for disclosure of any wrongdoing to the police or appropriate regulatory or statutory body, the public policy reasons in favour of upholding the obligation are likely to tell with particular force, and may well outweigh the article 10 rights of the party who wishes to publish the confidential information.

A number of the breach of confidence cases concern celebrities and intrusions into their life by the press. Public figures must expect and accept that their actions will be subject to increased scrutiny by the media. As shown in *A v B & C*, this will be particularly so where the individual has actively 'courted' the publicity and notoriety.

A v B (a company) [2002] EWCA Civ 337, [11], [2003] QB 195, 208

In this case, a married footballer wanted to stop the publication of information about two affairs. This was originally granted but was overturned by the Court of Appeal, which commented that he had actively sought public profile and interest, therefore reducing his rights to privacy.

Woolf CJ handed down the judgment of the Court, providing a number of guidelines that judges should use when considering whether an injunction should be awarded. This included Guideline xii, which stated:

Where an individual is a public figure he is entitled to have his privacy respected in the appropriate circumstances. A public figure is entitled to a private life. The individual, however, should recognise that because of his public position he must expect and accept that his actions will be more closely scrutinised by the media. Even trivial facts relating to a public figure can be of great interest to readers and other observers of the media. Conduct which in the case of a private individual would not be the appropriate subject of comment can be the proper subject of comment in the case of a public figure. The public figure may hold a position where higher standards of conduct can be rightly expected by the public. The public figure may be a role model whose conduct could well be emulated by others. He may set the fashion. The higher the profile of the individual concerned the more likely that this will be the position. Whether you have courted publicity or not you may be a legitimate subject of public attention. If you have courted public attention then you have less ground to object to the intrusion which follows. In many of these situations it would be overstating the position to say that there is a public interest in the information being published. It would be more accurate to say that the public have an understandable and so a legitimate interest in being told the information. If this is the situation then it can be appropriately taken into account by a court when deciding on which side of the line a case falls. The courts must not ignore the fact that if newspapers do not publish information which the public are interested in, there will be fewer newspapers published, which will not be in the public interest.[5]

Children of celebrities create interesting challenges. Generally, children should be afforded additional privacy protection, and this is outlined in the IPSO Guidelines discussed above. However, if celebrities are seen to forego some of their rights to privacy, how does that impact their children? In *Murray v Express Newspapers Plc*, JK Rowling prevented the publication of a photo of her 19-month-old child being pushed down the street in a pushchair.

Murray v Express Newspapers Plc [2008] EWCA Civ 446, [2008] 3 WLR 1360, [45]–[46], [55]–[57] (Sir Anthony Clarke MR)

45. ... In our opinion it is at least arguable that David had a reasonable expectation of privacy. The fact that he is a child is in our view of greater significance than the judge thought. The courts have recognised the importance of the rights of children in many different contexts and so too has the international community: see e g *R v Central Independent Television plc* [1994] Fam 192, 204–205, per Hoffmann LJ, and the United Nations Convention on the Rights of the Child (1989) (Cm 1976), to which the United Kingdom is a party. More specifically, clause 6 of the Press Complaints Commission Editors' Code of Practice contains this sentence under the heading 'Children': '(v) Editors must not use the fame, notoriety or position of a parent or guardian as sole justification for publishing details of a child's private life.' There is also a publication called the Editors' Codebook, which refers to the code and to the above statement. Although it is true that the codebook states, at p 51, in a section headed 'Intrusion' that the Press Complaints Commission has ruled that the mere publication of a child's image cannot breach the code when it is taken in a public place and is unaccompanied by any private details or materials which might embarrass or inconvenience the child, which is particularly unlikely in the case of babies or very young children, it seems to us that everything must depend on the circumstances.

---

5 This does, however, appear to go against the approach taken by many European countries which provide protection for public figures and their sexual lives: *Craxi (No 2) v Italy* (2004) 38 EHRR 47; *Tammer v Estonia* (2003) 37 EHRR 43.

46. So, for example, in *Tugendhat and Christie, The Law of Privacy and the Media* (2002) the authors note, at para 13.128, in connection with a complaint made by Mr and Mrs Blair, that the PCC has stated that

> 'the "acid test" to be applied by newspapers in writing about the children of public figures who are not famous in their own right (unlike the Royal Princes) is whether a newspaper would write such a story if it was about an ordinary person.'

It seems to us to be at least arguable that a similar approach should be adopted to photographs. If a child of parents who are not in the public eye could reasonably expect not to have photographs of him published in the media, so too should the child of a famous parent. In our opinion it is at least arguable that a child of 'ordinary' parents could reasonably expect that the press would not target him and publish photographs of him. The same is true of David, especially since on the alleged facts here the Photograph would not have been taken or published if he had not been the son of JK Rowling.

...

55. We recognise that there may well be circumstances in which there will be no reasonable expectation of privacy, even after *Von Hannover v Germany* 40 EHRR 1. However, as we see it all will, as ever, depend upon the facts of the particular case. The judge suggests that a distinction can be drawn between a child, or an adult, engaged in family and sporting activities and something as simple as a walk down a street or a visit to the grocers to buy the milk. This is on the basis that the first type of activity is clearly part of a person's private recreation time intended to be enjoyed in the company of family and friends and that, on the test deployed in *Von Hannover v Germany*, publicity of such activities is intrusive and can adversely affect the exercise of such social activities. We agree with the judge that that is indeed the basis of the European court's approach but we do not agree that it is possible to draw a clear distinction in principle between the two kinds of activity. Thus, an expedition to a café of the kind which occurred here seems to us to be at least arguably part of each member of the family's recreation time intended to be enjoyed by them and such that publicity of it is intrusive and such as adversely to affect such activities in the future.

...

57. It seems to us that, subject to the facts of the particular case, the law should indeed protect children from intrusive media attention, at any rate to the extent of holding that a child has a reasonable expectation that he or she will not be targeted in order to obtain photographs in a public place for publication which the person who took or procured the taking of the photographs knew would be objected to on behalf of the child. That is the context in which the photographs of David were taken.

14.4.2.2 STAGE TWO: 'UNAUTHORISED USE'

The second element of a breach of confidence action is whether there was unauthorised use or publication of the private information. This involves a balancing of the interests protected by Article 8 against those protected by Article 10 and s 12, both of which were discussed above at 14.2. A short but effective summary of this exercise is outlined in *In re S (a child)*, which provides four clear propositions when considering the interplay between Articles 8 and 10.

In re S (a child) [2004] UKHL 47, [2005] 1 AC 593, [16]–[17] (Lord Steyn)

16. ... By section 12(4) of the Human Rights Act 1998 Parliament made special provision regarding freedom of expression. It provides that when considering whether to grant relief which, if granted, might affect the exercise of the convention right to freedom of expression the court must have particular regard to the importance of the right.

17. The interplay between articles 8 and 10 has been illuminated by the opinions in the House of Lords in *Campbell v MGN Ltd* [2004] 2 WLR 1232. For present purposes the decision of the House on the facts of *Campbell* and the differences between the majority and the minority are not material. What does, however, emerge clearly from the opinions are four propositions. First, neither article has *as such* precedence over the other. Secondly, where the values under the two articles are in conflict, an intense focus on the comparative importance of the specific rights being claimed in the individual case is necessary. Thirdly, the justifications for interfering with or restricting each right must be taken into account. Finally, the proportionality test must be applied to each. For convenience I will call this the ultimate balancing test. This is how I will approach the present case.

A more detailed discussion is outlined by the European Court of Human Rights in *Von Hannover v Germany (No 2)*. In this case, the court held that photos of Princess Caroline and her family during a family skiing vacation were not private or confidential, largely on the basis that she was an 'undeniably very well known' person. In coming to this conclusion, the European Court of Human Rights provided multiple relevant criteria.

Von Hannover v Germany (No 2) (App Nos 40660/08 and 60641/08) [2012] ECHR 40660/08, [108]–[113]

(iv) The criteria relevant for the balancing exercise

108. Where the right to freedom of expression is being balanced against the right to respect for private life, the criteria laid down in the case-law that are relevant to the present case are set out below.

(α) Contribution to a debate of general interest

109. An initial essential criterion is the contribution made by photos or articles in the press to a debate of general interest (see *Von Hannover*, cited above, para 60; *Leempoel & S.A. ED. Ciné Revue*, cited above, para 68; and *Standard Verlags GmbH*, cited above, para 46). The definition of what constitutes a subject of general interest will depend on the circumstances of the case. The Court nevertheless considers it useful to point out that it has recognised the existence of such an interest not only where the publication concerned political issues or crimes (see *White*, cited above, para 29; *Egeland and Hanseid v Norway* [2009] ECHR 34438/04, para 58, 16 April 2009; and *Leempoel & S.A. ED. Ciné Revue*, cited above, para 72), but also where it concerned sporting issues or performing artists (see *Nikowitz and Verlagsgruppe News GmbH v Austria* [2007] ECHR 5266/03, para 25, 22 February 2007; *Colaço Mestre and SIC – Sociedade Independente de Comunicação, S.A. v Portugal* [2007] ECHR 11182/03 and 11319/03, para 28, 26 April 2007; and *Sapan v Turkey* [2010] ECHR 44102/04, para 34, 8 June 2010). However, the rumoured marital difficulties of a president of the Republic or the financial difficulties of a famous singer were not deemed to be matters of general interest (see *Standard Verlags GmbH*, cited above, para 52, and *Hachette Filipacchi Associés (ICI PARIS)*, cited above, para 43).

(β) How well known is the person concerned and what is the subject of the report?

110. The role or function of the person concerned and the nature of the activities that are the subject of the report and/or photo constitute another important criterion, related to the preceding one. In that connection a distinction has to be made between private individuals and persons acting in a public context, as political figures or public figures. Accordingly, whilst a private individual unknown to the public may claim particular protection of his or her right to private life, the same is not true of public figures (see *Minelli v Switzerland* [2005] ECHR 14991/02, 14 June 2005, and *Petrenco*, cited above, para 55). A fundamental distinction needs to be made between reporting facts capable of contributing to a debate in a democratic society, relating to politicians in the exercise of their official functions for example, and reporting details of the private life of an individual who does not exercise such functions (see *Von Hannover*, cited above, para 63, and *Standard Verlags GmbH*, cited above, para 47).

While in the former case the press exercises its role of 'public watchdog' in a democracy by imparting information and ideas on matters of public interest, that role appears less important in the latter case. Similarly, although in certain special circumstances the public's right to be informed can even extend to aspects of the private life of public figures, particularly where politicians are concerned, this will not be the case – despite the person concerned being well known to the public – where the published photos and accompanying commentaries relate exclusively to details of the person's private life and have the sole aim of satisfying public curiosity in that respect (see *Von Hannover*, cited above, para 65 with the references cited therein, and *Standard Verlags GmbH*, cited above, para 53; see also point 8 of the Resolution of the Parliamentary Assembly – para 71 above). In the latter case, freedom of expression calls for a narrower interpretation (see *Von Hannover*, cited above, para 66; *Hachette Filipacchi Associés (ICI PARIS)*, cited above, para 40; and *MGN Limited*, cited above, para 143).

(γ) Prior conduct of the person concerned

111. The conduct of the person concerned prior to publication of the report or the fact that the photo and the related information have already appeared in an earlier publication are also factors to be taken into consideration (see *Hachette Filipacchi Associés (ICI PARIS)*, cited above, paras 52–53, and *Sapan*, cited above, para 34). However, the mere fact of having cooperated with the press on previous occasions cannot serve as an argument for depriving the party concerned of all protection against publication of the photo at issue (see *Egeland and Hanseid*, cited above, para 62).

(δ) Content, form and consequences of the publication

112. The way in which the photo or report are published and the manner in which the person concerned is represented in the photo or report may also be factors to be taken into consideration (see *Wirtschafts-Trend Zeitschriften-Verlagsgesellschaft m.b.H. v Austria (no. 3)* [2005] ECHR 66298/01 and 15653/02, para 47, 13 December 2005; *Reklos and Davourlis*, cited above, para 42; and *Jokitaipale v Finland* [2010] ECHR 43349/05, para 68, 6 April 2010). The extent to which the report and photo have been disseminated may also be an important factor, depending on whether the newspaper is a national or local one, and has a large or a limited circulation (see *Karhuvaara and Iltalehti*, cited above, para 47, and *Gurgenidze*, cited above, para 55).

(ε) Circumstances in which the photos were taken

113. Lastly, the Court has already held that the context and circumstances in which the published photos were taken cannot be disregarded. In that connection regard must be had to whether the person photographed gave their consent to the taking of the photos and their publication (see *Gurgenidze*, cited above, para 56, and *Reklos and Davourlis*, cited above, para 41) or whether this was done without their knowledge or by subterfuge or other illicit means (see *Hachette Filipacchi Associés (ICI PARIS)*, cited above, para 47, and *Flinkkilä v Finland* [2010] ECHR 25576/04, para 81, 6 April 2010). Regard must also be had to the nature or seriousness of the intrusion and the consequences of publication of the photo for the person concerned (see *Egeland and Hanseid*, cited above, para 61, and *Timciuc*, decision cited above, para 150). For a private individual, unknown to the public, the publication of a photo may amount to a more substantial interference than a written article (see *Eerikäinen*, cited above, para 70, and *A. v Norway*, cited above, para 72).

14.5 Remedies

If the claimant can establish a breach of confidence claim, the next question to consider is the appropriate remedy. If the information has yet to be published, it is highly likely that an injunction will be sought. As seen in *Venables & Thompson v News Group Newspapers Ltd*,[6] the court can award an injunction *contra mundum* (against the world at large) in order to protect against the publication of private information. Whilst the courts are generally hesitant to award interim injunctions, there is an increasing acceptance of this if the information is in respect of personal information and where damages may be an inadequate remedy.[7]

If the information has already been published, an injunction is not needed or relevant. Therefore, damages will need to be considered. Determining an appropriate level of damages is complicated – how does the court put a monetary amount on privacy rights? This issue was considered by the court in *Richard v British Broadcasting Corporation*. In 2014, the South Yorkshire Police commenced an investigation of Sir Cliff Richard in relation to allegations of a historic sex offence, resulting in a search of Sir Cliff's residence. The BBC became aware of the investigation and search, giving it prominent and extensive television coverage both in real-time and after the event. This included filming his home from both the ground and by helicopter and taking photographs of the officers searching the apartment. No charges were laid, and the investigation was dropped in 2016.

Sir Cliff commenced an action for damages against the BBC. He claimed that the broadcasting of the police search of his residence breached his right to privacy under Article 8 of Sch 1 to the HRA 1998. Mann J held that there had been an infringement and that Sir Cliff was entitled to damages, awarding him £190,000 in compensatory damages and £20,000 in exemplary damages.

Richard v British Broadcasting Corporation [2018] EWHC 1837 (Ch), [2018] 3 WLR 1715, [349]–[351]

When determining an appropriate level of compensation, Mann J commented:

> 349. I acknowledge the need to keep damages claims within bounds so as not to contribute to an illegitimate chilling effect on legitimate journalism, but that does not mean that Sir Cliff should not have proper compensation for the wrongs committed against him. I shall bear that in mind when reaching my figure. So far as *Mosley* is concerned, I find it of limited assistance because of the very different nature of the victim, the publisher and the publication in this case (nationwide instant transmission,

6 [2001] EWHC 32 (QB).
7 *Coco v AN Clark (Engineers) Ltd* [1969] RPC 41, 50.

by a national broadcaster, to large numbers of people, several times in a day), the triggering of publications by others, the nature of the facts published, and the identity and attributes of the claimant, and the huge consequential publicity given in the rest of the media. But if one is comparing the two cases, I can say at this stage of the reasoning that, contrary to the submission of Mr Millar, I regard the present case as much more, not less, serious than *Mosley*, and worthy of a much greater sum, not a lesser sum, than *Mosley*.

350. The following factors should be taken into account in assessing general damages in this case:

(a) Damages can and should be awarded for distress, damage to health, invasion of Sir Cliff's privacy (or depriving him of the right to control the use of his private information), and damage to his dignity, status and reputation. (Gulati in the Court of Appeal [2017] QB 149 at para 45; Gulati at first instance, supra; and the discussion above about reputation.)

(b) The general adverse effect on his lifestyle (which will be a function of the matters in (a)).

(c) The nature and content of the private information revealed. The more private and significant the information, the greater the effect on the subject will be (or will be likely to be). In this case it was extremely serious. It was not merely the fact that an allegation had been made. The fact that the police were investigating and even conducting a search gave significant emphasis to the underlying fact that an allegation had been made.

(d) The scope of the publication. The wider the publication, the greater the likely invasion and the greater the effect on the individual.

(e) The presentation of the publication. Sensationalist treatment might have a greater effect, and amount to a more serious invasion, than a more measured publication.

351. Those factors clearly inter-relate with each other but it is useful to separate them out as being relevant factors. Applying those factors yields the following results. In taking them into account I have been careful to take an overall view, and have not double-counted their respective effects.

This case highlights that the balancing of competing rights enshrined in Article 8 with those in Article 10 and s 12 is relevant for both the finding of a breach of confidence and determining the appropriate remedy.

14.6 Tort of privacy?

The shocking actions of the journalists in *Kaye v Robertson* highlighted the significant limitations of the current legal protections. In this case the claimant was a well-known actor who had a car accident, needing extensive surgery and ongoing hospitalisation. The defendants, two employees of 'The Sunday Sport' tabloid, gained access to his private hotel room despite notices prohibiting any unauthorised entry. They interviewed the claimant at length and took flash photos of him before being removed by security staff. The claimant sought an injunction against the publication of any story based on the interview or photos on the basis of malicious falsehood, libel, passing off and trespass to the person. The defendants argued that the claimant had consented to the interview, despite the fact that he clearly had not been in a fit state to consent, and a short time after the 'interview' he could not recall the incident. The Court of Appeal granted an injunction against the publication.

Kaye v Robertson [1990] EWCA Civ 21, [1991] FSR 62 at 66 and 70

Glidewell LJ held that there was no actionable right of privacy in English law but that all elements of malicious falsehood had been made out, thereby justifying an injunction. He emphasised that this should be a role for the Parliament:[8]

> It is well-known that in English law there is no right to privacy, and accordingly there is no right of action for breach of a person's privacy. The facts of the present case are a graphic illustration of the desirability of Parliament considering whether and in what circumstances statutory provision can be made to protect the privacy of individuals.

Bingham LJ used the case as an opportunity to express his dissatisfaction with the state of the law, commenting that:[9]

> This case nonetheless highlights, yet again, the failure of both the common law of England and statute to protect in an effective way the personal privacy of individual citizens ...
>
> The defendants' conduct towards the plaintiff here was 'a monstrous invasion of his privacy' ... If ever a person has a right to be let alone by strangers with no public interest to pursue, it must surely be when he lies in hospital recovering from brain surgery and in no more than partial command of his faculties. It is this invasion of his privacy which underlies the plaintiff's complaint. Yet it alone, however gross, does not entitle him to relief in English law.
>
> The plaintiff's suggested cause of action in libel is in my view arguable, for reasons which Glidewell LJ has given. We could not give interlocutory relief on that ground. Battery and assault are causes of action never developed to cover acts such as these: they could apply only if the law were substantially extended and the available facts strained to unacceptable lengths. A claim in passing-off is hopeless. Fortunately, a cause of action in malicious falsehood exists, but even that obliges us to limit the relief we can grant in

---

8 [1991] FSR 62 at 66 and 70.

9 ibid at 70.

a way which would not bind us if the plaintiff's cause of action arose from the invasion of privacy of which, fundamentally, he complains. We cannot give the plaintiff the breadth of protection which I would, for my part, wish. The problems of defining and limiting a tort of privacy are formidable, but the present case strengthens my hope that the review now in progress may prove fruitful.

In light of the piecemeal and incomplete protection of privacy rights under the existing legal framework, there are ongoing calls to increase this protection through the development of a freestanding tort of privacy.

Paula Giliker, 'A Common Law Tort of Privacy?: The Challenges of Developing a Human Rights Tort' (2015) 27 *SAcLJ* 761, [19], [32], [39] (footnotes omitted)

19 In developing tort law, the common law has traditionally demonstrated a reluctance to engage in radical legal development. In the words of Brennan J, '[i]t is preferable, in my view, that the law should develop … incrementally and by analogy with established categories'. One sees, therefore, emphasis on categorisation and the identification of tests which are able to determine the scope and limits of liability without undermining the stability of the current legal position. This approach is reflected in the case law examined above: the courts rejecting a tort of privacy per se as far too vague and broad-ranging, but accepting that aspects of privacy are worthy of protection, notably the publication of private or personal information and intrusion into the private affairs of another. Lisa Austin has identified in the context of privacy a palpable 'containment anxiety' in which courts try to juggle an obvious need to provide some action against privacy invasion against its fears of an ill defined and amorphous action which unduly restricts freedom of expression. This leads, in her view, to a preference for protecting privacy rights by expanding existing causes of action or at least by proceeding incrementally. In particular, she finds a general distrust of high-level principle.

…

32 The move towards formal recognition of misuse of private information as a tort has led a number of scholars to contemplate how such a tort would fit within the existing tort law framework. Roderick Bagshaw has argued that, in reality, the post-Campbell privacy tort is at odds with the design of English tort law. If, he argues, one of the aims of tort law is to regulate behaviour, how is this to be achieved by a cause of action which simply balances competing rights and where it may be difficult for an ordinary individual to determine the precise balance between freedom of expression and the right to privacy? Donal Nolan further argues that the introduction of human rights principles into private law threatens to undermine the structural underpinnings of the law of tort. Such a view has received some support in recent case law. In Michael v Chief

Constable of South Wales Police, for example, the majority of the Supreme Court found that: Convention claims [have] different objectives from civil actions … Whereas civil actions are designed essentially to compensate claimants for losses, Convention claims are intended to uphold minimum human rights standards and to vindicate those rights. Jenny Steele comments that the current approach, which favours 'shoehorning' claims into an existing cause of action, is far more appealing to common lawyers who prefer not to deal with broad general principles, in particular those deriving from that most diverse and elusive of ECHR rights: Art 8. Such views are important. They indicate that even if the English courts do expressly acknowledge the action of misuse of private information as a tort, this will not resolve the current conceptual confusion as to the interests this tort will seek to protect, its content or future direction.

…

39 The time has come to recognise that there is a need to stabilise the centre of gravity of the tort of misuse of private information. A Law Commission report would provide a valuable first step, but this will need to be followed by judicial or legislative intervention if the current situation is to improve. Failing this, it is likely that the courts will continue to take small incremental steps to develop the tort, but that progress will be slow and at the expense of conceptual clarity. Evolution in tort law can be unpredictable and create uncertainty, but it is argued here that it is the role of the law to provide victims injured by unwarranted intrusions into their personal life with a clear basis on which to seek a remedy for the wrong committed against them.

Table 14.2: Arguments against privacy developments

Argument against privacy development	Limitations of argument	Case examples/other resources
Importance of freedom of speech	The common law has developed effective ways to balance privacy protection against freedom of expression.	*Re S* [2004] UKHL 47; *PJS v News Group Newspapers Ltd* [2016] UKSC 26
Adequate protection is already provided by existing legal mechanisms	Whilst breach of confidence (also known as misuse of private information) protects confidential or private *information*, other privacy rights, such as the right to privacy of your bodily autonomy, are not covered by this cause of action.	*Wainwright v Home Office* [2004] 2 AC 406

Argument against privacy development	Limitations of argument	Case examples/other resources
Difficulties in defining privacy	Many legal concepts are hard to define. Workable definitions of privacy have been provided by academia ('the right to be left alone'[10]) and the government ('right to determine for oneself how and to what extent information about oneself is communicated to others'[11]). The common law can develop these definitions further.	Warren and Brandeis 'The Right to Privacy' (1890) 4 *Harvard LR* 193; The Committee on Privacy, Younger Report (Cmnd 5012, July 1972)
The potential for claimants to bring frivolous or vexatious claims	The law already has mechanisms to deal with frivolous or vexatious claims, as this concern is not limited to privacy. As with defamation, a 'serious harm' requirement could be included in the requirements for any breach of privacy claim.	Defamation Act 2013, s 1; Civil Procedure Rules, Practice Direction 3A – Striking Out a Statement of Case, para 7 (Vexatious Litigants)
Complexities of awarding remedies	The complexity of awarding remedies is an issue in many areas of tort law.[12] To prevent the publication of confidential information, the court has the power to award injunctions, as well as issue interim injunctions and injunctions to the world at large. If the information is already in the public realm, an injunction can be awarded to stop further publication, and if that will not assist, damages can be awarded to the claimant.	*Venables & Thompson v News Group Newspapers Ltd* [2001] EWHC 32 (QB); *RocknRoll v News Group Newspapers Ltd* [2013] EWHC 24 (Ch); *Douglas v Hello! Ltd* [2001] 2 WLR 992; *ABC v Telegraph Media Group Ltd* [2018] EWCA Civ 2329

Question to consider: Should the courts develop a tort of privacy? If yes, what should this look like? If no, why not?

Other resources: H Kalven Jr, 'Privacy in Tort Law – Were Warren and Brandeis Wrong' (1966) 31 *Law & Contemporary Problems* 326; *Kaye v Robertson* [1991] FSR 62; G Philipson, 'Transforming Breach of Confidence? Towards a Common Law Right of Privacy under the Human Rights Act' (2003) 66(5) *MLR* 726; *Wainwright v Home Office* [2004] 2 AC 406; *PJS v News Group Newspapers Ltd* [2016] UKSC 26.

10 S Warren and L Brandeis, 'The Right to Privacy' (1890) 4 *Harvard* LR 193, 193.

11 Committee on Privacy, Younger Report (Cmnd 5012, July 1972), 22.

12 For further discussion, see Chapter 17 (Damages).

14.7 When privacy should not be protected

Similar to defamation, privacy rights can be misused by people with knowledge and resources to prevent the publication of their wrongdoing that is harmful or embarrassing for them. The question is – as usual – a situation of balancing different rights and obligations.

An example of a case where the applicant was unsuccessful in protecting their privacy rights is *Sutherland v Her Majesty's Advocate*. In this case, Sutherland was convicted of various child sexual offences after being entrapped by members of the public acting as 'paedophile hunters'. He appealed against his conviction on the basis that the evidence obtained by these paedophile hunters was in breach of his right to private life and respect for correspondence under Article 8(1). The Supreme Court upheld the criminal convictions on two separate bases. First, the appellant's sexual communications (with a person he believed was a 13-year-old boy) were not worthy of respect for the purposes of the ECHR. Second, the appellant had no reasonable expectation of privacy in relation to these communications and, therefore, enjoyed no protection under Article 8(1). Consequently, the communications could be disclosed and used by public authorities in criminal proceedings, and the convictions were upheld.

Sutherland v Her Majesty's Advocate [2020] UKSC 32, [2021] AC 427, [31]–[32], [40]–[43], [51], [56] (Lord Sales)

31. In my judgment, there are two reasons why the appellant's rights under article 8(1) in relation to respect for private life and respect for his correspondence were not interfered with in the circumstances of this case: (i) the nature of the communications from the appellant to the decoy, whom he believed to be a child, was not such as was capable of making them worthy of respect for the purposes of the application of the ECHR; and (ii) the appellant had no reasonable expectation of privacy in relation to the communications, with the result that he enjoyed no relevant protection under article 8(1) as regards their disclosure to and use by the respondent and the other public authorities referred to above. I develop these points below.

(i) The nature of the communications by the appellant

32. An individual's rights under article 8(1), so far as relevant here, are to 'respect for' his private life and his correspondence. In my view, it is implicit in this formulation that the features of his private life and his correspondence for which protection is claimed under article 8(1) should be capable of respect within the scheme of values which the ECHR exists to protect and promote.

...

40. In the present case ... the conduct which is made the subject of the criminal offences that are in issue involves direct, sexually motivated contact between a paedophile and a

child. In my view, in the absence of any question of state surveillance or interception of communications, and where all that is in issue is the balance of the interests of a person engaging in such conduct and of the children who are the recipients (or intended recipients) of the relevant communications, the reprehensible nature of the communications is such that they do not attract protection under article 8(1). They do not involve the expression of an aspect of private life or an aspect of correspondence which is capable of respect within the scheme of values inherent in the ECHR.

41. This view is supported by three matters. First, the conduct in question involves contact between a paedophile and a child which is criminal in nature and is capable of affecting the child more immediately …

42. Secondly, as observed above, the state has a positive obligation under article 8, owed to children, to enforce these provisions of the criminal law effectively. That obligation reflects the protection which article 8 requires to be accorded to fundamental values and essential aspects of private life in relation to children, who are recognised to be vulnerable individuals. Accordingly it is clear that, under the scheme of the ECHR and for the purposes of article 8, the interests of children in this field have priority over any interest a paedophile could have in being allowed to engage in the conduct which has been criminalised by these provisions.

43. Thirdly, article 17 of the ECHR (prohibition of abuse of rights) supports the conclusion that the criminal conduct at issue in this case is not such as is capable of respect for the purposes of article 8(1).

…

(ii) No reasonable expectation of privacy

51. According to the Strasbourg case law, an important indication whether the right to respect for private life and correspondence is engaged in relation to an individual's communications is whether the individual had a reasonable expectation of privacy in relation to them: see e g *Halford v United Kingdom* 24 EHRR 523, para 45; *Garamukanwa v United Kingdom* [2019] IRLR 853, paras 22 and 29; *Benedik v Slovenia* 24 April 2018, paras 98, 101 and 115–116; and *López Ribalda v Spain* 71 EHRR 7, paras 89–90 and 93.

…

56. In the present case … the appellant's communications were sent directly to the decoy, a private individual believed by the appellant to be a child of 13. Their contents were not a matter in relation to which the recipient could be thought to owe the appellant any obligation of confidentiality. There was no prior relationship between the appellant and the recipient from which an expectation of privacy might be said to arise between them (contrast the position in *López Ribalda v Spain*, in which the applicants had a reasonable expectation that they would not be subjected to covert video surveillance by their employer; and contrast the position which might arise in relation to intimate

letters sent in the course of an established romantic relationship between adults). The appellant's contact with the decoy came out of the blue and exhortations by the appellant in messages sent to the decoy that he should keep their communications private did not establish a relationship of confidentiality. Furthermore, the appellant believed that he was communicating with a 13-year-old, a child of an age in relation to whom it was foreseeable that he might well share any worrying communications he received with an adult.

Another example is *Linklaters LLP & Anor v Mellish*, where a magic circle firm was successful in preventing the publication of harmful information about sexual harassment and unfair treatment of women at the firm on the grounds that the firm had a 'legitimate interest' in preventing the publication of this information. This case, in addition to *ABC v Telegraph Media Group Ltd* discussed above, creates significant concerns about the rich and powerful using privacy laws to silence victims and prevent disclosure of their own wrongdoing.

Linklaters LLP & Anor v Mellish [2019] EWHC 177 (QB), [2019] All ER (D) 18 (Feb), [27], [32]–[35] (Warby J)

27. Whenever a person threatens or intends to publish information, the Convention right to freedom of expression must be considered by the Court. An injunction which restrains publication is an interference with that right, which can only be justified if it pursues one of the legitimate aims identified in Article 10(2) of the Convention, and is necessary to and proportionate for the pursuit of such aim(s). The method by which the Court should strike the balance between competing considerations in this field is discussed in the *ABC* case, which emphasises the weight to be given to obligations of confidence which are assumed under a contract, freely entered into, for good consideration. There is, as the Court of Appeal emphasised, an important public interest in upholding contractual bargains which cannot be impeached for fraud, undue influence or any other vitiating factor. That aspect of the matter is highlighted in *Mionis v Democratic Press SA* [2018] QB 662, a case on which the Court of Appeal drew heavily in *ABC*. The authorities indicate that the right approach for the Court to take, when faced with a contest between public interest considerations and a contractual duty of confidence, is to ask itself not just whether the information is matter of public interest but 'whether in all the circumstances it is in the public interest that the duty of confidence should be breached': *HRH Prince of Wales v Associated Newspapers Ltd* [2006] EWCA Civ 1776 [2008] Ch 57 [68].

…

32. I was satisfied that the likelihood that the claimants would succeed at a trial was sufficient to justify the relief that I granted. There was clear evidence of a threat or intention to give interviews for publication about matters that came to the attention of the defendant in the course of his employment. Whether that threat was likely to be

carried out was unclear. But there was clear evidence of a risk. It may well be possible to speak publicly in general terms about the 'culture' at Linklaters, or any other large firm or organisation, without breaching duties of confidence.

...

33. The rights of the third parties involved, and in particular those of the individual complainants, bolstered the case in favour of granting an injunction. I see the force of Mr Caldecott's submission, that internal grievance processes are confidential in nature. Those interviewed as part of such a process are entitled to expect that what they say will be kept confidential. There are strong policy reasons for upholding those legitimate expectations, to encourage genuine complainants to come forward rather than risk having sensitive material of the kind in issue here made public by a third party, against their wishes and (on the evidence) without consultation.

34. It is accepted by the claimants that there is, in general terms, a legitimate public interest in the due performance by large firms such as Linklaters of their social and moral duties towards their staff. But the existence of such an interest cannot justify indiscriminate disclosure of otherwise sensitive confidential information which others have a legitimate interest in keeping confidential. A general desire to talk publicly about the 'culture' of a large firm is not enough to justify the disclosure of such details. There may be cases in which the details of individual acts of alleged or establish misconduct, combined with one another, create a compelling picture of persistent or habitual wrongdoing, serious enough to satisfy the tests to which I have referred. In some cases, the public interest in correcting misleading public statements could come into the picture. But nothing of that kind emerges from the evidence presented to me in this case at this stage.

35. The claim is partly motivated by concern for the reputational harm disclosure might cause, but that is not the sole or main purpose behind this application, which I did not regard as an abuse of process. Damages would not be an adequate remedy. I saw no reason to doubt that the injunction, if granted, would be effective against the defendant. Its effects on third parties will depend on where they are, what they know, and the local laws. But this was not a case in which it was apparent that the Court's decision was likely to be defeated or undermined by third party conduct over which the Court had no jurisdiction or control.

Question to consider: When, if ever, should privacy laws be capable of preventing the publication of moral or legal wrongdoing?

Other resources: T Aplin, 'The Development of the Action for Breach of Confidence in a Post-HRA Era' [2007] *IPQ* 19; J Richardson, 'If I Cannot Have Her Everybody Can: Sexual Disclosure and Privacy Law' in Richardson and Rackley (eds), *Feminist Perspectives on Tort Law* (Routledge, 2012) 145; N Moreham, 'Unpacking the Reasonable Expectation of Privacy Test' (2018) 134 *LQR* 651.

14.8 Conclusion

Considering that there is no 'tort of privacy', it could be expected that this would be a very short and simple chapter. As you have probably worked out by now, the exact opposite is true. The piecemeal nature of the current legal regime creates significant complexities and confusion. Privacy rights have wide-ranging support across society, the legislature, and the court; however, this support has not resulted in the development of a freestanding privacy-based tort; rather there is a patchwork of different protections – from the common law, statute, human rights, and self-regulatory mechanisms by the press. These provide protection in certain situations but leave others, for example, physical privacy infringements, underdeveloped. The tort of breach of confidence has provided some level of protection for information that has the requisite level of privacy and was used without authorisation. However, this is limited in its application and leaves significant gaps where the privacy infringement is not information-based, such as unwanted touching or overlooking. Whether this situation will change in the future is yet to be determined, and it is something you should consider as you go through the readings.

Chapter 15 VICARIOUS LIABILITY

15.1 Introduction

Vicarious liability is liability imposed on one person for a tort committed by another. This might seem at first blush to be an extraordinary thing for the law to do, and so the justifications for it have been examined at length, particularly by academics. It usually occurs in situations in which one party has some form of control or power over the party committing the tort (such as the employment relationship) and where the controlling party is in a better position to provide compensation to the claimant. Given its clear policy implications, it is a topic that lends itself very well to essay questions, not least because there has been a significant amount of appellate litigation over it in recent years. That considerable body of case law, however, also makes it a subject ripe for problem question analysis. So, as ever with tort, you need to know the common law authorities very well.

For vicarious liability to arise, there needs of course to have been a tort committed by somebody. This would give rise to primary liability in the tortfeasor. For secondary (vicarious) liability to follow, two more elements need to be established. First, there needs to be between the primary wrongdoer and the vicarious defendant a relationship recognised by the law as being capable of giving rise to vicarious liability. Historically, this was arguably an easier inquiry to conduct because it largely tracked the employer–employee relationship, so that employers could be liable for the torts of their employees but not for the torts of independent contractors. In recent years, however, the recognised relationship has expanded to cover relationships that would better be described as quasi-employment relationships. This partly reflects the changing patterns of working life in general, but might also be said to reflect a legal recognition that a broader range of claimants should be able to succeed in recovering for harms caused by non-employees. This is particularly so since the definition of 'employee' is in legal terms both technical and multi-faceted and does not cover a significant number of people who are nonetheless placed by organisations in positions that can facilitate harmdoing (and sexual abuse in particular). The second stage of the inquiry is then to ask whether the wrongdoer's action was sufficiently closely connected to that relationship.

In the first decision extracted below, the Supreme Court arguably began the modern expansion of the category of relationships which can give rise to vicarious liability, and clearly set out the requirement to engage in the two-stage inquiry referred to above.

Catholic Child Welfare Society v Various Claimants [2012] UKSC 56, [2013] 2 AC 1, [85]–[87], [91]–[94] (Lord Phillips)

The Institute of the Brothers of the Christian Schools (an unincorporated association of lay brothers of the Catholic Church) had provided staff to a residential school managed by the claimant board. The board had already been held vicariously liable for alleged physical and sexual abuse carried out against pupils at the school, and it was appealing against the finding of the Court of Appeal that the Institute was not also vicariously liable.

85. The precise criteria for imposing vicarious liability for sexual abuse are still in the course of refinement by judicial decision. Sexual abuse of children may be facilitated in a number of different circumstances. There is currently concern at the possibility that widespread sexual abuse of children may have occurred within the entertainment industry. This case is not concerned with that scenario. It is concerned with the liability of bodies that have, in pursuance of their own interests, caused their employees or persons in a relationship similar to that of employees, to have access to children in circumstances where abuse has been facilitated.

86. Starting with the Canadian authorities a common theme can be traced through most of the cases to which I have referred. **Vicarious liability is imposed where a defendant, whose relationship with the abuser put it in a position to use the abuser to carry on its business or to further its own interests, has done so in a manner which has created or significantly enhanced the risk that the victim or victims would suffer the relevant abuse.** The essential closeness of connection between the relationship between the defendant and the tortfeasor and the acts of abuse thus involves a strong causative link.

87. These are the criteria that establish the necessary 'close connection' between relationship and abuse. I do not think that it is right to say that creation of risk is simply a policy consideration and not one of the criteria. Creation of risk is not enough, of itself, to give rise to vicarious liability for abuse but it is always likely to be an important element in the facts that give rise to such liability.

...

91. The relationship between the Institute and the brothers enabled the institute to place the brothers in teaching positions and, in particular, in the position of headmaster at St William's. **The standing that the brothers enjoyed as members of the institute led the managers of that school to comply with the decisions of the Institute as to who should fill that key position. It is particularly significant that the Institute provided the headmasters, for the running of the school was largely carried out by the headmasters. The brother headmaster was almost always the director of the Institute's community, living on the school premises. There was thus a very close connection between the relationship between the brothers and the Institute and the employment of the brothers as teachers in the school.**

92. Living cloistered on the school premises were vulnerable boys. They were triply vulnerable. They were vulnerable because they were children in a school; they were vulnerable because they were virtually prisoners in the school; and they were vulnerable because their personal histories made it even less likely that if they attempted to disclose what was happening to them they would be believed. The brother teachers were placed in the school to care for the educational and religious needs of these pupils. Abusing the boys in their care was diametrically opposed to those objectives but, paradoxically, that very fact was one of the factors that provided the necessary close connection between the abuse and the relationship between the brothers and the institute that gives rise to vicarious liability on the part of the latter.

93. There was a very close connection between the brother teachers' employment in the school and the sexual abuse that they committed, or must for present purposes be assumed to have committed. There was no Criminal Records Bureau at the time, but the risk of sexual abuse was recognised, as demonstrated by the prohibition on touching the children in the chapter in the Rule dealing with chastity. No doubt the status of a brother was treated by the managers as an assurance that children could safely be entrusted to his care. The placement of brother teachers in St William's, a residential school in the precincts of which they also resided, greatly enhanced the risk of abuse by them if they had a propensity for such misconduct.

94. This is not a borderline case. It is one where it is fair, just and reasonable, by reason of the satisfaction of the relevant criteria, for the Institute to share with the Middlesbrough defendants vicarious liability for the abuse committed by the brothers. I would allow this appeal.

STAGE 1: THE RELATIONSHIP

Lord Phillips identified five factors that make it fair, just and reasonable to impose liability on an employer:

(1) The employer is more likely to have the means to compensate the victim than the employee and can be expected to have insured against that liability.
(2) The tort will have been committed as a result of activity being taken by the employee on behalf of the employer.
(3) The employee's activity is likely to be part of the business activity of the employer.
(4) The employer, by employing the employee to carry on the activity, will have created the risk of the tort committed by the employee.
(5) The employee will, to a greater or lesser degree, have been under the control of the employer.

STAGE 2: THE CONNECTION

The judgment recognises that this is still a developing concept, but held that vicarious liability should be imposed where the abuser has been given their position for the purposes of furthering the defendant's own interests, and where this has been done so as to generate a significantly increased risk of abuse being perpetrated.

15.1.1 The requisite relationship

Cox v Ministry of Justice [2016] UKSC 10, [2016] AC 660, [15], [16], [22], [24], [30], [40], [41] (Lord Reed)

The Ministry of Justice appealed against a decision of the Court of Appeal that it was vicariously liable for injury caused by the negligence of a prisoner undertaking work in the prison kitchen, arguing that the relationship between the Prison Service and its prisoners was distinct from an employment relationship because its primary function was prisoners' rehabilitation, rather than commercial profit for the Prison Service. The Supreme Court found that *Catholic Child Welfare Society v Various Claimants* (*CCWS*) extended the scope of vicarious liability beyond employment relationships. In order to be held vicariously liable, therefore, it was enough that a defendant was acting in the furtherance of its own interests, profit-related or not. Defendants could not, therefore, avoid liability by reference to technical distinctions between employees and non-employees.

It found that the facts of the case met the *CCWS* criteria, rendering the Ministry vicariously liable. Prisoners working in the kitchens were integral to the operation of the prison, and had been placed in positions that generated the risk that they would commit torts. Significantly, the Court recognised that the *CCWS* criteria were designed to ensure that vicarious liability was imposed where it was fair, just and reasonable to do so, regardless of whether a relationship of employment existed.

15. Vicarious liability in tort is imposed upon a person in respect of the act or omission of another individual, because of his relationship with that individual, and the connection between that relationship and the act or omission in question. Leaving aside other areas of the law where vicarious liability can operate, such as partnership and agency (with which this judgment is not concerned), the relationship is classically one of employment, and the connection is that the employee committed the act or omission in the course of his employment: that is to say, within the field of activities assigned to him, as Lord Cullen put it in *Central Motors (Glasgow) Ltd v Cessnock Garage & Motor Co* 1925 SC 796, 802, or, adapting the words of Diplock LJ in *Ilkiw v Samuels* [1963] 1 WLR 991, 1004, in the course of his job, considered broadly. That aspect of vicarious liability is fully considered by Lord Toulson in the case of *Mohamud*.

16. It has however long been recognised that a relationship can give rise to vicarious liability even in the absence of a contract of employment. For example, where an employer

lends his employee to a third party, the third party may be treated as the employer for the purposes of vicarious liability. In recent years, the courts have sought to explain more generally the basis on which vicarious liability can arise out of a relationship other than that of employer and employee.

...

22. The remaining factors listed by Lord Phillips were that (1) the tort will have been committed as a result of activity being taken by the tortfeasor on behalf of the defendant, (2) the tortfeasor's activity is likely to be part of the business activity of the defendant, and (3) the defendant, by employing the tortfeasor to carry on the activity, will have created the risk of the tort committed by the tortfeasor.

...

24. Lord Phillips's analysis in the Christian Brothers case wove together these related ideas so as to develop a modern theory of vicarious liability. **The result of this approach is that a relationship other than one of employment is in principle capable of giving rise to vicarious liability where harm is wrongfully done by an individual who carries on activities as an integral part of the business activities carried on by a defendant and for its benefit (rather than his activities being entirely attributable to the conduct of a recognisably independent business of his own or of a third party), and where the commission of the wrongful act is a risk created by the defendant by assigning those activities to the individual in question.**

...

30. It is also important not to be misled by a narrow focus on semantics: for example, by words such as 'business', 'benefit', and 'enterprise'. The defendant need not be carrying on activities of a commercial nature: that is apparent not only from the cases of *E* and the *Christian Brothers*, but also from the long-established application of vicarious liability to public authorities and hospitals. It need not therefore be a business or enterprise in any ordinary sense. Nor need the benefit which it derives from the tortfeasor's activities take the form of a profit. It is sufficient that there is a defendant which is carrying on activities in the furtherance of its own interests. The individual for whose conduct it may be vicariously liable must carry on activities assigned to him by the defendant as an integral part of its operation and for its benefit. The defendant must, by assigning those activities to him, have created a risk of his committing the tort. As the cases of *Viasystems*, *E* and the *Christian Brothers* show, a wide range of circumstances can satisfy those requirements.

...

40. ... it was argued that it was always necessary to ask the broader question whether it would be fair, just and reasonable to impose vicarious liability. In that regard, reliance was placed on the fact that the prison service acts for the benefit of the public, and on the fact that any liability would have to be met out of scarce public funds. It was also argued that

there was no justification for imposing vicarious liability on the prison service in addition to its common law duty of care towards Mrs Cox, and its various statutory duties.

41. I do not consider that it is always necessary to ask the broader question. The criteria for the imposition of vicarious liability listed by Lord Phillips in the Christian Brothers case are designed, as he made clear at paras 34, 35 and 47, to ensure that it is imposed where it is fair, just and reasonable to do so. That was the whole point of seeking to align the criteria with the various policy justifications for its imposition. As I have explained, the criteria may be capable of refinement in particular contexts. But in cases where the criteria are satisfied, it should not generally be necessary to re-assess the fairness, justice and reasonableness of the result in the particular case. Such an exercise, if carried out routinely, would be liable to lead to uncertainty and inconsistency.

The Supreme Court extended this analysis in the following case.

Armes v Nottinghamshire CC [2017] UKSC 60, [2018] AC 355, [59]–[65] (Lord Reed)

The appellant argued that the appellant local authority should be liable for the physical and sexual abuse she suffered at the hands of her foster parents. She made no argument that the authority had been negligent in its selection of her foster parents. In finding in her favour, the Supreme Court considered that the principles outlined in *Cox v Ministry of Justice* pointed towards the imposition of vicarious liability on the local authority. Specifically, this was because the foster parents committed the relevant torts in the course of an activity carried on for the benefit of the local authority, and because the local authority exercised a significant degree of control over how the foster parents carried out their responsibilities. Significantly (particularly for essay questions about the policy underpinning of vicarious liability), the Court also considered it relevant that most foster parents would have insufficient means to be able to meet a substantial award of damages, and that victims are therefore far more likely to receive compensation from local authorities for their harm.

59. Applying the approach adopted in *Cox* to the circumstances of the present case, and considering first the relationship between the activity of the foster parents and that of the local authority, the relevant activity of the local authority was the care of children who had been committed to their care. They were under a statutory duty to care for such children. In order to discharge that duty, in so far as it involved the provision of accommodation, maintenance and daily care, they recruited, selected and trained persons who were willing to accommodate, maintain and look after the children in their homes as foster parents, and inspected their homes before any placement was made. They paid allowances to the foster parents in order to defray their expenses, and provided the foster parents with such equipment as might be necessary. They also provided in-service training. The foster parents were expected to carry out their fostering in co-operation with local authority social workers, with whom they had at least monthly meetings. The local

authority involved the foster parents in their decision-making concerning the children, and required them to co-operate with arrangements for contact with the children's families. **In the light of these circumstances, the foster parents with which the present case is concerned cannot be regarded as carrying on an independent business of their own: such a characterisation would fail to reflect many important aspects of the arrangements.**

60. Although the picture presented is not without complexity, nevertheless **when considered as a whole it points towards the conclusion that the foster parents provided care to the child as an integral part of the local authority's organisation of its child care services. If one stands back from the minutiae of daily life and considers the local authority's statutory responsibilities and the manner in which they were discharged, it is impossible to draw a sharp line between the activity of the local authority, who were responsible for the care of the child and the promotion of her welfare, and that of the foster parents, whom they recruited and trained, and with whom they placed the child, in order for her to receive care in the setting which they considered would best promote her welfare.** In these circumstances, it can properly be said that the torts committed against the claimant were committed by the foster parents in the course of an activity carried on for the benefit of the local authority.

61. Considering next the issue of risk creation, the local authority's placement of children in their care with foster parents creates a relationship of authority and trust between the foster parents and the children, in circumstances where close control cannot be exercised by the local authority, and so renders the children particularly vulnerable to abuse. Although it is generally considered to be in the best interests of children in care that they should be placed in foster care, since most children benefit greatly from the experience of family life, it is relevant to the imposition of vicarious liability that a particular risk of abuse is inherent in that choice. That is because, if the public bodies responsible for decision-making in relation to children in care consider it advantageous to place them in foster care, notwithstanding the inherent risk that some children may be abused, it may be considered fair that they should compensate the unfortunate children for whom that risk materialises, particularly bearing in mind that the children are under the protection of the local authority and have no control over the decision regarding their placement. In that way, the burden of a risk borne in the general interest is shared, rather than being borne solely by the victims.

62. So far as the issue of control is concerned, it was explained earlier that the local authority selected foster parents and inspected their homes prior to the placement of children with them. The local authority were required under the Regulations to arrange regular medical examinations of fostered children, to ensure that the children were regularly visited, to carry out regular reviews of their welfare, health, conduct and progress, and to remove them from the foster parents forthwith if the visitor considered that their health, safety or morals were endangered. It was also explained that foster parents had to agree that they would allow the children to be medically examined at such times and places as the local authority might require, that they would inform the local authority immediately of any

serious occurrence affecting the children, that they would at all times permit any person authorised by the local authority to see the children and to visit their home, and that they would allow the children to be removed from their home when so requested by any person authorised by the local authority. It was explained that a number of aspects of the lives of children in foster care were decided by the local authority, reflecting the fact that it was the local authority, not the foster parents, which possessed parental powers in relation to the children. The arrangements made in practice for the monitoring of placements were described earlier. Accordingly, **although the foster parents controlled the organisation and management of their household to the extent permitted by the relevant law and practice, and dealt with most aspects of the daily care of the children without immediate supervision, it would be mistaken to regard them as being in much the same position as ordinary parents. The local authority exercised powers of approval, inspection, supervision and removal without any parallel in ordinary family life**. By virtue of those powers, the local authority exercised a significant degree of control over both what the foster parents did and how they did it, in order to ensure that the children's needs were met.

63. In relation to the remaining issue, that of the ability to satisfy an award of damages, **vicarious liability is only of practical relevance in situations where (1) the principal tortfeasor cannot be found or is not worth suing, and (2) the person sought to be made vicariously liable is able to compensate the victim of the tort. Those conditions are satisfied in the present context.** Most foster parents have insufficient means to be able to meet a substantial award of damages, and are unlikely to have (or to be able to obtain) insurance against their own propensity to criminal behaviour. The local authorities which engage them can more easily compensate the victims of injuries which are often serious and long-lasting.

64. Consideration of the factors discussed in *Cox* therefore points towards the imposition of vicarious liability. What, then, of the reasons given by the Court of Appeal for reaching the opposite conclusion (prior, it should be said, to the decision in *Cox*)? As was explained earlier, Tomlinson LJ rejected vicarious liability principally on the basis that the local authority did not exercise sufficient control over the foster carers. The provision of family life 'by definition' could not be an activity of a local authority or part of the enterprise on which it was engaged, since inherent in it was a complete absence of external control over day to day routine. The local authority's control was at the 'higher or macro level', rather than 'micro-management'. Control at that level was irrelevant to the risk of abuse occurring. Black LJ similarly considered that the provision of the experience of family life through fostering precluded the degree of control required for the imposition of vicarious liability. Burnett LJ agreed with both judgments.

65. It is important not to overstate the extent to which external control was absent from the fostering with which this case is concerned, as explained earlier. The local authority controlled who the foster parents were, supervised their fostering, and controlled some aspects of day to day family life, such as holidays and medical treatment. More fundamentally, it is important not to exaggerate the extent to which control is necessary

in order for the imposition of vicarious liability to be justified. The possibility that vicarious liability may arise in relation to the provision of elements of family life is consistent with such cases as *Lister v Hesley Hall Ltd* [2001] UKHL 22; [2002] 1 AC 215, where vicarious liability was imposed for the abuse of children by the warden of a school boarding house, and the Canadian case of *Bazley v Curry* [1999] 2 SCR 534, where it was imposed for abuse committed by a 'father figure' employed to perform parental tasks at a children's home. It is not necessary for there to be micro-management, or any high degree of control, in order for vicarious liability to be imposed. There are countless cases where vicarious liability has been imposed for torts committed by professional persons who carry out their work without close supervision.

Given that *Armes* contains explicit judicial consideration of distributive issues, but also gave rise to a fairly open-textured inquiry, it is perhaps unsurprising that, in *Barclays Bank Plc v Various Claimants*, the Supreme Court was asked to consider the issue once again.

Barclays Bank Plc v Various Claimants [2020] UKSC 13, [2020] AC 973, [24], [27]–[29] (Lady Hale)

The defendant bank appealed against a finding of vicarious liability in relation to alleged sexual assaults perpetrated by a doctor who carried out medical examinations as part of its employment process. The bank referred candidates to the doctor, paid a fee for each examination and provided the paperwork. The examinations themselves were, however, carried out on the doctor's own premises and no retainer was paid. The bank argued that there should be no liability for independent contractors. The claimants, on the other hand, argued that the factors outlined by the Supreme Court in recent cases (*CCWS, Cox* and *Armes*) had the effect of bringing the inquiry closer to one that asked whether it was fair, just and reasonable to impose vicarious liability according to a particular set of facts.

In agreeing with the defendant, the Supreme Court stated that the essential legal distinction is one made between those who are acting in the furtherance of their *own* business, and those whose actions are integral to *another's* business. The Court went on to clarify that the five policy considerations outlined in *CCWS* would only be required in borderline cases in which the distinction between an employee and an independent contractor was not clear. On the facts of the instant case, it was clear that the doctor had been acting in the furtherance of his own business. He was not, therefore, in an employment relationship with the defendant bank or one that was 'sufficiently akin' to that for vicarious liability to be imposed.

24. There is nothing, therefore, in the trilogy of Supreme Court cases discussed above to suggest that the classic distinction between employment and relationships akin or analogous to employment, on the one hand, and the relationship with an independent contractor, on the other hand, has been eroded. Two cases decided by common law courts since *Christian Brothers* and *Cox* have reached the same conclusion.

…

27. **The question therefore is, as it has always been, whether the tortfeasor is carrying on business on his own account or whether he is in a relationship akin to employment with the defendant. In doubtful cases, the five 'incidents' identified by Lord Phillips may be helpful in identifying a relationship which is sufficiently analogous to employment to make it fair, just and reasonable to impose vicarious liability.** Although they were enunciated in the context of non-commercial enterprises, they may be relevant in deciding whether workers who may be technically self-employed or agency workers are effectively part and parcel of the employer's business. But the key, as it was in *Christian Brothers*, *Cox* and *Armes*, will usually lie in understanding the details of the relationship. Where it is clear that the tortfeasor is carrying on his own independent business it is not necessary to consider the five incidents.

Application in this case

28. Clearly, although Dr Bates was a part-time employee of the health service, he was not at any time an employee of the bank. Nor, viewed objectively, was he anything close to an employee. He did, of course, do work for the bank. The bank made the arrangements for the examinations and sent him the forms to fill in. It therefore chose the questions to which it wanted answers. But the same would be true of many other people who did work for the bank but were clearly independent contractors, ranging from the company hired to clean its windows to the auditors hired to audit its books. **Dr Bates was not paid a retainer which might have obliged him to accept a certain number of referrals from the bank. He was paid a fee for each report. He was free to refuse an offered examination should he wish to do so. He no doubt carried his own medical liability insurance, although this may not have covered him from liability for deliberate wrongdoing. He was in business on his own account as a medical practitioner with a portfolio of patients and clients. One of those clients was the bank.**

Comment

29. **Until these recent developments, it was largely assumed that a person would be an employee for all purposes – employment law, tax, social security and vicarious liability. Recent developments have broken that link, which may be of benefit to people harmed by the torts of those working in the 'gig' economy.** It would be tempting to align the law of vicarious liability with employment law in a different way. Employment law now recognises two different types of 'worker': (a) those who work under a contract of employment and (b) those who work under a contract 'whereby the individual undertakes to do or perform personally any work or services for another party to the contract whose status is not by virtue of the contract that of a client or customer of any profession or business undertaking carried on by the individual' (Employment Rights Act 1996, section 230(3)). Limb (b) workers enjoy some but by no means all the employment rights enjoyed by limb (a) workers. It would be tempting to say that limb (b) encapsulates the distinction between people whose relationship is akin to employment and true independent contractors: people such as the solicitor in *Bates van Winkelhof v Clyde and Co LLP* [2014] UKSC 32; [2014] 1 WLR 2047, or the plumber in *Pimlico Plumbers Ltd v Smith* [2018] UKSC 29; [2018] ICR

1511. Asking that question may be helpful in identifying true independent contractors. But it would be going too far down the road to tidiness for this court to align the common law concept of vicarious liability, developed for one set of reasons, with the statutory concept of 'worker', developed for a quite different set of reasons.

15.1.2 A sufficiently close connection?

This, as we have seen, is the second stage of the vicarious liability inquiry. Two decades ago, the House of Lords moved away from the traditional Salmond test[1] for establishing vicarious liability. This test had required:

(1) a wrongful act authorised by the master; or
(2) a wrongful and unauthorised mode of doing some act authorised by the master.

The problem with this test, as highlighted in the case that follows, is that it will exclude some of the most serious wrongs committed by an employee, even where their commission depended upon the employment relationship. For instance, an employee of a teacher supply agency, who uses her position to take and misuse client banking information, is clearly not doing an act authorised by her master. Her access to that information, however, depends entirely on her employment. This was the point addressed in *Lister*, a set of facts concerned with a far more heinous wrong.

Lister v Hesley Hall Ltd [2001] UKHL 22, [2002] 1 AC 215, [50], [54], [59], [60], [61] (Lord Clyde), [65], [82], [83] (Lord Millet)

The claimant's case was that that the owner of a care home in which he had been a resident was vicariously liable for the sexual abuse inflicted upon him by its warden (who was an employee of that owner). The Court of Appeal had been bound by *T v North Yorkshire CC* [1999] to find that sexual abuse could not be considered to be an unauthorised means of carrying out an authorised act. In considering the appeal, the House of Lords in *Lister* made it clear that the important question was whether there was a close connection between the employee's duties and the wrongful act. Since, on these facts, the warden had been entrusted with the welfare of the children, it would be fair and just to impose vicarious liability on the owner for the intentional torts committed as a result.

[Lord Clyde] 50. I turn finally to the facts of the present case. It appears that the care and safekeeping of the boys had been entrusted to the respondents and they in turn had entrusted their care and safekeeping, so far as the running of the boarding house was concerned, to the warden. **That gave him access to the premises, but the opportunity to be at the premises would not in itself constitute a sufficient connection between his wrongful actings and his employment. In addition to the opportunity which access gave**

1 Formulated by John William Salmond: RFV Heuston and RA Buckley, *Salmond and Heuston on the Law of Torts* (Sweet & Maxwell, 1996) 443.

him, his position as warden and the close contact with the boys which that work involved created a sufficient connection between the acts of abuse which he committed and the work which he had been employed to do. It appears that the respondents gave the warden a quite general authority in the supervision and running of the house as well as some particular responsibilities. His general duty was to look after and to care for, among others, the appellants. That function was one which the respondents had delegated to him. That he performed that function in a way which was an abuse of his position and an abnegation of his duty does not sever the connection with his employment. The particular acts which he carried out upon the boys have to be viewed not in isolation but in the context and the circumstances in which they occurred. Given that he had a general authority in the management of the house and in the care and supervision of the boys in it, the employers should be liable for the way in which he behaved towards them in his capacity as warden of the house. The respondents should then be vicariously liable to the appellants for the injury and damage which they suffered at the hands of the warden.

…

54. … a situation where the employer has assumed a relationship to the plaintiff which imposes specific duties in tort upon the employer and the role of the employee (or servant) is that he is the person to whom the employer has entrusted the performance of those duties. These cases are examples of that class where the employer, by reason of assuming a relationship to the plaintiff, owes to the plaintiff duties which are more extensive than those owed by the public at large and, accordingly, are to be contrasted with the situation where a defendant is simply in proximity to the plaintiff so that it is foreseeable that his acts may injure the plaintiff or his property and a reasonable person would have taken care to avoid causing such injury. The category into which the present cases fall is recognised by the agreed facts and the useful summary of Judge Harry Walker adopted by Swinton Thomas LJ:

> 'The defendant admits it had a duty of care towards the plaintiffs. That duty of care was to take all reasonable steps to safeguard the plaintiffs (and other pupils) in their physical, moral and educational development whilst at the school. In carrying out that duty of care the defendant, a limited company, necessarily had to appoint a hierarchy of responsible agents … each of whom had either general or particular responsibilities which bore upon this duty of care. Mr Grain in particular was responsible for the boys while at Axeholme House …'

The fact that sexual abuse was involved does not distinguish this case from any other involving the care of the young and vulnerable and the duty to protect them from the risk of harm.

…

59. The classic Salmond test for vicarious liability and scope of employment has two limbs. The first covers authorised acts which are tortious. These present no relevant problem and

the present cases clearly do not fall within the first limb. The defendants did not authorise Mr Grain to abuse the children in his charge. The argument of the respondent (accepted by the Court of Appeal) is that Mr Grain's acts of abuse did not come within the second limb either: abusing children cannot properly be described as a mode of caring for children. The answer to this argument is provided by the analysis which I have set out in the preceding paragraphs. **Whether or not some act comes within the scope of the servant's employment depends upon an identification of what duty the servant was employed by his employer to perform. (Diplock LJ *sup.*) If the act of the servant which gives rise to the servant's liability to the plaintiff amounted to a failure by the servant to perform that duty, the act comes within 'the scope of his employment' and the employer is vicariously liable. If, on the other hand, the servant's employment merely gave the servant the opportunity to do what he did without more, there will be no vicarious liability, hence the use by Salmond and in the Scottish and some other authorities of the word 'connection' to indicate something which is not a casual coincidence but has the requisite relationship to the employment of the tortfeasor (servant) by his employer**: *Kirby v National Coal Board* 1958 SC 514; *Williams v A & W Hemphill Ltd* 1966 SC(HL) 31.

60. My Lords, the correct approach to answering the question whether the tortious act of the servant falls within or without the scope of the servant's employment for the purposes of the principle of vicarious liability is to ask what was the duty of the servant towards the plaintiff which was broken by the servant and what was the contractual duty of the servant towards his employer. The second limb of the classic Salmond test is a convenient rule of thumb which provides the answer in very many cases but does not represent the fundamental criterion which is the comparison of the duties respectively owed by the servant to the plaintiff and to his employer. Similarly, I do not believe that it is appropriate to follow the lead given by the Supreme Court of Canada in *Bazley v Curry* 174 DLR (4th) 45. The judgments contain a useful and impressive discussion of the social and economic reasons for having a principle of vicarious liability as part of the law of tort which extends to embrace acts of child abuse. But an exposition of the policy reasons for a rule (or even a description) is not the same as defining the criteria for its application. Legal rules have to have a greater degree of clarity and definition than is provided by simply explaining the reasons for the existence of the rule and the social need for it, instructive though that may be. In English law that clarity is provided by the application of the criterion to which I have referred derived from the English authorities.

61. It follows that the reasoning of the Court of Appeal in *Trotman v North Yorkshire County Council* [1999] LGR 584 and the present cases cannot be supported. On the undisputed facts, the present cases satisfy the criteria for demonstrating the vicarious liability of the defendants for the acts of Mr Grain.

[Lord Millet] 65. Vicarious liability is a species of strict liability. It is not premised on any culpable act or omission on the part of the employer; an employer who is not personally at fault is made legally answerable for the fault of his employee. It is best understood as a loss-distribution device: (see Cane's edition of *Atiyah's Accidents, Compensation and the Law* 6th ed (1999), p 85 and the articles cited by Atiyah in his monograph on *Vicarious Liability in the Law of Torts*, at p 24. The theoretical underpinning of the doctrine is unclear. Glanville Williams wrote ('Vicarious Liability and the Master's of Indemnity' (1957) 20 MLR 220, 231):

> 'Vicarious liability is the creation of many judges who have had different ideas of its justification or social policy, or no idea at all. Some judges may have extended the rule more widely, or confined it more narrowly than its true rationale would allow; yet the rationale, if we can discover it, will remain valid so far as it extends.'

Fleming observed (*The Law of Torts*, 9th ed, p 410) that the doctrine cannot parade as a deduction from legalistic premises. He indicated that it should be frankly recognised as having its basis in a combination of policy considerations, and continued:

> 'Most important of these is the belief that a person who employs others to advance his own economic interest should in fairness be placed under a corresponding liability for losses incurred in the course of the enterprise ...'

Atiyah, *Vicarious Liability in the Law of Torts* wrote to the same effect. He suggested, at p 171:

> 'The master ought to be liable for all those torts which can fairly be regarded as reasonably incidental risks to the type of business he carries on.'

These passages are not to be read as confining the doctrine to cases where the employer is carrying on business for profit. They are based on the more general idea that a person who employs another for his own ends inevitably creates a risk that the employee will commit a legal wrong. If the employer's objectives cannot be achieved without a serious risk of the employee committing the kind of wrong which he has in fact committed, the employer ought to be liable. The fact that his employment gave the employee the opportunity to commit the wrong is not enough to make the employer liable. He is liable only if the risk is one which experience shows is inherent in the nature of the business.

...

82. In the present case the warden's duties provided him with the opportunity to commit indecent assaults on the boys for his own sexual gratification, but that in itself is not enough to make the school liable. The same would be true of the groundsman or the school porter. But there was far more to it than that. The school was responsible for the care and welfare of the boys. It entrusted that responsibility to the warden. He was employed to discharge the school's responsibility to the boys. For this purpose the school entrusted them to his care. He did not merely take advantage of the opportunity which employment at a residential school gave him. He abused the special position in which the school had placed him to enable it to discharge its own responsibilities, with the result that the assaults were committed by the very employee to whom the school had entrusted the care of the

boys. It is not necessary to conduct the detailed dissection of the warden's duties of the kind on which the Supreme Court of Canada embarked in *Bazley* and *Jacobi*. I would hold the school liable.

83. I would regard this as in accordance not only with ordinary principle deducible from the authorities but with the underlying rationale of vicarious liability. Experience shows that in the case of boarding schools, prisons, nursing homes, old people's homes, geriatric wards, and other residential homes for the young or vulnerable, there is an inherent risk that indecent assaults on the residents will be committed by those placed in authority over them, particularly if they are in close proximity to them and occupying a position of trust.

It could be argued that there was, following *Lister*, a period during which the vicarious liability inquiry could be described in relatively simple terms. The next case, however, brought that to an end. It is not a judgment that has been particularly favourably received, either in judicial or academic circles.

Mohamud v WM Morrison Supermarkets Plc [2016] UKSC 11, [2016] AC 677, [44]–[46] (Lord Toulson), [50], [53], [54] (Lord Dyson)

The defendant supermarket employed K to run its petrol station and to serve its customers. The claimant was a customer who was violently physically assaulted by K. At both first instance and in the Court of Appeal, the connection between K's role and his abuse of the customer was insufficiently close to found vicarious liability: whilst his job was a customer-facing position, there was nothing inevitable about including abuse of customers. In allowing the customer's appeal, the Supreme Court expressly approved the close connection test, but also set out to simplify it by identifying two basic questions, as set out in Lord Toulson's judgment below:

[Lord Toulson] 44. In the simplest terms, the court has to consider two matters. **The first question is what functions or 'field of activities' have been entrusted by the employer to the employee**, or, in everyday language, what was the nature of his job. As has been emphasised in several cases, this question must be addressed broadly; see in particular the passage in Diplock LJ's judgment in *Ilkiw v Samuels* [1963] 1 WLR 991, 1004 included in the citation from *Rose v Plenty* at para 38 above, and cited also in *Lister* by Lord Steyn at para 20, Lord Clyde at para 42, Lord Hobhouse at para 58 and Lord Millett at para 77.

45. **Secondly, the court must decide whether there was sufficient connection between the position in which he was employed and his wrongful conduct to make it right for the employer to be held liable under the principle of social justice which goes back to Holt.** To try to measure the closeness of connection, as it were, on a scale of 1 to 10, would be a forlorn exercise and, what is more, it would miss the point. The cases in which the necessary connection has been found for Holt's principle to be applied are cases in which the employee used or misused the position entrusted to him in a way which injured the third party. *Lloyd v Grace, Smith & Co*, *Petterson* and *Lister* were all cases in which the

employee misused his position in a way which injured the claimant, and that is the reason why it was just that the employer who selected him and put him in that position should be held responsible. By contrast, in *Warren v Henlys Ltd* any misbehaviour by the petrol pump attendant, qua petrol pump attendant, was past history by the time that he assaulted the claimant. The claimant had in the meantime left the scene, and the context in which the assault occurred was that he had returned with the police officer to pursue a complaint against the attendant.

46. Contrary to the primary submission advanced on the claimant's behalf, I am not persuaded that there is anything wrong with the Lister approach as such. It has been affirmed many times and I do not see that the law would now be improved by a change of vocabulary. Indeed, the more the argument developed, the less clear it became whether the claimant was advocating a different approach as a matter of substance and, if so, what the difference of substance was.

…

[Lord Dyson] 50. As Lord Toulson has explained, the test for holding an employer vicariously liable for the tort of his employee has troubled the courts for many years. The 'close connection' test (whether the employee's tort is so closely connected with his employment that it would be just to hold the employer liable) was first articulated in this jurisdiction by the House of Lords in *Lister v Hesley Hall Ltd* [2002] 1 AC 215. It has been subsequently followed in many cases, including several at the highest level: see para 42 above. As Lord Nicholls said in *Dubai Aluminium Co Ltd v Salaam* [2002] UKHL 48; [2003] 2 AC 366, para 26, the test is imprecise, but that is inevitable given the infinite range of circumstances where the issue of vicarious liability arises. The court, he said, has to make an evaluative judgment in each case, having regard to all the circumstances and to the assistance provided by previous court decisions on the facts of other cases.

…

53. The close connection test has now been repeatedly applied by our courts for some 13 years. In my view, it should only be abrogated or refined if a demonstrably better test can be devised. Far from being demonstrably better, the proposed new test is hopelessly vague. What does 'representative capacity' mean in this context? And by what criteria is the court to determine the circumstances in which the reasonable observer would consider the employee to be acting in a representative capacity? I do not see how this test is more precise than the close connection test or how it better reflects modern views of justice. The attraction of the close connection test is that it is firmly rooted in justice. It asks whether the employee's tort is so closely connected with his employment as to make it just to hold the employer liable.

54. It is true that the test is imprecise. But this is an area of the law in which, as Lord Nicholls said, imprecision is inevitable. To search for certainty and precision in vicarious liability is to undertake a quest for a chimaera. Many aspects of the law of torts are inherently imprecise.

For example, the imprecise concepts of fairness, justice and reasonableness are central to the law of negligence. The test for the existence of a duty of care is whether it is fair, just and reasonable to impose such a duty. The test for remoteness of loss is one of reasonable foreseeability. Questions such as whether to impose a duty of care and whether loss is recoverable are not always easy to answer because they are imprecise. But these tests are now well established in our law. To adopt the words of Lord Nicholls, the court has to make an evaluative judgment in each case having regard to all the circumstances and having regard to the assistance provided by previous decisions on the facts of other cases.

As we can see from this, liability was based here on the fact that the defendant had *entrusted* the wrongdoer with a position in which he was dealing directly with the general public. The Supreme Court's view was that this generated a risk of K abusing that position, and the fact that K had been motivated by personal inclination did not detract from their finding that it was fair, just and reasonable to impose vicarious liability on the defendant. Importantly, however, that approach must now be understood in the light of the following case, in which the Supreme Court returned to the point.

WM Morrison Supermarkets Plc v Various Claimants [2020] UKSC 12, [2020] AC 989, [16], [17], [25], [31]–[35], [47] (Lord Reed)

The defendant appealed against a finding that it was vicariously liable to its employees in respect of the disclosure of their personal information by a former employee. Whilst employed, he uploaded the personal data of a large number of employees to a publicly accessible file-sharing website. In allowing the appeal, the Supreme Court closely analysed the reasoning of Lord Toulson in *Mohamud* in relation specifically to the connection between the employee's conduct and his employment, which the lower courts in this case appeared to have regarded as referring to an unbroken temporal or causal chain of events. Were such an interpretation to be correct, *Mohamud* would have effected a major change in the law. In the view of the Supreme Court, this was not its consequence, and the general principle remained that the wrongful conduct had to be so closely connected with acts the employee was authorised to do that, for the purposes of the liability of the employer to third parties, it might fairly and properly be regarded as done by the employee while acting in the ordinary course of his employment. Lord Toulson's 'an unbroken sequence of events' did not refer to the temporal or causal connection between employment and action, but rather between the capacity in which the employee was acting and the events which took place.

The Supreme Court also reiterated that this case concerns the close connection stage, rather than the relationship stage, of the vicarious liability inquiry.

16. The courts below applied what they understood to be the reasoning of Lord Toulson in *Mohamud* [2016] AC 677. They treated as critical, in particular, his reference in para 45 of his judgment to 'the principle of social justice which goes back to Holt CJ', his references in para 47 to the connection between the employee's conduct in that case and

his employment ('an unbroken sequence of events', or 'a seamless episode'), which they appear to have regarded as referring to an unbroken temporal or causal chain of events, and his statement in para 48 that 'Mr Khan's motive is irrelevant', Mr Khan being the employee whose conduct was in question in that case. The resultant approach, if correct, would constitute a major change in the law.

17. **Lord Toulson's judgment was not intended to effect a change in the law of vicarious liability: quite the contrary. That becomes clear if the judgment is read as a whole, as I shall explain.** The judgments below focused on the final paragraphs, in which Lord Toulson summarised long-established principles in the simplest terms and applied them to the facts of the case then before the court. A few phrases in those paragraphs, taken out of context, were treated as establishing legal principles: principles which would represent a departure from the precedents which Lord Toulson was expressly following.

...

25. ... Lord Toulson summarised the present law in paras 44–46 of his judgment ([2016] AC 677). 'In the simplest terms', he said, the court had to consider two matters. The first question was what functions or 'field of activities' had been entrusted by the employer to the employee. In other words, as Lord Nicholls put it in *Dubai Aluminium* at para 23, it is necessary to identify the 'acts the ... employee was authorised to do'. Secondly, Lord Toulson said at para 45, 'the court must decide whether there was sufficient connection between the position in which he was employed and his wrongful conduct to make it right for the employer to be held liable under the principle of social justice which goes back to Holt CJ'. That statement, expressly put in the simplest terms, was more fully stated by Lord Nicholls in *Dubai Aluminium* [2003] 2 AC 366, para 23: in a case concerned with vicarious liability arising out of a relationship of employment, the court generally has to decide whether the wrongful conduct was so closely connected with acts the employee was authorised to do that, for the purposes of the liability of his employer, it may fairly and properly be regarded as done by the employee while acting in the ordinary course of his employment. That statement of the law, endorsed in *Mohamud* and in several other decisions at the highest level, is authoritative.

...

31. It follows from the foregoing that the judge and the Court of Appeal misunderstood the principles governing vicarious liability in a number of relevant respects, of which the following were particularly important. First, the disclosure of the data on the Internet did not form part of Skelton's functions or field of activities, in the sense in which those words were used by Lord Toulson: it was not an act which he was authorised to do, as Lord Nicholls put it. Secondly, **the fact that the five factors listed by Lord Phillips in *Various Claimants v Catholic Child Welfare Society* [2013] 2 AC 1, para 35, were all present was nothing to the point. Those factors were not concerned with the question whether the wrongdoing in question was so connected with the employment that vicarious liability**

ought to be imposed, but with the distinct question whether, in the case of wrongdoing committed by someone who was not an employee, the relationship between the wrongdoer and the defendant was sufficiently akin to employment as to be one to which the doctrine of vicarious liability should apply. Thirdly, although there was a close temporal link and an unbroken chain of causation linking the provision of the data to Skelton for the purpose of transmitting it to KPMG and his disclosing it on the Internet, a temporal or causal connection does not in itself satisfy the close connection test. Fourthly, the reason why Skelton acted wrongfully was not irrelevant: on the contrary, whether he was acting on his employer's business or for purely personal reasons was highly material.

32. The question whether Morrisons is vicariously liable for Skelton's wrongdoing must therefore be considered afresh. Applying the general test laid down by Lord Nicholls in para 23 of *Dubai Aluminium* [2003] 2 AC 366, the question is whether Skelton's disclosure of the data was so closely connected with acts he was authorised to do that, for the purposes of the liability of his employer to third parties, his wrongful disclosure may fairly and properly be regarded as done by him while acting in the ordinary course of his employment.

33. Considering first the acts which Skelton was authorised to do, so far as relevant, he was given the task of collating and transmitting payroll data to KPMG. He performed that task on a date between 15 and 21 November 2013. The remaining question is whether Skelton's wrongful disclosure of the data was so closely connected with the collation and transmission of the data to KPMG that, for the purposes of the liability of his employer to third parties, the disclosure may fairly and properly be regarded as made by him while acting in the ordinary course of his employment.

34. The connecting factor between what Skelton was authorised to do and the disclosure is that he could not have made the disclosure if he had not been given the task of collating the data and transmitting it to KPMG. It was the provision of the data to him, so that he could perform that task, that enabled him to make a private copy of the data on 18 November 2013, which he subsequently used to make the disclosure on 12 January 2014.

35. Clearly, the mere fact that Skelton's employment gave him the opportunity to commit the wrongful act would not be sufficient to warrant the imposition of vicarious liability: see, for example, *Morris v C W Martin & Sons Ltd* [1966] 1 QB 716, 737, and *Lister* [2002] 1 AC 215, paras 25, 45, 50, 59, 65, 75, and 81–82. The courts below, however, treated it as important that Skelton's disclosure of the data on the Internet was, as the judge said 'closely related to what he was tasked to do' ([2019] QB 772, para 186): a remark which the Court of Appeal described as 'plainly correct' ([2019] QB 772, para 63). The fallacy in that approach was explained by Lord Wilberforce in *Kooragang Investments Pty Ltd v Richardson & Wrench Ltd* [1982] AC 462, which concerned an employee who was authorised to carry out valuations, and negligently carried out a valuation without authority from his employers and not on their behalf. Lord Wilberforce rejected the argument that so long as

the employee is doing acts of the same kind as those which it is within his authority to do, the employer is liable, and is not entitled to show that the employee had no authority to do them. He said at p 473:

> 'the underlying principle remains that a servant, even while performing acts of the class which he was authorised, or employed, to do, may so clearly depart from the scope of his employment that his master will not be liable for his wrongful acts.'

...

47. All these examples illustrate the distinction drawn by Lord Nicholls at para 32 of *Dubai Aluminium* [2003] 2 AC 366 between 'cases ... where the employee was engaged, however misguidedly, in furthering his employer's business, and cases where the employee is engaged solely in pursuing his own interests: on a "frolic of his own", in the language of the time-honoured catch phrase.' In the present case, it is abundantly clear that Skelton was not engaged in furthering his employer's business when he committed the wrongdoing in question. On the contrary, he was pursuing a personal vendetta, seeking vengeance for the disciplinary proceedings some months earlier. In those circumstances, applying the test laid down by Lord Nicholls in *Dubai Aluminium* in the light of the circumstances of the case and the relevant precedents, Skelton's wrongful conduct was not so closely connected with acts which he was authorised to do that, for the purposes of Morrisons' liability to third parties, it can fairly and properly be regarded as done by him while acting in the ordinary course of his employment.

This case does not represent the end of the line for judicial analysis of the close connection test. Very recently, that test was again examined at the highest level. In the next case, the Supreme Court was asked to tailor the close connection test to sexual abuse cases, thereby making it more expansive (and so, of course, more likely to allow victims to recover). In overturning the Court of Appeal on this point, however, the Supreme Court made it clear that the close connection test is *not* amenable to extension according to context, and that, therefore, it applies to sexual abuse cases in the same way as it does to other sets of facts.

Barry v BXB [2023] UKSC 15, [2023] 2 WLR 953, [58] (Lord Burrows)

The claimant had been raped by a Jehovah's Witness congregation elder. The relevant question for the Court was therefore whether that action was sufficiently closely connected to what the elder had been authorised to do so as to be regarded as having been committed in the course of his quasi-employment. The rape occurred whilst the victim was in the elder's home to provide him with emotional support as opposed to visiting him in his capacity as elder. Accordingly, the close connection test was not satisfied. The Supreme Court held that policy considerations were relevant only as a means of assessing the issue in the round and not as an active part of deciding whether a connection was sufficiently close to satisfy the test.

58. Having examined the main 21st century decisions on vicarious liability of the highest court, it is now possible to pull together the legal principles applicable to vicarious liability in tort that can be derived from those authorities particularly the most recent cases of *Barclays Bank* and *Morrison*.

(i) There are two stages to consider in determining vicarious liability. Stage 1 is concerned with the relationship between the defendant and the tortfeasor. Stage 2 is concerned with the link between the commission of the tort and that relationship. Both stages must be addressed and satisfied if vicarious liability is to be established.

(ii) The test at stage 1 is whether the relationship between the defendant and the tortfeasor was one of employment or akin to employment. In most cases, there will be no difficulty in applying this test because one is dealing with an employer-employee relationship. But in applying the 'akin to employment' aspect of this test, a court needs to consider carefully features of the relationship that are similar to, or different from, a contract of employment. Depending on the facts, relevant features to consider may include: whether the work is being paid for in money or in kind, how integral to the organisation is the work carried out by the tortfeasor, the extent of the defendant's control over the tortfeasor in carrying out the work, whether the work is being carried out for the defendant's benefit or in furtherance of the aims of the organisation, what the situation is with regard to appointment and termination, and whether there is a hierarchy of seniority into which the relevant role fits. It is important to recognise, as made clear in *Barclays Bank*, that the 'akin to employment' expansion does not undermine the traditional position that there is no vicarious liability where the tortfeasor is a true independent contractor in relation to the defendant.

(iii) The test at stage 2 (the 'close connection' test) is whether the wrongful conduct was so closely connected with acts that the tortfeasor was authorised to do that it can fairly and properly be regarded as done by the tortfeasor while acting in the course of the tortfeasor's employment or quasi-employment. This is the test, subject to two minor adjustments, set out by Lord Nicholls in *Dubai Aluminium*, drawing on *Lister*, and firmly approved in *Morrison*. The first adjustment is that, to be comprehensive, it is necessary to expand the test to include 'quasi-employment' as one may be dealing with a situation where the relationship at stage 1 is 'akin to employment' rather than employment. The second adjustment is that it is preferable to delete the word 'ordinary' before 'course of employment' which is superfluous and potentially misleading (eg none of the sexual abuse cases can easily be said to fall within the 'ordinary' course of employment) and was presumably included by Lord Nicholls because 'in the ordinary course of business' were the words in section 10 of the Partnership Act 1890. The application of this 'close connection' test requires a court to consider carefully on the facts the link between the wrongful conduct and the tortfeasor's authorised activities. That there is a causal connection (ie that the 'but for' causation test is satisfied) is not sufficient in itself to satisfy the test. Cases such as *Lister* and *Christian Brothers* show that sexual abuse of a child by someone who is employed or authorised to look after the child will, at least generally, satisfy the test. But, as established by *Morrison*, the carrying out of the wrongful act in pursuance of a personal vendetta against the employer, designed to harm the employer, will mean that this test is not satisfied.

(iv) As made particularly clear by Lady Hale in *Barclays Bank*, drawing on what Lord Hobhouse had said in *Lister*, the tests invoke legal principles that in the vast majority of cases can be applied without considering the underlying policy justification for vicarious liability. The tests are a product of the policy behind vicarious liability and in applying the tests there is no need to turn back continually to examine the underlying policy. This is not to deny that in difficult cases, and in line with what Lord Reed said in *Cox*, having applied the tests to reach a provisional outcome on vicarious liability, it can be a useful final check on the justice of the outcome to stand back and consider whether that outcome is consistent with the underlying policy. What precisely the underlying policy is has been hotly debated over many years by academics and judges alike. See, for example, PS Atiyah, *Vicarious Liability in the Law of Torts* (1967) chapter 2; Jason Neyers, 'A Theory of Vicarious Liability' (2005) 43 Alberta Law Review 287; Anthony Gray, *Vicarious Liability: Critique and Reform* (2018); *Vicarious Liability in the Common Law World* (ed Paula Giliker, 2022). As we have seen at para 38 above, Lord Phillips referred to five policies in *Christian Brothers* but, as Lord Reed recognised in *Cox*, a couple of those have little, if any, force. At root the core idea (as reflected in the judgments of Lord Reed in *Cox* and *Armes*: see paras 42 and 47 above) appears to be that the employer or quasi-employer, who is taking the benefit of the activities carried on by a person integrated into its organisation, should bear the cost (or, one might say, should bear the risk) of the wrong committed by that person in the course of those activities.

(v) The same two stages, and the same two tests, apply to cases of sexual abuse as they do to other cases on vicarious liability. Although one can reasonably interpret some judicial comments as supporting special rules for sexual abuse, this was rejected by Lord Reed in *Cox*. The idea that the law still needs tailoring to deal with sexual abuse cases is misleading. The necessary tailoring is already reflected in, and embraced by, the modern tests.

Barry, as this excerpt from Lord Burrows' judgment suggests, is a very helpful judgment in getting to grips with this area of the law; not only for its own substantive reasoning, but for the way in which it sets out and assimilates the other common law authorities on the issue.

Question to consider: Do you think the relatively recent expansion of vicarious liability is justified? What are the key policies behind the court's increasingly finding institutions responsible for the torts committed by individuals?

Other resources: Marco Cappelletti, *Justifying Strict Liability: A Comparative Analysis in Legal Reasoning* (OUP, 2022); Paula Giliker, 'Vicarious Liability in the Common Law World' (Hart Publishing, 2022); AJ Bell, '"Double, Double Toil and Trouble": Recent Movements in Vicarious Liability' (2018) 4 *JPI Law* 235–47; J Plunkett, 'Taking Stock of Vicarious Liability' (2016) 132 *LQR* 556–62.

15.2 Non-delegable duties

Strictly, non-delegable duties are not analogous to vicarious liability because they are a form of primary, as opposed to secondary, liability. As the name suggests, the defendant remains liable for the tort because, even though another has physically caused the harm, the duty and responsibility for it remains with the defendant. Essentially, the legal duty and the factual execution are separated. Since, however, the breach of a non-delegable duty results from the actions of a third party, it makes sense to discuss it here, not least because it is often litigated alongside vicarious liability. Whilst a defendant will not be vicariously liable for the actions of an independent contractor, they might, depending on the facts of the case, be found to be in breach of a non-delegable duty as a result of the contractor's action. This is what happened in the following case, an important authority on this point.

Woodland v Essex CC [2013] UKSC 66, [2014] 1 AC 537, [23]–[25] (Lord Sumption)

The claimant had suffered brain injuries during a swimming lesson that was taught by an instructor and supervised by a lifeguard, both of whom were independent contractors. The Court of Appeal had found that the local authority did not owe the claimant a non-delegable duty of care, but the Supreme Court disagreed and held the local authority liable for the claimant's injuries. Lord Sumption, below, sets out the five criteria necessary to give rise to a non-delegable duty of care:

23. ... cases are characterised by the following defining features:

(1) The claimant is a patient or a child, or for some other reason is especially vulnerable or dependent on the protection of the defendant against the risk of injury. Other examples are likely to be prisoners and residents in care homes.

(2) There is an antecedent relationship between the claimant and the defendant, independent of the negligent act or omission itself, (i) which places the claimant in the actual custody, charge or care of the defendant, and (ii) from which it is possible to impute to the defendant the assumption of a positive duty to protect

the claimant from harm, and not just a duty to refrain from conduct which will foreseeably damage the claimant. It is characteristic of such relationships that they involve an element of control over the claimant, which varies in intensity from one situation to another, but is clearly very substantial in the case of schoolchildren.

(3) The claimant has no control over how the defendant chooses to perform those obligations, ie whether personally or through employees or through third parties.

(4) The defendant has delegated to a third party some function which is an integral part of the positive duty which he has assumed towards the claimant; and the third party is exercising, for the purpose of the function thus delegated to him, the defendant's custody or care of the claimant and the element of control that goes with it.

(5) The third party has been negligent not in some collateral respect but in the performance of the very function assumed by the defendant and delegated by the defendant to him.

24. In *A (Child) v Ministry of Defence* [2005] QB 183, at para 47 Lord Phillips of Worth Matravers MR, delivering the leading judgment in the Court of Appeal, suggested that 'hitherto a non-delegable duty has only been found in a situation where the claimant suffers an injury while in an environment over which the defendant has control.' This is undoubtedly a fundamental feature of those cases where, in the absence of a relevant antecedent relationship, the defendant has been held liable for inherently hazardous operations or dangers on the public highway. But I respectfully disagree with the view that control of the environment in which injury is caused is an essential element in the kind of case with which we are presently concerned. The defendant is not usually in control of the environment in which injury is caused by an independent contractor. That is why as a general rule he is not liable for the contractor's negligence. Where a non-delegable duty arises, the defendant is liable not because he has control but in spite of the fact that he may have none. The essential element in my view is not control of the environment in which the claimant is injured, but control over the claimant for the purpose of performing a function for which the defendant has assumed responsibility. The actual result in *A (A Child)* was therefore correct. The Ministry of Defence was not responsible for the negligence of a hospital with whom it contracted to treat soldiers and their families. But the true reason was the finding of the trial judge (quoted at para 28 of Lord Phillips' judgment) that there was 'no sound basis for any feeling ... that secondary treatment in hospital ... was actually provided by the Army (MoD) as opposed to arranged by the army.' There was therefore no delegation of any function which the Ministry had assumed personal responsibility to carry out, and no delegation of any custody exercised by the Ministry over soldiers and their families. For exactly the same reason, I think that the Court of Appeal was right in *Myton v Woods* (1980) 79 LGR 28 to dismiss a claim against a local education authority for the negligence of a taxi firm employed by the authority to drive children to and from school. The school had no statutory duty to transport children, but only to arrange and pay for it. As Lord Denning MR put it, the authority was not liable for an independent contractor 'except he delegates to the contractor the very duty which he himself has to fulfil.' Likewise,

the Court of Appeal was right in *Farraj v King's Healthcare NHS Trust* [2010] 1 WLR 2139, to dismiss a claim against a hospital which had employed an independent laboratory to analyse a tissue sample for a patient who was not being treated by the hospital and was therefore not in its custody or care. As Dyson LJ put it at para 88, the rationale of any non-delegable duty owed by hospitals is that

> 'the hospital undertakes the care, supervision and control of its patients who are in special need of care. Patients are a vulnerable class of persons who place themselves in the care and under the control of a hospital and, as a result, the hospital assumes a particular responsibility for their well-being and safety.'

25. The courts should be sensitive about imposing unreasonable financial burdens on those providing critical public services. A non-delegable duty of care should be imputed to schools only so far as it would be fair, just and reasonable to do so. But I do not accept that any unreasonable burden would be cast on them by recognising the existence of a non-delegable duty on the criteria which I have summarised above. My reasons are as follows:

(1) The criteria themselves are consistent with the long-standing policy of the law, apparent notably in the employment cases, to protect those who are both inherently vulnerable and highly dependent on the observance of proper standards of care by those with a significant degree of control over their lives. Schools are employed to educate children, which they can do only if they are allowed authority over them. That authority confers on them a significant degree of control. When the school's own control is delegated to someone else for the purpose of performing part of the school's own educational function, it is wholly reasonable that the school should be answerable for the careful exercise of its control by the delegate.

(2) Parents are required by law to entrust their child to a school. They do so in reliance on the school's ability to look after them, and generally have no knowledge of or influence over the arrangements that the school may make to delegate specialised functions, or the basis on which they do so, or the competence of the delegates, all of which are matters about which only the school is in a position to satisfy itself.

(3) **This is not an open-ended liability, for there are important limitations on the range of matters for which a school or education authority assumes non-delegable duties. They are liable for the negligence of independent contractors only if and so far as the latter are performing functions which the school has assumed for itself a duty to perform, generally in school hours and on school premises (or at other times or places where the school may carry out its educational functions).** In the absence of negligence of their own, for example in the selection of contractors, they will not be liable for the negligence of independent contractors where on analysis their own duty is not to perform the relevant function but only to arrange for its performance. They will not be liable for the defaults of independent contractors providing extra-curricular activities outside school hours, such as school trips in the holidays. Nor will they be liable for the negligence of those to whom no control over the child

has been delegated, such as bus drivers or the theatres, zoos or museums to which children may be taken by school staff in school hours, to take some of the examples canvassed in argument and by Laws LJ in his dissenting judgment.

(4) It is important to bear in mind that until relatively recently, most of the functions now routinely delegated by schools to independent contractors would have been performed by staff for whom the authority would have been vicariously liable. The recognition of limited non-delegable duties has become more significant as a result of the growing scale on which the educational and supervisory functions of schools are outsourced, but in a longer historical perspective, it does not significantly increase the potential liability of education authorities.

(5) The responsibilities of fee-paying schools are already non-delegable because they are contractual, and the possibility of contracting out of them is limited by legislation. In this particular context, there seems to be no rational reason why the mere absence of consideration should lead to an entirely different result when comparable services are provided by a public authority. A similar point can be made about the technical distinctions that would otherwise arise between privately funded and NHS hospital treatment.

(6) It can fairly be said that the recognition of a non-delegable duty of care owed by schools involves imputing to them a greater responsibility than any which the law presently recognises as being owed by parents. Parents would not normally incur personal liability for the negligence of (say) a swimming instructor to whom they had handed custody of a child. The Appellants' pleaded allegation that the school stood *in loco parentis* may not therefore assist their case. The position of parents is very different to that of schools. Schools provide a service either by contract or pursuant to a statutory obligation, and while LEA schools do not receive fees, their staff and contractors are paid professionals. By comparison, the custody and control which parents exercise over their children is not only gratuitous, but based on an intimate relationship not readily analysable in legal terms. For this reason, the common law has always been extremely cautious about recognising legally enforceable duties owed by parents on the same basis as those owed by institutional carers: see *Surtees v Kingston-on-Thames Borough Council* [1992] PIQR 101, 121 (Beldam LJ); *Barrett v Enfield London Borough Council* [2001] 2 AC 550, 588 (Lord Hutton).

In the following article, Professor Giliker, who is an authority on vicarious liability, particularly in a comparative context, examines these recent developments, and puts them in the context of recent developments elsewhere in the common law world. You would be well-advised to read the full piece. This excerpt focuses on 'enterprise risk' liability and the interaction between vicarious liability and non-delegable duties.

Paula Giliker, 'Analysing Institutional Liability for Child Sexual Abuse in England and Wales and Australia: Vicarious Liability, Non-delegable Duties and Statutory Intervention' (2018) 77(3) *Cambridge Law Journal* 506–35

What we see is that the basis for the modern theory of vicarious liability is primarily one of risk management with institutions internalising the risk of abuse which is inherent in hiring workers to care for vulnerable children. Such reasoning notably overlaps with the focus of the public inquiries discussed above. We may also observe that the *CCWS* criteria are now being applied beyond abuse claims to those involving negligence (*Cox*) and non-sexual intentional torts (*Mohamud*). ... it is worth noting that UK law has developed a broad doctrine of vicarious liability, inspired by its fellow common law jurisdiction, Canada, which places on the institution/enterprise responsibility for the risks associated with its activities. Deakin has noted that nevertheless English judges have been hesitant to adopt a purely 'enterprise risk' approach. This is true, but at the very least we can say that enterprise liability has been a driving force to extend the doctrine to cover the inherent risks of child sexual abuse ...

UK commentators are now asking: if vicarious liability is increasingly giving rise to fears of over-extensive liability, are non-delegable duties the answer? ... Traditionally a non-delegable duty is one imposed directly on the defendant to ensure that reasonable care is taken. It is primary, not vicarious, liability and holds the institution personally liable to victims injured due to the torts of any employees or independent contractors to whom it has delegated its duty of care. As the UK Supreme Court commented in *Armes*:

> 'The expression thus refers to a higher standard of care than the ordinary duty of care. Duties involving this higher standard of care are described as non-delegable because they cannot be discharged merely by the exercise of reasonable care in the selection of a third party to whom the function in question is delegated ...'

... The common law non-delegable duty, revived in the UK in *Woodland* in 2013 ... has received some academic support as a means of dealing with abuse cases, but ... it remains unclear whether the *Woodland* duty will apply to intentional harm and there are unresolved questions of conceptual clarity. Notably if the non-delegable duty is treated simply as a means of *supplementing* vicarious liability, it is likely to offer little bar further complicating the existing law ... The paper recommends, therefore, adoption of an incremental approach at both stages of the UK vicarious liability test.

Question to consider: In light of the significant expansion of vicarious liability, is there still a role for non-delegable duties?

Other resources: P Giliker, 'Vicarious Liability, Non-delegable Duties and Teachers: Can you Outsource Liability for Lessons?' (2015) 31 *PN* 259; R Stevens, 'Non-delegable Duties and Vicarious Liability' in J Neyers et al (eds), *Emerging Issues in Tort Law* (Hart, 2007) 331; John Murphy, 'The Liability Bases of Common Law Non-Delegable Duties – A Reply to Christian Witting' (2007) 30(1) *UNSW Law Journal* 86.

15.3 Conclusion

Vicarious liability is an area in which there have been several recent and crucial developments; it is certainly a topic that has kept our highest courts very busy! Specifically, the limits and boundaries of this type of liability have been tested, expanded and, in some cases, reduced again. The headline point is that vicarious liability now involves a two-stage inquiry, looking first at the *nature of the relationship* between the wrongdoer and the defendant, and then the *closeness of the connection between that relationship and the wrong* itself. Policy discussion in this space somewhat inevitably focuses on the extent to which the imposition of liability on one party for actions committed by another can be justified. It is certainly something that requires justification, and arguments about it are best substantiated by reference to the aims and objectives of tort law as a whole; so do refer back to Chapter 1 when you are formulating your own.

Chapter 16 DEFENCES

16.1 Introduction

Once a cause of action in tort has been established, the defendant has the ability to raise a defence (or potentially multiple defences) that could defeat the claim or reduce the damages awarded by the court. There are many different defences in tort law, but this chapter will only focus on three – contributory negligence, *volenti non fit injuria* and illegality. Goudkamp, in his book, *Tort Law Defences*, discusses a total of 38 different defences, so these three are a mere drop in the ocean.[1] However, these defences are almost universally covered in tort law courses around the United Kingdom, so it is a good start. These three defences apply to almost every tortious cause of action, though students should still be aware of the specific defences that apply to specific torts, including:

- nuisance – prescription, acts of a stranger, and statutory authority;[2]
- trespass to the person – consent, necessity, self-defence, and lawful authority;[3] and
- defamation – truth, honest opinion, public interest, operation of websites, privilege and consent.[4]

Before we start looking at these three specific defences, it is important to at least try to provide a definition of a 'defence' in tort law. As you will see from Goudkamp's discussion below, this is a surprisingly difficult task.

James Goudkamp, *Tort Law Defences* (Hart Publishing, 2013) 5–7 (footnotes omitted)

> Describing any argument made by the defendant that he should not be held liable as a defence suppresses the difference between the claimant's cause of action and liability-defeating rules that are external to the elements of the claimant's action. Obscuring this distinction is undesirable. This is because it is one of the most basic organising devices in

1 James Goudkamp, *Tort Law Defences* (Hart Publishing, 2013).
2 See 10.2.3.
3 See 12.5.
4 See 13.4.2.

tort law. A sense of its significance may be gleaned from the fact that it is recognised not only in tort law but throughout the law of obligations. A corresponding distinction is also a central feature of the criminal law.

The third meaning of the word 'defence' is also unhelpful. If one uses the word 'defence' to include principles in the law of remedies, one conflates liability rules and remedial rules. These are fundamentally different types of rules and the one term should not be used to refer to them indiscriminately. It is routine for tort law textbooks to discuss rules that merely diminish the remedy to which a successful claimant is entitled (such as the apportionment provision for contributory negligence) alongside rules that prevent liability from arising. This is a significant error in classification induced by the careless use of the word 'defence'. The slipshod use of this term has also led to the frequent commission of the converse and equally bad error, which is to include analyses of rules that preclude findings of liability (such as the doctrine of abatement) in discussions of remedies.

It is difficult to support using the word 'defence' in the fourth identified way. A major problem with saying that defences are rules in respect of which the defendant carries the burden of proof is that it draws within its net many rules that no one would intentionally count as defences. Foreign matter that is identified as defences on this meaning of the word includes the very many procedural rules the applicability of which must be established by the defendant. Such rules encompass the provisions that enable defendants to obtain security for their costs, to obtain accelerated service of a claim form and to amend their pleadings after service. To apply the term 'defence' to any of these rules would be a gross distortion of language.

The fifth meaning of the word 'defence' is downright bizarre. It is doubtful whether those who use the word in this way really intended to do so. The idea that the absence of defences constitutes the final element of actions in tort (as opposed to the final question to be asked in deciding whether liability should be imposed) simply does not enjoy support in the case law. It is notable that those who claim that the absence of defences is the final element of torts do not cite any authorities that endorse this position. The fifth meaning of the word 'defence' should be assiduously avoided.

In contrast with the other definitions of the word 'defence', the second meaning of the word facilitates clear thinking about tort law. This definition, unlike all of the others, brings into focus the fundamental difference between rules that define torts and rules that release from liability a defendant whose conduct constitutes a tort. This is a conceptually sound way of organising that part of the law of torts that is concerned with specifying when liability arises. It also gives the concept of 'defence' sensible boundaries (it does not, for instance, encompass procedural rules that no one would count as defences). For these reasons, the second definition of the word 'defence' will be adopted in this book. Thus, a defence will be regarded as a rule that relieves the defendant of liability even though all of the elements of the tort in which the claimant sues are present.

Some readers will doubtlessly find this meaning of the word 'defence' to be rather odd. It excludes from the category of defences the provision for apportionment for contributory negligence. That provision is, as has been observed, widely referred to as a defence. Some might consider it to be the most important defence in the modern law of torts in terms of practical relevance. However, if confusion is to be avoided, basic distinctions, such as that between liability rules and remedial rules, should be reflected in the language that is used to discuss the law of torts. Principles that comprise the law of remedies should not be referred to as defences.

In light of these challenges, Goudkamp proposes a definition that a defence is 'a rule that relieves the defendant of liability even though all of the elements of the tort in which the claimant sues are present'.[5] If this is the accepted definition, it would mean that contributory negligence is not actually a defence but instead a rule on what remedy the claimant is able to receive. The complexities highlighted by Goudkamp are valid, and we recommend you reflect on the definition of 'defence' for legal coherency. However, this chapter will proceed on the orthodoxy that contributory negligence is a defence and, therefore, include it in the analysis and discussion.

16.2 Contributory negligence

Contributory negligence is a defence that works not by the defendant justifying or denying their negligent behaviour but by contending that the claimant has also been negligent – and that this justifies a reduction in the amount of damages to be paid. Steele highlights the importance and practical impact of contributory negligence.

Jenny Steele, 'Law Reform (Contributory Negligence) Act 1945: Collisions of a Different Sort' in TT Arvind and Jenny Steele (eds), *Tort Law and the Legislature: Common Law, Statute and the Dynamics of Legal Change* (Hart Publishing, 2013) 165–67 (footnotes omitted)

[I]t is worth considering some features of [the 1945 Law Reform (Contributory Negligence) Act's] operation today. In cases of tort liability involving personal injury, the reformed defence is used on a daily basis. It is applied regularly by courts, but is used much more frequently by parties (including of course insurers) negotiating settlements. Thus the statute's core provision that damages are to be reduced according to the judgment of 'the court' as to what would be just and equitable rarely reflects the impact

5 Goudkamp (n 1) 7.

of the modern defence. Far more often, 'contributory negligence' operates to reduce the level of settlements. It is therefore operated chiefly by lawyers and other negotiators, rather than by courts.

…

In terms of the pattern of compensation for the victims of tort, there is an added significance to reductions of damages because few personal injury claimants carry adequate first party insurance. Such reductions in damages therefore typically lead to uncompensated and uninsured elements of loss. In this respect, contributory negligence in its proportionate form is a striking embodiment of the fault principle, despite its heritage in a practical rule of maritime commerce, since it treats an element of uncompensated loss as justifiable on the basis of personal responsibility. But rarely is that judgment of responsibility made by a court. Rather, the chance of such a judgment operates to influence bargaining and decision-making positions. We can illustrate this by returning to *McLean v Bell*. It seems certain that such a claimant today would not be forced to take her case to the House of Lords in order to secure damages – nor, indeed, to court at all. On the other hand, it also seems certain that the claimant's damages would be reduced through settlement to reflect a degree of contributory negligence. The route taken by the House of Lords in that case, to secure full compensation, would be virtually unattainable. Practically, more claims are met since the 1945 Act, and few of these require a court to determine liability. But at least a substantial number of claims for personal injury are subject to reductions. And those reductions, unlike the defendant's liability, will tend to reflect the fault principle in their impact as well as in principle, because this portion of the loss will generally be uninsured. A full-blooded fault principle is wielded primarily by insurers and other negotiators and is not the precision instrument it may appear to be.

This point about the association with fault leads to a different aspect of the role of contributory negligence. It has already been pointed out that the partial defence is sometimes seen as quintessentially suited to the modern law of tort, or at least to the part of the law of tort which deals with personal injury. It offers a refinement of the fault principle, which it strongly reflects despite not being confined to cases of carelessness or deliberate harm, in that it allows division in a very wide range of circumstances according to relative responsibility. One result of this is that it gives courts the capacity to mediate between situations in which arguments based on individual claimant responsibility (for example in cases of drug-taking, suicide, and foolhardy risks) and arguments based on defendant responsibility (for example in cases involving protection of the dependent or vulnerable or health, safety and risk reduction more generally) may otherwise come into irreconcilable conflict. The way of making these positions commensurable is through adjustments to quantum of damage.

On the other hand, this outlook too may be susceptible to change. Reduction in damages is not always seen as sufficiently reflecting the responsibility of one party or the other, even if courts now have to find different routes (no duty, or *ex turpi causa*, for example) to avoid it. One perspective has been that the rise of contributory negligence in a relative form renders some complete defences less appropriate. Indeed it was suggested very soon after enactment that there ought as a consequence of the 1945 Act and its logic to be less willingness to reject a causal link between breach and damage, replacing legal causation questions with responsibility sharing, though as we will see there is conclusive evidence that neither the Law Revision Committee, nor Lord Simon, shared this view. But this is not always the approach taken. Reduction of damages frequently appears fair; and sometimes it provides a useful compromise position. But at other times it is still avoided, rather as the old total defence was avoided, though the available arguments have changed.

16.2.1 History of contributory negligence

The modern-day version of contributory negligence sees damages apportioned between the claimant and the defendant; however, this was not always the case. Historically, contributory negligence worked to bar the claimant from a claim, leaving them with no compensation at all. This created a system where both the claimant and defendant had acted negligently, but the defendant was able to get off scot-free. An example of this was in the 1809 case of *Butterfield v Forrester*. Current students of tort law will appreciate the simplicity of the two-paragraph case, with the judgment of Lord Ellenborough CJ coming in at 116 words in total!

Butterfield v Forrester (1809) 103 ER 926

This was an action on the case for obstructing a highway, by means of which obstruction the plaintiff, who was riding along the road, was thrown down with his horse, and injured, &c. At the trial before Bayley J. at Derby, it appeared that the defendant, for the purpose of making some repairs to his house, which was close by the road side at one end of the town, had put up a pole across this part of the road, a free passage being left by another branch or street in the same direction. That the plaintiff left a public house not far distant from the place in question at 8 o'clock in the evening in August, when they were just beginning to light candles, but while there was light enough left to discern the obstruction at 100 yards distance: and the witness, who proved this, said that if the plaintiff had not been riding very hard he might have observed and avoided it: the plaintiff however, who was riding violently, did not observe it, but rode against it, and fell with his horse and was much hurt in consequence of the accident; and there was no evidence of his being intoxicated at the time. On this evidence Bayley J. directed the jury, that if a person riding with reasonable and ordinary care could have seen and avoided the obstruction; and if they were satisfied that the plaintiff was riding along the street extremely hard, and without ordinary care, they should find a verdict for the defendant: which they accordingly did.

Vaughan Serjt. now objected to this direction, on moving ... for a new trial; and referred to Buller's Ni. Pri. 26(a), where the rule is laid down, that 'if a man lay logs of wood across a highway; though a person may with care ride safely by, yet if by means thereof my horse stumble and fling me, I may bring an action.'

Bayley J. The plaintiff was proved to be riding as fast as his horse could go, and this was through the streets of Derby. If he had used ordinary care he must have seen the obstruction; so that the accident appeared to happen entirely from his own fault.

Lord Ellenborough C.J. A party is not to cast himself upon an obstruction which has been made by the fault of another, and avail himself of it, if he do not himself use common and ordinary caution to be in the right. In cases of persons riding upon what is considered to be the wrong side of the road, that would not authorise another purposely to ride up against them. One person being in fault will not dispense with another's using ordinary care for himself. Two things must concur to support this action, an obstruction in the road by the fault of the defendant, and no want of ordinary care to avoid it on the part of the plaintiff.

As a result of the unfair outcome of the 'all or nothing' approach of common law contributory negligence, the Law Revision Committee was given the task of considering 'whether, and if so, in what respect the doctrine of Contributory Negligence requires modification'.[6] After reviewing the relevant case law, the Committee recommended 'that in cases where damage has been caused by the fault of two or more persons the tribunal trying the case (whether that tribunal be a judge or jury) shall apportion the liability in the degree in which each party is found to be in fault'.[7] This resulted in the enactment of the Law Reform (Contributory Negligence) Act 1945 (the '1945 Act').

Law Reform (Contributory Negligence) Act 1945

1 Apportionment of liability in case of contributory negligence

(1) Where any person suffers damage as the result partly of his own fault and partly of the fault of any other person or persons, a claim in respect of that damage shall not be defeated by reason of the fault of the person suffering the damage, but the damages recoverable in respect thereof shall be reduced to such extent as the court thinks just and equitable having regard to the claimant's share in the responsibility for the damage:

There needs to be *damage* suffered as a result of fault from both parties. If the claimant has acted negligently, but it did not contribute to the damage suffered, it will not be covered by the Act.

Section 1(1) removes the common law's 'all or nothing' approach.

The court has the obligation to reduce damages to the extent it thinks is 'just and equitable'.

When determining what is 'just and equitable', the courts should consider the claimant's share in the responsibility for the damage.

6 Law Revision Committee, *Contributory Negligence* (Cmd 6032, 1939) (LRC's 8th Report).

7 ibid 19. For an analysis of the Committee's recommendations, including some of the difficulties, see Jenny Steele, 'Law Reform (Contributory Negligence) Act 1945: Collisions of a Different Sort' in TT Arvind and Jenny Steeles (eds), *Tort Law and the Legislature: Common Law, Statute and the Dynamics of Legal Change* (Hart Publishing, 2013) 167–76.

Provided that—

(a) this subsection shall not operate to defeat any defence arising under a contract;

(b) where any contract or enactment providing for the limitation of liability is applicable to the claim, the amount of damages recoverable by the claimant by virtue of this subsection shall not exceed the maximum limit so applicable.

(2) Where damages are recoverable by any person by virtue of the foregoing subsection subject to such reduction as is therein mentioned, the court shall find and record the total damages which would have been recoverable if the claimant had not been at fault.

...

(5) Where, in any case to which subsection (1) of this section applies, one of the persons at fault avoids liability to any other such person or his personal representative by pleading the Limitation Act 1939, or any other enactment limiting the time within which proceedings may be taken, he shall not be entitled to recover any damages ... from that other person or representative by virtue of the said subsection.

(6) Where any case to which subsection (1) of this section applies is tried with a jury, the jury shall determine the total damages which would have been recoverable if the claimant had not been at fault and the extent to which those damages are to be reduced.

...

4 Interpretation

The following expressions have the meanings hereby respectively assigned to them, that is to say—

'court' means, in relation to any claim, the court or arbitrator by or before whom the claim falls to be determined;

'damage' includes loss of life and personal injury;

...

'fault' means negligence, breach of statutory duty or other act or omission which gives rise to a liability in tort or would, apart from this Act, give rise to the defence of contributory negligence.

This section does not apply to any defences arising under a contractual claim.

'Fault' is defined in line with the common law that existed when the Act was implemented. This has meant that contributory negligence does not apply to intentional torts (as discussed at 12.5.3 above).

16.2.2 Elements of contributory negligence

There are three elements to contributory negligence:

(1) Was the claimant contributorily negligent?
(2) Did the contributory negligence contribute to the damage suffered?
(3) By how much should the damages be reduced as a consequence of the claimant's actions?

16.2.2.1 WAS THE CLAIMANT CONTRIBUTORILY NEGLIGENT?

Just as you have a duty of care to those around you, you also have a duty of care to yourself. The first element to consider is whether the claimant was contributorily negligent, ie was the damage partly the fault of the claimant and partly the fault of the defendant under s 1(1) of the Law Reform (Contributory Negligence) Act 1945? The concept of 'fault' is defined in s 4 as: 'negligence, breach of statutory duty or other act or omission which gives rise to a liability in tort or would, apart from this Act, give rise to the defence of contributory negligence'. This has been defined broadly, for example in *Reeves v Commissioner of Police of the Metropolis.* In this case, the House of Lords held that both the intentional act of the deceased and the negligent actions of the police contributed to the deceased's suicide. The damages awarded to the deceased's partner were reduced by 50% on the basis that the deceased's suicide was contributory negligence under the 1945 Act. The majority of the House of Lords applied a 'common sense' test to determining fault, as opposed to requiring evidence of a specific negligent act.

Reeves v Commissioner of Police of the Metropolis [1999] UKHL 35, [2000] 1 AC 360 (Lord Hoffmann)

Plainly Mr. Lynch's act in committing suicide would not have given rise to liability in tort. That part of the definition is concerned with fault on the part of the defendant. The question is whether, apart from the Act, it would have given rise to a defence of contributory negligence. I recognise, of course, that it is odd to describe Mr. Lynch as having been negligent. He acted intentionally and intention is a different state of mind from negligence. On the other hand, the 'defence of contributory negligence' at common law was based upon the view that a plaintiff whose failure to take care for his own safety was a cause of his injury could not sue. One would therefore have thought that the defence applied a fortiori to a plaintiff who intended to injure himself. The late *Professor Glanville Williams*, in his book *Joint Torts and Contributory Negligence* (1951) (at p. 199) expressed the view that 'contributory intention should be a defence.' It is not surprising that there is little authority on the point, because the plaintiff's act in deliberately causing injury to himself is almost invariably regarded as negativing causal connection between any prior breach of duty by the defendant and the damage suffered by the plaintiff. The question can arise only in the rare case, such as the present, in which someone owes a duty to prevent, or take reasonable care to prevent, the plaintiff from deliberately causing injury to himself. Logically, it seems to me that Professor Glanville Williams is right.

Buxton L.J. took a different view and I must examine the reasons which he gave. First, he said, at p. 182 that there was no authority that the intentional act of the plaintiff could be 'fault' within the meaning of section 4 of the Act of 1945. This, as I have said, is true but, logically, I think it can be.

Secondly, he said that the conclusion that Mr. Lynch's act did not prevent the negligence of the police from being a cause of his death meant that his death could not have been partly as a result of his own fault and partly as a result of the fault of the police. The way he put it, at p. 182 was as follows:

> '... on the assumption that Mr. Lynch's alleged 'fault' is to have killed himself, did Mr. Lynch suffer death partly as a result of his killing himself and partly as a result of the defendants giving him an opportunity to kill himself, to adapt the terms of section 1 of the Act of 1945 to this case? The commonsense answer to a question posed in those terms is that given by the judge: that Mr. Lynch suffered death entirely as a result of his killing himself. That conclusion would however entail, and be the same as saying, that Mr. Lynch's act of self-destruction was in law a novus actus: which, as I have sought to demonstrate, is not the case.'

This reasoning seems to me fallacious. It is saying that because Mr. Lynch's own act did not negative the causal connection between the negligence of the police and his death, it would be inconsistent to say that he caused his own death at all. Neither logic nor common sense requires such a conclusion. Mr. Lynch's suicide did not prevent the breach of duty by the police from being a cause of his death but that does not mean that his suicide was not also a cause of his death. As I said in *Environment Agency (formerly National Rivers Authority) v. Empress Car Co. (Abertillery) Ltd.* [1998] 2 WLR 350, 358, 'one cannot give a common sense answer to a question of causation for the purposes of attributing responsibility without knowing the purpose and scope of the rule.' Because the police were under a duty to take reasonable care not to give Mr. Lynch the opportunity to kill himself, the common sense answer to the question whether their carelessness caused his death is yes. Because Mr. Lynch also had responsibility for his own life, the common sense answer to the question whether he caused his own death is yes. Therefore both causes contributed to his death and the Act of 1945 provides the means of reflecting this division of responsibility in the award of damages.

16.2.2.2 DID THE CONTRIBUTORY NEGLIGENCE CONTRIBUTE TO THE DAMAGE?

Once it has been established that the claimant had been contributorily negligent, the defendant must also show that the negligent act or omission contributed to the damage suffered. This is required by s 1(1) of the Law Reform (Contributory Negligence) Act 1945, which applies '[w]here any person suffers *damage as the result partly of his own fault* and partly of the fault of any other person or persons (emphasis added)'. This requirement is discussed further by Lord Denning in *Jones v Livox Quarries*.

Jones v Livox Quarries Ltd [1952] 2 QB 608, CA, 615–16 (Denning LJ) (footnotes omitted)

The facts are simple. The plaintiff rode on the towbar of a vehicle, which was a careless thing to do because of the danger that he might fall off. Later, whilst the vehicle was almost stationary, another vehicle negligently ran into him from the back as he stood on the towbar, and he was crushed between the two vehicles. The question is whether he was guilty of contributory negligence such as to reduce his damages. The case of *Davies v. Swan Motor Co. (Swansea) Ld.* has been much discussed before us. It has been said that the three judgments in that case do not proceed on precisely the same lines. That is true, but it is, I suggest, quite understandable, because the court was there feeling its way in difficult country. Since that time, however, the ground has been cleared considerably. It can now be safely asserted that the doctrine of last opportunity is obsolete; and also that contributory negligence does not depend on the existence of a duty. But the troublesome problem of causation still remains to be solved.

Although contributory negligence does not depend on a duty of care, it does depend on foreseeability. Just as actionable negligence requires the foreseeability of harm to others, so contributory negligence requires the foreseeability of harm to oneself. A person is guilty of contributory negligence if he ought reasonably to have foreseen that, if he did not act as a reasonable, prudent man, he might be hurt himself; and in his reckonings he must take into account the possibility of others being careless.

Once negligence is proved, then no matter whether it is actionable negligence or contributory negligence, the person who is guilty of it must bear his proper share of responsibility for the consequences. The consequences do not depend on foreseeability, but on causation. The question in every case is: What faults were there which caused the damage? Was his fault one of them? The necessity of causation is shown by the word 'result' in section 1 (1) of the Act of 1945, and it was accepted by this court in *Davies v. Swan Motor Co. (Swansea) Ld.*

There is no clear guidance to be found in the books about causation. All that can be said is that causes are different from the circumstances in which, or on which, they operate. The line between the two depends on the facts of each case. It is a matter of common sense more than anything else. In the present case, as the argument of Mr. Arthian Davies proceeded, it seemed to me that he sought to make foreseeability the decisive test of causation. He relied on the trial judge's statement that a man who rode on the towbar of the traxcavator 'ran the risk of being thrown off and no other risk.' That is, I think, equivalent to saying that such a man could reasonably foresee that he might be thrown off the traxcavator, but not that he might be crushed between it and another vehicle.

In my opinion, however, foreseeability is not the decisive test of causation. It is often a relevant factor, but it is not decisive.

…

In order to illustrate this question of causation, I may say that if the plaintiff, whilst he was riding on the towbar, had been hit in the eye by a shot from a negligent sportsman, I should have thought that the plaintiff's negligence would in no way be a cause of his injury. It would only be the circumstance in which the cause operated. It would only be part of the history. But I cannot say that in the present case. The man's negligence here was so much mixed up with his injury that it cannot be dismissed as mere history. His dangerous position on the vehicle was one of the causes of his damage just as it was in *Davies v. Swan Motor Co. (Swansea) Ld.*

16.2.2.3 HOW SHOULD THE DAMAGES BE APPORTIONED?

The final question for contributory negligence is how the damages awarded by the court should be apportioned between the two parties. The Law Reform (Contributory Negligence) Act 1945 highlights two issues that should be considered: (1) what is 'just and equitable', and (2) what was the claimant's share in the responsibility for the damage. This creates a relationship between the second and third element of the contributory negligent test, which is outlined by Lord Denning in *Davies v Swan Motor Co (Swansea) Ltd* where his Lordship stated:

> Whilst causation is the decisive factor in determining whether there should be a reduced amount payable to the plaintiff, nevertheless, the amount of the reduction does not depend solely on the degree of causation. The amount of the reduction is such an amount as may be found by the court to be 'just and equitable' having regard to the claimant's 'share in the responsibility' for the damage. This involves a consideration, not only of the causative potency of a particular factor, but also of its blameworthiness.[8]

Therefore, the courts will consider both the causative potency and moral blameworthiness. An excellent example of how these two factors work together is *Froom v Butcher*. In this case, the claimant was injured in a car accident with the defendant, which was a result of the defendant's negligent driving. The defendant admitted liability but argued that the injuries were largely the result of the claimant's failure to wear a seatbelt and damages should be reduced accordingly. The trial judge rejected this argument and held that a failure to wear a seatbelt is not sufficient for a finding of contributory negligence and the reduction of damages. The defendant appealed to the Court of Appeal where (again!) Lord Denning MR gave the lead judgment and provided very helpful directions for how to address apportionment in contributory negligence situations.

8 *Davies v Swan Motor Co (Swansea) Ltd* [1949] 2 KB 291, CA, 326 (Denning LJ).

Froom v Butcher [1976] QB 286, CA, 384, 387–88 (Lord Denning MR)

The cause of the damage

In these seat belt cases, the injured plaintiff is in no way to blame for the accident itself. Sometimes he is an innocent passenger sitting beside a negligent driver who goes off the road. At other times he is an innocent driver of one car which is run into by the bad driving of another car which pulls out on to its wrong side of the road. It may well be asked: why should the injured plaintiff have his damages reduced? The accident was solely caused by the negligent driving of the defendant. Sometimes outrageously bad driving. It should not lie in his mouth to say: 'You ought to have been wearing a seat belt.' That point of view was strongly expressed in *Smith v. Blackburn* [1974] R.T.R. 533, 536 by O'Connor J.:

> '... the idea that the insurers of a grossly negligent driver should be relieved in any degree from paying what is proper compensation for injuries is an idea that offends ordinary decency. Until I am forced to do so by higher authority I will not so rule.'

I do not think that is the correct approach. The question is not what was the cause of the accident. It is rather what was the cause of the damage. In most accidents on the road the bad driving, which causes the accident, also causes the ensuing damage. But in seat belt cases the cause of the accident is one thing. The cause of the damage is another. The *accident* is caused by the bad driving. The *damage* is caused in part by the bad driving of the defendant, and in part by the failure of the plaintiff to wear a seat belt. If the plaintiff was to blame in not wearing a seat belt, the damage is in part the result of his own fault. He must bear some share in the responsibility for the damage: and his damages fall to be reduced to such extent as the court thinks just and equitable.

...

The share of responsibility

Whenever there is an accident, the negligent driver must bear by far the greater share of responsibility. It was his negligence which caused the accident. It also was a prime cause of the whole of the damage. But in so far as the damage might have been avoided or lessened by wearing a seat belt, the injured person must bear some share. But how much should this be? Is it proper to inquire whether the driver was grossly negligent or only slightly negligent? or whether the failure to wear a seat belt was entirely inexcusable or almost forgivable? If such an inquiry could easily be undertaken, it might be as well to do it. In *Davies v. Swan Motor Co. (Swansea) Ltd.* [1949] 2 K.B. 291, 326, the court said that consideration should be given not only to the causative potency of a particular factor, but also its blameworthiness. But we live in a practical world. In most of these cases the liability of the driver is admitted, the failure to wear a seat belt is admitted, the only question is: what damages should be payable? This question should not be prolonged by an expensive inquiry into the degree of blameworthiness on either side, which would be hotly disputed. Suffice it to assess a share of responsibility which will be just and equitable in the great majority of cases.

> Sometimes the evidence will show that the failure made no difference. The damage would have been the same, even if a seat belt had been worn. In such case the damages should not be reduced at all. At other times the evidence will show that the failure made all the difference. The damage would have been prevented altogether if a seat belt had been worn. In such cases I would suggest that the damages should be reduced by 25 per cent. But often enough the evidence will only show that the failure made a considerable difference. Some injuries to the head, for instance, would have been a good dead less severe if a seat belt had been worn, but there would still have been some injury to the head. In such case I would suggest that the damages attributable to the failure to wear a seat belt should be reduced by 15 per cent.

16.3 *Volenti*

Volenti non fit injuria (*volenti*), unlike contributory negligence, provides a complete defence to tort claims. This means that if a defendant can establish *volenti*, the claim will be defeated, and no damages will be awarded. *Volenti* translates as 'to a willing person, no injury is done', and the defence was described by Lord Shaw in *Letang v Ottawa Electric Railway Co* as '[i]f the defendants desire to succeed on the ground that the maxim *volenti non fit injuria* is applicable, they must obtain a finding of fact that the plaintiff freely and voluntarily, with full knowledge of the nature and extent of the risk he ran, impliedly agreed to incur it'.[9]

16.3.1 Justifications for *volenti*

Volenti is a controversial defence that has been heavily criticised by academics and judges. The justification for the defence was discussed by the House of Lords in *Smith v Baker*.

Smith v Baker & Sons [1891] AC 325, HL, 360, 362 (Lord Herschell)

> It was said that the maxim, 'Volenti non fit injuria,' applied, and effectually precluded the plaintiff from recovering. The maxim is founded on good sense and justice. One who has invited or assented to an act being done towards him cannot, when he suffers from it, complain of it as a wrong. The maxim has no special application to the case of employer and employed, though its application may well be invoked in such a case. The principle embodied in the maxim has sometimes, in relation to cases of employer and employed, been stated thus: – A person who is engaged to perform a dangerous operation takes upon himself the risks incident thereto. To the proposition thus stated there is no difficulty in giving an assent, provided that what is meant by engaging to perform a dangerous operation, and by the risks incident thereto, be properly defined. The neglect of such definition may lead to error.
>
> …

9 [1926] AC 725, 731, citing *Osborne v London and North Western Railway Co* (1888) 21 QBD 220, 224 (Willis J).

Where, then, a risk to the employed, which may or may not result in injury, has been created or enhanced by the negligence of the employer, does the mere continuance in service, with knowledge of the risk, preclude the employed, if he suffer from such negligence, from recovering in respect of his employer's breach of duty? I cannot assent to the proposition that the maxim, 'Volenti non fit injuria,' applies to such a case, and that the employer can invoke its aid to protect him from liability for his wrong.

It is quite clear that the contract between employer and employed involves on the part of the former the duty of taking reasonable care to provide proper appliances, and to maintain them in a proper condition, and so to carry on his operations as not to subject those employed by him to unnecessary risk. Whatever the dangers of the employment which the employed undertakes, amongst them is certainly not to be numbered the risk of the employer's negligence, and the creation or enhancement of danger thereby engendered. If, then, the employer thus fails in his duty towards the employed, I do not think that because he does not straightway refuse to continue his service, it is true to say that he is willing that his employer should thus act towards him. I believe it would be contrary to fact to assert that he either invited or assented to the act or default which he complains of as a wrong, and I know of no principle of law which compels the conclusion that the maxim, 'Volenti non fit injuria,' becomes applicable.

It was suggested in the course of the argument that the employed might, on account of special risk in his employment, receive higher wages, and that it would be unjust that in such a case he should seek to make the employer liable for the result of the accident. I think that this might be so. If the employed agreed, in consideration of special remuneration, or otherwise, to work under conditions in which the care which the employer ought to bestow, by providing proper machinery or otherwise, to secure the safety of the employed, was wanting, and to take the risk of their absence, he would no doubt be held to his contract, and this whether such contract were made at the inception of the service or during its continuance.

16.3.2 Application of *volenti*

To establish *volenti*, the defendant must show that the claimant (1) voluntarily agreed to take the risk, and (2) knew the full nature and extent of the risk involved.

With regards to the first requirement, Lord Denning outlined the high level of proof required in *Nettleship v Weston* when he stated:

> Nothing will suffice short of an agreement to waive any claim for negligence. The plaintiff must agree, expressly or impliedly, to waive any claim for any injury that may befall him due to the lack of reasonable care by the defendant: or, more accurately, due to the failure of the defendant to measure up to the standard of care that the law requires of him.[10]

10 *Nettleship v Weston* [1971] 2 QB 691, CA, 701 (Lord Denning MR).

Whilst a high level of agreement is clearly needed, what this actually entails remains frustratingly vague, as outlined by Gordon.

DM Gordon, 'Wrong Turns in the *Volens* Cases' (1945) 61 *LQR* 140, 140

> Few branches of English case law are as confused and inconsistent as the decisions on a man's right to complain of physical injury after he has knowingly incurred danger. When knowledge of danger precludes complaint should be an elementary question. But the Courts have yet to find us convincing answers. Even text-writers who feel free to theorize on what the law should be, have been no more successful in giving us the answers.

Some cases have developed clearer principles in specific situations, for example:

(1) The risk associated with rescuing another will not suffice for a successful claim in *volenti*.[11]

(2) People engaging in inherently dangerous sporting activities will not voluntarily consent to injuries arising from actions 'which fell far below the standards which might reasonably be expected in anyone pursuing the game'.[12]

(3) Voluntariness will also not be found if the claimant had consumed so much alcohol and/or drugs[13] or was suffering from any sort of mental incapacity[14] that meant that they were unable to understand (and therefore accept) the nature of the risk.

(4) Generally, *volenti* will not apply in cases where the claimant committed suicide due to the negligence of the defendant (however, damages can be reduced on the basis of contributory negligence if appropriate).[15]

The second element, that the claimant knew the full nature and extent of the risk involved, is strict in requiring that the defendant must show the claimant was aware of *the specific risks*. This was highlighted by Asquith J in *Dann v Hamilton*. In this case, the claimant knowingly got into the car with a driver who had consumed significant amounts of alcohol. There was another passenger in the car who refused to go any further with the driver and warned the claimant that she should also get out of the car, but the claimant continued the journey. The driver then had an accident in which he was killed, and the claimant was injured. The court had to consider whether the *volenti* defence applied to the claimant's actions, especially as she had been specifically warned of the risk of continuing the journey with the driver.

---

11 *Haynes v Harwood* [1935] 1 KB 146, CA.

12 *Condon v Basi* [1985] 1 WLR 866, CA, 869 (Donaldson MR); *Wooldridge v Sumner* [1963] 2 QB 43, CA, 57 (Sellers LJ).

13 *Morris v Murray* [1991] 2 QB 6, CA.

14 *Kirkham v Chief Constable of the Greater Manchester* [1990] 2 QB 283, CA; *Corr v IBC Vehicles* [2008] UKHL 13, [2008] AC 884.

15 *Reeves v Commissioner of Police of the Metropolis* [2000] 1 AC 360.

Dann v Hamilton [1939] 1 KB 509, 515–19 (Asquith J.) (footnotes omitted)

The maxim [of *volenti*] undoubtedly applies in many cases of pure tort, but case law in this field is very scanty. This is not, perhaps, because its application is rare in this field, but because in a large class of cases its applicability is so obvious as not to be brought to the test of litigation.

…

Where a dangerous physical condition has been brought about by the negligence of the defendant, and, after it has arisen, the plaintiff, fully appreciating its dangerous character, elects to assume the risk thereof, the maxim has often been held to apply, and to protect the defendant. Instances are *Torrance v. Ilford Urban District Council* and the more recent *Cutler v. United Dairies (London), Ld.* Where, however, the act of the plaintiff relied on as a consent precedes, and is claimed to license in advance, a possible subsequent act of negligence by the defendant – and this, I think, was the case Beven had in mind – the case may well be different. Here, *Smith v. Baker* does not help as much as might be expected. In any case it turned on contract, which is not in question here.

…

I find it difficult to believe, although I know of no authority directly in point, that a person who voluntarily travels as a passenger in a vehicle driven by a driver who is known by the passenger to have driven negligently in the past is volens as to future negligent acts of such driver, even though he could have chosen some other form of transport if he had wished. Then, to take the last step, suppose that such a driver is likely to drive negligently on the material occasion, not because he is known to the plaintiff to have driven negligently in the past, but because he is known to the plaintiff to be under the influence of drink. That is the present case. Ought the result to be any different? After much debate I have come to the conclusion that it should not, and that the plaintiff, by embarking in the car, or re-entering it, with knowledge that through drink the driver had materially reduced his capacity for driving safely, did not impliedly consent to, or absolve the driver from liability for any subsequent negligence on his part whereby she might suffer harm.

There may be cases in which the drunkenness of the driver at the material time is so extreme and so glaring that to accept a lift from him is like engaging in an intrinsically and obviously dangerous occupation, intermeddling with an unexploded bomb or walking on the edge of an unfenced cliff. It is not necessary to decide whether in such a case the maxim 'volenti non fit injuria' would apply, for in the present case I find as a fact that the driver's degree of intoxication fell short of this degree. I therefore conclude that the defence fails, and the claim succeeds. I arrive at this conclusion with the less reluctance in that it would be unjust that the deceased man's estate should be protected from suit by the mere fact that he got drunk before committing the final act of negligence, whereas, if he had committed the same act when sober, his estate would have been liable. The deceased was in fact, at the material time, when the plaintiff re-entered the car, guilty of the criminal offence of being drunk in charge of a car, and, possibly, later, of the further criminal offence of manslaughter. According to some authorities this in itself would be sufficient to exclude the operation of the maxim 'volenti non fit injuria.' However, this seems to me to be open to question, and I prefer to base the present judgment on the grounds I have indicated.

Prior to 1988, a significant number of the *volenti* cases involved road traffic accidents – often when a passenger voluntarily got into a car with a drunk driver. However, this changed when s 149 of the Road Traffic Act 1988 was enacted, which removed the application of the common law *volenti* defence from motor vehicle accidents.

Road Traffic Act 1988

149 Avoidance of certain agreements as to liability towards passengers

(1) This section applies where a person uses a motor vehicle ...

...

(3) The fact that a person so carried has willingly accepted as his the risk of negligence on the part of the user shall not be treated as negativing any such liability of the user.

The defence of *volenti* is no longer relevant in the context of road traffic accidents. However, it is still applicable to other vehicles, and the defence was successfully pleaded in *Morris v Murray*. In this case, the claimant accepted a flight in a friend's light aircraft despite being aware that the friend had consumed a considerable amount of alcohol that day. The plane crashed, killing the pilot and seriously injuring the claimant. The autopsy revealed that the pilot had consumed the equivalent of 17 whiskies before flying. Fox LJ referred to Asquith J's comments about the extreme and glaring case in *Dann v Hamilton*, stating that '[t]he question before us … [is] whether this present case is one of them'.[16] After considering the facts of the case, he held that the facts in *Morris v Murray* did meet the requirements for the *volenti* defence.

Morris v Murray [1991] 2 QB 6, CA, 16–17 (Fox LJ)

If the plaintiff had himself been sober on the afternoon of the flight it seems to me that, by agreeing to be flown by Mr. Murray, he must be taken to have accepted fully the risk of serious injury. The danger was both obvious and great. He could not possibly have supposed that Mr. Murray, who had been drinking all the afternoon, was capable of discharging a normal duty of care.

16 [1991] 2 QB 6 at 13.

But as he himself had been drinking, can it be assumed that he was capable of appreciating the risks? The matter was not very deeply examined at the trial, but he was certainly not 'blind drunk.' In cross-examination, he agreed with the description 'merry.' He was capable of driving a car from the Blue Boar to the airfield; and he did so for the purpose of going on a flight with Mr. Murray. He helped to start the aircraft and fuel it.

...

In my opinion, on the evidence the plaintiff knew that he was going on a flight; he knew that he was going to be piloted by Mr. Murray; and he knew that Mr. Murray had been drinking heavily that afternoon. The plaintiff's actions that afternoon, from leaving the Blue Boar to the take off, suggest that he was capable of understanding what he was doing. There is no clear evidence to the contrary. I think he knew what he was doing and was capable of appreciating the risks. I do not overlook that the plaintiff's evidence was that, if he had been sober, he would not have gone on the flight. That is no doubt so but it does not establish that he was in fact incapable of understanding what he was doing that afternoon.

If he was capable of understanding what he was doing, then the fact is that he knowingly and willingly embarked on a flight with a drunken pilot. The flight served no useful purpose at all; there was no need or compulsion to join it. It was just entertainment. The plaintiff co-operated fully in the joint activity and did what he could to assist it. He agreed in evidence that he was anxious to start the engine and to fly. A clearer source of great danger could hardly be imagined. The sort of errors of judgment which an intoxicated pilot may make are likely to have a disastrous result. The high probability was that Mr. Murray was simply not fit to fly an aircraft. Nothing that happened on the flight itself suggests otherwise, from the take off downwind to the violence of the manoeuvres of the plane in flight.

...

I think that in embarking upon the flight the plaintiff had implicitly waived his rights in the event of injury consequent on Mr. Murray's failure to fly with reasonable care.

16.3.3 Criticisms of *volenti*

Despite *volenti* being an accepted common law defence for tort claims, it is rarely invoked and successful on even fewer occasions. The defence has been subject to significant criticisms and calls for reform, including recently by Gardner.

Jodi Gardner, 'Rethinking Risk-taking: the Death of *Volenti*?' (2023) 82 *CLJ* 110, 115–16, 118, 120, 136 (footnotes omitted)

[I]t is contended that the basis of *volenti* – that someone knowingly accepts the risk of being harmed – is an intrinsically troubling principle. A significant portion of the factual scenarios of the *volenti* cases involve imbalances of power; employee and employer, passenger and driver, doctor and patient, consumer and business. A tort law defence that allows people's claims to be denied on the basis that they agreed to the risk may involve turning a blind eye towards structural inequalities of power that exist in our society. Those who have less in life will more often be required to accept risks than others who have greater resources or power. People with less choice in their lives are, for example, more likely to accept work in inherently dangerous situations simply because they have few or no alternative choices.

The relationship between risk-taking and inequality is clearly shown in the (now thankfully abolished) doctrine of common employment. The policy implications of this principle were succinctly captured in *Thrussell v Handyside*, when Hawkins J. said: 'his poverty, not his will' accepted this risk.

…

The second limitation of the application of *volenti* relates to the tension between the common law of tort and developments in contract law. The defence is at odds with the current approach to exclusion of liability in contract law …

…

The third key concern of the *volenti* defence is that it accepts the notion of the claimant agreeing to the risk without adequate analysis of whether they were *genuinely* and *voluntarily* willing to run the risk of the defendant's negligence. Liberal tradition has conventionally placed great importance on people's freedom to undertake obligations voluntarily, valuing (and in turn shaping) the legal practice of recognising and enforcing these obligations. This is however an oversimplification and further critique is necessary. As outlined by Atiyah, agreeing to something 'without inquiry into the reasons for which the [agreement] was given, seems a barren thing. It is, indeed, an example of formal reasoning, which can easily become formalistic if not fetishistic, to insist that [agreement] must bind, no matter what the reasons'.

…

The final limitation of *volenti* is related to the practicalities of keeping such a defence as part of the current legal system. The utility of *volenti*, has been significantly circumscribed in three key ways. First, the enactment of the Law Reform (Contributory Negligence) Act 1945 has meant that cases are more likely to result in damages being apportioned on the grounds of contributory negligence than defeated by a successful plea of *volenti*. Lord Denning acknowledged as much when he said: 'now that contributory negligence is not a complete defence, but only a ground for reducing the damages, the defence of *volenti non fit injuria*… has been severely limited.' Second, the modernisation of employment rights and obligations has restricted the application of the *volenti* defence in dangerous workplaces. Finally, the Road Traffic Act 1988 removed the applicability of the defence to motor vehicle accidents on public roads. Between them, these reforms have had a profound practical impact on the application of the defence. …

…

The limitations of *volenti* are widely accepted and have been used to minimise the scope of the defence on many different levels. However, in light of the inherent difficulties associated with it, instead of renaming the defence, it would surely be better to abolish it completely. It will ensure a more appropriate approach and way of thinking about the cases and about risk-taking in society. This is the best of all worlds; providing more clarity and coherence, responding to the concerns about inequality and excluding the undesirable aspects of an inappropriate tort law defence, whilst also ensuring that if the elements of the tort are not made out, defendants will not be held liable.

Question to consider: '*Volenti* is based on unjustified notions of people agreeing to risks, leads to harmful outcomes, and does not fit modern approaches to tort liability.' Discuss.

Other resources: *Thrussell v Handyside & Co* (1888) 20 QBD 359, DC; *Bowater v Rowley Regis Corp* [1944] KB 476; DM Gordon, 'Wrong Turns in the *Volens* Cases' (1945) 61 *LQR* 140; *Imperial Chemical Industries Ltd v Shatwell* [1965] AC 656; *Nettleship v Weston* [1971] 2 QB 691, CA; Richard Kidner, 'The Variable Standard of Care, Contributory Negligence and *Volenti*' (1991) 11 *LS* 1.

16.4 Illegality

The final defence to consider is illegality. The defence of illegality is based on the maxim of *ex turpi causa non oritur actio*, which translates as 'no cause of action may be founded on an illegal act'.

16.4.1 Rationale for illegality

The exact rationale behind the illegality defence and when it should apply have been subject to ongoing debate. There has been significant academic and judicial commentary about the role of illegality, with the Law Commission publishing *The Illegality Defence: A Consultative Report* in 2009.[17] Six potential rationales were considered in this report: '(1) furthering the purpose of the rule which the claimant's illegal behaviour has infringed; (2) consistency; (3) the need to prevent the claimant profiting from his or her own wrong; (4) deterrence; (5) maintaining the integrity of the legal system; and (6) punishment'.[18] However, there is a significant focus on the

17 Law Commission, *The Illegality Defence: A Consultative Report* (Law Com CP No 189, 2009).

18 ibid [2.5].

rationales of consistency and integrity within the legal system,[19] alongside ensuring that the legal system does not 'give with one hand what it takes away with another, nor condone when facing right what it condemns when facing left'.[20]

Hall v Herbert [1993] 2 SCR 159, 1993 CanLII 141, 177–90 (McLachlin J)

There may be cases where the principle of *ex turpi causa* should be invoked to prevent tort recovery which do not fall under the category of profit from illegality. Professor Weinrib, *supra*, suggests that the defence of *ex turpi causa* may properly be invoked to prevent the 'stultification of the criminal law' or 'evasion of the consequences of the criminal law': at pp. 52–53. He gives the example of a burglar who, due to his partner's negligence, is caught and required to pay a fine. Such a person, he suggests, should be barred from recovering damages for the fine from his partner. Weinrib states that this result could be justified either by saying that one criminal owes no duty to another, or by recourse to the maxim *ex turpi causa non oritur actio*.

...

While this example cannot be explained in terms of profit, since the claim is one of compensation for a fine incurred, it does accord with what I have called the more fundamental rationale for the defence of *ex turpi causa*, that based on the need to maintain internal consistency in the law, in the interest of promoting the integrity of the justice system. Again we have a situation where permitting recovery in tort would amount to the law's giving with one hand what it takes away with the other. Again it can be said that to permit the claim would be to create 'an intolerable fissure in the law's conceptually seamless web.'

There is weighty authority which supports the proposition that the preservation of the integrity of the justice system is the true rationale for the defence of illegality associated with the maxim *ex turpi causa non oritur actio*.

...

Cory J. does not deny the importance of the integrity of the justice system as a rationale for the defence. He does, however, argue at p. 216 that such a rationale may be too broad, since it is difficult to distinguish in many cases between what Ford, *infra*, terms 'public and merely judicial outrage', and he adopts the warnings of Ford that 'moral indignation must not be mistaken for public policy'. On the other hand, he points out that tort awards have been properly made in many cases where the plaintiff's conduct might have offended

19 *Patel v Mirza* [2016] UKSC 42, [2017] AC 467, [120] (Lord Toulson).
20 *Hounga v Allen* [2014] UKSC 47, [2014] 1 WLR 2889, [55] (Lord Hughes).

a judge. It seems to me that the narrow form of the rationale which I have developed, premised on the need to prevent internal inconsistency in the law, does not attract this criticism. It is not the judge's outrage but a concern for the coherence of the legal system which he or she administers which is operative.

I add a comment on the criteria of 'joint criminal activity', which has sometimes been invoked as a condition of the application of ex turpi causa as a defence: see *Tomlinson v. Harrison*, [1972] 1 O.R. 670, and *Tallow v. Tailfeathers, supra*. Other courts have refused to adopt this requirement, arguing against its anomalous and 'paradoxical result': see, for example, the comments of Lambert J.A. in *Betts v. Sanderson Estate, supra*, at p. 12. When the *ex turpi causa* rule is understood to be based on the need to maintain the integrity of our system of law, it becomes clear that there is no reason to insist that both the plaintiff and the defendant have been involved in the criminal or immoral activity in order that the *ex turpi causa maxim* operate.

I conclude that there is a need in the law of tort for a principle which permits judges to deny recovery to a plaintiff on the ground that to do so would undermine the integrity of the justice system. The power is a limited one. Its use is justified where allowing the plaintiff's claim would introduce inconsistency into the fabric of the law, either by permitting the plaintiff to profit from an illegal or wrongful act, or to evade a penalty prescribed by criminal law. Its use is not justified where the plaintiff's claim is merely for compensation for personal injuries sustained as a consequence of the negligence of the defendant. I turn now to the question of the form in which this principle should be cast.

16.4.2 Elements of illegality

There are three elements to the illegality defence:

(1) the claimant has engaged in illegal or immoral behaviour;
(2) there was a sufficient link between the illegal behaviour and the tort; and
(3) when considering all the relevant factors, the claim should be defeated.

16.4.2.1 ILLEGAL OR IMMORAL BEHAVIOUR

The first element is that the claimant must have engaged in illegal or immoral behaviour. This does have to have a certain level of seriousness, as not every illegal or immoral activity should stop a claim in tort law. For example, what if an individual has parked illegally and a third party runs into their car because they were driving under the influence of alcohol? Most people would not believe that the illegal parking was sufficient to deny their claim for property damage and potentially personal injury.

Sir Murray Stuart-Smith highlighted in *Vellino v Chief Constable of the Greater Manchester Police* that criminal activities must be sufficiently serious for the defence to be applicable. When determining what would be 'sufficiently serious', his Lordship highlighted that '[g]enerally speaking a crime punishable with imprisonment could be expected to qualify'.[21] Therefore, it is important to first identify if the claimant had engaged in any illegal or seriously immoral conduct before proceeding to see if this conduct is sufficiently linked to their tort claim.

16.4.2.2 SUFFICIENT CONNECTION

The next element to show is that there was a sufficient connection between the illegal behaviour and the tort cause of action. This has caused ongoing confusion and difficulties, as the court has had to determine what is considered a 'sufficient connection' in a wide range of cases. Lord Asquith discussed this difficulty in *National Coal Board v England*.

National Coal Board v England **[1954] AC 403, HL, 428–29 (Lord Asquith) (footnotes omitted)**

The defendants relied on the maxim 'ex turpi causa non oritur actio' as absolving them of liability.

The short answer to this contention has no doubt been found by those of your Lordships who pointed out the definition of 'fault' in the Law Reform (Contributory Negligence) Act, 1945. But for myself I should have decided in the same sense in the absence of any such definition. The vast majority of cases in which the maxim has been applied have been cases where, there being an illegal agreement between A and B, either seeks to sue the other for its enforcement or for damages for its breach. That, of course, is not this case. Cases where an action in tort has been defeated by the maxim are exceedingly rare. Possibly a party to an illegal prize fight who is damaged in the conflict cannot sue for assault (*Boulter v. Clark*). But it seems to me in principle that the plaintiff cannot be precluded from suing simply because the wrongful act is committed after the illegal agreement is made and during the period involved in its execution.

The act must, I should have supposed, at least be a step in the execution of the common illegal purpose. If two burglars, A and B, agree to open a safe by means of explosives, and A so negligently handles the explosive charge as to injure B, B might find some difficulty in maintaining an action for negligence against A. But if A and B are proceeding to the premises which they intend burglariously to enter, and before they enter them, B picks A's pocket and steals his watch, I cannot prevail on myself to believe that A could not sue in tort (provided he had first prosecuted B for larceny). The theft is totally unconnected with the burglary.

---

21 [2001] EWCA Civ 1249, [2002] 1 WLR 218, [70] (Sir Murray Stuart-Smith).

16.4.2.3 BALANCING OF FACTORS

The final aspect to consider is the 'balancing of factors' requirement. Once the first two elements have been shown, the question arises – should every tort law claim be defeated (the 'rule-based approach'), or should the courts have discretion to consider the situation and only defeat claims where they think it is appropriate (the 'range of factors approach'). Both of these approaches have their own benefits and detriments; the rule-based test provides more certainty for parties, but the range of factors approach is arguably fairer and provides the courts with a level of discretion on when to apply a claim-defeating defence.

However, the Supreme Court could not agree on which approach should be taken. As a result, the English law's approach to the illegality defence was unsettled for a period. The lack of agreement resulted from an unusual situation, with the Supreme Court considering the matter in four cases within three years: *Hounga v Allen*,[22] *Les Laboratoires Servier v Apotex Inc*,[23] *Bilta (UK) Ltd v Nazir (No 2)*[24] and *Patel v Mirza*. These cases – and the different judgments in each case – went back and forth between the rule-based approach and the range of factors approach. The final case, *Patel v Mirza*, was heard with a bench of nine and provided some much-needed clarity to the situation. The Supreme Court was unanimous in relation to the case's result, and six judges came down strongly in favour of the range of factors approach.

Patel v Mirza [2016] UKSC 42, [2017] AC 467, [107]–[108] (Lord Toulson), [259], [261], [263] (Lord Sumption)

107. In considering whether it would be disproportionate to refuse relief to which the claimant would otherwise be entitled, as a matter of public policy, various factors may be relevant. Professor Burrows' list is helpful but I would not attempt to lay down a prescriptive or definitive list because of the infinite possible variety of cases. Potentially relevant factors include the seriousness of the conduct, its centrality to the contract, whether it was intentional and whether there was marked disparity in the parties' respective culpability.

108. The integrity and harmony of the law permit – and I would say require – such flexibility. Part of the harmony of the law is its division of responsibility between the criminal and civil courts and tribunals. Punishment for wrongdoing is the responsibility of the criminal courts and, in some instances, statutory regulators.

…

22 [2014] UKSC 47, [2014] 1 WLR 2889.

23 [2014] UKSC 55, [2015] AC 430.

24 [2015] UKSC 23, [2016] AC 1.

259. ... Professor Burrows has proposed that the same solution should be adopted by judicial decision, in his *Restatement of the English Law of Contract* (2016). He would make the application of the illegality principle dependent, at any rate in contract cases, on a 'range of factors' approach. This would require the judge to assess whether to deny a remedy would be an 'appropriate response' to the claimant's conduct, taking account where relevant of eight factors. These factors are for the most part derived from the Law Commission's Consultative report: paras 8.3, 8.11. They are: (a) how seriously illegal or contrary to public policy the conduct was; (b) whether the party seeking enforcement knew of, or intended, the conduct; (c) how central to the contract or its performance the conduct was; (d) how serious a sanction the denial of enforcement is for the party seeking enforcement; (e) whether denying enforcement will further the purpose of the rule which the conduct has infringed; (f) whether denying enforcement will act as a deterrent to conduct that is illegal or contrary to public policy; (g) whether denying enforcement will ensure that the party seeking enforcement does not profit by the conduct; (h) whether denying enforcement will avoid inconsistency in the law, thereby maintaining the integrity of the legal system. Lord Toulson JSC, in his judgment on the present appeal, supports this approach while suggesting that yet further factors may also be relevant.

...

261. The real issue, as it seems to me, is whether the 'range of factors' identified by the Law Commission and Professor Burrows are to be regarded (i) as part of the policy rationale of a legal rule and the various exceptions to that rule, or (ii) as matters to be taken into account by a judge deciding in each case whether to apply the legal rule at all. As matters stand, the former approach represents the law. The latter would require the courts to 'weigh, or balance, the adverse consequences of respectively granting or refusing relief' on a case by case basis, which was the very proposition that the House of Lords unanimously rejected in *Tinsley v Milligan*. ...

...

263. The reason why the adoption of a 'range of factors' test on a case by case basis would be uncertain is obvious in the light of these considerations. An evaluative test dependent on the perceived relevance and relative weight to be accorded in each individual case to a large number of incommensurate factors leaves a great deal to a judge's visceral reaction to particular facts. Questions such as how illegal is illegality would admit of no predictable answer, even if the responses of different judges were entirely uniform. In fact, it is an inescapable truth that some judges are more censorious than others. Far from resolving the uncertainties created by recent differences of judicial opinion, the range of factors test would open a new era in this part of the law. A new body of jurisprudence would be gradually built up to identify which of a large range of factors should be regarded as relevant and what considerations should determine the weight that they should receive. No one factor would ever be decisive as a matter of law, only in some cases on their

particular facts. The size of the authorities bundles in this and other recent appeals to this court on the illegality principle is testimony to the volume of litigation which the principle has generated in every period of its history.

The facts of *Patel v Mirza* are of limited assistance, as the case was based on a contractual claim and the application of the illegality defence on this basis. However, this approach does apply to illegality in tort law, as confirmed by the Supreme Court in *Henderson v Dorset Healthcare University NHS Foundation Trust.*[25] *Hounga v Allen* provides a helpful example of the balance of factors approach in tort law. In this case, the claimant was a young Nigerian girl who had assumed a false identity to gain entry into the United Kingdom to work as an au pair for the defendants. During her 'employment', the claimant was subject to 'serious physical abuse', harassment, and discrimination by the defendants. She sued the defendants in tort, and they raised the illegality defence. The question before the Supreme Court was whether the illegality of the claimant's entry into the country and her subsequent employment barred her claim in tort. Lord Wilson provided some helpful guidance for how the illegality defence works in the tort law context.

Hounga v Allen [2014] UKSC 47, [2014] 1 WLR 2889, [42], [44]–[45], [48], [52] (Lord Wilson)

42. The defence of illegality rests on the foundation of public policy. 'The principle of public policy is this ...' said Lord Mansfield by way of preface to his classic exposition of the defence in *Holman v Johnson* (1775) 1 Cowp 341, 343. 'Rules which rest on the foundation of public policy, not being rules which belong to the fixed or customary law, are capable, on proper occasion, of expansion or modification': *Maxim Nordenfelt Guns and Ammunition Co v Nordenfelt* [1893] 1 Ch 630, 661 (Bowen LJ). So it is necessary, first, to ask 'What is the aspect of public policy which founds the defence?' and, second, to ask 'But is there another aspect of public policy to which application of the defence would run counter?'

...

44. Concern to preserve the integrity of the legal system is a helpful rationale of the aspect of policy which founds the defence even if the instance given by McLachlin J of where that concern is in issue may best be taken as an example of it rather than as the only conceivable instance of it. I therefore pose and answer the following questions: (a) Did the tribunal's award of compensation to Miss Hounga allow her to profit from her wrongful conduct in entering into the contract? No, it was an award of compensation for injury to feelings consequent on her dismissal, in particular the abusive nature of it.

25 [2020] UKSC 43, [2021] AC 563.

(b) Did the award permit evasion of a penalty prescribed by the criminal law? No, Miss Hounga has not been prosecuted for her entry into the contract and, even had a penalty been thus imposed on her, it would not represent evasion of it. (c) Did the award compromise the integrity of the legal system by appearing to encourage those in the situation of Miss Hounga to enter into illegal contracts of employment? No, the idea is fanciful. (d) Conversely, would application of the defence of illegality so as to defeat the award compromise the integrity of the legal system by appearing to encourage those in the situation of Mrs Allen to enter into illegal contracts of employment? Yes, possibly: it might engender a belief that they could even discriminate against such employees with impunity.

45. So the considerations of public policy which militate in favour of applying the defence so as to defeat Miss Hounga's complaint scarcely exist.

...

48. In her claim form Miss Hounga alleged that the UK Human Trafficking Centre had accepted her as a victim of human trafficking. Before the tribunal she filed a report on herself made by Ms Skrivankova, Trafficking Programme Co-ordinator, Anti-Slavery International, which intervenes in this appeal. The report must be handled with care because Ms Skrivankova did not interview Miss Hounga and relied on written material, in particular her witness statement, which included disputed allegations in relation to which the tribunal made no findings. At all events Ms Skrivankova reported that all the elements in the definition of trafficking in the Palermo Protocol were present in Miss Hounga's case. She suggested that it was a classic case of the trafficking of a vulnerable child, lacking family support, by people known to her, who abused her natural trust in them with promises which were not kept and who subjected her to forced labour.

...

52. ... the decision of the Court of Appeal to uphold Mrs Allen's defence of illegality to her complaint runs strikingly counter to the prominent strain of current public policy against trafficking and in favour of the protection of its victims. The public policy in support of the application of that defence, to the extent that it exists at all, should give way to the public policy to which its application is an affront; and Miss Hounga's appeal should be allowed.

16.4.3 Forms of illegality

There are two 'forms' (also referred to as 'rules' or 'claims'[26]) of the illegality defence; these forms have different consequences and underlying rationales. The narrower form prevents the claimant from obtaining damages for losses that flow

26 See, for instance, the discussion in *Gray v Thames Trains Ltd* [2009] UKHL 33, [2009] 1 AC 1339 and *Henderson v Dorset Healthcare University NHS Foundation Trust* [2020] UKSC 43, [2021] AC 563.

from the *criminal punishment imposed*. The justification for this prohibition is the avoidance of inconsistency between the criminal law and tort law. In contrast, the wider form prohibits the claimant from recovering compensation for losses which they have suffered as a *consequence of their criminal actions* and is based on policy grounds and public notions of the fair distribution of resources. The difference between the two forms of the illegality defence was discussed by the House of Lords in *Gray v Thames Trains*.

Gray v Thames Trains Ltd [2009] UKHL 33, [2009] 1 AC 1339, [32]–[33], [51]–[53] (Lord Hoffman)

32. The particular rule for which the appellants contend may, as I said, be stated in a wider or a narrow form. The wider and simpler version is that which was applied by Flaux J: you cannot recover for damage which is the consequence of your own criminal act. In its narrower form, it is that you cannot recover for damage which is the consequence of a sentence imposed upon you for a criminal act. I make this distinction between the wider and narrower version of the rule because there is a particular justification for the narrower rule which does not necessarily apply to the wider version.

33. I shall deal first with the narrower version, which was stated in general terms by Denning J in *Askey v Golden Wine Co Ltd* [1948] 2 All ER 35, 38:

> 'It is, I think, a principle of our law that the punishment inflicted by a criminal court is personal to the offender, and that the civil courts will not entertain an action by the offender to recover an indemnity against the consequences of that punishment.'

. . .

51. I must therefore examine a wider version of the rule, which was applied by Flaux J. This has the support of the reasoning of the Court of Appeal in *Clunis's* case [1998] QB 978 as well as other authorities. It differs from the narrower version in at least two respects: first, it cannot, as it seems to me, be justified on the grounds of inconsistency in the same way as the narrower rule. Instead, the wider rule has to be justified on the ground that it is offensive to public notions of the fair distribution of resources that a claimant should be compensated (usually out of public funds) for the consequences of his own criminal conduct. Secondly, the wider rule may raise problems of causation which cannot arise in connection with the narrower rule. The sentence of the court is plainly a consequence of the criminality for which the claimant was responsible. But other forms of damage may give rise to questions about whether they can properly be said to have been caused by his criminal conduct.

52. The wider principle was applied by the Court of Appeal in *Vellino v Chief Constable of the Greater Manchester* [2002] 1 WLR 218. The claimant was injured in consequence of jumping from a second-floor window to escape from the custody of the police. He sued

the police for damages, claiming that they had not taken reasonable care to prevent him from escaping. Attempting to escape from lawful custody is a criminal offence. The Court of Appeal (Schiemann LJ and Sir Murray Stuart-Smith; Sedley LJ dissenting) held that, assuming the police to have been negligent, recovery was precluded because the injury was the consequence of the plaintiff's unlawful act.

53. This decision seems to me based upon sound common sense. The question, as suggested in the dissenting judgment of Sedley LJ, is how the case should be distinguished from one in which the injury is a consequence of the plaintiff's unlawful act only in the sense that it would not have happened if he had not been committing an unlawful act.

The 'balance of factors' approach in *Patel v Mirza* raises the question of the relationship between the House of Lords' approach in *Gray v Thames Trains Ltd* and the narrow/wider form of the illegality defence. This situation was clarified (to a certain extent) in *Henderson v Dorset Healthcare University NHS Foundation Trust.*

Henderson v Dorset Healthcare University NHS Foundation Trust [2020] UKSC 43, [2021] AC 563, [89]–[96] (Lord Hamblen)

89. The appellant argues that the decision in *Gray* [2009] AC 1339 is an example of the now discredited rule-based approach to illegality and is contrary to the flexible policy-approach endorsed in *Patel* [2017] AC 467. It does not allow for the court to take into account the particular circumstances of the case, such as the degree of the claimant's personal responsibility. Nor does it allow for consideration of proportionality.

90. In my judgment, the essential reasoning in *Gray* is consistent with the approach adopted in *Patel. Gray* did not involve the reliance-based approach, nor did it follow or apply *Tinsley v Milligan* [1994] 1 AC 340. Indeed, at para 30 of his judgment Lord Hoffmann stated that such an approach was not helpful in that case, that it had 'nothing to do with whether there is the rule of law for which the appellants contend' and that the maxim ex turpi causa expresses a policy.

91. The court in *Gray* examined whether the narrower and the wider rules were, as was contended, 'a special rule of public policy'. As already explained, both Lord Hoffmann and Lord Rodger considered the policy reasons for the rules and concluded that they were justified as a matter of public policy. Even though Lord Hoffmann endorsed a causation approach to the application of the wider rule, that involved a causal rule based on policy considerations. As the Court of Appeal said at para 64 of its judgment, it was a 'combination of public policy and causation'.

> 92. In *Patel* Lord Toulson JSC stated at para 28 that in *Gray* the House of Lords 'held that public policy precluded him from recovering damages'. As he further observed at para 32:
>
> > 'The Law Commission drew from the various judgments a readiness on the part of the judges to examine the policy reasons which justified the application of the illegality defence and to explain why those policies applied to the facts of the case.'
>
> 93. *Gray* was correctly seen in *Patel* as being an example of a decision on illegality based on policy considerations rather than reliance. It was cited with apparent approval not only by Lord Toulson JSC at paras 28–32, but also by Lord Kerr JSC at para 129 and Lord Neuberger PSC at paras 153 and 155.
>
> 94. In addition, the fundamental policy consideration relied upon in *Gray* was the need for consistency so as to maintain the integrity of the legal system, the very matter that was held in *Patel* to be the underlying policy question.
>
> 95. It is correct to observe that *Gray* involved no express consideration of proportionality. In *Patel* that did not, however, cause any doubt to be cast on the correctness of the decision and, for reasons explained below, the factual circumstances in *Gray* do not give rise to any issue of proportionality.
>
> 96. The approach adopted by the House of Lords in *Gray* therefore provides no reason why it should be departed from. If anything, it points to the contrary conclusion.

The wider/narrower approach in *Gray* was therefore held to be '*Patel*-compliant' and should be applied to tort law illegality claims, in addition to the balance of factors approach.

16.4.4 Concluding thoughts on illegality

Illegality has a number of similarities with *volenti*; it is a controversial, complicated defence that – if successful – will defeat the claim in its entirety. Whilst the initial justifications sound convincing, the entire basis of illegality can be questioned in the context of tort law, where the aim of damages is to compensate the individual for the harm suffered. As Green outlines, there are strong arguments towards removing the defence's application in tort law. If the claimant's actions will be penalised by the criminal law, should they really suffer a double punishment by being barred from compensation for the harm suffered as a result of another's tortious actions?

Sarah Green, 'Illegality and Zero Sum Torts' in Sarah Green and Alan Bogg (eds), *Illegality After Patel v Mirza* (Hart Publishing, 2018) 187–212

Consider, for example, 'pure' strict liability offences. The criminal law has its reasons for convicting those whose culpability might be very low or even absent:

> If the object of the criminal law is to prevent the occurrence of socially damaging actions, it would be absurd to turn a blind eye to those which were due to carelessness, negligence, or even accident ... [A]s much and more damage is done by negligence, or by indifference to the welfare or safety of others, as by deliberate wickedness ... If the law says that certain things are not to be done, it is illogical to confine this prohibition to occasions on which they are done from malice aforethought.

This is the obvious point to make against the creation of a caput lupinum, but the difficulties do not end there. Whilst strict liability offences lack at least some element of mens rea, murder, for example, is an offence for which no excusatory defences are allowed. It is also an offence of ulterior intent, so that one can be convicted of murder without having had the intention to kill. Responsibility and culpability, therefore, are not necessarily coterminous where the offence applies, and yet the label and consequences of this crime do not differentiate between grades of morality. Given that a murder conviction brings with it a mandatory sentence of life imprisonment, there may well be cases in which the punishment is not in truth proportionate to the defendant's culpability. And yet it is the gravest of offences, and so an application of the range of factors approach is likely to result in the claimant having her tort claim denied in addition to her heavy criminal penalty. The first and third of the Patel factors in particular are likely to have the effect that, the graver the crime, the less likely the claimant is to be successful in her tort claim. We can see, however, that, given the rich and complex nature of the criminal law, those whose actions result in the most serious of consequences are not necessarily the most morally deficient members of society. For anyone, the denial of a tort claim in addition to a criminal penalty is in effect a double penalty. For those already treated in a heavy-handed way by the criminal law, the result is even more disproportionate.

That is not to suggest that those whose actions seriously impinge on, or destroy, the lives of others do not deserve a measure of punishment and censure, whatever their moral standing, but that the complexities of that question are amplified, rather than reduced, by bringing the law of tort to bear on it.

Question to consider: Is the illegality defence justified in tort law? If so, what justification (or justifications) is the most compelling?

Other resources: *Tinsley v Milligan* [1994] 1 AC 340, HL; James Goudkamp, 'The Defence of Illegality in Tort Law: Wither the Rule in *Pitts v Hunt*?' [2012] *CLJ* 481; *Les Laboratoires Servier v Apotex Inc* [2014] UKSC 55, [2015] AC 430; Nicholas McBride, 'The Defence of Illegality: Not a Principle of Justice?' in Sarah Green and Alan Bogg (eds), *Illegality After Patel v Mirza* (Hart Publishing, 2018) 85–106.

16.5 Conclusion

There are several defences in the common law of tort, and they work in different ways; some mean that there is no successful claim, some reduce the amount of damages award and others defeat an otherwise successful tort claim. A full consideration of all the tort law defences is not possible in this chapter. We have therefore focused on the three most commonly considered defences - contributory negligence, *volenti* and illegality - and outlined the elements, key cases, and main challenges associated with these defences. An understanding of these issues is crucial for problem questions but can also help to enliven essay questions on a wide variety of topics.

Chapter 17 DAMAGES

17.1 Introduction

Once the claimant has established their tort cause of action and, assuming no liability-defeating defence applies, the courts will need to consider what remedy is appropriate. In the vast majority of cases, this remedy will take the form of damages, which is the focus of this chapter. However, there is the potential for other remedies, such as an injunction or potentially specific performance (ie requiring the defendant to perform a specific action) for particular torts. These other remedies are particularly relevant for nuisance, the Protection from Harassment Act 1997, defamation, and privacy.[1]

The aim of damages in tort law is to put the claimant in the position they would have been in had the tort not been committed; therefore, tort law aims to restore the status quo. This can be contrasted to the expectation damages in contract law, which aims to place the claimant in the position they would have been in had the contractual obligations been fulfilled. Whilst this sounds straightforward, the courts have encountered numerous challenges – especially in light of the wide range of tort actions and harms suffered. The courts have to place monetary figures on the loss of limbs, sexual assault and harassment, loss of reputation, pain and suffering … the list goes on.

One particularly challenging case was *XX v Whittington Hospital NHS Trust*. The court had to consider what the appropriate level of damages was for negligent infertility, as the NHS Trust had not detected signs of cancer from the claimant's cervical screening tests in 2008 and 2012. When the cancer was detected in 2013, it was so advanced that the treatment made the claimant, who was 29 at the time, infertile. She was able to collect and freeze some eggs prior to her treatment, and it was probable – with the use of surrogacy – that she would be able to have two children with her own eggs. Commercial surrogacy is illegal in the UK but occurs in a number of other jurisdictions, including California. The claimant and her partner always wanted four children, so she claimed damages for the cost of two further children through commercial surrogacy in California with donor eggs. The NHS argued that this cost should not be awarded as it was against public policy.

---

1 See, for example, 10.2.2, 12.6.2, Chapters 13 and 14.

The Supreme Court held that the claimant was entitled to damages for the physical injuries of surgery and chemotherapy, long-term disabilities, and psychiatric injury, as well as the complete loss of fertility. The claimant was also entitled to damages for the cost of surrogacy arrangements, using her own eggs, and the cost of using donor eggs. The majority of the Supreme Court held that the claimant was also entitled to the cost of international commercial surrogacy.

XX v Whittington Hospital NHS Trust [2020] UKSC 14, [2021] AC 275, [1] (Lady Hale)

The object of damages in tort is to put the claimant, as far as possible, back in the position in which she would have been had the tort not been committed. Money has to compensate, as far as it can, for those injuries that cannot be cured.

17.2 Types of damages

Whilst the majority of damages awarded are compensatory damages, aimed at putting the claimant back in the position they would have been in had the tort not been committed, there are other forms of damages that can be awarded by the courts, namely nominal damages, aggravated damages, and exemplary damages. These are highlighted in the table below, but the rest of the chapter will focus on the different approaches to compensatory damages.

Table 17.1: Summary of damages

	Explanation	When awarded	Relevant cases
Nominal damages	Tokenistic damages are designed to highlight that a legal wrong has been committed but that no substantive harm has been suffered by the claimant.	Nominal damages are most often awarded in trespass to the person cases, which are actionable *per se* (ie without the need to prove that damage has actually been suffered).	False imprisonment: *R (Lumba) v Secretary of State for the Home Department.*[2]
Aggravated damages	Damages, which are still compensatory in nature, but are awarded at a higher level to compensate for the manner in which the tort was committed. These damages	Aggravated damages are not applicable to every tort as they are limited to causes of action in which the claimant's feelings are closely linked with the	Trespass to the person: *Appleton v Garrett.*[3] Breach of confidence: *Campbell v MGN Ltd.*[4]

2 [2011] UKSC 12, [2012] 1 AC 245.
3 (1995) 34 BMLR 23.
4 [2004] UKHL 22, [2004] 2 AC 457.

	Explanation	When awarded	Relevant cases
	are awarded because the court finds that the actions of the defendant have aggravated the injury to the claimant (generally to their feelings, personal autonomy and/or dignity).	actions, for example, trespass to the person, breach of confidence, and defamation.	Malicious prosecution: *Rowlands v Chief Constable of Merseyside Police*.[5]
Exemplary (or punitive) damages	Damages which are not focused on compensation but instead are intended to punish specifically harmful conduct by the defendant. Unlike compensatory damages, exemplary damages focus on the actions of the defendant as opposed to the harm suffered by the claimant. The application of these damages in tort law is controversial.	Three situations justify the award of exemplary damages: (1) oppressive, arbitrary or unconstitutional actions by government services, (2) conduct calculated to make a profit exceeding the compensable payment under the tort, (3) where these types of damages have been expressly authorised by statute.	Economic torts: *Rookes v Barnard*.[6] Defamation: *Cassell & Co Ltd v Broome*.[7] Malicious prosecution: *Kuddus v Chief Constable of Leicestershire Constabulary*.[8]

17.3 Property damage

Compensating property damage is, generally, the most straightforward head of loss in tort law, as the court can receive expert evidence on the cost of rectifying the damage suffered. The one area where controversy can occur is the appropriate measure of damages – the cost of cure (ie fixing the damage) or diminution in value (ie compensating the claimant for the reduction in value due to the damage). These measures can vary dramatically depending on the nature of the property damaged and the parties' intention.

In *Dodd Properties Ltd v Canterbury City Council*,[9] the Court of Appeal held that there was no hard and fast rule; instead, the specific facts of each case should be considered – particularly the claimant's future intentions with the property and what was reasonable in the circumstances. This was applied in *Southampton Container Terminals Ltd v Schiffahrtsgesellschaft 'Hansa Australia' MGH & Co*, where a crane was negligently damaged and could no longer be used.[10] The claimants sought

5 [2006] EWCA Civ 1773, [2007] 1 WLR 1065.
6 [1964] AC 1129, HL.
7 [1972] AC 1027, HL.
8 [2001] UKHL 29, [2002] 2 AC 122.
9 [1980] 1 WLR 433, CA.
10 [2001] EWCA Civ 717, [2001] 2 Lloyd's Rep 275.

£2.35 million in damages for the cost of replacing the crane, whereas the defendants argued that it should only have to pay £665,000 as this was the approximate market value of the damaged crane. On appeal, Lord Clarke upheld the lower court's judgment, which awarded the lesser value on the basis that, prior to the accident, the claimant had already ordered a new, larger crane.

17.4 Personal injury

Personal injury is a lot more complicated to compensate. Damages for personal injury are divided into 'pecuniary' losses (measured in quantifiable monetary terms) and 'non-pecuniary' losses (non-financial losses that cannot be easily quantified).

Table 17.2: Heads of Damages

Pecuniary losses	Relevant legal principles	Applicable laws
Medical and related expenses	If private medical care is utilised by the claimant, these costs can be claimed as damages. Claimants can claim for medical expenses not covered by the NHS, for example, dental, physiotherapy, specialist services and speech therapy.	Law Reform (Personal Injuries) Act 1948, s 2(4); *Lim Poh Choo v Camden and Islington Area Health Authority*[11]
Loss of earnings	Claimants can recover loss of net earnings, including past and future losses. The multiplier method will be used – ie the court will multiply the claimant's annual income by the number of years they had expected to work until retirement. However, the amount will be reduced as (a) the court will assume that the claimant will invest the lump sum, and (b) the 'vicissitudes of life'. Claimants can also recover damages for difficulties in finding a new job or a reduction of their position in the labour market.	*British Transport Commissioner v Gourley;*[12] *Smith v Manchester Corp*[13] Actuarial tables for use in personal injury cases
Past and future care needs	Claimants can recover the cost of professional care. However, a complication arises when family or friends provide the care. In this case, the damages will be awarded to the claimant to be held in trust for the care provided. This rule (the '*Hunt v Severs*' rule) has been criticised by the Law Commission.	*Donnelly v Joyce;*[14] *Hunt v Severs;*[15] Law Commission, *Damages for Personal Injury: Medical, Nursing and Other Expenses; Collateral Benefits* (Law Com No 262, 1999)

11 [1980] AC 174, HL.
12 [1956] AC 185, HL.
13 (1974) 17 KIR 1, CA.
14 [1974] QB 454, CA.
15 [1994] 2 AC 350, HL.

Reduced life expectancy	Claimants can claim for 'lost years', representing the period in which their life expectancy was reduced.	*Pickett v British Rail Engineering Ltd* [1980] AC 136, HL
Non-pecuniary losses		
	Claimants can claim for pain and suffering, emotional distress, and loss of amenities. The value of lost amenities will be determined on an objective basis. The fact that a claimant may have been unconscious does not deprive them of the right to claim for non-pecuniary losses. The starting point is the Judicial College *Guidelines for the Assessment of Damages in Personal Injury Cases*, but the Court of Appeal in *Heil v Rankin* held that there should be an 'uplift' for serious injuries.	*Lim Poh Choo v Camden and Islington Area Health Authority*[16] Judicial College, *Guidelines for the Assessment of General Damages in Personal Injury Cases*, 16th edn (OUP 2022); *Heil v Rankin*[17]

The difficulties of awarding an appropriate level of non-pecuniary damages were outlined by Lord Wolff MR in *Heil v Rankin*; this was particularly challenging and left the court vulnerable to the criticism of encroaching into the role of the legislature.

Heil v Rankin [2001] QB 272, CA, [20], [39]–[40], [46]–[47] (Lord Wolff MR)

20. We start by making it clear that we do not consider it necessary for the purpose of this appeal to depart from any existing legal principles as to the assessment of personal injury damages. The task of the court if we intervene will be limited to providing fresh guidelines so as to give effect to well established principles as to the objective which should be achieved by an award of damages.

...

39. In determining what is the correct level of damages for PSLA [pain, suffering, and loss of amenity], it is not usual for the court to attribute differing sums for different aspects of the injury. The court's approach involves trying to find the global sum which most accurately in monetary terms reflects or can be regarded as reflecting a fair, reasonable and just figure for the injuries which have been inflicted and the consequences which they will have in PSLA.

...

40. We accept as well that the question of what is an appropriate award for general damages for PSLA is always a difficult task, and that to attempt the task of altering the

16 [1980] AC 174, HL.

17 [2001] QB 272, CA.

level of awards generally can involve the courts in highly controversial issues which it would be preferable for the courts to avoid if this is not inconsistent with the courts' responsibility. However, changing the current levels of damages, if they are no longer reflecting what should be the correct level of awards, is ... part of the courts' duty. A duty which the court should not shirk.

41. The level of awards does involve questions of social policy. But the questions are ones with which the courts are accustomed to deal as part of their normal role. Parliament remains sovereign. It can still intervene after the court has given its decision. The task would be a novel one for Parliament. However, Parliament's intervention in this instance would not necessarily result in a loss of flexibility or interfere with the ability of the court to craft an award to the individual facts of a case, which is a virtue of the present system.

...

42. Ironically, the arguments which are relied on for saying that the court should not embark on the task of re-evaluating the level of damages are in part based on the fact that the court has agreed to materials of a general nature being placed before the court so that the court is aware of the implications of its decisions for the insurance industry and the NHS. However, much of the material provided only underlines matters of which any reasonably well informed person would be well aware.

43. While we have in mind the arguments advanced by the defendants and the insurers based on the consequences of a change in the level of the awards, those arguments go to the question of whether it is appropriate to increase the level of damages and not, as is now accepted, to jurisdiction. The question of the level of damages has always been an issue for the judges and the correct approach has been expressed as well as it can be by Lord Diplock in *Wright v British Railways Board Railways Board* ... upon which we cannot improve:

> '[Where] judges carry out their duty of assessing damages for non-economic loss in the money of the day at the date of the trial ... this is a rule of practice that judges are required to follow, not a guideline from which they have a discretion to depart if there are special circumstances that justify their doing so ... My Lords, given the inescapably artificial and conventional nature of the assessment of damages for non-economic loss in personal injury actions ... it is an important function of the Court of Appeal to lay down guidelines ... as to the quantum of damages appropriate to compensate for various types of commonly occurring injuries ... The purpose of such guidelines is that they should be simple and easy to apply though broad enough to permit allowances to be made for special features of individual cases which make the deprivation caused to the particular plaintiff by the non-economic loss greater or less than in the general run of cases involving injuries of the same kind.'

46. ... in considering whether the level of the awards of damages for non-pecuniary loss is too low, there is no change in the law involved even if we come to the conclusion that a change in the level is required. The court is doing no more than considering the adequacy

> of the level of current awards by applying existing principles and, in so far as they are inadequate, bringing them up to date.
>
> ...
>
> 47. We emphasise this because we have no intention of seeking to involve ourselves with matters of policy-making which are more suited for Parliament than for the courts.

17.5 Compensating benefits

The aim of tort law is to place someone in the position they would have been in had the tort not been committed against them. What if they were potentially placed in a *better position* because of the commission of the tort? In these circumstances, how should the court approach the award of damages? This situation is called 'compensating benefits' and often occurs when the individual has an insurance policy, receives assistance from family and friends, or is provided with charitable support in their time of need. Whether courts should take into account these compensating benefits when awarding damages raises difficult policy questions. On one hand, if they are not considered, the claimant could be over-compensated and left better off because of the tort. On the other hand, if they are taken into account, it could deter people from assisting those in need, and it may seem unfair for government, friends, family or charities to subsidise the tortfeasor.

Hussain v New Taplow Paper Mills Ltd [1988] AC 514, HL, 527–28 (Lord Bridge)

The challenges of compensating benefits were highlighted by Lord Bridge:

> In *Parry v. Cleaver* ... Lord Reid, discussing the general principles applicable to the assessment of damages for financial loss said ...
>
> > 'Two questions can arise. First, what did the plaintiff lose as a result of the accident? What are the sums which he would have received but for the accident but which by reason of the accident he can no longer get? And secondly, what are the sums which he did in fact receive as a result of the accident? And then the question arises whether the latter sums must be deducted from the former in assessing the damages ... it is a universal rule that the plaintiff cannot recover more than he has lost. And, ... we must have regard to realities rather than technicalities.'
>
> ...
>
> This dichotomy, however, must not be allowed to obscure the rule that prima facie the only recoverable loss is the net loss. Financial gains accruing to the plaintiff which he would not

have received but for the event which constitutes the plaintiff's cause of action are prima facie to be taken into account in mitigation of losses which that event occasions to him. In many, perhaps most cases, both losses and gains will come into the calculation. Just as in a claim for damages for wrongful dismissal the plaintiff must, if he can, mitigate his damage by securing other employment, so also a plaintiff disabled by personal injury from continuing his pre-accident occupation mitigates his damage suffered by the loss of the whole of his earnings in that occupation by exercising some other skill, which he already possesses or acquires by training, to earn money in a new occupation which, but for the accident, he would never have pursued. One may ask either 'What is his real loss?' or 'Is the gain accruing from earnings in the new occupation deductible from the loss of earnings of the old occupation?' to arrive at the same answer. But to the prima facie rule there are two well established exceptions. First, where a plaintiff recovers under an insurance policy for which he has paid the premiums, the insurance moneys are not deductible from damages payable by the tortfeasor: *Bradburn v. Great Western Railway Co.* ... Secondly, when the plaintiff receives money from the benevolence of third parties prompted by sympathy for his misfortune, as in the case of a beneficiary from a disaster fund, the amount received is again to be disregarded: see *Redpath v. Belfast and County Down Railway* ... In both these cases there is in one sense double recovery. If the award of damages adequately compensates the plaintiff, as it should, the additional amounts received from the insurer or from third party benevolence may be regarded as a net gain to the plaintiff resulting from his injury. But in both cases the common sense of the exceptions stares one in the face. It may be summed up in the rhetorical question: 'why should the tortfeasor derive any benefit, in the one case, from the premiums which the plaintiff has paid to insure himself against some contingency, however caused, in the other case, from the money provided by the third party with the sole intention of benefiting the injured plaintiff?'

There are, however, a variety of borderline situations where a plaintiff may receive money which, but for the wrong done to him by the defendant, he would not have received and where there may be no obvious answer to the question whether the rule against double recovery or some principle derived by analogy from one of the two classic exceptions to that rule should prevail. Some of these problems have been resolved by legislation, sometimes in the form of a compromise solution providing that a proportion only of certain statutory benefits is to be taken into account when assessing damages. But where there is no statute applicable the common law must solve the problem unaided and the possibility of a compromise solution is not available. Many eminent common law judges, I think it is fair to say, have been baffled by the problem of how to articulate a single guiding rule to distinguish receipts by a plaintiff which are to be taken into account in mitigation of damage from those which are not. Lord Reid aptly summed the matter up in *Parry v. Cleaver* when he said ... 'The common law has treated this matter as one depending on justice, reasonableness and public policy.'

Given the inevitable divergencies of judicial opinion as to what justice, reasonableness and public policy require, it is not surprising that courts in different common law jurisdictions should sometimes have solved similar problems in this field in different ways.

As Lord Bridge commented, there are no hard and fast rules, as the court's approach should depend on justice, reasonableness, and public policy. However, some general statements can be gleaned from the relevant legal principles.

Table 17.3: Different Compensating Benefits

Who provided the benefit	Examples	Outcome	Case(s)
The claimant's own foresight	Payments from pensions,[18] or personal insurance policies.	Generally, the compensating benefit will not result in a reduction of damages.	*Bradburn v Great Western Railway*;[19] *Parry v Cleaver*[20]
Generosity of others	General assistance in the form of, for example, housekeeping, providing meals, childcare, or charitable donations.	The compensating benefit will generally not result in a reduction of damages.	*Jones v Stroud District Council*[21]
Actions of defendant	A negligent employer who gives an injured employee a lump sum of money or paid time off work.	The compensating benefit is normally deducted from the final quantum awarded to the claimant.	*Hussain v New Taplow Paper Mills Ltd*;[22] *Williams v BOC Gases Ltd*[23]
Social security benefits	Provision of unemployment benefits.	The government has the power to recover benefits paid by court judgments and out-of-court settlements.	Law Reform (Personal Injuries) Act 1948; Social Security (Recovery of Benefits) Act 1997; Social Security (Recovery of Benefits) Regulations 1997 (SI 1997/2205)

17.6 Legislation relevant to damages

17.6.1 Law Reform (Miscellaneous Provisions) Act 1934

In the unfortunate situation where the claimant has passed away by the time the tort claim is heard, the question arises regarding what damages are payable and to whom.

18 *Parry v Cleaver* [1970] AC 1. If the claimant did not contribute to the pension payments, then this will be a compensating benefit akin to sick pay and will result in a reduction in the amount paid by the defendant: see *Hussain v New Taplow Paper Mills Ltd* [1988] AC 514, HL.

19 LR 10 Exch 1.

20 Parry v Cleaver [1970] AC 1, HL.

21 [1986] 1 WLR 1141, CA.

22 [1988] AC 514, HL.

23 [2000] ICR 1181, CA.

> **Law Reform (Miscellaneous Provisions) Act 1934**
>
> **1 Effect of death on certain causes of action**
>
> (1) Subject to the provisions of this section, on the death of any person after the commencement of this Act all causes of action subsisting against or vested in him shall survive against, or, as the case may be, for the benefit of, his estate. Provided that this subsection shall not apply to causes of action for defamation …
>
> (1A) The right of a person to claim under section 1A of the Fatal Accidents Act 1976 (bereavement) shall not survive for the benefit of his estate on his death.
>
> (2) Where a cause of action survives as aforesaid for the benefit of the estate of a deceased person, the damages recoverable for the benefit of the estate of that person—
>
> (a) shall not include—
>
> (i) any exemplary damages;
>
> (ii) any damages for loss of income in respect of any period after that person's death;
>
> (b) …
>
> (c) Where the death of that person has been caused by the act or omission which gives rise to the cause of action, shall be calculated without reference to any loss or gain to his estate consequent on his death, except that a sum in respect of funeral expenses may be included.

All causes of action, except defamation and the right to bereavement damages, survive for the benefit of the deceased's estate.

Pain and suffering incurred before death may also be recovered, but it must have been more than momentary; see *Hicks v Chief Constable of South Yorkshire Police* [1992] 2 All ER 65, HL.

The deceased's estate cannot claim any exemplary damages or damages for loss of income prior to the deceased's death.

Funeral costs, if the estate incurred them, may be recoverable.

17.6.2 Fatal Accidents Act 1976

The next piece of legislation applies when someone has been negligently killed and provides a cause of action for the deceased's dependants. To claim successfully under the Fatal Accidents Act 1976, the party will need to show that (1) they fall under the definition of a 'dependant' of the deceased under s 1(3) of the Act, and (2) they were, in fact, financially dependent on the deceased.

> **Fatal Accidents Act 1976**
>
> **1 Right of action for wrongful act causing death**
>
> (1) If death is caused by any wrongful act, neglect or default which is such as would (if death had not ensued) have entitled the person injured to maintain an action and recover damages in respect thereof, the person who would have been liable if death had not ensued shall

The death has to have been caused by the defendant's negligence for the deceased's dependants to claim against them.

be liable to an action for damages, notwithstanding the death of the person injured.

(2) Subject to section 1A(2) below, every such action shall be for the benefit of the dependants of the person ('the deceased') whose death has been so caused.

(3) In this Act 'dependant' means—

The Act provides a limited and specific list of people who can claim damages.

(a) the wife or husband or former wife or husband of the deceased;

(aa) the civil partner or former civil partner of the deceased;

This includes a current or former wife, husband, and civil partner.

(b) any person who—

(i) was living with the deceased in the same household immediately before the date of the death; and

(ii) had been living with the deceased in the same household for at least two years before that date; and

(iii) was living during the whole of that period as the husband or wife or civil partner of the deceased;

(c) any parent or other ascendant of the deceased;

(d) any person who was treated by the deceased as his parent;

(e) any child or other descendant of the deceased;

(f) any person (not being a child of the deceased) who, in the case of any marriage to which the deceased was at any time a party, was treated by the deceased as a child of the family in relation to that marriage;

(fa) any person (not being a child of the deceased) who, in the case of any civil partnership in which the deceased was at any time a civil partner, was treated by the deceased as a child of the family in relation to that civil partnership;

(g) any person who is, or is the issue of, a brother, sister, uncle or aunt of the deceased.

…

1A Bereavement

(1) An action under this Act may consist of or include a claim for damages for bereavement.

(2) A claim for damages for bereavement shall only be for the benefit—

(a) of the wife or husband or civil partner of the deceased;

…

(b) where the deceased was a minor who was never married or a civil partner—

(i) of his parents, if he was legitimate; and

(ii) of his mother, if he was illegitimate.

...

(3) Subject to subsection (5) below, the sum to be awarded as damages under this section shall be £15,120.

An even smaller group of people are entitled to claim a 'bereavement payment' of £15,120. This is limited to the deceased's wife, husband, civil or co-habiting partner, or parents (if the deceased was minor.

...

3 Assessment of damages

(1) In the action such damages, other than damages for bereavement, may be awarded as are proportioned to the injury resulting from the death to the dependants respectively.

(2) After deducting the costs not recovered from the defendant any amount recovered otherwise than as damages for bereavement shall be divided among the dependants in such shares as may be directed.

(3) In an action under this Act where there fall to be assessed damages payable to a widow in respect of the death of her husband there shall not be taken account the re-marriage of the widow or her prospects of re-marriage.

This clause expressly excludes a *female*'s remarriage or the prospect of remarriage as a relevant consideration in determining awards for damages (but a male's prospect of remarriage is strangely not mentioned!).

...

4 Assessment of damages: disregard of benefits

In assessing damages in respect of a person's death in an action under this Act, benefits which have accrued or may accrue to any person from his estate or otherwise as a result of his death shall be disregarded.

The Act specifically states that compensating benefits should be disregarded in any claim.

The strict approach of the Fatal Accidents Act 1976 does not accord with modern notions of relationships and families. The limited category of people who can claim has been heavily criticised by academics, the courts, and the Law Commission; however, all the calls for reform have been ignored.

Question to consider: How should the Fatal Accidents Act 1976 be updated to better reflect modern-day families?

Other resources: SM Waddams, 'Damages for Wrongful Death: Has Lord Campbell's Act Outlived its Usefulness?' (1984) 47 *MLR* 437; *Shepherd v Post Office* [1995] 6 WLUK 107, CA; Law Commission, *Claims for Wrongful Death* (Law Com No 263, 1999); Richard Kidner, 'A History of the Fatal Accidents Acts' (1999) 50 *NILQ* 318; *Cox v Ergo Versicherung* AG [2014] UKSC 22, [2014] AC 1379.

17.6.3 Limitation Act 1980

The third piece of legislation that will be considered is the Limitation Act 1980, which provides strict statutory deadlines for when claimants can commence tort actions against tortfeasors. The specific time limit depends on the type of tort claim made.

Limitation Act 1980

2 Time limit for actions founded on tort

An action founded on tort shall not be brought after the expiration of six years from the date on which the cause of action accrued.

> A general tort law claim must be commenced within six years of the date on which the action accrued.

...

4A Time limit for actions for defamation or malicious falsehood

The time limit under section 2 of this Act shall not apply to an action for—

(a) libel or slander, or

(b) slander of title, slander of goods or other malicious falsehood,

but no such action shall be brought after the expiration of one year from the date on which the cause of action accrued.

11 Special time limit for actions in respect of personal injuries

(1) This section applies to any action for damages for negligence, nuisance or breach of duty (whether the duty exists by virtue of a contract or of provision made by or under a statute or independently of any contract or any such provision) where the damages claimed by the plaintiff for the negligence, nuisance or breach of duty consist of or include damages in respect of personal injuries to the plaintiff or any other person.

> Damages for 'negligence, nuisance or breach of duty' are afforded much more complex time limits, having a starting point of three years either from the date that the action accrued or the date of knowledge of the person injured.

(1A) This section does not apply to any action brought for damages under section 3 of the Protection from Harassment Act 1997.

> The Act does not apply to claims brought under the Protection from Harassment Act 1997.

(2) None of the time limits given in the preceding provisions of this Act shall apply to an action to which this section applies.

(3) An action to which this section applies shall not be brought after the expiration of the period applicable in accordance with subsection (4) or (5) below.

(4) Except where subsection (5) below applies, the period applicable is three years from—

(a) the date on which the cause of action accrued; or

(b) the date of knowledge (if later) of the person injured.

> Personal injury damage claims under 'negligence, nuisance or breach of duty' have a time limit that starts on either, (a) the date the cause of action accrued, or (b) the date of knowledge of the person injured – if this was later.

There are a range of exceptions provided by the Act under s 28. For example, the time limit is extended in cases of disability, which is defined to include infancy (see s 38(2)).

28 Extension of limitation period in case of disability

(1) Subject to the following provisions of this section, if on the date when any right of action accrued for which a period of limitation is prescribed by this Act, the person to whom it accrued was under a disability, the action may be brought at any time before the expiration of six years from the date when he ceased to be under a disability or died (whichever first occurred) notwithstanding that the period of limitation has expired.

(2) This section shall not affect any case where the right of action first accrued to some person (not under a disability) through whom the person under a disability claims.

(3) When a right of action which has accrued to a person under a disability accrues, on the death of that person while still under a disability, to another person under a disability, no further extension of time shall be allowed by reason of the disability of the second person.

(4) No action to recover land or money charged on land shall be brought by virtue of this section by any person after the expiration of thirty years from the date on which the right of action accrued to that person or some person through whom he claims.

...

Courts also have general powers to 'disapply' the specified time limits if 'it would be equitable to allow an action to proceed'.

33 Discretionary exclusion of time limit for actions in respect of personal injuries or death

(1) If it appears to the court that it would be equitable to allow an action to proceed having regard to the degree to which—

(a) the provisions of section 11, 11A, 11B or 12 of this Act prejudice the plaintiff or any person whom he represents; and

(b) any decision of the court under this subsection would prejudice the defendant or any person whom he represents;

the court may direct that those provisions shall not apply to the action, or shall not apply to any specified cause of action to which the action relates.

...

When determining whether the action proceeding would be equitable, the court must have regard to all of the circumstances, including the length of the delay and its reason, the delay's impact on the evidence adduced by the claimant, the defendant's conduct, whether the claimant acted promptly and reasonably, and any steps taken by the claimant to obtain medical, legal or other expert advice.

(3) In acting under this section the court shall have regard to all the circumstances of the case and in particular to—

(a) the length of, and the reasons for, the delay on the part of the plaintiff;

(b) the extent to which, having regard to the delay, the evidence adduced or likely to be adduced by the plaintiff or the defendant

> is or is likely to be less cogent than if the action had been brought within the time allowed by section 11, by section 11A, by section 11B or (as the case may be) by section 12;
>
> (c) the conduct of the defendant after the cause of action arose, including the extent (if any) to which he responded to requests reasonably made by the plaintiff for information or inspection for the purpose of ascertaining facts which were or might be relevant to the plaintiff's cause of action against the defendant;
>
> (d) the duration of any disability of the plaintiff arising after the date of the accrual of the cause of action;
>
> (e) the extent to which the plaintiff acted promptly and reasonably once he knew whether or not the act or omission of the defendant, to which the injury was attributable, might be capable at that time of giving rise to an action for damages;
>
> (f) the steps, if any, taken by the plaintiff to obtain medical, legal or other expert advice and the nature of any such advice he may have received.
>
> ...

Initially, the more flexible time limit available for actions in 'negligence, nuisance or breach of duty' was held not to apply to claims for trespass to the person torts. Unfortunately, in *Stubbings v Webb*, this resulted in the victims of trespass to the person torts (often being cases of serious sexual and physical abuse) generally being in a worse position when compared with the victims of negligence or nuisance torts. This is particularly concerning as many victims of serious sexual abuse understandably lack the strength or ability to commence actions until a significant period of time has passed.

In *Stubbings v Webb*, the claimant was a 36-year-old woman who alleged that her adoptive father sexually abused her and that her stepbrother had raped her when she was a minor. She wished to commence claims against both alleged perpetrators for trespass to the person; however, the defendants contended that any potential claim was statute-barred by the Limitation Act 1980. The House of Lords unanimously held that the claim was statute-barred as trespass to the person claims did not benefit from the more flexible time limitation that 'negligence, nuisance or breach of duty' cases received.

Stubbings v Webb [1993] AC 498, HL, 507–8 (Lord Griffiths)

But I cannot agree that the words 'breach of duty' have the effect of including within the scope of the section all actions in which damages for personal injuries are claimed which is the other ground upon which the Court of Appeal decided *Letang v. Cooper*. If that had been the intention of the draftsman it would have been easy enough to say so in the section. On the contrary the draftsman has used words of limitation; he has limited the section to actions for negligence, nuisance and breach of duty and the reason he did so was to give effect to the recommendation of the Tucker Committee that the three-year period should not apply to a number of causes of action in which damages for personal injury might be claimed namely damages for trespass to the person, false imprisonment, malicious prosecution or defamation. There can be no doubt that rape and indecent assault fell within the category of trespass to the person.

Lord Denning M.R. in *Letang v Cooper* ... was not prepared to assume that Parliament did intend to give effect to the Tucker Committee's recommendations, but we can now look at Hansard and can see that it was the express intention of Parliament to do so. The proposer of the Bill, Mr. John Peyton, in moving the second reading said:

> 'In its main provisions the Bill follows precisely the recommendations of the committee which sat under the chairmanship of Tucker L.J. There is only one comparatively minor point upon which the provisions vary from the recommendations of the Tucker committee.' ...

The minor point I have already identified, it was to substitute a fixed period of three years for a two-year period which might be extended to six years. This point was accepted by Lord Tucker: when commenting upon it in the second reading in the House of Lords he said:

> 'With regard to the period, I do not think I am revealing any secrets when I tell your Lordships that on the committee, once they came to the conclusion that the proper course was to limit the period in regard to personal accident cases, there was a difference of opinion about whether that period should be two years or three years. I think the acceptance of two years with discretionary power to the judge in Chambers, represented a compromise between the two views but for which we should not have had a unanimous report from the committee – and it is always valuable to have a unanimous Report. I have no strong views on this subject, but I incline to favour some fixed period:' ...

Even without reference to Hansard I should not myself have construed breach of duty as including a deliberate assault. The phrase lying in juxtaposition with negligence and nuisance carries with it the implication of a breach of duty of care not to cause personal injury, rather than an obligation not to infringe any legal right of another person. If I invite a lady to my house one would naturally think of a duty to take care that the house is safe but would one really be thinking of a duty not to rape her. But, however this may be, the terms in which this Bill was introduced to my mind make it clear beyond peradventure that the intention was to give effect to the Tucker recommendation that the limitation period in respect of trespass to the person was not to be reduced to three years but should remain at six years. The language of section 2(1) of the Act of 1954 is in my view apt to give effect to that intention, and cases of deliberate assault such as we are concerned with in this case are not actions for breach of duty within the meaning of section 2(1) of the Act of 1954.

The language of section 2(1) of the Act of 1954 was carried without alteration into the Act of 1975 and then into section 11(1) of the Act of 1980 where it must bear the same meaning as it had in the Act of 1954.

It thus follows that the plaintiff's causes of action against both defendants were subject to a six-year limitation period. This period was suspended during her infancy but commenced to run when she attained her majority: see section 28 of the Act of 1980. This period expired many years before she issued *her writ* in these proceedings. There are no provisions for extending this period and her actions are therefore statute-barred and cannot proceed.

This ruling was highly criticised and has produced some regrettable outcomes. In *S v W (Child Abuse: Damages)*, the rule in *Stubbings v Webb* meant that the victim could sue her mother for negligently failing to protect her from sexual and physical abuse by her father, but could not sue her father for the abuse itself. It was clear that the judges were unhappy with this outcome but had no alternative.

S v W (Child Abuse: Damages) [1995] 1 FLR 862, CA, 867 (Sir Ralph Gibson)

I agree that the appeal should be dismissed for the reasons my Lords have given. As has been pointed out, the result of the judge's ruling was, as he rightly said, illogical and surprising. That fact, in my view, is a good reason for inviting the attention of the Law Commission to the interrelation of these provisions and to the absence of any longstop limitation period of this and any other parts of the Act, for example, section 28 of the Act which deals with persons under a disability. It is not the basis on which this court could reach any other conclusion.

This provision and its outcomes were subject to significant criticism from the Law Commission, which recommended legislative reform.

Law Commission, *Limitation of Actions* (Law Com No 270, 2001) paras 1.4–1.8 (footnotes omitted)

1.4 In the Consultation Paper we identified the major problems of the current law: it is unfair, complex, uncertain and outdated.

1.5 Traditionally, the limitation period has started from the date the cause of action accrued, whether or not the claimant knows of the potential claim. This caused injustice where the injury suffered by the claimant did not become apparent for several years. Provision has been made for such cases of latent damage in actions for personal injuries, under the Consumer Protection Act 1987 and in some other cases. However, the provision for latent damage does not extend to most causes of action. Outside the areas of personal injuries and consumer protection, the limitation period will only run from the date the claimant knows the relevant facts if the claim is brought in negligence. Even where the claim is for personal injuries, provision for latent damage does not extend to deliberately caused injuries. Here the limitation period remains six years, running from the date of accrual of the cause of action. This has led to the anomalous result that a claimant who has been sexually abused by her father may have longer to bring a claim for damages against her mother for negligently failing to prevent the abuse than to bring a claim against her father for actually committing the abuse.

1.6 It is necessary to balance the interests of the claimant (who wishes to have as long as possible to bring a claim) and the defendant (who must be protected from stale claims) in setting a limitation period. It will never be possible to achieve complete fairness between the parties (indeed the imposition of any limitation period could be regarded as doing 'rough justice' to the claimant). However the balance struck under the present law does not give sufficient recognition to the interests of the claimant. And even though the changes referred to have resulted in some improvement, in each case a different regime has been adopted, introducing needless complexity into the law.

1.7 The law lacks certainty in some areas. For example, it is unclear precisely what 'actions to recover sums recoverable by virtue of an enactment' are under section 9 of the Limitation Act 1980. The correct interpretation of the provisions in the Limitation Act 1980 on breach of trust, on conversion and on actual and constructive knowledge is also unclear.

1.8 The law is outdated in some respects. The traditional limitation period of six years which applies to some actions founded on tort and actions founded on breach of (simple) contract originated in the Limitation Act 1623 when communication and gathering information was far more difficult than it is today. The law has also preserved some traditional distinctions which no longer have any relevance, such as the restriction of the concept of acknowledgments to claims for specified amounts and the distinction between actions on a simple contract (subject to the six year limitation period) and actions on a specialty (subject to a twelve year limitation period).

Despite the significant criticisms from the Law Commission, academic writings, and the judiciary's comments, the legislation recommended was not implemented by the government. However, the situation was rectified by the common law in the House of Lords' decision in *A v Hoare*.

A v Hoare [2008] UKHL 6, [2008] 1 AC 844, [21]–[22], [24]–[25] (Lord Hoffman)

This was a combined appeal of six separate cases of claims for sexual assaults and abuse, which appeared to be barred by the Limitation Act 1980. In deciding whether or not the cases were barred and if *Stubbings v Webb* was good law, Lord Hoffmann commented:

> 21. For some time after it was decided, I do not think that *Stubbings* gave rise in practice to much difficulty. That was because it was generally believed, on the authority of cases like *Trotman v North Yorkshire County Council* [1999] LGR 584, that an employer could not be vicariously liable for sexual assaults committed by his employee. They were inherently outside the scope of his employment. Only the abuser himself could be liable. But people who commit sexual assaults are seldom worth suing. In the appeal before the House of *A v Hoare* [2006] 1 WLR 2320, the claimant decided to sue only when she heard that the defendant had won the lottery. In *Stubbings*, where the plaintiff wanted to sue her adoptive father and step-brother for sexual abuse more than 20 years earlier, Lord Griffiths observed, at p 501G, that neither of them appeared to 'have the means to satisfy any significant award of damages'. The fact that the motive for the proceedings seemed to be something other than the recovery of compensation may have influenced the construction which the House gave to the statute.
>
> 22. The situation was radically changed when the House of Lords decided in *Lister v Hesley Hall Ltd* [2002] 1 AC 215 that sexual abuse was not necessarily outside the scope of an employment. It depended upon whether there was a sufficiently close connection between the work which the employee had been employed to do and the acts of abuse. A company which owned and operated a school boarding house was held liable for sexual abuse of pupils by a man employed as warden. After that, claims against the operators of schools, detention centres and similar institutions for sexual abuse by employees came thick and fast. And these threw into relief the anomalies created by *Stubbings*.
>
> …
>
> 24. The matter was considered by the Law Commission as part of a comprehensive review of the law of limitation of actions which was presented to Parliament in 2001: Limitation of Actions (2001) (Law Com No 270). The effect of *Stubbings* was described as anomalous, with particular reference to *S v W (Child Abuse: Damages)* [1995] 1

FLR 862: see para 1.5 of the report. The Commission recommended a uniform regime for personal injuries, whether the claim was made in negligence or trespass to the person: see the summary at para 1.14. There has not yet been any implementing legislation, possibly because the Commission's recommendations were not confined to the *Stubbings* anomaly but proposed a completely new law of limitation of actions.

25. Lord Reid's observation in *Ex p Hudson* [1972] AC 944, 966 that unsatisfactory decisions of the highest court can cause uncertainty because lower courts tend to distinguish them on inadequate grounds is also pertinent to the consequences of *Stubbings*. Claimants who have suffered sexual abuse but need to seek the discretion of the court under section 33 are driven to alleging that the abuse was the result of, or accompanied by, some other breach of duty which can be brought within the language of section 11. Thus, in addition to having to decide whether the claimant was sexually abused, the courts must decide whether this was the result of 'systemic negligence' on the part of the abuser's employer or the negligence of some other person for whom the employer is responsible. In the appeals before the House, the appellants put forward at least four alternative theories of liability on which they wish to rely if the rule in *Stubbings* is upheld. These are, in increasing degree of artificiality (1) breach of a direct duty of care owed by the employer to the claimant; (2) breach of a duty of care by other employees; (3) breach of a duty of care by the abuser himself and (4) breach of a duty by the abuser to notify the employer of his own wrongful acts. In *KR v Bryn Alyn Community (Holdings) Ltd* [2003] QB 1441, para 100 Auld LJ said that the need to frame a claim in one or other of these ways when the real cause of complaint was sexual abuse for which the employer was vicariously liable was causing 'arid and highly wasteful litigation turning on a distinction of no apparent principle or other merit'. I therefore think that it would be right to depart from *Stubbings* and reaffirm the law laid down by the Court of Appeal in *Letang v Cooper* [1965] 1 QB 232.

17.7 How damages can be awarded

Complex personal injury claims give rise to significant practical challenges, including how the court should award damages. The majority of awards are given as a one-off 'lump sum' payment, which the claimant is entitled to use as they see fit. This approach does give rise to a number of potential issues. For example, what if the claimant uses it all up without leaving sufficient funds for their future needs? What if the claimant needs access to the funds immediately and cannot wait for the end of a long and complex trial? Finally, what if the injury turns out to be more or less serious than originally anticipated? In response to these challenges, the courts have several powers to try to ensure that the claimant is adequately compensated and taken care of in the long term.

One such power is the right to order periodical payments instead of a single lump sum payment that may be difficult for the claimant to manage effectively.

Courts Act 2003

100 Periodical payments

(1) For section 2 of the Damages Act 1996 (periodical payments by consent) substitute—

'2 Periodical payments

(1) A court awarding damages for future pecuniary loss in respect of personal injury—

(a) may order that the damages are wholly or partly to take the form of periodical payments, and

(b) shall consider whether to make that order.

(2) A court awarding other damages in respect of personal injury may, if the parties consent, order that the damages are wholly or partly to take the form of periodical payments.

(3) A court may not make an order for periodical payments unless satisfied that the continuity of payment under the order is reasonably secure.

This provision amended s 2 of the Damages Act 1996, providing the courts with the power to award damages wholly or partly in the form of periodical payments, which will provide the claimant with a 'stream' of money.

The courts will only award periodical payments if they are satisfied that that payment is reasonably secure (ie that the defendant will continue to make the periodical payments).

The challenges of balancing current and future needs in large and complex personal injury cases were highlighted in *Eeles v Cobham Hire Services Ltd*. In this case, the claimant suffered a serious head injury as an infant. At the time of the hearing, he was 11 and had made a good physical recovery but retained ongoing difficulties with fine motor skills, cognition and intellect. The court held that he would need ongoing assistance, including physiotherapy, occupational therapy and speech therapy and that he would never have the capacity to manage his own affairs. The defendant did not dispute its liability, and the parties agreed they were unable to adequately quantify the claim until the claimant was older, when the extent of the injury was more accurately determined. Before a final hearing on damages, the parents requested an interim payment of £1.2 million for the purchase and refurbishment of a large house to assist with the claimant's therapy and development, which the trial judge awarded. However, the defendant appealed on the basis that this large award was not a reasonable proportion of the likely final sum, especially as it was appropriate to award a periodical payment order for the claimant's long-term care.

Smith LJ handed down the judgment of the court, emphasising that the court must not order an interim payment that exceeds a reasonable proportion of the likely amount of the final judgment. This involved considering a 'broad assessment' of the merits of both sides to make a preliminary estimate and allowing a 'comfortable margin' in case this estimate was too generous.

Eeles v Cobham Hire Services Ltd [2009] EWCA Civ 204, [2010] 1 WLR 409, [4]–[6], [43] (Smith LJ)

4. Before making an order, the court would not necessarily need to inquire as to what the claimant intended to do with the interim payment: *Stringman (A Minor) v McArdle* [1994] 1 WLR 1653. If of full age and capacity, the claimant would be entitled to do with it as he wished. If he was a minor or patient, control of the money would be exercised by the Court of Protection. None the less, claimants often wished to explain why they wanted a particular sum at the time. Typically, a claimant might want to demonstrate the need to buy or adapt accommodation or to provide a care regime. He might wish to demonstrate the need for such a facility in order to show that the final award would be of sufficient size to warrant the making of an interim payment of the amount sought. Judges were warned against making an interim award which would have the effect of creating a status quo in the claimant's way of life which might have the effect of inhibiting the trial judge's freedom of decision ...

5. With the rise in the value of claims for severe injuries, it has become quite common for very substantial interim payments to be made, based upon a reasonable proportion of the likely amount of the final capital award. However, under the amended Damages Act 1996 it became possible for a judge to make a periodical payments order (PPO) in respect of some or all of the heads of future loss, index-linked to reflect future changes in the value of money and continuing for the whole of the claimant's actual life. Since this court in *Thompstone v Tameside and Glossop Acute Services NHS Trust* [2008] EWCA Civ 5 affirmed that, when making a PPO, the court had the power to apply whatever index was most appropriate to the head of loss concerned, the benefits of a PPO have been generally recognised and such orders are now routinely made.

6. When considering how to allocate the various heads of future loss between a capital award and one or more PPOs, the trial judge has to consider what allocation will best meet the claimant's needs: ... The trial judge's task is to weigh the various aspects of the claimant's needs, in the light of the sums which are to be awarded under each head of loss and in the light of the available financial advice.

After reviewing the facts of the case and the arguments from both sides, Smith LJ gave the judgment of the court refusing the £1.2 million interim payment as it would not leave sufficient funds for the claimant's ongoing needs. His Lordship also provided a helpful summary of the approach that should be taken when determining whether to make an interim payment where a trial judge may also wish to make a PPO.

43. The judge's first task is to assess the likely amount of the final judgment, leaving out of account the heads of future loss which the trial judge might wish to deal with by PPO. Strictly speaking, the assessment should comprise only special damages to date and damages for pain, suffering and loss of amenity, with interest on both. However, we consider that the practice of awarding accommodation costs (including future running costs) as

a lump sum is sufficiently well established that it will usually be appropriate to include accommodation costs in the expected capital award. The assessment should be carried out on a conservative basis. Save in the circumstances discussed below, the interim payment will be a reasonable proportion of that assessment. A reasonable proportion may well be a high proportion, provided that the assessment has been conservative. The objective is not to keep the claimant out of his money but to avoid any risk of over-payment.

This case highlights the need for judges to carefully balance the current and future needs of claimants when determining how defendants should pay the damages, and how this can be particularly difficult when dealing with young claimants who will need to have long-term assistance.

17.8 Conclusion

It must be recognised that awarding damages in tort law is exceptionally complicated, and the process connects with a range of other topics. Multiple books have been written focused solely on tort law damages. This area is inherently linked with complex civil procedure rules, which can only be briefly discussed in this chapter. It is both unnecessary and beyond the scope of this chapter to go into detail about how damages are calculated, and, therefore, only the general principles have been discussed in this chapter. In light of the challenges associated with awarding appropriate damages, it is easy to criticise the tort law system for not fulfilling its underlying goal of providing compensation to individuals harmed by the tortious actions of others. This has resulted in some people calling for the abolition of the tort law system. Whilst these criticisms are valid on a number of levels, as outlined by Morgan, it is important to remember that damages in tort law have other goals, such as deterrence and accountability.

J Morgan, 'Abolishing Personal Injuries Law? A Reply to Lord Sumption' (2018) 34 *Professional Negligence* 122–42

Tort law is, considered solely as a compensation scheme, outstandingly badly designed (in theory) and staggeringly inefficient to operate (in practice). But compensation is not tort's only legitimate role. Once this is acknowledged, the case for abolition is uncertain. Tort's other social functions could rationally justify its survival – although dubious moral sentiments (in my view) cannot ...

To the extent that tort meets either of these goals, it does so incidentally rather than by design. To state the obvious, the criterion for tort compensation is that another person is legally responsible for the claimant-victim's injury. Inevitably that means that very many of those injured – we may say the great majority – are ineligible. Most accidents are *not* another's fault. Even in the two areas that generate the majority of tort claims between them – accidents on the roads and in the workplace – the proportion receiving tort compensation is relatively small ...

Thus only a small proportion of those who suffer injury and disease ever receive tort compensation. (The compensation that these 'lucky' few receive is, let us remember, generous – *restitutio in integrum* tailored to their individual needs, both financial and non-pecuniary, at significant expense.) To criticise tort for compensating such a small fraction might seem unfair – as idle as complaining that a case of champagne is not much use for putting out a fire. That is not what it is designed to do. But still, all victims of injuries and disease suffer equally – the *cause* of their misfortune (another's fault or not?) affects their needs not at all. From the perspective of *need*, it is unjustifiable that a small subset of victims has their needs expensively met in full while the great majority receive nothing. From this perspective, tort seems impossible to defend. With a fire raging, we need a fire extinguisher.

Tort is not so unsatisfactory when we consider its effect at *spreading* the costs of accidents. It is notorious that irrespective of the *nominal* defendant (who might be an individual), tort damages are usually paid by liability insurers. Yet this spreading phenomenon obtains in spite of the basic structure of tort law, not because of it. As a matter of corrective justice, the claimant's entire loss is shifted to the responsible defendant. It undermines this basic structure if the defendant is permitted (or in actually *compelled*) to offload the responsibility by insuring. But whether or not insurance is theoretically acceptable, it is undeniably widespread. Why sue an uninsured individual? Thus the losses of tort claims are in practice spread across the pool of insurance premium payers.

However (following on from the point above), it is of course only the cost of *tortious* accidents that is spread through liability insurance. Those who are injured by non-tortious causes (i.e. the vast majority) are excluded by the inevitable harsh logic that 'the loss lies where it falls' (i.e. on the victim). A rational loss-spreading scheme would cover *all* those who suffer loss. It could be part of an extended social security system, or first-party insurance, or a combination.

Seen from the compensation viewpoint alone, tort is an inevitable failure ...

Contrary to what is sometimes believed, tort law continues to have a significant deterrent effect. That is so notwithstanding the prevalence of liability insurance. However, although the deterrent effect is real, its precise impact is difficult to quantify. So while incentives of real social value would be lost if tort were replaced by an accident compensation scheme, entailing that the number of negligently-caused injuries would increase, predicting the effect appears impossible ...

Tort has other dimensions of social value. Even if we assume that some combination of compensation scheme and regulation could provide optimal accident deterrence and compensation, at lower administrative cost, society might still be impoverished by the abolition of tort claims for negligent personal injury. In particular, negligence claims can enable victims to hold powerful bodies to account for the harm that they do. The value of this cannot be quantified in cash terms.

Question to consider: Does the UK tort law system handle the difficulties associated with awarding damages adequately? If not, what amendments would you recommend?

Other resources: Craig Brown, 'Deterrence in Tort and No-Fault: The New Zealand Experience' (1985) *CLR* 976; Joanne Conaghan, 'Tort Litigation in the Context of Intra-familial Abuse' (1998) 61 *MLR* 132; Annette Morris, 'Spiralling or Stabilising? The Compensation Culture and Our Propensity to Claim Damages for Personal Injury' (2007) 70 *MLR* 349; Lord Sumption JSC, 'Abolishing Personal Injuries Law: a Project: *An Address to the Personal Injuries Bar Association*' [2018] JIRL 1.

INDEX

C

H

I

J

L

M

Q

R

W